A-Level
ICT
for Edexcel

A-Level

ICT

for Edexcel

K Mary Reid • Fraser Harrington • Dan Birkett
Gerry Enright • Alan Jarvis

Heinemann Educational Publishers, Halley Court, Jordan Hill, Oxford OX2 8EJ

A division of Reed Educational & Professional Publishing Ltd

Heinemann is a registered trademark of Reed Educational & Professional Publishing Limited

OXFORD MELBOURNE AUCKLAND JOHANNESBURG BLANTYRE GABORONE IBADAN PORTSMOUTH NH (USA) CHICAGO

First published 2002
2005 2004 2003 2002
10 9 8 7 6 5 4 3 2 1

A catalogue record for this book is available from the British Library on request.

ISBN 0 435 45495 1

Typeset by TechType, Abingdon, Oxon
Printed and bound in Great Britain by The Bath Press Ltd, Bath

CONTENTS

INTRODUCTION

Writing a textbook to support the Edexcel specification for A/AS Level ICT has proved to be a something of a challenge. The Edexcel specification is rather different from those offered by other examination boards, including, as it does, topics that are not normally dealt with at this level, but which engage students through the obvious relevance to their future working lives.

The inspiration for the style of this book came from the examiners, who invariably set questions placed firmly in realistic contexts. They, and we, believe that an understanding of technical matters grows best when it is firmly associated with solving real-life problems. Therefore, we have decided to create a virtual world of characters and organisations who create, support or use ICT solutions. The characters interact with each other in a number of realistic scenarios, which are themselves based on discussions we have had with professionals in the field. The technical knowledge emerges as it is needed to solve interesting problems.

This natural approach contrasts vividly with the traditional approach to the teaching of computing subjects, in which technical knowledge and skills, and their underlying basic principles, are studied in depth, and in which applications in the real world are only discussed when the fundamentals are understood.

We hope that the imagination of A Level students, and their teachers, will be captured by this book. We hope that it will inspire them to do some research of their own, by asking people that they meet about their work and their use of ICT.

How the specification is structured

The Edexcel specification for A/AS Level ICT can be downloaded from the board's website.

The specification includes four theory units:

AS theory units
Unit 1   System administration
Unit 2   The generation of applications

A2 theory units
Unit 4   Systems management
Unit 5   The implementation of event-driven applications.

There are two further coursework units:

AS coursework unit
Unit 3   Case study and problem solution

A2 coursework unit
Unit 6   Research and applications development project.

Each coursework unit consists of two tasks and each task is designed to partner one of the theory units.

How the book is structured

The book is structured into four main sections, each containing the theory and practical advice to support one unit and its related coursework task. Each section also contains examination-style questions and mark schemes.

Systems Administration – Unit 1 and Unit 3 (Task 1)

The Generation of Applications – Unit 2 and Unit 3 (Task 2)

Systems Management – Unit 4 and Unit 6 (Task 3)

The Implementation of Event-Driven Applications – Unit 5 and Unit 6 (Task 4)

One additional chapter is entirely devoted to the techniques of interpreting, and responding to, examination questions. The advice is illustrated with questions, and examiners' comments, from the pilot scheme. Our own students have found this material invaluable.

Websites

The book is supported by online resources on Heinemann's website at www.heinemann.co.uk/vocational/it. The password for accessing these resources is HEIN23. These resources include lists of books and links to websites that will provide background information to the topics. The website also provides downloadable materials, including tutorials in Visual Basic® and HTML and some sample coursework, as well as some notes on Key Skills. Over time we intend to update this site in order to bridge the gap that will develop, inevitably, between the information given in the book and the current technologies in the real world.

Teachers may like to join the A Level ICT Network, which has been created by fellow teachers to support the delivery of the Edexcel specification, by visiting the network's website.

ICT, IT and IS

The terms 'Information Technology' (IT) and 'Information and Communications Technology' (ICT) are used interchangeably throughout the book, as indeed they are in the real world. The term 'Information Systems' (IS) denotes a much broader category, which includes all the systems for storing and distributing information irrespective of whether they use modern technology.

Acknowledgements

The authors would like to thank the following people for the generous advice, information and support that they have given us:

Douglas Kay at Edexcel; Ian Cooper, Nader Moghaddam, Ray Brown, George Dyball and Lida Moghaddam at Kingston College; Mohammad Chowdhry (a former student at Kingston College); Maggie Roberts and Tim Parr at Warlingham School; Stephen Ball at ClubRunner; students at Kingston College and Warlingham School who acted as guinea pigs for some of our material; Neela Soomary for her invaluable help in preparing some of the A2 chapters; and to numerous colleagues and students who have enriched our professional lives.

Finally, we all want to express particular thanks to our spouses and partners, who gave us tireless support.

K Mary Reid
2001

The publishers would like to acknowledge Macmillan Computer Publishing. They would also like to thank the following organisations for permission to reproduce photographs and other material:

Mark Boulton/CEC – page 41
British Computer Society – page 111
Daily Telegraph – pages 107–8, 321
The Guardian – pages 104, 105, 114, 322, 324, 326
IBM Corporation – pages 61, 66, 70 and 75
The Image Bank/Sparky – page 334
The Image Bank/Xavier Bonghi – page 336
PC Magazine – page 7
Seaward Electronic Ltd/Chris Ridley – page 390
Telegraph in Colour Library/Jean Luis Batt – page 289

Screen shots reproduced with permission from Microsoft Corporation.

Every effort has been made to contact copyright holders of material published in this book. We would be glad to hear from unacknowledged sources at the first opportunity.

SYSTEMS
ADMINISTRATION

CHAPTER 1

The responsibilities of a systems administrator

This chapter introduces the role and responsibilities of systems administrators, using a real-life example. It will set the scene for the first part of this section and put your mind into frame as far as the practical management of ICT is concerned. You might be interested to return to this later in the course and see how your learning has developed. The rest of this section will cover in more detail the topics introduced here. This chapter will provide:

- an introduction to systems administration and computer systems

- a case study examining a real-life administration example

- an overview of the administration process

- an introduction to the operating system (OS)

- an overview of data representation in computers.

This chapter covers these Learning Outcomes in the specification:

L.O. 1.1 Define the responsibilities of systems administrators
L.O. 1.3 Demonstrate a knowledge of a range of common ICT applications (covered in Chapters 1–8)

It covers these Technical Knowledge topics:

T1.1.1 The purpose of an operating system (part)
T1.2.1 Data types (part)
T1.2.2 Internal representation of data types (part)
T1.3.1 Basic components

Introduction

Systems administration is sometimes referred to (as are many other aspects of computing) as a magic art. That is to say, much of its practice is rather obscure and has nothing to do with the precise, logical science of silicon technology, and more to do with guesswork, gossip and luck! Like many other aspects of life, it is often whom you know and not what you know that is most important.

Systems administration has the goal of putting together networks of computers, getting them going and then keeping them running. We refer to *networks of computers* because it is unlikely that any computer system runs without connection to others. Even if you have a standalone computer at home, it is unlikely that you use it without connecting to the Internet – and hence you become part of a global network of computers. A network is a community of users who may have competing or collaborative interests. Systems administration therefore has to deal with cultural, social, economic and political issues as well as technical ones.

Systems administration tries to service the needs of the users. The end-users are the *raison d'être* for the system but are, ironically, often seen as the fly in the ointment by some systems administrators.

You may have found in your own experience in various establishments where you are the end-user of a computer system that you are fairly low down in the pecking order as far as having your computing requests dealt with. That may be because your expectations are too high (e.g. you want to pursue your leisure activities too zealously); or your individual requests might jeopardise the community of users you share the systems with (e.g. you want to be able to download and run free software but security measures prevent you from doing this); or else your individual but perfectly reasonable request (e.g. you want to be able to join a discussion list of other students studying your course) is just too much trouble to implement.

Activity

You are the end-user of a computer system. Describe what you need to use the computer system for. Think what support you need, and how you might achieve this more easily, or more efficiently. Think of all the things that would need to happen for any improvements to be made to assist you (use headings such as technical, cultural, social, economic, etc.). Do not concern yourself with technical feasibility at the moment.

The challenges of systems administration are therefore to support communities of users who have work to accomplish and have different needs. Systems administrators have to:

- design networks that are logical and efficient
- deploy computer systems so that they can be used for as long as possible and kept up to date
- negotiate with end-users about their needs and keep them informed of what is possible and what is not
- plan and implement security for computer systems
- ensure a good, healthy environment for users
- develop ways of fixing errors and problems
- maintain an account of how systems are operating
- find ways to keep informed and make use of the huge amount of information available.

An outline of a computer system

You may be familiar with a computer system at home or in the wider world. However, it will be useful to summarise briefly what we mean by a computer system. It is an electronic machine made up from a number of devices that can store, retrieve and process data. Stored instructions or programs *control* how the data is to be processed, and electronic circuits *carry out* the processing. The programs can be changed in order to carry out different processing activities.

Take a look at the very simple outline system in Figure 1.1.

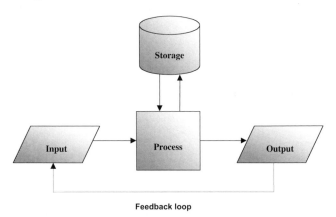

Figure 1.1 *A simple computer system*

Input:
Information or data have to be fed into the system so that it can do something useful. The data that is input may be used as part of a processing operation or it might be the instructions or program that controls the system. Either way the program or data has to be input by keyboard, bar code reader, scanner, etc.

Process:
Data that is input will be processed. That is to say, some kind of operation will be applied to it. If the data is text then it will most likely have to be put into sentences and formatted in a way so that the results are useful. If the data is numbers, we may want them processed by calculating with them or carrying out comparisons of them. The processing is carried out by the collection of hardware that includes memory and a central processing unit. The hardware is controlled by the instructions that form the program. The program says what operations need to be carried out, and collectively it is called 'software'.

Output:
Having processed our data we now want to use it, and so we have to get it out of the system. Much of the output is in printed form, but it may well be output that is sent electronically somewhere else.

Storage:
When we input data to the system we may want to use that data again and again. If the data makes up the computer program, then we do not want to keep inputting it. For that reason storage devices are attached to the system.

Feedback:
Computer systems, like many other systems, need data to be re-input. This may be because the output has to be compared with new input, or else errors have to be corrected. It may be that the system needs new instructions based on the results of processing, in which case it requires our intervention. It is useful to see the system as not simply linear but *cyclical*, as often we need to repeat steps that have already been taken.

An introduction to systems administration

The role of a systems administrator is one that must embrace a wide and thorough understanding of all aspects of computer systems and their operations. The rest of this unit will examine these matters in detail.

To help you understand the role more easily, we want to introduce a person who appears later in a case study about a college. His name is Bevan Hughes and he is in charge of administering a college-wide network. Each week Bevan makes a list of the tasks he has to carry out that week. Figure 1.2 shows an example of a task list for one week. You can see that Bevan has a range of duties to perform and these are summarised below.

- *Maintaining existing systems*
  - supporting new and existing users
  - supporting applications in use
  - supporting hardware in use
  - setting and controlling operating system performance
  - installing new or upgrade software
  - installing new hardware
  - monitoring network and communication systems
  - auditing resource use and exploring performance optimisation
  - troubleshooting and error detection

- *Security*
  - controlling access to all resources, be it data, programs or equipment
  - backup and restoring data
  - securing hardware resources
  - preventing malicious intrusion by external agents, including viruses

- *Planning or preparing changes*
  - providing data used for forecasting technical changes and user requirements
  - analysing technical requirements, researching solutions, investigating designs
  - tendering for services or equipment

- *Upgrading systems*
  - project management
  - acceptance testing
  - maintenance

- *Training technical staff.*

Activities

1 What is the difference between data and information? What kinds of data are there?

2 Define hardware and software, stating clearly the difference.

3 Describe at least five computer systems you have used, saying in each case what input, processing, storage and output is done.

4 Find out what is meant by application software and system software.

5 Imagine yourself (your brain and body) as a computer system. Describe a case of input, processing, storage, output and feedback you have performed in the last 24 hours.

6 Describe all the places where communications might take place in a computer system.

The responsibilities of a systems administrator

Mon	Tues	Wed	Thurs	Fri
Check e-mails and allocate work from repair job cards and requests to technicians. Troubleshoot urgent network problems	Confirm prices for Dell network computer from suppliers, and order new computer	Research best network monitoring software – must be compliant with ISO standards	Installation of new network computer – all day. Configure network software on new machine	Helpdesk training session 9.30–16.30
Interview potential technician	Consult with helpdesk software suppliers on training programme for helpdesk operators	Research network requirements for new media studies software		
Lunch				
Helpdesk software upgrade – go through contract with supplier	Prepare report on infrastructure upgrade and decision on network computer	Instruct technician on installation of new media studies software		
Find out why network computer keeps crashing. Look at network traffic log and talk to network maintenance contractors	Meeting with Head of ILT on current infrastructure upgrade and strategic developments	Check on maintenance work to date and meet with technicians on other site	Restore backup of admin data to new network computer	

Figure 1.2 *Task list*

Activities

1. *Working in small groups, look at Bevan's week and say which part of the systems administrator's job he has to do for each of the activities mentioned. Explain in simple terms what they mean.*

2. *Suggest what activities you do or should perform if you have to administer a computer at home.*

Service you deserve

This case study is taken from an article on network support written by Phil Crewe who is a network administrator. (Network administrators are systems administrators who work on computer networks.) In it, he describes how software applications can be set up or rolled out. He looks at different kinds of approaches to the way applications are used on a network. Read through the case study and try and work out what is being said. Words in italics may be new to you and they are explained in the text. Try and think what problems are being discussed and the solutions to them.

We've been doing a lot of *application roll-outs* this month, and clients and users have asked us a lot of questions about how we approach this kind of problem. While the approach you take will always be based on individual requirements and circumstances, here are some guidelines we use to develop our practice.

When installing applications, the interaction between a *file server* and its *clients* or applications is just one of many elements to be considered, but it's crucial if you're to get the optimal system at the end of it all. Most companies will be primarily concerned with *fat client* applications, such as Office 97 or Office 2000, although many cases also call for *thin client* and *client/server installations* – so I'll look at both.

Historically, when the core *operating system* was *DOS* and *NetWare* powered 95 per cent of networking, installing a *client-site application* that was hosted off the server was relatively simple. Managing it was easy because any changes in the application just needed to be applied to the server version. No application information was held on the client machine itself.

Windows changed all that. There are three basic differences from the old days: modern fat applications are much bigger than their DOS counterparts; parts of the application – DLLs – are only loaded when required; and some of the application invariably has to be installed in the client's Windows system.

The first two issues mean that a much greater strain is placed on the network infrastructure when loading and using these applications across a network. If the file server is used for all users' storage requirements, then this stresses it harder, resulting in demand for additional disk space, more RAM and better processor investment.

On the plus side, however, you usually end up with fewer support problems. Another advantage of server-based applications is that local disk space requirements are reduced from 150MB to around 25MB for Office 97.

What's clear is that you need an alternative to the tangled web of server-hosted applications and one that allows you to manage the process. Here, the development of sophisticated tools, such as *SMS*, has presented many organisations with an alternative to server-based applications, purely for management purposes.

Whichever route you decide to take when installing and managing applications, remember that it's not practical to run office applications over a *WAN link*, because of speed. This means you'll need some kind of server at each local point on the network if you're either going to run applications from the server or use the server as a distribution point.

For the current breed of office suites, running from a server isn't recommended. Instead, plan to install and upgrade from server-based distribution points, but run the application locally from the client machine.

Source: PC Magazine, December 1999

Some definitions

In Figure 1.3 you can see that PCs connected to a network are called 'clients'. They access information stored across the network on the file server. Read the explanation of what various terms mean.

- *Application roll-outs* – the installation or upgrading of software packages that are needed by users. So client applications are the software used by people sitting at individual PCs or workstations connected to a network. The applications might be database, spreadsheet or word-processing packages.

- *File server* – a computer that shares its hard drive and file storage with users connected to it by a network. Users are given access to their own file storage areas and to common areas that they share. The file server manages the interaction between users and file access using a network operating system. The file server may be used to run a file-processing application whereby a request for information on a particular set of records is received and processed. The particular records that are fetched are sent back to the client computer (see below) for further processing – such as to produce a total of goods supplied to a particular customer group over a period of time.

- *Client* – the other half of the client–server partnership. The client requests service from the server. The server carries out the processing request and passes the results back to the client for further processing or as a completed operation.

- *Fat client* – large applications package where most of the program is stored on users' machines and the rest is stored on a file server. When a user runs an application program it will load from the local machine but some parts of the program (DLLs) are stored across the network on the file server.

- *Thin client* – all or most of a software package is stored centrally on the file server. When a user wants to run the program it has to be sent across the network to the local machine, where it is stored in memory and then executed.

- *Operating system and Novell® NetWare* – software that manages the computer system such as file storage, program execution, memory and peripherals. Novell® NetWare is a type of network operating system that manages users' access to a network and the resources available on it.

- *DOS* – acronym used to describe Microsoft's disk operating system (MS-DOS®). This was the operating system used for IBM-compatible personal computers, before newer versions of Microsoft's operating system replaced it.

- *Client-side application* – an application or part of an application that runs on the user's personal computer – sometimes called a workstation on a network.

- *SMS* – Systems management server, a piece of software designed to assist the administrator of a network.

- *WAN link* – computers that are connected over any area greater than a few miles are said to be in a wide-area network. Usually the network will cover a country but, as in the Internet, may be global. Therefore a link to a wide-area network is any computer with software that can access computers remotely using a communications link such as a phone line.

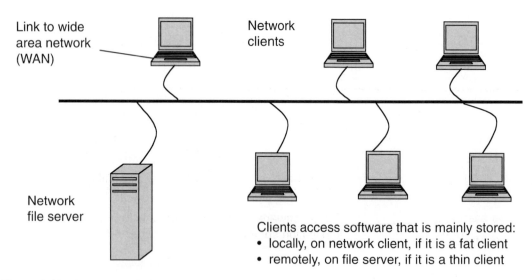

Figure 1.3 *A local area network (LAN): network clients and network file server*

Comparison of fat and thin clients

Thin clients are stored on the network file server. When a user of a PC wants to run this kind of application, the operating system must request that it be sent from the file server. When application software loads across the network, network traffic increases and that may slow down overall network response times. However, if an upgrade is developed for the application, the systems administrator has to carry out changes on only one machine, the central file server.

In contrast, fat clients make more use of their local hard drive to store the program code, so that network traffic is not increased when a user runs the program unless part of it is stored centrally. However, when installing or upgrading software that is stored on client machines, the operation is much more difficult because centralised administration breaks down.

Therefore the main benefit of a thin client is that applications can be upgraded centrally because they are stored on a central server. The main disadvantage is that when a user wants to use a piece of software it has to be sent across the network to a workstation. This increases network load.

The main benefit of a fat client is that the software is loaded locally and so has little impact on network performance. There are two disadvantages:

- Applications that need upgrading will require the system administrator to change the software on all the machines.
- Fat clients still use the network for some of their processing code.

Activity

Read the case study again and then answer these questions:

1. *What aspect of fat-client applications is most likely to lead to increased network traffic?*

2. *What, besides the operation of the software itself, leads to increased network traffic on a client machine?*

3. *Why do fat clients lead to centralised administration breaking down?*

4. *What is meant by a 'DLL'?*

5. *Work out again which list of administrator roles need to be performed for this case study. Make sure you can explain the terms you use. For example, does Phil Crewe have to ensure that system security issues are dealt with?*

In order to facilitate the management of software installation and upgrading, administrators tend to favour the use of server-based application distribution points. These distribution points are likely to be managed by an SMS, or systems management server (see Figure 1.4).

The case study you have just looked at describes one small problem, but it touches on the whole subject of

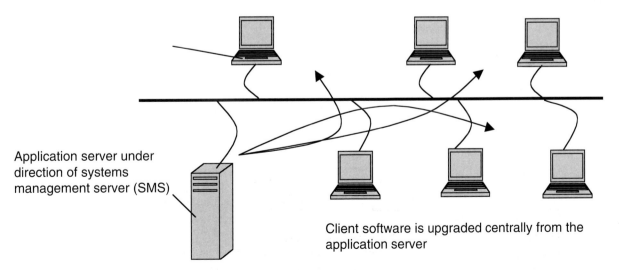

Application server under direction of systems management server (SMS)

Client software is upgraded centrally from the application server

Figure 1.4 *Management of distribution points by SMS*

systems administration. In this one case, references are made to the following:

- *Management* – approaches, installing applications, upgrading applications, optimising systems, testing
- *Hardware* – processor, RAM, file server, disk space, WAN link
- *Software* – OS and client applications (DLLs), systems management tools (systems management server)
- *Overall* – network infrastructure, WAN links, user requirements, client–server architecture.

Activities

1. *Your friend wants to connect her computer to the Internet. Imagine you are her systems administrator. Find out what needs to be done (using the list of administrator's duties) to fulfil her wishes effectively and securely.*

2. *Using a computer on the Internet is similar to a client–server partnership. What are the roles of the client and server in this set-up?*

3. *How might a systems administrator weigh up the benefits and advantages of a particular course of action?*

The purpose of an operating system

The systems administrator role is quite complex and varied, as you have seen. In particular, he or she will need to become an expert at using the *operating system* (OS) that controls their computer system. So just what is an operating system?

The purpose of the OS is to manage the *resources* of a computer system so that it (a) works at its optimum capability, (b) is able to respond flexibly to changing conditions, and (c) is able to make adjustments in a robust, predictable and reliable way.

We have all experienced sufficient computer crashes to know that the last point is both vexing and, it seems, difficult to achieve.

Activity

Keep a record of when computer crashes happen to you. Try to build up a picture of the actions and operations you were doing when crashes occurred. See if you can make your computer crash. Normally teachers don't tell you to do this sort of activity – but for the purpose of investigating IT, it is useful to find the flaws in your system.

For example, crashes sometime occur when using a floppy disk drive. If you swap disks when an application is using a file from one disk, a system error often occurs. Although this should not cause a crash, sometimes it does.

The OS has to achieve another goal as well. It must be able to deliver the resources organised on the computer system in a way that makes the life of the user – operator, programmer and administrator – as easy as possible. It must provide a friendly, accessible *interface* between us and the complexities of the computer system.

So, to summarise, the operating system should:

- manage resources
- hide complexity.

Figure 1.5 shows levels of components in a computer system. At the bottom of the diagram are the actual physical devices – memory, input/output (I/O) ports, processor, various specialist electronics (e.g. sound card), etc. These are the electrical and electronic components – the *hardware*.

Above that are the *micro programs* that directly operate the hardware. These are usually hard-wired into electronic circuits and represent the electronic logic for operating the hardware.

The next layer is where low-level *programs* written in a computer system's own *machine language* sit. The machine language is made up of commands that can be directly executed by the computer's processor without any translation. Device controllers are programs written in machine language that can directly interface with hardware connected to the system. The programs are usually coded into electronic chips and use electronic logic to carry out low-level

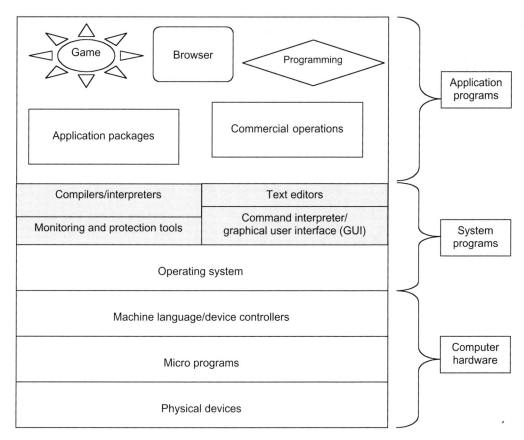

Figure 1.5 *Layers of a system*

operations with the hardware (e.g. reading data from a disk drive).

The OS sits on top of that layer and is the interface between the hardware below and the user programs above.

The layer above the operating system is usually part of the OS package, although it is not strictly part of the OS itself. It comprises software that is oriented towards one of three things:

- the process of creating programs to run on a particular system (compiler/interpreter)
- useful utilities that assist either the user or administrator (disk defragmentation, disk repair, calendar)
- the interface which provides user direct access to the system (GUI/command interpreter).

The final layer is the actual user programs which run on a particular machine.

Managing resources

Let us now look more closely at what we mean by the resources of the computer system. Figure 1.6 shows the architecture of a basic computer system. The main resources shown are the CPU, memory, a backing store where the file system is organised, and input/output (or I/O as it is commonly called).

Central processing unit (CPU)

This is where the code for running a computer system is executed. It can be called either the processor or central processing unit. The CPU operates by fetching instructions from memory, decoding them and then carrying out the operations indicated by the code. The instructions will lie somewhere in the memory address space and a program will execute by having its instructions brought one after the other from memory using a numbered address code.

The instructions executed by the CPU are in binary form – that is, they are made up of zeros and ones. An instruction may vary in size depending on the CPU being used. For example, a typical Intel Pentium CPU uses an instruction length of 32 bits. This means that

The responsibilities of a systems administrator

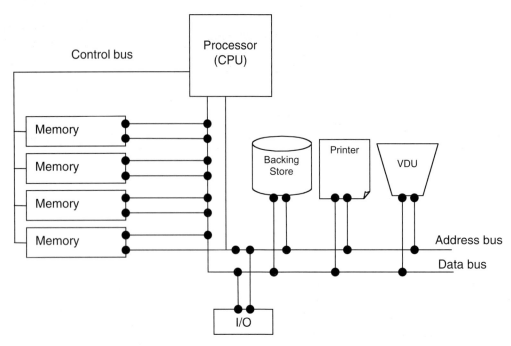

Figure 1.6 *System architecture*

the CPU can have a large range of different instructions because 32 bits gives many different code combinations. Alternatively a 32-bit instruction allows a number of smaller instructions to be coded and then fetched in one memory transfer. That speeds up processing.

The OS ensures that programs are loaded and run correctly and that any changes in the system operations that require other programs to be loaded and run happens smoothly.

Memory

This is usually referred to as *random-access memory* (RAM). It is made from integrated circuit components and is connected to the computer processor by a fast data circuit called a *bus*. Memory locations, where all kinds of data are stored, are numbered sequentially from 0 up to the maximum size of the address space. A single address will allow the processor to fetch a unit of data from one location in memory. A unit of data is made up from several memory switches. Each switch holds a charge that represents a single number, either 1 or 0. When the computer is switched off the memory contents are lost.

Notice also that there is also an address bus. The data bus carries data around the system, while the address bus carries the location of the data to the system.

The OS allocates memory space to programs running or needing to run on a machine. It ensures that allocation to all the programs using memory is efficient and error-free.

Backing store

The file system is usually physically located on a disk drive attached to the bus via a controller unit, which is simply a specialised input/output port. A port is place where data comes into or out of the system, just like a seaport in our world. The OS sends requests to all kinds of backing stores for files to be read, written, opened or closed.

Input/output

The computer system must interface with the rest of the world. Special I/O ports connect the outside world to the internal buses, memory and processor. The OS oversees the free flow of information between the inside and outside of the system. Common devices connected by I/O are the printer and visual display unit (VDU), which provides graphic output.

Activity

What other resources may have to be managed by the operating system? Try to think of three other things that may have to be managed.

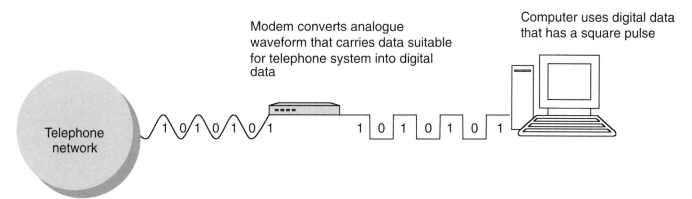

Figure 1.7 *The operation of a modem*

Hiding complexity

The OS is a layer of software that lies between user applications and the machine it manages. Below the operating system are the physical devices and the control languages, which directly operate them (see Figure 1.5). The machine language, sometimes called low-level or *assembly language*, allows systems programmers to write programs to carry out functions around the system. These programs are called 'low-level' because they deal with the physical logic of the integrated circuits that make up the computer system.

In the example shown in Figure 1.7, a low-level program is used to control the operation of a modem. (A modem is a device that allows digital data from a computer to travel up or down a telephone wire that carries analogue data.) The operating system oversees the whole procedure. This example is complex because it illustrates how the OS is hiding the complexity! You don't need to follow it all to see that as a user you shouldn't have to know about the detail.

When a telephone rings a modem, the modem has to negotiate with the rest of the computer system to use resources. The following simplified steps gives you an idea of how devices interact and how the OS manages them.

- A program takes control of the modem. For example, the computer system runs a communications program.
- An incoming telephone call causes the modem to respond and set up a communications channel with the remote caller. The modem stores low-level control routines on an onboard processor to do these operations.
- The modem sends a signal, called an *interrupt,* via a control circuit to the processor to indicate that it wants to carry out data input.

- The OS responds by stopping its current processing jobs and stores the state of the current program so it can be restarted later.
- The OS then calls the communications program which will manage the transfer of data from the modem to the computer's memory.
- When data has been transferred, the modem lets the communication process know that it has finished.
- Control is picked up by the operating system, which restarts the jobs it has halted.

This can be represented as in Figure 1.8.

In this example it is an external signal that triggers a system call – that is, a signal to the operating system to deal with an event that involves some action being taken. Part of the computer's memory space is set aside for the operating system's main program – called the *kernel*. The kernel operates in a protected part of memory and is the central control program. It determines where signals come from, and therefore how to respond.

In this case it is alerted to a call from an interface (serial), and tied to that is a corresponding communications process that handles operations from that interface. The communications program may also use a special *device driver,* which is a program written in a low-level language that deals with operations between hardware components. In this case a program that is specially written for the particular modem is being used.

Let us recap at this point:

- The OS is software designed to hide the physical complexities of hardware from the user.
- To engage the OS for particular events occurring inside the computer, a system of signals or interrupts triggers it to act.

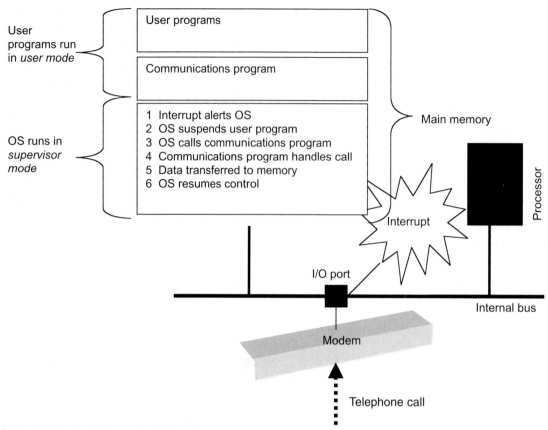

Figure 1.8 *How the OS manages a telephone call*

- Signals may be generated by external or internal *events*.
- The signals or interrupts initiate the OS to run software procedures that deal with various interrupt requests. In this case the event is a call for an input/output operation. Interrupts from software are called *system calls*.

Figure 1.9 shows system information for a typical PC. The system has a list of devices each of which has an 'interrupt request' (IRQ) number. Taking our previous example, you can see that the modem would signal an

interrupt number 10, and the OS would know which program to use to handle that request.

You might still be thinking: 'How does the modem example show the OS hiding complexity?' The answer is that the person using the communications program (such as fax software) need have *no knowledge* of how the computer system will actually handle the receipt of an incoming file. Similarly, the programmer who writes the communications software need not know the complexities of how the modem will work. Instead, he or she writes a code which deals with certain logical operations – such as opening a channel for input, writing data for output, etc. – and the OS passes this information on to lower-level routines.

One other point to be aware of is that software programs or processes may themselves generate interrupts. For example, if a program requests a file, that generates a call to the OS to find and open the file for processing by the program.

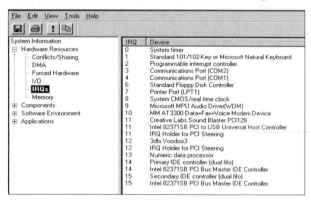

Figure 1.9 *Interrupts used on a particular PC*

1. *There are plenty of new terms you need to have an idea about. Working with another person, decide what the following terms mean: devices, communications channel, onboard processor, software routine.*

2. *You are buying a sandwich in a shop when your mobile phone rings (if you don't have a mobile phone then imagine what you would do). Draw a diagram showing the stages of the process from when you request a sandwich through to finishing your purchase. You are interested in the signals (interrupts) that you receive and send out, and the effects of those signals and how you or others deal with them.*

3. *Take one example from a computer system you use and describe how the system manages a resource you use (e.g. find or open a file). How user-friendly are the messages to you about what you are doing? How might the activity be made easier for you?*

Data representation

So far we have looked at data and processing. In this section we want to examine data and how a computer system represents it. Refer back to your discussion on the difference between data and information to recall the different kinds of data.

Imagine that a computer's memory is made up of consecutive storage locations where many different types of data need to be stored. One problem is that the way in which the data is stored uses one thing – a small electric charge that is either there or not. This is the way semiconductor transistor memory works, and it is usual to say that if a charge is present in a single memory switch (or cell) then it is ON or equal to 1; if a charge is not present then the cell is OFF or equal to 0. Using this series of on/off switches, all data has to be represented.

In the location N in Figure 1.10 there are 16 single cells that may represent a 1 or 0. These are *binary digits*, also called *bits* (a bit is a single digit, either 1 or 0). But what do these digits represent? That is the subject of this section.

The two most basic types of data representation are text and numbers. Of these there are sub-categories and different versions (see Figure 1.11).

Text	26 letters, numbers and punctuation	A–Z, a–z, 0–9, !<'{=# etc.
Extended text	As above but with special graphic characters	¶ ☻ ♪ Ữ
Symbols	❶⑥✲☎☎✌	Special graphical characters only
Different alphabets	The Chinese alphabet has 3000+ symbols	
Whole numbers	0, 1, 2, 2342870	Called integers
Decimal numbers	0.12, 56.45, 123.9999	Fixed or floating point
Negative or positive numbers	+12, −150, −12.34	Called signed numbers

Figure 1.11 Data types

Memory addresses — Memory bank of cells 16 spaces wide

First address	0															
	1															
	2															
	N	0	1	0	1	1	0	1	0	1	0	0	0	0	1	0	0
	N+1															
Last address															

Figure 1.10 The principle of storing data

Basic number representation

In a *binary* system only two digits can be used – as the name implies. Each bit can represent only two states, and so to be able to count, for example, we have to use more and more bits. Because the counting system is using two numbers, it is said to be a 'base-2 number system'. Although binary numbers can get a bit complicated, the purpose of this section is to introduce you to ideas on how they are used in computers. For a full account you will need to go to a specific computer science book.

Binary representation			Decimal count
Three bits	Two bits	One bit	
000	00	0	**0**
001	01	1	**1**
010	10		**2**
011	11		**3**
100			**4**
101			**5**
110			**6**
111			**7**

Figure 1.12 *Using bits to represent numbers*

In the table in Figure 1.12, you can see that a single bit might be 0 or 1, and so a single bit allows us to count up to decimal one. If we want to count higher than one we need another bit with which we are able to count another two numbers (decimal two and three).

Each binary bit that is added doubles the amount of decimal numbers that can be represented. An easy way of working out how much a binary number represents in decimal is to put the binary digits under column headings which show their value doubling:

128	**64**	32	**16**	8	4	**2**	1
0	1	0	1	0	0	1	0

In this example, you add together the column heading where each binary digit is 1:

$$64 + 16 + 2 = 82.$$

Activity

Convert the following three numbers to decimal:

11111111   10101110   00110011

and these three to binary:

189   256   99.

Each column allows us to double the size of the decimal number that can be stored. This can be written down as follows: $2 * 2 * 2 * 2 * 2 * 2 * 2 * 2$, so for eight columns the total number that can be stored is 256. However, because the first digit stores only one and not two, we have to subtract one from the final total. So the largest eight-bit binary number is $256-1 = 255$. Another way of representing this is to say that eight bits can store 2^8 (8 being the number of 2s multiplied by each other) different numbers.

Activity

Work out the highest number that can be stored by the following binary numbers:

- *12-bit number*
- 2^{16}
- 2^{32}

You can use this method to work out how many memory addresses or instructions a computer has to play with. A 32-bit processor means that it is capable of having 2^{32} different instructions, or a 64-bit memory space means there can be 2^{64} different storage locations. Figure 1.13 shows a table of common computer data storage sizes.

Storage size	Amount	Abbreviation	Notes on amounts
1 bit	1 or 0	1 b	
1 byte	8 bits	1 B	
1 kilobyte	1000 bytes	1 KB	It actually means 2^{10} which is equal to 1024 bytes, but as a shortcut we refer to the metric kilo which means 1000
1 megabyte	1 million bytes	1 MB	1000 * 1000 bytes
1 gigabyte	1 billion bytes	1 GB	1000 million bytes
1 terabyte	1 trillion bytes	1 TB	1 million million bytes
1 exabyte	1 quintillion bytes	1 EB	1 billion billion bytes

Figure 1.13 *Data storage sizes*

So far we have looked only at whole numbers, or integer numbers as mathematicians call them. How can positive and negative integer numbers be represented? The simplest way is to use what is called the *signed method*. This uses the first digit in front of a number to indicate whether it is plus or minus. A 1 indicates a minus number, and a 0 indicates a positive number. An example is 10000011, which represents a minus three.

Activity

Work out what the following binary numbers represent as signed integers:

- *0101101010000100*

- *1110000101100001.*

The architecture of the computer's *arithmetic logic unit* is able to carry out calculations using binary arithmetic. The more bits that can be handled, then the larger the numbers that can be processed. The fastest operation that can be performed is adding, because the logic circuit to do this can be very easily built using electronic switches – called gates.

Representing decimal numbers

In the decimal number system, fractions are represented by using a point to separate the whole and fractional parts. For example, the decimal number 123.45 can be depicted thus:

100	10	1	.	$\frac{1}{10}$	$\frac{1}{100}$
1	2	3	.	4	5

The whole number part, 123, represents 1 unit of 100, 2 units of 10 and the digit 3. The fractional part represents $\frac{4}{10}$ and $\frac{5}{100}$. Every place to the left of the decimal is multiplied by 10 while every place to the right is divided by 10.

The binary number system is similar in principle. Every number to the left of the point is multiplied by 2 while every number to the right is divided by 2. For example, the binary number 011001.1100 can be depicted as:

32	16	8	4	2	1	.	$\frac{1}{2}$	$\frac{1}{4}$	$\frac{1}{8}$	$\frac{1}{16}$
0	1	1	0	0	1	.	1	1	0	0

This binary number is equivalent to the decimal number $16 + 8 + 1 + \frac{1}{2} + \frac{1}{4} = 25\frac{3}{4}$.

It is a lot easier to use fractions if you use a table like that shown in Figure 1.14.

Binary fraction	Fraction	Decimal fraction
0.1	–	0.5
0.01	–	0.25
0.001	$\frac{1}{8}$	0.125
0.0001	$\frac{1}{16}$	0.0625
0.00001	$\frac{1}{32}$	0.03125
0.000001	?	?

Figure 1.14 *Some useful conversions*

Activity

Using Figure 1.14, convert the following binary fractions to decimal fractions:

- *01101.001*

- *00111010011.00110*

- *00111010110.011101.*

Note that it is a lot harder to store accurate decimal numbers in binary form. For example, consider a builder who is measuring a wall in metric units. The builder takes a measurement of 2 metres and 65 centimetres, or 2.65 metres. If we convert this to binary form using two places after the point, we can store only 01, 10 or 11. That is, we can store only 0.25 (.01) or 0.5 (.10) or 0.75 (.11) of a metre. We can't store 0.65. We can of course increase the accuracy by having more digits after the binary point, but still most decimal numbers cannot be *exactly* represented.

Text representation

All the letters of the alphabet as well as text characters have to be represented in binary. The best-known character set is *ASCII*, and a sample is presented in Figure 1.15. The letters stand for American Standard Code for Information Interchange. The coding scheme uses seven or eight bits assigned to up to 256 characters, including letters, numbers, punctuation marks, control characters, and other symbols. ASCII was developed in 1968 to standardise data transmission among different hardware platforms and software systems, and it is built into most

Decimal	Hexa-decimal	Octal	Character	Description
0	00	000	NUL	null
1	01	001	SOH	start of heading
2	02	002	STX	start of text
3	03	003	ETX	end of text
4	04	004	EOT	end of transmission
5	05	005	ENQ	enquiry
6	06	006	ACK	acknowledge
7	07	007	BEL	bell
......	....	....	......	....
48	30	060	0	digit zero
49	31	061	1	digit one
56	38	070	8	digit eight
57	39	071	9	digit nine
58	3A	072	:	colon
59	3B	073	;	semi-colon
60	3C	074	<	left angle bracket
61	3D	075	=	equal-to
62	3E	076	>	right angle bracket
63	3F	077	?	question mark
64	40	100	@	at sign
65	41	101	A	uppercase A
66	42	102	B	uppercase B
67	43	103	C	uppercase C
68	44	104	D	uppercase D
69	45	105	E	uppercase E

ASCII control characters (rows 0–7)

Figure 1.15 *Sample of ASCII control codes, some punctuation, numbers and characters*

minicomputers and all PCs. The 8-bit extended ASCII includes special graphic characters that you saw before in Figure 1.11.

Owing to the fact that an 8-bit character set cannot represent all alphabets, new character codes have been introduced. The 16-bit UNICODE, and Double Byte Character Set (DBCS) which is used in Asia–Pacific countries, are designed to extend the range of characters that can be represented and allow for standardisation between systems.

Activity

Find out which of the two standards, UNICODE or DBCS, is the most widely used.

Data representation is a fundamental part of computer systems since the computer system has only one way to store data and therefore must know what kind of data is stored in its memory. Various systems have been devised to represent different numbers and characters. Calculations on numbers will be dependent on the accuracy of the representation and this will depend on the number of bits available to store and process numbers.

Conclusion

In this chapter you have been introduced to the role of the systems administrator and some of the basics of a computer system. In particular you looked at:

- the overall goal of systems administration
- the basic processing cycle of a computer system
- the role of the systems administrator
- an introduction to a systems administrator's work through a case study
- the purpose of the operating system, especially to manage resources and hide complexity
- the representation of data in computer systems.

CHAPTER 2

Evaluation of an ICT solution

This chapter looks at how a user can decide what model of computer system is right for their needs. It identifies an application requirement and shows how a system chosen for this can be evaluated to see whether it meets the requirement.

In particular, this chapter covers:

- analysing user requirements

- evaluating systems

- selecting vendors

- determining which OS to use.

The chapter covers the following Learning Outcome in the specification:

L.O. 1.2   Demonstrate knowledge of the way in which a developed ICT system that provides a specific service should be evaluated

It covers the following Technical Knowledge topic:

T1.1.2   The types of operating system

Introducing 'Wessex County Hospital'

'Wessex County Hospital' is a large teaching hospital situated in the south-west of England. It provides a range of general surgery and outpatient services. The use of ICT is a primary concern in an effort to modernise the hospital. Peter Harris, the Head of Administration, is very aware that ICT will play an ever-greater role in patient care and has, as one of his strategic aims, the goal of increasing the application of ICT in the hospital. One area where new initiatives are being developed is the research faculty.

The research faculty of the hospital is equipped with one rather old standalone computer. This is used primarily for logging experimental data and printing hard copies. There are plans to eventually link the faculty to the hospital network, but with the planned budget there is enough finance to purchase only one

new standalone. However, Peter Harris is very keen for the research faculty to evaluate systems that help doctors to diagnose patients. This fits in with a major review of the hospital services in response to NHS initiatives to provide faster and more effective treatment for patients.

To this end, the hospital has been accepted as a partner to test a new 'expert system' that has been designed to predict the likelihood of a patient having a heart attack. Dr Lars Edenbrandt of the University Hospital in Lund, Sweden, carried out the main research. His research team has developed an expert system based on a revolutionary way of building up information profiles using artificial neural networks.

The expert system has been provided with thousands of electrocardiogram (ECG) readings – equivalent to one or more than one cardiologist could read throughout his or her professional career – along with actual patient histories that match the ECG tests. In this way, the computer emulates the way an expert might examine and analyse an ECG. In testing the system, researchers had it evaluate 1120 ECG results from patients who had heart attacks and almost 10,452 normal ECG results. Scientists found that the computer was 10 per cent more accurate at identifying heart attacks, than their most experienced cardiologist. The next requirement is to test the system across different regional and national borders to see whether similar results can be achieved.

Muriel Orgreave works in the research faculty and has overall charge of its hardware requirements. She also carries out systems administration duties. Muriel has been asked to investigate the system specification for a standalone PC capable of being used to run Dr Edenbrandt 's system (called ECGspect). She has been provided with a minimum system specification from Dr Edenbrandt's team (see Figure 2.1).

- Fast processor (central processing unit)
- At least 64MB of random-access memory (RAM)
- Large hard drive
- VGA colour monitor (VDU)
- CD-RW drive or DVD drive capable of reading compact disks
- Backup device or CD-RW
- Scanner or form reader
- Printer
- Mouse and keyboard

Figure 2.1 *Minimum system specification required for the ECGspert system*

• *Fast processor*	Any intensive processing operation will benefit from a fast processor. Word-processing is not highly intensive, but graphics and number-crunching are. Also, if the system is going to be used to run several programs at the same time, then speed will affect this.
• *Motherboard*	One that has a well-specified chipset will work at optimum speed with the components that are being used.
• *At least 64MB of (RAM)*	Memory has an important impact on performance because programs and data are stored there during processing. If data or programs cannot be held in immediate access store, then when they are required data and code not currently being used have to be moved to a backing store in order to make room for new data and program code. This slows down operations. Muriel will need to make sure she gets a system that supports fast memory modules that are compatible with the motherboard.
• *Large hard drive*	The data used by ECGspert come from thousands of patient records and ECG readings. These files are large. Besides their size, it may be necessary to think in terms of how fast a particular backing drive system can work in transferring them from drive to RAM.
• *VGA colour monitor*	ECGspert, as with most software applications, will use graphical output at some point; e.g. for graphs and colour-coding as well as for the graphical user interface. It is not being used for intensive graphical operations, but having a good amount of onboard video RAM may still affect overall performance.
• *Scanner or form reader*	ECGspert needs to have hundreds of ECG readings and patient medical histories input. The Swedish team have decided that, as they are collecting patient histories from a number of different sites, a form reader or scanner is suitable. The completed forms are then input by using optical mark recognition. ECG recordings are captured direct from ECG machines and saved as digital files.
• *CD drive or DVD drive capable of reading CDs*	Most software is distributed on CD, and ECGspert is no exception.
• *Backup device or CD system that allows CDs to be created*	Backup can be carried out either using a tape drive or a writable CD-ROM drive. The benefit of using a CD-RW drive is that CDs can be produced which can be read on other computers with a compatible CD reader.
• *Modem*	The modem allows the computer to transmit data along a phone line. It is therefore necessary for connecting to the Internet or e-mail system.
• *Printer*	For hard output.

Figure 2.2 *Hardware requirements*

Muriel Orgreave is well aware of the technical issues that will influence her choice of computer for the department. However, she also has to consider a range of other factors when making a selection. She starts with the requirements that have been sent by the Swedish research team, and then addresses the other factors.

Step 1: Analysing the requirements

The specification

Muriel already knows some of the characteristics of the system she needs, having been given a minimum specification for the ECGspert software. However, she is going to buy a machine that will be an asset for all the work of the research department. She therefore needs to list all possible uses that she can envisage. Figures 2.2 and 2.3 show her lists for hardware and software, respectively.

Making the choice of computer

Muriel needs a computer capable of running the programs the faculty will be using, so that will guide her choices. Most popular applications today have versions that run on *either* a PC using Microsoft®

Windows or on a Macintosh® computer. There are also versions available for other operating systems such as Unix® or Linux®. Most choices still depend on what has traditionally been used in an organisation, and on what technical skills exist to support and maintain its computers. Usually there has to be a strong cost-benefit case for a company to change from a system where experience, software and usability are well understood to a new system that comes out better in a straight technological comparison.

There are also portable computers, which might be an important factor. However, portable computers are currently more expensive than desktops having the same specification.

Deciding on how much needs to be spent depends mainly on the required performance and system components. However, an interesting comparison of costs shows that it is not always best to buy the very latest processor based on speed performance. For example, Figure 2.4 shows a snapshot of Intel® Pentium III prices taken in the year 2000. The slower clock speeds are now coming to the end of their commercial life – that is to say, they are not being sold in large numbers in new machines, although they are still being used for much cheaper machines and for upgrades.

•	*ECGspert*	Expert-system software works by processing 'facts' according to a rule-based processing system. This involves comparing values, and branching to different processing paths depending on the outcome. It might be that this kind of processing will go down many levels of detail as profiles are constructed. A fast processor will move through this processing complexity quicker.
•	*Data logging*	Existing data-logging software should be able to run on the new machine and support any sensor interfaces being used. Muriel also needs to ask: 'Will existing experiments using monitoring equipment need to run concurrently?'
•	*E-mail and Internet*	It makes sense for the research faculty to connect to the Internet via a dial-up connection. In this way data and messages can be shared with the Swedish research team. Muriel will probably use a standard browser but may wish to use an e-mail program that is already used in the hospital. If not, she will probably want an e-mail program capable of being used by a number of users.
•	*Statistics*	The research team already uses software statistical analyses. Again, it may be necessary to check compatibility.
•	*Office applications*	Muriel wants to upgrade the faculty's existing office applications. She will need to check the system specifications for this.
•	*System software and utilities*	Besides an operating system, Muriel needs to have software for backing up files, antivirus software, and drivers for the various hardware she will be using.

Figure 2.3 Software requirements

	Processor clock speed in MHz	System bus speed in MHz	Price in dollars	Value rating (MHz per dollar)
1.	667	133	193	3.5
2.	700	100	214	3.3
3.	733	133	219	3.3
4.	750	100	262	2.9
5.	800	100	294	2.7
6.	850	100	455	1.9
7.	866	133	465	1.9
8.	933	133	669	1.4
9.	1000	133	990	1.0

Figure 2.4 *Pentium characteristics in 2000*

(The processor clock speed determines how quickly instructions can be executed, and the system bus speed determines how quickly transfer occurs between memory and the processor. These are covered in detail in the next chapter.)

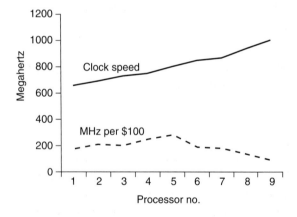

Figure 2.5 *Processor speed and value-for-money*

The figures in the last column of Figure 2.4 are obtained by dividing the processor clock speed by the price, which gives a performance ratio of clock cycles for every dollar spent. When these figures are plotted on a line graph (Figure 2.5), you can see that the best performance/price ratio is obtained just before the steep rise for processor 8. The performance obtained from an 866MHz processor would not be much less than from a 1GHz processor, although the price difference is substantial. For a company buying

hundreds of new computers, this performance/price ratio will be very significant.

Other factors to consider are:

- expandability or upgradeability
- reliability
- warranty and service
- ergonomics.

Step 2: Evaluating the system

Basics

Evaluating the system involves looking at how the components the system uses meet the needs of the user – in this case Muriel's requirements. This is where a good knowledge of how a computer's sub-systems work will guide choices. Muriel may want to research different components to make sure she has an up-to-date knowledge of component performance. The main components are, of course, the processor and motherboard, the display, the memory (RAM), the hard disk space, communications hardware and printer.

> **Activity**
>
> *Study the box 'Examples of performance choices'.*
>
> *Which of these general categories have influenced the choice of hardware you have used?*

Muriel has also to check and see what the evaluation issues are for particular operating systems, and whether a machine has sufficient resources to operate the OS effectively. She may also check a 'hardware compatibility list' provided by the software designers. As an example, the *minimum* requirements shown in Figure 2.6 are recommended for Windows® 2000 Professional (standalone or network client) and Windows 2000 Server (e.g. provides file or print services on a network).

Examples of performance choices

Have a look at the ways in which various uses affect system evaluations.

- *A gaming system.* Because of the calculations required to redraw the video frames, CPU and video performance are the most important. Memory is important, but because separate video RAM provides the essential storage space it is not the most important consideration. Storage performance is a secondary matter, as most of the graphics is determined by calculations.
- *A graphics workstation.* Graphics designers build up complex images using layers, and graphics applications are multipart, so memory is important. Then, video, CPU and hard disk storage performance are the next most important factors.
- *Network file servers.* These machines need to have good memory capacity because they are keeping track of many user processes and file operations. They also need to have large and fast hard drives for capacity and transfer speed. Network reliability requires that systems have redundancy built in, and this means several hard drives performing the same read and write operations. A good interface such as SCSI is important (covered in the next chapter). CPU performance is not such an important issue. Video performance is irrelevant for servers.
- *Internet use.* Essentially this depends on the connection speed. This is affected by the modem speed if comparing a 28.8Kbps modem against a 56Kbps one, but is much more influenced by the connection type available (e.g. ISDN, ADSL).
- *Multimedia (audio and video).* The most important performance considerations are system memory, CPU speed and storage. If multimedia includes the preparation of videos, then the video card is important. Audio performance depends mostly on having a good-quality CD or DVD drive in the system, and decent speakers.
- *General home or office use.* No component has to be specified to the highest performance, although the hard disk is the slowest component that directly affects overall performance.

Resource	Windows® 2000 Professional	Windows® 2000 Server
CPU	Pentium 133 MHz or equivalent compatible processor	
	Up to two processors	Up to four processors
Memory	64MB	256MB
Hard disk	2GB with 1GB free space	2GB with 1GB free
Display	VGA	VGA
CD-ROM	12x speed	12x speed
Network adaptor card	Any compatible card	

Figure 2.6 *Minimum requirements for two OS*

Activity

Find out whether an operating system you use has a hardware compatibility list accessible through the Internet. If so, are the components you use (or might like to add) on that list?

Methods of evaluation

When evaluating an ICT system there need to be criteria against which the system will be judged. It is fairly self-evident that an organisation will want to know whether changes will improve their current or proposed system. The criteria will form part of a requirements definition document, where the various customer requirements are set out. The requirements definition is like a 'wish list', in that the customer describes what they want the system to do.

So how can a system be evaluated? There are essentially three different approaches. The methods are not mutually exclusive, and the choice will depend a great deal on the experience and values held by the people carrying out the evaluation.

Metrics or measurements

These are numerical data gathered from existing systems, usually in the form of *baselines* that establish the 'normal' operating load for a system depending on factors such as time and demand. These help to ensure that any proposed changes will show advantages over existing operating conditions, and give suppliers parameters against which they must show justifiable evidence for their own claims. See Figure 2.7 for an example.

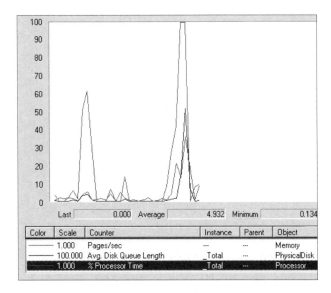

Figure 2.7 *Example of the measurement of computer activity*

Simulations, test benches or benchmarks

These are undertaken on test rigs in a laboratory or workshop. A system is built from components that are under investigation. Factors such as communication links and network conditions, as well as the performance of software, are simulated to mimic the real system. Measurements are taken of how well an application performs under various conditions. These form benchmarks against which other system configurations can be compared.

Case studies and user surveys

Existing systems that use particular technologies are investigated for performance, and users can be asked

to rate specific aspects of systems on a scale. Competing suppliers might be evaluated against various categories and given a score on how their system performs against those categories. The various scores can be compared and an organisation can see where particular strengths and weaknesses lie for different proposals. Industry analysts exist to give independent information on products, and newsgroups (on the Internet) are also used extensively to discuss the pros and cons of technologies.

Activities

1. *You want to buy a new game for your computer and you want to know whether it will run effectively. What numerical information might you use to evaluate your system with the proposed software?*

2. *Investigate the word 'benchmark' and present a discussion of your findings of its uses in ICT.*

3. *Try to find an example of a case study that examines the effectiveness of certain ICT. As well as understanding the case study you also need to know who the authors of the case study are and whether their information is reliable, valid and independent.*

Hardware evaluation issues

- *Performance*
  - Speed, capacity and throughput of hardware?

- *Cost*
  - Buy or leasing costs?
  - Operational costs?
  - Maintenance costs?

- *Reliability*
  - Risk of failure (mean time between failure)?
  - Ease of maintenance?
  - Error or diagnostic tools?

- *Compatibility*
  - Meets open-platform standards (other manufacturers)?
  - Compatible with existing hardware and software?

– Likely to stay compatible (future-proofing)?

- *Scalability*
  - Can be expanded with 'add-ons' if current needs change?
  - Has an upgrade path?
  - A flexible solution for wide range of processing needs?

- *Technology*
  - Tried and tested?
  - At what point in the product life cycle is it?
  - Is it obsolete?

- *Ergonomics*
  - Easy to use?
  - Engineered with human–computer interface in mind?
  - Is it safe?

- *Connectivity*
  - Designed to function on local or wide-area networks?
  - Supports a range of protocols?
  - Easy to connect with standard devices?

- *Software*
  - System software available that best integrates this device?
  - What application software has been tested with it?

- *Support*
  - Does the vendor provide and will continue to provide hardware support?

Software evaluation issues

- *Efficiency*
  - How much memory does it use?
  - How much disk space does it require?
  - Is it compatible with the advanced features of hardware and operating systems?

- *Flexibility*
  - Works with a variety of user loads?
  - Will continue to function in a changing hardware environment?

- *Security*
  - Provides control procedures for errors, malfunction and improper use?

- *Connectivity*
  - Is it network enabled so it can easily access networks on its own, or by working with network browsers or other network software?

- *Language*
  - Software can be tailored to a user's needs?
  - Uses industry standards that allow programmers to modify it easily?

- *Documentation*
  - Is the software well-documented?
  - Does it include full user instructions?

- *Hardware*
  - Do existing systems work effectively with it, or do modifications need to be made?

Activities

1. *In a small group, suggest a hardware component you would like to be able to use in your normal computer classroom, and evaluate its suitability using the hardware evaluation list.*

2. *You need to extend the software issues to include criteria present on the hardware evaluation list. Look at the categories that might also be used for software, and write bullet points on what they are for. Use this list to evaluate a piece of software you would like to purchase.*

System issues other than performance

The most important issues that are not based on system performance are quality, industry standards, expandability/upgradeability, ergonomics and reliability.

Quality

This is an issue to do, of course, with whether components that are being bundled together into a PC are from a branded source that has evidence to support claims concerning quality. Perhaps the most important quality is whether components are built to the highest specification – and the 'mean time between failure' ranks amongst the highest. Ever since the IBM

PC was 'cloned' and a plethora of manufacturers started making all the various electronics that go into computers, there has been a tension between the original equipment manufacturers (OEMs) and other sources. OEM components have usually been built to complement a specific design and are tested within it. Non-OEM components may well work perfectly satisfactorily, but it may not be known whether their performance is as good.

Industry standards

In some ways this follows from the issue of quality. Most parts of a computer system are now built according to recognised industry standards that are documented and agreed by manufacturers. This ensures that a standard will be well supported and not liable to erratic changes that leave consumers and manufacturers uncertain whether their machines will work.

Having a standard means that designers know they are working within parameters that are well-documented and understood. They can create new devices with an expectation that they will work reliably and predictably within the whole system. Proprietary designs *may* work well, but they may try to do something in a way that means the rest of the system does not work. Proprietary designs also lead to users becoming tied into a particular company, which may use this situation to reap unfair advantages.

Expandability and upgradeability

After purchasing a machine, a user may wish to make enhancements in a year or two as developments occur or as their needs mature. They may simply want to add more memory as their needs grow or as part of their budgeting strategy. This is why it is important to try to specify machines that will allow growth and support changes. For example, a user may not have any USB (universal serial bus) devices at the moment, but in a year or two the market may have become dominated by this standard. In order to take advantage of it, new machines bought now should have this capability.

Ergonomics

This is part of the human–machine interface. A computer may be used intensively by one person or require a range of personnel to use it. It should be designed to be usable over extensive periods without being detrimental to health (mental or physical), and should be flexible and transparent in application so that different people using it are not disadvantaged by bizarre complexities or quirks.

Reliability

Computer systems are often installed and then turned on and remain switched on for a long time. One of the main considerations is protecting the investment an organisation makes and ensuring that maximum work throughput can be maintained for long periods. Loss of data is one of the greatest risks to a user, and so ensuring reliability is one way of protecting against this.

Activity

Identify computer-industry standards organisations. Then choose one and give a rundown of what it does.

Step 3: Selecting vendors/suppliers

Vendors can provide a valuable service in orienting a potential customer towards the current 'best practice' and industry standards that are around. A vendor should be able to give an accurate picture of state-of-the-art technology. The vendor's reputation depends on giving good service, competitive prices and good backup provision.

However, in a market where demand outstrips supply, vendors may not worry so much about keeping customers satisfied. If a transaction goes wrong the vendor can simply move on to the next deal and make little effort to satisfy customers who have already paid.

Activities

1. *From the vendor's viewpoint, what are the advantages and disadvantages of providing a full customer-care package?*

2. *If you decide to buy a fairly expensive product like a mobile phone or music player, what criteria do you use and where do you find out about them?*

Vendor evaluation issues

- *Performance*
  - Performs according to the standards it sets?
  - What quality assurance provided?

- *System development*
  - Use own systems analysis and programming consultants?
  - Does vendor contract out?

- *Maintenance*
  - What is provided for maintenance?
  - Is the service agreement competitive?

- *Conversion*
  - What systems development, programming and hardware installation services will be provided during the conversion period?

- *Training*
  - Provides comprehensive training of personnel?
  - What is its quality and cost?

- *Backup*
  - Facilities provided for backup?
  - Services provided for emergency and disaster recovery?

- *Accessibility*
  - Service provided for telephone support?
  - An up-to-date electronic information resource provided?
  - How long to respond to e-mail queries?

- *Business reputation*
  - Vendor has good market position?
  - What is its reputation?

- *Hardware*
  - Has a good knowledge of the hardware choices available?
  - Tied into specific suppliers?

- *Software*
  - Has a good knowledge of the software choices available?
  - Tied into specific suppliers?

Activity

Carry out research for a machine that would meet the requirements of the Wessex County Hospital research faculty you read about earlier. You should list the various components that are required and then find out what components might meet the requirements. Your research should identify the choices you have made and why you have made those choices. You are required to choose a system that meets the system requirements but should give value for money. (Don't just pick the best specification system you can find, as that will be very expensive – you are trying to balance performance against value.)

Remember to consider the other non-performance factors that have been discussed.

Step 4: Determining which OS to use

Choosing an operating system depends on a number of factors. Quite often it will depend on the knowledge base, professional experience and brand loyalty vendors or system managers have. However, there are still operational factors to consider when choosing an operating system.

Figure 2.8 is a simplified decision chart for selecting a personal-computer OS based on an understanding of the architecture on which it will run and the role it might play in an organisation's computing infrastructure. It is simplified because, as with all technology, there are overlaps owing to historical or market-oriented reasons. For example, an architecture might mimic or emulate a CISC machine in order that it can work in the PC world although its underlying architecture is actually RISC. It is also simplified because the architecture of PCs is more complex than whether it is RISC or CISC. The choice will also depend on comparing like with like – for example the commonly acceptable factors for comparing a mid-range processor with another.

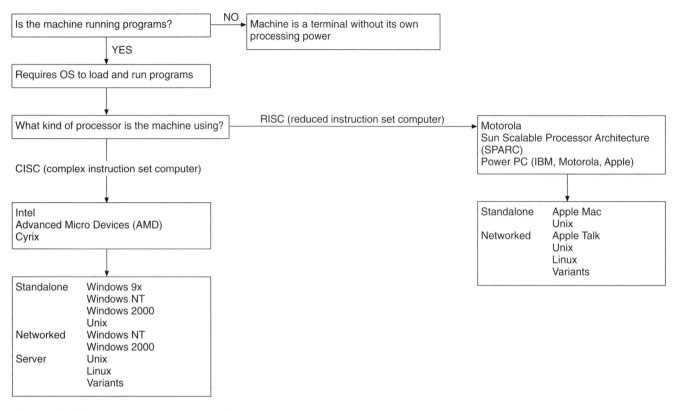

Figure 2.8 *Decision chart for selecting a computer/OS*

The first decision box isolates machines that are not going to be used for processing, such as terminals attached to a mainframe system. The next decision box determines the kind of OS based on the architecture of the machine. Essentially the Apple® Macintosh® world uses a different type of processor from Microsoft® Windows® and hence there is a fundamental split between them. Unix® and Linux® are 'open platform' operating systems, which means they are designed to run on a wide variety of computer systems with different hardware standards without problems. The software is produced so that it will run on different platforms.

Finally, there are listed two broad operational differences: the standalone or client networked machine, and the machine which will provide resources to others by providing file or print services, for example. Machines that are providing a network service require higher specification because they need to process network requests at a fast response rate.

There are other criteria for selecting an OS once it has been established that it is compatible with the hardware platform on which it will operate.

- Does it have a good user interface?
- Does it have good supporting documentation, online help and customer support?
- What levels of security does it provide?
- What peripherals will it support, and is it easy to add new hardware?
- What systems will it connect with?
- Does it support an efficient file system?
- What resources does it require (e.g. memory, expansion cards, drive space)?
- Is it easy to configure?
- Does it have useful utility and debugging programs?
- How reliable is it? Is it robust?

Activity

Investigate the built in security facilities of a standalone OS you use. Explain what they are for and how to set them up.

Conclusion

Choosing a system requires a good understanding of how various systems operate – some are better at one type of application than others. The user requirements must be well understood before systems are evaluated. Having established requirements, various systems need to be evaluated. The user can gain a good understanding of how a system performs from metrics, benchmarks and case studies.

Hardware and software can be evaluated by using rating indicators obtained from knowledge of the market, vendor information and other users. For this reason selection of a vendor also needs to be considered carefully.

The choice of operating systems will depend on the hardware system you are likely to use. Again this needs to be evaluated according to user requirements.

CHAPTER 3

The elements and performance of a standalone system

This chapter aims to give you a thorough understanding of a standalone computer system. It identifies the system components, describes what they are and how they relate to the rest of the system. You will learn how a computer system operating performance is established.

It particular, this chapter covers:

● internal PC components, their operation and performance criteria

● how 'technological progress' is measured.

This chapter covers the following Technical Knowledge topic:

T1.3.2   Internal components

Performance criteria for PC systems

How can one decide what components are required for the expert system (ECGspert) described in the previous chapter? Besides having a system compatible with the operating system, and the software a user wants to run, what are the criteria for assessing a PC's operating performance? Here we shall examine the different components that make up a PC and how they operate together.

Figure 3.1 builds on the representation used in Figure 1.6 in Chapter 1. Notice that the I/O has been split into parallel and serial data (see later for an explanation), and new components – internal expansion cards – have been added.

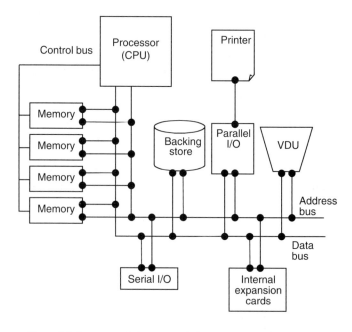

Figure 3.1 *Arrangement of components in a computer system*

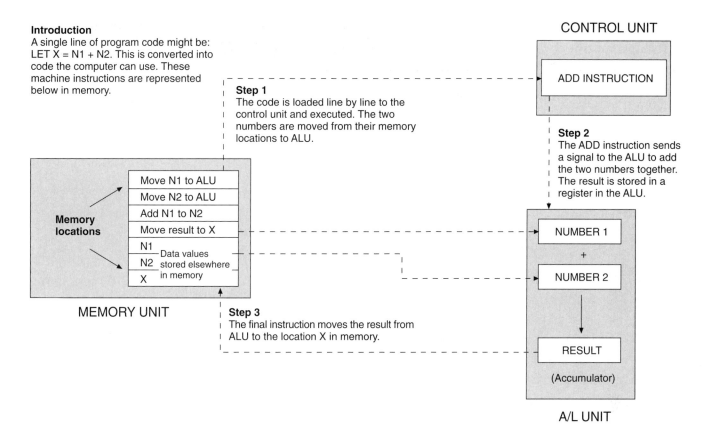

Introduction
A single line of program code might be: LET X = N1 + N2. This is converted into code the computer can use. These machine instructions are represented below in memory.

CONTROL UNIT

ADD INSTRUCTION

Step 1
The code is loaded line by line to the control unit and executed. The two numbers are moved from their memory locations to ALU.

Step 2
The ADD instruction sends a signal to the ALU to add the two numbers together. The result is stored in a register in the ALU.

Move N1 to ALU
Move N2 to ALU
Add N1 to N2
Move result to X

Memory locations

N1
N2 — Data values stored elsewhere in memory
X

MEMORY UNIT

NUMBER 1
+
NUMBER 2

RESULT

(Accumulator)

A/L UNIT

Step 3
The final instruction moves the result from ALU to the location X in memory.

Figure 3.2 *What goes on in a central processing unit (CPU)*

Inside the central processing unit

The central processing unit (or just 'processor') in a computer carries out the execution of instructions, and in turn it depends on the rest of the system to function. The processor receives instructions by addressing them in memory. It transfers them to an instruction register (temporary store) in the control unit, from where it executes them. Figure 3.2 will give you an idea of the steps involved in the execution of a simple program. ALU is an acronym for the arithmetic and logic unit – where calculations and logical operations are performed in electronic circuits.

The CPU and buses

The choice of processor usually comes down to a number of things:

- the price, which is related to the speed and power that a user needs
- the speed of a system which, as in many other systems, is dependent on the slowest component.

For example, a processor may be able to operate at speeds up to 1GHz (gigahertz) – meaning it is able to carry out execution of instructions at one billion cycles per second. In practice the actual speed will depend on the number of operations the processor has to do in order to fetch and execute an instruction – see the information box 'Processor speed ratings'. If the other components cannot keep up this blazing speed, then the processor's high performance is made redundant. An analogy is driving a high-performance car through a busy city centre at rush hour on a Friday – the car's top speed is unobtainable because the communication channels (streets) are too busy.

Instructions are executed according to a digital clock that operates by pulsing timing signals to the processor's components. The timing pulses mean that operations occur at the right time and in the right order. The speed of the processor's clock will have an influence on the speed of the rest of the system. However, no matter how fast the processor can execute instructions, it will still depend on the speed at which it can receive instructions and data from memory.

Processor speed ratings

A common misunderstanding about processors is their different speed ratings

A computer system's clock speed is measured as a frequency, usually expressed as a number of cycles per second, called hertz. The hertz was named after the German physicist Heinrich Rudolph Hertz. A typical computer system runs millions of these cycles per second, so speed is measured in megahertz (MHz).

A single cycle is the smallest element of time for the processor. Every action requires at least one cycle and usually multiple cycles. To transfer data to and from memory, for example, an 8086 chip needs four cycles plus wait states. (A *wait state* is a clock tick in which nothing happens to ensure that the processor is not getting ahead of the rest of the computer.) A 286 needs only two cycles plus any wait states for the same transfer.

The time required to execute instructions also varies. The original 8086 and 8088 processors took an average of 12 cycles to execute a single instruction. The 286 and 386 processors improve this rate to about 4.5 cycles per instruction; the 486 drops the rate further to two cycles per instruction. The Pentium includes twin instruction pipelines and other improvements that provide for operation at 1 cycle per average instruction.

Different instruction execution times (in cycles) make it difficult to compare systems based purely on clock speed, or number of cycles per second. One reason the 486 is so fast is that it has an average instruction-execution time of 2 clock cycles. Therefore, a 100MHz Pentium is about equal to a 200MHz 486, which is about equal to a 400MHz 386 or 286, which is about equal to a 1000MHz 8088. As you can see, you have to be careful in comparing systems based on pure MHz alone; many other factors affect system performance.

The speed of random-access memory (RAM) depends on how quickly an address can be translated into a location in the millions of storage transistors that make it up. Then data from a memory location has to be placed on an internal communications highway called the *data bus* and transferred to the processor. If the electronics of the memory and the bus are not able to work fast enough to keep up with the processor's execution speed, then the processor will idle while awaiting new instructions or data.

Speeding up the selection and transfer of instructions from memory modules to the processor via the bus has been an area where engineers have strived to build improvements. You can see in Figure 3.1 the addresses to the memory modules are carried on an address bus and data passes to and fro along a data bus. A control signal pass along another circuit and determines whether a memory operation is reading or writing data to a memory address. One way in which speed

differences between the memory and CPU have been evened out has been to connect memory to a bus used only by the CPU and memory – called the system bus. This means that it has been easier to improve RAM–CPU performance because the connections between them are more streamlined (see Figure 3.3).

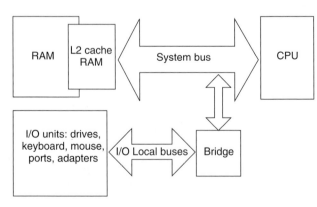

Figure 3.3 *Buses at work*

The elements and performance of a standalone system

Processor	Chipset	System bus speed (MHz)	CPU speed (MHz)
Intel Pentium II	82440BX		
	82440GX	100	350, 400, 450
AMD K6-2	Via MVP3ALi Aladdin V	100	250, 300, 400
Intel Pentium II Xeon	82450NX	100	450, 500
Intel Pentium III	i815		
	i820	133	600, 667 and up
AMD Athlon	VIA KT133	200	600–1000

Figure 3.4 *Processor speed readings*

The table in Figure 3.4 compares the speed in megahertz of the CPU with the speed of the system bus of several well-known processors.

As well as the speed at which clock and circuits can physically work, there is another factor which determines speed. You might call it 'throughput'. It is the amount of data that can be stored, transmitted and processed at the same time or in parallel. For example, a memory location may be 16, 32 or 64 bits in size. This means that with larger store sizes, a single address operation is able to fetch more data. (Turn back to Figure 1.13 on page 16 to remind yourself of bits and bytes.)

Address	1 byte	1 byte	1 byte	1 byte	1 byte	1 byte	1 byte	1 byte
0001								
0002								
0003								

Figure 3.5 *Fetching data from a memory location (address)*

In Figure 3.5, address 0001 points to a single memory location that can store two bytes, whereas addresses 0002 and 0003 point to memory locations that double the previous amount. A program fetching data from a memory location that can store eight bytes of data will work faster than a program that has to address four locations for the same amount of data.

Similarly with bus sizes – if a bus can carry 64 bits of data at once then it can move data faster between CPU and memory or between memory and the external peripherals. There is little gain in speed if the system bus can transfer 64 bits of data at a time if the slowest bus, such as the ISA bus (described in detail later), is capable of transferring only 16 bits at a time.

Activities

1. Read the information box 'Processor speed ratings'. Create a chart that compares the system bus speed against different processor models and their CPU speed. You might want to investigate newer processor models and compare their speeds with the ones discussed.

2. You want to upgrade your computer to make it run faster. Find out whether you would be better improving the internal bus speed or upgrading the processor.

Traditionally the slowest components in a system are the peripherals, and this is again an area where much development has been concentrated. As before, the performance depends on how quickly data can be transferred across the boundaries of the computer to the processor. The boundaries of the computer are where the internal buses stop and external devices start. So, for example, the printer cable plugs into the computer and connects the printer from the outside to the internal communication channels (buses) on the inside.

That is one reason why one of the main ways of improving performance has been to add memory to external components such as printers and graphics cards, and to include more processing power on the control circuits (adapters) that operate the peripherals. It cuts down the amount of transfer across slow buses to the processor. In Figure 3.6 you can see the relationships of external components to the CPU and system bus. These will be covered in more detail later.

The elements and performance of a standalone system

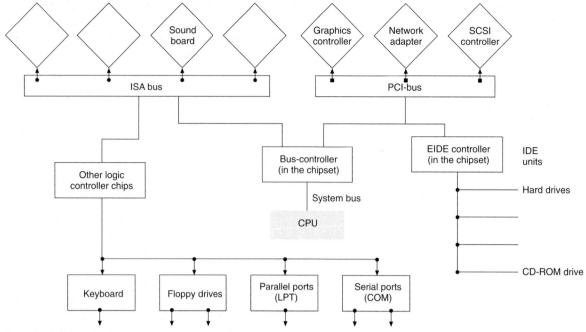

Figure 3.6 *Relationship of external components to the CPU and system bus*

The CPU is an integrated circuit that is made up of millions of tiny transistors which act as switches. The CPU is able to take instructions in the form of 1s and 0s and carry out operations based on them. The CPU manufacturer decides what the processor will do when different binary codes are loaded for execution. One instruction may load data from memory, another instruction may add a number from memory to one stored within the processor's temporary stores (called registers). Figure 3.8 shows a typical layout inside the CPU (don't be concerned about the details).

The basic components of a processor are complex but include the following.

- *Registers.* These are data storage locations used by the processor to hold the data being processed or the results of processing.

- *Onboard cache.* This is an area of memory storage actually on the chip that allows for code (instructions) and data to be stored right next to

Technology	Theoretical Maximum Throughput Megabits	Used For
Serial Port	0.23 Mbps or 230 Kbps	Printers, telephony devices, modems, etc
USB at low data transfer rate	1.5 Mbps	Most devices
10Base-T	10 Mbps	Laser printers, network connections, etc
USB at high transfer rates	12 Mbps	Most devices
SCSI	40 Mbps	Hard drives, removable storage, scanners, etc
Fast SCSI	80 Mbps	High performance drives
100Base-T	100 Mbps	Laser printers, network connections, etc
Ultra SCSI	160 Mbps	High performance drives
Wide Ultra SCSI	320 Mbps	High performance drives
Ultra2 SCSI	320 Mbps	High performance drives
FireWire	400 Mbps	Hard drives, scanners, digital video
USB 2.0 (Intel)	480 Mbps	Standard due in late 2000 or early 2001
Wide Ultra2 SCSI	640 Mbps	High performance drives
FireWire	800 Mbps	Hard drives, scanners, digital video
Ultra3 SCSI	1280 Mbps	High performance drives
FireWire	1600 Mbps	Hard drives, scanners, digital video

Figure 3.7 *Theoretical throughput of a range of data bus technologies*

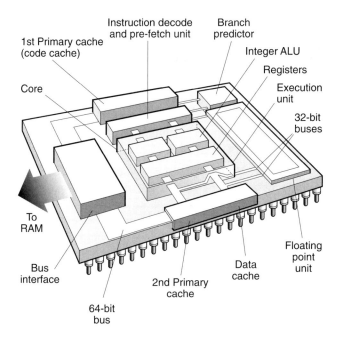

Figure 3.8 *The internal layout of a typical PC processor*

Labels on figure: 1st Primary cache (code cache), Instruction decode and pre-fetch unit, Branch predictor, Integer ALU, Registers, Execution unit, Core, 32-bit buses, To RAM, Floating point unit, Bus interface, Data cache, 2nd Primary cache, 64-bit bus

- *Bus interface.* This is the logic unit that ensures data and addresses are placed on the correct system buses so that transfer of data to and from the processor flows unimpeded.

- *Floating-point unit.* This is the place where decimal number calculations are carried out.

- *Arithmetic and logic unit.* This calculates the outcome of integer or whole-number operations and makes logical decisions based on inputs.

- *Pipelines.* This is rather like a factory production line. In order to execute an instruction a number of stages have to be passed through. The first stage would be decoding the instruction, the next stage might be transferring data from memory to a register, and then there might be an operation like adding the contents of one register to another. One stage in the pipeline is dedicated to each of the stages needed to execute an instruction, and each stage passes the instruction on to the next stage when it is finished with it.

the execution unit. Cache can be used as part of a pre-fetch process – in other words the processor can fetch instructions and data in anticipation of their being needed. This speeds up execution time. A level 2 cache is also used to speed up execution time, but this is outside the CPU chip.

The motherboard and chipset

The *motherboard* contains all the electronics and communication channels to bind the computer together into a fully functioning device. Early motherboards essentially held just the memory and

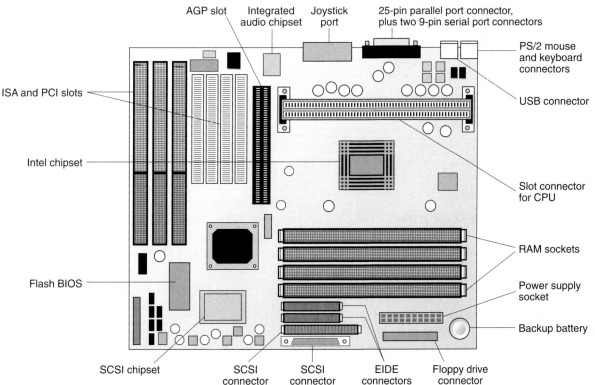

Figure 3.9 *A typical modern motherboard*

Labels on figure: AGP slot, Integrated audio chipset, Joystick port, 25-pin parallel port connector, plus two 9-pin serial port connectors, PS/2 mouse and keyboard connectors, ISA and PCI slots, USB connector, Intel chipset, Slot connector for CPU, Flash BIOS, RAM sockets, Power supply socket, Backup battery, SCSI chipset, SCSI connector, SCSI connector, EIDE connectors, Floppy drive connector

The elements and performance of a standalone system

the processor, and many of the other devices plugged in using *expansion cards*. These are electronic circuit cards that contain all the components for the operation of a device such as a hard drive or visual display unit. The motherboard then provided the pathways to memory and the processor. Today the motherboard has on it rather more circuitry, but the essential parts are described below (see Figure 3.9).

Controller chips for buses and ports

The chipset of a motherboard comprises the integrated circuits (IC) devised for specialised tasks and the connections between them. This means that the operation of a particular component is built into IC units, thus removing the processing burden from the CPU. In effect many transfer tasks can now take place at the same time, for example between a peripheral and memory or between memory and the CPU.

The main chip controls the transfer of data between the system bus and the other buses such as PCI and ISA (of which more later). This control chip is also called a 'bridge' because it connects together dissimilar components and allows them to work together. So the interface between the system bus and the PCI bus is a chip that bridges different components together.

There is also a controller for the hard drives (called the EIDE controller) and one for the floppy disk drive. Recent additions have given support for the specialised graphics interface, AGP, and for the universal serial bus. The chipset also supports the read and write operations to memory, so compatibility is an issue that has to be considered. Finally there are support operations concerned with keyboard, mouse and other serial and parallel ports. The main thing to remember is that the transfer of data around the system requires it to be transferred across different boundaries. The controller chips are the interfaces between these different boundaries.

Read-only memory (ROM) and BIOS

These are chips that have system software burnt permanently on to them. That is why it is called 'read-only' memory. Sometimes a chip called 'erasable programmable ROM' can be used that can be modified when, for example, infrequent updates of software are required (also called flash memory). ROM is used to hold the software for handling a range of devices, from CD-ROM to graphics and sound cards.

The motherboard has a ROM that holds the basic input/output system (BIOS) software. This is a vital layer of system software that carries out several operations:

- POST (power on self test) tests that the system is working when you switch it on. For example, it checks that memory is functioning (you can see this test on your screen).
- The PC's setup instructions connect with a special memory chip called complementary metal-oxide semiconductor (CMOS), where user start-up instructions are stored. A low-power battery can maintain the CMOS chip when the computer is switched off. User instructions include the system time and date, power management and the order in which different drives can be used for boot-up.
- BIOS instructions connect with the various hardware peripherals
- The boot instructions load the operating system from a hard disk.

The BIOS software provides a layer of software between the operating system and hardware. When the computer starts, essential routines must be loaded in order for the monitor and keyboard to work, for example. After the operating system takes over it communicates with the BIOS in order to send and receive data from devices.

Activity

Find out how to make changes to your basic system setup configuration.

Power supply

The power unit needs to provide a steady and uninterrupted current as power surges or spikes can cause the computer to crash. Voltage levels in the mains electrical supply are much greater than those used on PC motherboards and so need to be transformed to a lower level (5 and 12 volts).

Ports

Serial and parallel ports

These are standard ports used to connect peripherals

to the computer. The mouse is an example of a device that sends serial input to the system. Serial I/O is a stream of bits sent down a single wire by a device. Usually additional control signals are sent down other lines.

The *serial ports* are controlled by a UART (universal asynchronous receiver transmitter) chip that transfers data from an external connection on to the internal bus. Serial devices are low speed and data is usually stored in a buffer on the UART before being transferred to memory, to be processed by software designed to use this data stream.

Figure 3.10 illustrates an 8-bit data block arriving simultaneously (in parallel) down an 8-bit bus to the serial UART port.

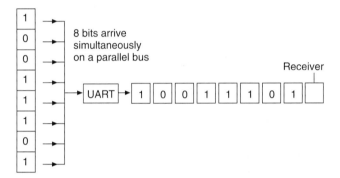

Figure 3.10 *Converting parallel to serial*

Control signals are used to signal when a system is ready to receive data, and a return signal will indicate whether the sender is ready to send data. Modern systems have a dedicated port for a mouse (called PS/2). Transmission speeds can be up to 115,200 bits per second.

Parallel ports are generally used for printers. As their name implies, they can receive data simultaneously along a series of parallel wires. In Figure 3.11 you can see an 8-bit data block arriving on an 8-wire bus and then being transmitted out on another 8-wire cable.

Although this means that more data can be transmitted, there are weaknesses because the length of the parallel cable cannot go beyond about five metres before the signal becomes degraded.

Although usually used to connect the printer an enhanced bi-directional parallel port has meant other devices can be used on this interface; for example:

- Zip drives
- portable CD-ROM drives
- SCSI adapters
- digital cameras
- scanners.

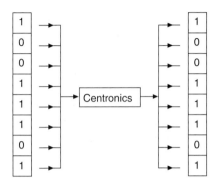

Figure 3.11 *The standard parallel interface called Centronics that accepted a 25-pin connector*

USB

A new type of serial port, called a USB, is now more or less standard on new computer systems. USB stands for *universal serial bus* and is a cheap bus that can transfer data at 1.2MBps and above (see Figure 3.7).

USB follows an open system approach to standards, which means it can be used by any manufacturer without paying royalties. Units can be plugged and unplugged very easily using a simple interface for a number of PC devices:

- keyboard
- mouse
- joystick
- modem
- scanner and camera
- external drives

All these units can be connected using one single plug at the computer. USB holds up to 127 units in one long chain. As an example, the VDU could potentially hold a central connection interface (hub) where other USB units could be connected, as in Figure 3.12.

The elements and performance of a standalone system

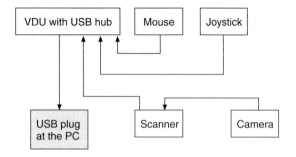

Figure 3.12 *Connecting several USB peripherals*

Random-access memory

The internal working memory (random-access memory, or just RAM) is where data and instructions are stored for processing. RAM is volatile – which means that the transistors that hold the binary values making up a memory word (a single addressable location) have to be constantly supplied with power to keep the bit set for each 0 or 1 in a location.

RAM is another part of computing technology that has been the subject of intense research. It can determine the type of motherboard you can use, the speed at which the system bus can transmit data, and the speed at which data can be selected and placed on the data bus.

RAM usually comes provided on modules that plug into sockets on the motherboard. The older type of memory module was called a SIMM (single inline memory module) and had 72 pins. This type of module had to be fitted as pairs of equal size memory (e.g. you had to install two SIMMs of 16MB each). The newer type of module is called a DIMM (dual inline memory module). It has two rows of 168 pins and does not have to be fitted in pairs.

There are basically two types of RAM, static RAM (SRAM) and dynamic (DRAM). Static is very high-speed memory, expensive to build and used for the external cache. DRAM is cheaper to build and comes in various types:

- FPM (fast page mode)
- ECC (error correcting code)
- EDO (extended data output)
- SDRAM (synchronous dynamic RAM)

In order to use RAM, an address is placed on the address bus. The control chips use this to select the memory location indicated by the address. The row and column number, just like a spreadsheet, determines the address of a memory location. In Figure 3.14 you can see that the right-hand digits of the address are being used to select row 01 and the left-hand digits are being used to select column 10. These coordinates select the memory location. The data are placed on the data bus and a write signal would change address 1001 from 0 to 1. This is a simplified drawing because each memory address refers to only one digit, whereas on a modern system an address would locate 32 bits of storage.

RAM speed is measured in nanoseconds, but there is a strong relationship between the speed at which data can be actually read from the RAM circuits and how fast the system bus can move data into and out of the processor. Motherboards will specify the type of RAM that a system can support, including the total amount of RAM the system can use.

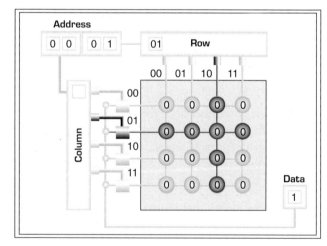

Figure 3.14 *Diagram showing simplified logic array of memory*

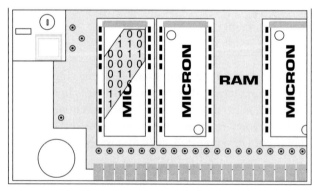

Figure 3.13 *Drawing showing part of a DIMM module, holding RAM chips*

The elements and performance of a standalone system

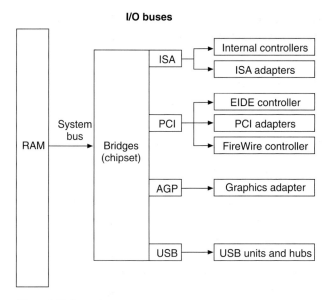

I/O buses

Figure 3.15 *A summary*

Activities

Review what you have already learnt. Refer to Figure 3.15.

1. What is the function of the system bus?

2. What is the purpose of expansion or adapter cards?

3. What is meant by the chipset, and why can it be referred to as a bridge?

4. What does the EIDE controller control?

5. When choosing a PC, what are the factors that might influence your choice of motherboard?

Local buses and adapter cards

You have seen how the system has a lot of electronics built into the motherboard, as a chipset. One area that has been touched on is the expansion or adapter cards used to control external devices, and the buses on which they connect.

Buses

Figure 3.16 shows the relationship between different external devices (peripherals) and their connections to local buses on the motherboard.

ISA stands for *industry standard architecture* and has been the mainstay for many years – the 16-bit version has been standard since 1984. Because it has remained

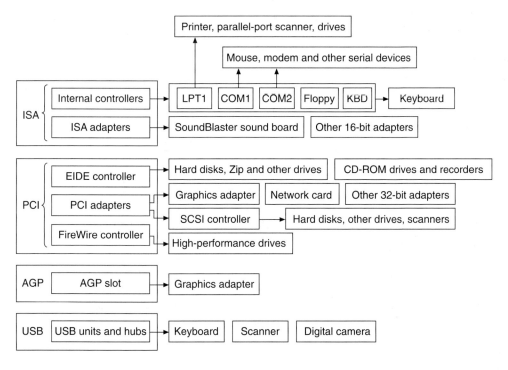

Figure 3.16 *Buses and devices*

a standard for so many years there are plenty of companies making adapter cards that fit it. Typical cards are modems and sound boards.

PCI stands for *peripheral component interconnect*. This local bus was developed by Intel and introduced in 1993. The rationale was, of course, to improve performance within the computer and with external devices. That is why it has a higher throughput (you can also use the term 'bandwidth') and works at a higher speed than the ISA bus. The PCI bus implements two enhancements not available on the ISA: bus mastering and burst mode. *Bus mastering* is when the control chips for the bus are able to transfer data directly from an adapter card or other device to memory without intervention by the CPU. It can control which devices can use the bus at any particular time and ensure there are no mishaps over sharing it. In *burst mode* a whole block of data can be transferred using a single start address and the size of the data block to be transferred.

The PCI bus also introduced the *plug-and-play* capability used on modern PC systems. Intel developed it, with cooperation from Microsoft and many other companies. The PCI chipset circuitry handles the identification of cards and works with the operating system and BIOS to automatically set resource allocations for compatible peripheral cards. This has made the installation of devices much easier, as the system sets up internal settings, locates, and installs device software.

AGP stands for *accelerated graphics port*. This is the newest addition to the bus standards and is devoted to

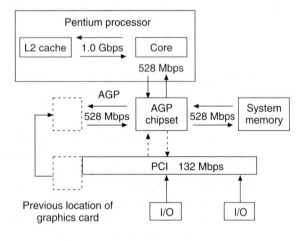

Figure 3.17 *Attaining more speed with AGP*

what is says. With the advent of more and more graphics-intensive applications and virtual 3D game-playing, the speed at which the picture on your monitor could move was being held back by the speed at which data could move across the PCI bus. The big change has been to move the graphics capability from the local bus on to the system bus, as Figure 3.17 shows.

The move on to the system bus means that data transfer between the AGP and system memory occurs at speeds up to 528Mbps as opposed to the maximum possible of 132Mbps achieved with the PCI bus.

Activities

1. *Explain the difference between the system bus and the local bus.*

2. *Investigate at least three types of RAM that are commonly used today. What are their advantages and disadvantages?*

Adapter cards

These are cards that plug into buses using various connection configurations. Adapter cards expand the capability of the system because they allow for other devices to be plugged into specialised circuitry on the card. The cards' electronics can improve system performance because the software built into them is designed for specific devices, and because more processing can be carried out on the card with less movement across the system to the CPU.

The graphics card

For a VDU to display output it must be connected to a graphics card. The graphics card contains a processing chip that creates the signals used by the monitor to form an image. It also contains a RAMDAC chip. RAMDAC stands for *random access memory digital-to-analogue converter*. A chip built into some video adapters that converts the binary representation of a pixel into the analogue waveform used by the monitor to display it.

The graphics card needs to contain enough memory to hold at least one frame of video image for the screen. The video image is made up from tiny dots on the screen called *pixels*, and each one has to be mapped to a memory location. So one screen of image is mapped to thousands of memory locations and is known as a *bit-mapped image*.

The amount of video memory required to hold a complete screen image can easily be calculated. For example, an 800 x 600 pixel display requires 480,000 bytes. But that is assuming only one byte of memory is used for each pixel, and one byte can store only up to 256 different colours. So assume that you want to have better colour definition and are using two bytes for every pixel. This would double the amount of RAM for one screen image from 480,000 to 960,000 bytes.

Now imagine that this amount of data has to be updated as a screen image changes and then transferred from system memory to the graphics adaptor, and thence to the VDU. As you can guess, this would slow the system down excessively – which is why the display adapter stores images using video RAM. The more video RAM your adapter has, the quicker it can build new bit-maps and transfer them from the card direct to the monitor.

The system and video card work together. The CPU may be running a games program. As your heroine rushes headlong into another dangerous affray, the picture has to change (video frame refresh rates need to be in the range 20–25 frames per second to avoid a jerky picture). The program calculates what aspect of the display needs to change and passes these instructions to a program called a *device driver*, which readies them for the particular display adapter you are using. The device driver then sends these instructions to the graphics card, which converts the instructions into new bit-mapped images it stores in its video RAM. It then passes the bit-mapped image through the RAMDAC chip (see above) that sends the finished video signal to the VDU.

Network cards

In order for a computer to use a network, it needs a network adapter card (also known as a network interface card). Just like other adapter cards, this fits into one of the onboard expansion slots. The network cable can then be attached to the external socket on the card. The card provides the electronics for detecting and reading transmissions from the network and preparing and sending data from the computer.

Like many other cards, the network adapter card will contain software instructions (firmware) for carrying out these routines on ROM. It will also have processing power to execute its interface and transmission roles, as well as RAM to hold data either being removed from the network or about to be sent.

The communication stream on a network is usually by packets of data each having the sender's and receiver's address. The packet will be generated by the network software in the sender's computer and then converted by the network card into a stream of analogue signals that can be picked up by network cards on the rest of the network. The conversion is similar to the serial port above (see Figure 3.10) where the internal parallel transmission from the local bus is converted into a bit stream for transmission along a cable.

Figure 3.18 shows a typical network card with the external connector and onboard electronics.

Figure 3.18 *A network card*

Each network card has a unique address that is hardwired on to the card when it is manufactured. When a computer is running in network mode – that is to say, the user has access to resources beyond the physical boundary of the PC – a request for a remote resource will be processed into packets and put into memory. The adapter card will then transfer the data across the local buses on to the adapter card, where it will be further processed before being converted into appropriate signals for transmission. The network card will access the network infrastructure according to an access *protocol* that determines how many users can share a cable. This is like flow control on a single-track road or footpath: if only one person can cross a footbridge and many people want to use it in both directions, then some form of control would be needed.

The network card has also to receive data packets from the network that are addressed to it. There are different ways in which the card reads transmissions on the network cable, but essentially they involve removing data streams and then converting them into a form that will be processed further by the network software resident on a user's machine.

EIDE controllers, UltraDMA and SCSI cards

Access to instructions and data maintained on secondary storage is a constant feature of any operation. The most common internal control chip for storage drives (hard drives, tape drives and CD-ROMs) is called the EIDE (enhanced integrated drive electronics) controller. It allows for four devices to be connected using two channels where each channel can have a master and a slave device. Data transfer rates are up to 16.6Mbps and can use the same bus mastering techniques described earlier. The drive controller acts as a bridge between the drives and the local bus, negotiating when data can be put on to the bus and controlling its flow. Figure 3.19 shows a typical configuration for the EIDE controller.

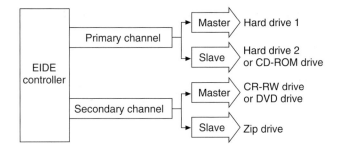

Figure 3.19 *The EIDE drive controller*

The controller works in a *multitasking* mode between channels; i.e. it is able to deal with requests on two devices at the same time between channels. However, interaction between the master and slave devices on one channel is single-tasking – only one device can be used at a time.

Activity

What are the consequences for this arrangement?

The operation of the drives is controlled by *firmware* processed on board the drive. When data needs to be

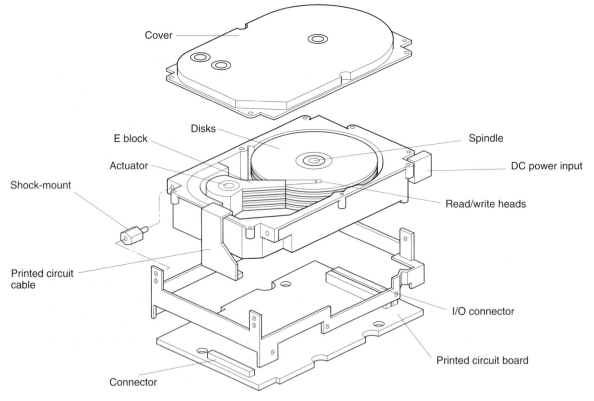

Figure 3.20 *Exploded drawing of a hard disk*

SYSTEMS ADMINISTRATION

The elements and performance of a standalone system

stored or retrieved, the operating system passes the cylinder, track and sector identification to the hard drive, which converts the logical information into electro-mechanical instructions. Once the read/write head has been moved into position over the right cylinder and sector, then data transfer takes place.

In Figure 3.20 the hard drive has five disks or *platters* on which data can be stored. Each surface of the platter has a read/write head capable of transferring data. Once the correct head or disk surface has been selected, then the drive instructions have to know where on the surface to access data (see Figure 3.21).

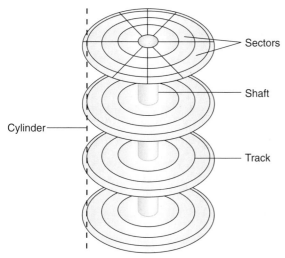

Figure 3.21 *Tracks, cylinders and sectors of a hard drive (see also Figure 3.20)*

The *cylinder information* locates the correct disk surface, *track information* locates where data are stored from the outside perimeter of the disk to the inner spindle. The *sector information* determines on which part of the concentric circle to access data.

The continual demands for higher speed and performance have recently seen the addition of two other standards: UltraDMA (direct memory access) and SCSI.

- UltraDMA is an improved data transfer protocol that can see speeds of up to 66.6Mbps.
- SCSI (small computer system interface) is a technology that provides the means for data exchange among a range of different hardware devices (e.g. drives, tape streamers and scanners). It is a more expensive technology and so is especially used in high-end systems such as network servers.

A SCSI system is built around a central, intelligent controller called the *host adapter*, which can be connected to the PCI bus as an expansion card. The host adapter can control several SCSI units at the same time:

- up to 15 devices on the same host adapter
- many types of drives: hard disks, CD-ROMs, Zip drives
- tape backup drives
- scanners.

The host adapter has its own separate BIOS and possesses its own processing power, thus freeing the CPU from workload. Because SCSIs have high throughput and intelligent control, they provide an excellent way of adding high-performance drives.

Technological progress

It is important to realise that technological developments do not take place in a vacuum where all that is objectively rationale takes place. For example, Intel released a Pentium processor where in some circumstances the floating-point maths co-processor would come up with slightly flawed results. This was not a problem for most people who perform simple calculations and was brought to light only by a professor of maths who wanted to use a PC for serious number-crunching.

Pentium floating-point division bug

The message below is extracted from an Internet discussion list about the Pentium floating-point bug. It illustrates how communities of users have built up around different technologies, and how they interact to share a range of information. You are not expected to understand all of this, but you might like to try out one of the equations on your own machine. For example, the following equation should compute to zero:

$x = 4195835$

$y = 3145727$

$z = x - (x/y)*y$

Open up a spreadsheet program and enter the x and y values to different cells. Then enter the formula for z in a different cell, substituting the x part of the formula with the cell reference for the x value you have put in and the y part with the cell reference for the y value. Does the formula compute to zero?

There has been a flurry of activity the last few days on the Internet news group, comp.sys.intel, that should interest MATLAB users. A serious design flaw has been discovered in the floating-point unit on Intel's Pentium chip. Double precision divisions involving operands with certain bit patterns can produce incorrect results.

The most dramatic example seen so far can be extracted from a posting by Tim Coe of Vitesse Semiconductor. In MATLAB, his example becomes

$x = 4195835$

$y = 3145727$

$z = x - (x/y)*y$

With exact computation, z would be zero. In fact, we get zero on most machines, including those using Intel 286, 386 and 486 chips. Even with roundoff error, z should not be much larger than eps*x, which is about 9.3e-10. But, on the Pentium, z = 256.

The relative error, z/x, is about 2^(-14) or 6.1e-5. The computed quotient, x/y, is accurate to only 14 bits.

An article in last week's edition of Electronic Engineering Times credits Prof. Thomas Nicely, a mathematics professor at Lynchburg College in Virginia, with the first public announcement of the Pentium division bug. One of Nicely's examples involves p = 824633702441. With exact computation

$q = 1 - (1/p)*p$

would be zero. With floating-point computation, q should be on the order of eps. On most machines, we find that

$q = eps/2 = 2^(-53) \sim= 1.11e-16.$

But on the Pentium

$q = 2^(-28) \sim= 3.72e-09.$

This is roughly single precision accuracy and is typical of most of the examples that had been posted before Coe's analysis.

We are not sure yet how many operands cause the Pentium's floating-point division to fail, or even what operands produce the largest relative error. It is certainly true that failures are very rare. But, the real difficulty is having to worry about this at all. There are so many other things than can go wrong with computer hardware and software that, at least, we ought to be able to rely on the basic arithmetic.

The bug is definitely in the Pentium chip. It occurs at all clock rates. Intel has recently made changes to the on-chip Program Logic Array that fix the bug and is now believed to be producing error free CPUs.

However, here was a fundamental design error. It has been suggested that the flaw would not have happened if Intel had tested more thoroughly and, this is the important point, had not been in a rush to keep ahead of competitors.

According to Moore's law (Gordon Moore was one of the founders of Intel), the number of transistors that can be placed on the same area of a microprocessor doubles every 18 months. This has meant that processing power has constantly been increasing, and equally that processing power has got cheaper.

However, in order for this law to work a company like Intel must stay ahead of the game by spending heavily on research and development. At the same time Intel aggressively defends its market share from intruders and so, for example, has launched many lawsuits where it thinks a competitor is infringing its patents. In this way Intel had, until quite recently, an almost monopolistic control over the processor industry. Today there are serious competitors, such as AMD, and Intel are being pushed to keep on top. So products are developed in highly competitive, often secretive, circumstances where commercial pressure may influence developments more than the scientific ones.

Another example was IBM's attempt to introduce a new bus architecture, called 'micro channel architecture'. The MCA bus was technically superior to the ISA bus but was not backwardly compatible (it would not support components built for other older architectures, either because the electronics was radically different or you simply can't plug the components into the MCA bus). All those ISA adapter cards would have had to be thrown away and replaced by MCA-compatible ones. This would have been a coup for IBM because they would have specified and controlled a major industry standard. However, the consumers didn't want to replace their adapter cards and the MCA bus fell into the backwaters of history and became irrelevant and ultimately superseded by the PCI bus. The history of the PC and IBMs involvement is a salutary reminder for hi-tech businesses everywhere.

Activity

In the last chapter you were asked to specify a system for Muriel Orgreave in the research faculty of Wessex County Hospital. You need to review your specification and provide technical description of all the components you have chosen. This should be like a briefing paper for someone who has some computer knowledge but needs to know what the technology terms mean.

Conclusion

This chapter has given you a thorough insight into the internal operations of a computer system. The purpose was to provide you with technical knowledge so that you can assess how the internal operations affect choices when specifying a system. In summary, the following factors influence the specification of a machine:

- speed
- throughput or bandwidth
- ongoing technical developments (CPU, buses, RAM)
- controllers, bridges, interfaces and distributed resources (adaptor cards)
- peripherals
- cost
- compatibility.

CHAPTER 4

The facilities of current operating systems

This chapter presents a range of information on how a computer system is set up and how the facilities of the system are configured.

It particular, this chapter covers:

- the system command interface
- stages of operation system installation
- configuration of the OS environment
- determining disk requirements
- file systems and file organisation.

The chapter covers the following Technical Knowledge topic in the specification ('security' is discussed in Chapter 7):

T1.1.3   The OS interface, setup, software installation, hardware installation, file management, peripheral management, embedded applications

The command interface

The user of a computer system has to issue commands to and receive status information back. A typical operation would be clicking on a window icon in order to run a program associated with the graphical link (or shortcut). However there are different ways of issuing commands that are dependent on the job being done and the technical level required. We shall look at three ways in which a user interfaces with the computer system in order to issue commands:

- command-line interfacing
- graphical user interfacing
- shell scripts and job control languages.

Command-line interfacing

The command-line interface is the simplest form of user interface to provide, although it is not the easiest way for a novice to issue commands. For someone with technical expertise, the command line is often a quicker and more powerful way of interrogating the system and issuing commands.

A command-line is entered as a series of characters at the keyboard when the system is in its command-line 'listening' mode. The system usually provides a *prompt* to show the user that he or she is in this mode. Most commands refer to file names of programs held on the OS; by typing their name the file executes and carries out the purpose of the command. Let us look at a few examples:

● MS-DOS®	move a:\myproj.doc c:\mydocs\a_lev_ICT.	This command *moves* the file *myproj.doc* from the A: drive to a subdirectory on the C: drive.
● UNIX®	find /usr/ndusers/nduser0 -type -f -size +20 –print.	This command will *find* all the files in the */usr/ndusers/nduser0* directory that are *greater than 20 blocks*, and *print* their names.
● Windows® 2000	winnt /u:adminfile /s:I386.	This command automates installation of Windows 2000 by using the install command *winnt* with a file *adminfile*, which contains the switches necessary for installation using files from the *I386* directory.

Notice that the *format* is the command name followed by additional information necessary to tailor the command to particular parts of the system. This additional information can be called *operands*, *switches* or *parameters*.

The command has to be typed in exactly the right way for the system to understand what the user wants. This is called the *command syntax* and is usually set out in the OS reference manual.

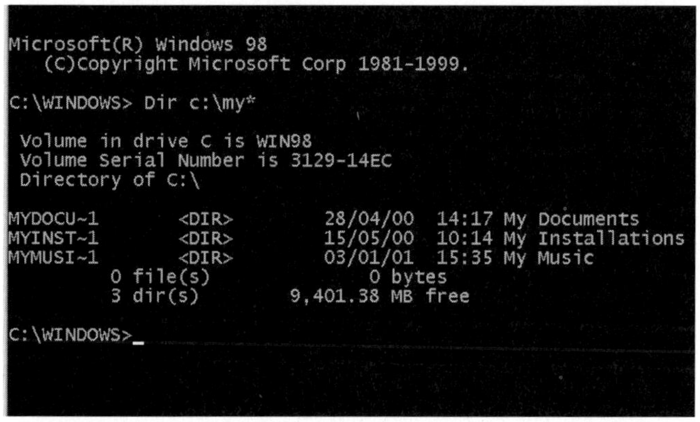

```
Microsoft(R) Windows 98
   (C)Copyright Microsoft Corp 1981-1999.

C:\WINDOWS> Dir c:\my*

Volume in drive C is WIN98
Volume Serial Number is 3129-14EC
Directory of C:\

MYDOCU~1     <DIR>        28/04/00  14:17 My Documents
MYINST~1     <DIR>        15/05/00  10:14 My Installations
MYMUSI~1     <DIR>        03/01/01  15:35 My Music
       0 file(s)             0 bytes
       3 dir(s)       9,401.38 MB free

C:\WINDOWS>_
```

Figure 4.1 *A screen shot in MS-DOS®*

Figure 4.1 shows the command-line prompt 'C:WINDOWS>' followed by the command 'Dir' and the parameter 'c:\my*'.

Activities

1. What is the purpose of the information in the prompt?

2. What do you think the command Dir does?

3. What information has the user requested with the parameter?

Graphical user interface (GUI)

GUI has become the standard for many OS interfaces. First implemented on the Apple® Macintosh® machine it soon became adopted by Microsoft in various Windows® versions and in other OS such as Unix®, which uses a system called X Window. In Microsoft's version, the user's base view of the computer system they are using is the *Desktop*. This is known as a 'metaphor' because it supposedly represents a physical desktop that has various storage locations containing papers and procedures, tools and devices such as calculator or telephone.

Activities

The screenshot in Figure 4.2 comes from the Windows® 98 Help tutorial. Examine the Desktop closely and answer the questions below. You should make sure your answers include descriptions for the following terms: title bar, menu bar, toolbar, focus, drag and drop, slide bar, active window.

1. What does a 'window' mean, and what are the standard features you find on a window (e.g. for opening, moving, navigating, issuing commands etc.)?

2. The interface is sometimes called a 'WIMP' interface. Find out what the term WIMP refers to.

3. Why are GUI interfaces described as 'intuitive' and 'user-friendly'?

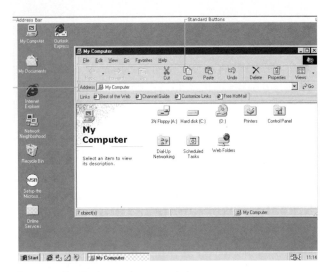

Figure 4.2 *The Desktop and an open window*

Although the GUI has significant advantages for the user, it doesn't come without disadvantages. The presentation of screens of bit-mapped information requires powerful graphics cards and requires large amounts of memory to allow changes to the output to appear seamless. The software is more complex to implement, although methodologies now exist that streamline the creation of windows-based applications. The most powerful way of assisting the development of these kinds or programs is by using shared libraries of windows 'objects' such as a toolbar, drop-down menu or command button. Nevertheless, the software requires better resources and a well-developed use of I/O routines to work smoothly.

Also, for the advanced user, complex operations require a user to navigate a series of dialogue boxes selecting various options, whereas the command line achieves this much more quickly and is more efficient in its execution.

Shell scripts and job control languages

Scripts are like mini programs of system commands packaged together in a file. Any often-repeated operation can be built up from a series of commands and stored in the script file.

A common use of the script file is for user logon. This allows the various options available to a user to be implemented from one place and different user levels can use different logon scripts. For example, some users require permission for a particular printer and want to have their personal directory, where they store their files, as the place they see when they request a

file operation. These options are placed in the logon script that is run straight after they type their logon name and password. Any changes to a user's login requirements can be quickly implemented by changing their logon script.

Job control languages (JCL), too, provide a series of commands for controlling the operation of a routine operation. For example, a master file has to be updated every week with new transaction data, so the JCL file will instruct the system in the various stages of operation to complete this action.

Installation of the operating system

Running setup

For most OS, running a setup program that is contained on a CD starts the installation process. A completely new machine requires some kind of boot-up program from a floppy disk. This loads the 'bare bones' of an operating system, enough so that the user can load an installation program from the CD drive. If an older version of the OS is being upgraded, the new OS can be launched from the CD and it will make the necessary changes to the OS configuration, replacing the old version with the new.

Once the setup program starts, then it is usual for the user to follow setup instructions that configure the basic system settings. These will include agreeing to the *software licence*, selecting the *disk partition* on which to install, and choosing the *file system*.

Installing the keyboard and mouse

The system will detect standard devices connected and configured using the typical ports and hardware settings determined by BIOS (as described in the previous chapter). These include the keyboard and mouse.

It will also prompt you to install regional settings:

● numbers

● currency

● date

● time (in the UK we use Greenwich Mean Time)

● locales.

Entering a computer name

Computer names are used as identifiers within local area networks (LANs). A computer in that case has to belong to a logical group that is controlled by a master network server, or *domain controller*. The domain controller stores security and other information about each resource registered in its area. Alternatively, the computer can be set up in a workgroup (see Figure 4.3).

You can choose a name for your computer, or your network administrator can tell you what name to use. This is entered in a dialogue box. You are also asked for a password, which again can be one you choose or one the administrator gives you. This password determines who can configure and adjust system settings.

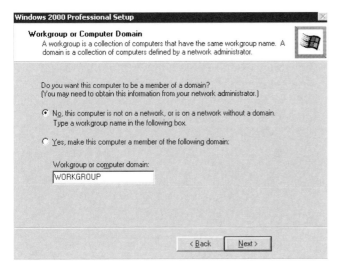

Figure 4.3 *Choosing a workgroup or computer domain*

Determining accessibility options

A modern operating system such as Windows® 2000 provides options to magnify the screen display and to narrate commands using a speech synthesiser.

Determining language options

Options include choosing a primary and a secondary language, such as English (UK) and Somali.

Choosing a network setting

Standard settings for a PC running Windows® 2000 are installing client software for using a network, creating options for file and print sharing, and setting up 'transmission control protocol/Internet protocol' (TCP/IP). This is the protocol used for communicating with the rest of the network and the Internet.

Configuring the OS environment

Certain environment settings can be configured. These deal with things like the directory used for temporary files, or the directory where certain files are located.

Installing hardware

The typical way of installing hardware for the first time is to attach the device to the correct interface. For example, a drive is connected to the EIDE controller and has a power connection. A CD drive connects to the EIDE controller and additionally is connected to the sound card, if there is one. A printer connects to the parallel port or USB port. Once the hardware is physically connected the system is rebooted, then the correct driver software is loaded, and properties for the device are configured.

Plug-and-play

This refers to the ability of the OS to locate hardware configuration information from a device's onboard ROM and the system BIOS. When a system boots, the OS scans its various buses and I/O ports to find out what devices are attached and fetch operating information about them. If the hardware is new, the OS will configure the device into its various resource management tables (see Figure 4.4). It will need to know how to respond to an interrupt call from the device, by setting up software routines. The OS will also need to build an interface between its system commands and the device driver that actually operates a new piece of hardware.

Typically, configuration of system resources involves the following.

- *Interrupt request numbers.* A hardware line is tied to particular I/O ports, disk drives or expansion cards. The hardware line sends an interrupt signal to the OS when it wants to carry out an I/O operation.
- *Direct memory access.* This is a way of allowing a device to transfer data into or out of memory without using the CPU.
- *I/O port addresses.* These are special memory addresses through which data move to and from the device.
- *Memory address range.* Parts of a system memory can be uniquely allocated to data from the device.

Figure 4.4 *In this screenshot, the system has detected a new piece of hardware*

Having detected the hardware, the OS searches its own database for *device drivers*. Most OS hold drivers for a range of common hardware. However, if the device driver is not found you will be asked if you want to install the file from another location – usually the floppy disk or CD drive. The system will then update its hardware list and make the necessary changes to its I/O control systems. Usually a reboot completes the operation.

Manual setup

Installing a device driver

Where plug-and-play is not a feature of the OS, installation of hardware needs to be done manually. Then you need to use a system tool such as 'Add new hardware'. You select the type of device and then the device driver that runs the device.

Figure 4.5 shows a wizard from Microsoft Windows 2000 that does this. The user has selected 'modem' as

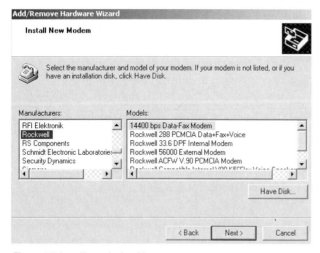

Figure 4.5 *Installing a device driver*

the type of device and is then able to choose which device model to install. Notice the option to choose an installation disk, because the manufacturer should have supplied configuration software and a device driver with the equipment.

You may at some point in the future want to change a device driver used by the system – particularly when the equipment manufacturer produces an improved driver. You then need to use a tool that allows you to change the device driver. Usually, you select the hardware properties of the device and then choose a command to update the driver.

Setting up hardware profiles

An OS may allow the system administrator to create more than one hardware profile. This means the system can be run with a different set of hardware for different occasions without the user having to keep installing/removing hardware controls. For example, in Figure 4.6 you can see that two profiles exist for different monitors. When the flat screen is available, the user can plug it in and switch on the system, which then offers the choice of profiles to use.

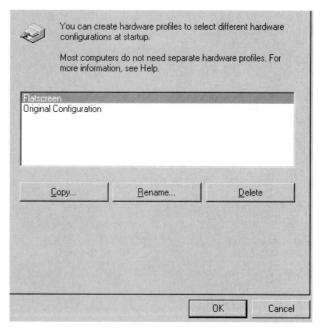

Figure 4.6 *Installing more than one hardware profile*

Configuring display options

The user or systems administrator can modify the display settings. This usually involves changing the type of monitor or graphics adapter registered for a

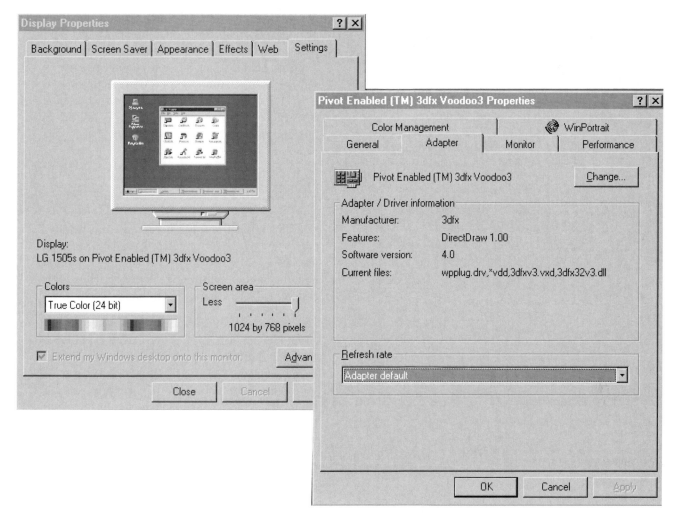

Figure 4.7 *Configuring the display*

particular display. As well as this, the display can be fine-tuned to give the best combination of screen resolution, colour depth and refresh rate. It is important not to make a mistake when changing the refresh rate. If a change is made that makes the screen totally distorted, there is the problem of not being able to see how to make corrections to get it back again!

In Figure 4.7 you can see the settings for a display that uses a high resolution and a very wide colour spectrum.

Other settings allow the administrator to change background images, the appearance of colour and font for window objects, the size of icons, the choice of screensaver, and so on.

Configuring a printer

On a network system the user has to be given permission to access a printer, but once that has been

Activities

1. *What would be the total amount of display memory required for the setting shown in Figure 4.7?*

2. *What balance needs to be achieved when setting display options?*

3. *Certain websites display a notice stating that their site is best viewed using 800 × 600 pixel resolution. Why is that?*

done the same printer setup needs to be performed as for a single-user system. First of all the system has to know which printer device driver to use, so that data sent from an application are formatted according to the printer being used. A setup operation in Windows® is very straightforward:

- choose Settings | Printer | Add printer
- indicate whether it is a network or local printer
- choose the make and model of printer
- indicate which I/O port it is using (e.g. parallel port)
- decide whether this is the default printer.

Once the printer driver has been installed, it is possible to tailor particular properties of the printer for the user (see Figure 4.8).

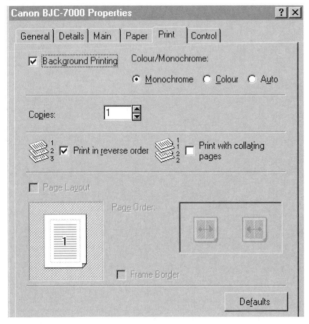

Figure 4.8 *Setting a printer's properties*

> **Activity**
>
> *Find out what properties have been set for your printer. Are you satisfied with these settings?*

Installing software

Application software is installed from its distribution disk. Usually the software comes with setup instructions for the system it is going to run on. Installation of software requires the OS to store a range of information about its operating requirements. This information is stored in a *database*.

For that reason, if the software is going to be changed or removed, an *uninstall* operation has to be performed. This is meant to leave the application database held by the OS free from unnecessary references to software that has been removed. However, this operation is not always successful and registration information remains. Some utilities can attempt to locate these irregularities and fix them.

Using embedded applications

The OS administrator can use a range of software that comes embedded (or bundled) with the OS. This is useful for configuring the system, reading Help files and manuals, or controlling devices attached to the system and operating through the OS layers.

The distinction between OS core applications and additional applications has become blurred. For example, the simple text editor used in most OS has been backed up by a fairly well-featured word-processing system in Windows®. There are also applications for playing media files, adjusting sound levels, recording sound files, creating bit-maps, playing games etc.

Other applications, such as *utilities*, are essential in helping maintain the system either by scheduling jobs, recovering disk errors or helping to back-up the system.

Determining disk requirement

The hard disk size required depends, first of all, on the minimum requirement for the installation and operation of the OS. Clearly, a much larger drive will be required for a computer if it is to store user and application files, as well.

In Figure 4.9, various estimates and provisions are used to come up with an idea of the minimum requirement for a network disk storage system.

The following parameters are used: four applications at 45MB each and four applications at 20MB each; and users are allocated 100MB each and there are 35 users.

Storage factor	Hard disk space (MB)
Windows® 2000 server advises 2 gigabytes	2000
Four applications @ 45MB	180
Four applications @ 20MB	80
Budgeted disk space per user = 100MB Number of users = 55 Multiply by 110% to give an extra margin	3850
Total disk storage recommended for this configuration (minimum)	6110

Figure 4.9 *Calculation of minimum hard disk size*

> ## Activity
>
> *Carry out research for a typical computer classroom you use. Try to get an idea of the amount of disk space your network requires for this classroom. Find out how much actual disk space is allocated to the network.*

Hard disk partitioning

Another consideration is whether the disk is going to be *partitioned*. Partitioning occurs when a physical drive is divided into smaller *logical drives*.

Some systems administrators recommend that a disk be partitioned so that each logical drive (C, D, E etc.) can be used for different functions. C could be used by the network operating system files, D could be used by the application programs being used on the network, and E could store user directories and files. The purpose of this would be to aid administration such as backup or management of disk space.

Partitioning means that the operating system will identify the partitions as though they are *separate* hard drives. They will appear in file management software such as Windows® Explorer with separate drive identifiers.

Partitioning allows for several conditions to be addressed.

More efficient disk space allocation

In older operating systems such as Windows® 95, partitioning allowed disk space to be allocated more efficiently. Figure 4.10 shows that as the partition gets larger then the minimum unit of storage, the *cluster*, also gets larger. This reflects adopting an addressing scheme that uses a 16-bit number.

Partition sizes (MB)	Minimum required cluster size (KB)	Percentage wasted space (approx.)
16–127	2	2
128–255	4	4
256–511	8	10
512–1023	16	25
1024–2047	32	40
2048–4096	64	50

Figure 4.10 *Calculation of minimum cluster size*

> ## Activities
>
> *To find out how many addresses can be supported using a 16-bit number, try this activity. Use the calculator that comes with Windows® to do the following:*
>
> - *click on View on the menu bar*
> - *change to Scientific view*
> - *click on the 2 button*
> - *click the x^y button*
> - *click on the 1 and 6 buttons (for 16)*
> - *click the = button (result = 65536)*
> - *click on the – button*
> - *click on the 1 button*
> - *click the = button (result = 65535)*
> - *click on the Bin radio button.*
>
> *You should get the result 1111111111111111. This tells you that a 16-bit number can store up to 65535 addresses.*
>
> *If one number equals an address and each address can store 64KB of data, what is the largest drive that this system can use?*

The early file systems reflected this fixed number of addresses, so as disk space increased, cluster size had to grow. However, this approach to storage is wasteful, as you have seen in Figure 4.10. Why is this so? Cluster size is the *minimum* unit of storage, so if a file is being stored on a hard disk of 512MB it uses *at least* 16KB of space. If the file were 20KB in size then it would require two clusters, meaning that 12KB of space would be wasted. Partitioning the drive into smaller sizes means that the overall space stays the same but the cluster size can be reduced.

Activity

Imagine a hard drive of 1023MB is being partitioned into four logical drives. What will be the size of each partition (assuming they are of equal size), and what will be the minimum cluster size? Calculate what percentage of waste there is for a 20KB file when stored using 16KB clusters and the new cluster size you have just determined.

Use of different file systems

The next reason to partition a drive is in order to use different file systems. For example, Windows® NT Network Server uses a file system called NT File System (NTFS). This means the directory information for the files and the way the files are stored on the disk are different from the way the file information is stored by Windows® 95 (FAT file system) or Windows 98 (FAT or FAT32 file system). NTFS is able to read data from an older file system, but if older programs in FAT format need to be stored on an NTFS drive then they have to be stored on a partition setup using the older file system such as MS-DOS.

Use of more than one OS

Finally, partitioning is used if a machine is to be operated with two different OS. This allows the system to be 'dual-booted' into either of the two operating systems (but not at the same time!).

File systems and file organisation

You have already seen how different file systems may affect the space taken up by files, and how it is

necessary to use a file system that is compatible with the software applications and data files being used on a system. Newer file systems generally have a more efficient structure and include more facilities. However, they have to address the issue of 'backwards compatibility', so that if a system is being upgraded older files are still usable. In this section, you will look at how file systems work, the facilities they offer and a comparison of different types.

At the lowest level (i.e. immediately after formatting), a hard disk contains sectors numbered 0, 1, 2, etc. and concentric tracks similarly numbered (see Figure 3.21 on page 44). This forms the basic organisation of a disk. Without additional support, each disk would be one large storage area. Operating systems allow the addition of *directory structures* to break the disk up into smaller collections of files, assign names to each file, and manage the free space available to create new files.

The directory structure and methods for organising a disk or partition is called a *file system*. Different file systems reflect different operating system requirements or different performance assumptions. Some file systems work better on small machines, while others work better on large servers.

Files

Most traditional operating systems for small machines are not concerned with the content of files but see them as a group of bytes. What the bytes represent is determined by the software which will use them, so they may be bit-mapped graphics, MP3 files, numbers etc. Microsoft file systems use extensions such as .exe (executable) to differentiate from .txt (text) files, but this is more custom and practice rather than a real difference recognised by the OS. File extensions can be used to match files with applications so that it easier to open a file directly into the program that created it. Other OS do have file types that control the way a file is internally structured.

What the OS has to do is be able to manage files so they can be stored and retrieved from the disk. In order to do this, the file system uses directory records or entries that store information about the file, and a table that stores information about where on the disk files are allocated too.

Figure 4.11 shows an example of a directory record. Note that the record says which cluster the file starts

File name	File extension	A	D	V	S	H	R	Time	Date	First file cluster	File size
Assignment 1 MW-2	doc	✓						23:34	07/03/2001	2922	45
Snmpapi	dll	✓						16:23	03/03/1999	12345	456

Figure 4.11 *Example of a directory record or entry*

in. Later on you will see how the cluster information is organised to access files. This example also shows that the record includes special attribute bits that mean the following:

- A: archive – file needs to/not be included in a backup
- D: directory – a system file that holds information about groups of files or directories
- V: volume label – describes the disk partition
- S: system files – can't be deleted from within the OS
- H: hidden – won't show up in a listing of files
- R: read – can't be written to

Most OS (but not MS-DOS®) allow long file names. In order that Windows 9x and above can use long file names and be backward compatible with MS-DOS®, the file name portion of the directory entry points to a special file where the remaining portion of the name is stored. (This is known as a *fix.*)

Directories

As files are created their names are entered in directories (folders in Windows®). However,

directories may be limited in the number of file entries they can hold, so sub-directories are used to increase the number of files that can be stored. Even if an OS is not so restricted in the number of entries, sub-directories make the organisation of files for users much easier as they can be grouped according to different uses and for different people. The structure of directories, starting from the *root directory,* is called a *directory tree* (see Figure 4.12).

To find a file in a directory or folder, it is easy to use a graphical interface to click on directory names that open up and display the files they have inside them. However, sometimes it is useful to know the address of a file in applications that do not offer a graphical interface. In order to tell the OS where to find the file, we type in the path to the file, starting with the drive and root directory. For example, the path to the directory highlighted in Figure 4.13 is:

C:\Program Files\JBuilder3\samples\com\
borland\samples\jbcl\cardlayout.

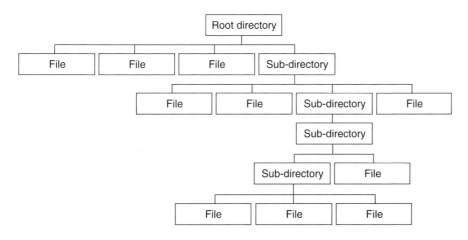

Figure 4.12 *A directory tree starting at the root and branching into sub-directories.*

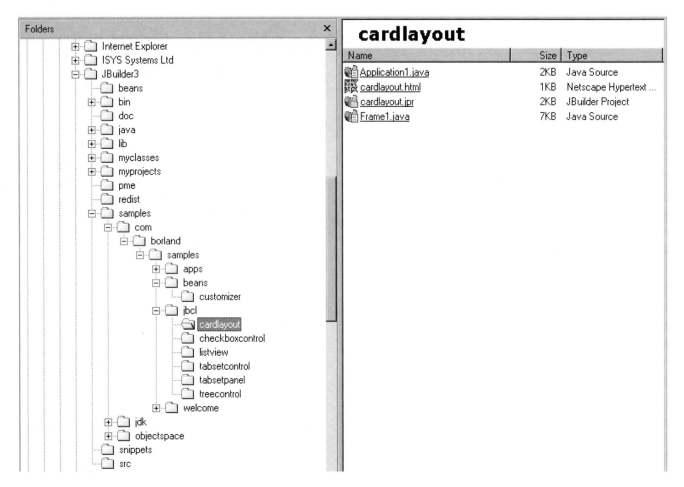

Figure 4.13 *Typical multi-branching tree of directories and files as seen through file management software*

Activities

1. *Open a text editor, write a few short sentences, and then save the file as myfile.exe. Using a file manager, locate the file and find out what kind of file type the operating system has decided it is. Try opening the file and see what happens.*

2. *You have finished a piece of work and saved it in a file. In order that you don't accidentally erase it, you set its attribute to read-only. Have you successfully protected the file? Create a small text file and try this out. Also try editing the file and saving it.*

Organising hard disk space

As new files are created, they have to be allocated space on the hard drive and given an address based on the sector, track and cylinder being used.

Activity

To remind yourself what the terms sector, track *and* cylinder *mean, sketch a hard drive with three disks and draw them in. Note: don't confuse this with clusters; they are covered again later in this section.*

As files are added they will be given physical space that forms a *block*. When a file is able to reside in one space on a drive it is said to occupy *contiguous space*.

However two problems arise as more and more files are added.

The first problem is with *file allocation*. The files depicted on the first line in Figure 4.14 all occupy blocks of contiguous space on a disk. Notice that they are not the same size – file A is using two units of space and files B and C are using one unit of space. In order for File A to be able to grow, it is going to have to use free space that is not next to it. So the problem is: how is the file system going to keep track of the space allocated to a file that is not contiguous?

Space 1	Space 2	Space 3	Space 4	Space 5
File A		File B	File C	Free Space
File A.1		File B	File C	File A.2

Figure 4.14 *File allocation*

In Figure 4.14 you can see that file A on the second line now occupies two physically separate parts of the disk. The file system has to be able to access these parts, and in the right order.

The second problem concerns *fragmentation*. As time goes by, files are deleted and gaps appear all over the disk space – this would be fine if other files took over the space completely, but what happens is that smaller and smaller gaps are scattered over the disk and new files are broken up to fill them. The file system has become fragmented (see Figure 4.15). This means that when files are in use the OS has to keep track of where all the different parts of a file are stored, thus slowing down access time.

Solutions to allocation and fragmentation

File allocation

In order to keep track of space and the location of files, system designers decided to use a table to store information about all the locations on the disk. Because some systems could not address the actual physical unit (sector x, track y, cylinder z) the file system was divided into allocation units or *clusters*. You have already seen how disk size is matched to cluster size. A file must use a minimum of one cluster but can use more if necessary.

The table (or array) stores the file allocation for every cluster on the disk (see the activity at the end of this section to see how many clusters this is). Each file name says which cluster it starts from and the table stores the remaining clusters it occupies (see Figure 4.16). The same is true for all the other files. This system allocates space dynamically as the file organisation changes, using this linked list (also known as *file chaining*).

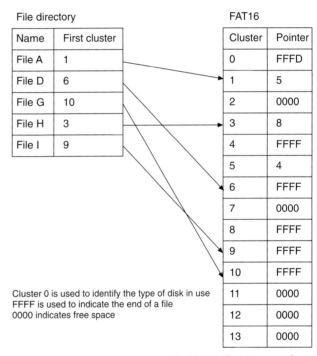

File directory

Name	First cluster
File A	1
File D	6
File G	10
File H	3
File I	9

FAT16

Cluster	Pointer
0	FFFD
1	5
2	0000
3	8
4	FFFF
5	4
6	FFFF
7	0000
8	FFFF
9	FFFF
10	FFFF
11	0000
12	0000
13	0000

Cluster 0 is used to identify the type of disk in use
FFFF is used to indicate the end of a file
0000 indicates free space

Figure 4.16 *File allocation table as used by MS-DOS® and Windows®.*

Time	Space 1	Space 2	Space 3	Space 4	Space 5	Space 6	Space 7	Space 8	Space 9	Space 10	Space 11	Space 12
T1	File A		File B	File C								
T2	File A.1		File B	File C	FileA.2	File D		File E	File F	File G		
T3	File A.1			File C	FileA.2	File D			File F	File G		
T4	File A.1		File H.1	File C	FileA.2	File D		File H.2	File F	File G		
T5	File A.1		File H.1		FileA.2	File D		File H.2		File G		
T6	File A.1		File H.1	File A.3	FileA.2	File D		File H.2	File I	File G		

Figure 4.15 *Fragmentation table*

The facilities of current operating systems

Fragmentation

To sort out files which become scattered across the disk and non-contiguous, special utilities are used to *defragment* the disk. Windows® uses a program called defrag.exe to do this. Files that occupy non-contiguous clusters are reorganised so that they occupy contiguous ones.

File systems

The system of file allocation described in earlier sections is essentially how MS-DOS® works. Originally it used a 12-bit then a 16-bit FAT table, until later versions of Windows® used a 32-bit file allocation table that allowed much larger drives to be used without having unduly large cluster sizes.

Microsoft then introduced VFAT that incorporated several enhancements to the disk management capabilities. Access to the file system can be done using high-speed 32-bit drivers, or for compatibility, the older MS-DOS® 16-bit routines. Support was added for long file names and also for better control over such matters as disk locking – so utilities could access the disk in 'exclusive mode' without fear of other programs using it in the meantime.

Windows® NT and now Windows® 2000 use a file system called NTFS. This also uses clusters but the largest is a 4KB one that means much less disk space is wasted. NTFS creates a table of logical cluster numbers that are used for addressing the disk. It assigns cluster numbers from the start to the end of the disk. Taking the logical cluster number and multiplying it by the size of a cluster establishes a physical disk 'offset' – where in the disk a file starts.

Unlike file systems described already, NTFS files are not simply streams of bytes that are then organised by an application. A file is a *structured object* consisting of *attributes*. Each attribute of a file is an independent stream of bytes making up the file's characteristics. Attributes include the file name, the creation date and security descriptor that specifies access control. Directory attributes include an index of the files stored in it, and then there is the data attribute that is the data stored in the file. All the information relating to the attributes is stored in a master file table. 'Methods' are described for the various structures that comprise the file object (see Figure 4.17).

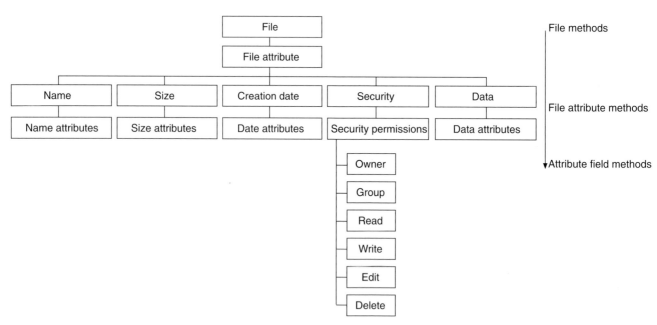

Figure 4.17 *NTFS structured file objects*

Conclusion

In this chapter you have learnt that the installation and configuration of an operating system requires keen attention to detail and careful work.

Drive space can often be better organised by breaking it into a number of logical partitions. Early file systems saw high wastage as disk size increased, and the fixed maximum address size meant that file clusters became inefficient. More recent file systems such as FAT32 and NTFS have bigger address sizes and allow for smaller, less wasteful cluster sizes. File organisation makes use of directory structures and file allocation methods using linked lists in tables.

CHAPTER 5

An introduction to mainframe computing

This chapter deals with a number of related matters. First we shall be looking at the commercial operations of banking, and in particular at the way banks use large mainframe computers. Banks have to process a huge number of transactions. Some are processed immediately whilst others are collected for batch processing.

You will see how the development of different processing needs has pushed the evolution of operating systems.

Finally, the chapter looks at how a bank can carry out training for systems administration staff when changes are undertaken.

We shall be covering:

- the commercial application of mainframes
- mainframes and their development
- transaction batch and online processing
- operating systems: background on processing modes
- specifying training needs.

The chapter covers the following Learning Outcomes in the specification:

L.O. 1.4 Indicate how an organisation should prepare for the changes that could result from the installation of a new ICT-based solution

L.O. 1.7 Specify training needs for ICT systems administration staff

It covers the following Technical Knowledge topics:

T1.1.1   The purpose of an operating system (part)
T1.2.1   Data types (part)
T1.2.3   Object types
T1.2.4   The storage implications of objects

Background on banks and banking

Banks are a dominating feature of everyday life. There are speciality banks offering a wide variety of different services, and most building societies now function as banks, having previously offered mostly investment and mortgage services.

The vast majority of the adult population have a bank account. The largest organisation has more than 15 million customers. It offers a wide range of financial services, including long-term savings, home and motor car insurance and share dealing.

The high street banks are going through a period of transition, involving streamlining of services and the way in which these organisations operate. There are certainly fewer branches in rural areas. Although the general public use the facilities at a bank for paying bills, cashing cheques and arranging loans, there are many people who bank online.

Banks still use the traditional system of gathering data from the public during the day, and transactions are either processed inhouse at the branch or relayed electronically to a centralised area. The processing makes use of a *mainframe computer*. Mainframe computers are used by many, if not most, large organisations such as insurance companies and airlines. Many terminals (up to 10,000) may be connected to a mainframe computer.

Bank ICT requirements

Transactions take place every day. From Monday to Saturday branches are open, and electronic transactions are possible 24 hours per day every day.

Batch processing usually takes place at the end of the working day, involving the millions of transactions that have taken place during the day. There is also online transaction processing where banking requests are processed immediately. The hardware requirements are vast, so a fully functioning mainframe is the key to an efficient service. However, each branch will contain at least a minimum requirement involving a network of machines.

Software is especially written for the bank, and support staff are required to ensure that it functions without error.

Automatic teller machines (ATMs) enable customers to withdraw money from the 'hole in the wall'. They are located outside most high street banks, and in the case of busy branches inside too. ATMs appear around busy supermarkets and in well-populated shopping areas.

EPOS (electronic point of sale) terminals are payment points inside supermarkets – you pay for your goods and have the option of 'cashback'.

Credit cards, direct debit, standing orders and salary payments are other aspects that should be considered. Clearly a bank is a complex organisation that is heavily dependent on the use of ICT.

A banker's story, Switzerland

Banc One Financial Card Services Corporation, a subsidiary of Banc One Corporation, is the nation's third largest third-party card processor. It provides services to a broad array of banks, savings and loans, credit-card finance companies and brokerage firms across the country. Triumph, a state-of-the-art application, processes over 16 million of the credit-card accounts and offers a variety of functions and services for third-party card processing, from product management and customer service, to risk management and collections processing. DB2® Batch processing is fundamental to the Triumph application process.

Customer services

Many new services have become available to customers with the growth of Internet banking. Quotations are given online, account balances are available and bills can be paid. There are current accounts, investment accounts and mortgages on offer.

Privilege speciality accounts are available to customers whose income from work exceeds a certain amount. This can allow cheaper loan rates, higher investment rates, savings on home shopping, car leasing, extended warranty on household appliances and free holiday insurance.

It is clear that banking is adapting to the technological revolution and incentives are given at different levels. The younger 16-year-old is encouraged to 'open an account' with arrangements for percentage discount offers from popular high street shops.

Business banking

Banks offer a number of services to the business world including:

- Insurance
- Money transmission
- Pension scheme advice
- Foreign currency services
- Business-related publications.

Banks will also offer support and advice to charitable organisations and to environmental and ecological groups.

Introducing 'GBW Bank'

The 'GBW Bank' is a large national bank created from a building society that 'de-mutualised' in the early 1990s. It engages in all the traditional banking activities but still has particular specialisms in mortgages, property, insurance and loans.

GBW is to merge with 'BS', a small regional building society that currently has 85 branches scattered over the north west of England. It has a centralised mainframe system that is used to batch process client transactions generated through terminals at branch offices. Most of its work is with mortgages, loans and insurance that requires careful preparation of user details before being entered into the batch system.

ICT aspects of the change

Merger will have many implications for the work of BS, not least as its computer systems will have to be brought into line with those of the GBW bank. The challenge of the merger, for the ICT systems, is how different systems can be brought together and integrated into one coherent operation. A strategic decision is that the newly merged building society will have its operations brought into line with those of the GBW bank. The proposals for change are as follows:

- All new branch offices will be upgraded to local area networks (LANs) running Windows® 2000 Server and Professional.
- Mainframe operations will be switched to the GBW computer centre.
- GBW's current transaction processing applications will be installed on the new LANs.
- Banking systems (current accounts, loans, overdrafts, mortgages and insurance) will be brought into line with GBW.
- Computer centre staff will be relocated, some to the GBW national computing centre. The rest will be trained to act as regional support staff for the branches.

The reasons for carrying out the changes in this way are (a) to ensure continuity of service and (b) to avoid the inevitable problems when two incompatible computer systems are merged. The process will be rolled out as follows:

- Each branch will have their new LAN implemented and their new OS installed. Existing applications will continue to be used on the PCs, which will act as dumb terminals to the current mainframe. In the next stage, GBW's applications will be setup on PCs so they can operate in dual operating mode either as terminals to the old mainframe or as clients of GBW's mainframe. Training of staff will be carried out inhouse on new applications.
- Once LAN hardware and communications have been shown to be reliable, and training has been undertaken, applications using GBW's mainframe will go live. Customer transactions will be processed online and in real time.
- Branches that wait to be included will continue to use the current system.

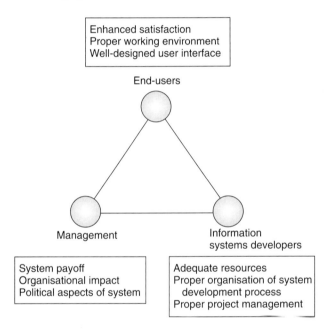

Activity

Prepare a timeline showing the activities required for the changes to take place.

The Head of Information Systems, Jane Morgan, has overall charge of introducing changes to the bank's ICT operations. She has to ensure that three key agents to the change process are satisfied (see Figure 5.1). They have different perspectives and interests and these have to be managed. In the diagram you can see how the agents might view what is important for them in the change process.

Enhanced satisfaction
Proper working environment
Well-designed user interface

End-users

Management

Information systems developers

System payoff
Organisational impact
Political aspects of system

Adequate resources
Proper organisation of system
development process
Proper project management

Figure 5.1 *Three key agents in a change process*

Introduction to mainframe computing

The Senior Systems Administrator for GBW Bank is James Harris. He originates from the financial sector and so has considerable experience in the operation of large mainframe centres. He needs to ensure that as part of project management he can commission new equipment to extend the operation of the existing mainframe while still allowing existing GBW banking operations to continue. This section introduces you to the operation of mainframes in organisations.

Mainframe systems are used widely in large organisations where mission-critical data processing is required. This includes airlines, manufacturing or financial institutions where loss of computer processing would have a severe impact on the functioning of the business. When it is a matter of controlling millions of transactions and integrating the flow of data between systems coupled together, then it is no good the computing centre saying 'The server's down and we're just rebooting it now. You might be able to use it quite soon.'

Connecting

In the past a company would buy a single computer, to which their terminals would connect using various channels. One way would be to connect terminals through a 'multiplexor' that allowed many terminals to share a single high-speed link. Another way would be for remote users to connect through a modem using the phone lines. A third way was for computer terminals to connect to the mainframe by cables running direct to the system.

Today's mainframe environment is much more mixed although access to the mainframe still involves the public telephone system, using dedicated leased lines. There are many more solutions being employed and therefore many more suppliers of these solutions. A mainframe is likely to be connected to different kinds of network and needs to be able to offer *open systems interconnectivity* – which means different commercial products use the same standards, so they can work together.

Reliability

In order for the system's operations to be very robust, computer designers build in high-capacity components which will have the ability to switch to mirror systems without loss of function. This switching is controlled by the operating system and allows for 'graceful degradation'. Another technique that may be used is to switch demand from one part of the system to another – this is known as 'load balancing'.

Systems like this also allow for new peripherals to be added or removed while the machine is functioning. This is known as 'hot-plugging'.

Altogether a system that allows for work to be passed to other parallel machines and to tolerate system 'outages' is called *fail-safe* or *fault-tolerant*.

Specification

A modern mainframe setup might have a specification like this:

- capable of supporting between one and 12 processors
- support for 512MB or 1, 4, 8, 12, 16, 24, 32 gigabytes of internal memory
- support for several types of high-speed network adapter cards which can work at from 100 to 155Mbps
- support for multiple storage disks on high-speed input/output buses – these are known as RAID (redundant array of inexpensive disks) systems
- support for a variety of operating systems which might run concurrently, such as Unix®, Windows® 2000, Linux® as well as its own OS
- ability to process different languages such as Java, C, C++ and its own job control language
- dual-power system to cover for loss of power
- ability to manage a range of local-area network types, such as Ethernet and Token Ring
- high-speed fibre-optic channels to a number of communication routers.

There will also be a coupling facility that links several mainframe computers together, allowing them to share data and programs. This facility is used to present the

Activities

1. *What does it mean to have 'mirror systems'?*

2. *Explain 'load-balancing', 'hot-plugging and 'graceful degradation'.*

3. *Explain the elements of Figure 5.2 in as much detail as you can.*

combined processing power as a single logical computing system. It also means that they can take over processing if one system becomes disturbed. Each system may be many miles away from its sisters.

In Figure 5.2 you can see a typical layout of this kind of system. The mainframes are used here for batch-processing jobs as well as interactive time-sharing applications accessing data stored in databases. It will also be running an e-commerce system for the company's intranets, including online banking. Remember that although only one branch is shown, this system will be connected to hundreds of other computer systems, whether they be local-area networks or ATMs. Communication channels are fed through the 'data centre router' that controls I/O to the rest of the world.

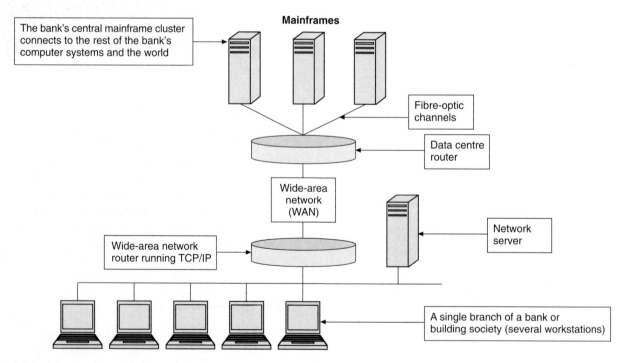

Figure 5.2 *A modern mainframe setup*

Upgrading

James Harris has to carry out a projection of the consequences of delivering additional traffic to the mainframe cluster used by GBW Bank. From this he can plan where and what new equipment is needed to deal with the increased demand. The information box 'Full service banking' illustrates how changes to an existing system can improve company operations.

Full-service banking

At Tri Counties Bank, community partnership is the key to gaining a competitive advantage in a marketplace dominated by banking giants. Founded 20 years ago in Chico, California, Tri Counties has grown from its initial $1 million investment to $630 million in assets by serving predominantly rural communities throughout Northern California.

Tri Counties works hard to maintain personal service and accessibility for its customers. In addition to locating branch offices in rural communities – some as small as Bieber, with a population of fewer than 1000 – the bank has been a leader in developing supermarket branches. The bank's 21 offices provide a variety of agricultural and community development loans and makes significant donations to community organizations and schools.

One of the greatest challenges that Tri Counties has faced in its growth has been managing a communications network that spans several telephone companies. Connections were difficult and often unreliable, limiting the bank's ability to take advantage of new technology. When Pacific Bell offered Frame Relay service in the Tri Counties area, the bank looked to IBM for a networking solution that could take advantage of the new communications services.

Its marketing and technology partnership with Bell Pacific enabled IBM to provide a complete, end-to-end networking solution across Tri Counties' service area. "We knew that we were building our business on whatever networking solution we chose," says Ray Rios, Tri Counties' information systems manager.'

With many of its branches in remote locations, consistent and reliable service played a critical role in the vendor selection. "IBM can provide on-site service in all of our offices," says Ray Rios. "And the service is consistent at every location. Whenever problems arise, IBM is very responsive – their service has been outstanding."

Tri Counties' WAN is a multiprotocol network, supporting the bank's existing SNA communications as well as new applications over a Novell NetWare LAN. In addition to equipment, IBM provided network design, installation and implementation services for Tri Counties. The WAN uses IBM 2210 Nways Multiprotocol–Application Network infrastructure to support operations distributed over an extensive service area

An enabling environment

Although Tri Counties only recently installed the new network, results are already evident. Within two months, the bank's new electronic mail system reduced the amount of paper being transferred between locations by 50 per cent. Loan processing will also get a boost from the new network. Today paper-based loan processing averages 30 days. In the future Tri Counties' loan officers will create, route and approve loan documents electronically. The bank's goal is to reduce loan turnaround to one week, significantly increasing customer satisfaction. "Every time we simplify our internal processes, we reduce the time it takes to get an answer back to the customer," says Rios.

The bank's principal business application, FiServe from Comprehensive Banking Systems (CBS), can now be distributed to local servers in the branch offices, reducing processing time. And because power outages are a fact of life in the Tri Counties' service area, the network will increase system reliability and availability by enabling unaffected areas to continue processing locally.

As part of the networked FiServe system, Tri Counties will be implementing a new teller application that provides online signature verification. The bank anticipates that this feature alone will eliminate a significant amount of fraud. Distributing information via an intranet, the bank plans to publish internal documents. For example, interest rate schedules will no longer be faxed to the branch offices. Instead the information will be posted on the intranet, where it can be accessed easily from all locations.

"The intranet can be used to distribute a wide variety of information that is currently being printed and delivered to each user," Rios explains. "For example, instead of printing 1200 manuals, we can publish bank procedures and system documentation on an intranet page. Users can pull the information they need, when they need it. It is more efficient and it will dramatically reduce printing and distribution costs."

Rios stresses the value of a single-source network solution. "A WAN is too big a project to build by yourself, and there are too many variables in a multi-vendor solution. With a single-source solution, you have clearly defined accountability. You have one person to call. And with IBM as our supplier, as soon as we make that call, someone is working on our problem immediately."

Activities

1. *What were the challenges to Tri Counties' ICT services, and what was the proposal for overcoming them?*

2. *How was Frame Relay going to be used to assist Tri Counties, and what did it mean in terms of the networking solution?*

3. *List all the gains that were made in using the new system.*

4. *Think about what you have learnt about mainframe systems. Suggest some of the types of changes James Harris might adopt to prepare the GBW mainframe centre for additional capacity.*

Transaction processing in organisations

Any business operation is likely to produce information relating to the changing state of people's relationships to it. A bank has to maintain information about the flow of money throughout the system and between external and internal bodies. *Transaction processing* is about capturing, processing and storing these activities.

Transactions make up the mainstay of a bank's processing system as they record the individual activities of money moving around the system. Many banks still use programs developed to record and process transactions from the earliest days of their computerisation. These are often referred to as *legacy systems* because they are a legacy from the bank's earliest IT investments and are kept running on new machines because they essentially need little adjustment.

The basics

Data is captured about an operation from many different avenues and in many different forms. The most efficient data capture is recording a transaction electronically so that it can be processed immediately by the ICT system. For example, data might be captured using a bar-code reader at a point-of-sale terminal or by a credit card scanner at a retail store. It might be data generated from an e-commerce website when, for example, a user makes a purchase. In banks, the flow of cheques is an important part of data capture.

Once data is captured it has to be processed. There are two ways in which transactions are processed: batch and online. Batch processing happens when transaction data are accumulated over a period of time and then processed at regular intervals. In contrast, online processing (OLTP) happens in 'real time', so the transaction is dealt with immediately by the computer applications maintaining company data.

A typical bank batch-processing job might be creating monthly statements of current accounts. Information on transactions may come from the ATM transaction file, cheques that have been issued, cheques that have been received and electronic data interchange through electronic funds transfer (this would include such things as pay, direct debits and standing orders).

The data files that record a company's activities must be kept up to date. New transactions must be processed so that the database reflects the current balance of resource flows. Transaction processing updates the company database.

Transaction processing systems must also produce documents and reports that reflect the state of different aspects of an organisation's work. These may be invoices, timesheets, purchase orders and summary documents.

Transaction processing systems may allow users to produce queries of the company database to find out the current state of transactions. Using a web browser or other input system, queries can be generated and the results displayed in a suitable format.

Specifics

Transaction files

Figure 5.3 shows how transaction data from paper-based records are used to update the files that maintain the account for whatever activity the records are for. A transaction file would consist of a record for each of the transactions committed by a bank's customers in a specified time period.

The following table shows an example of a transaction file record:

Field name	Data type	Size in bytes
Account number	String	9
Date	Date	4
Amount	Numeric (float)	4
Transaction type	String	3
Transaction description	String	45

The account number of the bank's customer identifies the transactions in a file. Records in the file will be stored in the order in which they were created. Usually, as in the example here, the length of the record is fixed and this is used by the system to determine the start and end point of each record – known as a *fixed-length record*. Field sizes can vary, in which case each record needs to have an additional field to indicate the length of the record.

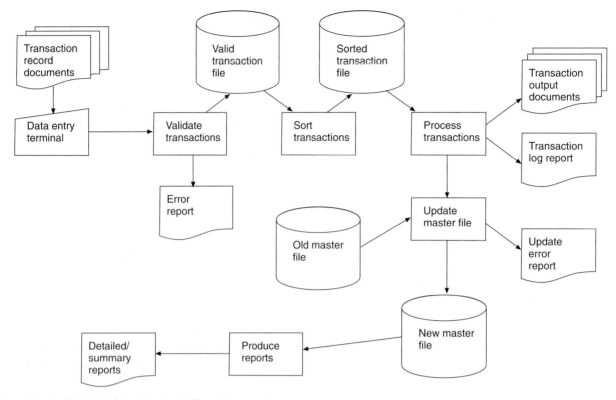

Figure 5.3 *System flowchart of batch processing: file update*

Activities

1. *Why does the account number identify the transactions in a file? How is it used?*

2. *Give examples of information that might be stored in this transaction record?*

3. *Describe the process of customer file update by cheques being processed through the system flowchart in Figure 5.3.*

The following is a typical layout of a transaction file on disk:

Each *record* consists of *fields* determined by the application programmer. The fields allow for each record structure to be composed of data representing the different *types* that are being processed. The field types may be defined by the programming language or else will be constructed by the programmer into a *user-defined type*.

Figure 5.4 shows some of the commonly used data types that are built into a programming language. These are also known as the language's *primitive or built-in data types*, and they can be converted directly into a binary representation by the program compiler.

Start of file	*Header Record*						*End of file*
8 bytes	255 bytes	Record 1	Record 2	Record 3	Record 4	Record 5	Record 6	8 bytes

Type	Name	Size	Description
Numeric	Byte	8 bits	Very small signed integer (-128 to +127)
	Short	16 bits	Short signed integer (-32768 to+ 32767)
	Int	32 bits	Large signed integer
	Long	64 bits	Very large signed integer
	Float	32 bits	Large decimal-point number
	Double	64 bits	Very large decimal-point number
Character	Char	8 bits	One of the ASCII character codes
Boolean	Boolean	1 bit	True or false

Figure 5.4 *Typical primitives*

Programming languages also have *composite types* that allow more complex data structures to be created. The most common are the *array* and *string* types. They both allow a programme to use data made up of lists of similar types – such as a list of temperatures, of prices or of characters (this is so that textual data can be accessed in the same operation):

Example of Integers (Short)	-9	22	65	3990	1192	4357
Example of Floats	12.33	122.00	863.32	933.45		
Example of characters (string)	'C'	'y'	'b'	'o'	'r'	'g'

The transaction record stores information made up from primitive, composite and user defined types.

Activity

Why do you think the account number is defined as a string?

In the transaction record, the date is an example of a user-defined type. This means that the programmer has created his or her own data structure which has been called 'date'. It is made up from the language's primitives and might be defined in the following way:

Date:
  Day: byte
  Month: byte
  Year: short

Activity

Try designing a user-defined type for a field called 'personal id' that is going to be used to store a person's initials, postcode and gender.

It is also worth pointing out that record structures are themselves user-defined types, because it is the programmer who builds up their storage characteristics from primitives and other user-defined types.

Programming systems do vary on which data types are represented in them as primitives. Some applications may allow you to use *date or currency types*, and others have types that are particularly useful for system programming – such as accessing memory.

Online real-time processing

With the development of the Internet, many banks are starting to provide comprehensive online transaction processing for their customers. Figure 5.5 shows the system flows that are required.

Activity

Imagine an input screen for a bank customer setting up an online account to be used over the Internet. What do you think needs to be checked at the validation stage?

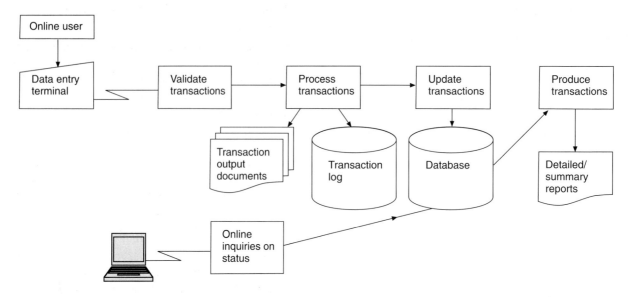

Figure 5.5 *System flowchart of online processing*

The WORLDSPAN reservation system

Maintaining continuous global operations 24 hours per day, 365 days per year of the WORLDSPAN computer reservation system is no easy feat. For one thing, the sheer volume of data is staggering: 15 IBM transaction processing facility (TPF) transactions for each reservation, with more than 2200 transactions received each second during peak periods (over 90 million per day). And while 80 per cent of the transactions are fairly simple, the other 20 per cent are extremely complicated.

To balance this huge workload and ensure quick processing, WORLDSPAN originally connected its network to one IBM mainframe computer that functioned as a communications front-end. This mainframe operated as a traffic cop, feeding transactions to seven additional mainframes over channel-to-channel connections to ensure that each carried its proper share of the workload. (The actual transaction processing was done on these additional mainframes.) At the same time, this configuration ensured fast processing. Because each mainframe ran TPF software, any system could process the transactions.

Reproduced with permission from IBM's T. J. Watson Research Laboratory. Copyright International Business Machines Corporation, 1999.

Online operation is definitely the future for financial institutions, but an important issue for consumers and banks is to ensure that transactions can take place securely and confidentially. One approach to this is the *secure electronic transaction* (SET) standard for electronic payments.

The development of the SET standard is an interesting example where it is possible to see how real-time transaction processing works. It concerns security between an online customer, an online shop or merchant and a credit card company.

An overview of SET

SET has been developed by Visa and MasterCard, along with a number of other companies providing technical input. It defines an architecture and a set of protocols, providing an open standard that is now widely accepted for use in e-commerce. Briefly, SET provides:

- *Encryption* of information, to allow confidentiality of information being transmitted
- *digital signatures* and *certificates* to allow the means to authenticate other participants in the transaction (digital signatures are used to detect tampering of data while a transaction between participants is being undertaken)
- *an open set of protocols* to provide *interoperability* between the systems of different vendors.

The participants in a SET e-commerce application are:

- the card holder – the consumer doing the purchase
- the credit card company – the financial institution that issues the card to the card holder
- the merchant – the online store providing the goods

- the acquirer – the financial institution of the merchant
- the *payment gateway* – the system, operated by the acquirer, that handles the financial requests from the merchant and interacts with the credit card company on the merchant's behalf
- the *certificate authority* – a website that can generate and validate certificates.

The relationships between these participants are shown in Figure 5.6 (the solid lines indicate protocol flows defined in SET, the dashed lines indicate some possible non-SET protocol relationships). Figure 5.7 takes you through a typical transaction process.

The example demonstrates several important aspects of online transaction processing. It is likely to involve a number of participants. It requires software that may have to work across networks and between different software. It needs to use unique methods of program design.

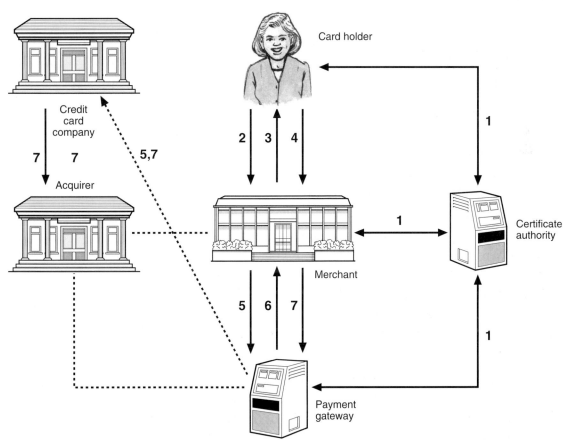

Figure 5.6 *Making an online purchase (see also Figure 5.7)*

Step	SET scenario	Real-life scenario
1	Participants request and receive certificates from certificate authority.	–
2	Card holder browses online catalogue, selects items, and sends order to merchant.	Consumer goes into store, selects items to purchase, and takes them to sales desk.
3	Merchant sends its certificate to card holder for verification.	–
4	Card holder sends its certificate to merchant.	Consumer hands credit card to sales clerk.
5	Merchant requests payment authorisation from payment gateway, which checks with credit card company of the payment card.	Sales clerk swipes card through device.
6	After payment, gateway verifies with credit card company; it returns the result to the merchant.	An authorisation code is returned through the device, which the sales clerk records.
7	Some time later, the merchant requests payment capture from the payment gateway for one or more credit transactions. The payment gateway sends the request to the financial network to have the amount transferred from the credit card company to the acquirer.	At the end of the day, credit card slips are sent to the credit card company, requesting payment.

Figure 5.7 *A guide to Figure 5.6*

Interoperability

The SET standard is a fully documented and open specification. This is so that software developers can use the SET protocols and write software that will be able to work with software they have not designed. The *SET data types* give both sets of designers a common interface through which their software can work. A message that is created at one end of the transaction chain will be expected to work in a well-defined way and have data values meaningful to both parties engaged in the transaction.

Figure 5.8 demonstrates how *part* of the SET messaging definition has been designated. It indicates which parts are global (i.e. shared between the card-holder and the merchant systems) and which parts can be used solely for one party to the transaction.

Object-oriented design

One way in which systems such as SET are represented is as objects with a real life of their own operating in a collaborative and distributed world. Processes on different computers have to be able to work together to deliver a service, and must do so in a busy, sometimes conflicting, world.

Version	Version of SET message
Revision	Minor revision of SET message
Date	Date and time of message generation
MessageIDs	{[LID-C], [LID-M], [XID]}
RRPID	Request/response pair ID for this cycle
SWIdent	String identifying the software (vendor and version) initiating the request
LID-C	Local ID: convenience label generated by and for the cardholder's system
LID-M	Local ID: convenience label generated by and for the merchant's system
XID	Globally unique ID generated by the merchant in **PInitRes** or by the card holder in **PReq**

Figure 5.8 *SET message wrapper*

This approach to program design is called *object-oriented programming* and is a way of producing programs using a 'real-world' model. Things that make up a program are modelled as though they were real objects. A customer account in a bank may be one such object. Each object is made up of a *class* that defines the data it uses, and *methods* that describe what activities can be carried out on the data. Objects communicate with each other by sending *messages* and responding to messages. The messages are passed to the object through its *interface* with the rest of the world.

In the SET example, an object may be a customer credit card account. Part of this class is the data about the credit card and what activities (methods) that credit card can do. The most important activity is the payment one and involves the owner exchanging information with a service provider. The card holder needs to ensure the transaction is safe and the amount is correctly deducted. The service provider wants to ensure that the card holder is genuine and the credit card valid. They communicate their data to each other using a common interface such as the XID identifier listed in Figure 5.8

Another example is the bank account object made up from the data it defines and the methods that work on it. Data would include an account number and an account name, for example. Methods might include actions such as 'debit account' or 'credit account'.

Figure 5.9 shows how an object may receive a message from an external object or sender. Based on the

contents of the message the receiving object may initiate actions formed from the methods. These methods will act on data local to the object and may pass messages back to the rest of the system where other objects will do things.

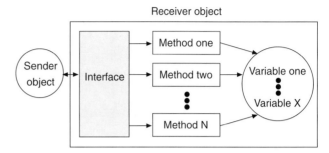

Figure 5.9 *The sender/receiver relationship*

Activity

Imagine you are deciding the characteristics of a program object called 'printer'. Discuss in small groups what messages the object can receive, what methods it might have and what responses it can make to messages. You might want to summarise your findings on a diagram showing the object printer, the messages it receives, the actions or methods it performs, the data it needs to hold and the responses it can make.

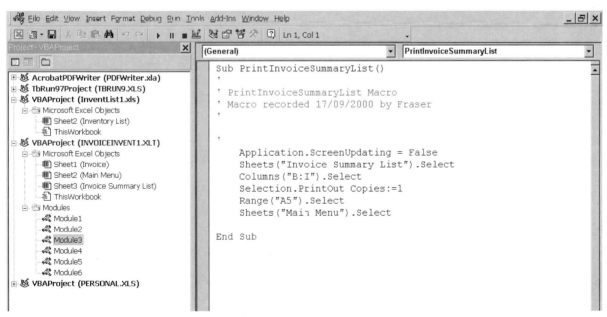

Figure 5.10 *Objects in Excel, represented in Visual Basic®*

This programming approach is called a *paradigm* and is widely applied to many programming environments and applications. For example, you are probably familiar with Microsoft® Office applications that have an object-oriented model beneath them. Every part of an application is made up of objects. In Figure 5.10 you can see how some of the common objects of an Excel spreadsheet are referred to in a program.

An Excel worksheet is made up of cells, ordered in columns and rows. The cell as a basic unit holds data that can be set to a number of types. A cell also has properties such as its location in a sheet, the type of data it holds, its size, background colour and so on. A cell also has methods that act on it; an example of a method for a cell might be to change the type of data it holds from a number to text or to delete its contents. Similarly, worksheets have methods, data and properties. In the screenshot in Figure 5.11, an object of type 'Sheets' is selected, and then an object within the sheet 'Columns' is selected from column B to I, then a method 'PrintOut' is used.

Also in Figure 5.11 you can see part of a list of methods that can be used by Excel. In this case the picture shows Columns has a number of methods. The PrintOut method is shown, and at the very bottom of the picture you can see the messages it uses to control its behaviour.

Because objects are coherent units made up of all facets of their identity, they require more complex storage and manipulation. When a worksheet in Excel is opened, all the information about the columns, rows and cells that make it up must be restored, as well as any settings about their current appearance and state.

However, although the storage implications for objects means larger and more diverse files, software designers are able to use well-defined descriptions of objects saved in *software libraries*, to build new applications using existing objects and their characteristics. So, for example, a developer who wants to create a program to run in Windows® can use code already written to create windows with their familiar menus, toolbars and buttons. They add new functionality to core libraries of objects and their classes.

As stated before, object-oriented design has particular relevance to the Internet because the global collection of computers can be thought of as lots of objects receiving messages from each other and carrying out operations based on those messages. The information box describes this feature in more detail. Read and discuss the questions that follow.

Figure 5.11 *Methods in Excel*

The Tao of e-business services

Collaborating services on the Web resemble collaborating objects in an object-oriented (OO) system, especially in a distributed OO system. So the lessons learned from two decades of experience with OO systems can help us to understand systems of collaborating services.

An economy of collaborating services will consist of many service providers and many service requesters. This economy will become powerful only when we provide organising principles and structures, at design time and at runtime, to make the overall computing process understandable to individuals and to the social and business groups that need to embrace it.

Services represent yet another new form of computing that will require new organising principles. Each individual service, unlike an individual function or object, is designed to satisfy a business agenda of an individual organization while collaborating with applications or services from other organizations. So the organization of services must serve a constituency far larger than the technical professionals within a single company.

Runtime is when the carefully scripted and rehearsed sequence of collaborations among the various services plays out. Service requesters must find and bind to the right instance of one or more other services and then carry on the dialog needed to get the job done. Those services may, in turn, need to take advantage of still other services on other servers. The collaboration itself, not the behavior of any one machine, provides the value. For a decade or so, the consensus notion of computing has been undergoing a transformation from "computing happens in a single CPU" to "the network is the computer". We have seen architectures based on distributed object systems communicating through remote method calls and marshalled or demarshalled objects (for example, CORBA). This approach stems from a desire on the part of architects to tame the complexities of collaborating computers by making them look more like a problem with which we are more familiar: object systems running in a single computer. Collaborating services in the vast untamed chaos of the Internet is another beast entirely.

The business reasons for using e-services, in general, will be as varied as the reasons for using IT. The *killer* application for e-business services today is supply chain integration. Others will emerge as well. What we expect to happen is that a marketplace of e-services will open opportunities for outsourcing some work that is now done in monolithic applications. Another obvious application is splitting monolithic internal applications into multiple services that can more easily be specialised. This sort of thing is already common in high-volume Web sites.

Activities

1. *The article describes 'collaborating services'. Give examples of what might fit the author's description. Also what is meant by 'supply chain integration'. Draw a diagram showing the flow of data through collaborating services that make up this chain.*

2. *Imagine you are setting up an online auction. Think what services your website will have to provide to users. What transactions will you need to store? What administration issues will have to be considered?*

Operating systems: background on processing modes

The first computers using electronic components evolved from the experience of the Second World War, when scientific development was concentrated into producing more sophisticated weapon and control systems. Electronic equipment was built using parts called thermionic valves (or vacuum tubes). Up to the 1950s, huge machines comprising thousands of 'valves' were laboriously constructed in research institutes around the world.

To program a machine, the raw binary code (zeros and ones) had to be fed into the machine using a bank of switches. Simple calculations were the only thing performed, and the processing power was on a par with a basic handheld calculator today.

By the middle of the 1950s peripheral equipment was being designed to progress the way in which people could get input (programs, data) and output from a machine. One of these was a punched-card reader. This allowed binary code to be punched as holes, and a light-sensitive device could read in the columns of binary numbers. This not only meant it was easier to read in programs, but they were also stored for re-use. The electronics were now being built using transistors. The transistor was a much smaller component and a much more stable one. It was now possible to build commercially viable computers that were capable of doing serious work. The decades 1960–1970 were the heyday of the mega mainframe – huge computing devices operated by a team of specialists in special air-conditioned rooms, and supplied by a tiny handful of firms, such as IBM, and costing many millions of pounds.

Programs were still being written using punched cards or tape, but instead of feeding in one program at a time and then reading in the program which would translate the first into code, a system that became known as *batch processing* was developed. This used smaller computers devoted to reading a series of programming jobs held on card and writing them to magnetic tape. The tape was then loaded on the main computer and processed using a simple operating program that was the forerunner of today's operating system. This was called a *job control language*.

Job control languages are still used today and because they were developed in the era of the punched card that could hold 80 columns of binary code they still work to an 80-character format.

The job control process would identify the first job from tape noting the programmer's details, load the program translator, load the program to be translated, then translate the program and run it. Output would be written back to an output tape. Then the next job would be run. When all the jobs were run, the output tape would be taken to the smaller computer where results could be printed and a new batch loaded on to the mainframe.

It was during the 1960s that the integrated circuit took over the computer industry. This allowed many thousands of transistors to be built on to one circuit made from a silicon slice. More powerful computers could be made, which were smaller and cheaper. It also meant that computers could be placed in a range of environments: scientific, commercial and academic. IBM introduced a general-purpose range of computers starting with the 360. IBM wanted a flexible system where a family of computers existed that fitted different requirements but had a range of compatible software. They also wrote an operating system that could work on different platforms and satisfy the diverse requirements expected of it. The code was enormously complex, required legions of programmers to maintain it and was never rid of bugs.

Several new techniques were developed, of which *multiprogramming* was the most important. Multiprogramming allowed several jobs to be run at the same time so that when a job stopped using the processor (because it was doing something else such as input/output) another job could be started. This meant the CPU time was being fully utilised. The memory was *partitioned* into several portions and each portion held a job. When a job stopped using the processor, another job started. Special hardware was used to ensure that one job didn't interfere with the memory partition of another job (see Figure 5.12).

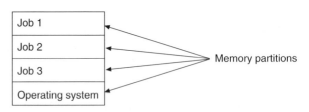

Figure 5.12 *The early concept of partitioning*

Another technique that was developed was *spooling*, which stands for 'simultaneous peripheral operation on-line'. Jobs were brought to the computer on cards that could be read and saved to disk while the computer was running other jobs. When one job finished it could load another from disk. Output to disk was also handled in this way.

A third development was to break out of the straightjacket imposed by batch processing. Programmers were tied to the cycle of waiting for their job to be entered into the system, processed and the results passed back to them. Instead, a system of *timesharing* was conceived. This is similar to multiprogramming but users could now use terminals to issue commands over their processes and the CPU time was divided between them. This provided for greater interactivity while still allowing selected jobs priority when necessary.

During this growth period in the use of computers, their size, price and processing power was constantly being revised. Not surprisingly smaller and cheaper machines meant departments in an organisation could buy into their own systems. The DEC PDP-1 was one such machine and started a generation of minicomputers, essentially stripped-down versions of mainframes. Big operating systems such as MULTICS were written to try to provide timesharing operations to hundreds of people – with mixed success. At the Bell Labs in America, a computer scientist, Ken Thompson, designed a simple one-user system that laid the foundation in 1974 for the Unix® operating system that is still widely used today.

To bring this historical journey up to date, we need to move on to the development of the very large-scale integrated circuit – the microprocessor chip that allowed all the necessary electronic components for a central processing unit to be held on a silicon wafer. This made it possible for computer companies to develop the personal computer or workstation. Though not dissimilar to a minicomputer, the microcomputer was cheap enough to be made available to individuals. It heralded the growth of new software that enthusiastic programmers would write. One of these was VisiCalc, the first spreadsheet, which became the 'killer app' of its day and made its author one of the new technology tycoons.

Programmers aimed to produce highly interactive and user-friendly software. The potential for more graphically oriented interfaces was continuously being pushed. The earliest operating system for early microcomputers was called CP/M, but Microsoft's DOS quickly superseded this when Bill Gates got the contract to supply the new IBM XT PC with its operating system. The XT was a phenomenal success and the rest, the story of MS-DOS®, is history. The first operating systems for PCs operated as single process systems because the single user would be running a single program at a time.

In the mid-1980s a further development was the *network operating system*. This allowed standalone machines to operate as though the rest of the world was part of their computing domain. People can access their own resources (disks, files, applications, printers) or resources on other computers. The growth of the Internet also means that any PC connected to a telephone line can operate with global links, using appropriate communications software. Operating systems now have to work in an environment that is widely distributed across the globe – hence the development of *distributed operating systems*.

Training needs

One of the most powerful ways of building satisfaction with a system is adequate training that enhances users' ability to work and is beneficial to their working life. At GBW Bank, Jane Morgan intends to tackle training in the following ways.

Senior managers will have to be briefed so they can understand the benefits and problems that the changes are likely to bring. They will need to understand:

- how the new systems will fit into corporate information systems strategy
- how added value can be gained from the investment by improving customer services
- how resources will be allocated and what level of resources will be needed to complete the changes
- which ICT developments are related to specific senior management functions.

Middle managers need to be fully aware of the computer system's functions so that corporate strategy is matched by the information system of the bank. They need to be kept closely informed of ICT projects and operations to ensure that they are working satisfactorily, and to decide where changes are needed.

Middle managers also need to be able to define security levels and policy, and so will need to be trained in requirements definition, how systems can be integrated, and how systems can be developed and utilised fully. They will also require training on specific software relevant to them, and the functions of the computer system.

For *general bank staff*, full training will be needed on all the various applications that will be used. When staff are working on the counter they will need to be able to carry-out the many functions required to manage accounts – such as checking balances, taking in money, authorising cheques etc. When working in back-office functions they may need to carry out searches and queries, tally accounts and ensure monthly returns are fulfilled.

Training-needs analysis

One way in which Jane can ensure training needs are fully met is to carry out *training needs analysis*. It is an approach that provides a rigorous set of criteria to training needs and outcomes. It may comprise the following steps:

- *Context analysis*. What is the setting where a training programme is proposed? A context analysis is used to define what the company hopes to accomplish through the training and why it has been proposed – this might be summarised by producing suggested *performance outputs*. This may seem obvious but unless management are clear why it is being implemented then it may not come about in a way sympathetic to the complex make-up of the organisation.
- *User analysis*. User analysis is about finding out who will be the learners and instructors. These are the people who will access the program in whatever format – a classroom setting, a self-study program or a multimedia format. Factors such as education, age, gender and mother tongue influence how people learn. Negative experiences with certain instructional methodologies can create resistance to some approaches to training. A solid user analysis will identify current levels of knowledge, attitudes and skills.
- *Work analysis*. This is an overall term used to group job study, task analysis, performance analysis and competency studies. All are variations on the training-needs analysis approach of

analysing the job, the required levels of performance and the ability of individuals or groups to perform at the required level.

- *Content analysis*. With this approach, material such as administrative procedures, laws and computer application documentation are used to identify topics of instruction. Content analysis may include existing courses that need to be updated, new policies and procedures that need to be taught, or material that a group of experts has brought together. The analysis of content helps to ensure that courses are designed in the most suitable way with, for example, a logical flow; definitions are found for key terms, and the level and clarity of the content are appropriate to the needs of the users – as established in the user analysis.
- *Training-suitability analysis*. Is non-performance due to a lack of knowledge and skills or are there another reasons? This is the essential question of a training-suitability analysis. Training is often seen as a quick fix for changing individual and organisational performance, but in reality the impact of training is limited to providing knowledge and skills and practice to develop them.
- *Cost–benefit analysis*. In a cost–benefit analysis, an instructional designer takes a long, hard look at the financial side of training, to determine whether training makes economic sense.

Once this analysis is carried out, the best available solutions to providing training can be sought.

Approaches to training

There are a number of approaches to training that can be provided. Usually a mixture of them will fit the availability of staff and their learning needs. Examples of different methods are:

- instructor-led courses using specialist bank staff or external training providers
- computer-based training using simulation programs or multimedia on CD-ROM
- intranet-based online training using browsers
- video training
- team-based training using manuals and other materials
- software training using Help facilities and special training modes such as training login and practice files.

Some staff may go on more extensive professional development courses to give them additional qualifications – such as Microsoft Certified Systems Engineer, Certified Novell Netware Engineer or Cisco qualifications.

Activities

1. *Suggest performance outputs that might be used to judge a training programme for GBW Bank.*

2. *Comment on what you think are the strengths and weaknesses of different training methods.*

Specific ICT training

Besides training programmes for all levels of the organisation, specific training will need to be provided for the ICT system staff. Jane identifies the following training needs:

- overview of the ICT infrastructure: LAN, LAN/WAN communications, and mainframe operations
- LAN administration: adding, removing and maintaining LAN hardware and network OS
- ICT system account policy and system security: workgroups, user account maintenance, security protocols and firewalls.
- mainframe operations: OS administration and configuration, applications development and management, and system integrity.

Conclusion

This chapter has introduced you to the use of ICT in banks, and in particular the range of business transactions that are processed by them. You read about a bank that was restructuring and the possible changes required to the ICT systems.

You went on to look at the use of mainframe computers in banks where millions of transactions are being processed daily. You saw the organisation of mainframe operations, how they related to a bank's overall operations, and the importance of good networking arrangements.

The importance of transaction processing was illustrated by two approaches: batch and online real-time processing. With batch processing, programmers organise data types and data structures. With online transaction processing, you saw how Internet security might be achieved using collaborating processes and how this kind of system was modelled using object-oriented design. This system uses a real-world approach that defines objects, their data and methods.

You have been introduced to the history of transaction modes as they developed in operating systems. The need for sharing the processor became implemented first in batch processes with multiprogramming, then through to multi-user, multitasking timeshared systems.

Finally, you have read about the role of training in bridging the competing interests of the many ICT users of the system. One way of investigating training needs is to carry out a training-needs analysis that gives a thorough understanding of the training cycle.

CHAPTER 6

Maintaining a networked system

This chapter looks at the operations of a water company and how its computer system is set up as a local-area network (LAN). You will read about the role of the systems administrators in maintaining the overall system.

In particular, the chapter covers:

- the computers connected to a company network
- network configurations (called topologies)
- network maintenance
- PC maintenance.

The chapter covers the following Learning Outcome in the specification:

L.O. 1.6 Critically appraise defined maintenance procedures for a specified ICT system

It covers the following Technical Knowledge topic:

T1.3.3 Networks

Introducing EauCo Water Company

'EauCo Water Co.' is based in South Shields, Tyne and Wear. During 1999 the company moved to Gateshead, a distance of eight miles, into temporary premises, while the old building was demolished and replaced with a new modern design.

Andrew Jones, the Operations Manager, runs all IT within the company at this site. He is not directly employed by EauCo Water, but works on a contract from a company called Direct Control. Two other people are responsible to Andrew; they are Kevin and Trevor, who carry out all the routine system administration. Andrew briefs Kevin and Trevor at weekly meetings, and he has overall control of the network and other computer applications within EauCo. This is not the only company that he works

with; he also works with Durham Spring Water, which is another large water company.

Some of Andrew's responsibilities are as follows:

- maintain computer operations within EauCo Water
- make sure that all the company's systems are secure
- offer support on the company's computer systems
- purchase new software
- purchase new hardware
- evaluate the company's computer equipment.

The computer system at EauCo Water

The computer system at EauCo comprises the local-

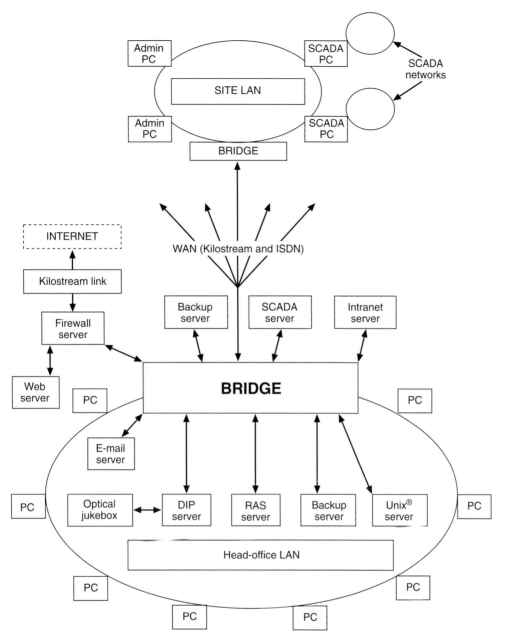

Figure 6.1 *The EauCo network*

area network (LAN) in Figure 6.1 and its connections to the outside world.

In the building there are approximately 120 PCs in use at any one time, in a network made up of six legs. There are over 400 metres of cable joining up the computers just within this office; however, if the distance of cable between individual machines becomes too large, then the signal that is sent between them will become distorted. Two main networks run in this office – a LAN and a WAN.

- The LAN allows workers to communicate with each other within the office, through a suitable cable.

- The WAN (wide-area network) allows employees to communicate between other sites of the water company, through the public telephone network. They have a dedicated line that is used only by their company to link to other offices – this ensures that data transfers between each site are reliable and open all the time. They also subscribe to a digital ISDN line from the phone company, which allows voice, data and video to travel over the same line at 128Kbps.

Within this office there are seven main servers, which are described in detail below.

Servers

The Unix® server

This is used for customer billing, payments and the payroll, which are the main administrative activities of the business. Unix® is an operating system that has been used since the 1970s. It is used mainly in medium to large businesses. They do not use Windows® NT or any other similar Windows® operating system because Andrew Jones does not think they are reliable enough with the large amount of data the company processes each day, and he has the most knowledge and experience with this system.

Some of the individual PCs within the company use Windows® as their operating system instead of Unix® because they do not have to deal directly with the amount of information that the server handles.

There is a backup server that is used to back up the above and the other servers within the building.

The RAS server

A remote-access service server is used for people who want to connect to the network using a laptop, for example, and a modem. The idea is that people should be able to connect to the network when they are working away from the office – as though they were still physically linked to the network.

The DIP server

A document-imaging processing server is connected to the 'optical jukebox'.

The optical jukebox stores images on a compact disk. It stores images in the format 'write once, read many' – this means that files can be written once only and then not changed (i.e. read-only). An example of information stored on this disk are letters that have been sent to them by customers. They currently have 1,500,000 documents stored on this disk, taking up 50GB of disk space. Their main reason for using this is because it is a cheap and economical way of storing a large amount of data. It also means documents can be readily accessed and used without storing large amounts of paper.

The e-mail server

The program that is used on this server is called Microsoft® Exchange. It acts like a central post office,

receiving e-mails and distributing them to their respective recipients as well as sending company e-mails out to the rest of the world. Just at this office, they can receive anything up to 1000 e-mails each day.

The SCADA server

SCADA stands for supervisory control and data acquisition. This server is in charge of the testing of water for extremes of chemical content and the general quality of the water. There are sensors at all of the water reservoirs. If a sensor detects an abnormality in the quality of the water, it sounds an alarm and shows up on a computer screen what the fault is. There is constantly somebody watching these screens 24 hours a day every day. If there is a fault the person who is watching the screen alerts the relevant person, so the problem can be fixed at once, before the infected water reaches homes and businesses. This ensures there is never a risk to the health of the customers.

The Web server

This is how employees connect to the Internet. The connection goes via the firewall server (see below) and uses a Kilostream link. The web server stores frequently used Web pages in its cache. The cache memory speeds up the use of websites because, when pages are stored locally, they don't have to be fetched from across slow Internet links. The Web server also ensures that pages are sent to the right Web client on the network. Each time a user connects to the Internet, their computer receives a unique address or domain name. In that way, requests for information will be sent to the right computer in the right organisation and in the right country.

The firewall server

This server is situated between the company's computers and the outside world (the Internet). It uses security parameters to decide who can access the Web server. For example, e-mails that do not carry attachments in a prescribed format are not allowed through the firewall.

Activities

1. *If possible, investigate the different types of server used on a network you use, and what their purposes are.*

2. *Does your network use a firewall? If so, find out what it does.*

Network communications

Each computer is connected to the LAN network by a *network adapter card* that sends and receives packets of data travelling along the cable connecting computers. Each adapter card has a unique address, so that data sent from it has a specific origin and it can receive data addressed to it.

The network operating system running on each computer has to organise the flow of data between its processes and the resources it is using. To do this it uses *protocols*. These are 'rules of communication' that govern how all the computers talk to each other. At EauCo they use a protocol called TCP/IP to establish links. This protocol is becoming the choice for many networks because it has been developed to ensure *open system interconnectivity* – that is, many different computers can talk to each other because TCP/IP is a common language they 'speak'. The best example of interconnection using TCP/IP is the Internet.

TCP/IP controls where data are sent by attaching the correct address – this is similar to the way a postal service reads the address on an envelope and makes sure it is delivered to the correct house. It breaks up the data into small, easy-to-handle sections called *packets*, and then puts it all back together again at the other end of the connection. The packets and their addresses are different from the packets and addresses added by the network adapter card.

All the servers are linked to the *bridge*, which allows them to be connected. The main job of this is to point requests from one computer to another quickly and easily. The bridge is also able to link together computer systems that may be using different protocol.

In this case the computers are all using TCP/IP and the bridge acts as an intelligent router. Each site office has a bridge of its own that is connected, by the phone system, to other bridges in the water company.

Network topology

When EauCo implemented its system it was necessary to choose a configuration, and in networking terms this is called a *topology*. A topology refers to the physical layout of computers, cables and other components comprising the network. A network topology is more than just a physical layout, however, because it originates from very fundamental design characteristics that networks have and these refer to the underlying electronic and transmission logic that is used.

A topology defines:

- the different types of cables used in connecting network components
- the types of network interface card and their connections to the cable
- the method of communication used to establish, send and receive data across the network.

There are three basic types of LAN topology: bus, star and ring.

Bus topology

The bus topology (Ethernet) is the simplest and most common method of connecting computers. It consists of a single cable (which can be called a *backbone* or *segment*) that connects all the computers in a single line, as in Figure 6.2. (A bus network should not be confused with the system bus that is internal to the PC.)

Figure 6.2 Bus topology

Computers communicate on a bus by addressing data to a particular computer and putting that data on to the cable as electronic signals. In a bus system, the signals bounce down the cable in both directions from the sending computer, and all computers on the cable 'sniff' the signal to see whether it is addressed to them. If it is then the signal will be read. When two computers want to transmit, they look to see whether the cable is free and then transmit. Sometimes two computers transmit at the same time and this causes a collision. When that happens all computers must wait a random amount of time and then try to retransmit. At the end of the cable are *terminators*. These are electronic components that stop signals bouncing back down the cable.

Because only one computer at a time can use the cable, a network will slow down as more and more computers are waiting to get on the cable. The faster the signal can travel, the faster will be the network performance overall. That is also why bus networks are divided into different groups.

Star topology

In this topology, computers are connected by cable segments to a central component, called a *hub*. To transmit, a computer sends a data signal to the hub that in turn forwards the transmission to the computer using the address on the data signal.

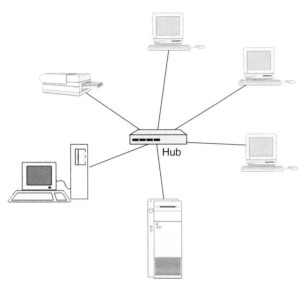

Figure 6.3 Star topology

With a star network a lot of cable is needed to connect computers to the hub. Also, if the hub fails then the whole system fails. However, if a single computer or connection line fails the rest of the network can continue to operate.

Ring topology

In this topology, the cable that joins the computers makes up a single unbroken circle. A data signal travels around the cable in one direction, passing through computers. The computers can boost the signal, so improving connections over a distance. However, if one computer fails the ring can be broken, and that can affect the whole network.

One common access method for a ring network is *token passing*. This is a small packet of data that circulates from computer to computer. When a computer wants to send a message to another computer, it takes the token and sets it to 'send' mode. It then attaches its data packet to the token and sends

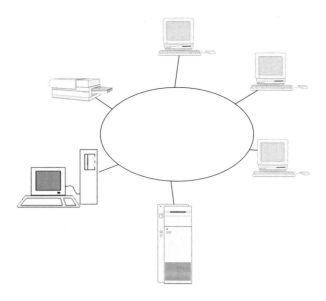

Figure 6.4 Ring topology

the packet as a signal along the ring. The other computers detect that the token is in use and look to see whether the data packet is addressed to them. If it is, then the relevant computer will read the data signal, and send a message to the sending computer indicating that it has received its data packet. The sending computer will then regenerate a new token and set it off circulating the network again.

Token ring networks are technically more difficult and therefore more expensive. However, because a computer must have a token to transmit, every computer will have a turn in a known time frame – making it more predictable. This is important for real-time settings where a known response time must be known (e.g. on an airplane control circuits).

EauCo Water uses a ring topology because the company needs to ensure that monitoring equipment can sample water quality on a regular and predictable basis.

Network applications

The main database is held on the Unix® machine and has to hold information on 225,000 customers who are billed twice a year. The company uses a multi-user application running on the Unix® machine that carries out all the standard customer business functions. The other main applications used are word-processing and spreadsheets produced by Microsoft.

Information stored on computers has to comply with the Data Protection Act. This includes customer bill data (e.g. telephone numbers, addresses and other personal data).

Kevin is responsible for ensuring that billing runs are performed using a batch-processing method. Data files on customers are brought up to date in the month before billing, and then bills are printed in one session.

Backing-up of files

Files at EauCo Water are backed-up every night. The system is backed-up twice for extra security. Extremely important data can be backed-up four times! The data is copied on to magnetic disks, which are then copied on to magnetic tape. This process takes approximately six hours every night. Once a week these magnetic tapes are transported to a secure site five miles away, in a fireproof safe. The company's backup procedure runs a five-week cycle. This means that there can be five weeks' worth of data stored at any one time. The backup cycle is carried out automatically, although the systems administrators must manage the rotation of tapes and keep backup documentation up to date.

This amount of data takes up approximately 50GB of disk space on the backup server.

In the event of the servers being either stolen or destroyed, it would take three or four days to get them replaced; they can cost up to £250,000 each.

It is the responsibility of Trevor to ensure that all the company's files have been backed-up correctly and to read the automatic printed report each morning that gives details on how successful the backup was. If any faults are found he has to make sure they are corrected as soon as possible.

Security of access

Each user must log on to the Unix® server using a user name and a password. Each user is allocated to a user group that has had its security policy set. The policy for each group controls which directories they can view, which applications they can run and what level of administration they can accomplish. Each user has his or her own file area in which to save work. A similar procedure is used to log on to the general PCs, although for convenience the same user name and password are used.

There is also a system on the server that is known as DMZ, which stands for demilitarised zone. This prevents people from outside accessing any data that they should not be looking at.

Finally, all 120 PCs in the building have virus protection which is regularly updated.

Network maintenance

Kevin and Trevor are responsible for computer system maintenance at EauCo Water.

There are three main areas of system maintenance:

- *User administration.* Each user on the network must have access to an account. Each account must be set to allow access to network resources. New users must be added, existing users may change their status and users may leave.
- *Performance management.* This is to ensure that network activity is monitored and logged and system performance is maintained and enhanced.
- *Configuration and resource management.* Network configuration must be planned, and may need adjustment, for example, when the network expands. Configuration information needs to be documented and maintained. Various hardware and software resources must be suitably managed.

In addition, *troubleshooting* involves the prevention, detection and solution of network problems.

User administration

When a user logs on to the network it is common for that person to be a member of a group. Each network users' group will have a *security profile* set up for it that controls the environment each user in that group has. Profiles are used to control a *user's logon environment*, including the resources they can access and the appearance of their desktop. Other settings that may be controlled by profiles are printer connections, regional settings, display settings and system tools.

Group accounts make the maintenance of many user accounts much easier, because group settings can be set just once instead of for each user. One of the most important aspects of a group profile will be its *permissions* – that is, what programs and directories and other network resources members have permission to use. Group accounts and permissions may need to be adjusted from time to time. The process for determining groups is based on what functions they perform; so, for example, all the people in the accounts department might have access to resources they particularly need. Once the accounts group is set up, then the relevant user accounts are added. These users then inherit the permissions allocated to that group.

At EauCo, Kevin has been asked to set up four different group profiles: one for senior management, another for the engineering department, another for finance, and one for the sales and marketing people. In Figure 6.5 you can see the types of permission that Kevin might use. Each server is a network resource that performs a function. Some servers store data and programs related to the activity that takes place on that server. For example, the Unix® server holds the programs and data for performing billing, payroll and a number of other administrative functions. Some users may have access to programs that only read data from files on the server (Read and Execute (Xcute)) while others have access to programs that add data to the files (Read, Write, Xcute).

Files that are used by groups are saved in shared directories. That is, the permissions to use a directory are set for particular users. They may not have access to other parts of a server's storage area.

Other servers perform functions for groups that have permission to use them. So, for example, some users are allowed to dial in to the RAS server where they can access the rest of the network. They may use the same login name and password they normally use, but they must have remote-access permissions to be accepted by the RAS login authentication.

Activities

1. *Look at all the permissions in Figure 6.5 and think about why they have been set thus.*

2. *Imagine three groups of students: a group studying marketing, another studying graphic design and a final group that studies programming. Would it be sensible to use different account groups for these three types of student? If so, why? What type of permissions might each group use?*

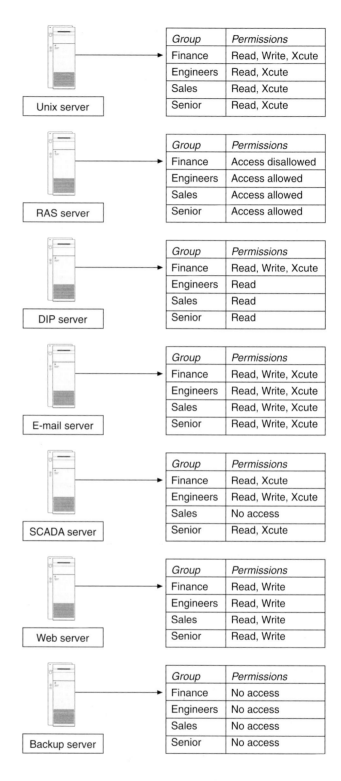

Figure 6.5 *Server access at EauCo Water*

Performance management

Once a network is operational it is important to maintain its operations effectively. To do this the administrator must keep track of the network's performance. The network administrator must be aware of the overall function of the network, and this will depend on the monitoring tools used. Monitoring performance is carried out to improve performance based on the existing configuration, to plan for increased capacity, and to detect areas such as bottlenecks that are degrading the system.

Bottlenecks occur when a device on the network is holding back operations because it is either too slow, or takes up a lot of the system resources, or is being used beyond its capacity, or is faulty in some way. Examples of devices that can cause bottlenecks are CPUs, memory, network cards, disk controllers, and network cabling. In order to track system performance most networks have software that will automatically monitor the system. The first thing to establish is how the network manages under a normal load in optimum conditions. To do this a network administrator will create a *baseline of system performance* against which comparisons can be made if new equipment is added, or for some reason the system is not performing as well as it should.

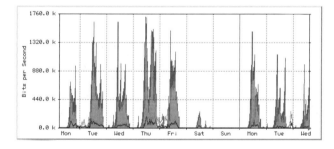

Figure 6.6 *Data traffic on an Internet connection*

> ## Activity
>
> *Figure 6.6 shows the amount of data passing through an Internet connection at particular times in the day throughout a time period. The connection speed is 2Mbps. The baseline for acceptable performance is that the amount of data passing through the connection must remain below 80 per cent of capacity for 90 per cent of the time. Is the traffic on this line exceeding the acceptable amount established by the baseline?*

Baselines establish the normal acceptable conditions, and if generated over time allow trends to be established and allow for network planners to forecast when changes may need to be made. If the network degrades for some reason, new performance logs can be taken and compared with known good baselines to see where problems have arisen.

System management software should be designed to conform to a software protocol, such a *simple network management protocol* (SNMP). This protocol uses small programs called agents loaded on to devices being managed. Here they monitor network traffic and behaviour and maintain the information in a *management information base* (MIB). SNMP components may include servers, network interface cards, bridges and other equipment.

When a network administrator wishes to check performance of components, he or she will use a performance management console to download data from agents' MIBs and present the results in the form of graphs, or analyse the data using specialist software.

Configuration and resource management

Maintaining a network history

It is important for the network administrator to maintain excellent documentation that shows where changes have been made to the original specification or configuration. The documentation sets out what the changes were intended to do and what the outcome was. Again this acts as a record to see how the system has been developed and why particular decisions were made. Of course, future employees will then be able to learn fully about the development of the system.

Examples of the issues that need to be recorded are:

- growth
- equipment purchases
- maintenance schedules
- system configuration changes.

> ## Activity
>
> *Think about what information needs to be recorded about each of the items in the above list.*

Maintaining data

The network administrator also has to ensure that all necessary data is backed-up. Although this is more of a security issue, the network administrator has to make sure that the backup schedule is appropriate and effective. Various backup options are possible:

- full backup: backs-up the complete system or all selected files
- copy: takes a copy of a file, meaning it is not marked as being backed-up
- incremental backup: backs-up files only if they have changed since the last backup
- daily copy: again makes copies of files on a particular day, but the files are not marked as being backed-up
- differential backup: backs-up files that have changed since their last backup, but does not mark them as being backed-up.

A backup schedule may involve a full backup once a week, and an incremental backup on a daily basis. Tapes can be rotated as it becomes clear that a later backup has superseded their contents. In order that backup rotation occurs in a systematic and rigorous way, detailed *backup logs* need to be maintained.

Activities

At EauCo, the following backup cycle is used. On the first night a full backup is made and this is duplicated to a second tape. On the following day, an incremental backup is performed using the duplicate tape. This too is duplicated, and on the third night, this tape is used to perform another incremental backup. The cycle then starts again using new tapes for all parts of the cycle. After this cycle the old tapes from the first backup are re-used.

1. *How many tapes are used for this backup cycle?*

2. *Design a form for recording where in the backup cycle a network administrator is. Your form should allow a new person to identify what tape should be used next, and which part of the cycle has been reached.*

Maintaining service

Huge investments are made in computer systems, so it is important that they are running at optimum efficiency with minimum downtime. One way in which systems can be provided with a better guarantee of service is to build in *fault tolerance*. Essentially this means building into a system a means for alternative processing if there is a crash. In mainframe systems this may mean having entire computer centres able to mirror processing if another computer has to be taken out of service. On networks, servers can be duplicated so that processing and vital system data are maintained at all times by creating clusters (groups) of servers that act as one machine. Should a system within the cluster fail, cluster software will disperse the work from the failed system to the remaining servers.

This redundancy is also built into resources vital for system operation. So, for example, groups of disks can be used to ensure that if a disk becomes faulty then no data are lost as copies are maintained on other disks. This disk organisation is called RAID (redundant array of inexpensive disks).

When regular maintenance is required, for example to take a printer offline, users need to be kept well informed. Downtime is chosen to occur at the least disruptive time.

Activity

Look at the main diagram of the EauCo network (Figure 6.1). Which part of the network is the most vulnerable? How might this be overcome?

Maintaining software

Applications and OS are continually being revised and 'improved'. It is important again that changes to software do not impinge on the work of the network users. The approach should follow these guidelines:

- Plan and announce upgrades well in advance, and issue a date when changes will be implemented. Pick a time that is least disruptive.
- Test the upgrade on a small section of the network, and ensure recovery procedures are clear if the system has to be returned to its previous state.

- Ensure upgrades are necessary and compatible with current operations. Examine their rationale and cost/benefits.

Activity

Think about changes to software you have used or upgrades you have performed. What difficulties or problems have arisen from this?

Monitoring PC system performance

There are many utilities that can help a system administrator to do this. Windows® has its own monitoring tool called System Monitor. This allows the system administrator to set up line charts that record the fluctuations of a system at regular intervals. A person can choose which resources to monitor and record the ongoing changes to a log file. The system administrator can then decide which data make up the baseline, and later make comparisons.

One way in which *benchmark* testing works is to take a system and then get it to undertake some intensive tasks (e.g. redraw a complex graphic) to see how system performance is affected.

For example, look at Figure 6.7, which shows graphics taken off the dial-up connection to two different ISPs. Each ISP was activated and then the same call was made to a website where an e-mail application was used in exactly the same way. Connection speed was the same, the second ISP (on the right) was not a reliable connection as incomplete frames and CRC (cyclic redundancy check) errors

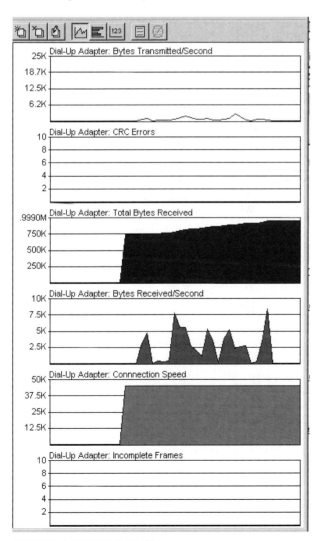
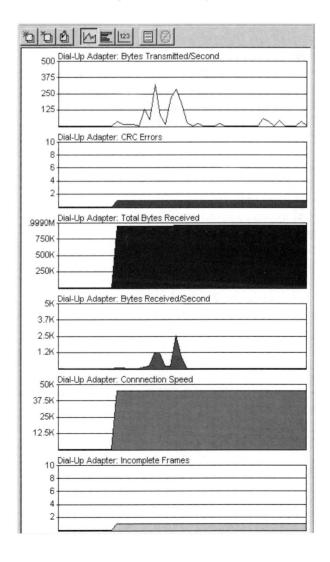

Figure 6.7 *Comparison of two ISPs*

were recorded. This meant the sending computer had to send requests for corrupted frames to be retransmitted. Observe how much more data had to be transmitted to the second ISP (bytes transmitted per second).

Activity

Set up a system performance monitor on your system. Create a baseline of data, stored in a log file. Carry out performance challenges and record new data. Compare the new logs with the baseline.

PC system maintenance procedures

A good network administrator will try to pre-empt system problems or failure by carrying out preventative maintenance. This is in contrast to diagnostic or corrective maintenance, which is performed to correct an already-existing problem.

Preventative maintenance will vary. A PC that is in a very dirty environment will need to be cleaned frequently. Cleaning removes build-up of dirt on components, which may lead to poor electrical performance and eventually to the cooling properties of the system being compromised. If the CPU is not kept cool it can cause erratic processing cycles and eventual burnout. A PC that is used for heavy Internet traffic may be exposed to virus attack more frequently. Therefore regular upgrading of virus definition files will be normal.

Because human beings tend to be imperfect at keeping up tasks, especially ones that may be regulated over many months, software utilities for scheduling work are important. These allow for various tasks to be given times when they will be run. Most OS have built-in scheduling agents for this. But what kinds of regular tasks need to be carried out?

- **Checking the file system for errors**. Poor software applications, system crashes or bugs can corrupt file systems. In order to check the file system structure – directories, directory file entries and linked lists in allocation tables – utilities like Scandisk or Disk Doctor need to be run regularly.

- **Checking all hard disks for read errors**. Hard disks are incredibly reliable but they *can* develop faults. Normally they don't have catastrophic failures, but they may develop areas on their surface that are termed *bad clusters*. In order to detect areas of the disk that may be developing this kind of error, disk surfaces need to be checked. Again a utility like Scandisk will do this.

- **Scanning all hard disks and files for viruses**. Viruses can have highly destructive effects and so a hard drive needs to be scanned regularly. Because new viruses are constantly being introduced, virus definition tables need to be kept up to date and the utility run to scan files. Different levels of scanning can be used and different file types can be included.

- **Defragmentation of all hard disk volumes**. You learnt about this in a previous chapter (see pages 57–58).

A good network administrator will maintain a *maintenance log* that contains amongst other things:

- details of contractors who are paid to deliver a maintenance service, and the relevant contracts
- details of contractors who provide a call-out service, their prices and expertise
- log of faults that have been repaired (what, when, why, solution)
- log of faults that are outstanding
- details of jobs and who is attending to them
- maintenance procedures and schedule.

Figure 6.8 shows a possible maintenance schedule for a PC.

Activities

1. *Investigate scheduling software on a system you use, and set up scheduling tasks.*

2. *Configure an antivirus program to scan a system and update the virus definitions from the Internet.*

Preventive maintenance activity	Recommended frequency	Auto?
Scan hard disk file systems for errors	Daily	Yes
Scan for viruses	Daily	Yes
Back-up data	Daily	No
Clean CRT screen	Weekly	No
Defragment hard disks	Weekly	Yes
Scan for hard-disk read errors	Weekly	Yes
Clean mouse	Monthly	No
Check for full hard-disk volumes and remove unnecessary files	Monthly	No
Update virus definition files	Monthly	Sometimes
Check power protection devices to ensure they are still protecting the system	Monthly	No
Clean keyboard	Quarterly	No
Check power supply fan for ventilation and dirt build-up and clean if necessary	Quarterly	No
Back-up CMOS information	Quarterly	No
Update emergency boot floppies	Quarterly	No
Clean floppy disk drive internals and read/write heads	Quarterly (depending on use)	No
Check processor temperature, inspect heat sink and fan to ensure they are working	Annually (or whenever case is opened)	No
Check hard disk for temperature and vibration	Annually (or whenever case is opened)	No
Clean exterior of case	Annually	No
Clean exterior of monitor	Annually	No
Check and clean interior, motherboard and expansion cards if necessary	Annually	No
Check internal connections and cables	Annually	No

Figure 6.8 PC maintenance schedule

Conclusion

In this chapter you have read about the network structure of a water company. You have been introduced to the wide-area and local-area connections and a range of network devices – particularly the servers. You have also learnt that communication on the network uses a particular protocol, in this case TCP/IP.

The layout of a computer network follows certain topologies, which may be a bus, ring or star network.

Having learnt about network basics, you then studied the main aspects of network maintenance. The most important aspects of this are users, performance, network security, network history and keeping service to an optimum level.

CHAPTER 7

Setting up security processes for a network

This chapter is designed to help your understanding of computer systems that deliver a specific service. The service examined is a metropolitan-area network used to deliver teaching and learning resources to the higher and further education sectors in London. The case study will give you further insight into how computers are connected, and how that connectivity can be used.

In particular, the chapter covers:

- an introduction to a metropolitan-area network (MAN)

- the services delivered to a MAN

- an introduction to security issues and how they can be tackled

- achieving your own computer security.

The chapter covers the following Learning Outcome in the specification:

L.O. 1.5   Demonstrate the knowledge required to set up defined security processes for a specified ICT system

It covers the following Technical Knowledge topic:

T1.1.3   The facilities of current operating systems (security)

Introduction to metropolitan-area networking

Highgate College is a medium-size establishment in north-west London. It has spent a large amount of money on a local-area computer network (LAN). Initially the network was used for Computing and Business Studies courses, to teach IT-related knowledge and skill components. However, computer resources were expanded to give all the students a foundation in the use of computers and to provide facilities for staff. Recently, with the development of the Internet, and with government interest, the college has been expanding facilities so that all students can routinely use computers to prepare their work, use resources on the LAN and college intranet, and have access to the Internet.

The college has in fact *two* main networks: an academic network with many workshops and learning centres wired up, and an administration network that links together offices and staff rooms. Connection to the Internet is through a leased line from the local exchange. It is capable of delivering 64Kbps of Internet traffic from the college to its Internet service provider (ISP). An ISP is an organisation that provides connectivity to the rest of the Internet. The college connects to the Web servers of the ISP using a *router*, a device for sending data to an address on the World Wide Web. An ISP has high-speed connection to main communication highways of the Internet, and may provide user services such as Web hosting or e-mail post boxes.

Recently the Principal of Highgate, Peter Cohen, received a visit from the manager of the London Regional Support Centre (RSC) of the Joint Information Systems Committee (JISC). The RSC is a partnership between further and higher education, funded by their respective funding councils. Its objective is to provide access for FE colleges to the London metropolitan-area network (MAN) that joins together all the regional higher education institutes.

The London MAN is in turn connected to the national academic wide-area network (WAN) (SuperJANET®). Colleges themselves will not have to find additional money for this. The initiative is to give FE colleges a relatively high-speed access to services provided on the MAN, these being:

- 2Mbps (megabits per second) link (voice, data, video)
- access to newsgroups
- access to datasets such as government census data and health statistics
- e-mail and discussion facilities
- access to the World Wide Web
- video-conferencing
- access to resources at HE institutes
- participation in ICT teaching and learning developments.

To summarise, a MAN is a regional network that covers a particular area such as a city or county where a community of users wish to enhance their connectivity to each other and collaborate on the costs of doing so. It is something between a LAN (a small, fast, locally managed network) and a WAN (a widespread connection of different networks). The MAN has a single management infrastructure although it joins together networks that are different. Different MANs may be connected to form a WAN (see Figure 7.1). A MAN will provide high-speed connection within the community connected to it. The benefits of MANs are to provide a locally managed and jointly resourced fast network. It may also make connection to the Internet easier and quicker.

The Principal of Highgate College sets up a working group to take advantage of this new opportunity. He decides it should be a cross-college interdisciplinary team chaired by the senior manager in charge of ICT

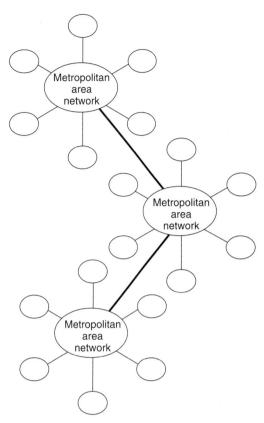

Figure 7.1 A group of three interconnected MANs

developments, Margaret Roberts. Besides Margaret it will include the network administrator, Bevan Hughes, a member of staff from the learning resources centre and the college's curriculum development manager. Bevan is in charge of technical services and has five network technicians working for him. The committee will have the following brief:

- to investigate the technical aspects of connecting the college to the London MAN
- to report on security issues of the connection
- to create and activate a strategy for the development of new teaching and learning opportunities afforded by the MAN connection.

Technical aspects

Bevan Hughes contacts the HE agency responsible for providing connection of the college computer networks to the MAN – and hence to the Internet and to the rest of the higher education WAN. It is a straightforward process of installing a router on the college network (see Figure 7.2). The college's Internet traffic will then travel over a communication line provided by a telecommunications company to a router on the MAN. The MAN team will have the experience to easily connect and configure the local router to work on the college's LAN.

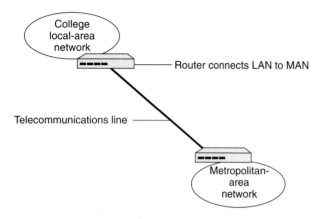

Figure 7.2 *Router between LAN and MAN*

Security issues

Bevan Hughes has to consider security implications very carefully. The college already has a security policy implemented for its network and an 'acceptable-use' policy that includes security considerations.

The *security policy* lays down what security measures should be taken by users of the network, and the threats the network administrator will protect against. The security policy has to take account of the following possibilities:

- malicious attacks
- illegal access that threatens the confidentiality of data held on the network
- accidental erasures of data
- hardware failures such as disk crashes
- untrained users.

The *acceptable-use policy* informs users what activities are deemed acceptable on the college's network, including maintaining security of their accounts. Also, the access or transmission of defamatory or offensive material is unacceptable.

Protecting against the various security risks identified in the bullet points above requires *proactive measures* as well as damage control and limitations after breaches have occurred. Special security is required for mission-critical systems where reliability is paramount (e.g. with control systems on planes and railways). 'Mission-critical' means that the operations of a service or process cannot be performed without the system.

Fundamental dangers

Computers are connected by networks to other computers and servers where resources can be accessed. Potentially any communication between users is insecure. One of the easiest ways of reading information is by interception of e-mails or the transfer of files. Another vulnerable area is using programs to log in to a remote network.

Common programs for transferring files, such as file transfer protocol (FTP), do not encrypt the password, user name or data during transfer. So one of the first points of protection is the network *firewall*. This aims to isolate the external world from the internal operation of the network.

Most network systems adopt a login procedure that requires a password and user name. The administrator can set certain characteristics expected of a password – for example, any password that can be found in a dictionary might be disallowed. Also, setting the length of a password makes guesswork harder. It is also usual practice to make sure that users change their passwords on a regular basis. Some large corporations actually use once-only password systems.

The identity of users is maintained in the network users' database. This checks whether a login request is coming from a valid user, and if so, what resources that person is trusted to use. The trust settings are created by the network administrator.

User security

This can be based on the following guidelines. Users should:

- know who to contact if they suspect a security hazard or breach
- be bound to keep passwords secret at all times
- have access to a password-locked screensaver, or should log out when they leave their workstation
- control closely who has physical access to their computer
- know that downloading software from unknown origins is highly risky
- report security problems to the systems administrator as soon as possible.

Viruses

These are essentially malicious programs that can execute (i.e. run) on a user's machine, or other machines connected to it, without the user's knowledge or permission. Some viruses wait until certain dates are reached; others remain silent in the system until a particular afflicted program is activated.

Administrators will normally restrict the numbers of people in their charge who can install software on computers . Users quite often try to access hard drives so that they can install games that employers do not normally make available.

Antivirus software can be effective at detecting and removing viruses before they inflict damage. This special software must be kept up to date to ensure unusual disk activity is monitored and prevented. For example, certain system files and disk areas would not normally be accessible to users, so any activity happening on them can be considered to be suspicious.

Activity

Outline a set of procedures a systems administrator should employ to protect a computer system from attack by viruses.

The dangers of downloading

Programs that are downloaded from the network or Internet may appear to be innocent enough and carry out what they say they will do. However, the program may be a *Trojan*, allowing unknown network activity to occur in the background. One type of malicious program waits to catch people logging on and then transmits their details to another computer. Administrators will often prevent any software downloading by either blocking known sites or examining downloaded files for tell-tail pointers to *executable files*.

Recently, e-mails have been used as carriers of dangerous programs such as the 'Love' and 'Melissa' viruses. These work by tricking the unwary recipient into believing someone they know has sent them a message. When they look at the attachment it turns out to contain a computer virus.

Activities

1. *Find out what is meant by a 'Trojan'.*

2. *Investigate the security settings of a network you use. Does the network allow software to be downloaded?*

Web page dangers

Besides being able to execute programs, Web pages also contain *forms*. Unless the Web browser is using a security level such as *secure socket level* (SSL), then all information being transmitted by the forms is readable by an interceptor. SSL *encrypts* data sent between the user's browser and the Web server, so no-one along the way can read it.

Another security threat is sites that are forgeries. People are then misdirected to sites that are not the genuine sites that are expected. This is where Web *certificates* are useful. These work by sending you a special key that encrypts everything that you send to that site. The data you return can then be decrypted by a private key the website uses. Certificate authorities that check the authenticity of the receiver can only issue certificates, but of course it is possible for certificates to be stolen and reused illegally.

Activities

1. *Give a one sentence explanation of the term 'encryption'.*

2. *Investigate sites that transmit user details by means of forms (e.g. shopping, banking or travel). How do they prevent private information being read by someone who intercepts pages containing these details?*

File protection

Data files and directories on shared systems or networked file systems require care and maintenance.

Shared files

Users may work in groups where shared access is necessary and desirable. System administrators can set sharing privileges for these groups. If a file is kept in a public area, then sharing permissions may need to be set and users must be aware of their own.

Protected files

Usually, a user's personal files are kept in a directory to which only they have access. Permissions to this area are also controlled by the administrator, who will not allow any other user access. Further security to personal files can be gained by encrypting data files. However, strict password discipline needs to be maintained in order not to forget passwords or to write them down.

Activity

Find out how you can encrypt and protect your own documents.

Software dangers

Application software has become more powerful in recent years by giving users the ability to write *program extensions* within their application documents. These are sometimes known as *macro facilities*. Because application files seem so common and friendly, is possible to include macro code that is damaging to the user's files or computer. System administrators sometimes make application extensions inaccessible, particularly in areas that are vulnerable.

Similarly, *Web plug-ins* are programs used to enhance the features of a browser. Because they are so common it is possible for a user to believe that the plug-in he or she is using is from a trusted source, when it may not be.

As well as this, it is very easy to write programs or *scripts* that download with Web pages. These scripts are then executed on the receiving computer by programming facilities installed with the Web browser. A script written in a language such as JavaScript could then carry out a damaging attack. Again administrators might disable the processing capabilities of browsers to prevent this.

Social factors

Confidences can be broken when passwords are shared. People can overhear matters not concerning them that they then exploit. Other people are forced to reveal details by manipulation or coercion. Examples of this have been people contacting the systems administrator pretending to be authentic users: the 'helpless' person who would like to be reminded of his or her password, or the big boss who makes threats of dire consequences if not told a password 'immediately'.

Site security policies and acceptable-use guides will make it the responsibility of all users to guard their passwords and login details. Failure to comply could lead to a person having computing access removed.

Security procedures

At Highgate College, Bevan Hughes and his team need to set up a security procedure that implements protection to the college's network resources. He decides to call in a security consultant from the MAN team. He receives advice on general protection principles, as follows.

1. Ensure all computers added to the network fulfill security requirements

New equipment needs to be brought up to a standard that fulfills security needs. Unnecessary software may have to be removed; the system should be configured to minimise access to its operating system; virus protection should be installed; and login authentication should be activated for all potential users. The system should enable authorised users to access the resources they need to use but prevent them damaging vital system areas.

2. Ensure network servers fulfill network security

Servers from different vendors need to be assessed to see whether they provide the optimum conditions for running the network operating system that will protect the network. Certain server hardware provides enhanced features for this. The server should be sufficiently powerful to run the system and to allow for services such as regular backups to be handled easily.

3. Keep operating systems and applications software up to date

Software manufacturers often provide enhanced security to their products as new threats emerge or bugs in their software are discovered. Manufacturers often fix known problems by releasing security patches. Patches are small parts of a program's source code that have been re-engineered to remove problems. The systems administrator will have to keep abreast of changing conditions by visiting manufacturers' websites and joining suitable discussion lists.

4. Offer only essential network and OS services on the server host machine

Network operating systems come with a wide range of options to meet the needs of a range of users. However, installing the full range of system tools can make the server vulnerable. For example, hackers can use certain system programs to access other parts of the system. The function of the server should be tailored to meet the minimum requirements to achieve the service required. This is known as a 'deny all, then allow' approach. If, for example, the server is going to be used for internal database access, any access should be configured with the most stringent protection, including password encryption.

5. Configure computers for user authentication

The network's security is maintained by careful application of authorisation levels to all users. Account groups need to be determined and specific resources allocated to them. Users added to these groups should have passwords that meet secure criteria, and passwords should be changed on a regular basis. Inactive logins should be closed. Failed logins should be logged and access denied after a few attempts. Only designated people should have access to computer systems.

6. Configure computer OS with appropriate access controls

The server will hold several types of resource that need careful access. The systems administrator must have a good knowledge of the rights and permissions that are available as default in an operating system environment, and make sure that they are secured or disabled. A careful map needs to be drawn of the files, directories, programs and devices that are available from the system. From this, an access control list can map resources to specific users and groups. For example:

System files

- All system files should be in directories that are blocked to all but the administrator.
- Unnecessary system files and utilities should be disabled or deleted.
- System logs should be protected from access.
- Execute permissions for system programs should be granted only to the administrator.

User files

- Files containing sensitive information should be encrypted.
- Data files for different parts of the organisation should be controlled. 'Write' privileges should be set for only specific users.

7. Identify and enable system and network logging mechanisms

System logs track all the activity on the network and so allow the detection of intruders or activity that is suspicious. Log files help to trace the identity of a security breach – which systems have been tampered

Setting up security processes for a network

with – and they also allow for solutions to be proposed and remedial action to be taken.

Log files can be set to track user logins, the execution of programs, which system settings have been changed, where network traffic is directed, and what devices have been used. User activity can be logged for files and programs that have been used.

8. Configure computers for file backups

All network data should be regularly backed-up according to a rigorous schedule. The system should be properly documented and attempts to restore data undertaken. This will ensure that the whole process is as reliable as possible.

9. Protect computers from viruses

Antivirus software should be installed and regular updates made to virus definition files.

10. Configure computers for secure remote administration

Computers that are administered from other parts of the network should be set up to authenticate the system administrator using a secure login procedure, particularly an encrypted password. The computer on which the administrator is working should have a known fixed address. Any information passing between the administrator and a remote server should be secure.

Steps to protect your system

Use the following table to review the procedures you have in place to protect your own computer.

Security hazard	Response
Do you share your PC?	You may want to create separate login options so that different users have different file access.
Who acts as PC administrator, and is it clear what his or her responsibilities are?	If your system is shared, someone must take on the responsibility of allocating file or directory access rights. Investigate options for securing file and directory information on your PC.
Are passwords in place and secure?	Users' passwords should be secret and effective.
Do you share your password with anybody?	Your friends must be trusted not to disclose this to anybody. The more people who have it the more vulnerable you are to accidental disclosure. Don't get yourself in a compromising situation with friends.
Is your PC *physically* secure?	You may want to lock away items or access to your PC to prevent damage to it.
Do you have a policy on downloading software?	Software you download may not be from a secure source. Do you have measures in place to scan software for viruses?
Is your antivirus software effective and kept up to date?	Ensure you regularly update software and antivirus definition files.
What is your policy on opening unknown e-mails or attachments in e-mails?	A common way of transmitting harmful programs is to put them in seemingly innocuous e-mails. Never open attachments from an unknown source.
Do you send sensitive information from your Internet browser?	You should configure your browser to use a secure layer, or transmit information only to secure sites. Make sure sensitive data are encrypted.
Do you use a personal firewall with your PC when you open a connection to the Web?	Free firewall software provides some basic protection from online sniffers and snoopers.
Do you keep your OS and software up to date?	Some software has been found to have security loopholes. Check websites for patches or upgrades.
Do you make regular backups?	Make sure your vital files are kept regularly backed-up. Prepare recovery disks for your computer.

Activities

At a recent educational conference, a discussion group examined a certain establishment and raised the following issues:

- *Where is your data stored? What protection can you offer against natural disaster, fire, stealing or any other physical difficulty?*

- *Are there security measures in place for virus checking, passwords, levels of data being accessed, and back-ups to the system?*

- *Who is responsible for security and how often are checks carried out? Have staff received the necessary training?*

1. *What other issues can you raise, and how would you attempt to resolve them?*

2. *What might be the consequences of a breach of security?*

Conclusion

You have seen how a college might benefit from being connected to a community of academic users. A regional MAN provides fast, locally managed connections that share resources effectively.

Connections can be installed easily using a router, and the MAN can provide central support for this.

Security threats can come from a number of directions, but a security policy should help to manage these threats. Linked to the security policy is an acceptable-use policy. Security measures can be undertaken to protect systems from attack.

CHAPTER 8

Social, moral and ethical implications of ICT solutions

This chapter describes:

- social, moral and ethical implications of the exploitation of ICT solutions
- the effect that ICT has on individual employees
- the wider effects on a global society of the use of major ICT systems.

The chapter covers the following Learning Outcome in the specification:

L.O. 1.8 Demonstrate a critical understanding of the social, ethical and moral implications of the exploitation of any ICT-based solution to a problem

ICT and society

In this chapter we will be considering *the effect that ICT has on employees* who work in the ICT industry or who use IT facilities at work. We will also think about the *impact of ICT on the public at large*.

Computers were first used by business in the early 1950s. Since then, the impact of ICT on society has rivalled that of the invention of the internal combustion engine. Entirely new industries have grown up whose very existence was unthinkable before cars or computers came along.

As a direct result of the growth of ICT, relevant skills are required of almost every employee today; new career structures have opened up; the difference between the costs of luxury and basic consumer goods has narrowed; entertainment has changed dramatically; and our access to knowledge has been freed from the constraints of time and place.

Activity

Consider a typical day in the life of an adult member of our society. List all the ways in which she or he will use, or be affected by, ICT solutions.

Issues raised by new technologies

Often a new medical or scientific breakthrough is followed by public concern about whether and how it should be exploited. For example, the cloning of human tissues has been hotly debated. The debate touches on the morality of experimenting with human tissues, the social impact of exploiting the techniques, and the implications of the high costs involved – together with the ethical dilemma of doctors who have to decide which patients will benefit.

A similar debate occurs amongst ICT professionals. Their technology has also raced ahead of the debate. Current technology makes possible widespread and immediate access to data, and the public wants to know whether this is always in their best interests. As new technology is developed, and more becomes possible, so new issues are raised.

Here are some examples of technological advances which raise social, moral, ethical and legal issues:

- The *growth in capacity of storage media* means that very large databases, some on a national scale, can be created. For example, a supermarket chain can log data about customers who use their loyalty card. They can analyse buying preferences and spending habits. The use of this data can raise civil liberty issues, such as privacy.

- The *speed at which data can be processed* means that 'artificial intelligence' (AI) techniques can be exploited widely. Many AI systems are very beneficial, but they can also be used to control military weapons to devastating effect.

- The *speed at which data can be searched and accessed* has resulted in demands for immediate access to information which was not possible in the past. For example, until 2001 it was possible, and legal, for anyone to find out the name and address of any person in the UK who is on the electoral register. Indeed, anyone could buy the lists. Limited access is still possible, and the social significance of this becomes apparent as we move towards electronic balloting in elections.

- The *improvements in data communications* since the 1980s have encouraged the widespread use of the Internet, which raises concerns about the availability of material that would be illegal in many countries. It is not clear how the suppliers, hosts or viewers of material which is racially offensive, drug-related or pornographic could be prosecuted, or which country's laws would apply.

Administration systems in hospitals

Many of these issues are raised in hospitals like Wessex County (to which you were introduced in Chapter 2). Completing the computerisation of hospitals has been a major undertaking of governments. It has been a highly complex task because of the many different ways in which patients interact with health professionals.

A member of the public in Britain may see their general practitioner (GP) or the practice nurse about a problem and be treated satisfactorily, or the GP may refer the person to a consultant at a hospital, or perhaps to a specialist hospital that is farther away. In hospital a patient will be assessed and treated by a number of professionals, and after discharge may need the services of a district nurse, midwife or physiotherapist. There is, of course, parallel provision for dental and eye care.

All these health professionals keep records of each patient's medical history, diagnosis and treatment, and one of the major debating points in the past has been how much of this information should be transferred as the patient moves from one stage to another.

The intention is that eventually each citizen should have a lifelong health record which would be held centrally by the National Health Service, so that all health professionals could access it through a wide-area network (WAN). GPs would be able to use this network to refer patients directly to hospitals and to receive the results of tests. All health workers would be able to use national databases about treatment. Patients would be able to get advice from their doctors online, and there would be direct links from surgeries to pharmacies.

Until all this is achieved the patient administration system at Wessex County is designed to ensure that all the data about a patient is collated and accessible to those who need to know. At the same time, the data is protected and secure.

The system at Wessex County also manages outpatient appointments, waiting lists for operations, prescriptions, bed booking, payroll and stock control for equipment and drugs.

Activity

Patients in one area of the country have been trying out a Virtual Hospital as part of a research project. They stay at home, and are given all the equipment they need, such as thermometers and heart monitors, to take readings. These are linked through a computer network to the specialist caring for the patient, who could be based anywhere in the country. Local community nurses and doctors can be called out if necessary.

1. *What are the advantages of the Virtual Hospital from the points of view of (a) the patient, (b) the specialist, and (c) the National Health Service?*

2. *What sort of technology is needed to support this project?*

Social, moral and ethical implications of ICT solutions

The social impact of ICT solutions

Employment

The rapid spread of ICT technologies from the 1970s has undoubtedly changed employment patterns. Initially, concerns were expressed that jobs would be lost as tasks became automated. But in practice there has been an explosion of new job opportunities in the ICT field.

The main issue here is the type of employment that is now available and the level of skill required in order to carry out the work. For example, in the past some office workers had a high level of technical skill (e.g. a shorthand typist) whilst others required just general skills (e.g. a filing clerk). Today, all office workers are expected to have IT skills, and many of them are expected to have advanced skills as well.

Employees today tend to have broader and more demanding job descriptions than many had in the past. More employees are now 'knowledge workers'. There has also been a switch from the production of goods to the provision of services. Couple these factors with the new industries that have emerged – software houses, network management, integrated ICT solutions, e-commerce, independent IT training – and we can see that the changes have had a noticeable impact on training for work and on general education.

Training

Within any one organisation, such as the GBW Bank you met in Chapter 5, the changes may have happened gradually over a period of time. James Harris, the Senior Systems Administrator, needs to employ personnel who already have a high level of technical skill, and he looks to universities and colleges to provide the prior training. But he knows that many of the longstanding staff in all departments of the Bank were educated before IT tools were commonplace, and he is aware of their needs for training and sympathetic support.

Wessex County is a teaching hospital where doctors are trained. Medical students learn some of their skills through watching senior professionals doing their job and joining in discussions about the options. Eventually they will have to diagnose and treat patients on their own. The hospital has invested in some virtual-reality (VR) systems to help students build up their skills and confidence in diagnosis and treatment.

The teaching department has also used the VR systems to give the trainee doctors some insight into the experience that a patient has when undergoing treatment. Certain therapies cause extreme fatigue, and software that simulates the frustration suffered by patients can help the doctor to understand how the patient reacts.

Activities

1. Look through job advertisements in the local and national press and note down the proportion of jobs that are (a) in the ICT field or (b) require IT skills.

2. Look at degree courses offered at universities, and training courses offered by private companies. How is the need for IT skills being met by education and training?

3. Find out other industries where virtual-reality systems are used for training people to do complex tasks.

Environmental issues

One area of concern that all systems administrators must face at some point is the disposal of old equipment. Computers contain toxic heavy metals and non-biodegradable PVC, which are safe whilst the machines are in use, but which could contaminate landfill sites and create a major pollution problem. At present there is no legislation governing the problem, although proposals are probably going to the European Parliament. In the USA it has been suggested that over 300 million computers will have been discarded by 2004.

The Data Protection Act 1998

The first Data Protection Act was introduced in 1984. It dealt with *personal data* that was stored on a computer system. The 1984 Act did not apply to any other data, such as business information, nor to data stored only in document form.

Personal data is identifiable information about living persons. Data that is aggregated so that individuals cannot be identified does not count as personal data. Examples of aggregated data are a statistical analysis of census data for a region, and market research findings based on postcodes.

The Data Protection Act 1998 incorporated much of the earlier Act, but updated it to take account of the European Data Protection Directive. It also extended the earlier Act to include personal data held in any format at all. It refers to non-computer based storage, such as folders in a filing cabinet or lists held on paper, as 'personal data filing systems'. In practice, organisations have until 2007 to ensure that these manual personal data filing systems comply with the law.

The 1998 Act places obligations on the *data controller* (the person who is responsible for the storage or access to personal data) and it also gives rights to the *data subject* (the person the data refers to).

There are eight *Data Protection principles*. Personal data must be:

1. processed fairly and lawfully
2. obtained and processed for limited purposes
3. adequate, relevant and not excessive
4. accurate
5. kept no longer than necessary
6. processed in accordance with the data subject's rights
7. secure
8. transferred to countries outside Europe only with adequate protection.

Principle 1 has some additional rules about processing sensitive data. Sensitive data is information about a person's ethnic origin, religious beliefs, physical or mental health, sexual life or criminal record. This data can only be processed if the data subject has given explicit permission, but there are a number of exceptions. For example, relevant sensitive data can be processed by a health professional without the consent of the data subject.

Principle 2 implies that data must normally be obtained with the knowledge and consent of the data subject.

Principle 6 ensures that data subjects have the right to be given a copy of the data about them, although they may be charged a small fee for this service. They also have the right to prevent processing for direct marketing purposes, or if it is likely to cause damage or distress.

The Data Protection Commissioner is responsible for regulating data controllers. Every organisation or individual who processes personal data, with certain exceptions, must *notify* the Commissioner.

The main exemption to this Act applies to data held for 'personal, family or household purposes', so you can rest assured that you do not have to notify the Commissioner about your personal address book! Other exemptions apply to data collected for, amongst others, national security, investigation of crime and taxation.

Activity

The article 'Grounded by the fiasco in cyberspace' highlights some of the problems connected with the Data Protection Act. How can they be resolved? You may like to do some research to find out whether there have been any changes in the regulations since the article was written.

Grounded by the fiasco in cyberspace

It's the ultimate nightmare scenario for many Internet users – someone else being able to access your bank account details without your knowledge and then raiding your finances and embarking on a fraudulent spending spree.

The nightmare became a reality this week – at least the first part of it – when Barclays was forced to shut down its online banking service for several hours after customers were confronted with details of other people's accounts when they logged on.

Social, moral and ethical implications of ICT solutions

Barclays, which claims to be the UK's largest online bank with 1.25 million users, says only seven people were able to see other customers' details and insists it would not have been possible for them to actually carry out transactions on these accounts.

Barclays described the security flaw as 'unacceptable'. Ironically, the problems seem to have stemmed from an upgrade to its service which included the introduction of a new layer of security, adding an extra stage to the login process. As a result of the problems Barclays ripped out the new software and reinstated the old system.

This week's incident is the latest in a series of Internet security scares. Last month gas and electricity supplier Powergen agreed to pay £50 compensation to up to 7000 online customers after an error allowed their names, addresses and credit card details to be accessed by an unauthorised person.

And just a few months ago the Halifax was forced to temporarily close its online share-dealing service after a technical fault led to worries that some customers had been able to access other people's accounts. It also comes hard on the heels of technical problems that blighted the launch of two new online banks, Intelligent Finance (IF) and Cahoot. . . .

In an attempt to improve the situation, the National Consumer Council is calling for a number of improvements, including more secure payment systems which provide a decent safety net when problems occur; beefing up the existing protection for credit card transactions that go wrong; higher standards of customer service; and a government-backed publicity campaign to promote greater awareness of your rights and how to get redress.

©*The Guardian*, from an article by Rupert Jones on 5 August 2000

The Computer Misuse Act 1990

The Computer Misuse Act is designed to deal with unauthorised access to computer systems. Some of this unauthorised access could be described as 'hacking', but you need to distinguish between the three kinds of offence that are made illegal by the Act:

- *Unauthorised access to computer material.* The key issues here are whether someone was *authorised* to access a computer system, and whether they deliberately did something *with the intention of* gaining unlawful access. If someone accidently gains access to a system then they are not guilty of an offence, although they would be if they continued to explore the system once they realised what had happened. Notice that gaining access as an experiment or 'for a laugh' is still a criminal act. Examples of offences under this section include logging on to a system with someone else's user name and password, or altering, deleting, copying or simply reading programs or data when not authorised to do so.
- *Unauthorised access with intent to commit or facilitate commission of further offences.* This is more serious, and deals with cases where the person intends to commit another crime, such as theft or blackmail, and is gaining unauthorised access in order to do so.
- *Unauthorised modification of computer material.* This section outlaws the intentional alteration or deletion of data when the person does not have authority to do so. It also covers the deliberate introduction of a virus to a system.

Social, moral and ethical implications of ICT solutions

Hacker threat to Whitehall revealed

The security of government Internet and e-mail services is a shambles, raising serious questions about national security, according to one of the government's most senior advisers on electronic protection.

Deri Jones, the head of Europe's biggest Internet security testing company, which supplies services to a series of government departments as well as the Bank of England, Powergen and British Gas, said tests had revealed gaping holes at the heart of the government's computer services. He said hackers – and unauthorised government officials – would find it easy to get into many of the government's most sensitive Internet sites.

Jones accused officials of being complacent about security issues. They were too busy fighting turf wars over who has the most complex Internet sites to realise that threats from outside individuals were real and that malevolent insiders could be having a field day.

The government's supposedly secure intranet service, GSI, which links departments, is thought to be particularly vulnerable. . . .

Jones's company, NTA Monitor, which provides security advice and equipment for the Cabinet Office, the Office of Fair Trading, the Department for Education and the government's publishing arm, the Stationery Office, surveyed 16,000 organisations in Britain last month. Of the groups tested, more than a third of government departments and linked organisations failed the most basic security test – the e-mail relay vulnerability test. That compared with just one in five university sites and one in four commercial sites.

©*The Guardian*, from an article by Kamal Ahmed on 23 July 2000

The moral impact of ICT solutions

We all have our own views about what is morally right and wrong, but we do not all agree with each other over them. Some people derive their moral views from their religious convictions whilst others base their morals on fundamental beliefs about what it is to be human. Many people choose to adopt a single principle, such as "Always treat others as you would like to be treated", and use that to decide what is morally right.

Whatever the basis for our moral views, *almost everyone agrees that morality is essential in human society*. Most people would also agree on a list of actions that they consider to be wrong. This list would include harming other people (physically or emotionally), telling lies, damaging property, and theft.

When dealing with moral issues people often talk about our 'moral duties'. *A moral duty is something that we ought to do, because we are human.*

Confidentiality

At Wessex County all the data on the hospital's systems is accessible to authorised users only. As far as personal data is concerned this is a legal requirement of the Data Protection Act. But the repercussions of errors could go far beyond the legal consequences, because people can be seriously harmed if confidential information is passed to the wrong people. Does the hospital have a moral duty, as well as a legal one, towards its data subjects?

There has been concern in the past that patients' notes may have been copied to health authorities, universities and local councils. In some cases the medical records are used by universities and drug companies to carry out research into the spread of diseases and the effectiveness of treatments. This use is quite legitimate but only if all the features of a medical record that would identify the subject are erased.

Censorship

Computer users can, if they wish, acquire a large amount of unpleasant material, in both textual and graphical formats. Most of this is accessible through the Internet which, because of its global nature, cannot be effectively regulated.

Some of this material is pornographic, excessively violent or racially offensive, and would be shunned by most fairminded people. However, there may be a divergence of views about other items, especially political material which may be judged as subversive

by oppressive governments but as liberating by those in opposition.

Most organisations have a policy of forbidding employees to use their computers for non-work-related activities. Others do not forbid the use of computers for personal matters during lunch breaks, but would still forbid the storage of inappropriate material.

EauCo Water, which you met in Chapter 6, has a strict policy of not allowing users to use their computers for anything other than work activities. Andrew Jones, the Operations Manager, has configured the user access privileges so that users are unable to install any new software. This not only prevents games from being played, but also ensures that the company stays within copyright legislation.

But a number of users, particularly in the Marketing Department, have Internet access. 'Nanny' software has been installed which filters out Web pages that contain certain key words which would suggest that the material is offensive. Unfortunately, this also *filters* out some sites dealing with sewerage management. Andrew has had to disable the filter for some trusted users.

Andrew's department is able to carry out random checks of Internet usage, but does give it a rather low priority compared with all the other pressures on his staff.

Activities

On 25 June 2000, The Observer *newspaper reported a number of cases where medical records had been passed to unauthorised people. Discuss the social effects of these mistakes, as outlined below. Are any of them morally defensible uses of data? What could be done to prevent security lapses like these at Wessex County Hospital?*

- *A 68-year-old man was refused a place in a care home when social services found from his medical records that he was gay.*

- *An uncle found out that his niece had a secret abortion when the company he worked for was asked to do a financial audit of the local health authority. He told her parents, who are very religious.*

- *A woman was sacked after her GP sent her records to her employer. The notes revealed that she had a history of mental health problems.*

- *Patients with medical conditions have been approached by researchers who have had access to their records.*

- *The medical histories of everyone living in Oxford are used without their knowledge by Oxford University for research. Names are removed, but patient groups claim individuals are identifiable through postcodes.*

- *A Member of Parliament was sent the medical records of a constituent without her consent. She found out only when the MP passed on the records to her.*

Resigning issues

Under what circumstances, if any, should an employee disobey instructions given by a senior?

Many people believe that some moral duties are more significant than others and that certain moral duties must take priority. They may consider that moral duties to tell the truth, to preserve life, to prevent harm to others must take precedence over keeping faith with an employer. If they are asked by a senior to undertake activities which go against such moral duties, then they must follow those higher values and disobey.

For example, a famous case recently drew attention to the practice in one or two hospitals of retaining, for research purposes, the organs of patients who had died. This should normally only be done with the permission of relatives, or where the patient had previously indicated that it was their wish. But organs are needed to advance our knowledge of medical conditions and to train doctors and researchers. As insufficient organs were available by the normal route, organs were routinely removed without relatives being informed. Some of the medical staff involved believed that the practice was morally wrong.

What should an employee do in these circumstances? In many cases the only solution is for the employee to resign, even though he or she has not done anything improper.

Results confusion in Scotland

MORE than 1400 pupils will suffer the frustration of not learning their full exam results when certificates are received in homes throughout Scotland today. The Scottish Qualifications Authority (SQA) said that around one per cent of candidates who sat Higher, Standard Grade and Intermediate exams could have some part of their results missing.

It is the first time in more than 100 years that the Higher results have been sent out without complete certificates.

The pupils will find that the school assessment portions of their exams, which count towards their final grades, are missing. However, the Scottish Executive said the final results would be posted within a week.

The SQA has set up a telephone helpline to answer questions from pupils and schools, and has contacted universities, whose admissions departments will be without the same information. A spokesman for the Universities and Colleges Admission Service, said that the problem meant universities would not be able to confirm immediately that students had won the places they had applied for.

The Chief Executive of the SQA blamed the situation on a new computer system that had been introduced, without full testing, to deal with a range of new exams introduced under the government's education reforms. He said: 'We accept full responsibility for everything that has happened in the course of this year. We had to introduce a whole range of new qualifications which means the documents and all the systems concerned with it.'

The computer system was almost as complex as those used for air traffic control. It was understandable that a small number of the 140,000 pupils sitting the exams had been affected. The Chief Executive defended the Authority's record on its new system and said there was no question of the accuracy of the results being released today. He said: 'Over 99.5 per cent of results are complete. There are gaps and this comes to one per cent of candidates. We regret that.' Pass rates were said to be broadly in proportion to last year's results.

Source: taken from an article by Auslan Cramb in *Daily Telegraph*, 10 August 2000

Social, moral and ethical implications of ICT solutions

The problems were illustrated by the case of 16-year-old Kirsty Anderson, who received a Higher pass certificate for a mathematics paper she did not sit, but no results for the drama and biology exams that she had taken.

Source: taken from an article by Martin Bentham in *Sunday Telegraph*, 13 August 2000

Activity

Read the two newspaper extracts in the box 'Results confusion in Scotland'. On 13 August 2000 the Chief Executive resigned. Some students waited four weeks for their results. Whose fault was it? Was the Chief Executive right to resign?

The ethical impact of ICT solutions

In this section we will be looking at the moral duties that a person might have as an employee in the ICT industry. These duties are sometimes referred to as *professional ethics*.

The massive growth of ICT during the last quarter of the twentieth century resulted in radical changes in the kinds of job available and in the way people work. This has forced employers to reconsider what they should expect of their employees.

Common law duties

Anybody who works for an employer has certain duties. These have developed out of good practice over a long period and are now commonly accepted. For example, if an employee falls down on certain duties, and loses his or her job as a result, then that person cannot sue the employer for unfair dismissal.

Employees have to act in good faith towards their employer

This means that employees should not do anything that might harm the employer's business. Here are some examples of breaches of good faith:

- deception – misrepresenting information to the employer
- fraud – deception in order to gain a personal advantage
- theft – taking something which belongs to the employer or a client (including money transferred electronically)
- falsification of documents
- deliberate concealment of information which may harm the business
- unlawful use of insider information.

Activity

John has just started working as an assistant to the network administrator at Highgate College. A student complains to him that someone has gained access to her workspace and has deleted important coursework files. John realises that he made a mistake when setting up the accounts for the students on her course – he gave everyone access to the directories of all the other students. He does not know how to fix this problem, but does not want to be blamed for the loss of coursework.

Discuss all the possible ways, good and bad, in which John could behave in this situation. Which of those ways would be ethical and which unethical?

Employees have a duty of confidentiality towards their employers and clients

Employees should not pass on any information that they have gained through their work. Of course, this has to be taken in a reasonable way – most employers would not mind if an employee told a friend outside the company about the high quality of food served in the staff restaurant, although technically that breaches confidentiality. This duty of confidentiality applies even when someone has left a job.

A whistle-blower is someone who decides to reveal to the general public wrong practices that are going on inside an organisation. It can be difficult for them to do this without putting their own job at risk, so they should always go first to a formal authority, such the police or the Health & Safety Executive.

Employees have a duty of care

All employees should use reasonable care in what they do for their employer. This means that they should not be negligent, and they should not be careless about safety in the workplace.

Activities

1. Sara used to work for a subsidiary of WorldWise that supplied software to the travel industry, and she had developed for them some particularly neat techniques for solving real-time programming problems. She recently joined a large tour operator as an analyst programmer. Although she now does not have printouts of her programming code, she can easily remember what she did in her previous job and discusses with her new project manager how she could use the techniques in her new work. In order to impress him with her skills, she also tells him about the sales success of the software she had helped to write. Is Sara acting unethically?

2. Hassan works in the accounts department of a college. He has discovered that his manager has used access privileges to set up an account for a unfamiliar supplier and that substantial sums of money are being transferred regularly into this account. When the accounts manager buys an expensive new car Hassan becomes convinced that the accounts manager is stealing the money. Hassan has explained his fears to the human resources manager of the college, but was told that he must have misunderstood what was going on.

   Hassan has a friend who works as a reporter on the local paper, and he has discussed the problem with him. His friend now says that he wants to publish the story, but that Hassan's name will not be mentioned. What should Hassan do, and why?

Activity

Kara drives a company van to deliver computer supplies to customers. One day, as she was on her way to deliver new computers to Whittle Valley Leisure Centre, she stopped at some traffic lights and then noticed an elderly pedestrian collapse on the pavement. As she had some first-aid training Kara got out of the van quickly and went to help. Eventually the ambulance arrived and the woman was taken to hospital. When Kara returned to the van she found that all the valuable stock had been stolen.

What would be the reaction of Kara's boss? Did Kara behave morally and ethically?

Misconduct

All employees are entitled to a written contract, which will spell out the expectations of the employer. An employer can always dismiss someone for gross misconduct, and a contract will sometimes list examples of what this could mean.

Gross misconduct includes all the breaches of common law mentioned already. But it could also reasonably include telling lies to the employer, damaging company property, behaving violently towards anyone, or sexual harassment.

Misconduct is less serious wrongdoing and will usually result in disciplinary action but not dismissal. But what counts as misconduct? Some actions, such as the use of obscene language to customers, may be obvious cases of misconduct. But in other areas the definition of misconduct may vary from organisation to organisation. For example, some companies forbid employees to make personal telephone calls from work, whereas others allow them. In general, the employer should make any house rules clear to employees. If the employer wants to change a rule, then reasonable notice should be given.

Activity

Chris works as a personal assistant to a head of department at Highgate College. During his lunch break Chris usually uses his office computer to catch up on his personal e-mail and newsgroups. He has a particular interest in Formula 1 racing cars and belongs to a number of mailing lists. One lunchtime he received an e-mail which promised him a picture of a fast car, but it was only after he had saved the attachment that he realised that it was pornographic material. When his PC crashed later in the day one of the IT technical staff told him that a virus had wiped all the word-processed files from his hard disk. This included an urgent report that he had just completed for his boss.

Has Chris done anything unethical? Could he be disciplined for misconduct? What should he do next?

Professional ethics

Many areas of work are governed by *professional bodies*. Generally speaking, we call someone a professional if they have achieved a high level of qualification and expertise in their chosen field.

For example, doctors cannot practice in the UK unless they are members of the General Medical Council, which is their professional body. They can become full members only after they have qualified as doctors. The council lays down standards that members must abide by, and it can suspend anyone who does not meet those standards.

The ICT industry is not as straightforward as medicine. It covers people working in a wide variety of jobs at differing levels of skill. But it does have its own professional body, the *British Computer Society* (BCS), which was incorporated by Royal Charter in 1984. You can visit its website at www.bcs.org.uk.

The BCS advises Parliament and acts as the public voice on ICT issues. Members can attend informative meetings, join special interest groups and develop their professional skills through the society.

Becoming a member of the BCS is not simply a matter of filling in a form. Members must have a sufficient combination of qualifications and/or experience. A typical new member might be a Computer Science graduate with at least four years of relevant experience in the industry.

You may be interested to know that student membership is open to people studying for a degree or HND in a relevant subject. Full members of the British Computer Society can use the title 'Chartered Information Systems Practitioner'.

Activity

All members of the BCS agree to be bound by the Society's code of conduct (see page 111). Compare this code of conduct with the common law duties of an employee.

British Computer Society

Code of Conduct (extract)

The Public Interest

1. You shall carry out work or study with due care and diligence in accordance with the relevant authority's requirements, and the interests of system users. If your professional judgement is overruled, you shall indicate the likely risks and consequences.
2. In your professional role you shall have regard for the public health, safety and environment.
3. You shall have regard to the legitimate rights of third parties.
4. You shall ensure that within our professional field/s you have knowledge and understanding of relevant legislation, regulations and standards, and that you comply with such requirements.
5. You shall conduct your professional activities without discrimination against clients or colleagues.
6. You shall reject any offer of bribery or inducement.

Professional Competence and Integrity

7. You shall seek to upgrade your professional knowledge and skill, and shall maintain awareness of technological developments, procedures and standards which are relevant to your field, and encourage your subordinates to do likewise.
8. You shall not claim any level of competence that you do not possess. You shall only offer to do work or provide a service that is within your professional competence.
9. You shall observe the relevant BCS Codes of Practice and all other standards which, in your judgement, are relevant, and you shall encourage your colleagues to do likewise.
10. You shall accept professional responsibility for your work and for the work of colleagues who are defined in a given context as working under your supervision.

©British Computer Society

Many professionals in the world of ICT work as *consultants*. Consultants offer their services to clients on a short-term basis in order to solve particular problems for them.

A client may be worried about offering a contract to a consultant who is self-employed, as the consultant will not be answerable to a manager. But if the consultant is a member of a professional body then the client will be reassured because that body's code of conduct applies and it can discipline the member if necessary.

Activity

Hannah works as a self-employed IT trainer and is a full member of the BCS. She has provided training for the GBW Bank many times in the past, and one day they ask her to put on a three-day course for six members of staff on a newly released graphical software package. She agrees to do this and books the dates for the course in a month's time.

Hannah intends to buy the package, develop her own skills in using it and write some training materials during the next four weeks. Unfortunately, she is involved in a car accident and takes two weeks to recover. She then does not have enough time to develop her materials properly and the course is a bit of a disaster. Has Hannah violated the BCS code of conduct? What should she do next?

Social, moral and ethical implications of ICT solutions

Political issues

Politics is about power and decision-making in government. Political activity is essentially directed towards making laws and managing public resources. Governments are uniquely placed in having to balance social, moral and ethical issues when framing laws and spending public funds.

Normally when we talk about government we are referring to our democratic institutions. In the UK these authorities are:

- the European Parliament
- the Westminster Parliament
- regional Assemblies and Parliaments
- local authorities (county, metropolitan borough, district, parish).

Voters elect representatives to these bodies, and give them authority to design policies, laws and regulations which then apply to us all as citizens.

The power that is given to members of these authorities, such as Members of Parliament and local councillors, derives from the fact that they are elected periodically. Electors can always choose other representatives at the end of the term of office if they are not satisfied with the way in which their representatives have exercised their power.

In addition, members of the public can contact (lobby) their representatives and explain why they want them to take up a particular position on an issue.

In practice, politicians usually group together in political parties, and the party will decide, after detailed debate, the line that they will take on an issue. The decision will depend on a mixture of basic principles and an assessment of what is possible and practical to achieve.

Law-making and social, moral and ethical issues

The laws and regulations generated by parliaments and by local authorities clearly fit into the political arena. Some of these laws relate directly to ICT systems, whilst others have an indirect impact.

Individual politicians decide on their position on a proposed law by considering the social and moral issues surrounding it. They often have to compare one moral position with another. For example, legislation on data protection has always had to recognise that a balance needs to be kept between freedom of information and personal privacy.

Politicians also have to understand professional ethics. They usually encourage professions to regulate themselves through their professional bodies, rather than by the law. However, sometimes laws are needed.

The Internet is very difficult to regulate because it is a global phenomenon. If a website makes false or defamatory claims, or contains offensive material, should it be subject to the laws of the country where it is written, where it is hosted or where it is downloaded? What can be done about a site that contains information which has a high security rating in another country, such that the disclosure of the information could cause considerable harm to that country? What laws protect consumers who purchase goods online from a company based in another country?

The governments of countries around the world have differing views about these issues, and some have made laws which seem to be in direct conflict with those of other nations.

Activities

1. *Research news and parliamentary archives on the Internet to trace the development of a piece of legislation that has an impact on ICT systems.*

2. *Carry out some research to discover what protection a consumer has when buying goods online from an overseas company.*

Managing public resources and social, moral and ethical issues

Parliaments and local authorities have to manage very substantial budgets. Politicians have to decide how to allocate finance, and once again these decisions are based on a mixture of policy and practicalities.

In order to make these decisions it is usually necessary to prioritise a number of possible projects. The task of putting several different claims on the public purse into descending order of priority will be governed by social and moral considerations.

For example, a local authority has a limited budget and has to choose between upgrading the ICT systems at the public libraries or providing tourist kiosks (touch-sensitive screens giving tourist information) at key points in the town centre. Some local politicians argue that upgrading the library system will make the libraries more accessible to the general public, and to children and the elderly in particular. Others claim that the town needs to encourage tourists in order to boost the local economy, which would benefit everyone eventually.

Activity

Read 'Billions wasted on computers' in the box. Comment on the technical and political causes of the problems. How can problems like these with large public contracts be avoided in the future?

Wessex County Hospital has been trying out a new software system to handle waiting lists in the Ear, Nose and Throat department. A patient first sees a consultant. If the consultant recommends surgery the patient is put on the waiting list. In the past urgent cases were given priority, but everyone else had to wait in the queue. Some patients waited for up to two years for non-urgent surgery.

With the new waiting list system, patients are scored according to several factors, including the type of disease, the pain they are suffering, the level of disability and the time they have been waiting. Patients with the highest scores are seen first.

This system does not mean that more operations are performed, but it does ensure that patients will not have to wait so long for surgery for the more disabling and life-threatening conditions.

Waiting lists have considerable political significance. The government tends to concentrate funding on the longest lists. The Wessex County system still has a long waiting list for relatively trivial operations, but the hospital management argues that the quality of the lists is much better. They believe that waiting lists should be measured by taking both the score and the

Billions wasted on computers

Government is wasting billions of pounds on ineffective and useless information technology systems, a committee of MPs says in a report published today. The government is spending some £7 billion a year on new systems, and the Commons public accounts committee draws together a decade of blunders – from the National Insurance contributions system to the debacle at the Passport Agency, which disrupted tens of thousands of applications. . . .

The report highlights 25 projects which have failed to deliver the promised improvements to the public and in some cases had to be abandoned because they did not work properly.

One of the worst ministries was the Home Office which is condemned for making a mess of a new system to deliver passports; for signing an unenforceable contract over processing nationality and immigration claims; and for introducing a computer system that actually delayed payments for people handing in guns after the Dunblane massacre.

The Home Office blunders led to the cost of processing passports increasing from £12 to £15.50. A new passport now costs £28. The section on the Home Office's failings concludes: 'It is essential that departments learn from their past mistakes and consider how they can co-ordinate better their considerable resources to ensure better

Social, moral and ethical implications of ICT solutions

value for money from IT development.'

Other departments heavily criticised include the NHS Executive, the Ministry of Defence and the Contributions Agency.

- The NHS was attacked for years of errors in co-ordinating information on hospital patients and failing to co-ordinate a system so different hospitals could share the information.
- The Ministry of Defence had to abandon a top-secret computer system never used at a cost of £40million and spent millions of pounds on a faulty computer system to handle the sale of surplus equipment.
- The Benefits Agency and the Contributions Agency are attacked for trying to implement computer systems that were not capable of doing the job. The Contributions Agency has still not sorted out a new system to record National Insurance payments, with the result that people are still not being paid. The failure in the National Insurance recording system meant 172,000 pensioners were underpaid by between one penny to £100 a week because their contributions had not been collated.

The report calls for widespread changes in the way computer contracts are handled, ensuring that departments employed skilled project managers to run them properly.

©*The Guardian*, 2 May 2000

time waiting into account. This is a debate that will undoubtedly continue in the public arena.

Activities

1. *Find out the policy of the main political parties on a current issue. Try to choose a topic that has some relevance to ICT.*

2. *What is the role of the media in influencing political decisions?*

CHAPTER 9

How to do Task 1

This chapter gives advice on how to tackle coursework **Task 1.** The task requires you to produce a detailed written report describing the ICT administration processes of a major actual application.

A sample report, with comments, can be viewed on the Heinemann website at www.heinemann.co.uk. Do not forget that the examiners will have read this book, so do not attempt to use any of the material from the sample in your own report (see the section below on plagiarism).

This chapter covers the following Learning Outcome in the specification:

L.O. 3.1 Produce a written report of the ICT administration process

Selecting your subject

For Task 1 you should prepare and write a report on the *IT administration processes of a major actual application* from one of these areas :

- industry
- commerce
- government
- society
- academia (education).

The emphasis in this coursework task is on the processes carried out by the systems administrator to support the application. You will have to carry out research in order to write this report, and this will be both through direct contact and through background reading.

It is essential that you speak to a real systems administrator when carrying out your research. In order to do this effectively you will have to have some understanding of the responsibilities of that role. The chapters in this section of the book should give you most of the background information that you need, but you may also want to use other books and sources on the Internet.

How do I find a suitable application?

You are required to investigate a *major* application. This is usually interpreted as one that is run on a multi-user system which needs the specialist support services of a systems administrator. A systems administrator may have a different job title – such as network manager, computer support or IT technician. Alternatively, the person may not actually describe himself or herself in any of these ways, and the systems administration tasks may be only part of the job the person does.

When selecting a subject, then, the most important consideration is that you actually know someone, or can be put in contact with someone, who does the work of a systems administrator, whatever their job title.

It is a good idea to start by thinking about your personal contacts amongst your family and friends. It is very likely that a number of them will work in some way with an IT application. Your teacher may also be able to introduce you to a local organisation. It is probably a mistake to begin by selecting a local business out of the blue and then trying to make a contact – they are unlikely to be very cooperative for a complete stranger – so an introduction is always a good first step.

The person you contact initially may work as an end-user of a major application rather than as a systems administrator. Find out whether you can be introduced to the systems administrator.

Here are some ideas for possible subjects:

- shops and mail order companies – sales or ordering applications
- schools, colleges and universities – academic or administrative software
- GP and dental surgeries, or hospitals – patient records and/or appointments systems
- service industries, such as insurance companies and banks – customer records databases
- manufacturing companies – production systems
- local government – council tax and benefits
- call centres – call logging software
- voluntary organisations and charities – advice systems or fundraising databases.

Preparing your report

The coursework task should be developed in two stages:

- **Preparation for the report**
  - Plan
  - History of information gathering
- **The report**

If you were reporting to an employer you would normally hand in only the final report, but in this case the examiners want to see the preparation as well. Half the marks are allocated to the preparation stage!

How do I plan my coursework?

The syllabus requires you to include the following elements in your plan:

- basic details of the application to be researched
- the main sources of information
- a checklist of investigation topics
- initial ideas of the main headings of the report.

You will have to select a subject before you begin your plan, and to obtain permission from the organisation to carry out your research.

In the meantime, find out some general background about the application and the organisation that uses it. Write an outline, at least, of the first three sections of the Plan (as explained later) before you start investigating in depth. You should ask your teacher to check your Plan at this stage.

What are my sources of information?

You can obtain information for your report from:

- **primary sources** – by talking directly to people who work with the application
- **secondary sources** – by reading documents that tell you more about the application and the organisation
- **background research**.

The main primary sources will be employees of the organisation, such as systems administrators (or people who do the systems administration, whatever their job titles), end-users of the application and their managers.

You may be able to obtain some secondary source documents, such as manuals, charts, reports and other inhouse documentation.

Whilst working on this coursework task you can build up your background knowledge of computer systems, software applications and the procedures that systems administrators carry out. This knowledge can be obtained from a variety of sources, including books, magazines and the Internet.

How do I get the information from primary sources?

You will have to make contact with your primary sources in the organisation. The main methods you will use to gather the information will be interviews and observation. You may also write letters or send e-mails.

Any conversation or discussion, however informal, with one of your chosen sources is referred to as an *interview*. Some interviews may have to be carried out over the telephone. It is important to prepare the questions that you want to ask in advance of the interview.

What information do I need?

You are required to identify the systems administration processes that have to be carried out in order to keep an application working effectively for its end-users.

Note that you are not being asked simply to describe a hardware or software system, although you will have to include a description at some point. You must write about the day-to-day procedures that have to be done to keep an application working successfully. These will include procedures that relate to the hardware, to the system software and to the application itself.

If you scan through the Technical Knowledge topics and Learning Outcomes for Unit 1 you should be able to identify a number of possible topics that could form the basis for your investigation. For example, you could investigate the security requirements of the application, or the regular file management procedures. You could find out how the hardware is serviced, what consumables are needed, and how minor repairs are carried out. The system and application software and their associated data files will have to be maintained; and the hardware and communication links will have to be tested and monitored. These and other topics can be explored in your interviews and research.

How do I provide evidence of my research?

Your history of information gathering should include full evidence of all your research. You should keep a *research log*. This is a list of all the research activities you have carried out, presented in chronological order. It should include information about:

- visits – when and where
- interviews – when and where the interview took place, who you spoke to and the main topics of discussion
- observations – when and where you observed the system in action
- correspondence – dates when correspondence (letters, telephone calls and e-mails) was sent or received
- reading – when you found the material and the book title or website address
- other research – dated entries for any other research that you carried out.

The entries in your research log should be backed up with *detailed evidence of the information collected*. For example, it could include:

- notes taken at interviews and on visits
- copies of relevant documents provided by the organisation
- copies of correspondence
- photocopies/printouts of relevant extracts from books or websites
- photographs.

The evidence can be provided in its original form. For example, if you interview someone include the rough notes that you took – this is much more convincing evidence than a neatly printed version. But if you have taped an interview (which you should only do with the express permission of the subject) then you should provide a transcription or notes, rather than the actual audio tape.

Documents, photocopies and printouts should be annotated – that is, you should hand-write notes on them, drawing attention to the relevant parts.

When you hand in your coursework task, do not submit large documents. Your work will not be assessed by its weight! In fact, you will be judged by your ability to identify and extract relevant material from the mass of documents that you may find. A succinct selection of carefully annotated, highly relevant extracts will gain you more marks than bulky documents which lack comments.

Writing the report

How should I present the main report?

In business contexts a report is always written with a specific reader in mind. This will often be a more senior person within the organisation, or it may be a client of the company. In the case of this coursework task, the intended audience for your main report is, perhaps, a manager in the organisation who wants to know what exactly the systems administrators do in their work. You may imagine this person to be intelligent but not technically minded, so you need to explain all the computer terminology clearly.

You must also assume that the Plan and History of Information Gathering will not be seen by the imaginary reader of the report, so the report must make sense *on its own*. You may feel that there is some repetition between these two sections and the report itself, but the information should be addressed to different audiences so should not be presented in the same way.

In practice, of course, the examiner will see and assess both the preparation for the report and the report itself.

How should I identify my sources of information?

All sources of information in your report must be identified and recorded. Failure to give credit to a person who helped you is considered discourteous; failure to give credit to a written source amounts to plagiarism.

When quoting from documents you should always give:

- the title of the work
- the author of the text or article
- the reference to where it was found (e.g. book, paper etc.)
- the date of publication.

When quoting from websites you should always give:

- the name and/or domain name of the website
- the author (if possible)
- the date it was published (if possible) and the date it was viewed.

How will the contents of my report be assessed?

- **Depth of treatment of the identified issues**. Have you really investigated a topic in depth, or have you simply repeated what you have been told? Do you understand everything you have written? Have you tried to find out alternative ways of carrying out procedures?
- **The overall structure and layout of the report**. The structure should include the main headings that you identified in the Plan, but you should also show that you can break down broad issues into subsidiary points in a coherent manner.
- **Content**. The actual content of the report carries the most marks. Is it an interesting read? Will your reader learn something by reading it? Is it accurate, comprehensive and coherent?

Quality of language and presentation

It goes almost without saying that you will use the spelling and grammar checkers on your word-processor. If you are not sure which of several alternative spellings is the one you need, then check their meanings in a dictionary. You should ask someone else to read through your report to ensure that it is intelligible.

If English is not your first language then you may want to discuss the vocabulary and sentence construction with a language teacher. They should not help you directly with the wording, but should be able to point out errors.

Pay some attention to the visual appearance of your report. You may use a preset template or design one of your own.

Here is a checklist to use when your main report is complete:

- ☐ Have I checked the report for spelling and grammar?
- ☐ Have I checked that the report is readable and makes sense to a new reader?
- ☐ Have I numbered the pages (preferably in a footer)?
- ☐ Have I included my name in a header or footer on each page?
- ☐ Have I selected suitable text styles for headings, the main body of the text, headers and footers? The styles should be consistent throughout the report, and should be clear and businesslike.
- ☐ Have I included a contents page?

Assessment of Task 1

How does the mark scheme work?

Maximum marks are shown in square brackets. The maximum possible total is 40 marks.

- **Preparation for the report**
  - Plan [10]
  - History of Information Gathering [10]

- **The report**
  - Quality of presentation and language [2]
  - Depth of treatment of the identified issues [3]
  - Structure [5]
  - Content [10]

Writing up Task 1

This coursework task should be presented in two parts.

The preparation for the report will contain all your planning, and should provide evidence of the information gathering you have done. It may include rough notes and copies of some of your source material.

The report itself should be presented attractively as a standalone document. It should be possible for a reader to understand the report without referring to the preparation section. You are expected to divide your report into sections, using headings and subheadings. All pages should be numbered.

The notes on the mark scheme have been extended to provide you with additional guidance. The sentences in *italics* are quotes from the mark scheme.

Preparation for the report [20 marks]

1. Plan [10 marks]

The student should produce an outline plan for the task ahead. The plan should include:

- *basic details of the application to be researched*
- *the main sources of information*
- *a checklist of investigation topics*
- *initial ideas of the main headings of the report.*

Each of these four elements of the plan will be given equal weighting.

1.1 Application to be researched

- Describe the application and explain your interest in it.
- Describe the organisation that uses the application.
- Describe the end-users of the application.

1.2 Main sources of information

- Identify the systems administrator(s) you intend to contact, and the structure of their department.
- Identify the end-user(s) you may intend to contact and their role in the organisation.

- Identify other possible sources of information that you plan to use.

1.3 Investigation topics

- List all the topics you plan to discuss with the systems administrator.
- List all the topics that you plan to discuss with other people.
- Identify which topics you will want to do further research on.

1.4 Main headings for the report

- Give an overall plan of the final report.

2. History of information gathering [10 marks]

A significant part of this task will be the process of gathering raw information. Students are likely to produce notes from observations, interviews and reading. It is therefore important that they are given credit for these processes irrespective of the quality of the final report.

2.1 Research log

- Include dated entries of all your research.

2.2 Information collected

- Include notes on interviews and observations.
- Include notes on other research findings (from book and Internet sources).
- Provide annotated copies of original documents (where relevant).
- Present any other research evidence.

The report [20 marks]

Title page

- Give your report a suitable title.

Contents

- List sections and page numbers.

Acknowledgements

Main sections

You should structure the main sections of your report using the headings identified in the Plan.

CHAPTER 10

Examination questions and mark schemes for unit 1

This chapter provides examination questions and mark schemes for Unit 1: Systems Administration. Edexcel has given permission for the use here of this copyright material.

You are also advised to read Chapter 20 which provides hints on how to succeed in examinations, and examples of how to tackle exam questions.

Specimen examination questions

1. Adrian is the systems administrator at a large law firm. The firm has a network of computers connected to one file server. Each room has access to a shared laser printer.

    (a) Wendy, one of the secretaries, telephones Adrian at the helpdesk to complain that when she tries to print from her word-processor, nothing happens. Adrian visits her and finds that the printer driver has been removed.

        (i)   Describe the purpose of a *printer driver*.
              [2 marks]
        (ii) Name *three* other drivers that may be present on Wendy's computer   [3 marks]
        (iii) Describe steps that Adrian could take to prevent Wendy from accidentally removing any of her drivers again.
              [2 marks]

    (b) Adrian installs the printer driver and does a test print from one of Wendy's documents. A message appears on screen, which says *The printer is out of paper*. Describe how the printer interacts with the operating system in order to produce this message.   [4 marks]

    (c) When Adrian installed the driver, he put the operating system installation disk into the CD drive of Wendy's machine. He then looked for the folder (directory) containing the drivers.

The drivers were located in a sub-folder in the *system* folder.

    (i) Explain why, from Adrian's point of view, folders are a sensible way of organising and storing files.   [3 marks]
    (ii) Explain how the operating system is able to access files that are organised in a hierarchical tree structure.   [5 marks]

Edexcel pilot specification, Summer 2000

2. *Images* is a film production company that makes extensive use of IT. Cleo is the systems administrator and, with the growth of the use of IT in the company, she is finding that she has too much to do. It is decided that a person experienced in IT should be appointed to act as Cleo's assistant. Cleo will have to retain the following responsibilities:

    *   negotiating contracts with suppliers
    *   ensuring that the general IT strategy is consistent with the needs of the company.

    (a) Explain why Cleo must continue to exercise these responsibilities.   [4 marks]

    (b) Tony is appointed as the deputy systems administrator to Cleo. Although Tony is experienced in IT he has not worked in a film production company before. Cleo will have to devise a training programme for Tony. Detail

three aspects of this training programme.
[6 marks]

(c) Tony will receive many requests each day to solve users' routine technical problems.

Give *four* questions that Tony will have to ask about a problem in order to make sensible decisions about the day's priorities. [4 marks]

(d) Tony is responsible for documenting the solution to any problem that he solves.

(i) List *two* items of information that will be recorded in this documentation.
[2 marks]

(ii) Explain why such documentation is necessary. [3 marks]

Edexcel pilot specification, Summer 2000

---

3. In the country of Datalia, several different companies run train services. A separate company, Trackside, owns and administers the tracks and the stations. Trackside publishes an interactive website where potential passengers can enter details of their intended journey. The information given by the passenger is used to query a database. The result of the query gives the times of the trains and the connection details.

The train companies periodically give details of the changes to their services to the Trackside webmaster who looks after the timetable website. Trackside receives no payment for timetable enquiries but offers the website facility as a service.

(a) Mary has an interview for an important job, 100 miles from her home. She consults the website timetable to plan her journey. One of the main train operators has changed the timetable and the details have not yet been passed on to the webmaster. As a result, she misses her connection, is late for the interview and does not get the job. Discuss the extent to which Mary has a grievance against Trackside and the train company. [4 marks]

(b) Trackside wants to be sure that Mary's problems are rare.

(i) Describe ways in which information can be gathered to determine how often such problems occur. [3 marks]

(ii) Outline procedures that Trackside could put in place to ensure that the information given to passengers is as accurate and as up to date as possible.
[4 marks]

(c) Access to the Internet and the World Wide Web is obtained by opening an account with an Internet service provider. Many private individuals publish information about a wide range of interests on the Web. Discuss:

(i) how far it should be the moral and legal responsibility of such individuals to ensure that the material that they publish is accurate and appropriate.

(ii) how far it should be the moral and legal responsibility of the Internet service provider to ensure that such information is accurate and appropriate. [8 marks]

Edexcel pilot specification, Summer 2000

---

4. Below is a quotation from a computer sales person who is talking to an ICT systems administrator.

'A modern computer system is nothing without its operating system and you will love this new OS because of its improved graphics user interface.'

(a) Give *two* reasons why the sales person believes that the improved graphics user interface will be attractive to the systems administrator.
[2 marks]

(b) Explain why the phrase '*is nothing without its operating system*' is **not** true. [2 marks]

(c) The sales person continues:

'Another great feature of this operating system is that it will automatically make all the adjustments if you insert an additional internal board.'

(i) Describe *two* circumstances when a systems administrator might want to add an internal board to a system. [4 marks]

(ii) Describe what the systems administrator would have to do if the operating system did not support this automatic feature.

[2 marks]

(iii) Describe how *one* aspect of the systems administrator's responsibilities would be made easier due to this automatic feature. [2 marks]

(d) Annabel uses her computer system to store and retrieve many documents. She is very disciplined about deleting unwanted files from the hard disk. She is unhappy to find that file access has become slower.

(i) Explain why Annabel's system has become slower. [2 marks]

(ii) Describe what Annabel should do to improve the speed of file access. [2 marks]

(iii) Explain how the operating system would carry out the process that you have suggested in your answer to (d) (ii). [3 marks]

Edexcel specimen paper

5. A medium-sized company has plans for expansion. The company sells cosmetics by mail order. Although all sections of the company use similar ICT systems there is no overall organisation and control of ICT provision. The management decides to appoint an ICT systems administrator to evaluate the ICT systems of the company.

(a) Describe how the systems administrator could carry out this investigation. [4 marks]

(b) The management of the company decide to appoint an ICT systems administrator to deal with this problem. Describe *three* areas of expertise that a systems administrator should have in order to be effective in dealing with any ICT-related problems of the company. [6 marks]

(c) The management of the company is concerned about their lack of market share and the Advertising Section is asked to react to the concern. At present the Advertising Section does not use ICT for publicity purposes. The head of the section seeks advice from the ICT systems administrator. Describe *two* aspects of an ICT solution that the systems administrator might propose. [4 marks]

(d) The head of the Advertising Section agrees to invest in the ICT solution proposed by the ICT systems administrator, but is concerned about the processes of the implementation and the possible effects on the department. Discuss how the head of the Advertising Section should prepare the section for the proposed ICT approach to their publicity responsibilities. [5 marks]

Edexcel specimen paper

6. (a) Democratic governments are responsible for providing a range of services for the citizens of a country. Governments make spending decisions based upon statistical information that they are given. Specialist ICT-based companies collect data and use computer programs to analyse the data. The results of the analysis are presented to government.

(i) Describe *two* detrimental effects that could have been due to the government being given incorrect information. [4 marks]

(ii) Describe *two* distinct ways in which such incorrect information could be generated by such a specialist ICT-based company. [4 marks]

(iii) Describe the technical mechanisms that the ICT-based company could put into place to minimise the generation of incorrect data. [3 marks]

(b) A manager is interviewing a candidate for the post of ICT systems administrator. The manager says:

'If I have an accident with my car due to inadequate maintenance by the garage, I could take the garage to court. If our computer systems fail due to lack of software maintenance which results in danger to our users, we might find ourselves in court.'

(i) Describe *two* situations in which the lack of software maintenance of a computer system could lead to dangerous situations. [4 marks]

(ii) Discuss the validity of the comparison between a car accident and a computer systems failure. [4 marks]

Edexcel specimen paper

7. Sarah works as a systems administrator for Kingsmond Sofa Designs. The company manufactures and markets sofas and chairs. One of Sarah's responsibilities is to maintain the laptap PCs used by the sales staff. The sales personnel visit stores around the country and record any orders on a spreadsheet on their laptops. They also use them to compose reports and letters. The hard disk on each laptop PC is partitioned into two drives. The files are then organised into a heirarchy of folders on each drive.

(a) Draw a diagram to show a sensible way of organising the files. [3 marks]

(b) Mohammed, a member of the sales team, has a visual impairment. Explain how Sarah could configure Mohammed's laptop to meet his needs. [2 marks]

(c) Describe *two* other ways in which the graphical user interface could be configured to meet any user's specific needs. [4 marks]

(d) Sarah is asked to install a new application on to Mohammed's laptop. When she runs the Install program an error message appears, and the installation is not completed. Give *one* possible reason why the installation program failed. [2 marks]

(e) Mohammed returns to the headquarters in Kingsmond once each week. He then plugs an office printer into his laptop and completes his sales reports. One day he plugs in a new printer but it does not respond. He reports the fault to Sarah. Explain what checks Sarah should carry out to determine why the printer is not responding. [4 marks]

(f) Sarah decides to defragment the hard disk in Mohammed's laptop. Explain how defragmentation can improve the performance of the system. [4 marks]

Mark schemes

1 (a)
(i) Software used by the operating system; to communicate/control/interface with the printer. [2]
(ii) Three peripheral names; e.g. video, scanner, mouse, disk drive, speakers. *Allow only one type of disk drive driver.* [3]

(iii) A brief description will suffice, such as hide the driver file, make the access rights read-only, educate the user of their importance. *Two methods, one mark each.* [max 2]

1 (b)
When a **sensor in the printer detects that the paper has run out,** the printer **sends an interrupt (signal); to the computer's processor;** which causes **redirection of program control;** to the relevant **interrupt service routine;** which **displays the message.**
One mark for each sensible reference to the concepts in bold. [max 4]

1 (c)
(i) Ensure that answers are relevant to technical support. Any of: similar files grouped together – faster to locate files rather than having to search through a single folder with all of the files in it; facilitates block operations (copy/delete/move); allows use of same file names in different locations.
One mark each for two reasons, with a third mark available for one of them described in depth. [3]
(ii) A **hierarchical tree structure consists of folders contained with other folders.** The **root folder directory** is accessed and contains **pointers (cluster numbers)** to the relevant sub-directories and contained files. **Following the pointers leads to the file required.** The **directories form a linked list.**
One mark each for sensible reference to the concepts in bold. [max 5]

2 (a)
● Cleo has experience of the global company needs and strategies, hence has an overview.
● A position of seniority is required to negotiate with department heads and other senior personnel.
● Systems administrator needs to control overall direction and has not the time to carry out many routine tasks.
● Contract negotiation is a managerial job not a technical job and so will be done by Cleo.
Two convincing well-argued points at two marks each. [max 4]

2 (b)
● Needs training for the film production specific software that he has not met before.

- Needs training in any systems/networking software that he has not met before.
- Needs training for the film production specific peripherals that he has not met before and the network layout.
- Needs training in the company-specific work practices, such as how they run their helpdesk, and the level of security required.

Three qualified points at two marks each. [max 6]

2 (c)

- How important is the job currently being done?
- How many people does the problem affect?
- Is the problem currently damaging hardware or software?
- Is there alternative hardware/software that can be used for the time being?
- How long since the problem was reported?
- Do parts have to be ordered, or is outside specialist help required?

Four reasonable distinct points at one mark each. [max 4]

2 (d)

(i) Date attended, parts used, method of solution, testing procedures, testing results, outside help used, time taken.
Any two for one mark each. [max 2]

(ii)
- If the problem re-occurs, useful data may be recorded to help produce a quicker solution.
- If Tony leaves then the solution will be useful to his replacement.
- There is evidence that the fault has been fixed for his boss Cleo, or if there are complaints.
- There is evidence that can be used when returning hardware to a manufacturer for replacement/repair.
- Analysis of the faults fixed may identify users needing extra training.
- Analysis of the faults may identify extra procedures needed for hardware or software, e.g. security measures.

Two reasons at one mark each, but with an extra mark for one of them being detailed. [max 3]

3(a)

Comments could be made along the lines of: If a service is placed in the public domain, it is reasonable to expect every effort to be made to ensure its accuracy and reliability. In this case, the provider of the enquiry service is part of the overall business that runs the trains, so a moral responsibility exists. On the other hand, the train operators are independent and Trackside cannot necessarily be held responsible for their shortcomings.
Two sensibly argued reasons for two marks each.
[max 4]

3 (b)

(i)
- Surveys can be carried out among passengers.
- Surveys can be carried out among train drivers.
- Ability for passengers to e-mail problems from website.
- Monitor complaints made to operators or to other agencies.

Three methods, one mark each. [max 3]

(ii) Accuracy
- Data validation routines such as checking for impossible times.
- Return timetable proofs to train companies for verification.

Two commented points for one mark each. [max 2]

(iii) Up to date
- Automatic update of the website from the train companies' databases.
- Direct link between the train companies networks and Trackside's so that automatic update is possible.
- Contract/policy implemented to send timetable changes to Trackside immediately.

One reasoned method for two marks. [max 2]

3 (c)

(i)
- A discussion of how the general responsibilities of citizens not to mislead or offend can be extended into Internet publishing.
- Laws such as Libel, Copyright Act and Data Protection Act 1984 can be applied to material on the Internet.
- A discussion of freedom of speech.

- A discussion of the material being available internationally but the laws not being the same in each country.

Two well-reasoned points of view at two marks each.   [max 4]

(ii)
- It can be argued that an ISP is simply a provider of access and has no responsibility regarding content because that lies with the author.
- Comparison can be made with (e.g.) newspaper publishing, where the newspaper commissions articles but also can be sued for libel etc., but the ISP does not necessarily commission the content on its servers and so should not be responsible.
- A discussion of the material being available internationally but the laws not being the same in each country. (Not in both answers.)
- A discussion of actual cases where ISPs have been taken to court and have had to remove offensive material.

Two well-reasoned points of view at two marks each.   [max 4]

---

4 (a)
- Ease of use for the customers of the service that the SA provides; this would enhance the image of the system and thus his/her administration.
- The mechanisms of administration of the system will be eased and hence the SA will be able to be more responsive.

One mark for each reason that clearly relates to a GUI and is qualified.   [max 2]

4 (b)
The candidate should show some understanding based on any two of:

- a raw system nevertheless has some boot-up software built in
- a raw system is a fully integrated working machine of communicating components
- a raw machine is capable of decoding machine-code instructions
- it can't be 'nothing' for how else could the OS be loaded?

The candidate cannot be awarded marks unless there is an indication of an understanding of the nature of a raw machine.   [2]

4 (c)
(i)
- To provide some new facility such as sound because of the requirements of some new software.
- To add a new means of outside communication, such as an additional parallel port because of the need to communicate with an external control device.

For each circumstance: one mark for a sensible board and another mark for any reasonable context. [max 4]

(ii) The SA will first have to study the appropriate technical documentation and then make the OS/hardware modifications by hand.   [2]

(iii) There are several SA responsibilities that could be the basis of this answer.
Full marks can be awarded if the candidate makes a connection with the responsibility and the advantage of the automatic facility. For example: the responsibility of training staff and the reduction of the skills to be tested.   [2]

4 (d)
(i) The hard disk will have become fragmented. Thus the OS will take longer to locate free space and files that are not stored in contiguous areas.
Marks are for these concepts; detailed technical descriptions are not required here.   [2]

(ii) Use some utility such as Defrag to tidy up the data on the disk.
Any reference to a 'Garbage Collection' utility would suffice.   [2]

(iii)
- The OS deals with fragmentation by using a linked list data structure whereby each free area points to the next free area and each 'fragment' of a file points to the next.   [1]
- The 'tidy up' utility would detect the existence of the non-deleted files and with the use of the IAS and the stored pointers join them together and restore them in contiguous areas on the disk. Free space would be dealt with in the same way.   [2]

5(a)

The candidate must bring out the prime nature of any evaluation that is the view of the customer, in this case the WP users. Hence there can be two marks for describing how reliable information from the users could be obtained: questionnaires; observation.

The next stage is to investigate products that would solve the problems. Thus another two marks for such as: information from suppliers; observing the facilities of other companies. [4]

5(b)

- Diplomatic communication skills with people that enable the non-contentious collection of information and the eventual imposition of standards.
- A sound technical understanding of hardware and software systems in order to be able to make informed judgements about systems.
- An understanding of the implications for staff with a view to designing training programmes.

For full marks, the candidates must make it clear that they understand three distinct areas of expertise; just meaningful headings would gain only half marks. [6]

5 (c)

The candidate must clearly identify the area of activity – for example 'Advertise on the Internet'; this would gain one mark. Such a statement should be followed by some reasonable detail of the processes actually required to achieve the activity; this would gain the second mark.

For each aspect, the role of ICT must be clear – for example 'Get feedback from present customers' is a good idea but there is no reference to ICT. 'Use OMR questionnaires to get feedback from customers' would be worth one mark; to get the second mark there must be some detail of how an ICT system will be used to analyse the customer responses. [4]

5 (d)

For four marks there should be the expectation of a detailed discussion that takes on at least two main areas of possible concern. An extra one mark can be awarded to candidates who present aspects of preparation that deal with both the physical and the intellectual problems of implementation. [5]

6 (a)

(i)
- Under or over provision of medical or education services resulting in either waste of funds or crises for individuals.
- Unexpected effects on the economy of the country resulting in problems with the export and import trade.

Responses must indicate the reasons for the detrimental effects; simple statements of situations would only gain half marks. [4]

(ii)
- Inadequacies in the data collection processes.
- Mistakes in the software that analyses the data. [4]

(iii)
- Professional questionnaire design coupled with questionnaire testing and ICT-based data validation.
- Complete testing of the analysis software involving normal, extreme and exceptional data.

There must be reference to both data capture and its processing. [3]

6 (b)

(i)
Out-of-date or incorrect software could affect information being acted upon by people or machines. There are an unlimited number of situations that could be described; for example:

- the police being led to make a mistaken identity and possibly harming an innocent person
- the control software on a train protection system not being updated, resulting in a fatal accident
- a hospital patient not being given the latest drug because new treatment regimes have not been entered into the system.

Candidates must qualify two distinct situations to gain full marks; a heading that is meaningful would gain half marks. [4]

(ii) There is a very direct association between a car accident and a life-or-death situation. If a piece of software is controlling an aircraft then the comparison with a computer system's fault is just as stark, *but the candidate's response should lead to the conclusion that very many computer systems' failures can result in serious consequences for people. Some indirect consequence examples should be given; for example the inappropriate billing for gas that has resulted in the suicide of elderly people.* [4]

---

7 (a)

One mark for a tree diagram showing a hierarchy of directories and files.

One mark for remembering to include system files.

One mark for showing the two drives with a sensible distribution of directories. [3]

7 (b)

Two sensible suggestions (one mark each), such as:

- adjust screen resolution
- reset default font sizes
- adjust colour display (especially contrast)
- configure system to read back text. [2]

7 (c)

Two further suggestions – one mark for idea, one mark for description of type of user who would benefit, such as:

- <List above>
- change colour values to suit colour blind person
- adjust clock to show a different time zone (for user doing business in another country)

- add words to large icons for a new user
- switch off Office Assistant for experienced user. [4]

7 (d)

Two marks for explanation of one reason such as:

- out of memory because of insufficient RAM
- out of memory because disk is fragmented
- virus detection software on laptop detects a virus
- new application requires a more recent or different operating system. [2]

7 (e)

One mark each for description of up to two checks, such as:

- Is the printer switched on?
- Is the cable properly installed? [2]

Two marks for:

- Is the correct printer driver installed on the laptop? [2]

7 (f)

To get your full marks should explain (probably with a diagram): how fragmentation occurs (two marks) and how defragmentation reorganises the files and frees space (one mark) thereby speeding up the processes of finding and saving data (one mark). [4]

THE GENERATION
OF APPLICATIONS

CHAPTER 11

Applications and how they are generated

This chapter introduces the underlying concepts of software development.

It will describe:

- what an application is

- what an application developer does

- the tools an application developer uses.

This chapter covers these Technical Knowledge topics in the specification:

T2.2.1   The distinction between an application and an applications generator
T2.2.2   Common interface units
T2.2.3   Macros

Basics

In this section of the book you will be reading about how software is created, and who creates it.

The term *software* is often used as an alternative for 'program'. A *program* is a set of instructions to a computer system. For a program to be activated it has to be loaded into internal memory from a hard disk or other medium and then *executed* (or run).

Many years ago each piece of software consisted of just one program. Whenever computer users wanted to use some software they simply had to load the program from tape or disk, and then run it. Sometimes computer users still imagine that to be the case.

But today, most software consists of many components which interact with each other. If you have ever installed some new software on a PC you will be aware that many separate files are copied during the installation process. Each of these files is either a program file or a data file. Program files are often referred to as *modules*.

Types of software

All software falls into one of three main types.

Application software is software that carries out a specific task for an organisation or individual. Examples include a hospital patient records system, a railway signal control program, an arcade game or an Internet browser. Applications software may be bought ready-made, or may be designed specifically for one organisation. This kind of software is used by an *end-user*.

System software is the software that controls a computer system. It includes the operating system, together with supporting programs known as *system utilities*. The end-user is not usually aware of the system software, as the application software works directly with it. However, the main task of a *systems administrator* is to interact with the system software. System software is described in the first section of this book.

Software tools are pieces of software that enable someone to develop (that is, create or write) new software. They are used by *software developers*, sometimes also known as *software engineers*. Software developers may write application software or system software, and they may be known as *application developers* or *system developers*. There are various software tools, including programming languages which are used by *programmers*.

The term *application* is often used as though it means the same as application software. Strictly speaking, the application is the actual task (such as booking and issuing a ticket) and the application software is the software which allows the end-user to carry out the task. But in practice, we tend to use the terms interchangeably.

There are a few other terms to note. An application or software *package* is, as the name implies, an extensive collection of programs which form one software application, and this description applies to most ready-made application software these days. The term 'package' does imply that the end-user will be able to choose which components to install, and it also suggests that full documentation is given to make the package immediately usable.

Generic (general-purpose) *software* is application software that can be used for many different tasks. Word-processing, spreadsheet, presentation, computer-aided design or desktop-publishing applications are examples of generic software. Generic software usually includes templates which can be used as the basis for the end-user's own output.

Many companies now offer *ICT solutions* to organisations. These are usually complete packages which include hardware, system software and application software.

Activity

Use Windows Explorer (or its equivalent) to identify the software installed on a PC that you use. Identify system software, software tools and application software. Investigate how you can tell whether a file is a program or a datafile.

Applications

Although all software has to be developed by someone, you will be concentrating on the development of application software, rather than system software.

You will be familiar with a range of applications that are commonly used on stand-alone PCs and office networks. But these are only a small proportion of the applications that are used across the world. Many applications are not immediately visible to the ordinary person. However, as you will see, you do interact frequently with applications, directly or indirectly, every day.

Applications fall into several distinct categories. Here are some of the more important types.

- *Production applications* are used to produce manufactured goods. They control production lines in factories.
- *Transaction processing applications* are used to manage all the day-to-day operations of most organisations. These include software such as that used for handling shop sales, club membership, customer orders and billing by service providers like mobile phone networks. A 'transaction' is a single action such as a purchase, enrolment, order or phone call.
- *Office automation applications* are used in an office setting to help employees to carry out their day-to-day tasks more efficiently. They are sometimes known as *productivity tools*. Many office automation applications are generic packages, such as word-processing software, but some are simply useful applications like diary managers, Internet browsers or voicemail systems.

Activity

Consider a normal day for an adult in our society and list all the points at which they come into contact with an IT application (other than at work). In each case, decide which type of application it is from the list above.

Off-the-shelf applications

Off-the-shelf software is ready-made, and can be installed and used immediately. It is normally sold as a complete package and can be bought either through a high street store, from an Internet retailer or through a mail-order software supplier. It is often supplied on an optical medium, such as a CD-ROM or DVD-ROM, or it can be downloaded from the Internet.

Off-the-shelf applications can be used in many different kinds of organisation, so the market is

Applications and how they are generated

potentially large. As the developers will plan to sell many copies of the software they can keep the price low. There are many other advantages in purchasing an off-the-shelf application. In particular it can be examined by a potential customer before purchase, and it will have been thoroughly tested by the software house. The main drawback is that it may not meet the precise needs of the customer.

In chapters 16 and 17 you will meet a case study about a software house which produces and markets an off-the-shelf package called 'Fitness matters'.

Bespoke applications

Bespoke, or custom-made, software is developed to meet the needs of a single client organisation. A large organisation like a bank may employ its own software developers who will devote thousands of person-hours to producing a substantial bespoke software product, such as a system for handling all the transactions at its automatic teller machines (ATMs, or cash machines).

A smaller organisation may call on the services of consultants or software houses to develop bespoke software for them. Bespoke applications are necessarily expensive as the development costs cannot be shared across a large market. The client will also have to wait some time whilst the application is being developed and tested, and there is always a possibility that the finished product will not come up to expectations.

Chapters 12 and 13 introduce a case study which describes how an IT consultant develops a bespoke room-booking application for a motel.

Customised software

This is a third option, which has some of the advantages of both off-the-shelf and bespoke systems. *Customised* software is often sold by specialist software houses into specific 'niche' markets.

For example, all libraries require substantial software systems to handle book loans, returns and reservations, as well as readers' catalogue enquiries and the purchasing and disposal of stock. But each library will have specific needs which may not be shared with all other libraries. They may stock videos, newspapers, software or even toys, and they may want to be able to find items in stock at neighbouring libraries. An off-the-shelf solution is then not appropriate as it will not be flexible enough to meet all these various needs, while a bespoke solution would probably be too expensive for a single library.

A customised solution can be purchased from a software house, who will be able to modify a package to meet a library's individual needs by selecting from a range of pre-written components. They will then add individual touches to the user interface, so that it will give the appearance of a bespoke system.

The case study in chapters 14 and 15 describes how a modular software package for managing leisure centres can be customised to meet the client's exact requirements.

Choosing the appropriate type

From the customer's point of view, there are a number of factors to be considered when deciding whether to purchase off-the-shelf, bespoke or customised application software.

- What is the required functionality of the application? That is, what functions or processes can it actually carry out for the end-user, and are these specific enough and comprehensive enough to meet the needs of the organisation?

- What is the required user interface? That is what the user sees on the screen (together with any devices that are needed, such as special keyboards). It should enable the expected users to get the best out of the application.

- What level of help is offered to the user through manuals, online help, training, telephone helplines, etc.?

Activities

1. *Collect some examples of customised and bespoke applications that you (or people you know) use. You may like to start with the administration systems at your school or college, and you could ask family and friends about the applications they use at work. Try to find out why the organisations chose to use a bespoke or customised solution.*

2. *Use the Internet to research companies that sell customised applications and the products they offer. Alternatively you can look through trade papers, which are newspapers and magazines distributed within a specific industry rather than sold by a high street newsagent.*

Application developers

Application developers are IT professionals. They have between them a wide range of skills, which include systems analysis, programming and software testing. When a large software application is being developed, a project team will be created consisting of specialist analysts, programmers and testers. In comparison, on a small project a single person could work as an analyst programmer carrying out all the tasks required to develop the software.

Application developers may be employed:

- as inhouse software developers in the IT development department of an organisation
- as analysts, programmers or testers in an independent software house
- as freelance consultants.

A consultant is a person with a high level of skills and knowledge who is hired by an organisation on a short-term contract to do a specific task.

Software tools

An application developer has to use one or more *software tools* in order to create an application. Today the main software tools fall into two categories: programming environments and application generators.

Programming environments

A *programming environment* allows a programmer to write an application using a programming language such as Visual Basic®, C++, Java, Pascal, etc. The programming environment brings together a number of software tools, including a *text editor* which allows the programmer to write the program code, a *compiler* which converts the program code into machine code, and a *debugger* which helps the programmer to trace errors.

The following is a very simple program written in the programming language Pascal. It asks the user to key in a set of test marks given to a class of students and then works out the average mark. Although you do not need to be able to understand the program code in

detail, you will be able to see that it uses ordinary English words.

```
PROGRAM Average(input, output);

VAR
  ThisMark, TotalMarks, NumberOfStudents, Count : INTEGER;
  AverageMark : REAL; BEGIN
  TotalMarks := 0;
  writeln('How many students are in the class?');
  readln(NumberOfStudents);
  FOR Count := 1 TO NumberOfStudents DO BEGIN
    writeln('Enter the mark obtained by the next student');
    readln(ThisMark);
    TotalMarks := TotalMarks + ThisMark;
  END;
  AverageMark := TotalMarks / NumberOfStudents;
  Writeln('The average mark is ', AverageMark:5:2)
END.
```

Figure 11.1 shows what appears on screen when this program is run. The numbers in *italics* are entered by the user. You will notice that the programmer has to write a lot of program code to implement a quite simple process. The code has to be absolutely accurate, as quite minor errors – such as leaving out punctuation – can cause the program to fail. Compare this with the effort required to set up a spreadsheet to perform the same process.

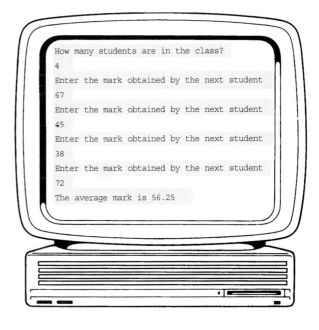

Figure 11.1 *The screen output of the simple example in the text*

You will learn more about programming in Chapter 16.

Application generators

An *application generator* allows a developer to produce an application with little or no formal programming. The developer creates an application by designing forms, reports and other components in a *graphical environment*.

However, it would be wrong to assume that an application produced in this way is not written in program code. The application generator cleverly 'writes' the program code in response to the choices that the developer makes.

Microsoft® Access is an application generator. It provides tools that enable an application developer to create a new database, together with all the forms and reports that are associated with it. In fact, an application consists of a complete set of forms and reports, with their underlying tables and queries, which can then be used by an end-user to carry out a specific task.

For example, the training manager of a company may want to keep records of all the courses they have run and who attended them. In response, an application developer employed by the same company can use Access to create a complete stand-alone application. The training manager will then be able to use the application to store all the data, to search for information and to print out the reports. The end-user (the training manager in this case) will never need to have any knowledge at all about Access, because the application will offer all the *functionality* that is required to carry out the tasks.

Other application generators on the market can be used to create production applications that control manufacturing processes, or to generate simulations, or to create computer-based learning materials.

Activity

If you have not yet developed an application in Access, you can look at one of the sample databases that are provided with it, or you can use the database wizard to generate one for you (see Figure 11.2).

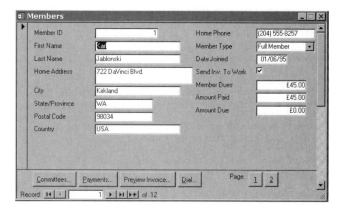

Figure 11.2 *One of the forms in an application created by the database wizard in Access*

Families of application generators

Microsoft® Office is a family of application generators. Although we have seen that Access is an application generator, it may surprise you to learn that other components of Office, namely Word, Excel and PowerPoint®, are also application generators. Although they were described earlier as generic applications, they do have additional functions which mean that they can also be used to generate complete, stand-alone applications.

So Word, Excel and PowerPoint® can be used as generic applications by an end-user and also as application generators by an application developer. What would be the difference in the output in each case?

An end-user would write a letter, create a simple spreadsheet to record attendances at an event or design a presentation for a talk – none of these outputs is an application in itself.

On the other hand, an application developer could use Word to create a mass mailing system that would store a list of names and addresses, plus templates of standard letters, and would then automatically use the mail-merge functions to print out personalised letters to all or a selection of people on the list. The end-user would be provided with a customised toolbar or drop-down menu offering all the options for the application. Alternatively, the developer could provide a series of forms and dialogues in Web page format that would guide the end-user through the various options. A well-developed application will include help facilities as well.

The question to ask is this: Can the end-user run this application without knowing anything at all about the application generator that produced it? If the answer is 'Yes' then the product really is an application.

Applications developed using one of these application generators will usually make use of some or all of the following features:

- templates
- forms for data entry
- command buttons or hyperlinks
- macros
- customised toolbars or drop-down menus.

Since Microsoft® Office is an integrated family, it is also possible to develop an application which draws on the facilities in more than one of its components. For example, data can be imported from an Access table, or from an Excel spreadsheet, into a mailmerge application in Word.

Common interface units

You will have noticed that many of the features of Word, Excel, PowerPoint® and Access are very similar. For example, if you select *Save As* in Word, Excel or PowerPoint® you will be presented with what appears to be an identical dialogue box in each case. In fact, there are some minor differences in the dialogue boxes and you might like to investigate what these are. However, the layout, wording and appearance of the buttons remains consistent.

The *Save As* dialogue is a *common interface unit* in Microsoft® Office. When the programmers developed this software they did not write three *Save As* program modules for Word, Excel and PowerPoint®. Instead they wrote one module that could be called upon by any of them. When the module is used by the parent software, data is passed to the module which determines which buttons are actually displayed.

Other common interface modules, which are used by one or more of the members of the Office family, include the New, Open, Page Setup, Insert Picture and Spelling dialogues.

There are many advantages to using common interface modules.

- The software developer need only create the program module once. Once this has been

thoroughly tested it can be used with confidence in other components.
- The end-user will meet familiar dialogues when using another member of the family. This will speed up their learning, increase confidence and reduce training requirements.
- The systems administrator will require less memory to store the software than would otherwise be the case.

Activity

Investigate and list the common interface modules in Microsoft® Office.

Macros

One of the features common to most application generators is the facility to create *macros*. A macro is a series or set of commands that can be created by an application developer. In fact, a macro is a very short program procedure, but no programming skills are required in order to write it. The commands trigger a number of actions, any of which could have been selected individually from one of the menus available to the end-user.

A macro can be used to automate a series of actions which are frequently carried out. By assigning a button or menu item to the macro, the complete sequence of actions reduces down to one action, as far as the end-user is concerned. For example, a macro developed in a word-processor could consist of the following actions:

1. Check the open document for spelling and grammar.
2. At the beginning of the document insert, in red, the words 'Document checked for spelling and grammar'.
3. Insert today's date.
4. Save the document.

The end-user responsible for checking documents would only have to call up this macro in order for all four actions to be carried out automatically in sequence on a document. The end-user would still have to respond to the spelling and grammar dialogues, as it would not be wise to automate those processes entirely, but as soon as the checking was complete the remaining actions would be carried out.

Creating a macro

A macro can be created in any one of three main ways:

- by using a macro recorder – this method can be used in Word, Excel and PowerPoint®
- by using a macro window – this method can be used in Access
- by using a programming language (Visual Basic®) – this method can be used in all four application generators.

A macro recorder allows the application developer to simply 'record' a series of actions, using the analogy of recording a message on audio tape. Once the macro recorder is selected from the Tools menu, a floating toolbar appears which has a Stop button on it. Every action taken from now on is 'recorded' as a macro command, until Stop is pressed. Any action that can be carried out using the normal menu and toolbar selections can become one of the sequence of commands in the macro. The macro recorder converts these commands into program code in the underlying programming language. In the case of Microsoft® Office, that language is Visual Basic®.

Access does not offer a macro recorder but does allow you to construct a macro by selecting a series of actions, in sequence, on a grid in the macro window. Each action is selected from a list of all the possible actions that are available from the toolbars and menus. Once again, the macro is converted into program code in Visual Basic®. The advantage of this method is that you can easily edit your macros in the same macro window, without going into Visual Basic®.

You can also use the programming language Visual Basic® to write macros (procedures) directly for Office. This is discussed later in the book.

Calling up a macro

There are several ways of calling a macro. The standard way is to select *Macro* from the Tools menu, and then select the correct macro from the list presented. A much more effective solution is to create a button to represent the macro and to place it on one of the toolbars. A suitable icon or label must be attached to the button. Alternatively a new item that calls the macro may be added to one of the existing menus, or a 'hot key' can be assigned to it, or a button can be placed on a form. Access provides some particularly helpful features for creating macros and their associated buttons.

If several macros have been developed for a user, then a new toolbar or menu can be created containing the relevant buttons or menu items. Customising the user interface in this way is one important aspect of developing an application in an application generator.

Learning to use application generators

As part of your study for the AS level modules, you should develop your skills in a number of application generators. You should have experience of developing applications using word-processing, spreadsheet and database software, as a minimum.

You will certainly need to have advanced skills in at least one application generator in order to undertake the practical coursework Task 2. There are many books and tutorials that can help you with learning these skills.

CHAPTER 12

The life cycle of an application

This chapter introduces the stages in the development of an application, using, as a case study, the creation of a bespoke application for a motel.

It will describe:

- the start of a project
- the development of a project from the requirements stage through to maintenance.

This chapter covers the following Learning Outcome in the specification:

L.O.2.1   Describe the life cycle of an application

The birth of a project

The IT consultant

Petra Richardson is a freelance IT consultant. Some years ago she graduated from university with a degree in Business Information Systems. Her course gave her a broad range of IT development skills, including systems analysis, database design and programming. It also taught her about the fundamentals of business management.

For her first job, Petra went to work for an IT company that specialised in developing solutions for small businesses. She gained excellent experience during this time, mainly developing databases for clients. But she began to realise that the partners who had founded the IT company did not have sufficient business acumen to steer the company through the lean times as well as the good. So when they suffered a quiet period with few projects on hand, Petra's job was declared redundant.

Petra decided to go it alone as a freelance consultant. She now has to find her own clients and convince them of her ability to produce IT solutions to meet their needs. She needs to spend 40 per cent of her time finding work and 60 per cent actually doing it. Most of

the time she works from home, where she has established a small office.

Some of Petra's projects take just a few days. One large project lasted five months, and in that case she was allocated office facilities at the client's headquarters. When Petra agrees to take on a project, the client draws up a contract which specifies the outcomes they are expecting. She knows that if the solution that she develops does not meet the client's exact requirements then they may withhold payment.

The client

One day an old university friend of Petra's, called Sean Casey, phones her. Sean also studied Business Information Systems, but although he understood the significance of ICT he was more interested in the entrepreneurial aspects of business. Sean says that he remembers how clever she was at developing software and wants to discuss some ideas with her, so they arrange to meet for a drink.

At their meeting, Sean explains to Petra that he tried several jobs after graduating, and eventually found himself working as the assistant manager at an American-style motel in Rutland, called Greensleeves. The owner-manager, Manuel Cortes, has already added an extension to the motel and has ambitious plans to go on to build a chain of similar ones around the country. Sean is excited by this possibility and wants to be a core member of the team as the business grows.

Sean has persuaded Manuel that he should have a good computer-based room booking system in place before he goes any further. Although he does not understand computer systems much, Manuel does not want to appear out-of-date, and he has asked Sean to look into the feasibility of this idea. Manuel has been fully occupied with overseeing the construction aspect of the site and ensuring that the guests who continue to use the facility are treated well, so is happy to pass this responsibility on to the younger man.

Petra listens with interest. If she can get this contract, then there might be a lot more work coming her way in the future.

The stages in the project

Petra arranges to meet Sean and Manuel at Greensleeves to discuss the whole project. Manuel is very interested to hear about projects she has worked on, including one for a residential conference centre. He asks her to explain what exactly she will have to do if awarded the contract by Greensleeves.

Petra explains she would produce a bespoke application for them; that is, the software would be designed specifically to meet their needs. She would also sort out their hardware requirements. In order to achieve this, she would have to do quite a bit of research at the motel before deciding how to design and make the application, and she would provide all the necessary help and support to the motel's staff when they started using it.

She then goes on to explain that all IT projects follow a similar pattern. However big or small, the project will break down into four main stages:

1. *Requirements stage* – understanding the problem and working out what is required.
2. *Design stage* – designing the solution to the problem.
3. *Implementation and testing stage* – building the solution and checking that it meets the requirements.
4. *Operations and maintenance stage* – running the solution as intended.

In fact, creating an IT solution is very similar to managing a building project like the one Manuel had just completed at the motel.

When Manuel started planning the new extension to the motel, he wrote down his ideas and worked out roughly how much it would cost and how long it would take. He then discussed the figures with his accountant and decided it was worth going ahead. Only at that stage did he employ an architect, who asked him lots of questions about what sort of building he wanted. All of this made up the *requirements stage*.

At the *design stage*, the architect drew up some plans, which Manuel eventually agreed. The architect then helped Manuel to find a suitable builder who was awarded the contract to build the extension. The building process is the equivalent of the *implementation stage* of an IT project. Throughout the building stage, and at its completion, the architect checked that the building met the requirements; this is a form of testing and it often overlaps with the building (implementation) stage.

Finally, the building was handed over to Manuel. The builder gave Manuel some instructions about *maintaining* the heating and plumbing systems. The architect arranged to come back a month later to check that everything was still functioning well, and he reassured Manuel that he would be available by telephone if there were any problems.

In this case two people were directly involved in the project – the architect and the builder – and the builder sub-contracted some of the work out to other specialists, including electricians and plumbers.

An IT project may be developed by many people, if the project is very large, with members of the software development team taking specialist roles – such as analyst, software engineer, programmer or tester. In the case of a relatively small project, one IT consultant like Petra may carry out all the tasks.

The system life cycle

Processes

The term *process* crops up frequently when discussing the development of an IT solution. A process is a task or procedure that is carried out, usually involving the handling and/or changing of data. Examples of processes include recording the sale of a ticket in a cinema box office, or adding a new name to an address book. Processes may be carried out manually (without the use of a computer system) or electronically (using a software application), or with a combination of the two.

In general, a process takes a batch of data as input, processes it in some way, then produces some form of data as output. For example, when a cinema ticket is bought, the date and time of the performance constitute the input data, which is then processed in order to allocate a specific seat. The output is twofold – a ticket is printed and the transaction data is stored in a data file.

Sometimes an application developer is asked to create an IT solution to enable a user to switch to using a computer for the first time. All the processes currently performed are carried out manually. The new solution may still include some manual, clerical processes, but most of the processes will become computer-based.

On other occasions the application developer deals with a client who already uses IT facilities to carry out some or all of the processes. The new solution will be designed to improve the way in which the processes are performed. It could also introduce new, computer-based processes which were not undertaken before.

A software application usually enables the user to carry out several different, but related, processes.

Systems

The term 'system' is used in a number of ways. You are familiar with the concept of a computer system, which is a combination of system software and hardware that enables the devices to be used as a computer or network. But in the context of a system life cycle, the term 'system' has a much wider meaning.

A *system* is a set of processes that are carried out within an organisation in order to achieve an objective. For example, a college student enrolment system consists of a number of processes. The processes might include recording information about students who apply for places, arranging to interview them to offer suitable courses, and registering them for classes at the beginning of the academic year. Taken together, these processes make up the enrolment system. The enrolment system exists as a system whether or not it is carried out using computer technology. Although all colleges today use software applications to carry out most of the processing in an enrolment system, in the past the systems were completely manual.

Large systems often consist of several related systems. The college enrolment system is really only a sub-system within the student management system. The whole system includes a timetabling sub-system and an examination entry sub-system, amongst others.

In this chapter we are examining how systems can be improved by using IT solutions. A new system will be implemented by the combined use of application software, systems software, hardware and manual processes.

The life cycle

The *system life cycle* is a term used to describe the stages in an IT project. As you have seen, these are: requirements, design, implementation and testing, operations and maintenance.

The phrase 'life cycle' implies some circularity in the process of providing IT solutions for organisations, and that is because the requirements of organisations are changing all the time. As they change, so the software and hardware themselves need to be updated, or even completely replaced. A life cycle suggests a process of continual change and renewal.

The requirements stage

Proposal, or user requirements specification

This is a report written by the client, outlining their requirements. This specification defines the proposed application in terms of the problem that has to be solved and the needs of the potential users. In practice the client may employ an outside specialist to help formulate exactly what they need and to put together the user requirements specification.

As this specification is written by (or for) the client it is written in non-technical language, and it describes the project from the point of view of the end-users. It explains, in general terms, what processes the software should carry out. It may specify how fast the processing should be and how much data it should handle. It may also describe the preferred type of user interface. Any new hardware requirements that are needed to run the application will also be covered in the specification.

The user requirements specification is put as a proposal to an application developer and it forms the basis of a contract between the parties.

Analysis

The application developer now has to use professional skills to analyse the requirements expressed in the user's specification, and turn this into a document that can form the basis for a detailed design.

For example, suppose the client company is a foodstore and they have stated in the user requirements specification that they want the system to speed up the throughput of customers at checkouts. The developer will want to know how many items are processed per hour at present (both in an average hour and at peak times), the average number of items per customer, how long the payment stage takes, etc. The developer will also want to quantify (put into figures) what kind of improvement the client wants.

The first part of the analysis of requirements is the *investigation*, the purpose of which is to discover how the client carries out the processes at present and what the detailed requirements are for the proposed system.

In many cases the client is already doing the processes with another application but it is not proving to be very effective, so the software will simply replace those processes. In other cases the client is carrying out all the processing manually – that is, without the benefit of IT systems. In some cases the client may want to start a completely new line of business and will not yet be doing the processes.

The developer will refer to the *current system* and to the *proposed system*. The current system is the set of processes that the client carries out at present, and these could be manual, computer-based, or a mixture of the two. The proposed system is the new IT solution that will be produced at the end of the project.

The developer will investigate many aspects of the current system, such as:

- What documents or on-screen forms are used?
- Who enters data on documents or on-screen forms?
- What data items are entered on documents or on-screen forms?
- When are data items entered on documents or on-screen forms?
- What happens to documents after they have been written?
- Who reads data, and why?
- What data items are captured by non-written methods, such as card swipe readers, data logging?
- Are there are any problems with entering or retrieving data?
- Are there any times or situations when the current system cannot cope?
- How long does it take to carry out a process?

The application developer can draw upon several standard methods of investigation:

- *Interview*. The application developer should always plan an interview (or discussion) with the client in advance. It should concentrate on the processes that the client carries out at present, either manually or on a computer, and should avoid subjective assessments. All users involved in the current system should be interviewed, unless the system is very large and it is only possible to interview a representative sample.
- *Questionnaire*. A questionnaire can be sent to the client, or end-users, in advance of the interview. This will give the client time to think about the questions, and to do any research that may be needed.
- *Document survey*. Copies of all documents that are currently in use are collected. These should include copies of blank and completed forms, as well as letter templates and instructions.

- *Observation.* The application developer should observe the current processes, and record what was done, who did it, how long it took and with what frequency.

The application developer will then need to define the processes that will be used in the proposed system. For each process, the application developer will specify:

- the input data requirements
- the sources of the input data
- the processing that will take place
- the data outputs
- the destination of the output.

The final part of the analysis is the *requirements document*. This is a summary of the findings of the investigation and the requirements of the proposed system. The requirements document will specify all the processes that will be included in the new system, and will indicate which of those processes will continue to be carried out manually. It will describe the optimal and minimal hardware configurations necessary to support the application. It will also outline the software and hardware maintenance needs.

The requirements document can then be used to judge the final product. The system produced at the end of the project can only be said to be successful if, when tested, it does everything that the requirements document states that it should do.

The design stage

System design

The system design will give an overall picture of all the aspects of the proposed system. In particular, it will

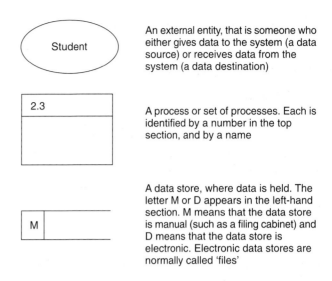

Figure 12.1 Elements in a data-flow diagram

show how the manual and computer-based processes interact with one another.

If any specialist hardware has to be designed, such as a card reader, then it will be identified at this stage. The design stage will then include hardware design sections as well as software design sections.

Normally application developers use a *top-down approach* to system design. They begin by looking at the overall problem and then break it down into its component processes. There are many ways of describing the system design, and a number of these make use of diagrams.

One well-known method is the *data-flow diagram*. This makes use of differently shaped boxes, although if you read widely around this subject you may come across a number of variations in the shapes of boxes. The ones we will use are shown in Figure 12.1.

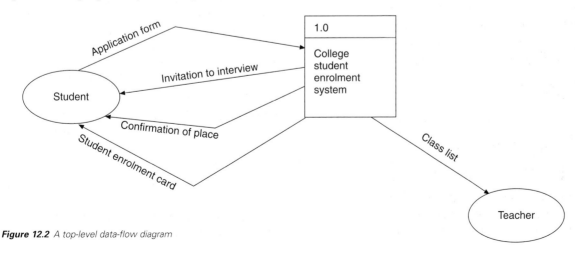

Figure 12.2 A top-level data-flow diagram

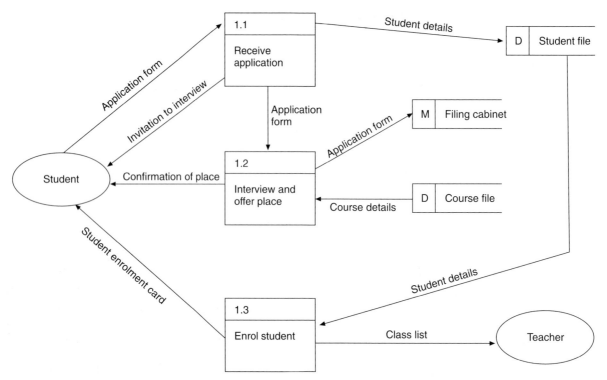

Figure 12.3 *A second-level data-flow diagram*

A top-level data-flow diagram is the simplest type and uses one process box for the whole system. The top-level diagram for the college student enrolment system described earlier could look like Figure 12.2. Note that data store boxes are not used in a top-level data-flow diagram.

The top-level data-flow diagram can be developed further to give a second-level diagram. In Figure 12.3 the college student enrolment system (1.0) has been broken down into three processes, numbered 1.1, 1.2 and 1.3. All the information about the processes and their data requirements will have been identified earlier in the requirements document.

Sometimes individual processes are then broken down into sub-processes. A third-level data-flow diagram should be drawn for each of the processes that can be broken down in this way.

The system design should also consider the relationship between all the computer-based processes and how the user can access them. This is normally achieved through one or more menus. Each selection from a menu should lead to another process. A diagram can be drawn to illustrate the menu structure (see Figure 12.4).

Software design: the user interface

The usability of the final application will depend on the quality of the user interface, so it needs to be designed in detail.

First, *data capture methods* will be designed. These may involve the use of specialist hardware devices or may be paper-based forms. The application developer will then draw sketches of all the screen layouts, or alternatively will use an application generator to create a prototype which can then be discussed with the client. The design of screens that are to be used for the manual input of data from data capture forms must be carefully related to the design of the forms themselves. Designs will also be drawn of the layout of any reports that will be produced by the new system.

There are many factors which have to be considered when designing a user interface, including:

- data to be included
- size and type of font
- colour of text and background
- use of graphical elements, such as logos
- positioning of elements such as text, data fields, labels, buttons and hypertext links

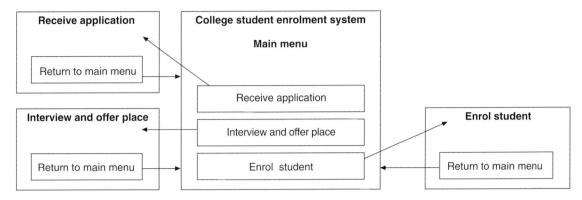

Figure 12.4 *A menu structure*

- provision of instructions and help
- access to menus
- events that will trigger changes.

The user interface design has to cover the mechanisms by which the user gains access to the menus. A menu can be a simple screen menu (also known as a 'switchboard'), a pull-down menu or a toolbar.

Software design: processing

Each process and each electronic data store (file) that has been identified in a data-flow diagram will now be designed in more detail, beginning with the data stores.

The developer must first sort out the *data structures* that will be used to store the data in the files. There are many types of data structure but the most common ones are *records* and *tables*. Files themselves are data structures, so the developer will need to consider what type to use, such as text files, files of records, and files for graphics and sound.

In many systems, data structures are described as *objects*. But an object is more than a data structure and has a program code associated with it. Examples of objects are buttons, text boxes and forms, and these should be described.

A relational database is a very complex object in itself, and if a database is to be used then the data model will be designed at an early stage. Data modelling for a relational database is considered in detail in the next chapter; but to summarise, the data model should include an entity relationship diagram and normalised table definitions.

Whatever data structure is used, decisions must be made about the data type of each of the basic data components, such as fields. The data type will specify the actual type and its length. Data types include text (also known as strings), integers, real (also known as floating point number), and boolean (also known as logical or yes/no). Special types, such as date or time formats, are offered by some application generators.

Finally, the developer will have to specify the *validation tests* that will be used on the data when it is input by the user. There are several types of validation test:

- A *presence check* ensures that a required field has not been left empty (e.g. a primary key field).
- A *type check* ensures that the data items entered are of the correct data type (e.g. that no characters have been entered into a numerical field).
- A *range check* ensures that the entered data items fall within a specified range (e.g. that a date lies after a particular one or an age is less than 120).
- A *code check* ensures that a code is of the correct format (e.g. an order code which has been designed with two letters followed by four numbers).

The developer will then turn to the *processes* which, as the data-flow diagram will show, draw on the data stored in the files. In a large and complex project the design of the processes will go through several stages, continuing to use the top-down approach.

There are a number of graphical techniques used by designers to help them to design processes, but the simplest technique is to simply list all the actions that have to be taken within a process. This method is known as *structured English*. For example:

```
Receive application:
    Assign student a student record number
    Input student details from application form
    Select interview date and time
    Send interview letter
```

Using structured English it is possible to specify alternative actions, the choice of which will depend on whether a condition is met. For example:

```
Receive application:
    Check whether student already exists on
    database
    IF student exists on database
    THEN
        Check details on application form
    ELSE
        Assign student a student record number
        Input student details from application form
    END IF
    Select interview date and time
    Send interview letter
```

If the application is to be programmed in a programming language, then the structured English will be further refined into pseudo-code, which looks very much like program code.

If the application is to be developed in an application generator, then structured English will be used to design any macros that will be used. Of course, the developer can also use the programming capabilities within an application generator, and if this is planned then the program code will have to be designed.

Individual functions within a process may need further design. For example, if a spreadsheet function is to be used then it must be defined. Similarly, queries to be used with a database must be specified.

Before the design is implemented it should be subjected to a design review. Normally this will involve another developer who will 'walk through' the design to check that it meets the requirements.

The implementation and testing stage

Implementation

When the design for a piece of software is complete, and has been subjected to a design review, the implementation can begin. As we saw in Chapter 11, software is implemented using one or more software tools. In practice this means that the developer uses either a programming environment or an application generator. Many application generators have a programming environment embedded within them.

If a database system is being used that underpins the whole application, then the database structures (tables and relationships) must be implemented first.

The implementation of the processes must, of course, match the design; but whereas the design is developed in a top-down fashion, the processes are often implemented bottom-up. In other words, the individual processes are implemented first, then they are combined to create the complete application. In the case of our example, first the structure of the student database would be created, then the three processes. Finally these would be linked by the top level menu.

The user interface is developed as the processes are being implemented and should not simply be tacked on at the end. Indeed, in many applications, the user interface is completely integrated with the processes and one cannot be created without the other.

Although the user interface will have been designed in detail, it is often difficult to judge the suitability of the screen designs in particular until they have been transferred on to screen. The developer will often create a *prototype* of the system and use this to get feedback from the client. A prototype is a cut-down version of the final application in which only certain aspects will be functioning. A prototype can be created to check how the processes function, but it is more common to set up a prototype to check the user interface. Comments from the end-users can be used to adjust the design. This means that, for some aspects of the application, the design and implementation can be repeated more than once until the outcome is satisfactory.

Technical testing

The processes will be tested continuously as they are being developed. Errors – also known as *bugs* – are detected and corrected. Errors can be of three types:

- *Syntax errors* occur if the statements used in a program are not legitimate statements in the programming language. Syntax errors are normally highlighted (literally) by the editor in the programming environment. This problem does not arise if the software is being developed using an application generator (unless the programming environment is used).

- *Logic errors* occur if the implemented processes do not match the design, with the result that the processes do not behave as they should. Alternatively, the design itself may have been faulty and may not have matched the requirements. Logic errors are more difficult to find, as the application may appear to be running as expected, but the data may not be processed correctly. Logic errors do not usually result in error messages.

- *Run-time errors* occur when the application is run, but are not due to logic errors. They are the result of external factors, such as insufficient memory, and usually result in system error messages. Some run-time errors may occur when incorrect data is input by the user, and could be eliminated with better data validation techniques.

The application developer will eliminate as many errors as possible as soon as they are detected. Once a process is complete it will be subjected to formal technical testing. Finally, when all the processes are linked – possibly through a menu system – the whole application will be tested.

The purpose of testing is to find any remaining errors in the application, not to prove that it works correctly under normal circumstances. The tester must assume that the application contains errors and must set out to unearth them.

Before testing begins a *test plan* should be drawn up. The test plan will be based upon the original requirements of the application, and will be designed to show that the finished product meets the client's specification. The test plan will specify data that should be entered, a sequence of actions that should be undertaken and the expected outcomes. The test data, and the test actions, should be carefully selected so that all possible options are covered.

Test data may be:

- *normal data* – this can be based on real data, if it is available

- *extreme data* – this is data which lies at the outer extremity of valid data that the user might enter, such as very long names

- *invalid (erroneous) data* – this is incorrect data, which may be entered by mistake, and should be trapped by validation tests.

In a large project the technical testing will be carried out by specialists. If a single consultant is carrying out the whole project then they will have to do their own testing. It is sometimes difficult for the original developer to test their own software in an objective way.

The operations and maintenance stage

When the application has been fully tested and corrected it is ready to be passed to the client for installation, or to be marketed. But before the new application can 'go live' the client has to prepare for the changeover. End-users will have to be trained; systems administration procedures will have to be defined; the changeover period itself will have to be planned; consideration will have to be given to the maintenance of the software. Many of these topics are treated in detail later in this section of the book or in the A2 units of this course, so are just touched on in this chapter.

Documentation for the systems administrator

Software on its own is insufficient; it must be accompanied by documentation to support its use. As you have seen, reports and other forms of documentation are written at all stages of the project, but two important documents are essential for the effective use of the completed application. These are the manuals for the systems administrator and for the end-user.

When you are using your own PC you act sometimes as a systems administrator, sometimes as an end-user and sometimes as a software developer, and it is easy to blur the distinction between the different activities.

When you buy off-the-shelf software for use on a home PC, the manual usually covers both systems administration and end-user tasks. However, for most applications in a business context the tasks undertaken by the systems administrator are rather different from those of the end-user.

The systems administrator should be provided with information to assist in the installation of the software and with providing support for end-users. It should include:

Systems Administration Manual

1 *Software licence.* This may be for a single user, for a specified number of users, or may be a network licence for an unlimited number of users.

2 *Hardware requirements.* This should specify the minimum hardware required in order to run the application, and could refer to the speed of the processor, the size of internal memory (RAM), the capacity of the hard disk, plus any network requirements.

3 *Operating system requirements.* This should specify which operating system the application is designed for.

4 *Software requirements.* This should specify if any other software applications need to be installed; for example, the application may interact with a common word-processor.

5 *Installation.* This will give complete instructions for installing the application and will list any configuration options offered.

6 *Testing.* This will explain how the systems administrator can test the application once installed to ensure that it performs as intended.

7 *Security.* This will describe how the security of data can be maintained, with instructions for defining access privileges (if relevant) and for backing up and recovering files.

8 *Troubleshooting.* This provides a list of possible problems that may occur and suggests how they can be solved.

9 *Technical support.* This identifies how the systems administrator may obtain support from the developers of the application.

Documentation for the end-users

The end-users also need information in order to use the IT solution properly. This is often supplied in a paper-based manual, but can also be provided through a computer-based format such as a Help file. (The term 'documentation' is used, whatever the medium.) End-user documentation should always describe the application from the perspective of a non-technical person and should relate to the real-life tasks that they are employed to carry out. This topic is discussed in detail in Chapter 15.

Installation

The process of installation should be described in detail in the documentation. It is normal for an *installation program* to be provided with an application. When this is run, the files that make up the application are installed in the correct directories on the hard disk.

The installation program will normally automatically detect hardware and software that is already installed and will install the relevant files. For example, it will detect the types of printer connected to the system and install the right printer drivers.

Sometimes the installation program offers the systems administrator some choices. A complete application, especially if it is an off-the-shelf package, may contain many modules, some of which are not required by all the end-users.

Training

It is normal for all end-users to be trained in the use of a new application. Before a new application is first launched, the potential users should be thoroughly prepared. Once it is in use, any new employees who join the organisation should also be trained in the use of any applications that they have not used before. End-user training is discussed in detail in Chapter 15.

Changeover

In many cases a new software application replaces a system that is already in use. The existing system may be completely manual or may be computer-based (or a mixture of the two). In all cases the changeover to the new system has to be handled with care. During the changeover period the end-users will need to be supported, because they will still be familiarising themselves with the new system and will not be as productive as they will become eventually.

As the changeover can be risky it is normally planned in detail by a systems manager. This is discussed in some detail in a later section of the book, dealing with systems management.

Evaluation and maintenance

The effectiveness of the IT solution will be evaluated by the client. The new system will be judged against the initial user requirements. This is covered in Chapter 17.

IT solutions are designed to meet the needs of an organisation at a particular moment in time. However, all organisations have to respond to change, so the software may eventually have to be adapted to meet new requirements. Changes can happen as a result of internal pressures such as expansion (or cutbacks) in a company, or the development of new lines of business. External pressures, such as changes in legislation, may also force the organisation to review its working methods, which will include its use of IT systems. 'Maintenance' refers to the constant process of reviewing and renewing software and hardware over time. Software maintenance is covered in Chapter 14.

Large and small projects

All IT projects follow the pattern described in this chapter. However, the time taken over each stage, and the quantity of documentation, will depend on how large the project is.

In a large project many people will be involved in its development. The project tasks may be shared between:

- *analysts* – analysis
- *software engineers* – design, implementation and testing of software
- *hardware engineers* – design, implementation and testing of specialised hardware
- *technical authors* – documentation for the systems administrators and end-users
- *trainers*
- *maintenance programmers* – upgrades to the software.

In a small project, such as the one for Greensleeves Motel, one person may carry out all the tasks. Petra Richardson works as a freelance IT consultant, and she could describe herself as an analyst programmer. The next chapter examines some of her tasks at the analysis and design stages of the project.

CHAPTER 13

Developing a relational database

This chapter explains how a relational database is designed, using the context of Greensleeves Motel that was introduced in Chapter 12.

It will describe:

- the key features of a relational database

- how to design a data model

- how queries and indexes are used in a relational database.

The chapter covers the following Technical Knowledge topics in the specification:

T2.4.1	Base tables
T2.4.2	Redundancy and normalisation
T2.4.3	Relationships and foreign keys
T2.4.4	Indexes

It also covers some related topics from one of the A2 units. Students who intend to implement a relational database for their coursework Task 2 will need to understand these topics, so they have been included at this level:

T5.4.1	Relationships and foreign keys
T5.4.2	Referential integrity

Databases

A *database* is a collection of information held on a computer system. Databases can be very large indeed – for example, the database at the Driver and Vehicle Licensing Agency (DVLA) contains information about every single vehicle registered in the UK and also about the owners of all the driving licences that it has issued. But a database can also be very simple and short – an example might be the phone book on a mobile phone.

Strictly speaking, the details held on a database are known collectively as *data*. Individual entries are referred to as *data items*. The term *information* should be used to refer to data that has been presented to a user in a usable fashion. For example, the data on the DVLA's database is stored as a series of numbers and codes which identify, amongst other things, the registration of a car and its current owner. The mass of data in the database, if viewed as it is stored, would be largely unintelligible to a user. But the database system also includes screen formats which can be used to present the data as information, so that the user can understand it and make use of it.

Most databases today fall into one of two types:

- A *flat-file database* is a simple database, where all the information can be easily presented to the user in a table or list. Examples of flat-file databases include the phone book mentioned above, a restaurant menu (with prices) or a list of members of a club.

- A *relational database* is a complex database, where it is not possible for all the information to be presented in a single table. Normally, a relational database will include data about a number of related things. For example, a large relational database for a furniture shop may hold information about all the products that are in stock, about all the orders and about the customers who have placed the orders.

This chapter concentrates on relational databases, but you will meet some fundamental concepts in the sub-section below on flat-file databases.

Flat-file databases

Many software packages include simple database features. For example, your e-mail processing software will include an address book, in which you can store details of people and organisations. Each entry in the address book – that is, the data about each person – is a *record*. The e-mail address book will store the data in categories, such as the name of the person and the e-mail address; these categories are known as *fields* (see Figure 13.1). If you use an address book that can be linked to other packages then it may well also contain other fields, such as telephone number, fax number and postal address.

The user is not allowed to change the fields in a built-in database like an address book, but many generic software applications allow you to create your own databases and to define the fields that you want to use. You can create a list (in Excel), a datasource (in Word), a table (in Access), or a file (in a programming language). All of these can be called *flat files* and all can be regarded as simple databases.

Any software that includes a flat file will normally provide facilities for sorting the data. All the records will be put into order, based on the data in one of the fields. This field is known as the *sort key*. For example, the e-mail address book allows the user to sort the records using name as the sort key, or alternatively, using the e-mail address as the sort key. Records can be sorted in ascending or descending order. Similarly, if you create your own list (flat file) in a spreadsheet and include the names and dates of birth of all your friends, then you will be able to sort the list into alphabetical order by name, or alternatively, in age order using date-of-birth as the sort key.

Files can also be *searched* (or *queried*, or *interrogated*) for data using a *query*. The query could be searching for all the records with data in one particular field that matches some specified text. Alternatively, it could search for data that meets a condition; for example, a search could be made in the date-of-birth field to find all the records of people born after a specified date. More complex searches can be carried out that check the data in several fields.

Flat-file databases often offer you a choice between two ways of viewing the data. The most usual way is to view all the records in a table format, with the field

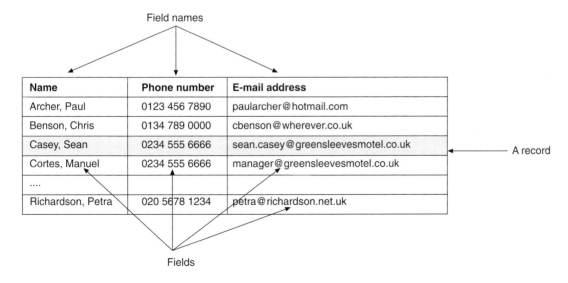

Figure names

Name	Phone number	E-mail address
Archer, Paul	0123 456 7890	paularcher@hotmail.com
Benson, Chris	0134 789 0000	cbenson@wherever.co.uk
Casey, Sean	0234 555 6666	sean.casey@greensleevesmotel.co.uk
Cortes, Manuel	0234 555 6666	manager@greensleevesmotel.co.uk
....		
Richardson, Petra	020 5678 1234	petra@richardson.net.uk

A record

Fields

Figure 13.1 *A simple address book*

names across the tops of the columns and the records arranged in rows, as shown in the example in Figure 13.1. An alternative is to view one record at a time, presented as an on-screen *form*. Some packages allow you to design your own forms.

Finally, you can usually print out the data in a file. Any printout of this sort is known as a *report*. A report can list all the data in the file or can use a query to select specific records and to present data in certain fields only.

Often a flat file will have one field, the *primary key*, which uniquely identifies each record. Examples of primary keys would be membership number in a file of club members, account number in a customer account at a bank, or stock code in a file of stock held in a shop.

A flat-file database feature in a package can be very useful if the data to be stored is quite simple. It will let the user set up any number of databases, each with its own record structure. However it has one overriding problem, namely that the same data may appear in two databases. So data, such as a person's address, may be changed in one file, but be left unchanged in another file. If this arises then the database lacks *data consistency*.

Relational databases

A relational database is a much more complicated structure than a simple flat-file database.

In a relational database, data may be stored in a series of *tables,* each of which has a similar structure to a flat-file database. Referring to the furniture shop example given earlier, such a database could have one table with data about stock, another of orders, and another of customer details. Note that in some software, the tables are referred to as 'files'.

The crucial added feature of a relational database is that it links the tables together. This means that one table can refer to data in another table – so a table of orders could link to the table of stock.

In a commercial organisation, the database should hold centrally all the data required by all the users, so that no separate files need be stored elsewhere. Normally each user will be able to view only those parts of the database which directly affect his or her work. For example, each of the shop salespersons will be able to view some of the data in the stock file when

they make a sale, but only the manager will be able to handle the orders to suppliers.

The task of the database developer is to create an underlying database structure that supports all the needs of all the users, and also to provide each type of employee with access to the exact data they need, and no more.

Relational databases are the natural method for handling online transaction processing applications. They are commonly used in a multi-user environment, such as a network. The database will be stored on the network server, and several users may be able to access the database at the same time.

Advantages of a relational database

A relational database has many advantages over the alternative, which is a set of independent flat files.

- *It reduces data redundancy*. It ensures that each item of data need be stored only once in the whole system. There is no danger of, say, the name and address for a person appearing in two flat files. Data which is repeated is redundant, that is, unnecessary.

- *It improves data consistency*. The data stored in a database should be accurate, reflecting the information in the real world. This is easier to achieve if there is no data redundancy.

- *It improves search times*. All the data is held in one large database, rather than in several independent files, so the database can be searched quickly for any required information.

- *It provides different views of the data to different users*. This means that the employees can view all those parts of the database that affect their work.

- *It can incorporate data security*, so that users view data only on a 'need to know' basis. It can also ensure that the system complies with the law and maintains confidentiality.

- *It can centralise all the data requirements of an organisation*. This makes it much easier for the systems administrators. Often a database manager will be appointed to maintain the software and ensure that it meets the current requirements across all departments in the organisation.

- *It can be used in a multi-user environment*. However, it is perfectly possible to set up a relational database for a single user on a standalone computer.

Greensleeves Motel

Ideal traveller's stopover or a base for a longer stay
Close to Rutland Water and the A1

At this American-style motel nightly rates are based on room size, not guest numbers, allowing you to select the accommodation in which you feel most at home.

If you do not wish to use the self-catering facilities, a healthy continental-style breakfast can be provided in your room on request. Alternatively, a cooked breakfast can be found in various cafes nearby, including one on the same site. The surrounding area boasts an abundance of good restaurants, catering for a wide variety of tastes.

There is a self-service laundry and games room for the use of guests.

NIGHTLY RATES per room
Double Ensuite   £42
Double Ensuite & Mini Kitchen   £46
Family Suite (4 people) – two separate sleeping areas & Mini Kitchen   £65

As you read in Chapter 12, Petra Richardson, a freelance IT consultant, has been asked to develop a software application for Greensleeves Motel. Sean Casey, the Assistant Manager, sends her a copy of an advertisement for the motel (see the extract). He then explains that it has recently been overhauled and their site has been expanded quite significantly.

At present there are 32 rooms available, but because of extensive building work this will rise to 80 rooms within a year. There are, in total, 14 members of staff involved in the running of the motel, but this will increase when the new building is opened.

Guests may phone or write in advance to book a room for any number of nights. They are asked to pay a deposit by credit card at the time of booking. They check in when they arrive at the motel, and they pay the balance of the bill when they check out.

Greensleeves' main aim over the next year is to improve the service to guests. The company also realises that, although it is sometimes possible to run a

small business without full ICT facilities, it is going to be very difficult to manage a larger business without them. At present they use PCs in the office simply for word-processing, but they know they can make much better use of this equipment. There are catering facilities at the motel offering breakfast and evening meals, bar service, self-service laundry and games room.

Activity

List all the processes (tasks) undertaken at the motel which could be carried out with ICT systems in the future. If you were the manager, which processes would you want to computerise first, and why?

Greensleeves has already decided that their first priority is for a computer-based room booking system, although in the long term they would like to add software for handling staff work rotas and holidays, payroll and the ordering of supplies. They also intend to add a full bar and restaurant, and will want to use IT applications to manage stock and accounts.

Sean lists the main objectives that he wants the room booking application to achieve. It should:

- speed up the booking process
- speed up the checking-in process
- produce bills quickly and accurately when a guest checks out
- be easy for a beginner to use, with a graphical interface and clear on-screen instructions
- reduce the amount of paperwork
- reduce the time spent on clerical work.

Petra carries out a careful investigation and records a great deal of information. She interviews all the relevant employees, produces questionnaires for employees and guests, collects samples of all the documents that are used, and observes the present system in operation. She asks many questions, such as:

- How exactly do guests make a booking, and how are bookings recorded?
- How are guests allocated a room?
- How do guests check in, and how is this recorded?
- Who produces the bills?
- How do guest check out, and how is this recorded?
- What are the responsibilities of each of the employees in relation to booking, checking in and checking out?
- What happens if a guest does not arrive as expected?
- What happens if a guest leaves without paying?
- Where are booking documents stored?
- What are booking documents used for once a guest has departed?

Petra discusses her findings with the Manager, Manuel Cortes, and Sean, and checks that she has understood everything correctly.

Data requirements

During the course of the investigation Petra has identified a number of processes that will be needed in the new application, each with their own data requirements. The main processes are:

- advanced booking of a room (including payment of deposit)
- checking in a guest
- checking out a guest (including production of bill and payment of balance)
- dealing with defaulters – that is, guests who do not arrive, or do not pay.

Petra has been listing all the data that is used by all the staff when carrying out these processes manually.

She now considers, in turn, each of the processes in the new application. For each one she prepares a list of all the kinds of data that need to be input into the system as part of that process. She then writes another list of all the data that the system should output. Some processes require input but do not produce any output. Some processes produce output with little or no input, but most processes have both input and output associated with them. For many processes some fields appear in both the input and the output list.

Petra identifies the following data requirements for the new application:

- room number and type (double, double with kitchen, family)
- nightly room rates
- name and address of guest
- arrival date of guest, number of nights booked and size of party
- amount of deposit paid for a booking
- amount of balance paid for a booking
- room allocated to a booking.

There are some particular problems associated with the storage of names, addresses, telephone numbers and dates, so Petra spends some time considering the needs of her client. She also thinks about the codes that could be used in some fields.

Names

Names can be stored in a database in a variety of ways. It is very common to have separate surname and forename fields, as the surname field is often used as a sort key. The client should be asked these questions:

- Do you need to address people by their title? If so, will Mr and Ms be enough, or should you also be prepared to use alternatives like Mrs, Miss, Dr, Rev, Sir or Rt Hon?

- Do you need to know the forename, or will initials be enough?
- Do you need the full set of forenames, the first name alone, or the known name where this is different from the first name?
- Do you ever need to use the name of a company or organisation, and if so, do you also need the name of a department, or the name of a contact person?

Addresses

How long is an address? The answer to that question varies from locality to locality. It also depends on whether the name of the town, county or country needs to be recorded. Consider these two addresses:

'The Elms'	145 Station Road
Woodlands Road	Richton
Lower Hook	KM5 2ER
nr Wandleton	
Middleshire	
KM4 8FT	
United Kingdom	

If all the addresses are in the same town, then the town name does not have to be input by the end-user, although it will, of course, have to be output if a letter is produced. Similarly, it may not be necessary to input the county or country. Each line of the address should be stored in a separate field, although some fields may be left blank.

If the application is going to be linked to a postcode database, then all that is needed to identify an address is the house number (or name) and postcode. In the UK each postcode identifies a part of a street within a particular town. A short street may have only one postcode, whilst a long street may have many postcodes. No postcode refers to more than one street.

Telephone numbers

The way in which telephone numbers are stored again depends on how they are to be used. The client should be asked:

- Do you need to store the national and international dialling codes for each number?
- Will the phone numbers be used for an automatic dialling system?

Telephone numbers are usually stored as text, partly because most numbers are printed with a space or hyphen somewhere in them. Also, if a number beginning with 0 were to be stored as an integer then the leading zero would simply be lost.

Dates

If a date is to be used within a calculation, for example to see whether a payment is overdue, then the date must be entered as three separate integers. In other cases it can be entered as text.

Application packages often look after the technicalities of dates by providing a date type. The package will handle dates correctly provided they are entered in a standard format. You are sometimes offered a choice of date formats, such as 03/12/2002 or 3.12.02 or 3rd December 2002. Be careful if you are using an American version of software, as dates are usually presented with the month first; for example 03/12/02 would mean March 12th 2002.

Codes

In some fields the data is best stored as a code. For example, the motel already uses codes to distinguish between the three room types: DB is used for a double room, DK is used for a double room with kitchen, and FS for a family suite. Some codes encapsulate some of the information about a record, especially where they are being used in a primary key. As an example, examine the code format of a person's driver number on a driving licence.

Activity

In the future Petra may be asked to develop an application for handling the staff work rotas and holidays.

1. *Write down a list of questions that she should ask during her investigation.*

2. *List the data requirements for that application.*

Petra decides that the application is best treated as a relational database. She has not yet decided which software tool to use when developing the database, but she turns her attention to the data model.

Developing a relational database

Data modelling

When you create a database you are designing a model, or representation, of facts in the real world. This model is composed of files or tables. For a simple flat-file database this is usually a straightforward process, and it is easy to work out which fields you want to use.

A relational database is a much more complex structure, and it is necessary to take considerable care in designing the data model. There are many ways of designing a relational database badly, and a bad data model can make the database inoperable, so it is essential that you design the model on paper and check it carefully before you start developing the system.

The data model for a relational database has two components:

- an entity-relationship diagram
- a set of base tables.

The entity-relationship diagram

An *entity* is simply something in the real world that is represented in a database. Examples of entities might be an employee, stock item, course of study, customer or book, though it is unlikely that they would all be found in the same database. Each entity will (eventually) be represented by a table in your database.

Step 1: Identify the entities

Reading the input and output data requirements for all the processes will help you to identify the underlying entities that you need to consider in your design. In the Greensleeves project Petra had identified the data requirements (see the bullet list in the previous section, beginning with room number and type). The data seem to relate to three kinds of thing – rooms, bookings and guests. She draws a rough diagram, as shown in Figure 13.2.

Figure 13.2 *Petra's rough diagram*

Step 2: Identify the relationships

Now link any related entities with a line. Do not attempt to draw in every possible relationship, but select only those that are direct and permanent. Petra's modified diagram is shown in Figure 13.3. Note that she has not drawn a line between the guest and room entities. That is because the relationship between rooms and the guests who occupy them is constantly changing. On the other hand, once a booking is made it remains as a permanent record of the transaction.

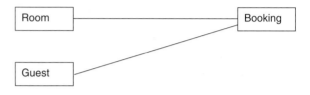

Figure 13.3 *Petra's modified diagram*

Step 3: Determine the type of relationship

Consider each relationship on the diagram in turn and decide which type it is from the explanations in Figure 13.4. Note that MANY means 'one or more'.

Indicate the MANY end of the relationship. Finally add a verb next to the line that describes the relationship.

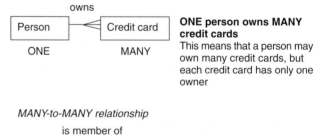

ONE-to-MANY relationship

ONE person owns MANY credit cards
This means that a person may own many credit cards, but each credit card has only one owner

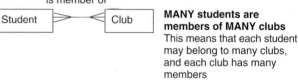

MANY-to-MANY relationship

MANY students are members of MANY clubs
This means that each student may belong to many clubs, and each club has many members

Figure 13.4 *Relationships*

You may identify a many-to-one relationship on your entity-relationship diagram. For example, you could have used the verb 'is owned by' for the first relationship and then read it as 'MANY credit cards are owned by ONE person'. Any many-to-one relationship can always be read as a one-to-many relationship in the opposite direction. We always use the one-to-many version in a relational database, and indeed most of the relationships in a relational database are one-to-many.

You will see below that many-to-many relationships do pose a problem in a relational database.

In the Greensleeves case, each guest may make many bookings, as they can return after their first visit. So the relationship between the guest and booking entity is one-to-many. Also each room is booked in many bookings. Although a room can be booked only once for any particular night, nevertheless over time there will be records of many bookings made for that room, so the relationship between the room and booking entities is one-to-many (see Figure 13.5).

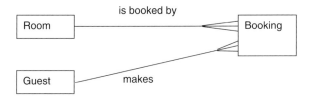

Figure 13.5 *Petra's diagram develops*

Step 4: Deal with many-to-many relationships

A relational database cannot handle many-to-many relationships, even though they do exist in the real world. If you find you have a many-to-many relationship in your diagram, then you will have to add a new entity. Each of the original entities will now have a one-to-many relationship with the new entity, which should be given a suitable name. This new entity is sometimes called an *allocation entity*.

Consider the many-to-many relationship between students and clubs given above. This will become as in Figure 13.6. Think of the new entity as a membership card or, if cards are not issued, as a list showing all the clubs that each student belongs to and all the members

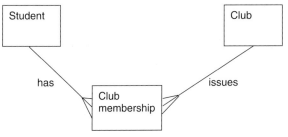

Figure 13.6 *Dealing with a many-to-many relationship*

of each club. So one student has many club memberships, and one club issues many club memberships. Remember to read each relationship in the one-to-many direction.

Step 5: One-to-one relationship

You may believe that there is a one-to-one relationship between two entities in your diagram. In practice, these very rarely occur. Most one-to-one relationships are really many-to-many.

Figure 13.7 shows two relationships which both appear to be one-to-one.

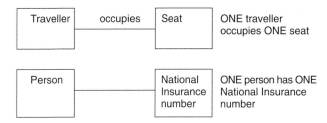

Figure 13.7 *One-to-one relationships*

Does the first relationship correctly illustrate the seats occupied by travellers on a flight?

The answer is 'no', because this relationship describes what happens on one flight only. Over a period of time, any one seat will have been occupied by many travellers, and travellers who use the route regularly will occupy many seats. The airline will keep records of all flights over a period of time, so the relationship is better considered as many-to-many and should be handled as described previously.

Figure 13.7 also shows another relationship which you may think is one-to-one. It is certainly true that each person has one NI number and each NI number is allocated to one person. But the NI number is just one of the pieces of data that will be held about the person, along with name, address, date of birth etc. A separate entity containing the NI number is not really needed. The next section will show how all these pieces of data are incorporated into one entity.

Designing a set of base tables

An entity has a number of *attributes*. An attribute is a data item that relates to an entity. For example, a Student entity may have these attributes: forename, surname, address line 1, address line 2, town, postcode, course, previous school.

The concepts of an entity and its attributes are rather abstract. When a relational database is actually implemented, each entity will be represented by a table or file. Similarly, each attribute will be represented by a field in the table or file. The simplest way to distinguish between them is to remember that the terms 'entity' and 'attribute' are used when you *design* a data model, and the terms 'table' (file) and 'field' are used when you *implement* a database.

The tables that represent the entities are known as the *base tables* for the database. Once set up they are a permanent part of the database. Between them they should contain all the basic information that is needed by the system. We will see later that it is possible to use queries to create temporary tables, but these are not base tables.

Throughout this chapter the term 'table' will be used instead of file. Eventually tables will be populated with data, and each row in a table will be a record.

Step 1: Identify the informational fields in the tables

Look carefully at your final entity-relationship diagram. For each entity on the diagram, check through the data requirements for the project and try to identify all its attributes. These will become the *informational fields* in the tables.

Begin by defining one table for each entity. A *table definition* consists of the name of the entity followed by a list of all its attributes in brackets. Write down (in draft form at this stage) the table definition for each entity, listing all the relevant attributes that you can find.

Petra checks her data requirements again (see the bullet list on page 152) and then writes down these three table definitions:

- room (roomnumber, roomtype, nightlyrate)
- booking (arrivaldate, numberofnights, sizeofparty, depositpaid, balancepaid)
- guest (forename, surname, title, addressline1, addressline2, addressline3)

At this point she does not include the nightly rate in the booking table as it belongs to another table.

> Each informational field should appear in one, and only one, table.

Some software tools do allow spaces in the names of the fields, but it is good practice not to use them.

Step 2: Include primary keys

Each table must have a *primary key* field. A primary key uniquely identifies each record in the table. If there is no obvious primary key among the informational fields then you must create one. A primary key is an *identification field*. The primary key is underlined in the table definition.

In theory a primary key can be any kind of data, but in practice it is often a code or number, such as a membership number, an account number, a stock code etc. One word of warning – do not use a person's name as a primary key, as several people can have the same name!

You may find that one of the tables does not have an obvious primary key, but that two or more fields taken together could be used to form a *composite primary key*. In theory it is permissible to use composite (or joint) primary keys, but they can be a bit tricky to work with, so you are strongly advised to avoid them. If necessary, add a new field as the primary key.

When she looks at information fields in the Greensleeves tables, Petra decides that the room number can act as the primary key in the room table, but that she needs to create primary keys for the other two tables. Her table definitions become:

- room (roomnumber, roomtype, nightlyrate)
- booking (bookingreference, arrivaldate, numberofnights, sizeofparty, depositpaid, balancepaid)
- guest (guestID, forename, surname, title, addressline1, addressline2, addressline3)

The primary key is often placed at the beginning of the list of fields, but it can appear anywhere in the list.

Step 3: Include foreign keys

Relational databases allow us make links between tables – this is how the relationships in the entity-relationship diagram are implemented. The tables are linked by taking the primary key from one table and adding it as an extra field to the linked table. It will then be known as a *foreign key* in the second table. A foreign key is also an identification field.

Examine each relationship in the entity-relationship diagram in turn. Copy the primary key from the table definition of the entity at the ONE end of the relationship and add it to the table definition of the entity at the MANY end.

Petra needs to look again at the entity-relationship diagram (Figure 13.5).

> Copy the primary key from the ONE end to the MANY end of the relationship.

She considers the relationship between the Room and Booking entities. The two tables look like this:

- room (<u>roomnumber</u>, roomtype, nightlyrate)
- booking (<u>bookingreference</u>, arrivaldate, numberofnights, sizeofparty, depositpaid, balancepaid)

The Room entity is at the ONE end of the relationship and the Booking entity is at the MANY end. So she copies the primary key of the room table to the booking table:

- room (<u>roomnumber</u>, roomtype, nightlyrate)
- booking (<u>bookingreference</u>, arrivaldate, numberofnights, sizeofparty, depositpaid, balancepaid, *roomnumber*)

The roomnumber field in the booking table is a foreign key – so-called because it is a primary key, but in another (foreign) table. Roomnumber is not the primary key in the booking table but acts as a link to the room table. In fact, its role is to identify the room that each booking refers to.

Petra now looks at the relationship between the Guest and Booking entities and copies the primary key of the guest table to the booking table. The tables now look like this:

- room (<u>roomnumber</u>, roomtype, nightlyrate)
- booking (<u>bookingreference</u>, arrivaldate, numberofnights, sizeofparty, depositpaid, balancepaid, *roomnumber, guestID*)
- guest (<u>guestID</u>, forename, surname, title, addressline1, addressline2, addressline3)

The foreign keys have been identified in the table definitions by italics.

Step 4: *Normalise the tables*

The tables in a relational database are subjected to a process known as *normalisation* in order to make it work as efficiently as possible. The main purpose of normalisation is to reduce data redundancy – in other words, to cut down on unnecessary duplication of data. By preventing the same data from appearing in several tables we can ensure that the data remains consistent for all the applications that use it.

A normalised database will also deal with queries much more efficiently, although the real advantages of this only really show up when there is a large amount of data.

Do not be tempted to simply remove redundant data or create new tables intuitively at this stage, as you may lose some of the structure you have already developed.

The rules of normalisation

You need to check each table against the three rules of normalisation.

> Rule 1: No repeating fields (First Normal Form)
>
> Rule 2: No partial dependencies (Second Normal Form)
>
> Rule 3: No non-key dependencies (Third Normal Form)

You should first check that each of the tables passes the first rule. If they do then they are in First Normal Form (1NF). Next check if they pass the second rule; if so, they are in Second Normal Form (2NF). Finally check whether they are in Third Normal Form.

If you have followed the instructions so far your tables should already be in 2NF, and may well be in 3NF as well. However, you should still go through the process of checking that your tables meet all three normal forms.

Rule 1: *No repeating fields*

Check whether any fields are repeated within a *single* table definition. If there are no repetitions then the table is already in 1NF.

Generally speaking, a table will fail this test if the designer is trying to make a flat file do the job of a relational database. For example, suppose Petra had tried to meet all the data requirements in one table, called guestvisits:

- guestvisits(<u>guestID</u>, forename, surname, addressline1, ... , roomnumber, arrivaldate, numberofnights, sizeofparty)

Some guests will return and stay again, so space would have to be made in the table definition for all past and future visits. The table would begin to look like this:

- guestvisits(<u>guestID</u>, forename, surname, addressline1, ... , roomnumber, arrivaldate, numberofnights, sizeofparty, roomnumber, arrivaldate, numberofnights, sizeofparty, roomnumber, arrivaldate, numberofnights, sizeofparty, roomnumber, arrivaldate, numberofnights, sizeofparty, roomnumber, arrivaldate, numberofnights, sizeofparty)

There are four repeating fields in this table definition: roomnumber, arrivaldate, numberofnights, sizeofparty. So this table is *not* in 1NF.

If there is a repeating field, then you must go back to the entity-relationship diagram and create a new entity. Petra has in fact avoided this problem by creating separate Booking and Guest entities.

Continue checking all the table definitions, amending them where necessary.

Rule 2: No partial dependencies

You must now remove any field that is partially dependent on the primary key (in other words, depends on only part of the key). This can only happen if the primary key is a composite key – that is, one that is made up of more than one attribute. Since we have suggested that you do not use composite primary keys, all your tables should be in 2NF.

None of the tables in the Greensleeves project has a composite key, so they are all in 2NF.

Rule 3: No non-key dependencies

In a table definition a *non-key* is any informational field that could not act as the primary key. You should identify any non-key fields in a table definition. If a table has no non-key fields or only one non-key field then it is already in 3NF.

If a table has more than one non-key field then check to see whether any two or more of these fields are dependent on each other. If they are, then you will probably have to create a new entity. The table definition for this new entity will contain all the fields that were dependent on each other in the original table. You will need to draw another version of the entity-relationship diagram at that stage.

Petra reviews her table definitions one at a time, starting with:

- room (<u>roomnumber</u>, roomtype, nightlyrate)

In the room table definition, roomtype and nightlyrate are both informational fields. Neither could act as the primary key so both are non-keys. The question is: are these two fields dependent on each other? The answer is 'yes', because all rooms of the same type are charged at the same rate.

The rooms are numbered in the traditional way. All room numbers consist of three characters. Rooms on the ground floor begin with G, and those on the first floor begin with 1. The data about the rooms looks like this:

room table

roomnumber	roomtype	nightlyrate
G01	DB	£42
G02	DB	£42
G03	FS	£65
G04	DK	£46
G05	DK	£46
G06	FS	£65
G07	FS	£65
G08	DK	£46
.....		
115	DB	£42
116	DB	£42

DB = double ensuite; DK = Double with kitchen; FS = family suite

Figure 13.8 The 'room' table

You can see that every single time the room type is given as DB, the nightly rate is £42. This means that the pairing of DB with £42 is duplicated many times. Similarly, the pairings of DK with £46, and of FS with £65, are duplicated. So the nightly rate is dependent on the room type.

To put this table into 3NF, Petra creates a new entity called Room Rate. Each nightly rate applies to many rooms, but each room has only one nightly rate, so the relationship between Room Rate and Room is one-to-many, as shown in Figure 13.9.

The new table definition for the Room rate entity is designed. It will simply contain the two dependent

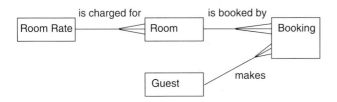

Figure 13.9 *The revised entity-relationship diagram*

fields. As the nightly rate is dependent on the room type, it is the room type that becomes the primary key in the new table. The room table now loses the nightly rate field, and room type becomes the foreign key linking it with the Room rate table:

- roomrate (<u>roomtype</u>, nightlyrate)
- room (<u>roomnumber</u>, *roomtype*)

The tables will now be as shown in Figure 13.10.

roomrate table

roomtype	nightlyrate
DB	£42
DK	£46
FS	£65

room table

roomnumber	roomtype
G01	DB
G02	DB
G03	FS
G04	DK
G05	DK
G06	FS
G07	FS
G08	DK
.....	
115	DB
116	DB

Figure 13.10 *Petra's two revised tables*

The room rates now only need to be entered once, so there is no possibility of error when entering the rates as might have been the case before. It is also easy for the room rates to be updated when charges change, as they only have to be entered once.

You can see that these two tables will take up less room than the original table on its own. This saving would be even more marked if there were many more records in the room table.

Petra checks the other two table definitions. First:

- booking (<u>bookingreference</u>, arrivaldate, numberofnights, sizeofparty, depositpaid, balancepaid, roomnumber, guestID)

All the informational fields are non-keys, but none is dependent on another, so this table is in 3NF. Then:

- guest (<u>guestID</u>, forename, surname, title, addressline1, addressline2, addressline3)

Similarly, all the informational fields are non-keys and there appear to be no dependencies, so this table is in 3NF. So, the final version of the tables reads like this:

- roomrate (<u>roomtype</u>, nightlyrate)
- room (<u>roomnumber</u>, roomtype)
- booking (<u>bookingreference</u>, arrivaldate, numberofnights, sizeofparty, depositpaid, balancepaid, roomnumber, guestID)
- guest (<u>guestID</u>, forename, surname, title, addressline1, addressline2, addressline3)

These are the base tables of Petra's database.

Advantages of normalisation

A database which has been put into 3NF will be far more effective in use than one which is not normalised. The advantages of normalising are:

- Data integrity can be maintained because each piece of information is entered and stored only once.
- It is easier to update the data, whether amending, deleting or adding new data.
- Interrogation of the database will be faster.
- Memory space will be saved because redundant data will have been removed.

A mail order company often sends out advertising literature to past customers. The relevant table definition is:

- customer (<u>customernumber</u>, title, initials, surname, housenumber, street, town, postcode, county)

Is this normalised? If not, explain what changes could be made to normalise the database.

Creating a database application

This section assumes that you are familiar with Microsoft® Access or another database applications generator. It is not a tutorial.

Petra Richardson decides which software tool she will use to implement the database you read about in the previous section. She could use a traditional high-level language, but she has decided instead to use a *database management system.*

A database management system (DBMS) is an application generator that is designed specifically for developing relational databases. Access is an example of a DBMS that can be used successfully on a PC.

The end-user is not normally expected to develop database applications using a DBMS; instead a database developer like Petra will create an application for an end-user. In practice, some end-users do become proficient at using Access to set up databases, at which point they cross the boundary between being an end-user and being a developer! Unfortunately, if the end-user-turned-developer does not understand the theory of relational databases and data modelling, then they can find themselves in some difficulty.

Referential integrity

Petra has set up a new database in Access and she has implemented the four base tables – roomrate, room, booking and guest. She now has to implement the relationships to match the entity-relationship diagram.

One of the strengths of a relational database is that it helps to maintain data integrity – that is, it supports the end-user's need to keep the data as accurate as

possible. This is largely achieved by normalisation, which ensures that none of the informational fields is duplicated anywhere in the database.

But where there is a relationship between two tables, the foreign key in one table does, necessarily, duplicate the primary key in another. There is a danger that an end-user will enter data in a foreign key field that does not correspond to an entry in its corresponding primary key field. For example, in Petra's booking table, *roomnumber* is a foreign key. When the end-user records a booking, the room number has to be entered, but this is not going to be very useful if the number that is entered does not belong to a real room. Since all the room numbers are already stored in the room table, the system should check that the room number that is entered (as a foreign key in the booking table) refers to one of the room numbers already stored (as a primary key in the room table). If the data matches we say that we have achieved *referential integrity.*

When a relationship is set up in Access the developer can specify that referential integrity must be enforced (see Figure 13.11). If the end-user tries to enter a room number in the booking table that does not already exist in the room table, then a warning message appears.

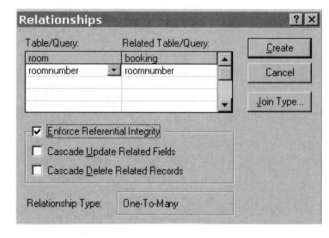

Figure 13.11 *How to enforce referential integrity in Access*

Petra now sets up all the relationships to correspond to the entity-relationship diagram. In Access, the ∞ (infinity) symbol indicates the MANY end of a relationship.

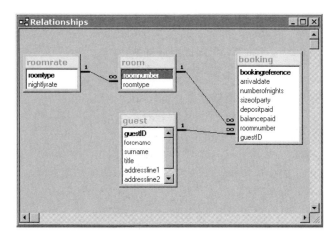

Figure 13.12 *The entity-relationship diagram implemented in Access (note the infinity symbols)*

Petra now sets about implementing all the processes that she had to consider at the design stage. This will require her to interrogate and manipulate the data in many ways.

A database application is only really of any value if it turns the large amount of data stored in the database into useful information. This is done by carefully picking out exactly the right data from the base tables and presenting it in a way that makes it intelligible to the end-user. As we shall see, the trick is to use *queries* to create temporary recordsets.

Recordsets

Any table that has data in it is a *recordset*. When a data model has been designed carefully, the base tables will between them include all the fields that are needed for the application. Each base table, when populated with data, is a recordset.

But the data in these base tables can be extracted, combined, sorted and output in many different ways. Each time data is selected from the database a new temporary table, or recordset, can be formed.

For example, in the Greensleeves application, the end-user may want to access a list of all the guests booked into the motel on a particular night. This recordset can be extracted from the booking and guest tables. Alternatively, the end-user may need to print out a simple list of rooms on the ground floor and what type each one is; to obtain this recordset only one table has to be used, as all the required data is in the room table. Yet again, the end-user will, at some stage, want to find the address of a particular guest who stayed at the motel recently.

In each of these examples, a recordset is created on demand by the application. These temporary recordsets are held in memory whilst in use, but are not saved permanently in the database. The base tables, on the other hand, are permanent recordsets.

Some recordsets are read-only; that is, the data can be viewed by the end-user but it cannot be changed in any way.

In comparison, some recordsets can be viewed on-screen and the end-user is able to amend the data. Any changes made to data in the temporary recordset will also change the original data in the base tables. Equally, any changes made to the data in the base tables will immediately be changed in the temporary recordset. This kind of recordset is also known as a *dynaset*.

Queries

When the term 'query' is used in the context of the design of a database, it does not mean quite what you might imagine. A query is not a question asked of the database by an end-user. Instead, it is a technical function, used by a database designer, in order to manipulate the data. To be precise, a query is the method used to create a temporary recordset from the base tables.

Using queries, the data can be manipulated in many different ways for different processes, and this can give tremendous flexibility and power to an application.

Queries select and combine data from different tables in three main ways.

Select fields

A query can be used to select the data in certain fields only. For example, Petra wants a list of the names of guests who have stayed at the motel. The guest table has several address fields as well, which she does need on this occasion, so she creates this query using the *Standard Query Language* (SQL):

```
SELECT DISTINCTROW guest.title,
guest.forename, guest.surname
FROM guest;
```

The SELECT line selects the title, forename and surname fields, and the FROM line identifies the table where they can be found. The fields will be output in the order in which they are listed in the query. Figure 13.13 shows part of the large recordset generated by this query.

Developing a relational database

	Mr	John	Rogerson
	Mrs	Sara	Patel
		M	Gibbs
	Rev	Robin	Redgrave
	Ms	Sian	Morris
		L K	Khan
	Mr	Leslie	Jones

Figure 13.13 *An extract from a query recordset*

Almost all DBMS systems use SQL. Some software, like Microsoft® Access, also offer the developer a graphical way of creating a query. In Access, the Design View of the query above looks like Figure 13.14. The top part of the window shows the table that is being used, and the bottom part is the *Query By Example* (QBE) grid. When a query is created by placing fields in the QBE grid, the software automatically generates the SQL statement.

If you create a query in Access using the QBE grid, you can also look at the SQL by choosing SQL from the View menu.

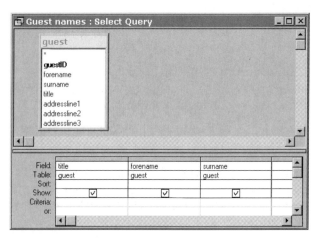

Figure 13.14 *Design View of a query in Access*

Select records

A query can also be used to select the data in a table that matches one or more conditions, or *criteria*. (Note that criteria is the plural of criterion.)

For example, if Petra wants to select all the rooms on the ground floor from the room table, she knows that the criterion will be that the data in the roomnumber field must begin with G. She creates a query in the SQL, which looks like this:

```
SELECT DISTINCTROW room.roomnumber,
room.roomtype
FROM room
WHERE (((room.roomnumber) Like "G*"));
```

The first two lines select the fields and base table as before. The WHERE line gives the criteria for selection – namely, that the data in the roomnumber field must begin with G. The * symbol can be read as 'anything', that is, the G can be followed by any characters or numbers.

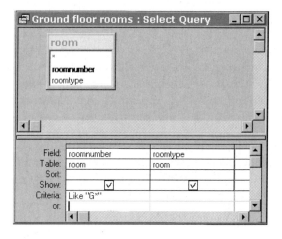

Figure 13.15 *Recordset and QBE grid*

The recordset created by this query looks like Figure 13.15. It shows only the ground floor rooms and omits those on the first floor. This recordset is a dynaset as it is possible to add new rooms, or change their room types, and any changes made will be reflected in the base table. Figure 13.15 also shows the QBE grid for this query.

Join tables

A query can combine the data from two tables. This can be done only if there is a relationship between the two tables. The primary key in one table will be linked with the foreign key in the other.

For example, in the Greensleeves database it would be useful to join the room table with the roomrates table in order to see exactly what is charged for each room. This is achieved with the query in Figure 13.16 (QBE version).

The roomtype field makes the join between the two tables. It appears as a primary key in the roomrate table and as a foreign key in the room table. *When you join two tables in a query, always use the foreign key.* You will see from the illustration that the roomtype field has been dragged down from the room table, where it is the foreign key, and not from the roomrate table. The system will recognise that the two tables are related and will automatically join the primary key to the foreign key.

The SQL generated is this:

```
SELECT DISTINCTROW room.roomnumber,
room.roomtype, roomrate.nightlyrate
FROM roomrate INNER JOIN room ON
roomrate.roomtype = room.roomtype;
```

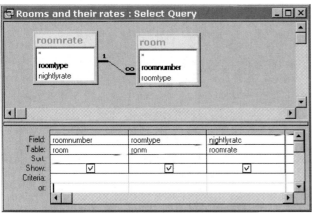

Figure 13.16 *Another QBE grid and its recordset*

Figure 13.16 also shows part of the recordset produced. Note that the rooms have been sorted by *room type* (DB, followed by DK then FS) as that is the join field.

You may remember that in the initial data model for this database, a single table had all three fields (on page 158). This was then split into two tables in order to put the database into 3NF. So why have they been combined again in this way?

You have to distinguish between the way in which the data is stored (in tables) and the way it is manipulated and used (in queries). A properly normalised database has great flexibility and can be used to generate very many queries.

Complex queries

Queries can select fields, can select records and can join tables, and they can do any combination of these at the same time. A query can even be based on another query (and its temporary recordset) instead of using a base table.

To give an idea of what a complex query might be used for, look again at the processes that are needed in the Greensleeves application:

- advanced booking of a room (including payment of deposit)
- checking in a guest
- checking out a guest (including production of bill and payment of balance)
- dealing with defaulters – guests who do not arrive, or do not pay.

Each of these processes calls on data stored in more than one of the base tables. For example, when a guest arrives at the motel and checks in, the end-user will want to see data in all these fields on the screen:

bookingreference	arrivaldate
forename	numberofnights
surname	sizeofparty
title	depositpaid
addressline1	roomnumber
addressline2	roomtype
addressline3	roomrate

All four of the base tables will contribute to this output. All four tables will be joined and all the fields will be needed except balancepaid. The SQL query is:

```
SELECT DISTINCTROW booking.bookingreference,
booking.guestID, guest.forename,
```

```
guest.surname, guest.title,
guest.addressline1, guest.addressline2,
guest.addressline3, booking.arrivaldate,
booking.numberofnights,
booking.sizeofparty, booking.depositpaid,
booking.roomnumber, room.roomtype,
roomrate.nightlyrate

FROM roomrate INNER JOIN (room INNER JOIN
(guest INNER JOIN booking ON guest.guestID
= booking.guestID) ON room.roomnumber =
booking.roomnumber) ON roomrate.roomtype =
room.roomtype;
```

This query produces detailed information about each of the room bookings that have been made at the motel.

Views

Base tables and queries form the core of any relational database. But these are the tools that the database developer uses, rather like the languages used by programmers. The end-user should never be expected to look at either the base tables or the queries directly.

Instead, the developer will design a series of forms or windows for the end-user. These forms will provide the user with a user interface which will hide the underlying system from the user, whilst making it easy for the user to carry out the processes.

Each process will require a form, or possibly a set of linked forms. These forms provide the end-user with a *view* of the database. Usually a form will display only a selection of data from the database, so each form will be based on a query.

In our Greensleeves example, the end-user has to carry out four processes on the database, so each will have its own view. Essentially, a view is a 'window' on to the database which selects and displays exactly the data needed for the process, and nothing else.

In a larger organisation, with a much more complex database, the various processes may be carried out by totally different employees. This means that each employee will have their own view of the database.

For example, a factory may include a wide range of data about its staff in its database – employment details, personal details, qualifications, pay rates, training undertaken, holidays taken, days off sick etc. The training manager may need a view of the database which shows him or her the names of staff and the training they have done. The payroll clerk's view will show details about the salaries of staff. A department manager will need to arrange the holiday rota, so will need to see what holidays have already been taken by staff and how many days holiday they are entitled to have. In each case, the end-user sees only a selection of the data in the database.

By using forms to provide views of the data, the developer can also build some security into the system. Each view can be password-protected, or can be linked to the user's network access privileges.

Indexes

An *index* is a special table which is used to speed up the querying and sorting of records in a database. Indexes will always remain hidden from the end-user, and will often not be viewed directly by the database developer either.

Records in a table or recordset are often sorted into a particular order. The primary key of a table is the *default sort key*, and when the records are output in the table they will normally be sorted in primary key order. But it is always possible to use other fields as sort keys as well.

Any field can be indexed. When this is done, an index table is created which lists all the records in the table sorted using that field as the sort key. The primary key is always indexed, and the index for the primary key is known as the *primary index*.

Returning to our Greensleeves example, each new guest at the motel is automatically allocated a guestID by the database system when they make a booking. The guestID consists of a year letter (A for 1998, B for 1999 etc.), followed by four digits. The guestID field is the primary key of the guest table in the Greensleeves database, so the data in the table is normally output in guestID sequence. The primary index is created automatically.

Sometimes the motel will need to list all past guests in alphabetical order, using the surname as the sort key, so Petra has set up an index on the surname field. The entries in the index table identify the records in the main table by their guestIDs but in surname order.

To follow how this is done, you have to realise that each record has a record number, which is normally hidden from the end-user or developer (see Figure 13.17).

guest table

record number	guestID (primary key)	forename	surname	title	address...
1	C2314	John	Rogerson	Mr	
2	C2315	Sara	Patel	Mrs	
3	C2316	M	Gibbs		
4	C2317	Robin	Redgrave	Rev	
5	C2318	Sian	Morris	Ms	
6	C2319	L K	Khan		
7	C2320	Leslie	Jones	Mr	

primaryindex

record number
1
2
3
4
5
6
7

surname index

record number
3
7
6
5
2
4
1

Figure 13.17 *How indexes are created*

You may wonder why it is necessary to have an index on the primary key. Often, as in this case, the primary keys are allocated to records in a defined sequence, when the records are first entered. But it is possible to allocate primary keys in any sequence at all, provided they are all different.

When the index method is used the actual records never have to be reorganised, but remain in the base table in the order in which they were entered. When the end-user asks for records to be output sorted by surname, the system uses the surname index to pick each record in turn from the main table and thus output the records in the correct order.

It is possible to output data using a sort key that is not indexed. But the system will have to employ a *sort algorithm*, which is a short program that sorts data on the spot. There are many sort algorithms, and some are faster than others. However, if the table of data is large the user may have to wait a noticeable length of time whilst the sort is being performed.

The use of an index is not simply to provide fast output of data sorted by the required sort key. In a large database it is even more significant when the database is being searched for a particular record. It is much easier to find a single record when the data is sorted by the field used for the search. Consider how difficult it would be to find an entry in a telephone directory if they were sorted by the primary key (the telephone number) instead of by surname!

When to use an index

Indexes can be set up for any number of fields, but this should be done with some caution.

If a field is indexed then the index table is kept up to date every time a record is added to or deleted from the base table. This requires a little processing time every time the table is amended. If many fields are indexed then the processing time can be noticeable as all the indexes will have to be updated. The time taken may become a problem if the table is large.

If a user wants to sort the records using, as a sort key, a field that is not indexed, there may be lengthy processing when the records are sorted. But, on the other hand, no processing takes place each time the base table is altered.

In general, you should index only these fields:

- all primary keys
- all fields that are likely to be used as sort keys
- all fields that are likely to be used as criteria in queries.

Finally, do not use indexes in a table that is going to contain only a few records, as the time taken to carry out sorts and queries is minimal anyway.

CHAPTER 14

This chapter explains how an ICT solution provider interacts with a client in order to provide the best service. To do this it uses the context of a supplier who develops customised applications for a niche market.

It will describe:

- how a modular package can provide a flexible ICT solution

- how an application is maintained

- how an application can be customised to meet the needs of clients.

The chapter covers the following Learning Outcomes in the specification:

L.O. 2.2 Specify the procedures for maintaining a specific developed application

L.O. 2.3 Understand and comment on the sensible use of a developed ICT-based solution to a defined

Providing ICT solutions

Leisure Systems Ltd specialises in producing ICT solutions for the leisure industry. There are many small companies like them who successfully focus on one sector – they are aiming at *niche* markets. They usually offer a high level of personal support to their clients, both before and after purchase.

Leisure Systems made its name in the 1980s with a software application called ClubManager, written by its founder, Stephen Bell. This is a software system for managing private health clubs and leisure centres. ClubManager covers all aspects of running a club, from enrolling a new member, checking in members as they arrive, subscriptions and sales, as well as providing reports for managers.

Stephen was the original application developer. He wrote the original software in a programming language called Pascal. In 1996 Stephen worked on a completely new version of the software to run on Microsoft® Windows. This time he used the visual language Delphi, which is based on Pascal.

Since then the company has enjoyed some considerable success, so Stephen now concentrates on his role as Managing Director, and leaves the application development to two younger employees. They are both qualified software engineers and between them they design, program and test the software. Stephen now takes responsibility for marketing ClubManager, with the help of two sales personnel.

Stephen has also built up a team of eight employees who between them carry out all the support and training, which has been such an important factor in their success. This team works flexibly according to demand, and they can cover each other's work when necessary. Most clients opt to take out a support contract with Leisure Systems and this gives them unlimited access to the support team.

Although their main product is software, Leisure Systems will also provide and install hardware to support the application, using a preferred hardware supplier.

A modular package

ClubManager consists of four main modules. These can be thought of as separate applications, but they interact with each other and are based on a common database (see Chapter 13). The main screen of ClubManager looks like Figure 14.1.

Figure 14.1 *The main (home) menu screen for ClubManager*

- The ReceptionManager module is used at the front desk of a club. Each member has a card on which a membership number has been printed in bar-code format. When a member arrives he or she hands over the membership card and the receptionist passes it under a bar-code reader. The member's details are displayed on screen and the person is normally allowed to proceed into the club. In some clubs the receptionist will record what facilities the member wants to use, such as the gym or swimming pool.

- If a new person wants to join, then the receptionist switches to the MemberManager module and goes through the process of entering the name, address and date of birth of the new member. They can then determine what type of membership is required (this varies from club to club) and how the person intends to pay the membership fee.

- The ShopManager module is used if the club has its own sales point, or can be used by the receptionist if they sell only a few items from the front desk.

- The ReportManager module is normally only used by the manager, and provides him or her with a large choice of report formats. Reports can inform the manager of attendance figures, use of facilities, sales, membership levels and subscriptions etc.

This modular approach allows Leisure Systems the flexibility to add new modules in response to demand. A few years ago, one of their major clients wanted to be able to pre-book facilities for members. Club members were no longer satisfied with simply turning up to use facilities such as the sauna or squash courts. At peak times these were often full, so instead they wanted to book in advance. Leisure Systems identified the need and developed a new module, called BookingManager. As not all clubs need this, BookingManager is sold as an add-on module to the original package, and it then, of course, is an option on the main menu.

Customising the application

ClubManager is not a simple off-the-shelf package as it can be customised to meet the client's requirements.

When a club purchases ClubManager they are provided with all the four basic modules, even though their needs may not be the same as those of another club. But the software can be customised in many ways. For example, printed receipts at the shop will give the name of the club, membership categories can be defined, and access security can be set up.

A further module, the OptionManager, is included in the package and this allows Leisure Systems to customise the software for a particular client when it is installed. Later, a manager may want to change some of these settings, or may ask the support team to make adjustments.

Maintaining software

The term *software maintenance* can easily be misunderstood, perhaps because most people associate maintenance with repairing their house and car. Software applications do sometimes exhibit faults and have to be 'repaired', but that is only a very small part of what we mean by software maintenance.

But the house is not an unhelpful analogy, as home maintenance is not just concerned with repair, but also covers a number of jobs that enable the house to continue to meet the owner's needs. These could include major changes such as installing a new kitchen, converting the loft into a bedroom or building an extension.

When a software application is first acquired it may suit the client's needs exactly. But as time goes on the client may require additional functionality, or may want to run it on a different operating system, or may demand a more up-to-date user interface. External changes may also produce a change in the client's needs; for example, changes in taxation that are announced in the government's Budget have to be reflected in the applications used by tax advisers and accountants.

> Software maintenance is the process of ensuring that a software product continues to meet the needs of end-users.

Changes made to an existing software product are usually known as *upgrades*. Each upgrade should be numbered, so that clients and developers can identify which version they are looking at. So the first version is usually known as version 1.0, and subsequent upgrades as versions 2.0, 3.0 etc. In the case of popular off-the-shelf applications, minor changes are usually issued with version numbers like 3.4, 3.5, or even 3.47. The change from, say, version 3.0 to 4.0 will usually indicate a major redesign of the software, with many new features incorporated.

Sometimes an interim change is made in order to correct an error. This will be provided in the form of a small program to be installed alongside the current version, which will sort out the problem. This is known as a *patch*. A patch is not always the most efficient way of dealing with the error, but it sorts it out temporarily until the next version of the software is released.

Activity

Check all the software that you normally use, and identify which version you are using. You can consider systems software and software tools as well as applications.

Have later versions been produced? If so, how do they improve on the version you use?

Types of software maintenance

Leisure Systems has released many upgrades and patches for ClubManager since it was first written. These have been developed for a number of reasons.

Corrective maintenance

Corrective (or remedial) maintenance is carried out when there are errors in the software. Errors can be of two types. A *programming error* occurs when the programmer has actually made a mistake, but this should be discovered and corrected before the software is released. The kind of error that slips through the testing stage is usually a *logic error*. The program appears on the surface to work correctly but it does not process the data as intended or does not produce the required output. Both types of error are commonly known as *bugs*.

Corrective maintenance is usually handled with patches. The millenium bug (the Year 2000 problem) triggered off widespread corrective maintenance and was largely solved with software patches.

Each time a new version of ClubManager is produced it has a few bugs. This is not supposed to happen, as the software is tested thoroughly inhouse, not just by the software engineers, but also by the training and support staff. But errors do get overlooked, especially when Leisure Systems is in a hurry to get the new version on the market. They always provide free patches to clients. These were provided on disk in the past, but today clients are encouraged to download them from the company's website.

Perfective maintenance

Perfective maintenance turns a good product into a better one. This is done in response to the demands of clients (or potential clients). A new version could make it easier for an end-user to carry out the processes, could include an improved screen design, or could offer more online help. Perfective maintenance does not, however, change the functions that the software carries out.

ClubManager has been through several improvements of this kind. Feedback from customers in the early days suggested that users did not like using the cursor keys to move between choices, and would prefer to select a choice by pressing a single hotkey. Also the screen colours were too bright for lengthy use. The software engineers made some changes and checked them out with one client's end-users before launching the new version.

Adaptive maintenance

Adaptive maintenance covers changes that are made in response to changes in the real world. For example, new legislation may mean that some of the functions, such as a tax calculation, have to be changed. A newly released version of a popular operating system may mean that an application must then be adapted to take advantage of the additional features that it offers. There may be widespread changes in the way that a company operates which will create a demand for adaptations to the software.

When digital cameras became readily available, one of the clients of Leisure Systems remarked that it would be good if they could take a photo of a new member and print it on the membership card. Stephen thought this was an excellent idea and the next upgrade included it as an option in the MemberManager module. That is an example of an application adapting to meet new demands and to take advantage of new technology.

Compatibility

When a new version of an application is released, customers want to be sure that the new version will be *compatible* with the old. You may be familiar with this issue when you install a new version of a word-processor. You expect it to be able to load documents that you wrote using the old version. Normally a software developer would be very foolish to market a new version which did not work with old files. The new version is *backwardly compatible* with the old version.

A problem can arise if you revert to an older version of an application and then try to load a file that was prepared in the newer version. This often causes difficulties. When the older version was developed the programmers could not anticipate the changes that would be made in the next version. The older version is not *forwardly compatible* with the new version.

Monitoring use to identify maintenance needs

Leisure Systems uses a number of methods for finding out what their customers need.

Helpline log

Leisure Systems provides high levels of support to clients. Clients who have taken out a support contract may use the 24-hour helpline to get advice. Every call on this line is logged. Leisure Systems has developed its own helpdesk software, and the person who takes the call records details of the problem and the solution given. Most of the calls are for help with understanding and using existing features of the application, but some of them are asking for functions that are not included in the application. This helpdesk log can be used to identify shortcomings in the application as well as newly emerging needs.

Planned callback

A member of the support team phones each client with a support contract at least once a month to check that everything is still satisfactory. They take the opportunity to ask whether the application does everything they want it to do, and note any suggestions for improvements.

Satisfaction survey

Not all their clients have taken out support contracts, so roughly once a year Leisure Systems posts out a client satisfaction survey to them. This is a questionnaire, which asks the manager to rate the software on such factors as ease of use and functions covered, and then asks what additional functions could be useful. To encourage a high return rate they put all returned questionnaires into a prize draw.

Marketplace analysis

Leisure Systems keeps a careful eye on its competitors, as there are two other rival applications on the market. Since Leisure Systems wants to remain the market leader, it monitors upgrades produced by the other two companies, and tries to keep one step ahead. Leisure Systems also watches out for social trends in the way people spend their leisure time and tries to predict the effect of these changes on clubs.

Sales intelligence

However much it wants to make a profit out of its software, Leisure Systems will not sell it to a club if the application does not meet their needs. It knows that if it did so, the support team would not be able to provide the right level of assistance, and the company's reputation would suffer. But the sales team always report back the reasons for not being able to sell the software. This information is very valuable as it can suggest possible improvements.

Marketing upgrades

An upgrade will not earn Leisure Systems any money until it is sold, so it has several strategies for marketing upgrades.

- *Mailshots*. Upgrades are advertised in a mailshot, which is sent to everyone on the marketing mailing list. This mailing list includes all clients and everyone who has enquired about the application in the past. It also holds the names and addresses of very many clubs across the country who have not yet made contact with Leisure Systems.

- *Press*. As Leisure Systems is selling into a limited market it does not advertise in the general press or even in computer magazines. Instead it restricts its advertisements to trade magazines that are targetted directly at the leisure industry. It also submits copies of its software to relevant publications, in the hope that they will give it a favourable review.

- *Client newsletter*. The sales team at Leisure Systems keeps in touch with all its past clients. They produce an annual newsletter which features a number of the clubs that are successfully using the application. The newsletter also includes profiles of the sales and support teams, and is presented in a friendly, informal manner.

- *Website*. The newsletter, and all correspondence from Leisure Systems, draw attention to the website. The site does not change a great deal, but it does have a useful support section for users. But the main purpose of the website is to market the application. Whenever an upgrade is released, full details are given on the site. Visitors are also able to download a demonstration.

- *Exhibitions*. Leisure Systems puts up a stand at the main trade exhibitions. All visitors to the stand are given a CD-ROM which uses multimedia techniques to explain what the application can do, illustrated by animated screenshots. Visitors are also enticed by a free draw to leave their business cards, and the names and addresses are added to the marketing mailing list.

Creating a maintenance policy

After the first version of the application was successfully released in the 1980s, Stephen Bell at Leisure Systems realised that he would have to develop a *software maintenance policy*. This would cover how frequently upgrades would be released, and the charging policy. After much discussion within the company, Stephen adopted the following standards, which have been updated from time to time:

Patches
- Patches are used for corrective maintenance.
- Patches are provided free to all users and are available for downloading from the website.
- All clients are informed by post when patches are released.

Upgrades
- New versions of the application are issued at intervals of between six months to one year. These address both perfective and adaptive needs.
- All clients with support contracts receive free upgrades. Other clients are charged the market rate.
- Upgrades are distributed on DVD-ROM.
- All upgrades are backwardly compatible.

New modules
- New modules, to cover completely new areas of functionality, are issued on an occasional basis.
- These are marketed to all clients, and are normally supplied at an add-on price.

One change that Leisure Systems had not anticipated in its policy was the introduction of Microsoft® Windows®. The original product was DOS-based. So once Windows® was widely established on PC networks around the country, the company released a Windows® version. This gave Leisure Systems an opportunity to completely rewrite the software, and to incorporate all the additional modules into the main application. This was a major upgrade. Since then the company has launched the bookings module and is currently working on a payroll module.

Two 'laws' of software evolution

As you have seen, applications grow and change in response to changes in the environment in which they are used. In 1980, M. M. Lehman suggested that there are five laws that apply whenever software is developed. The first two laws are worth mentioning here:

1. *Law of continuing change*. A program that is used in a real-world environment necessarily must change or become less and less useful in that environment.

2. *Law of increasing complexity*. As an evolving program changes, its structure becomes more complex unless activities are made to avoid this phenomenon.

Activity

Do you agree with Lehman's first two laws? Can you give examples of software to illustrate these laws?

Solutions for clients

When an organisation decides to acquire a new ICT solution, the description of its needs is often referred to as a 'problem'. This does not necessarily mean that the current system is problematic and causing serious difficulties (although that may indeed be the case). Instead the term is used in much the same way as it is used in mathematics, where a problem is taken to mean a challenge or a puzzle to be solved.

A problem looking for a solution

Whittle Valley Health Club has existed for approximately ten years. The facilities on offer include a swimming pool, multi-gym, squash courts, sauna and a sports hall for team sports and badminton. A number of franchised businesses also operate within the club, including a cafe, sports clinic, hairdresser and beauty therapist. The club is open from 7 am to 9 pm on Monday to Saturday and from 8 am to 6 pm on Sunday.

The manager of Whittle Valley is Winston Hall. He has been very successful in attracting new members of all ages from the town and surrounding villages. But Winston recognises that the local community is changing, and he wants to ensure that the club can respond to increased demand for its services. New younger residents have been moving to the area because of a recent spate of house building. This has provided the area with 600 new houses built on the site of a closed hospital and a transportation depot. The club is likely to expand its membership, and with the introduction of new

facilities, Winston is sure that there will be much to offer the members.

The health club is open only to paid-up members and their guests. Members can use any of the core facilities at no charge, although they do have to pay for any of the services offered by the franchised businesses. Membership is renewed on an annual basis, dated from the month in which a person joined. Members are charged an annual subscription, although they are encouraged to pay by monthly direct debit.

There are eight different categories of membership:

Weekday	(5 day admission, Monday to Friday)
Weekend	(Saturday and Sunday only)
Full Week	(7 day)
Junior Weekday	(5 day)
Junior Weekend	(Saturday and Sunday only)
Junior Full Week	(7 day)
Concession Weekday	(5 day, for the retired and unemployed)
Employee	(7 day)

Anyone under the age of 18 is classed as a Junior member. Each category of membership has a different subscription rate, except for employees who are granted free membership.

The current membership system does not make use of a computer and the tills in operation are the only electronic method of recording income. If members wish to book facilities in advance then they can telephone the club or book on a prior visit and this is entered on a booking sheet.

Each month the membership secretary, Terese Vozeler, writes to all those members whose annual membership is coming to an end. She requests their renewal subscription, which can be paid at the centre or by a cheque in the post. But she also sends them a direct debit form to encourage them to switch to this method of payment. When a member pays by direct debit, Whittle Valley's bank automatically requests the payment each month from the member's bank using BACS, the Bankers' Automated Clearing System.

Terese keeps a club book to record members' names, membership number and subscriptions due. A record of payments is maintained and a receipt and new membership card is either handed to or posted to the member. This is recorded in the club book. When new members join the club they are issued with a form to fill in, asking for their personal details and which category of membership they want.

Terese finds all these tasks time-consuming. She also has other administrative tasks to perform, including organisation of fitness training programmes, and working on the reception desk. She discusses this with Winston, and he agrees that the club needs to make a major investment in ICT. The club does use computers for some tasks, but they need to be integrated into a single management system. The hardware could be upgraded at the same time.

Criteria for selecting a solution

When an organisation decides to introduce a new software application there are certain questions that have to answered early on.

- *Should we use an inhouse or an externally developed solution?* Large organisations, like banks, have their own IT development team. The analysts and programmers work throughout the year maintaining existing applications and developing new ones. Most of their time is spent working on the kinds of applications that are specific to the industry. But even here, the organisation sometimes buys in externally developed software, such as popular office automation applications and standard software tools.

- *Should we buy an off-the-shelf, bespoke or customised solution?* The answer rather depends on whether there are very many other organisations with similar needs. If so, then there is probably an off-the-shelf product already on the market. If the software is going to be unique then a bespoke solution may be the only way of achieving the objectives. Customised solutions usually offer flexible solutions in niche markets.

Cost is also an important factor. Bespoke software can be very expensive as a well-paid professional (or team of professionals) will be working solely on the solution for a considerable time. The costs can run into tens of thousands of pounds, or millions in the case of very large projects. Customised solutions are usually priced at a few thousand pounds, whilst off-the-shelf software is comparatively cheap, usually costing a few hundred pounds, or even less.

Some purchasers prefer to buy customised or off-the-shelf software that has been on the market for some time, as any initial bugs in the application will have been ironed out. But it is also true that each new major upgrade will carry new errors.

Activities

For each of the problems below, discuss which would be more appropriate: (a) an inhouse or externally developed solution, (b) an off-the-shelf, bespoke or customised solution:

- *photo manipulation system for a magazine publisher*

- *financial management for a small manufacturing company*

- *payroll system for a large insurance company*

- *kitchen design system to allow customers to view design before purchase*

- *student enrolment system at a college*

- *statistical analysis tools for a government department.*

Since Whittle Valley Health Club is a relatively small business it cannot afford to employ its own inhouse software developers, so Winston knows he must look for an externally produced solution. The health club cannot afford the fees involved in commissioning a bespoke system, and Winston is not aware of any off-the-shelf packages that would be specific enough for his purposes. He accepts that the best solution will be a customised package.

Winston takes time out to attend a trade show aimed at the leisure industry. He finds three exhibitors who offer ICT solutions for health clubs, and he spends some time talking to the people managing the stands.

At the Leisure Systems stand he meets Charlotte Bone, who explains that she is the Support Supervisor for the company. She demonstrates ClubManager using a full working version of the software. Charlotte listens to Winston and says that he needs a transaction processing system that will handle membership and will check in members as they arrive. She then explains how other modules within ClubManager could be useful to him.

Charlotte wants to convince Winston that ClubManager is the best solution, but she will not try to sell it to him if it is unsuitable. Many new clients contact Leisure Systems as the result of a recommendation from a satisfied customer. The company relies heavily on the level of personal support it gives to clients, so cannot afford to lose credibility by providing a poor service to even one client.

Winston asks about the costs and is given the price list shown in Figure 14.2.

As you saw in Chapter 11, the customer should consider a number of factors before deciding whether to purchase off-the-shelf, customised or bespoke application software. These factors, together with a consideration of cost, also act as useful criteria for deciding *between* competing products.

- *Functionality*. Charlotte has demonstrated to Winston that ClubManager will carry out all the functions associated with membership and admissions. But he has also seen that it can be used to manage sales at the front desk, which would make another task simpler. He is impressed by the large variety of reports that can be generated by the system and thinks that they

ClubManager

'The total management solution for the leisure industry'

ClubManager includes:
    ReceptionManager
    MemberManager
    ShopManager
    ReportManager
    OptionManager
	£925 for first licence at a site
	£155 for each additional licence

Booking module	£195 for first licence at a site £45 for each additional licence
Support contract	£750 per annum for small site (up to 5 machines) £950 for larger sites

Add-ons – hardware and software packages
fully integrated into ReceptionManager
    Membership card printer
    Bar-code reader
    Digital camera
	
	£165
	£125
	£430

Installation and on-site training On-site consultation	£895 (3 days) £395 per day

All prices exclude VAT
Please enquire about our competitive deals for hardware and network solutions
Leisure Systems Ltd
www.leisuresystems.com

Figure 14.2 *A software price list*

will help him to make better management decisions.

- *Quality of the user interface.* Over the years many improvements have been made, in response to users' comments, to ClubManager's user interface. Winston can see that it would be easy for a beginner to learn, and that an experienced user would be able to carry out tasks accurately and rapidly.

- *Support available.* This is a very strong point in ClubManager's favour. Leisure Systems offers a support contract, which covers access to a 24-hour helpline, e-mail support and free upgrades. Members of the support team will visit on-site if necessary. Training is available immediately following installation and whenever it is needed afterwards. Winston believes that a support contract and adequate training are essential.

- *Costs.* Winston has been comparing the costs of the systems marketed by the three companies (including Leisure Systems), always bearing in mind the differences in the functionality offered.

Winston is convinced by what he has seen and believes that ClubManager will be exactly right for Whittle Valley. He leaves his business card with Charlotte, who promises that a member of the sales team will contact him shortly.

Sensible use of an ICT solution

Installation and configuration

A few weeks later, Charlotte Bone, the Support Supervisor at Leisure Systems, arrives at Whittle Valley to oversee the installation of the new system. A new network with six terminals, including a point-of-sale (POS) terminal with cash drawer, has already been set up and tested by a specialist network supplier.

Charlotte starts by installing ClubManager on to the system. She has told Winston that she will need to spend most of the day with him, customising the package to his requirements.

Charlotte first opens the OptionManager module. This presents her with a large number of options, and she works through them, one at a time, explaining their significance to Winston. They begin with the output options. Winston is able to specify the wording that will appear at the top of each screen – Whittle Valley Health Club. This will be printed on each receipt

produced at the POS terminal. Winston also decides what slogan should appear at the bottom of each receipt – 'Keep fit, keep happy'.

The next set of options relate to membership. Charlotte enters the eight categories of membership, and the times each is allowed to visit the club, and the current subscription rates for each. She checks that the member enrolment screen displays the fields that Winston needs. Winston has chosen to buy the digital camera package, so that photos can be taken of new members and included on the card and on-screen. He has also purchased the card printer. Charlotte activates the camera and card printer software, and they both decide on the wording and layout of the membership card.

Winston now has to specify which reports he wants, and these are configured on the system. At this stage he thinks he will need weekly reports on attendance and sales, and monthly membership reports. He also wants to be able to check, each month, which members are behind with their subscriptions. Charlotte sets these reports up for him and shows him how to generate his own reports in future.

Finally, Charlotte takes him through all the security aspects of ClubManager. First she sets up named users on the system. Each of the employees at Whittle Valley is given a username and password. She also creates a username called 'Boris' which can be used by any temporary agency staff. She is then able to assign access privileges to each of these users. For each module she can specify whether the user has 'no rights', 'read-only rights' or 'all rights'. She can also specify rights for individual tasks within each module. The reception staff have all rights to most of the ReceptionManager module, but when it comes to the MemberManager module they have read-only rights to most of the tasks apart from the one that deals with enrolling a new member, where they have all rights. Winston is the only person at Whittle Valley with any rights of access to the OptionManager.

Another security issue concerns backups. Charlotte advises Winston to create a backup every night, using a tape unit on the network server. They set the backup for 3 am every morning. Charlotte reminds Winston that he will have to change the tape every morning and to rotate the usage of the seven tapes that he has bought. All the tapes should be stored in a safe.

Although ClubManager is run as a real-time direct access system, it can be used from time to time to do a complete 'sweep' of all the members' records, rather like traditional batch processing. Once a month it checks all the members and identifies those who pay by direct debit. It then automatically passes the direct debit instructions to BACS. During the sweep it also picks out those members whose subscriptions are due in the next month, and prints reminder letters. Charlotte and Winston agree that this action should take place at 11.55 pm on the 28th of each month.

Activities

1. *Can you suggest some other ways in which ClubManager could be customised to meet the specific needs of a client?*

2. *Why is it necessary to set access privileges for different users? What access rights should Terese Vozeler, the membership secretary, be given?*

3. *Why does the sweep of all the members take place before the nightly backup?*

For the next one and a half days, Charlotte trains the rest of the staff in the use of the new system. Terese is particularly pleased with the way in which it seems to be working, but some of the receptionists complain that the membership cards use too small a font and are difficult to read quickly. Charlotte changes some of the settings in the OptionManager module to meet their objections.

Going live

Finally, on the third afternoon, the ClubManager system goes live, and Charlotte checks that everything is working as expected and that all the staff are happy with it. She then obtains a report from ClubManager listing all the options that she and Winston have set up in the OptionManager. She gives a copy to him and keeps one herself.

Before she leaves she asks Winston to sign a form stating that he is satisfied with the way the system is working. The list of option settings enables them both to track any problems that might develop later on. It also helps to determine where the responsibility lies for any mistakes.

After giving some final instructions to Winston, Charlotte leaves reminding him that he can call the support team at any time. He does call them, every day to begin with, but less frequently as time passes. Each time he calls, the support team log the nature of the problem and list the action that they advise him to take. Winston also logs all these calls, and prints out the options report whenever he changes an option. All these reports are dated, and he stores them safely.

Although Winston is not an ICT professional, he does have the level of competence with computers that you would expect of a manager these days. But it came as quite a shock to him to realise that he would be acting as systems administrator at Whittle Valley!

In practice, he does not have to do anything to the network itself as the network supplier is under contract to maintain it, but he does have to carry out some systems administration tasks in relation to the ClubManager software. All these tasks are performed through the OptionManager module. He now knows how to use it to change the content and appearance of screens, reports, membership cards and receipts. He can change the frequency and timing of backups, and he can add new users to the system and allocate access rights to them.

Leisure Systems Ltd provides an excellent support service, so whenever Winston needs help, or forgets how to do something, he gives them a call or e-mails them. He knows that although Charlotte and the other members of the support team will help him as much as they can, nevertheless, as manager he is ultimately responsible for the wellbeing of his staff and members.

CHAPTER 15

Empowering the end-user

This chapter uses the context of an ICT solution provider to explore how the end-user can be helped to make the most effective use of an application.

It will describe:

● how end-users can be trained to use an application

● the qualities of good end-user documentation.

The chapter covers the following Learning Outcomes in the specification:

L.O. 2.4 Understand the user training requirements for a developed ICT-based solution to a defined problem

L.O. 2.5 Understand what user documentation is required for a developed ICT-based solution to a defined problem

Who is the end-user?

The end-user is the person who uses an application, such as a bank assistant, a ticket clerk at a railway station, an administrator in a large organisation or an employee at a call centre. Many managers are also end-users as well. End-users may have general IT skills, but they are not usually expected to have any technical skills with computers.

The success of many organisations depends on how well the end-users carry out their tasks. In order to enable their employees to achieve the best they can with the software they are using, organisations invest time and money in training. They also need to ensure that the applications they use are supported with adequate user documentation.

In this chapter you will *not* be looking at the training for systems administrators, which is covered in Chapter 5.

Training

A software application is only as good as the people who use it.

If you have a part-time job working in a shop you will probably have been trained to use the electronic point of sale (EPOS) terminal. You will be the end-user of the software application which drives the EPOS, and the purpose of the training is to familiarise you with the various options and to make you efficient (that is, fast and accurate) in its use. This training may well have consisted of a brief introduction by the supervisor, or you may have been sent to a training centre for a few days.

There are, in fact, many ways of providing training for end-users, and the choice depends on the complexity of the software and the initial competence of the trainees.

New employees are normally given an induction programme which introduces them to the organisation and includes all the training they need to become immediately effective. More experienced end-users may need refresher training from time to time or may be ready to embark on advanced training. When a new software application is introduced then all the relevant employees will have to be trained, probably at the same time.

Learning objectives

Training should always be planned in the light of *learning objectives*. These are statements of what the training should achieve. That is, they state the actual skills that the trainee should have acquired by the end of the training period. For example, a training programme for new sales staff in a shop might have learning objectives to enable an employee:

– to log on and log off at any EPOS
– to process normal sales and returns
– to process cash, cheque, debit and credit card payments.

A training programme should also state the *prior knowledge and skills*, if any, that the trainee should have before embarking on it.

Often the learning objectives include descriptions of intended *outcomes*, which is the evidence that the trainee has met the learning objective. The training could be judged to be successful if the trainee passes a test, or is observed to use the application correctly. The learning objectives for a training programme for sales staff could include a checklist like the one in Figure 15.1.

When training is complete it can be *evaluated*. The trainee can be given an evaluation feedback form which asks questions about the usefulness and effectiveness of the training received, and its success in achieving the learning objectives.

Activity

Have you ever been trained to use a software application? If so, identify the circumstances and the learning objectives.

```
Name of employee _____

Name of trainer _____

Date of training _____


Employee can

☐   log on successfully

☐   log off successfully

☐   process a normal sale of several items

☐   process a cash payment

☐   process a cheque payment

☐   process a debit card payment

☐   process a credit card payment

☐   process the return of an item


Signed _____(Trainer)

Signed _____(Trainee)
```

Figure 15.1 *Sample checklist for induction training of sales staff on EPOS*

Training providers

Formal training

End-user training can be provided by the *software supplier*. This may be an extra cost, or may be included in the total cost of the package provided by a solutions provider.

A organisation may employ its own *inhouse trainers*. These will be qualified and experienced teachers who will themselves be highly competent at using the applications. When the task to be learnt is relatively straightforward, a colleague who is not a qualified trainer will show the trainee what to do.

There are also a number of *training companies* that offer short training courses. These can be provided on-site, or alternatively off-site at the training company's premises. This kind of training is limited to standard applications.

Informal training

In addition to the planned types of training, end-users may learn skills from a number of informal sources. They may join an Internet-based newsgroup or mailing list dedicated to the needs of end-users of a particular application. This will offer them the opportunity to post comments and to share their problems and expertise with others.

There are also many books and magazines on the market which provide advice and guidance to users. Some of these are designed as self-teaching training courses.

Training methods

Group training

This is traditional classroom-based learning, usually in groups of no more than six trainees. One trainer will use a mixture of teaching techniques – presentations, demonstrations, handouts, individual help, exercises and tests – to ensure that all the members of the group achieve the learning objectives. Group training requires a skilled trainer if all the members of the group are to succeed.

Individual training

Sometimes one-to-one training is the most appropriate method of training, especially if the skill is very difficult to learn. One-to-one training is necessarily more costly per person than group training. Intense tuition sessions will often be interspersed with periods of self-teaching.

Self-teaching

The trainee is given training materials and expected to work through them at his or her own pace. This does mean that training can be fitted around other commitments, but the trainee can feel isolated. Self-teaching methods work best when the trainee has access to a helpline or similar source of personal support.

Training materials

There are many training materials that can be used in different combinations for group training, individual training and self-teaching purposes. Here is a selection.

Training manuals

Books have traditionally been used to take the trainee through a training programme, step by step. The trainee can easily refer back to earlier sections, can repeat sections that are difficult, and omit sections that are already understood. Training manuals are most

successful when their intended outcomes closely match the learning objectives of the training programme. They should also state the prior knowledge and skills which it is assumed the reader has.

Video

Non-interactive media such as video (or audio) tape can still be a useful means of demonstrating how to use an application. A video can be viewed over and over again.

Computer-based training

This uses multimedia techniques to demonstrate skills to the end-users and to test their progress. Normally the tutorial is provided on CD-ROM or similar, but data about an individual user is also kept on a file. Information about the training outcomes of trainees can be reported to a supervisor or trainer.

The main advantage of computer-based training is that the system is interactive, and can respond in an individual way to each trainee. Some widely used packages include tutorial materials.

Online training

Trainees practise with a training copy of the real application. This will contain dummy data in a database, but will work exactly like the real application. The training copy will be stored separately from the real application so there will be no danger of the training exercises affecting the live data.

Training programmes

A training programme can be planned using whatever combination of training providers, training methods and training materials seems most appropriate. One key factor in deciding the structure of a training programme will be whether the application is off-the-shelf, bespoke or customised.

- There are very many end-users for *off-the-shelf applications*, so it is not surprising that there are many ways of learning to use them. Training companies usually concentrate on providing training for popular packages; their training courses will have been finely tuned over time and will usually provide a cost-effective solution. Training materials are readily available for these packages, and tutorial books can be bought in high street stores.

- When a *bespoke application* is commissioned, the initial provision of training by the software provider is normally built into the contract. This will usually be carried out on-site, and will draw on any of the methods and materials that have been mentioned above. If new employees join later, the organisation will usually provide inhouse training – their trainers will have been trained themselves by the software provider.

- Suppliers of *customised solutions* see training as an essential part of the service they offer, so they tailor their training programmes to meet the needs of their clients.

As you saw in Chapter 14, Leisure Systems Ltd sells customised solutions to health clubs and leisure centres. It offers its clients a three-day installation and training package for its main product, ClubManager. This offer, not surprisingly, is taken up by all the new clients. The first day is used for installation and customisation. The next two days are spent training the staff. Where possible this includes a period when the system goes live.

Charlotte Bone installed ClubManager at Whittle Valley Health Club and then customised it with the advice of the club's manager, Winston Hall. This was also a period of training for Winston in the systems administration tasks for which he would be responsible.

Charlotte now makes a complete copy of ClubManager, with all the customised settings, and installs it as a training copy on the network.

Charlotte then spends one day training the reception desk staff, accessing the training copy through terminals in the back office. She trains half the staff in the morning and the other half in the afternoon. She could not train all of them at once, as there must always be at least one person on duty at reception, and she never trains more than five people at once, anyway. Terese Vozeler, the membership secretary, joined one of the groups.

Some months ago Charlotte revised the training programme and she rewrote the handouts that she now gives to the staff. She now works her way through a familiar sequence of demonstrations and exercises. She covers the processes for checking in a member by scanning the bar-code on their membership card, viewing information about a member, recording and passing on messages to a member, enrolling a new member, using the digital camera and printing a membership card. She also shows how to record the sale of items that are sold from the reception desk.

Throughout the training session she encourages the users to use the Help file supplied with the application. This is styled as a tutorial, but also has a troubleshooting section and a searchable index.

Once the ReceptionManager module has been understood by the end-users, Leisure Systems finds that most clubs, like Whittle Valley, are confident enough to carry out their own training for any new employees. However, clients may then choose to buy in further training in the other modules from Leisure Systems. Often the manager of a health club will want to learn more about the options in the built-in report generator, ReportManager.

Activity

Outline a training programme for each of the three contexts below. You should include:

- *the learning objectives*
- *the training provider*
- *the training method*
- *the training materials.*

1. *A medical charity which employs around 30 staff in its head office decides to upgrade to the latest version of a popular office product, which includes word-processing, spreadsheet and e-mail applications. This will be the first upgrade for five years, and they will be 'jumping' several versions of the software.*

2. *A chain of estate agents runs a customised version of a package in all its branches. The application is used by the agents and records the details of houses for sale, and matches suitable properties to prospective customers. New agents need to learn how to use the software.*

3. *A multinational manufacturing company has a number of assembly plants in this country where televisions are built from imported components. They have recently contracted out a large software project. This is for an application that will track each component from its original manufacture abroad to its use in a finished television and then on to its eventual sale. All the supervisors will have to be trained in its use.*

User documentation

User documentation is a manual that is provided for the end-user of an application. It should not be confused with the documentation for a systems administrator.

When you purchase an application for a home PC, you usually receive some documentation with it. The owner of a standalone PC acts both as systems administrator and application end-user, so the documentation will usually contain material intended for both. Unfortunately, it is often not easy to distinguish between the two.

The documentation for the systems administrator should include the software licence, technical information about the system requirements and instructions for installing the software. The documentation for the end-user should include instructions on how to run and use the application.

The format of user documentation

'Documentation' traditionally referred to printed material. Today, much that we would call documentation is supplied in a paperless form.

- *Bound books or booklets*. Users may write notes on books but, like all paper-based products, they are susceptible to physical damage. Books are portable, and can be passed from one user to another, but as a result they can easily be mislaid. The production costs of books are quite high, so it is often not possible to provide a copy for each user. Books cannot be updated easily.

- *Ring-bound sheets*. Ring books have all the advantages and most of the disadvantages of bound books, but can be updated easily if corrections have to be made or when new versions are produced. This is the preferred form of paper-based documentation for bespoke and customised applications. The documentation is divided into sections and the pages are independently numbered in each section. New pages or sections can be inserted, along with a revised contents page, without disturbing other sections. End-users can be informed when new pages are available and these can be distributed across the Internet.

- *CD/DVD-ROM*. The documentation can be supplied on the same medium as the software itself. This is a very cheap means of distribution.

The end-user can view the documentation on screen, or can print out a paper-based copy.

- *Help files integrated into the application*. Most applications today provide on-screen help which can be accessed through a Help menu. Normally this consists of an introduction to the facilities of the application, presented in sections rather like a book. The contents can be searched using an index. Some Help systems include an interactive tutorial (that is, training) as well. Help pages usually use hypertext conventions, with hyperlinks linking one page with another. Some are developed in a Web format.

- *Web-based help*. Help pages can be placed on the supplier's website, and these can contain the latest versions of the documentation. The link to the website is usually given on the Help menu. If the user is permanently online to the Internet, they may not even be aware that they are viewing Help pages on the Internet rather than contained within the application. In future it is very likely that most Help facilities will be provided in this way.

Activity

What format is used for the user documentation of the applications that you use? Consider leisure as well as business applications.

Most of the software that you use will be off-the-shelf applications. Bespoke and customised solutions require user documentation as well, and it will have to be prepared to reflect the very specific way in which the software is to be used.

Stephen Bell, the Managing Director and founder of Leisure Systems Ltd, has always recognised the importance of providing good, clear user documentation to clients. There is an interesting relationship between the contents of the user documentation and the use of the helpline. Mistakes or omissions in the documentation result in an over-use of the helpline; but an analysis of the use of the helpline helps Stephen to identify shortcomings in the user documentation which can then be corrected.

Producing user documentation for a customised solution is not as easy, or as cheap, as producing it for an off-the-shelf application. Leisure Systems provides extensive Help facilities within the application and encourages all the end-users to become familiar with the contents.

Some of Leisure Systems' clients also ask for customised printed user documentation. Stephen addressed this problem some years ago, and worked with his support and training team to produce a set of templates for ClubManager. These covered the effects of all the possible settings in the OptionManager module. They also described all the report formats that could be produced. The client arranges for a consultancy day on-site with Charlotte, or one of her colleagues. She then uses these templates to construct and print the sheets for a user manual that exactly matches the customisation of the software.

The structure of user documentation

Whatever format is employed, user documentation will normally contain some or all of these features:

- *Contents*. This provides an overview of the user documentation, with an indication of what is contained in each section. Users may want to read the documentation in the sequence in which it is presented, or may wish to browse, so the contents page should be suitably informative.

- *Description*. This should describe what the application is designed to do, and who should use it.

- *'How to' sections*. These should be systematic instructions for using the software, starting with the most used functions and progressing to the more advanced features or less used functions. The instructions should contain screenshots which show clearly what a user has to do at each stage. Users who have not been given initial training may use these sections to familiarise themselves with the application.

- *Reference section*. This should be a mini-encyclopaedia of all the facilities in the application. This section will mainly be used by experienced users.

- *Troubleshooting*. This section provides the user with help in solving some of the problems that may occur. It begins with the problem, and works back to the solution. This section may also contain a list of all the error messages that may appear when using the application, with advice about what they mean and what the user should do.

- *Index*. A good index is invaluable in helping the user to find what they are looking for. It should always contain the reference to the first time a technical term is used, as well as all related entries.

- *Search*. This facility can be incorporated only into computer-based documentation. It allows the user to open a Find dialogue box in order to enter a term that they want to locate in the documentation.

The customised documentation provided by Leisure Systems to some of its clients includes both user and systems administrator documentation. The 'How to' part of the user documentation is divided into sections corresponding to the application modules. As the documentation is provided in loose-leaf format, each user can be given the documentation for the modules that they use.

Criteria for appraising user documentation

User documentation is essentially a business document, not a technical manual. It should be written for a real user to use – that is, someone whose main job is to carry out the tasks required by their employer. Most end-users, quite properly, simply see the software application as a tool they use to do their work. They do not wish to know how it works. But they do need to know how the functions in the application relate to the tasks they have to do. These real-world tasks should be the starting point for any user documentation.

User documentation can be judged by answering a number of questions:

Design and layout
- Is it easy to read? (This refers to font colours and sizes, not the language.)
- Are the contents listed in sufficient detail?
- Are the pages numbered properly?
- Are the sections easy to locate?

Content
- Does it include all the sections listed earlier?
- Does it show users how to carry out their work tasks using the application?
- Does it help a new user to get started?
- Is it easy for an experienced user to find what they want?
- Does it cover all the functions in the application?
- Is the language suitable for its audience (not too chatty, and not too technical)?

Empowering the end-user

- Are there enough illustrations of screen and printed output?
- Are the illustrations clear?
- Does the troubleshooting section cover all the problems the user might meet?
- Is the index comprehensive?

Activity

Collect examples of user documentation and use the questions above to appraise them. You might like to score and rank each example.

CHAPTER 16

Programming an application

This chapter explores some issues surrounding the programming of off-the-shelf applications, in the context of a large software house.

It will describe:

- how an off-the-shelf application is developed by a software house

- the software tools used by programmers

- the range of file types that can be used in programmed solutions.

The chapter covers the following Technical Knowledge topics in the specification:

T2.1.1   Languages and translation
T2.1.2   Load libraries
T2.3.1   File types

It also covers a related topic from one of the A2 units. This topic is better dealt with alongside related topics here, rather than in isolation later:

T5.3   File processing

Developing off-the-shelf applications

Off-the-shelf applications can be purchased through high street computer stores, through computer magazines or on the Internet. These range from games, through lifestyle applications (e.g. garden design) to reference materials (e.g. route finders). The major office automation packages, such as those from Microsoft and Lotus, are all off-the-shelf products.

These applications are often very large, and are the result of many years of development time. A substantial number of employees may be involved in developing and marketing an application, including software designers, programmers, testers, graphic designers, technical authors and marketing staff. By using many people on a product, each contributing months of their time, the actual time taken to produce an application may be reduced to a relatively short period. These people will use a variety of IT applications and software tools, so systems administrators will be employed to support all of them.

As the development costs will be high, off-the-shelf applications have to be widely marketed in order to get a return on the investment.

Off-the-shelf applications will be very thoroughly tested before being launched. At an early stage the programmers will produce a *prototype* of the final application. The marketing staff will test out the prototype with a selected group of typical end users, and will note their comments and suggestions.

Application development strategies

Most off-the-shelf applications are implemented using a programming language, instead of an application generator. There are many advantages in this:

- Programming languages give the programmer total flexibility in the design of the user interface. In comparison, most application generators allow the developer to create windows-style user interfaces, which are very satisfactory for normal office applications. But other applications may be better implemented with a less standard 'look' to the screens. For example, many multimedia products, like encyclopedias, and almost all games, have their own design styles and layouts which do not correspond to the Windows conventions.
- Programming languages also allow the programmer to implement a very wide range of functions.
- The programmer can, as you will see later, choose how data will be stored and accessed in data files.
- The code produced by programming languages can be optimised to speed up the processing. This is particularly important in real-time systems, such as booking systems, and in software that relies heavily on graphics, such as games.

Large projects are normally developed in a *modular style*. That means that at the design stage the application is broken down into a set of independent modules. Each module is then developed and tested by a single programmer, and all the modules are linked together as they become ready.

You saw in Chapter 14 that the ClubManager application is built up using several distinct modules. Those modules could themselves be constructed out of smaller modules. Each module and sub-module was programmed in the programming language Delphi.

Software houses

A software house is a business that specialises in producing software. These may be bespoke systems, or off-the-shelf packages, but the main activity of the software house will be the creation and marketing of software.

'Full Solutions Ltd' is a software house that has specialised in producing large applications for public bodies such as local authorities and hospitals. A couple of years ago it took on a substantial contract for Wessex County Hospital. The project covered the provision of a booking system for patient operations and a bed allocation system. As this was the first stage of a major effort to modernise the hospital, Full Solutions is now hoping to win further contracts to supply systems to support payroll for all staff, stock control for equipment and drugs, and for temperature, humidity and atmosphere control of the buildings.

Ian McPherson works for Full Solutions as a project manager and he was given the task of overseeing the Wessex County project. Ian was trained as a software engineer and joined Full Solutions ten years ago as a programmer. He was proficient in a number of programming languages, such as C++ and Pascal. Following a successful period as a software designer, he moved into project management. He now leads the team assigned to a project, coordinates their work and ensures that all the jobs are completed on time.

Developing applications using a programming language

At AS level in this subject you are not required to have any skills in programming. If you continue with the A2 modules then you will be expected to program using an event-driven programming language, such as Visual Basic®.

At this stage you do need to have some appreciation of the activities involved in programming an application, and the implications for the maintenance of the software. You also need to be aware of the implications for systems administrators, both at the software house and at the client company.

Programming languages

Full Solutions Ltd, like many other software houses, uses programming languages to develop its software. The programmers between them have skills in a number of programming languages and for each project they select the one that is most appropriate to the task. The end-users of their applications will be completely unaware of the programming language used to develop the software.

A program, as mentioned before, is a series of instructions to a computer system. The instructions are often written as statements in a programming language which bears some resemblance to ordinary English. The central processing unit (CPU) of a computer runs a program by loading each instruction in turn from internal memory into the control unit, then executing it.

Programming languages go back almost to the beginning of computer history in the 1940s, but not quite. Before programming languages came along computer operators still had to make a computer carry out a series of instructions. How did they manage it?

The actual program instructions stored in memory are in a pure binary form, known as *machine-code*. Each machine-code instruction is represented by a specific binary code. An instruction code uses up one or more bytes, and each byte consists of a sequence of eight binary values, which we usually represent as 0 or 1. It is possible for a programmer to learn all the binary codes for all the instructions, but this is not very easy. Before programming languages were invented that is exactly how programmers did write their programs.

The first programming languages were very simple and replaced each machine-code instruction with a program code, which consisted of a number or a couple of characters that were easier to remember than the binary machine codes. The programmer was able to enter the program codes in this format, which became known as an *assembly language*. Assembly languages are also known as *low-level languages*.

One of the problems with machine code is that each type of processor has its own individual set of codes, so that programmers who worked on different processors had to learn different machine codes for each. Assembly languages made this task a little easier, but there were still different codes, and hence different assembly languages, for each processor.

The programs written in an assembly language have to be translated into machine code. The translation was carried out by the very first software tool, known as an *assembler*.

As more people began to use computers and the demands for commercial software grew, new programming languages were invented. These tended to use ordinary English words such as IF, BEGIN and REPEAT, and to use familiar mathematical operators

like + and -, so that the program code became more readable. At the same time, the simple one-to-one correspondence between the machine-code instructions and the program code broke down.

Program code today consists of a series of statements that look quite like English, and each statement corresponds to several machine-code instructions. These languages are called *high-level languages*, and you may be familiar with the names of some of them: COBOL, FORTRAN, BASIC, Pascal, C, C++, Java, Visual Basic® and Delphi.

Activities

1. *Find out about the history of some well-known programming languages. When did they first appear? What kind of software is developed with each one?*

2. *Check through job advertisements to discover which languages are most in demand today.*

Programs written in a high-level language still have to be translated into machine code before they can be used. The software tools that carry out the translation are known as *compilers* and *interpreters*.

Compilers and interpreters translate the program code written in a high-level language into the machine code of a particular processor. But a programmer can choose which processor to use and can select the correct compiler or interpreter for that processor. This means that the program code is portable from one processor to another, provided the right compiler or interpreter is available. The programming language itself is *processor independent*.

High-level languages are much easier for a programmer to use than low-level languages. Nevertheless assembly languages are still in use, as they can be used to produce very efficient, or *optimised*, machine code. The programmer has far greater control over where data is to be stored whilst a program is running, and this can speed up the execution.

Once a program has been translated into machine code it will run on any computer that uses the same processor. In practise, that means any member of a family of processors. Generally speaking a program compiled for one of the Intel® Pentium® processors will run on any processor in the Pentium series, and will also run on any other make of processor that is compatible with the Pentium series.

When a user executes (runs) a program, the machine code is loaded into memory and the instructions are executed one by one. At this stage it is impossible to tell whether the original program was developed in a low-level language or a high-level language, and if the latter was used it is impossible to determine which language was used. It is not necessary for the user to have a copy of the software tools in order to run the program.

Software tools and programming environments

We have met three software tools so far: *assembler, compiler* and *interpreter*. There are a number of other software tools that a programmer will use; these include an *editor, debugger* and *link loader*.

A *programming environment* is a collection of software tools that can be used by a programmer to write and test a program. A programming environment will always include, as a minimum, an editor and a translator (compiler, interpreter or assembler).

When a programmer writes a program there are several steps that have to be followed. We will start by exploring the development of an application using a high-level language compiler (interpreters are described later).

There are three main steps to be followed in order to create a program, and these are illustrated in Figure 16.1.

Step 1: Use the editor to create source (program) code

Source code is the term used to describe the program-code file that is produced in the editor. Look again at this example of program code written in the programming language Pascal:

```
PROGRAM Average(input, output);
VAR
  ThisMark, TotalMarks, NumberOfStudents, Count : INTEGER;
  AverageMark : REAL;
BEGIN
  TotalMarks := 0;
  writeln('How many students are in the class?');
  readln(NumberOfStudents);
  FOR Count := 1 TO NumberOfStudents DO
  BEGIN
    writeln('Enter the mark obtained by the next student');
    readln(ThisMark);
    TotalMarks := TotalMarks + ThisMark;
  END;
  AverageMark := TotalMarks / NumberOfStudents;
  Writeln('The average mark is ', AverageMark:5:2)
END.
```

Each line in this program is a Pascal *statement*.

The source code is saved as an ordinary text file, consisting of no more than the ASCII codes for each of the characters used.

An editor is a simple word-processor which allows the programmer to enter the text and to cut and paste sections of it. It usually includes a Find function, because programs can be very long and the programmer may not remember where statements are located. An editor does not need to provide the page and font formatting functions that are to be found in a full word-processor, although, the tab key may be used to lay out the program on the page.

Step 2: Use the compiler to translate the source code into object (machine) code

Object code is the machine-code file produced by a compiler. The compiler analyses the source-code file statement by statement and produces a new file which

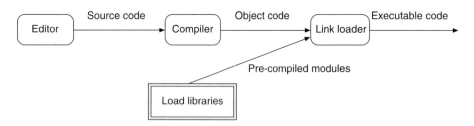

Figure 16.1 *Creating a program*

contains all the machine-code instructions in their binary format. This object code is normally unreadable by people.

The compiler goes through two stages:

- *Syntax analysis*. Syntax means *grammar*. Each statement in the source code is checked to see whether it is a legal (grammatical) statement in the language. The programmer may have made a typing error when editing the source code and this will be picked up at the syntax analysis stage. Or the programmer could have made a genuine mistake and entered a statement that did not match the rules (syntax) of the language. In either case, the compiler stops and reports the error to the programmer, who can then correct it and compile the source code again.

- *Code generation*. If the source code passes through the syntax analysis stage without any errors being detected, it is then converted to machine (object) code at the code generation stage.

Step 3: Use the link loader to combine the object code with pre-compiled modules and produce executable code

Applications often consists of several modules. Each of these modules may themselves contain a number of smaller modules. Within a program, links are made to the required modules.

Sometimes a programmer will find that the same modules are used over and over again in different applications. For example, the common interface units in Microsoft® Office are all modules that are used more than once. In another context a programmer may find that the code for, say, sorting a file by the record key is needed in several quite distinct programs. It makes sense, therefore, to create this as a module and then include the module whenever it is needed in a program.

Re-usable modules like these are written, tested and compiled. They are then stored with other pre-compiled modules and made easily available to programmers. The collection of pre-compiled modules is known as a *load library*.

Programming environments often provide the programmer with a set of load libraries for them to use. Programmers can also create their own libraries.

The link loader follows the links to the modules that are to be included in a program. It then combines the object code produced by the compiler with the object code of the pre-compiled modules. The final version of the machine code is now complete and can be executed on its own, which is why it is called executable code.

Activity

You may not yet have realised that the application generators in the Microsoft® Office suite all include a programming environment. You can enter the programming environment through Word, Excel, PowerPoint® or Access. It includes an editor, a Visual Basic® compiler and a debugger.

Have a look at the Visual Basic® programming environment in Office. The way in which you can enter the programming environment depends on which version of the software you are running, but you normally go through the Tools and Macro menus.

Find out what the editor, compiler and debugger offer to the programmer.

Compilers and interpreters

The compiler is the most commonly used type of translator, but sometimes an interpreter is used instead.

The main feature of an interpreter is that it translates the program code at run time – that is, when the program is executed. It does not translate and save the whole program in machine code, as a compiler does.

When a program is executed using an interpreter, the source code is loaded into memory. The first program code statement is compiled into machine-code and is immediately executed. Then the second statement is compiled and executed, and so on, until the program is completed.

The process of alternating between compiling and executing means that the program runs very slowly in comparison with executing a compiled machine code program. This effect is particularly marked if sections of the program code are repeated over and over again. For example, look at this fragment of the Pascal program:

```
FOR Count := 1 TO NumberOfStudents DO
BEGIN
   writeln('Enter the mark obtained by the next student');
   readln(ThisMark);
   TotalMarks := TotalMarks + ThisMark;
END;
```

The statements between BEGIN and END are repeated for each of the students in the list. The interpreter compiles these statements each time, so if there are 30 students, each of these statements will be compiled 30 times. This considerably extends the time taken to execute the program.

You will see that in order to run a program in this way the end-user must have access to a copy of the interpreter from their machine.

With so many disadvantages, you may wonder why an interpreter is used at all. In fact, it is a very useful tool in two contexts.

- Interpreters are sometimes used when people are learning a programming language. The student starts by writing a program in the editor. If a compiler is then used, the student will probably be presented with a long list of syntax errors, and these will all have to be corrected before the program can be compiled successfully. If an interpreter is used the program can actually be executed right up to the point where the first error occurs. This makes it much easier for the student to check how the program is behaving. The programming language BASIC was designed for beginners, and has always been used with an interpreter.

- An interpreter can be built into a debugger, which is a software tool that allows the programmer to identify and correct all the errors (bugs) in the program. These days, most BASIC and Visual Basic® programming environments include both an interpreter (debugger) and a compiler. They allow the programmer to use an interpreter whilst developing the program code; when the program is finished it can then be compiled into a complete standalone machine-code version.

Apart from these two circumstances it is normally preferable to use a compiler.

Implications of using load libraries

At Full Solutions, substantial libraries of pre-compiled modules have been developed over time. Some of these modules were supplied along with the programming environments, some have been specially purchased, whilst many others have been developed by the programmers themselves. These have all been documented so that all the programmers know what is available.

All modules, like all other compiled programs, are compiled to run on a specific processor. It is possible to use a cross-compiler which will run on one machine but produce machine code that will run on a different processor. This means that modules can be created for a variety of processors. These can then be used to create different versions of an application to run on different hardware platforms.

Like all software, load libraries have to be maintained. New modules are added to meet new requirements. New versions are created for new processors. Old modules developed for obsolete systems are discarded.

Susan Edwards is the systems administrator at Full Solutions, and she understands the needs of programmers very well. She ensures that all the load libraries are stored correctly and that all the programmers have access rights to them. When a programmer wants to make a link within a program to a pre-compiled module, they will include the full pathname of the module, in order for the link loader to locate it. Susan knows it is important that she does not move the load libraries to a new directory, or they will appear to the link loader to be 'lost'.

A mass market enterprise

For some time Ian McPherson has been suggesting to his boss, Jane Winter, that Full Solutions Ltd should consider entering the mass market with an off-the-shelf application. She agreed, in principle, and Ian has been casting around for the 'killer' application that would make Full Solutions' name.

Ian has maintained his contact with the Head of Administration at Wessex County Hospital, Peter Harris. Peter has been applying for grant funding to subsidise a new fitness programme for the over-50s.

The idea is that by encouraging a healthy lifestyle in members of the local community, the demands on some of the hospital services will be reduced. The participants would agree to attend at least once a week, when their fitness would be monitored by physiotherapists and nutritionists and a programme of exercise and diet would be suggested.

Peter had been very impressed by the work done by Full Solutions, so when the funding comes through he contacts Ian again. Peter wants to know whether it would be possible to produce an application that could be used by each of the participants on their weekly visit. They would start by answering, on screen, a set of questions about their eating, drinking and smoking habits. The medical staff would then measure and enter pulse rate, blood pressure, weight and other data. Ideally the system would then print out a fitness analysis, a recommended diet and an exercise programme.

Ian knows that this is possible, but he can see that the application could have greater relevance. So he suggests that Full Solutions and Wessex County collaborate in producing an application that could be used at many hospitals and clinics. Peter thinks this is an excellent idea. He has read that the liaison between software houses and medical centres is common in the USA and is building up significantly in the United Kingdom.

When Ian goes back to his office he discusses the proposal with Jane Winter. Jane can see even wider uses, and that health clubs, sports clubs, schools and leisure centres might well be interested in buying this type of software. She realises that here is their opportunity to invest in a project which would allow them to enter the mass marketplace with a specific off-the-shelf software package. Ian is given the job of managing the project.

Data files

Files fall into two categories: *program files* and *data files*. You met the different types of program file earlier, and we will now concentrate on data files. When a program is executed it may well create one or more data files. For example, a word-processing application creates a data file that we normally call a document; a game may create a file containing the score and position of the player.

Back at Full Solutions, the fitness software project is now under way, with a working title of 'Fitness Matters'. The overall software design has been drawn up, and the programmers have been briefed.

Kannoush Amani is one of the programmers in the Fitness Matters team. He has been asked to develop the module that handles all the individual records – that is, the personal and health data about each individual who participates in the fitness programme. When the Fitness Matters application is run, this dataset will be stored in a data file.

The application will allow users to process the data in a number of ways. For example, they will be able to view and update the data, to analyse the data statistically and to print out a variety of reports about individuals and groups. For this to be possible, Kannoush has to consider what kind of storage medium to use, how the data files will be structured and how this will affect the ways in which the data can be processed.

Storage media

The medium in which a file is to be stored may limit the processing that can be done with it. There are two main types of media in use today.

Serial-access storage medium

This normally refers to magnetic tape. When a data file is stored on tape the data on it can be read only in the order in which it is stored, starting at the beginning and working through to the end. This is very similar to audio or video; if you want to listen to a particular track on a tape, or you want to watch a specific portion of a recorded TV programme, you have to work your way through all the recorded parts of the tape that precede it. This is true, even if you do fast-forward through the tape. Data is stored on magnetic tape in a similar fashion.

Magnetic tape is used for a number of IT applications. It is best suited to applications which require very fast scans of a complete set of data. It is normally used when the amount of data is large and speed of processing is important. A typical use might be for a monthly payroll run in a large organisation, or the nightly account update process at a bank. Tape is also commonly used for backup files, as the data can be copied very rapidly.

Direct-access storage medium

This usually means a magnetic disk. Each block on the surface of the disk has a disk address. It is possible to go directly to a specific block on the surface of the disk without reading through all the preceding data, but this can be achieved only if the address of the block is known. This is not unlike the way in which individual tracks can be played on an audio CD without having to listen to all the earlier ones. However, it is always possible to work through an audio CD from the beginning in a serial manner.

Disks are the most widely used storage medium and they offer great flexibility in the way in which data can be stored. A file can be spread over many blocks. Individual blocks of data within the file can be accessed directly, if the disk address is known, or the whole file can be read serially.

Although tape offers the fastest access to data, it does not offer the flexibility of disk. That is why most computer systems use disks in preference to tape. The main exceptions are for tape backup and for specialist high-volume serial processing.

Fixed- and variable-length records

In most data files, but not all, the data are organised into *records*. There are many types of data file containing records, and the three most common types are serial, sequential and direct-access files.

The records held in data files can be of fixed length or variable length.

- *Fixed-length records*. Most of the data files you have created will have had fixed-length records. Each field within each record is of a specific type and requires a specific number of bytes to store the data. For example, one field might be an integer, which requires two bytes of storage; another field might be declared as a text type, and require 256 bytes. So each record will require a fixed number of bytes. The storage space required for each record will be earmarked for that record, whether or not any data has been entered.

- *Variable-length records*. These try to squash together all the data in a file so that it takes up the least amount of space. There is no fixed length to each field, but at the end of each field a special character is introduced called an *end-of-field marker*. Similarly, at the end of each record, another special character is inserted, called an *end-of-record marker*. Variable-length records do not have any unused space within them.

Fixed-length records are easy for the programmer to work with as each record is the same length, but these records can take up much more space than is strictly necessary. In contrast, although variable-length records are economical on storage space they can pose some problems for the programmer. It may be difficult to access a specific record quickly, especially if the file is large.

Serial files

In a serial file the records are stored one after another in no particular order. Individual records can be accessed only serially, that is by reading the whole file from the beginning. The records stored in a serial file can be of fixed or variable length.

A serial file can be stored on a serial-access storage medium (tape) or on a direct-access storage medium (disk). If it is stored on disk then it can still be accessed only serially.

Serial files are used normally for the temporary storage of records before the data is subjected to full processing. For example, in some electronic point of sale (EPOS) systems, the records about each sale are collected and stored on a magnetic tape in the terminal. At the end of the day all the data is transferred from the EPOS terminal to the main computer system, and is used to update the store's stock files. The serial file created at the EPOS terminal is not sorted in any way, and simply holds the records of sales as they occur. Serial files that store the records of transactions (like sales) over a period of time are called *transaction files*.

Sequential files

A sequential file shares all of the features of a serial file, with one exception. In a sequential file all the records are sorted into order. Usually the record key acts as sort key, but in practice any field can act as the sort key.

Sequential files are often created as a step along the way to carrying out a process. Taking the EPOS example, once the serial file has been transferred to the main computer, it is then sorted, using the stock code for each item as the sort key. Once the records in the serial file have been sorted they are copied on to a new file, which is now a sequential file.

The master file of stock records held in the store contains data about each stock item, including the stock level (that is, the quantity of each item in stock). The master file is also sorted, permanently, into stock code order; indeed, the stock code is the primary key for the master file. The new sequential file and the master file are now compared, record by record, and the data in the sequential file is used to update the stock levels in the master file.

Direct-access files

You have seen that serial and sequential files can be accessed only serially – that is, by starting at the first record and reading through the file to the end. This is the ideal method if you need to read and process all the records in the file, as it can be achieved in the fastest possible time.

But if you need to access just one particular record in a serial or sequential file it can take a long time, as all the records that appear earlier in the file will have to be read first. For access to an individual record, direct access is preferred. A direct-access file allows you to go directly to a specific record.

There are two types of direct-access files: *random-access* and *indexed sequential*. Both types use the record key as the clue to finding where the record is stored on the storage medium. Both types can be implemented only on a direct-access medium (disk). Both types are best implemented with fixed-length records.

Random-access files

Random-access files are used for large collections of data. A substantial amount of space on a storage medium has to be permanently reserved for the random-access file. Often a whole drive (or virtual drive) is set aside for this purpose.

Random-access files use a rather clever method of providing direct access to records. To understand the method, we need to assume that each record takes up one block on a disk. (In practice, a record may be larger than this, but it simplifies the explanation at this stage.)

Each record then is allocated to a block, which has its own unique address. But the records are not arranged in a neat sequence on the disk. In fact, if you were able to examine the records in a random-access file they would appear to be allocated to blocks in a totally random fashion – hence the name. Of course, the allocation of block addresses to records is not completely random, but is the result of a mathematical formula known as a *hashing* (or address generating) *algorithm*.

The hashing algorithm takes the primary key of each record and calculates from that the address where the record should be located on the disk.

For example, suppose a disk has 100 blocks, with addresses from 0 to 99. Each block can store one record. (Again, this is a simplification, as the number of addresses would run into thousands.) Now suppose that the primary key of each record is a six-digit number. The hashing algorithm could calculate the address like this:

> From the primary key multiply the second digit by 1, multiply the fourth digit by 3, multiply the sixth digit by 7, then add the three numbers together to give the address.

The lowest value that the address could have is 0, and the highest value is 99. (Why?) The table in Figure 16.2 shows a set of record keys and the addresses that would be calculated by the hashing algorithm.

When the application writes the first record (with the primary key 126743) to the random file it is stored at the block with the address calculated by the hashing algorithm, namely address 44. The next record will be stored at address 6, and so on. When the application reads the record it uses the record key and the hashing algorithm to calculate the address at which it can be found. A record cannot be found in a random file unless its record key is known.

Record key	Address
126743	44
409220	6
348756	67
247652	36
128754	51
254376	56
978123	31
790345	53
307821	31

Figure 16.2 *Addresses calculated by a hashing algorithm*

Note that two of the addresses are the same. This is known as a *hash collision*. The first of these records to be processed (with key 978123) will be written at address 31. The second one (with key 307821) cannot be stored at address 31, so it will be stored at the next available address, in this case address 32. A perfect hashing algorithm will never produce hash collisions, but these are almost impossible to find.

The hashing algorithm is built into the program that handles the file, so the end-user will be unaware of how it works, or where the records are stored.

Indexed sequential files

As the name suggests, an indexed sequential file is essentially a sequential file which has one or more related indexes. Normally a sequential file can be accessed only serially, but an index allows the system to jump directly to one of the records anywhere in the file. This means that an indexed sequential file can be used with either serial or direct access, and has the advantages of both.

Indexed sequential files are used for applications where direct access to individual records is normally required, but where the full set of data has to be processed as a whole from time to time. Fixed-length records are usually used.

As an example, suppose Figure 16.3 is an extract from a large sequential file holding details of the customers

Card number (Primary key)	Surname	Initials	...
...			
7000	Roberts	C D	
7001	Malik	D R	
7002	Jones	T	
7003	Ward	P	
...			
8000	Andrews	E K	
8001	Rawlings	X E	
8002	Hooker	R	
8003	Major	J J	
...			
8367	Oliver	J	

Figure 16.3 *Extract from a large sequential file*

Activity

1. *In a spreadsheet, set up the table shown in Figure 16.2. Enter a random selection of six-digit numbers in the left column. Enter the formula for the hashing algorithm in the top cell in the address column, and copy it down.*

   The formula is: =MID(A2,2,1)+MID(A2,4,1)*3 + MID(A2,6,1)*7

   Did you get any hash collisions?

2. *Can you find another hashing algorithm that will generate addresses in the range 0 to 99? If so, does it produce a lot of hash collisions?*

of a video shop. Each member has a card with a unique four-digit code, and the card has to be used whenever a video is hired. The cards are issued in number sequence. The card number is the primary key, and the file is sorted using the primary key as the sort field.

As before, we will assume that each record takes up one block on the disk. The records in the file are stored sequentially on the disk. An index file contains the disk addresses of selected records in the file, which are identified by their primary keys only (see Figure 16.4).

Card number	Disk address (track-side-sector)
0999	02-03-2
1999	14-03-6
2999	27-03-0
3999	39-03-4
4999	51-03-8
5999	64-03-2
6999	76-03-6
7999	10-04-6
8999	23-04-0
9999	35-04-4

Figure 16.4 *The index for the sequential file in Figure 16.3*

The index effectively divides the sequential file into groups of records, with primary keys 0000–0999, 1000–1999, 2000–2999, 3000–3999 etc. The address alongside the card number 3999 is the address of the *first* record in the group 3000–3999; that is, it is the disk address for the record with primary key 3000. (It is *not* the address of the record with primary key 3999.)

When the card with number 8367 is presented, the system searches for the record in the sequential file with this as its primary key. But instead of searching the whole file serially by starting at record 0000 and working through until it is found, the system makes use of the index. It first checks whether the card number is less than or equal to the first entry in the index. Since 8367 is greater than 0999, it goes on to check it against the next entry. Eventually it reaches 8999. The disk address against 8999 is 23-04-0, and this is the address of the first record in this group, namely the one with record key 8000.

The system now jumps to this address and then searches the file serially from this point onwards until the record is found. This method has shortened the search time considerably. If the whole file had been searched serially, it would have checked 8367 records before it found the correct one. By using an index it first checks nine entries in the index, jumps to record 8000, and then checks 367 records before it finds its target.

The indexed sequential method does not give true direct access, as some serial searching is needed, but it is usually classed as a direct-access method as it gives relatively fast access to individual records.

Text and binary files

Although files of records are used a great deal, there are other types of file that can be created by the programmer. Some kinds of data, such as graphics, sound and simple text, do not fall easily into a record structure, and these are stored as *text files* or *binary files*.

Text files

A text file contains nothing but printable characters from the ASCII character set. These characters include almost all those that are included on standard keyboards – upper and lower case letters, digits and punctuation. They also include the space character and the enter (or return) character.

Each of these characters is represented by a different pattern of bits. Each bit can be set to either 0 or 1. Eight bits (one byte) taken together give 2^8 different combinations of 0s or 1s. Since $2^8 = 256$, this means that one byte can be used to store 256 different bit patterns (binary codes). So one byte can represent any one of 256 different characters. In fact, only seven bits are needed to represent the complete character set, but the data for each character is normally stored in a byte.

Text files have no formatting at all – they are the simplest type of file for storing textual information. The source code for a program is normally a text file, as it consists of nothing but simple characters. The main body of an e-mail message is always sent as a text file.

Binary files

A binary file (also known as a bin file) appears to have no structure at all – it simply consists of a set of bytes

Programming an application

of binary data. Machine-code files are actually binary files, but they are program files and we are interested in how a binary file can be used as a data file. We will consider how a binary file can be used as a data file for a bit-mapped graphic.

A bit-mapped graphic is made up of thousands, or millions, of tiny points of colour, called *pixels*. The data file for the graphic consists of nothing but a series of binary colour codes, each code representing the colour value of one pixel. Each colour code uses one, two or three bytes.

If one byte is used per pixel then it can represent any one of 256 different colours. This is quite a limited range of colours, and is suitable for simple graphics, but does not give photo-realistic images. If two bytes are used per pixel, then the number of colour codes rises to $2^{16} = 65,536$. Three bytes give over 16 million colour codes, which is more than the number of colours that can be distinguished by the human eye.

So the data file for a bit-mapped graphic will consist of a series of bytes, each containing an apparently random sequence of bits. These bytes will be interpreted into a graphic by the program which reads the file. The program will reassemble the coloured pixels to give a recognisable image. In order to use the data file, the program needs to know exactly how the data is organised within the file. For example, it needs to know how many bytes are used per pixel.

When a binary file is transferred from one computer to another, there is always the danger that the bytes stored in a binary file will be interpreted as ASCII character codes. It is therefore necessary to identify the files as binary files. Binary files can be sent via the e-mail system, but they are sent as attachments.

Activity

Find out how sound is coded into bytes in a data file.

Choosing the best type of file

Kannoush Amani has to decide which type of data files he should use for the Fitness Matters application. The physiotherapists and nutritionists will be the end-users of the system. They will use it to store data about the people who attend the hospital or health clinic, whom they are monitoring on a weekly basis. The data would cover personal details such as name and address, medical information such as past health problems, lifestyle information such as drinking and smoking habits, and fitness readings taken throughout the period the person is attending.

The data can easily be assembled into records, so Kannoush will not be using text or binary files for this purpose. When a person attends the fitness programme the physiotherapist will need to have immediate access to that person's record, so Kannoush thinks that a random-access file would be the best solution. But random-access files require a substantial amount of disk space which is dedicated to the application. The hashing algorithm has to be tailored to match the actual disk addresses that are available on the system. This means that random-access files can only really be used successfully in a bespoke or customised solution.

Fitness Matters is going to be sold on the open market as an off-the-shelf package, and Full Solutions will have no control over the storage space that will be available on the end-users' systems. Kannoush decides that he cannot use a random-access file, after all.

Instead, Kannoush decides to use an indexed sequential file to store the records. This means that it will take slightly longer to access an individual record than if he had used a random-access file, but he does not think that the files will be large enough for this to be noticeable to the end-user. An indexed sequential file also has the advantage that all the records can be accessed sequentially, and this feature could be used to carry out rapid statistical analysis of the data.

But this is not the only data file that Kannoush will use. He decides to create a text file that will hold the end-user's preferences for the module. For example, the physiotherapist or nutritionist will be able to choose the layout of the reports on individual people. These preferences can be stored in a *configuration file*, which is a simple text file.

Finally, Kannoush is going to include some bit-mapped graphics in his module. Some of these will be icons in the user interface, whilst others will be pictures of the human body which will be used to help identify the areas which need attention. These graphical images will be stored in binary files.

CHAPTER 17

Evaluating ICT solutions

This chapter concentrates on the evaluation of ICT solutions by users.

It will describe:

● how the suitability and effectiveness of an ICT solution can be assessed

● how an evaluation strategy can be developed.

The chapter covers the following Learning Outcomes in the specification:

L.O. 2.6 Describe how information can be captured to determine the suitability and effectiveness of a specified ICT-based solution

L.O. 2.7 Design a report on the suitability and effectiveness of a specified ICT-based solution

Update on the Fitness Matters project

In the last chapter you read that Ian McPherson, who works for a software house called Full Solutions Ltd, is the project manager for the Fitness Matters project, which is designed to improve the fitness of the over-50s. This is a joint project with Wessex County Hospital, and it has now 'gone live' at the hospital.

Members of the public who join the fitness programme are expected to attend the hospital once a week, when physiotherapists and nutritionists monitor their fitness levels and diet, and suggest how these could be improved. The Fitness Matters software stores data on each participant.

An *expert system* has been built into the application. This stores the diet and fitness recommendations and 'learns' to make similar recommendations for new participants. Over time the knowledge of the medical professionals is gradually being transferred into the application itself.

During its first year of operation Ian monitors the operation of the application carefully. He maintains

the software by making adjustments in response to feedback from the hospital users. After a year he feels confident that the expert system is fully functional and that the whole application is satisfactory.

Ian reports to his boss, Jane Winter. He tells her that the Fitness Matters project is on schedule, and that he is now ready to develop an off-the-shelf application, which Full Solutions hopes will sell to hospitals, clinics and health centres.

Some changes have to be made to the application. The main functional changes are in the expert system, as this will no longer capture the expertise of the physiotherapists and nutritionists, but is being presented in its final form, containing all the knowledge it has acquired at the hospital.

Then changes are made to the user interface. Members of the general public will be the end-users of the off-the-shelf application, so the user interface is redesigned. All references to Wessex County Hospital are removed, although the hospital's role in the development of the application will be acknowledged in the documentation. Security is added, so that individual users can log on and will be able to access only their own data.

Documentation is overhauled. End-users will not be provided with paper-based manuals, but all the user documentation will be accessible on screen through Help files, and this is written and checked. Documentation for the systems administrator is written by a technical author.

The new application is thoroughly tested and finally is renamed 'Fitness Matters for All'. However, before the software is launched on the open market Ian wants to get it evaluated by independent outside people. When an ICT solution is evaluated, it is used under normal conditions in a typical context, and the users report back their reactions. The marketing department at Full Solutions has drawn up a profile of typical purchasers of the software – the target market. Ian needs to find an organisation that matches this profile which will be willing to evaluate the product for him.

Ian decided to approach the Whittle Valley Health Club. He had come across it through a friend and thought that this venue would provide the ideal testing ground for the new product. The club manager, Winston Hall, was quickly sold on the idea and could see the benefits of the proposed software for the club's members.

Winston agrees to install the Fitness Matters for All application on a standalone PC located in the gym. The application will be evaluated for a period of three months, during which Ian will gather data about its suitability and effectiveness.

Activity

Can you suggest other methods that Ian could have used to evaluate Fitness Matters for All?

Evaluating suitability and effectiveness

An evaluation is an assessment of an ICT solution. It can be carried out only when the solution is in use, in a real context and using live data. The end-users are the main source of feedback during an evaluation phase.

An ICT solution can only really be called a solution if it solves a problem for a client or customer, so the key questions that need to be answered during an evaluation will focus on:

- *suitability*: Is this a solution to the client's needs?
- *effectiveness*: Is this a good solution to the client's needs (or even, is it the best solution)?

These questions can be asked of any ICT solution in use, whether it is provided as a bespoke or customised solution for a specific client, or whether it is released on the open market.

The same two questions can be asked throughout the lifetime of an application. Users' needs change, and so does the environment within which an application is used. A solution that is both suitable and effective at the beginning may appear to be less effective as time passes.

Who carries out an evaluation?

Evaluation of software can be carried out by the software developer (as in the case of Fitness Matters for All) or by a client or customer.

Evaluation by a software developer

This can be done as the final stage of a project for an off-the-shelf product. This means that it will be put to use in a live context, but before it is marketed widely. The end-users will provide feedback to the developer, usually in return for free software.

Evaluation by a software developer can also be undertaken as the final stage of a client-based project. This will be done after the initial changeover period is completed and when end-users are using it confidently.

In both cases, evaluation is the last stage of the system's life cycle, and will be built into the project planning.

Evaluation by a client or customer

This can be done by a potential purchaser of an off-the-shelf application, in order to establish whether an existing application will suit them. Such an application must already be openly on sale. The organisation will probably purchase one licence and evaluate the application before deciding whether to buy multiple copies. Alternatively, they could evaluate the use of the application by another organisation, but they will have to recognise that an application which is both suitable and effective for one customer may be quite unsuitable for another.

Evaluation can also be undertaken by the client of a bespoke or customised solution. This can be done at any time during the life of an application in order to check whether it is still meets the needs.

Criteria for judging suitability and effectiveness

The suitability and effectiveness of application software can be judged in relation to:

- system requirements
- functionality
- the user interface.

System requirements

The system requirements for an application will be stated by the developer. This will include the minimum hardware specification that can be used, and any compatibility problems with peripherals or other software.

If the ICT solution is bespoke or customised, then all the hardware and compatibility issues should have been resolved at an early stage. But over time the computer systems may have changed in many ways, so that when an evaluation is done it may be the case that the application is no longer quite so well matched to the existing hardware and system software.

If an off-the-shelf package is being evaluated, then the accuracy of the expressed system requirements can be challenged.

Compatibility is the main issue when evaluating system requirements:

- Is the IT solution compatible with existing computer systems (hardware and operating system) or will purchases have to be made?

- Is the IT solution compatible with existing application software, if relevant?

You may think that the most effective solution is one that works with existing computer systems, but that is not necessarily true. Many organisations acknowledge that "hardware follows software" – that is, that the priority is to get the best application software in place, and hardware will be purchased to support it.

Functionality

Functionality refers to the processes that the software can carry out.

If an application has been written to meet the specific needs of a client, then its functionality will have been laid down by the user-requirements specification and developed in the requirements document. An evaluation of the application soon after it goes live should show that all the requirements have been met; if not, then the developer should continue working on it. Sadly, many expensive large-scale software projects are based on over-ambitious or poorly specified requirements, which in the end cannot be met satisfactorily.

When a software house develops an off-the-shelf application they have to make assumptions about the users' needs, and the functionality that is implemented will reflect this. A potential customer will evaluate the end product in the light of their own specific needs, and they will be able to judge whether the application is suitable by checking whether it carries out some or all of the desired processes. Sometimes they may not have a driving need for the application, but may assess instead its suitability as an enhancement to their existing applications.

It is more difficult to judge the effectiveness of an application, as the evaluator has to decide whether the solution is a good one, and this involves some judgements of quality. Software developers and users have differing views about what constitutes 'good' software. For some users it is important that the application be robust, that it does not respond to unusual events by crashing. For others, quality is judged by how easy it is for a complete beginner to learn. Assessments of quality can sometimes be subjective and difficult to quantify.

The user interface

The purchaser of an application, whether it be bespoke, customised or off-the-shelf, will want to know whether the actual end-users will be able to use it satisfactorily. An application could have full functionality and yet be quite unsuitable if the end-users find it puzzling and are unable to make it work for them.

The layouts of screen displays should be clear and uncluttered, with helpful prompts. It should be obvious to the user what they have to do next. There should be consistency in the use of icons for buttons and their position on the screen. Help facilities should be provided.

Since the IT skills of end-users vary greatly, the software developer has to ensure that all potential users will be able to use it without difficulty. Software which is easy for a beginner to use is often described as 'user friendly'. But experienced users may become very annoyed with all the helpful features of a user-friendly interface and may prefer a fast and efficient interface, perhaps using hotkeys instead of mouse clicks. An evaluation of a user interface will relate to the needs of the actual expected end-users.

Some end-users may have disabilities which can be catered for within the user interface. For example, someone who cannot grip a mouse well may prefer to use a joystick. Or again, an end-user with limited vision may need to enlarge the characters on screen. The design should not depend on colour to convey meaning.

It is unlikely that all end-users will make exactly the same judgements about the effectiveness of the user interface.

Activity

Find an example of a software application designed for children within a specific age range. Assess the suitability and effectiveness of the application in terms of its user interface and functionality.

Evaluation strategy

As we have seen, evaluation can be carried out by the software developer or by the client/customer. In either case, an evaluation strategy is needed.

The evaluation strategy will have four main components:

- What information is required?
- How will the information be captured?
- How will the information be analysed?
- How will the evaluation be presented in a report?

What information is required?

As you have seen, the evaluation will assess the suitability and effectiveness of the ICT solution in relation to the system requirements, functionality and the user interface.

At Full Solutions, Ian has clearly specified the system requirements for Fitness Matters for All. The minimum processor speed, internal memory and hard disk capacity are stated, along with the size and resolution of the screen and the type of printer. He wants to be sure that Winston at Whittle Valley understands those requirements; Ian also wants some feedback about whether they are reasonable requirements for a target organisation to meet.

Ian wants both the staff and the members at Whittle Valley to tell him whether the software was useful for them, whether it came up to expectation and whether it was easy to use. He has to ask them specific questions like 'After the introductory screen was it clear to you what you had to do next?' rather than general questions like 'Did you find the software easy to use?' All users are asked for personal information and also about their IT experience, as this helps in the analysis.

Sources of data

The client (or purchaser) of an ICT solution is, of course, usually an organisation. In many cases, an ICT solution will be used by many people within an organisation. The client can only be sure that an ICT solution is suitable and effective if it works in use, and that means as it is being used by a range of users. Unfortunately, a solution that appears to be a good one by the IT specialists may be viewed less favourably by actual users.

The information required for an evaluation will come from the users and their use of the ICT solution. The users will normally be the systems administrators (who will assess the suitability and effectiveness of the system requirements) and the end-users (who will judge the functionality and the user interface).

It is not always easy to obtain reliable information from users. Users may not be the best people to judge how long they spend on a task or how often they use a certain feature of the application. They are sometimes busy employees who may resent taking time out to talk about the software. Their assessment of an application may be clouded by emotional reactions – perhaps they found the changeover trying, or believed that the old familiar application was good enough. End-users may be ordinary members of the public, and it is quite difficult to interrupt their activities in order to obtain feedback.

Information supplied directly by the users must be supplemented with factual information about use drawn from observation and log files.

How will the information be captured?

Information is *captured* when it is successfully extracted from the source and stored on a computer system. The source of the information is often a person, but the source could be a device of some kind, such as a sensor. As you will see, the computer system itself could even be a source of information.

Information-capture systems use various methods to ensure that accurate data is collected and stored. The data is then analysed to give useful information.

Two-step information capture

The most familiar method of information capture is through the use of a paper document that a respondent (the source) has to fill in. The document could be a questionnaire which poses a number of questions. The respondent can either write in answers, or tick boxes to indicate the response. A *data-collection document* is one that is used to gather information that will be eventually be entered into a computer (see Figure 17.1).

The information on a data-collection document has to be keyed in. The process of keying in data from a document is sometimes referred to as *transcription*. This stage is prone to error, as the data entry clerk may make keying errors, or may misread the writing on the document.

There are several techniques for minimising transcription errors:

- Respondents can be asked to use only capital letters, which are easier to distinguish.
- Guidelines drawn on the document can be used to separate out the spaces in which respondents can enter individual characters.
- Tick boxes on the document make the responses unambiguous.
- The person who enters the data can be forced to *verify* the input data by reading it back personally or getting someone else to check it.
- *Validation* checks can be used in the software to identify some incorrect data.

Transcription is not the only way in which data can be entered from a data-collection document, as there are a number of automatic techniques that can be used instead. For example, the data on the form could be read by an *optical character recognition* (OCR) device, which scans the page and identifies the written characters. The success of OCR depends on how clearly the letters are written, and the input would have to be verified by eye.

Data can also be input automatically if the responses on the document are marks, instead of characters. Marks entered into boxes on the document can be scanned using an *optical mark recognition* (OMR) device. You will probably be familiar with this method for marking multiple choice examinations. If OMR is used then the respondent has to choose between pre-set answers, so it is of limited usefulness and it cannot be used easily to gather subjective reactions.

One-step information capture

The two-step method of capturing information is quite risky, as inaccurate data can easily be entered on the

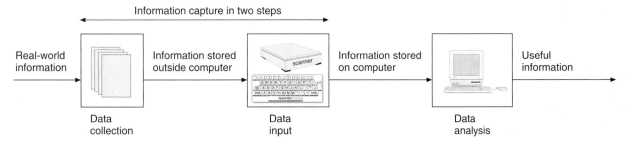

Figure 17.1 *Two-step information capture*

system, even when automatic methods of inputting are used. It is also costly as someone has to both enter the data and verify it. Sometimes a paper document is the only way in which information can be gathered from respondents, but alternative one-step methods can reduce the errors and cost dramatically.

A one-step information capture method will capture the information directly from the source. If the source is a person, then he or she could key in the information directly, instead of filling in a form. Alternatively, the person could input data on a swipe card or smart card by using an appropriate reader. A cash machine (ATM) uses both methods of information capture.

There are other ways of inputting data directly into a computer that require no human involvement at all. These are fully automatic in operation.

For example, software can be designed to generate *log files* which hold records of usage. So an operating system can create system log files which contain a history of the use of the system – for each access to the system it can record when it happened, which user logged on, which files they used and for how long. Similarly, application software can also generate usage files and these store information about which facilities within the application are most used and what errors are made by end-users. Both of these are one-step, automatic information-capture systems.

Another form of automatic information capture is used when sensors are embedded in a machine, or are set up to measure the results of scientific experiments. A sensor could measure temperature, humidity, light, movement or pressure. The data from these devices is transferred to the computer system in a constant stream. This process is known as *data logging*.

Although one-step methods of information capture reduce the chances of errors, they do not eliminate

them entirely, and data should still be put through a validation process.

Selecting the method of information capture

Ian McPherson has to decide which method of information capture to use. He chooses to produce two questionnaires, one for the gym staff and one for members who used Fitness Matters for All.

The club members are asked to complete their surveys immediately after using the application. They are asked some very specific questions about how they used the software, and at the end they are asked to rate it overall for usefulness, interest, and ease of use.

Club members are also asked for their telephone numbers so that a member of Ian's project team is able to contact them again a month later to see whether they have followed any of the recommendations given by the application. The data collected over the telephone is recorded on another data-collection form.

The gym staff are asked to record how many people use the software successfully, and how many start it but give up before completing it. They issue the questionnaires to members, collect them in, and post them each week to Full Solutions.

Ian then uses a spreadsheet package to design worksheets for storing all the feedback information from the club members and gym staff. The information collected on the data-collection documents is entered by an employee at Full Solutions and verified by a colleague.

Ian then looks at methods for gathering supportive data. He has already built a log-file-creation module into the application. This creates a log which identifies the name of each user, the date, time and duration of each session, and any error messages that are

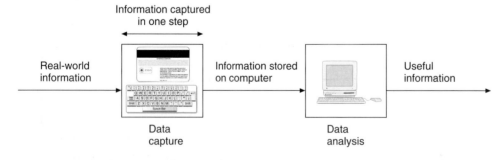

Figure 17.2 *One-step information capture*

displayed during the session. He arranges for a member of his team to visit Whittle Valley and copy this log file each month.

Finally, Ian arranges with Winston to spend a few days on-site observing the use that is made of the application. He sets up a video camera immediately above the PC in the gym. The camera switches on as soon as a member logs onto the system. Members have been warned that that is what will happen.

Back at Full Solutions, Ian previews the videos. He then asks one of his team to record on a spreadsheet worksheet how much hand and eye movement each user makes, and to time each session. He also asks for notes on any reactions to the software, such as smiling or signs of frustration.

Activity

Earlier you assessed a children's application in terms of its user interface and functionality. You now want to evaluate the application using real end-users. What methods of information capture could you use?

How will the information be analysed?

Ian has used:

- questionnaires completed by end-users and gym staff, which have been transcribed into a worksheet
- videos, which have been analysed and from which relevant data has been recorded on a worksheet
- log files, which he can also import into a spreadsheet and analyse statistically.

Since all the captured data is now stored on worksheets, Ian can analyse it and extract useful information about the suitability and effectiveness of the application.

If evaluation information is captured from a number of different sources and using different methods, then the results should be compared, as the direct responses from individual end-users may not give the full picture.

- Ian first of all checks the ratings given by club members. He finds that over 80 per cent of the members thought that the application was useful,

85 per cent found it interesting, but only 53 per cent said that it was easy to use.

- He checks on the responses made by end-users to questions about how easy it was to use, and he notes any difficulties they may have reported. He then compares their responses with the information extracted from the videos, and the usage statistics.
- He checks how much hand and eye movement each user makes, as he wants to ensure that these are kept to a minimum. He finds that users have to keep looking up at the screen and then down at a mouse or keyboard; he knows that this is likely to lead to errors being made.
- Ian also checks the questionnaire and video evidence to assess the relevance of the functions of the application. He finds that all the processes are used well and that users seems to find them interesting and useful to them.

Club members who have filled in questionnaires are phoned within a few weeks. Ian writes down a 'script' – that is, a list of questions to be asked. These focus on the difficulties that have been reported with navigation around the screens.

How will the evaluation be presented?

Ian has to report on the evaluation to his manager, Jane Winter. These are the headings in his report:

Introduction – short description of the Fitness Matters for All project

Evaluation strategy – what information was sought, and how it was captured and analysed

Analysis of findings – summary of main findings

Recommendations – including estimated costs

Ian recommends that the launch of the Fitness Matters for All application should be delayed for three months so that improvements can be made to the user interface. In particular, he wants to consider adding a touch screen to the package, so that users can select options easily. The delay will cost money, but as the final product will be more marketable, Jane decids to follow this course of action.

The second version of the application is developed and is then installed, with a touch screen, at Whittle Valley for further evaluation. This time users are very satisfied with the system, and the application is finally launched on the market.

As you saw earlier, an evaluation can also be done by a prospective purchaser. The report to management in this case will include recommendations about whether to purchase the application and for whom.

CHAPTER 18

How to do Task 2

This chapter gives advice on how to tackle coursework **Task 2**. The task requires you to produce and document an ICT solution to a significant problem that focuses on one area of application.

This chapter covers the following Learning Outcome in the specification:

L.O. 3.2 Document and implement an ICT-based solution

Throughout this section of the book you have been discovering how ICT applications are produced. Task 2 gives you the opportunity to create your own software solution to a problem.

The application you develop will be a relatively small one, but you will be expected to work in much the same way as a professional application developer. The complete project will take you through all the stages that you have studied:

- **requirements stage** – understanding the problem and working out what is required
- **design stage** – designing the software as the solution to the problem
- **implementation and testing stage** – building the software and checking that it meets the requirements
- **operations and maintenance stage** – running the software as intended.

You will write a project report which will describe all the stages that you go through. This should be word-processed and presented in a suitable binder or folder.

Although you will develop a software solution, you are not expected to submit a disk containing your application; instead you will provide, in the project report, full evidence of the implementation and testing of your application.

Needless to say, you must write the requirements and design stages before you start implementing the solution.

Selecting your problem

The Edexcel specification requires you to develop and document an application in one of these areas:

- modelling
- communications
- modern user interface
- multimedia
- data logging, involving significant file processing
- database manipulation.

Your teacher should advise you on suitable problems, and earlier chapters in this book may have already given you a number of ideas. You should normally select a problem that can be implemented on a straightforward standalone PC. Only tackle a network problem, or one that requires specialist peripherals, if you and your teacher are confident that you have the necessary background knowledge and that you have access to the facilities.

It is important that you have a potential end-user in mind. There are several ways of achieving this:

- You may select your problem by asking family and friends for ideas. If someone tells you that they could use some software to help them with an administrative task, then they can become a 'real' end-user for you. At the requirements stage you can ask them about the current system they use and their requirements for a new one. You can involve them in the design prototyping stage and again for the evaluation of the final system.

- You may be aware from your own experience of the need for a generic application to carry out a common task. It is not wise to act as your own end-user, as you will miss the opportunity for objective feedback. Instead, ask a friend, or a group of friends, to act as potential users for you. As before, they can then be involved at requirements, prototyping and evaluation stages.
- You may be given a simple one-line specification by your teacher, such as 'Develop a system for managing the newspaper rounds at a newsagent'. You should carry out some research, by talking to newsagents and by reading around the subject. It may not be possible for you to use a 'real' end-user at later stages in the project; if this is the case, then ask a friend to play the role of an end-user.

You may be tempted to revisit a project that you developed at GCSE. That is unwise, as it is unlikely that it will offer sufficient scope for a project at AS level.

Developing your solution

Once you have decided on a problem, you will have to do quite a bit of research into the problem itself and into possible solutions. The solution you select will be implemented using one or more application generators, and it is up to you to choose the most suitable tools to use.

Which application generator(s) should I use?

You may use any industry-standard application generator with which you are familiar, but you must be prepared to use advanced skills. However, you will not normally be expected to do any programming.

There are many teaching materials available, including books, that will equip you with the necessary skills. It is beyond the scope of this book to provide tutorials in the use of a wide range of application generators.

The skills that you have already acquired will probably limit your choice of subject for this task, but you should still aim to choose the application generator that is most appropriate for the problem that you are tackling.

What are advanced skills?

Here is a checklist of some advanced skills in the use of an application generator. The list is not exhaustive and you are certainly not expected to use all of them:

- implement mail-merge
- use a wide range of worksheet functions
- create paragraph and character styles
- customise the user interface
- create templates
- record macros and make them accessible from the user interface
- implement a relational database with relevant queries
- design forms and reports based on filters/queries
- create charts
- import and export data
- link and embed objects
- customise the properties of an object
- create 'What-if?' scenarios.

Below are some examples of project solutions which are *not* suitable for this coursework because they do not utilise advanced features:

- straighforward website design using a Web page editor
- a flat-file database solution, for example an address book
- a single-sheet budget
- a simple presentation using a presentation package.

Some of these could be developed into suitable projects. For example, the website or presentation could link to an underlying database.

Do not attempt projects which require specialist knowledge, such as an understanding of accounts or statistics, unless you are already studying the relevant subject.

Making a success of your coursework

Can I get help from teachers?

Although teacher supervisors should refrain from solving problems for the candidate, the candidate should be encouraged to have close consultative contact with the teacher supervisor at all stages of the work. Such contact and discussion should not be used as a reason to reduce the final marks awarded.

(from the Edexcel specification)

Your teachers are encouraged to give you plenty of support as you work on your coursework, so do not be afraid to ask for help. The examination board recognises the fact that you are still learning skills throughout the time that you are working on your coursework.

Teachers do, however, understand the difference between offering guidance and actually doing the work for you. If you do ask a teacher to complete part of the coursework for you, then you will lose some marks. You may reach a point where you believe this is the best way forward. Teachers should not give you that kind of help without warning you first that marks will be lost.

Can I get help from elsewhere?

You may ask other people to check your work for readability and to point out parts that could be improved. You must *not* ask another person to write any part of the report or to implement any part of the application.

Your teachers will be monitoring your work. The teacher who supervises your coursework is required to sign an authentication statement when it is submitted to the examination board. The wording for the Edexcel statement is:

'I declare that the work of each candidate for whom marks are listed is, to the best of my knowledge, the candidate's own.'

If your teacher cannot honestly sign this then you may be disqualified.

What resources can I use?

You might find sample applications in books, or as part of the examples provided with the software, and these may contain techniques that you want to use. It is quite legitimate to use techniques gained from any source, but you must say where they came from.

You may use any of the wizards and templates provided with application generators, but do check that they produce exactly what you want. You will probably find it best to start by using a wizard, and

then customise the application to meet your needs exactly.

If you explain in your report the origins of the techniques and ideas that you use, then you will be given credit for using your sources wisely. If you claim falsely to have invented a technique, then it will probably be very obvious to the examiner; you will lose credibility – and marks.

Working at home

Many candidates will have computing facilities at home and may wish to use these facilities for their coursework tasks. This can be allowed provided two conditions prevail:

- *the facilities are compatible with those at the centre*
- *the teacher is satisfied that the candidates are presenting their own work.*

(from the Edexcel specification)

You should discuss with your own teacher the appropriate use of computing resources. If you do work on your coursework at home you should ensure that:

- the software you use at home is compatible with that available at your centre
- your teacher sees your work at regular intervals and checks your progress
- you keep backups of all your files
- you have access to alternative computing resources in case your system fails.

Note that your centre cannot be responsible if your own computer system breaks down in any way.

Assessment of Task 2

How does the mark scheme work?

The four project stages that we have described are broken down in the mark scheme into ten sections. Maximum marks are shown below in square brackets. The maximum possible total is 60 marks.

Requirements stage

Specification (user specification, or proposal) [9]
Facilities [3]
Analysis [9]

Design stage

Design [9]

Implementation and testing stage

Implementation [9]
Testing [9]

Operations and maintenance stage

Documentation for the systems administrator [3]
Documentation for the user [3]
User training needs [3]
Evaluation [3]

Differentiation

As you might expect, the more demanding the problem you undertake, the better your chances of gaining the highest marks. To help you to understand this more clearly, the examination board puts problems into three categories of difficulty: foundation, intermediate and higher. The marks for each section are divided into three ranges, labelled F, I and H, to correspond to these categories.

	F	I	H
Specification	0–3	3–6	6–9
Facilities	0–1	1–2	2–3
Etc.	–	–	–

These are only guidelines and you can be awarded a mark outside the expected range if the section being marked is exceptionally good or weak.

Writing up Task 2

This coursework task should be presented as a formal report, with clear sections. The structure suggested below matches the mark scheme in the Edexcel specification. Although the structure may look rather long, you need to provide only a paragraph or two for many subsections.

The notes on the mark scheme have been extended to provide you with additional guidance. The sentences in *italics* are quotes from the mark scheme.

Your teacher may suggest alternative ways of presenting your work, depending on the type of problem you have chosen and the application generator you use.

- **Title page**
- **Contents**
- **Acknowledgements**

1. *Specification [9 marks]*

   Clear description of task to be attempted.

   Particular references to potential users and the type of processing that will be required.

   Statements that justify an ICT approach to the task and some consideration as to possible wider implications.

1.1 **Description of the task**
   - summarise the overall problem
   - identify which processes you intend to implement in your application

1.2 **Users and processing requirements**
   - describe the processing that the potential user requires
   - describe the existing IT skills of a potential user
   - describe the context in which the application is likely to be used

1.3 **Justification of ICT solution**
   - explain why an ICT solution is appropriate
   - consider wider (social, organisational, legal etc.) implications of providing an ICT solution to the problem

2. *Facilities [3 marks]*

   Discussion of the suitability of specific hardware and software required as they relate to the demands of the task in hand.

2.1 **Hardware**
   - discuss minimum and optimum hardware requirements

2.2 **Software**
   - discuss operating system requirements
   - identify software to þe used for implementing the solution
   - discuss suitability of software for generating the application, and identify alternatives

3. Analysis [9 marks]

Evidence that a thorough investigation of the background to the task has taken place in relationship to the potential users of the product. This should include, where appropriate, an analysis of any existing systems that are to be replaced and indications of from where the evidence has been gathered.

Description of the complete data requirements of the proposed system and indications of the sources of these data.

3.1 Investigation
- describe your investigation into the problem, using interviews, questionnaires, background research and observation, as appropriate, with evidence
- if an existing system is in use, describe it in detail, with evidence

3.2 Requirements of proposed system
- identify the objectives of the proposed system
- identify and describe each process in the proposed system, and identify whether it will be a manual or computer-based process
- describe the input and output data requirements for each process
- identify the sources of data for each process

4. Design [9 marks]

Top view of the proposed system showing the sources of the information, the information flow paths, the general nature of the processing required related to appropriate application generators and any remedial process that may be built in (data validation).

Complete design of all proposed input and output interfaces. For example, screen designs, report structures (or input signals if a real-time application).

Complete designs of any required processing structures, such as file structures, database structures, spreadsheet functions, hypertext connections, OLE sources and destinations.

4.1 System design
- draw a diagram showing the information flow in the proposed system

- describe how an application generator can be used to implement each of the computer-based processes
- draw a menu diagram to show how users will access the computer-based processes

4.2 Software design – user interface design
- sketch designs for paper-based data-collection forms (if needed)
- sketch designs for screen forms, including forms for inputting and/or displaying data, forms for providing instructions or help
- sketch layouts for customised pull-down menus, toolbars or menu (switchboard) forms
- sketch designs for printed reports

4.3 Software design – design of processing
- specify data structures and data types (including a full description of the data model for a relational database, if used)
- discuss data validation requirements and how these will be implemented
- design processes using structured English or similar
- design individual functions such as macros, spreadsheet functions and queries

5. Implementation [9 marks]

Detailed evidence of the implementation of the design. It is important that the relationship between the design and the implementation is clear and this may include reporting any iteration between design and implementation that often takes place (prototyping).

It could be an advantage to implement a system in a modular fashion and ensure that the documentation reflects this approach as it may assist in the awarding of deserved marks.

Annotated hard copy should be produced where appropriate.

This section provides the evidence for the way in which you have implemented your solution. All the printouts should be annotated (either by hand or in a word-processor).

You should build up Sections 5 and 6 at the same time. You should test each process as you complete it.

5.1 History of the implementation
- description of the sequence in which the solution was implemented
- description of any prototyping that took place and how the design was modified in response to feedback
- description of any technical problems encountered and how they were solved
- explanation for any variations from the original design

5.2 User interface
- printout of paper-based data-collection forms (if needed)
- screenshots of all screen forms
- screenshots showing customised pull-down menus, toolbars or menu (switchboard) forms
- printouts of printed reports

5.3 Processes

The content of this subsection will depend on the nature of the problem and the application generator used. Provide screenshots and printouts as evidence of the processing structures used. For example, in the case of a relational database you should provide evidence that all the tables, relationships, queries and macros were implemented as designed. You are not required to produce evidence of large datasets.

(*Warning.* Microsoft® Access has a built-in Documentor function which can give extremely detailed data about every object you have used. This should be used, if at all, with great caution. A carefully annotated screenshot fitting on to a single page will gain far greater credit than 20 pages of irrelevant technical data.)

6. *Testing [9 marks]*

It is good practice to perform technical testing as integral with implementation. Nevertheless to help students maximise credit for testing it is sensible for them to give evidence of what tests they have designed and tried out. They should include evidence of results that show that the components of their implementation work as expected.

6.1 Test plan
- a set of sample normal input data
- a sequence of actions that will demonstrate that all the processes in the application work under normal circumstances
- a set of abnormal (extreme and invalid) data
- a sequence of actions which demonstrate how abnormal data is handled

6.2 Testing
- annotated screenshots or printouts to show the effects of following through the test plan with normal data
- annotated screenshots or printouts to show how abnormal data is handled

6.3 Comments on testing
- comment on the success, or otherwise, of the testing procedures
- identify any limitations or shortcomings in the application

7. *Documentation for the systems administrator [3 marks]*

Documents that will assist a systems administrator install, test and troubleshoot the implemented system.

7.1 Installation
- outline the system requirements
- provide installation instructions
- describe security measures
- describe how to back up and recover files

7.2 Testing
- describe the testing that should be carried out prior to use

7.3 Trouble shooting
- common technical problems and their solutions

8. *Documentation for the user [3 marks]*

Students will have to demonstrate that they appreciate what is likely to be understandable to a potential user. They should use suitable software to produce an attractive guide to the product.

Produce a well-presented guide for the end-user. Include screenshots where appropriate. Do not duplicate information in Section 8 nor anything required for Section 9.

The guide may be in the form of a tutorial, or it could be related directly to each of the processes that the user has to carry out.

9. User training needs [3 marks]

Statements concerning any prior knowledge and skills the user may require.

A helpful walkthrough example of using the system.

A simple self-evaluation test for the user.

9.1 Prior knowledge and skills

– identify the knowledge and skills that the user should have before they start any training with the application

– describe the structure of a suitable training programme for end-users

9.2 Training materials – walkthrough example

– take an end-user through a straightforward session with the application

9.3 Training materials – self-evaluation test

– provide a set of questions (perhaps using a tick list) to enable the user to check whether they have used and understood the application correctly

10. Evaluation [3 marks]

Reflective statements on how the final system meets the expectations of the specification with reference to reported reactions of users of the system.

This section is not an evaluation of the way in which you carried out the project. Comments such as 'If I had more time I would have done …' are inappropriate. Instead you should be evaluating how successful your solution is in relation to the original specification.

10.1 Comparison of specification with final system

– compare the developed application with the specification in Section 1

10.2 Report on reactions of users

– provide a user with copies of the documents from Sections 9 and 10 and ask them to work through the software and comment on it

– ask other people to comment on the final system.

10.3 Evaluation of final system

– overall comments on the suitability and effectivenessof the implementation

CHAPTER 19

Examination questions and mark schemes for unit 2

This chapter provides examination questions and marking schemes for Unit 2: The Generation of Applications. Edexcel has given permission for the use here of this copyright material.

You are also advised to read Chapter 20 which provides hints on how to succeed in examinations, and examples of how to tackle examination questions.

Specimen examination questions

1. Just Do It is a company that sells do-it-yourself supplies. It is a company policy to train recruits so that they can answer customer enquiries. The training manager wants a computer-aided learning package so that trainees can quickly learn about the products. The trainees will work on the package at home using laptops provided by the company.

   The package should display pictures and details of all the products so that the trainees can learn and test themselves. A programmer named Nafisa is employed to produce the package.

   Nafisa chooses to produce the learning package using a general purpose high level programming language designed to produce programs that run in a *windowing* environment. The programming language has both an interpreter and a compiler.

   While she is working on the program, she uses the interpreter.

   (a) Give *two* reasons why Nafisa chooses to use the interpreter while she is developing the software. [2 marks]

   (b) When the program is complete, Nafisa compiles the source code.

       (i) Explain what is meant by source code. [2 marks]

       (ii) Explain why Nafisa compiles the completed source code. [4 marks]

   (c) Another programmer claims that he could have produced the solution in half the time by using an applications generator. Nafisa still thinks that using the general purpose high level language was better, especially as the software will often be used at home by the trainees on their own computers.

       (i) Explain what is meant by an applications generator. [2 marks]

       (ii) Explain why an applications generator could reduce development time. [2 marks]

   (d) The training manager wants to know how successful the home-based training has been.

       (i) Suggest ways that this can be evaluated. [2 marks]

       (ii) State *three* items of data that could be collected by the learning package to help with this evaluation. (3 marks)

       (iii) State *two* methods the training manager can use to ensure that the data collected is reliable. [2 marks]

   Edexcel pilot specification, Summer 2000

2. N&H Financial Management offers a variety of financial products to clients. These include investment funds and savings schemes. The products are managed for clients in order to provide them with profitable investments that take full advantage of market trends and tax benefits.

Micro Solutions plc provide N&H with software modules which keep track of client details and the performance of investment funds. Micro Solutions also provide support for the staff of N&H.

(a) Describe *two* ways in which the users at N&H might be supported by Micro Solutions. [4 marks]

(b) There is an IT user committee at N & H. They meet regularly to discuss their products. Describe *two* aspects of the information that N&H must obtain in order to evaluate the effectiveness of the software. [4 marks]

(c) Micro Solutions supplies new software modules from time to time. Describe *two* circumstances where such upgrades will be necessary. [4 marks]

(d) When major upgrades take place, the user documentation also needs to be updated. The new documentation may be supplied:

- as additional pages to a ring-bound manual
- on CD
- on a web site.

Comment on each of these methods in terms of:

- ease of user implementation;
- benefits to Micro Solutions. [6 marks]

Edexcel pilot specification, Summer 2000

3.

(a) A computer programmer wishes to develop a system in a high-level language called VISTA.

The systems administrator informs the programmer that there is no interpreter for VISTA, only a compiler.

(i) Describe the essential difference between the process of interpreting a computer program and the process of compiling a computer program. [4 marks]

(ii) Give *two* reasons why the programmer might not be happy to use a programming language that has no interpreter. [4 marks]

(b) After further consideration, the programmer decides that the system can be developed using an applications generator, in this case spreadsheet software.

(i) Describe *two* important advantages of using an applications generator from the programmer's point of view. [4 marks]

(ii) Give *one* important disadvantage of using an applications generator from the customer's point of view. [2 marks]

(iii) Describe *five* main features that are common to *all* applications generators. [5 marks]

Edexcel specimen paper

4. The life cycle of an ICT application includes the stages:

- proposal
- design
- implementation
- evaluation.

(a)

(i) State at what stages the users of the application should be involved. [1 mark]

(ii) Describe how the users should be involved at each of the stages given in your answer to part (i). [6 marks]

(b) Some application developers believe that the specification must be agreed and fixed in detail before any other stage is considered. Others believe that modifications to the specification should be considered during the development process. Discuss the relative merits of these two approaches. [6 marks]

(c) Distinguish between *technical testing* and *maintenance* and state at which stage they occur. [6 marks]

Edexcel specimen paper

5. Users of a large microcomputer network are able to report technical and software faults to the ICT department using a simple spreadsheet such as the following:

Fault no.	Login no.	Date	Time	Room	Device no.	Type sw/hw	Urgency	Problem	Fix notes	Fix dates
65	3305	23/3/97	12:55	M103	1256	hw	High	Toner low	Replaced	6/4/97

The spreadsheet cells contain only labels and data, i.e. no formulae or functions.

The requirements for the spreadsheet were:

- for users to be able quickly and easily to record faults
- for users to be able to look up the progress of fixing a fault
- for ICT technicians to view newly logged faults
- for ICT technicians to enter information on the progress of fixing a fault
- for the ICT manager to analyse faults to see if particular rooms, devices, or users were prone to error.

(a) Comment on the effectiveness of the spreadsheet, taking into account the requirements. [6 marks]

(b) Modern spreadsheet software has a range of user-interface screen objects available. For example, option buttons, list boxes, command buttons and many more. Design an improved user interface for the fault recording system, stating:
- the object type of each screen object
- the functions that the screen object would provide. [8 marks]

(c) Design a maintenance strategy for the computer fault logging system. [3 marks]

(d) The users of this system want to know whether this fault logging system has been effective. Describe what information is needed to determine how effective the system has been. [2 marks]

Edexcel specimen paper

---

6. A College management has decided that they need to change to a new system for handling student records. The system will handle the personal details of the students and include information about their courses, examination entries and results. The system will be used by course leaders and administrative staff.

The College considers buying a substantial application package called STUDENT+ which has already been sold to several other colleges. It also examines the alternative possibility of hiring a software consultant who would develop software for them.

(a) Give *two* advantages to the college of using an 'off-the-shelf' package like STUDENT+. [2 marks]

(b) List the documentation that should be provided with a package like STUDENT+ [3 marks]

(c) Give *two* advantages of hiring a software consultant to develop the application. [2 marks]

The College eventually chooses to use the software consultant. The consultant decides that the application should be developed as a relational database using an application generator, in this case a database management system.

(d) Explain the difference between an application and an application generator. [2 marks]

(e) Explain how a relational database differs from a simple flat-file system. [4 marks]

The software consultant is expected to provide documentation for the users of the new system.

(f) List the main sections that you would expect to find in the user documentation for this system. [4 marks]

---

7. William Rees works as a software consultant. He develops database solutions for small businesses and voluntary groups.

William is currently working on a relational database for a junior football club. The club runs six junior teams and each team is under the guidance of a number of adult leaders. William has already decided that he needs three tables, based on these entities: MEMBER, TEAM and LEADER.

(a) Draw an entity-relationship diagram to show the relationships between these entities.
                                            [2 marks]

(b) List the fields for each table. Indicate the primary key in each table.   [4 marks]

(c) Explain the purpose of a foreign key and identify any foreign keys that you have used in the tables.   [2 marks]

(d) Is your MEMBER table in first normal form (1NF)? Explain your answer.   [2 marks]

William discusses his data model with the manager of the football club. The manager is curious to know why the data model is so important.

(e) Give William's answer to this question.
                                            [4 marks]

William designs and implements a prototype of the database system and discusses it with the manager.

(f) What are the advantages to William of creating a prototype database?   [2 marks]

When new members enrol in the club they are immediately allocated to one of the six teams and introduced to one of the team leaders.

(g) Sketch a design for a screen form which will allow the manager to enrol a new member.
                                            [3 marks]

___

Mark schemes

1(a)
- An interpreter allows Nafisa to try out lines of code in interactive mode, e.g. to run a program and when it crashes make a change to the program code and then allow the program to continue executing from where it left off.   [1]
- An interpreter saves time not having to recompile each time a change is made before the program can be run again.   [1]

1(b)(i)
- Source code is the original text file that the programmer typed in.

- Source code is written in a high-level language.
- Source code is not executable.
                        [1 for each point; max 2]

1(b)(ii)
Nafisa will compile the completed program so that:

- it will execute faster because there is no need for interpretation
- there is no need for an interpreter/compiler on each user machine
- the program does not need to be reinterpreted each time it is run
- less memory will be needed when the program is run.   [1 for each point; max 2]

The reason for this is because a compiler **produces a machine code/object code file** that can be **directly run by the processor.**
                    [1 for each point in bold; max 2]

1(c)(i)
An applications generator is software that is used to create applications of different types. NB: *Not* to create a program – too general.   [2]

1(c)(ii)
- Less programming required because of built-in features such as mail-merge and tables in a word-processor, query editor in a database.
- They can contain templates, e.g. in a presentation/DTP package.
- They can contain wizards that automatically produce an application for you once you have made some choices.
- They can contain a toolbox of objects such as text boxes and option buttons for screen painting.

NB: *Not* because it won't need compiling – compilation time is minimal compared with development time.   [1 for each point; max 2]

1(d)(i)
- Surveys (interviews, questionnaires) on customer satisfaction.
- Surveys on staff views.
- Testing of staff.
- Record amount of use of the training package.
- Compare with an alternative form of training.
                    [1 for each distinct method; max 2]

1(d)(ii)

- Test results.
- Analysis of the test results.
- Amount of time used.
- Which areas have been accessed the most – indicating harder to learn.

[1 for each distinct type of data; max 3]

1(d)(iii)

- Retest staff.
- Ask employees how they thought they did.
- Put a password on the test results, that only the training manager knows.
- Data can be encrypted to stop the user editing them.
- Data can be made read-only.
- Data can be hidden.
- Data not stored as ASCII so not readable.

NB: *Not* data validation – the training manager is not the programmer. Also *not* data verification.

[1 for each distinct method; max 2]

2(a)

Micro Solutions may provide:

- user documentation for the software
- training in the use of the software
- a help desk
- on-line help
- training/support for the installation of modules
- training/support in converting and importing/exporting data from other systems.

NB: *Not* maintenance for their whole system – they provided only the financial software.

[2 for each reasoned point; max 4]

2(b)

- Comments on ease of use would help them to improve the user interface.
- Reports of bugs would help them improve the software performance. (Reliability)
- Comments on desired new features to assist product development.
- Degree to which solving original problems would help them improve software performance.

- Degree to which it is meeting their original requirements would help them improve software performance.
- The cost of using the software to see whether this is within budget and to decide any action to take if it isn't.

NB: *Not* if fast enough – more detail required. Also *not* . . . to make them more competitive.

[2 for each reasoned point; max 4]

2(c)

- To fix bugs.
- To improve design or add functionality.
- Government action might require new ways of working, e.g. changes in taxation. New products such as ISAs may require new modules.
- Inclusion of euro currency may require upgrades to modules.   [2 for each point; max 4]

2(d)

Ease of user implementation:

- Manual: Easy – just add/replace pages in binder
- CD: Easy – just replace/reinstall CD
- Web: Easy – none

Benefits to Micro Solutions:

- Manual: No need to reprint whole manual, so cheaper
- CD: Quick and cheap to reproduce CDs
- Web: No materials costs or copying costs. Can count hits on the site to see how much it is being used.

Also accept appropriate disadvantages of any of the methods for updating user documentation.

[1 for each category; max 6]

3(a)

(i) A compiler turns a high-level language program into a logically equivalent Run file [*1 mark*] that can be executed by the target processor without any reference to the source language [*1 mark*]. An interpreter executes the program statement by statement [*1 mark*] from the source code [*1 mark*].

[4]

(ii) A programmer spends much time in running debugging sections of program code [*1 mark*]. If there is only a compiler available then the programmer will have to initiate the compiling process [*1 mark*] for each test, no matter how small [*1 mark*]. Compared with using an interpreter, where a run can be initiated immediately after a source code edit [*1 mark*], this can be a lengthy process and adds to the development time [*1 mark*].　　　　[max 4]

3(b)

(i) An applications generator exists within a development environment [*1 mark*]. A range of complex facilities and functions are provided that can be integrated into the application being developed [*1 mark*], for example spellchecker, referential integrity checker, selection of predefined user interfaces [*1 mark*]. The development time is minimised owing to the high level in initial functionality [*1 mark*].　　　[4]

(ii) The customer will have to own a copy of the generator [*1 mark*] – for example the spreadsheet software – whereas an application developed into compiled code has no extra software overhead [*1 mark*].　　　　[2]

(iii) The candidate should give a brief description of any *five* common features that could include: functions related to the class of the generator; forms; toolboxes; macros; debug facilities; help systems; user-created procedures; class procedures.　　　　[5]

4(a)

(i) Proposal and evaluation (*no marks for one answer*)　　　　[1]

(ii) *Proposal:*

- Full involvement with the proposal for layouts on user interfaces (input and output).
- Agreement of the functionality of the project.
- Agreement of projected costs, estimated time scales and other contractual matters.　　　[3]

Evaluation:

- Structured feedback on technical performance.
- Structured feedback on the suitability of the user interface.
- Suggestions of bug fixes and upgrades.　　[3]

4(b)

A balanced argument would be appropriate here, with at least three marks for the presentation. For full marks there should be some reference to the influence that current development tools are having on the encouragement towards a prototyping approach.　[6]

4(c)

A full description of the process of technical testing is required including indications of the need of planning.　　　　[3]

It must be clear that maintenance is an ongoing process [*1 mark*] that requires input from users, implementers and software/hardware providers [*1 mark*]. Also there is a loop back to the mechanisms of technical testing [*1 mark*].　　　　[3]

5(a)

There are a host of comments that the candidate could make. Some short but relevant reference to six distinct points would gain full marks. Possible points could include:

- Users can fairly quickly enter faults.
- Users have to type in some data (fault no., log-in no., date, time) which could be provided automatically.
- The spreadsheet is wider than the screen so horizontal scrolling is necessary.
- The limited space for the problem does not encourage users to give full and accurate descriptions of the problem.
- Users can easily miss out important columns.
- Looking up the progress of a fault is slow because the user has to scroll through all faults previously logged, particularly if they did not make a note of the fault no.
- Technicians cannot easily find newly logged faults.
- Technicians can enter their progress on fixing a fault.
- The ICT manager can do simple searches to analyse the fault reporting.
- The ICT manager cannot do complex searches.
- Two or more users cannot enter a fault at the same time.
- System no good for logging faults that need to be fixed immediately.
- Users can delete other users' fault logs.　　[max 6]

5(b)

There are likely to be a variety of designs. Candidates can receive *four* marks for the names of four sensible objects that relate to stated application, and another *four* marks for a stated contextual use of the object.

- Type (hardware/software) could be entered by clicking option buttons.
- Searches by fault no. and log-in no. can be provided from command buttons.
- Only a single fault need be displayed on the screen.
- By default, only the user's faults should be displayed – move through them using scroll bar, latest logged viewed first.
- Error messages can be displayed if a compulsory item is missed out.
- A range of pre-programmed reports could be available from a drop-down menu.
- A message could appear on the technician's screen when a fault needs fixing immediately.
- Technicians should have access to separate screens which allow them to view all unfixed faults, new faults, urgent faults.   [max 8]

5(c)

Candidates can obtain *one* mark each for any three of the following:

- Back up hourly.
- Remove all references to fixed items a week after they have been fixed.
- Give new staff access.
- Train all new staff how to use the system when they first arrive.
- Remove unfixable items when the member of staff has been informed.
- Keep software and documentation up to date.
- Restore backup when necessary.   [max 3]

5(d)

The most fundamental information to generate is concerned with the time between the reporting and fixing of the fault. The candidate should indicate that there could be a delay between the fault being detected and the report being made.   [1]

The proposed system does not capture the data to generate this information and the candidate should indicate how this could be done.   [1]

6(a)

Possible advantages:

- Software will have been thoroughly tested.
- Finished version can be evaluated before purchase.
- Upgrades can be purchased as they become available.
- Relative cheapness.
                    [1 each for any *two* valid advantages]

6(b)

Documentation required:
- Software licence.
- Documentation for the systems administrator.
- Documentation for the user.   [3]

6(c)

Possible advantages:
- Customised to suit client's requirements.
- Quality control over finished product.
- Ease of maintenance (because full listings will be provided).   [1 each for any *two* valid advantages]

6(d)

An *application* is software designed as the solution for a particular IT problem. An *application generator* is a software development environment which can be used to develop applications.   [2]

6(e)

A *relational database* consists of a set of related base tables; the relationships are defined by the use of foreign keys. This method avoids data redundancy and hence promotes data integrity. Data in a relational system can be made available to any application that needs it. A simple *flat-file system* holds all the data for one application in one table (file) – if the data is at all complex this will result in repetition of data. Data cannot easily be shared between applications.
    [2 for explaining the difference, 2 for further descriptions]

6(f)

Features of Access might include:
- graphical interface to allow easy definition of objects
- facility to define tables and the properties of the attributes
- facility to set up relationships using a graphical representation of an ERD

- facility to define queries using a QBE grid related to a relationship diagram (rather than in SQL)
- facility to design forms using a graphical layout editor
- facility to build macros from a build list
- facility to write queries in SQL and modules in VBA if desired
- facility to transfer data between Access and other software in Microsoft® Office   [1 for each; max 6]

6(g)

User documentation could contain:
- contents
- introduction
- reference sections covering all the topics in the application
- tutorial
- trouble shooting
- glossary
- index   [4 for a reasonable coverage]

7(a)
Entity-relationship diagram as below.   [2]

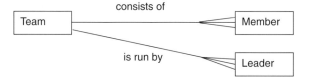

7(b)
Field lists may be given in any suitable format:

- team(<u>team ID</u>, team name, age range, ...)
- member(<u>member ID</u>, member surname, member forename, member address, dob, ... team ID)
- leader(<u>leader ID</u>, leader surname, leader forename, leader address, ... team ID)

One mark each for each table with a sensible selection of data fields. *One* mark for identifying all three primary keys. (Do not deduct marks in this question if foreign keys are missing.)   [max 4]

7(c)
A foreign key is a primary key in one table which is also included in another table to implement the relationship between the two entities.

One mark for correctly including and identifying the two foreign keys. [2]

7(d)
One mark for correctly saying whether the tables given are in 1NF. *One* mark for explanation.   [2]

7(e)
Points to make: A good data model increases the efficiency of a database – integrity of data and speed of interrogation etc. – by reducing data redundancy to the minimum. *Must be explained in non-technical language.*   [4]

7(f)
A prototype is a trial version of the database which can then be discussed by the client. [*1 mark*]. This provides feedback on negotiable aspects of the application, such as the design of the user interface, and can be used to determine additional functionality [*1 mark for anything similar*].   [2]

7(g)
Check the design for:

- all relevant fields present, including team details and leader names
- prompts/instructions to user
- navigation and other buttons.   [3]

TOWARDS
SUCCESS

CHAPTER 20

How to read and answer examination questions

This chapter will help you to present yourself in the best possible way in examinations. It discusses:

- how to read and analyse examination questions
- how to plan answers
- how to present your answers

All the sample questions quoted in this chapter are taken from the AS papers set by Edexcel for the pilot syllabus in IT in 1999.

Marking schemes and examiners' comments on the answers given by candidates are provided at the end of this chapter, and are reproduced here with their permission.

The structure of an examination paper

In this section we are referring to the exam papers set by Edexcel for their AS or A2 level ICT units. If you are studying for another examination board then you should refer to their specification for information about their examinations.

For the Edexcel specification you will take written papers for :

- **AS level**
  Unit 1: Systems administration
  Unit 2: The generation of applications

- **A2 level**
  Unit 4: Systems management
  Unit 5: The implementation of event-driven applications

The following is an extract from the Edexcel specification:

- *All examination papers last 1 hour 30 minutes*
- *All examination papers are marked out of 60*

marks (which will include 3 marks for the quality of written communication)
- *All questions will be compulsory*
- *All examination papers will consist of three structured questions that are approximately equally weighted*
- *There will be an incline of difficulty within each question*

Each question begins with a short description of a context in which ICT is used. This often describes an aspect of the work of a named IT professional.

Following the description there is a series of short part-questions, all of which relate to the context. Further background information may be provided at later points in the question. The part-questions increase in difficulty as you work through.

Most questions will be marked out of 19, but some variation is possible.

The first five minutes

When you are told you may begin an examination paper, you are probably still feeling nervous. Many students start by glancing through all the questions, but if they were then interrupted and asked what they had read they would probably recall very little.

This section explains how you can use the first few minutes productively.

Active reading techniques

When a professional reads a lengthy report or paper, he or she will normally annotate (write notes on) the document. This means that when the person returns to the document the notes will draw attention to the key points. We call this method 'active reading', as the reader is actively involved in analysing and commenting on the contents.

You can use active reading techniques in an exam. Start by reading right through the paper with a pen or highlighter in your hand, and use them to highlight all the key words and phrases in the questions.

You should identify key words of two types. You may like to use different coloured pens for each type.

Topic-related words or phrases identify *what the question is about*. These key words will be found in the context description, and also in the part-question itself.

Aim to pinpoint the specific topic, rather than the general area. For example, a question may talk about the work of the systems administrator in maintaining data security, but the part-question itself may specifically refer to making and storing backups. Make sure that you have highlighted the most specific reference.

Answer-related words or phrases identify *what sort of answer you should give*. These will be found in the part-question and will be phrases such as 'Discuss', 'Explain how', 'State two advantages of'. The meanings of these phrases are discussed in the next section.

Sample question

The answers to sample questions can be found at the end of this chapter.

1. Carry this out as a group exercise. Spend no more than a few moments reading the question on your own and identifying the key words. Then discuss your key words with the rest of your group.

   Premier Systems is a company that manufactures components for the electronics

industry, including the military. Premier Systems has grown rapidly during recent years. There are now several production departments, each with their own clerical and development sections. Each of these departments has been allowed to administer and control their own IT facilities.

(i)   Detail TWO reasons why it would be unwise for Premier Systems to continue to allow each department and section total administrative freedom with their IT facilities. [4 marks]

(ii)   The management of Premier Systems decides to advertise for an IT Systems Administrator. Each applicant for the post is sent a document outlining the responsibilities of the job and the experience required. Produce a draft for this document. [5 marks]

Understanding the question

After the first five minutes you will have settled down sufficiently to begin writing your answers. You will already have analysed all the questions, so will not need to do this again. Since you have given some initial thought to the whole paper, you may well find that as you write one answer your mind will be working away in the background on the other questions.

What is the question about?

The key words or phrases should point you towards a specific area or areas of the syllabus. Although your general knowledge of computers may prove to be useful, the questions are all derived directly from the Learning Objectives and Technical Knowledge topics in the specification.

For example, consider this question:

Distinguish between an application and an application generator. [4 marks]

This clearly refers to section T2.2.1 of the specification, and requires a detailed answer for four marks. The topic-related key words are obvious in this case. However, the following question needs a little more care:

The provision of user documentation on a website is increasingly the preferred option for the marketing divisions of companies that produce applications. Explain why this is so. [2 marks]

You will have no difficulty in picking out '*user documentation*' as topic key words. This refers to section L.O.2.5 of the specification.

But if those are the only topic-related key words that you highlight then you are in danger of writing a general answer about user documentation, which will be awarded no marks at all.

You should certainly also highlight the word '*website*'. And the '*marketing division of companies*' is important as well. The question is asking you to think about why a very specific area of a business (the marketing division) would prefer a very specific type of user documentation (web-based) for its products over other types of user documentation (paper-based or software-based). The question implies that perhaps other divisions in the company might prefer the other types of user documentation, but the marketing division may have good reasons for overruling them.

What sort of answer is required?

Here is a selection of answer-related key words.

▶ **Lists and descriptions**
  Name ...
  Give ...
  State ...
  Describe ...
  Detail ...

You may be tempted to give very brief responses to some of these questions. Be warned that one-word answers rarely gain marks at this level. All your answers should be framed as complete sentences, and should contain sufficient technical knowledge to convince the examiner that you have learnt something from your studies.

▶ **Definitions and explanations**
  Describe how ...
  Explain how ...
  Explain what is meant by ...
  Sketch ...

As a general rule, give examples to illustrate your answers whenever it seems appropriate, whether or not the question asks for an example. This is because the explanation or description that you give may not be as clear and unambiguous as you might like. If you

add in an example you are demonstrating to the examiner that you really do understand what you are writing about.

A diagram can be used to support a written answer. Occasionally a question specifically asks for a sketch or drawing, but *in all other cases the diagram should supplement the written answer and not simply replace it*. All diagrams should be clearly labelled.

▶ **Compare and contrast**
  Give advantages ...
  Give disadvantages ...
  Distinguish between ...
  Outline the relative merits of ...
  What are the benefits of ...

If a question asks for advantages you should ask (a) compared with what, and (b) for whom? Consider this question:

Describe one major advantage of common interface modules from the systems administrator's point of view.

Ask yourself:

● Compared with what? In this case you have to compare the use of common modules across a suite of applications with a set of unrelated applications that all use different interface modules.

● For whom? The question specifically mentions the systems administrator, so you are not being asked to comment on the advantages to the end-user, nor to the software developer.

▶ **Reasons**
  Explain why ...
  Justify ...
  Give reasons why ...
  Comment on ...

Reasons should always refer to an objective held by a person or organisation. Some of these may be technical objectives, others may be business objectives.

For example, you could be asked for the reasons for carrying out a particular security procedure. Your answer could refer to the need to meet the technical requirements of the Data Protection Act, or of ensuring that good disaster recovery systems were in place.

In another example, a software company may decide to produce an upgrade to a popular application, and you may be asked to justify this. The reasons given could refer to the business objectives of the software company, such as maximising profit, maintaining a market lead, upholding the reputation of the brand, or beating competitors.

▶ **Outline**
Outline ...
Produce a draft of ...

You are sometimes asked to produce notes for a presentation, or the first few sentences of a formal talk, or an outline for a report. This is an unusual way of asking an exam question, but it is favoured by the examiners of this syllabus. In preparing your answer you have to think about both the content and the method of communication.

You should ask yourself:

● Who is presenting the information?
● Who is receiving the information?
● What information is being conveyed?
● How is the information being communicated?

For example, consider this question:

Sean (a systems administrator in an insurance company) is preparing a training programme for the staff who use these IT facilities. Sean needs to explain the concepts of:

– an operating system
– a multitasking system
– a network.

Write down suitable opening comments that Sean could use to introduce each of these concepts in turn to the trainees. [6 marks]

Ask yourself:

● Who is presenting the information? This is the systems administrator, who has substantial knowledge of the systems.
● Who is receiving the information? These are trainee, non-technical end-users, who want explanations that they can understand.
● What information is being conveyed? This is defined in the question.
● How is the information being communicated? This is through speech, in a fairly formal setting.

Your answer should be written in speech mode, with a clear attempt to explain technical matters in non-technical language.

▶ **Discuss**
A later section in this chapter is devoted to questions which ask you to discuss a topic (see page 223).

How many answers should I give?

Some questions ask for a specific number of points – for example, *two* advantages or *one* situation. Do not be afraid to give more than required. Sometimes the examiners may consider that one of your points is irrelevant, or repeats another point you have given. By giving more than the requirement you increase your chances of obtaining full marks.

What does the examiner mean?

Here are some words commonly used in examination questions.

▶ **Feature**
A feature of a software package is a function that it can carry out or a tool that it offers. For example, features of a word-processing package include character formatting, spelling and grammar checkers, layout tools (such as page, column and paragraph formats), mail-merge etc. At this level do not expect to be given a mark for each minor feature that you mention; for example, you may list a number of ways of formatting fonts (selecting size, font, style, spacing and colour) but they would all count as a single feature.

▶ **Effectiveness**
The effectiveness of an application relates to whether it meets its objectives. For example, the specification for a point-of-sale system may have detailed the time taken for each transaction, or the level of detail required on the receipt. An effective application would have met those requirements. The application itself may have been designed to meet certain business objectives, such as to increase sales by reducing the time customers spend queuing at the checkout. Again, the effectiveness of the application can be measured.

▶ **Criteria**
Criteria are ways in which something can be judged; they are often written as specific questions. For example, a software house may want to establish criteria to decide whether to launch a new product. The software house will frame some basic questions, such as 'Can we expect over 10,000 sales of this product?'; 'Is the market free of any rival products?'; 'Can we develop the product within six months?'.

► Strategy

A strategy is a method and a plan for carrying out a policy, developed as a result of research. For example, the same software house may have a policy of releasing upgrades based on the feedback from customers. This policy applies to all its products. The actual strategy, or method of acquiring and assessing feedback, will vary from product to product. For a game it may decide to use feedback from focus groups of typical games users, whereas for an office product it may rely on monitoring feedback through the helpline.

What does the examiner expect?

Consider this question, which was mentioned earlier:

> *Distinguish between an application and an application generator.* [4 marks]

Your answer must show an understanding of ICT systems which goes beyond that required at GCSE level. Sometimes similar-looking questions are set in GCSE, AS and A2 papers, but you will be expected to give answers that match the level of the course. Here are two possible answers:

1. An application is software that does something useful. An application generator generates an application.

2. An application is a software package that has been developed to provide specific functionality for an end-user. An example might be a ticketing system used at a nightclub.

   An application generator is a software tool that can be used by a software developer to produce applications. Many applications generators are designed as development environments, offering a range of tools such as an editor, compiler, debugger, form designer and help facility. Examples would include programming systems or database management systems (such as Microsoft Access).

You can easily see which answer would meet the standards required at AS level. A student could probably have written the first answer before starting on the AS course – and anyone can guess that an application generator generates applications! The second answer draws on technical knowledge that will have been covered during the course and demonstrates that the writer has learnt to use the appropriate language and information.

Sample questions

2. This can be undertaken as a group exercise.

   (a) Read the question below, using active reading techniques.

   (b) Discuss how the marks would be allocated.

   (c) Discuss what the examiner expects as an answer.

   (d) Write complete answers to each part.

   (e) Discuss your answers.

   (f) Compare your answer with the solutions taken from the examiners' mark scheme, given at the end of the chapter.

   The staff of a major insurance company is provided with IT facilities via desktop workstations connected to a local area network. Sean has the responsibility of administering these IT facilities. The workstations have a graphical user interface.

   (i) Describe TWO advantages of a graphical user interface [2 marks]

   It is brought to Sean's attention that Barry is colour-blind and is having trouble using the graphical user interface of his workstation.

   (ii) Explain how Sean could use the facilities of the operating system to ease Barry's use of his workstation. [3 marks]

3. This question is an example of one which, although it is worth only two marks, can easily be misunderstood. Discuss what the examiners expect as an answer, and identify the kind of wrong answer that a student might give.

   Aisha makes her living by implementing computer-based solutions. A bookshop called Matts has contracted Aisha to develop an application that will store, on the company's existing computer system, the data about the books it sells. Initially, the management of Matts wants this new application to provide a facility for online customer enquiries.

   Aisha decides to use a relational database management system. She decides to represent the data about the books as three base tables named
   BOOK
   AUTHOR
   PUBLISHER

Aisha will have to decide what data fields will be needed in each table. Describe how Aisha should investigate which fields will be needed.

[2 marks]

4. This question follows on from the previous one. Discuss your answers with other students.

   Once the application is up and running, the senior management of Matts want to ensure its effectiveness.

   (i)Describe what the senior management mean by 'effective'. [2 marks]

   (ii)Aisha improves the system by making it store automatically the additional information that will assist in the evaluation of the system. Describe what that additional information might be.

   [2 marks]

5. This time, work on your own and allow yourself 15 minutes to analyse and answer the question.

   At a conference with the theme 'The Role of the Systems Administrator', the speaker said the following:

   'The management of most of your companies will be depending upon a comprehensive central database which you will be administering. The controlled access to selected parts of this database could be vital to the financial well-being of your company.'

   (i)   Explain what is meant by controlled access to selected parts of the database.

   [3 marks]

   (ii) Describe how the systems administrator could provide such access.   [4 marks]

   (iii) Describe one situation where controlled access to the database could be detrimental to the company.   [2 marks]

Planning your answer

Planning

It is a good idea to jot down your immediate thoughts and plans on the answer paper. A convenient way of doing this is to open the question booklet to a fresh double page for each question. Use the left-hand page for your notes and start the actual answer on the right-hand page. Do not worry about wasting paper; at such

an important time it is your convenience that is paramount.

You may not need to plan the answer to a simple question worth only two marks, but you should certainly create a plan for a question worth four marks or more, especially if the question asks you to discuss a topic.

There are many planning methods. Some people like to draw spider diagrams, which illustrate the main concepts and show the links between them. Others prefer to list the main points and develop an outline.

Structure

The most important element in your planning is the structure of your answer. You should list the main points in the sequence in which they will be mentioned, then identify any subsidiary points.

In an examination question on this subject you would normally be expected to adopt a report style. That means you may use numbered or bulleted points and may use headings and subheadings. The only exceptions to this would be if you are asked to discuss a topic, or if you are asked to give an extract from a talk. The next section deals with those questions.

How much should I write?

The number of marks awarded per part-question is a good indicator of the length of the answer. As a very rough rule, to obtain one mark you need to write at least one sentence, and you probably need to write two sentences.

Words to avoid

It is very tempting to use some general terms in an answer, hoping that the examiner will understand the technical details that you really mean. Here is a list of vague words and phrases – you should only use them if you then go on to explain in more detail exactly what you mean:

- fast
- big (when referring to capacity)
- cheap
- efficient
- user-friendly
- memory (if not qualified as internal or external)
- security.

6. This should be undertaken as a group exercise.

(a) Plan the answer to this question individually.

(b) Compare and discuss your plans in the group.

(c) Agree as a group on a good plan for an answer.

(d) As a group, compose an answer in accordance with the agreed plan.

During the implementation of any IT-based application, technical testing has to take place.

(i) Explain why it is important to document and keep the test plan and the results of the tests. [4 marks]

(ii) Once an application has been developed and is in use, the documentation of its technical testing can be regarded as historical documentation. Describe the circumstances where it would be necessary to add to this documentation. [4 marks]

7. On your own, analyse, plan and answer this question, then compare with other students. Finally check the answers given in the examiners' marking scheme, at the end of this chapter.

The staff of a major insurance company is provided with IT facilities via desktop workstations connected to a local area network. Sean has the responsibility of administering these IT facilities.

Sean is preparing a training programme for the staff who use these IT facilities. He needs to explain the concepts of:

- *an operating system*
- *a multitasking system*
- *a network.*

Write down suitable opening comments that Sean could use to introduce each of these concepts in turn to the trainees. [6 marks]

Discussing an issue

How do I answer a question that asks me to discuss an issue?

It is likely that at least one of your questions will require you to discuss a topic. Your answer should be modelled on a traditional essay, with an introduction and conclusion. In between you will argue your case in several clearly defined paragraphs.

You should expect to examine the issue from at least two points of view. You may be asked to look at it through the eyes of two different people – end-user and administrator, perhaps – or you may have to discuss the advantages and disadvantages of carrying out a task in a specific way. Your answer should balance the two, or more, viewpoints and try to treat each one fairly. In the conclusion it may be appropriate to state which of the alternatives you prefer.

Marks are awarded for answers in which the points you make are justified – that is, where reasons are given for each assertion.

How do I present the answer?

When a question asks you to discuss a topic you should write continuous prose. Do not use headings or numbered points.

This does not mean that you do not plan or structure your answer; in fact structure is most important. However, the structure should still be apparent through your use of paragraphs, and by the use of phrases like 'In conclusion'.

8. Carry this out as a group exercise.

(a) Plan and write an answer individually.

(b) Exchange the answers within the group and mark each other's answers.

(c) As a group, discuss what would be a good answer to this question.

At a conference, with the theme 'The Role of the Systems Administrator', the speaker said the following:

'Every time you install an application on your system you are providing a product for

your users. Your responsibility for that product is just like the responsibility that any supplier of a product has.'

Discuss the validity of the comparison between the responsibility for a physical product, for example a child's toy, and an information product, for example an Internet service. [4 marks]

9. Allow yourself 20 minutes to answer this question on your own, then compare your answers with other students.

   User documentation for a developed application could be in the form of:
   - *paper manuals*
   - *online help using hyperlinks*
   - *a website.*

   Discuss the relative merits of each of these media in the context of both the end-user and the applications developer. [9 marks]

Using the time well

How long should I spend on each question?

In the Edexcel specification, each examination lasts one and a half hours. Each paper consists of three questions, awarded 19 marks each. A further three marks are awarded for each paper for quality of written communication.

So the simple answer is to spend 30 minutes on each question. But you should also allow five minutes to read through the questions at the beginning, and five minutes at the end to review your answers.

If you allow roughly one minute of writing per mark, then you will use 60–70 minutes to write your answers, with the rest of the time given to reading and planning.

Make sure you have your own watch with you.

Tasks

10. This can be done as a group exercise. Select a question from this book or from an examination paper. Check the time on a watch, then write an answer to the question for exactly two minutes, without looking again at your watch. At the end

of what you believe to be two minutes, stop working and check to see how well you estimated the time.

11. Repeat the exercise with different periods of time.

12. Work through a past paper to time and, as far as possible under exam conditions. As you answer the part-questions jot down the time when you begin and end each one.

   Afterwards, analyse how you used the time and identify where you could have used it more effectively.

Quality of written communication

What are the criteria for awarding the marks for this?

Up to three marks can be awarded on each exam paper. The criteria used by Edexcel for awarding these marks are as follows:

- *1 mark:* The candidate rarely uses specialist vocabulary, but displays reasonably good spelling, punctuation and grammar to communicate with some clarity, relevance and coherence.
- *2 marks:* The candidate uses some specialist vocabulary and displays good spelling, punctuation and grammar to communicate, often with clarity, relevance and coherence.
- *3 marks:* The candidate uses appropriate specialist vocabulary and displays excellent spelling, punctuation and grammar to communicate consistently with clarity, relevance and coherence.

How can I improve my marks for this?

You have been presented with *specialist vocabulary* throughout this book. Use the terms you have learnt, in the correct context of course. Avoid the use of phrases like 'The computer thinks/knows' and 'The printer talks to the CPU'.

Spelling, punctuation and grammar have to be reasonably good to achieve even one mark. If these present you with problems then discuss with your tutor how they could be improved.

Clarity, relevance and coherence can be achieved by following the advice in this chapter.

What should I do if English is not my first language?

All exam papers will be marked according to the fixed criteria; there are no concessions for candidates for whom English is not their first language. However, it may be possible for you to use a dual language dictionary in the exam. You should check with the Examinations Officer at your centre and you must obtain permission in good time before the examinations.

What can I do about my handwriting?

Sadly, some candidates lose marks because their handwriting is indecipherable. Practice writing answers at some speed and then ask fellow students and teachers to read back to you. You may be surprised to discover that your handwriting is not as clear as you think it is. If necessary adopt a style of writing, purely for examination purposes, that is closer to simple printing. Alternatively, write unclear words again in capitals or print style.

What if I am dyslexic?

If you have been formally assessed as dyslexic then you may be allowed extra time to take each examination paper. You must see the Examinations Officer at your centre to arrange this well before the examinations take place.

Answers to the sample questions

Question 1

The key topic-related words are:

- 'several production departments'
- 'total administrative freedom with IT facilities'
- 'responsibilities of the job'
- 'experience required'.

The key answer-related words are

- 'Detail TWO reasons why it would be unwise'
- 'Produce a draft'.

Extract from the mark scheme

(i)   Possible reasons   [2 marks for any two reasons]

- no common standards of security
- no common standards of the user interface from the OS point of view
- diverse hardware and software that makes information transfer between sections less easy and could be uneconomic from a general maintenance point of view
- no general policy as to who is reposnsible for systems even within a section
- probable replication of effort resulting in unnecessary expense.

(ii) This is *not* the design of an advertisement. It is a prose document that describes to the applicant:

- some background of the company   [1 mark]
- what a systems administrator has to do (TWO well described responsibilities)
      [2 marks]
- what previous experience is needed (TWO specific areas of experience such as specific training or relevant work in a similar company for about two years)   [2 marks]

Comments from the examiners

(i)   Many reasonable attempts were made to account for the desirability of a unified IT approach across the company. Good points were made about data and hardware compatability and also confusion of responsibility.

(ii) Credit was given for any reasonable and identifiable role such as add users, perform or arrange security measures, but not for vague generalities such as 'maintain the system'. Training users is something that administrators might organise but not personally provide. Credit was given for any mention of sufficient relevant experience or qualifications, but this had to be specific. Just saying that the candidate had to have experience cannot be expected to gain credit.

Question 2

Extract from the mark scheme

(i)   Two marks for any sensibly described advantages.

(ii) One mark for the realisation of the Settings facility. Two marks for any specific reference to screen settings that are relevant to the problem that Barry has.

(i) Most candidates scored something for a basic understanding of what a GUI is. Full descriptions of how they assist the user to operate the computer without the need for memorising commands were less common.

(ii) Most candidates correctly discussed the alteration of screen colours in order to assist a colour-blind user. For full marks, some mention was needed of the Settings facility to execute such changes, such as the control panel utilities. Some candidates misread the question as being relevant to blind rather than colour-blind users and suggested the provision of sound or braille keys.

Question 3

Note that this question does *not* ask for a list of fields.

Extract from the mark scheme

It is assumed that Aisha has already defined the fields (keys) that will allow the appropriate relationships to be made.

She will have to question the appropriate staff to obtain a comprehensive view on the nature of the existing customer enquiries. In addition, she will have to discover what data about the books, authors and publishers is available as it may be worth including extra data in anticipation of future developments of the application.

Comments from the examiners

This question was usually well attempted, with a variety of suggestions made about how Aisha could decide upon suitable fields. Interviewing the bookshop staff was one good way suggested by many candidates.

Question 4

Extract from the mark scheme

(i) Effectiveness for Matts is about the sale of books. Thus any answer must make a connection between a customer making an enquiry and the sale or ordering of a book.

(ii) Two marks for any valid collectable information, e.g.:
 – the access rate to the system
 – the connection, if any, between specific book details accessed and the orders or sales associated with that book.

(i) Here, all that was required was for the candidate to realise what this system is for in a real world sense. The system exists to service the business (in other words, to sell books) and it is effective if it achieves all the aims expected of it.

(ii) This question referred to the evaluation of the system as a result of storing other data automatically. Thus it was not helpful to suggest other fields about books that could be put in to give customers more information. Successful candidates mentioned collectable data such as the time taken by customers, number of customers or connection with sales.

Question 5

Extract from the mark scheme

(i) This involves the concept that a DBMS can provide specific 'views' of the data to specific users.

(ii) Candidates could give any description that elaborates on the actual mechanism of the processes described in (i).

(iii) Two marks for any situation. Possible answers are:
 – access to other employees' salary details producing internal resentments
 – access to pricing policies that may give advantages to competitors
 – access to internal budget control policies that could produce tension between sections.

Comments from the examiners

(i) Most candidates managed the obvious point that *controlled access* referred to restrictions placed on users to certain parts of the database. It was expected that better candidates would also refer to the idea of views of data such as provided by objects as exemplified by dynasets. A realisation that certain users can be granted limited views of the underlying data was not often demonstrated.

(ii) This section was generally well understood, with a variety of security methods cited. It would be expected at this level that answers would include such ideas as read/write access, group permissions or the provision of selected aspects of data such as could be provided by specific queries.

(iii) Most candidates were able to come up with at least one good reason why controlled data access could be harmful to the company. Typical answers referred to industrial espionage or tensions resultant upon salary details becoming widely known. To gain credit, candidates had to mention something specific rather than vague generalities.

Question 6

(i) Two marks each for TWO well qualified points, for example :

- In the event of a fault then it must be known what tests were carried out and if, in fact, a test that relates to the faults was carried out.
- Was the outcome of the original test conclusive or did it not address the full range of possibilities?
- A corporate purchaser of the product may want evidence of the quality of the product via exposure to the results of system testing.

(ii) The examiner's agenda here is to expose the point that systems are often modified but the documentation is not. The candidate merely has to describe two circumstances out of :

- bug fixing
- additions to the system
- modifications due to a change of company or government policy
- modifications due to the discovery of initial inadequate testing.

Comments from the examiners

(i) This question was generally well answered. Most candidates were able to comment on how the test results could be useful in the event of later problems. Some better candidates were able to suggest that the testing strategy may need to be looked at again if there are doubts about its adequacy. Some also made the good point that purchasers of the system may require proof that the system has been adequately tested.

(ii) Most candidates successfully realised that documentation may need to be added to if bug fixes or upgrades are performed.

Question 7

Extract from the mark scheme

There are two main aspects to this question:

- the fact that Sean is preparing a training programme
- correct technical comments that explain each of the three concepts.

Thus one mark for a reasonable technical description of each concept, and one mark for the approach; for example:

'The operating system is most likely the computer program that greets you when you start to use your computer. In fact it is working all the time you are using the computer as it does jobs like organising files on disks, taking data from the keys as you press them, and refreshing the screen each time the data that you want displayed is changed.'

'You may have had both Word and Excel open at the same time and perhaps were transferring data from one to the other. This is possible because the operating system you were using was a multitasking OS. This means that the OS can direct the processor to give its attention to each application in turn, and because this swapping happens very quickly you have the illusion that the computer is doing both jobs at the same time.'

'Whenever several computers are connected together they are said to form a network. For the network to be useful it must be possible to pass data between specific computers that form the network, and for each member of the network to share such devices as printers and large data stores.'

Comments from the examiners

The issues covered in this question required at least some technical response to qualify for full marks. A good answer for the OS part would require at least two specific functions of an operating system, such as memory management, provision of user interface, or peripheral control.

Question 8

Extract from the mark scheme

This question tests the candidate's ability to make a consistent argument. The fact that the examiner does not agree with the argument is of no consequence when awarding marks. We should be looking for two, consistent, well-made points.

Comments from the examiners

Few candidates scored full marks here. It was expected that the candidates would make arguments comparing or contrasting the two examples. Most managed one, usually the idea of *fitness for purpose* applicable to each example. To score fully, more than one argument needed to be considered.

Question 9

Extract from the mark scheme

Each media type should be discussed from the points of view of:

- user convenience
- currency of information
- mechanism of production
- cost of production and maintenance.

Six marks should be allocated for the attributes of each medium and a further three marks for the quality of direct or implied comparison between the media.

Comments from the examiners

A wide variety of responses were encountered for this question. The better candidates made pertinent points about the characteristics of each medium and attempted to compare them on various criteria.

There were, however, some common problems. Many candidates misunderstood the concept of online help. This is help available from within the application as supplied by the developer. It is nothing to do with telephone support.

There was some confusion over the concept of the 'developer'. Some candidates took this to refer to some sort of super or power user who was looking at documentation for help rather than the person or organisation who wrote the documentation. There was perhaps a lack of realism from some candidates who suggested that an advantage of paper manuals is because people enjoy reading them!

SYSTEMS
MANAGEMENT

CHAPTER 21

The role of the systems manager

This chapter continues to explore the impact of ICT in the bank that was introduced earlier. It will describe:

● the role and responsibilities of the systems manager

● the relationship between the manager and the systems administrator.

This chapter covers these Learning Outcomes in the specification:

L.O.4.1   Demonstrate an understanding of the relationship between systems management and systems administration

L.O.4.2   Define the responsibilities of systems managers

Organisations and business

Earlier in this book we met the key people, James Harris and his staff, who keep the ICT systems running at GBW Bank. They are part of a large organisation, which is run as a profit-making business. Before we can understand how the people who run the ICT systems fit into GBW Bank's overall structure, we need to gain some background knowledge about organisations and business.

What is an organisation?

When people decide to work as a group to achieve something together, their social grouping can be described as an *organisation*. Examples of organisations include clubs, schools, shops, charities, airlines, theatres, law courts, and pressure groups. At a small level a family is an organisation, and at the large level a nation is an organisation.

How do organisations differ from a casual group of friends? One distinguishing feature is that members of organisations have a *common purpose* or *aims*. For example, all those who work for or support a medical charity do so in order to provide help for people suffering from a particular medical condition. This is the charity's main aim.

If you belong to an organisation you will notice that members take on different *roles*. Some people will be leaders, others will take on specific tasks. An amateur theatre group will have actors, musicians, stage crew, a programme designer and ticket sellers, and members will often take on different roles for different productions. A medical charity will have fundraisers, donors, publicists and administrators. GBW Bank is a substantial organisation with a large variety of roles.

Activity

List all the organisations that you belong to. What is your role in each organisation?

What is a business?

A business is a special kind of organisation. It is one in which *goods or services are provided to meet the needs of customers*. It does this by using a range of *resources*, such as raw materials and personal skills, which it converts into goods or services.

Goods are physical items such as computers, food and cars. *Services* are non-physical items such as insurance, banking, education, medical care, software development and entertainment.

Businesses can range in size from a consultant working alone, to a large multinational company. GBW Bank is a business that provides banking and financial services to customers.

What is a profit-making business?

All goods and services cost something to produce. The cost of producing a manufactured good is made up of the cost of the raw materials, the labour costs and the plant costs (machinery and buildings). The cost of providing a service is made up of the labour costs plus the premise's overheads.

Costs are usually paid for by the customer. But there are also businesses where the costs are met from other sources. For example, a college is a business that provides educational services, but most, if not all, of the costs are met by the government. This is an example of a *public sector* business.

If a business has to manage its own affairs without any financial support from outside, then it will normally need to make a *profit*. If its income is less than its outgoings then the business will not survive. If its income is more than its outgoings then the excess income (profit) can be used for any purpose it likes. In practice the profit is often used to pay senior employees a bonus, to provide a safety net for difficult times ahead, to pay shareholders who have invested in the company, or to invest further in the company by buying more machinery to increase production, to employ more staff, to buy larger buildings, etc.

Activities

1. *During each week you are a customer of a number of businesses. Identify as many as you can. Are any of these not-for-profit businesses?*

2. *Select one profit-making business and one not-for-profit business. What goods or services do they provide? What are their main aims? What are the resources available to these businesses?*

Some kinds of business, such as charities and public sector businesses, are not profit-making. Any excess income must be used to support the main aim of the organisation.

Business objectives

An *objective* is a kind of aim that can be used to judge whether a business is successful or not. There must always be a way of measuring whether an objective has been met.

For example, the general aim of a medical charity may be to relieve suffering for victims of a particular condition. One of its objectives may be to increase the money raised by 10 per cent in the coming year. This can be measured. GBW Bank has the aim of providing banking services to customers, but one of its objectives might be to reduce fraud by 25 per cent over the next two years.

A business does not exist in a vacuum. It exists in an environment which includes other businesses, which act on it and which it can influence. This means that the future success of a business can be somewhat unpredictable.

Activities

1. *What factors exist in the environment which may affect the success or otherwise of a business?*

2. *Identify some suitable objectives for GBW Bank.*

Business functions

Businesses, especially large ones like a bank with a head office and many branches, can be very complex organisations. At the top level, GBW Bank is run by the *board of directors* who decide the overall policy and direction of the company.

Some members of the board are *non-executive directors*, and do not work full-time for the company. They are asked to join the board in an advisory capacity. Other members are *executive directors*, and these will be one or more of the senior managers of the company. The leader of these executive directors is known as the *Managing Director*. In some companies, especially in the USA, the term *Chief Executive Officer* (CEO) is used instead.

Functional areas

The tasks that need to be done within a business are usually divided amongst separate *business functions*. The head office of GBW Bank has always followed a traditional pattern, dividing its workforce into these functional areas:

- *Finance Department* – budgets, stock control, costing, accounts, wages, cash. This deals with the internal costs of running the company and is separate from the banking services that it offers customers.
- *Banking Services Department* – customer services, account management, financial products, research and development, purchasing.
- *Marketing Department* – market research, advertising, public relations, sales, after-sales.
- *Administration Department* – legal, staff planning, human resources (personnel), training, office support services, security, estate management, catering.
- *Information Systems Department* – operations, communications, system development, user support. This covers all the technical ICT aspects as well as the development and support of information systems.

In a production company – one that produces goods the Banking Services Department would be replaced by a Production department. A Production department would carry out research and development, purchasing, storage, production planning, packing, quality control, dispatch and transport.

Each department at GBW Bank is run by a *senior manager*. Some or all of these senior managers may also be executive directors. The organisation chart in Figure 22.1 expresses the relationship between them.

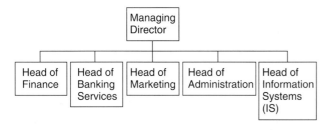

Figure 21.1 *The top of an organisation chart*

Jane Morgan, the Head of Information Systems at GBW Bank, is a senior manager of the company. She runs a large department and over 50 employees work for her. Some of those employees are also managers in their own right.

What is a manager?

Managers are responsible for the work of a number of other employees. They plan the work and they organise the procedures that they follow. Managers often have to co-ordinate work with colleagues in other departments and represent their department to other departments. Essentially their role is to make decisions and to control what happens in their areas, and they take responsibility for all the successes and failures.

Jane at GBW Bank knows that she has to be a leader within her department. This depends on her skills in motivating other people to carry out company policy. She has to support people and at times offer them advice and counselling. One of her main tasks is to ensure that people work together successfully.

Each day Jane spends some of her time sharing information with members of her department – she interprets new demands from the senior management team, and she listens to their concerns. She has to sort out any problems. Some of these are technical, others are more to do with personalities. Some problems relate to resources, and she has to sort these out using her tact and negotiating skills.

Levels of management

Businesses are traditionally organised with three levels of management, and GBW Bank is no exception.

Senior managers

The managing director and other senior managers like Jane are responsible for the overall direction of the business. They plan the long-term future of the company. Their major proposals are put forward to the board of directors who are ultimately answerable to the shareholders if things go wrong. The senior managers and directors establish the objectives of the business, and from the objectives work out a number of *policies*.

Military language is sometimes used to describe decisions taken within companies. The kind of important long-term decisions that senior managers make are known as 'strategic' decisions.

Jane is concerned with the overall management of information within GBW Bank. She has to consider the *information systems strategy* (information needs in line with overall business objectives, and what information is required) and the *information technology strategy* (what ICT systems are needed, and how to provide the information).

Middle managers

Large departments led by senior managers like Jane are usually divided up into smaller groupings. These are sometimes called sections, centres, units or divisions. The section managers ensure that the objectives of the organisation are carried out through the work of their sections.

At GBW Bank, Abdul Ahmed is the Systems Manager, a middle manager post. He runs the Systems Section and is responsible for the smooth running of all the ICT systems.

Carrying on with the military analogy, we say that middle managers make 'tactical' decisions. They check whether the procedures in place are working effectively and they make proposals for new developments. They are concerned with medium-term planning (up to one year, perhaps).

Abdul needs good information about how all the systems are running and is answerable to Jane if things go wrong. All the people who work for him have strong technical skills, so he needs to understand their problems, and find solutions. He also reports to Jane any problems that may need major expenditure. He recommends upgrades to the systems in the light of feedback from users and administrators, and also from customers.

Junior managers

These are often called front-line managers, operational managers, team leaders, supervisors or (traditionally) foremen. Their job is to make sure that the day-to-day

tasks are carried out efficiently. They are responsible for ensuring that all procedures are followed correctly.

At GBW Bank, James Harris is the Senior Systems Administrator, but that does not make him a senior manager. In fact, he is a junior manager and is answerable to the Systems Manager, Abdul. James has a team of systems administrators working for him. He works out their rotas, schedules their tasks, and encourages them to work as a team. Most importantly, he is highly trained in the work and gives technical support to less experienced members of his team.

The work of junior operational managers is absolutely crucial for the survival of the business. Jane may be away for a few days, but because her role is concerned with long-term goals her department will not fall apart without her. But if James is away, someone must cover his work, or the computer systems could grind to a halt.

Junior managers need information that is right up to date to make decisions about faulty hardware, for instance, or user problems. It is sometimes difficult for them to plan the work of the team, as much of the work done is in response to problems that arise. But they must be able to plan the installation and testing of upgrades. This is short-term planning – day by day or over a few weeks.

Line management

Each employee reports to a person who is more senior than them, known as their *line manager*. Jane is Abdul's line manager, and Abdul is James' line manager.

This relationship is best explained through an organisation chart. We will be looking at the structure of the IS department in the next section, so here we will concentrate on aspects of the Administration Department (see Figure 21.2).

A typical organisation chart, when filled out with all the people who work in the business, is shaped more like a pyramid, with the managing director at the top and the operational staff along the bottom. In a small business there will be fewer jobs, of course. This means that there will be fewer layers of management, and individuals will carry out a wider range of tasks.

Modern management styles

Towards the end of the twentieth century many organisations recognised that the traditional ways of

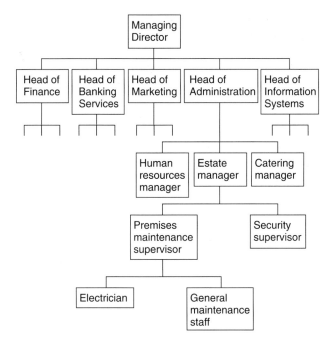

Figure 21.2 *A more extended organisation chart*

organising businesses were not always the most efficient. Although the traditional structures had the advantage that everyone was clear about their responsibilities, some people felt that they tended to stifle innovation.

There was also a growing understanding that the operational staff play an important part in the company, as many of them have direct contact with customers and other people outside the company. Companies started referring to them as the *front-line staff*, as they present the public face of the company. Front-line staff include sales persons, personnel assistants, switchboard operators, accounts staff, and security staff. Some managers also deal with the general public, so are also front-line staff.

At GBW Bank there are quite a lot of front-line staff – almost everyone who works at the high street branches of GBW Bank deals with customers. On the other hand, few of the employees at head office deal directly with customers, although many of them do have to communicate with other businesses who supply the bank with goods and services.

Several new approaches to managing businesses have been tried and combined in different ways:

- *Inverted pyramid.* In this approach the pyramid is drawn upside down, with the front-line staff at the top. This emphasises that the manager's role is to support and encourage the front-line work. When the business is seen in this way managers begin to value their staff more highly and try to organise their departments around the needs of the front-line staff.

- *Flatter structure.* If you ask some organisations why they have so many managers they may be unable to give a more persuasive reply than 'We have always done it like this'. Some businesses have undertaken a radical reassessment of why they organise themselves as they do, and have come to the conclusion that work would be more efficient if they removed many layers of middle management. This would then tend to reduce bureaucracy and speed up communications. For example, staff will often be organised into teams to tackle particular projects. When a project is completed then staff will be allocated to new teams. This gives employees at the lower level of the pyramid more decision-making power.

- *Business units.* A company may be subdivided into business units, each operating with its own budget and objectives. It is not always clear how IS fits into this. One solution is to have a central IS department that supplies services to all the business units. Another approach is for each business unit to have its own IT department.

> ### Activity
>
> *Think again about the organisation that you studied while working on coursework Task 1. Draw up an organisation chart for the areas that you were familiar with. Was the organisation structured in a traditional way, or had it developed one of the modern patterns of management listed in this section?*

The work of an information systems department

The success of GBW Bank depends entirely on the information that it has, and the information has to be with the right person at the right time. For example, a branch of GBW Bank must be able to tell a customer how much she has in her account, and a branch manager must have information about a customer's credit history in order to decide whether to grant a loan.

The IS department is responsible for the storage and distribution of information throughout GBW Bank. Whilst computer systems handle most of the information, the IS department must also consider other methods of distributing information, such as the telephone system and internal mail.

The term 'Information and Communication Technology' covers all the technical ways in which information can be stored and communicated, but GBW Bank also uses traditional, non-electronic methods, such as the post.

The IS department at GBW Bank is responsible for all the ICT and other information systems used throughout the company. These include:

- computer hardware and peripherals
- computer software
- network systems
- internal communications (internal mail, phone, intranet)
- external communications (external mail, phone, fax, Internet).

The IS department has to do these tasks:

- propose upgrades and new systems
- develop software applications
- purchase computer hardware, software and other items
- install and test systems
- administer systems
- train users and technical staff
- support end-users.

Many businesses today are highly dependent on their ICT systems. They can be dependent on ICT in one of three ways:

- It would be very difficult for the company to go back to paper-based methods of storing and processing all their information.
- Some of the services that the company offers would not be possible without ICT systems.
- The company would not exist at all without ICT systems.

GBW Bank falls into the second category.

Until recently, the IS function at GBW Bank had been part of the Administration department, and the Head of Administration has been Jane's boss. But as in many large businesses these days, the board of directors realised that IS was highly significant in the success of the company so restructured the company and created a new IS department. Today at least half of all IS managers are at senior level. This is because companies recognise that IS departments do not simply provide computer facilities for the rest of the employees, but are an integral part of the whole operation.

Activity

Study the accompanying job advertisement. Comment on the kind of work that the postholder will be expected to do and how the postholder will relate to the rest of the organisation.

Head of Management Information Systems

With the continuous growth of our technology-based information system, we as a charitable organisation are seeking to appoint a seasoned Head of Management Information Systems to be responsible for both IT strategy and the timely delivery of management systems throughout the UK. Reporting to the Director General and working across all functional areas, the postholder will develop and implement plans to fulfil the information needs of the organisation. The appointee will have the challenge of setting a new management information strategy and then delivering it.

Educated to degree level, the successful candidate will have at least five years' experience of designing and managing a complex multi-site system, managing a team of IT professionals, and working to tight budgets and deadlines. An extensive understanding of current technologies and best practices in information systems is essential, as is tenacity and exceptional communication skills. The new post provides an exciting opportunity to be both innovative and influential in developing a major IT system for the future.

Names and roles

If you look through job advertisements for managers in the IT field you will see a confusing array of *job titles*. Unfortunately, there is no simple way of telling from someone's job title what exactly their job entails.

Jane Morgan's job title at GBW Bank is Head of Information Systems, but she might just as well have been called the Information Technology Manager or, in an American company, the Chief Information Officer. Today most such senior people in large organisations have the word 'Information' somewhere in their job title. This implies that they are responsible for all the information that is stored and communicated within the organisation, and not simply for the hardware and software.

Abdul Ahmed is the Systems Manager. Again, his job title could have been IT Systems Manager or Computer Services Manager. In the past the managers in this area had titles like Operations Manager or Data Processing Manager. Abdul's line manager is Jane Morgan.

James Harris is the Senior Systems Administrator. In other companies someone doing a similar job might be known as the Network Manager or IT Systems Officer. The systems administrators that work for him could be called IT engineers or computer technicians.

Structure of the IS department at GBW Bank

Jane Morgan is responsible for four main areas of IS work:

- systems operation – administration and maintenance of systems
- support – help and training for end-users
- strategy – recommending new developments
- development – projects for producing new applications

There are two middle managers in the IS department who work for Jane. The three managers, including Jane, between them cover the areas of work listed above (see Figure 21.3).

Structure of the Systems Section at GBW Bank

Abdul Ahmed has a team of people working for him.

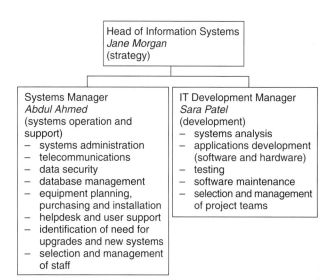

Figure 21.3 *The IS department at GBW Bank*

Some of these are junior managers in their own right. He drew up their job specifications and selected new staff, in conjunction with the Human Resources section.

All the members of the Systems Section have a high level of technical skill. Most have been educated to HND or degree level. Many are continuing their training by studying for specialist network engineer diplomas or other qualifications. GBW Bank encourages professional development and provides training opportunities where this clearly enhances the work of the IS department.

The organisation chart for the section (see Figure 21.4) does not show everyone working in the section.

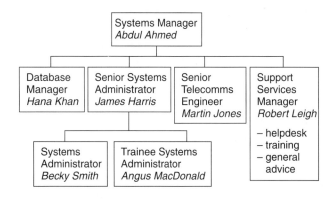

Figure 21.4 *The Systems Section at GBW Bank*

Structure of an IS department in a small company

In a small organisation the various roles we have described will be covered by fewer people, so some of the layers of management may disappear.

By far the most common feature of a small business is that it will not do any inhouse software development. It will buy in all its software or employ external consultants to carry out systems analysis and application development.

For example, at the water company EauCo Water, Andrew Jones combines the work of the IS manager and the systems manager. He is actually known as the Operations Manager. He is responsible for all the hardware and software, data security and user support, and he also draws up proposals for upgrades to the system. His team consists of five systems administrators, who work in shifts to give 24-hour coverage, and a database administrator. The systems administrators provide help to any other staff.

But ICT systems come on a smaller scale still. A firm of accountants has a small network of PCs and employs Jenny Chiu in an IT support role. Jenny has to provide support and training to all the users, maintain the computing and telephone equipment, install software and hardware, and research new products. In fact, Jenny is both a systems manager and a systems administrator.

Activity

Study the two accompanying job advertisements. For each one, where possible:

- *describe the responsibilities of the postholder*
- *draw up an organisation chart to show how the postholder will fit into the structure of the company.*

IT Services Manager

Location: Lincoln + travel

Benefits: £40K–£50K + car allowance + benefits

Role:
This newly created position is due to the continous growth of Bell Group. We currently require an IT Services Manager, who will be responsible for the management of IT services, IT strategies and IT support to both the HQ and all other Bell offices.

Skills:
Management of the IT support/services function
Best practices in IT support
Knowledge of the latest developments in IT and telecomms
Budget responsibility

Qualifications:
Degree or equivalent
Management experience

IT Helpdesk Manager (Network Services)

Location: Newcastle

Role:
The role, within the IT Department, is to serve as the point of contact for the helpdesk, providing advice, guidance and support on technical and personnel issues, while acting as a member of the Network Services management team.

Key responsibilities:
Day-to-day management of all NS-related issues for the UK helpdesk. Day-to-day task and personnel management of NS helpdesk personnel. Provide point of escalation for all user complaints and issues. Provide advanced technical support and reference for first- and second-line support. Contribute advice and resource to the development of site infrastructure.

Essential skills:
5+ years advanced working IT experience. Management in an autonomous role. Face-to-face customer service. Escalation resolution and customer service. Advanced working knowledge of Windows 98, Novell, Microsoft Office.

Systems manager

Relationship between the systems manager and senior management

Abdul Ahmed, the Systems Manager at GBW bank, knows that half of the Bank's annual capital expenditure is on ICT. Although Jane is the person who formulates strategy and makes proposals for new systems, Abdul plays an important role in identifying needs. He will know, better than Jane, where problems exist. Because he is able to monitor the performance of the systems, he is in a good position to recommend to her any upgrades that may be useful.

On the other hand, Jane realises that it is easy to assume that investment in ICT will benefit the company, but it is actually very difficult to measure the benefits. If she wants the bank to invest a large sum of money in a new system or an upgrade to the current system, she will have to put together a convincing case to the other senior managers and to the board of directors.

Jane will turn to Abdul to produce facts and figures about the systems. He should be able to give her answers to questions like:

- How many bank statements are produced each month, how long does it take to produce them, and how many staff are needed to produce them?
- How frequently does the main system go down, and for how long?
- Are the branch bank managers satisfied with the information they can access when deciding whether to grant a loan to a customer?
- Are any problems reported frequently to the helpdesk?

Relationship between the systems manager and systems administrator

One of Abdul's main responsibilities is to make sure that the systems administrators have clear procedures to follow when carrying out routine system maintenance. He discusses the procedures regularly with James Harris, the Senior Systems Administrator. James recommends new procedures to Abdul in the light of his own direct experience.

Abdul has to ensure that there are procedures for:

- carrying out any changes, however small, to the systems
- keeping records of any changes that are made
- monitoring the performance of the systems
- maintaining security
- handling downtime
- dealing with major breakdowns.

One day James told Abdul that a new member of the Human Resources section had asked Angus MacDonald, the Trainee Systems Administrator, for a user ID for the system and Angus had set up a new account for her. Later James discovered that the new 'member of staff' was in fact a student on work experience. Casual employees like this are allowed to have access to basic applications, such as word-processing, but are not entitled to have access to personnel records on the system.

James and Abdul discussed the best way to avoid mistakes like this in the future, and they also went over the problem with the Human Resources Manager. Eventually they suggested that middle managers should be asked to complete a form authorising computer access for new employees, and that this should state the appropriate level of access. All the systems administrators would be told that they should not set up any user accounts unless requested to do so on one of these forms. Abdul reported this proposal to Jane, then circulated copies of the new form to all the middle managers and explained the new procedure.

Murphy's law

After the Second World War, Edward Murphy was an engineer working for the US Air Force. He carried out experiments to test how the human body tolerates high accelerations. In one experiment he found that a technician had installed every one of the sensors the wrong way round, and he commented 'If there are two or more ways to do something, and one of those ways can result in a catastrophe, then someone will do it'. Someone summarised this as 'What can go wrong, will go wrong', which has become known as Murphy's Law.

This turns out to be a very sound approach to technical tasks of all kinds. The principle is that if any tiny flaw in a system could eventually lead to a problem, then at some time during the lifetime of the system the odds are that it will eventually cause trouble. Computer systems that go wrong can have a very serious impact on a business, and can, in some organisations, even cause loss of life.

Abdul approaches his work with Murphy's Law in mind. Not only does he ensure that procedures are in place for carrying out all the day-to-day tasks, but he is also on the lookout for places where things could, potentially, go wrong. For example, he gives highest priority to the security of data on the Bank's system. James and Abdul try to imagine all the possible ways in which people could gain unauthorised access to the system, because they know that if they can find the loopholes, then a criminal probably could too.

Relationship between the systems manager and end-users

The end-users at GBW Bank can be found in all departments and at all levels. The Managing Director is an end-user, as are all the managers, at all levels. Many of the front-line staff are also end-users.

Abdul's section provides end-user support to everyone in GBW Bank. Staff contact the helpdesk, usually by phone, and talk through their problems. The helpdesk staff use a manual which lists problems and then gives step-by-step instructions for solving them. If the problem is not listed, or is difficult to understand, then the helpdesk staff will visit the end-user personally.

Sometimes problems are reported that cannot be solved easily. These are reported to Abdul, so that he can investigate further. He may need to contact the hardware suppliers, or to talk to Sara Patel, the IT Development Manager. The user may have identified a shortcoming in the system that can be rectified only by an upgrade. Abdul must be aware of new technologies and new ways of using existing technology, so that he can prepare a proposal to Jane for an upgrade.

Sometimes managers in another department contact Abdul because they believe there is a need for a completely new application. Abdul is always the first person they speak to, as he may be able to point out to them that the task can already be achieved using existing applications. But if they have suggested an application which is genuinely new, then Abdul will do some preliminary research before putting a proposal to Jane.

Abdul sometimes has to *prioritise* proposals. That means that he has to consider proposals in the light of the objectives of GBW Bank, and to put them in order of importance.

The Systems Manager must have good relationships with other managers. Abdul is the direct interface

Activity

The sales manager in the marketing department of a large computer hardware company has suggested to the IT systems section that a new application is needed to track sales contacts and past customers. Identify which of these tasks is the responsibility of a) the IT systems manager and b) the systems administrator:

- *researching the options*
- *developing a costed proposal for the new application*
- *purchasing or commissioning the application*
- *installing and testing the application*
- *providing the sales team with access to the application*
- *training end-users*
- *providing support to end-users.*

between the technical IT personnel and the rest of the company.

Qualities of a good systems manager

A good systems manager:

- has good broad knowledge of ICT systems
- has an understanding of the whole business, and of the part that ICT systems play in it
- is a good communicator (listener, persuader, report writer)
- maintains good relationships with managers in other departments
- selects staff with good technical expertise and communication skills
- manages staff well
- proposes and prioritises projects that fit in with overall business objectives
- can be trusted
- enjoys working with others
- enjoys working in an changing environment.

A *hybrid manager* is someone who has good business knowledge as well as technical understanding. Many companies want to employ someone who really understands how businesses work and who is not just interested in technology for its own sake. This is reflected in the number of degree courses that combine business studies with IT.

Activity

The job description for a systems manager required some specific technical and managerial skills, but also included this lengthy list of personal requirements. Explain what each point means.

- *an effective change manager with a high degree of tolerance for change and ambiguity*
- *used to working in a complex technology environment*
- *ability to guide and delegate effectively and a strong commercial perspective*
- *excellent communication skills, both verbal and written*
- *effective and professional liaison skills*
- *ability to objectively assess situations*
- *ability to work to time-scales under pressure*
- *ability, through experience, to relate previous knowledge to current problems.*

This chapter continues to explore the impact of ICT in the bank that was introduced in Chapter 5 and discussed further in Chapter 21. It will describe:

● how the systems manager communicates with staff members across the organisation about their ICT needs

● the importance of communication skills in the ICT industry.

This chapter covers the following Learning Objective in the specification:

L.O.4.3   Define the communication process between all those concerned with the provision of ICT-based solutions

The provision of ICT solutions

In any large organisation the ICT needs are very varied. The Information Systems department may be asked to supply and support some or all of the following types of system.

Production systems are used by operational staff. In a manufacturing company they control the production of goods.

Transaction processing systems are also used by operational (front-line) staff and are used to record and manage all the day-to-day business operations of the organisation. Transaction processing systems are used in most functional areas, including marketing (sales and orders), finance (billing and accounting) and human resources (payroll and employee records). There may also be industry-specific transactional processing systems, such as reservation and tracking systems, or membership records.

Office automation systems are the familiar general packages for producing and viewing documents. They include word-processing, desktop publishing, graphics manipulation, Internet browser, e-mail management and calendar scheduling software. Some of these systems are now sometimes known as *knowledge*

work systems. Knowledge workers are professionals who create new information, and they include graphical designers, engineers, website designers and writers. They may use specialist software such as computer-aided design or Web design tools, but they could also use the standard office automation systems.

Management information systems are used by middle managers to summarise the data flowing through the production and transaction processing systems. The management information system will produce reports on a periodic basis (weekly, monthly or annually) which the managers can then use to plan for the future. The system will also generate reports on demand which can help the manager decide how to handle a specific problem. *Executive support systems* are management information systems used at the most senior level of the organisation and are designed to support long-term planning. They draw on data in the transaction processing systems, but they also use external information such as stockmarket reports.

The systems manager needs to understand how all these software systems function. But, more importantly, the systems manager needs to understand the business needs of all the employees in the organisation, so that good advice can be given about how software systems can help to meet those needs.

Communicating about ICT needs

With whom does the systems manager communicate?

The previous chapter outlined the organisational structure of GBW Bank. Abdul Ahmed, the bank's Systems Manager, has to communicate with people in all the functional areas of the company. He also has to communicate with people outside the company.

Internal communications

Abdul communicates on a daily basis with these fellow employees:

- his line manager (Head of Information Systems)
- the staff in his section
- the staff in the IT Development section
- end-users across the company
- managers of other departments.

Abdul communicates both internally and externally

External communications

Abdul regularly communicates with these people external to the organisation:

- maintenance service suppliers
- hardware suppliers
- consumables suppliers
- software houses
- consultants

What does the systems manager communicate about internally?

If we take, in turn, each of the people that Abdul communicates with, we can identify what they communicate about. Abdul communicates with ...

... his line manager
- to make proposals for new systems and upgrades
- to prioritise proposals in the light of costs and business benefits
- to discuss the implementation of new systems and upgrades

... staff in his section
- to set work priorities and discuss workload
- to discuss possible changes in procedures

... staff in the IT Development section
- to discuss possible solutions to problems
- to plan implementation of new systems, including testing, changeover and end-user training and support

... end-users across the company
- to discuss problems with the system that are difficult to solve
- to discuss possible improvements

... managers of other departments
- to discuss possible upgrades or new systems
- to negotiate the use of resources.

What does the systems manager communicate about externally?

Abdul also communicates with ...

... maintenance service suppliers
- to negotiate contracts

... hardware suppliers
- to discuss hardware solutions
- to negotiate prices for purchase or leasing
- for advice with hardware faults

... consumables suppliers
- to negotiate bulk prices
- to order and arrange delivery

... software houses
- to discuss possible projects
- to negotiate contracts
- to purchase off-the-shelf software

... consultants
- to establish terms of reference
- to negotiate contracts
- to monitor progress.

Human communication

Human communication is essentially concerned with passing messages from one person to another. In a business environment it is important that messages be received and understood correctly.

Sometimes we refer to the two people involved as the *sender* and the *receiver*. One person sends a message which is received by another. The receiver may then become the sender of a new message back to the original sender.

This simple description suggests that information can be transmitted easily from one person to another without any misunderstanding. In practice, communications often convey more than the straightforward factual information, and there is plenty of scope for the misinterpretation of messages. This is because communication usually occurs in a social context.

If two people meet face to face to discuss a problem, their communication will be two-way. The two-way communication will occur throughout the conversation, as they will each use facial expressions and gestures to communicate, as well as voice.

Similarly, a written communication, such as a memo or e-mail, can be couched in language to convey expressions of annoyance, anger, pleasure or enthusiasm. Although the communication is one-way, writers can use underlining, exclamation marks and emoticons such as :-) to express meaning and to engage the receiver in the issue.

People will also have shared knowledge because they work in the same environment. For example, the Systems Manager, Abdul, may make this comment to Sara: 'We've sorted out the ID problem', or he may ask simply 'Lunch?' Both are understood in the context of their work and previous conversations.

Communication networks

People who communicate with each other form a communication network perhaps like the one illustrated in Figure 22.1. Most of the communication in this particular network is two-way, but there is one area of one-way communication. These could be television viewers who receive broadcasts but cannot respond directly to them.

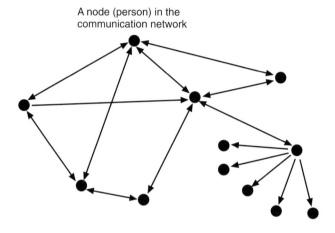

A node (person) in the communication network

Figure 22.1 *Schematic of a communication network*

The shape of the communication network in an organisation will be strongly influenced by the management structure. Various patterns of management were discussed in the previous chapter. For example, in a strict traditional organisation, such as the Army, people will communicate only vertically with their line manager, and their subordinates, and horizontally with their co-workers. In a flatter structure employees are more likely to communicate horizontally and vertically across the whole organisation.

So far we have referred to formal communications, but in practice many informal communication networks develop in organisations. These reflect friendships and common interests.

Communication networks become ever more complex as they grow larger. This can become a problem within a large organisation, such as GBW Bank. This is a particular issue for ICT staff, like Abdul, who need to communicate across the whole organisation. But as we shall see, ICT also provides some of the solutions to this problem.

Features of communication in an effective network

The medium of communication

The *medium* of communication is the means by which a particular message is conveyed from one person to another. Here are some examples of media that might be used in a business context:

- face-to-face conversation (formal or informal)
- telephone (direct contact, voicemail)
- Internet/intranet (e-mail, website)
- printed document (book, memo, report, letter)
- handwritten document (note)
- presentation (slide show, film, video).

The code of communication

A communication *code* is a system of meaning that is common to a certain culture. For example, spoken English is a code of communication, as is written English. We also use graphical codes, such as the icons in many graphical interfaces. Other codes are less obvious, and include tone of voice, conventions about dress, and body language.

Within a culture there may be many *subcultures*, with a bewildering variety of codes. This is easily understood if we observe the differences between the English spoken by Britons, Americans and Australians. But even within the United Kingdom, there are many cultural variants of spoken English, both geographical and social. Similarly, the codes of body language differ between cultures; for example, hand gestures have different meanings in different countries.

The important thing to remember about codes is that they enable people to communicate only if their meanings are shared by all the people involved.

Here are some examples of codes of communication which are relevant in a business context:

- conversational spoken language
- formal spoken language (e.g. at board meetings)
- informal written language (notes)
- formal written language (reports)
- graphics (photos, logos, warning signs)
- appearance (company's dress code, hair style)
- body language (tone of voice, facial expressions, posture, eye contact).

Frequency of communication

Communication may be *planned* or *unplanned*. Either may be written or spoken. Planned communication may be in the form of scheduled meetings between teams of people, or may be routine letters to customers. Unplanned communication may be conversations initiated to solve a problem, or memos about immediate events.

When communication is planned, the people involved should decide on the frequency of communication. At GBW Bank, this means that Abdul has to ask himself questions like these:

> How often should the systems administration team meet formally?
>
> How often should I report on helpdesk usage to Jane Morgan, the Head of Information Systems?
>
> How often should I be in contact with my preferred hardware supplier?

Written communications

A *report* is a formal written communication used to convey information within an organisation. A report is always written for a specific purpose and for a specific audience.

Often when an employee is asked to write a report it is to convey information to a person who is in a more senior position in the organisation's hierarchy. A report usually summarises a body of data. For example, the sales manager could write a report to the marketing director which describes and summarises the sales figures for the previous quarter.

Routine reports

A *routine report* is one that is produced at an agreed frequency. This could be weekly, monthly or annually. Routine reports are usually given to a manager as a summary of the raw data that is being gathered by an organisation – for example, production figures.

At GBW Bank, Abdul receives a short weekly report from James Harris, the Senior Systems Administrator. James summarises the problems that have occurred with the systems during the week and the action taken by his staff. All the data is gathered from the logs kept by the systems administrators. If necessary, James makes recommendations about new procedures, or possibly new purchases, which might help to reduce the problems.

Exception reports

An *exception report* is one that is written as a result of unexpected activity. It may warn a manager that something has gone wrong or is about to go wrong with the technical infrastructure. Or it may alert a manager to an unexpected increase in complaints, sales or enquiries. A report of an accident at work, or an unpleasant incident, would also be an exception report.

Abdul also receives a short weekly report from Robert Leigh, the Support Services Manager, who is responsible for the helpdesk. But if the number of requests for help suddenly rises mid-week, Robert will report to Abdul straight away. He may do this verbally in the first instance, but will follow up with a brief written report.

On-demand reports

An *on-demand report* is, as the name suggests, produced as a result of a request from a manager. A senior manager in a company may become aware of an increase in staff turnover. The initial indication of this may be included in a routine report. The manager may then ask for a more detailed report, which would analyse the reasons for the staff leaving. The report would then help the manager to assess the situation and take corrective action.

At GBW Bank, Abdul is sometimes asked by Jane Morgan, the Head of the Information Systems

Department, to produce a one-off report. She may ask for an assessment of the usage of the helpdesk, with a view to reducing the number of staff employed.

> **Activity**
>
> *Find examples of reports written for different purposes, and compare the styles of presentation.*

Quality of communication

Interpersonal skills

Abdul Ahmed is a good communicator. When he was appointed as systems manager the interviewing panel paid particular attention to the spoken and written communication skills of the applicants. They also tried to assess the quality of their *interpersonal skills*.

Staff, like Abdul, who deal with people have to possess good interpersonal skills. These skills are partly a matter of personality, but they can also be developed with training and experience. Abdul was previously employed as the Senior Systems Administrator at GBW Bank, so the managers were aware of his personal qualities.

People who are good at forming and maintaining relationships are usually good at listening to what others say to them and can understand the non-verbal signals that we all use. They respond to what the other person is saying, or what they are trying to say, and do not simply view a conversation as an opportunity to air their own views.

Managers also have to acquire *negotiating skills*. Negotiation is the process of coming to an agreement with someone. The agreement could be about the terms of a contract, or it could be about providing new ICT resources for another department. If people already agree about the outcome then there will be no need to negotiate. If there is a need for negotiation then at the beginning of a negotiation the people involved will, by definition, have differing views or demands.

Effective negotiating involves listening, accepting, responding and compromising by all the people involved. It should result in the satisfaction of needs that can be met, and the provision of explanations and support where needs cannot be met fully.

The culture gap

ICT specialists are often thought by others to be bad communicators. They have a high level of technical knowledge and they greatly enjoy talking about technical matters with others who share their enthusiasms. But they often find it difficult to talk about ICT in a non-technical way to ordinary users. This is sometimes called the *culture gap* between ICT and non-ICT people.

Some ICT professionals actually believe that they do not need to have good interpersonal skills as their work concentrates on solving technical problems. They also tend to enjoy the technology for its own sake, and do not understand that ICT is of value to the company only if it leads to business success.

But ICT staff have to solve problems for non-technical people, in order to make the business run as intended. If the ICT staff insist on using technical language that the end-user does not understand, then they will not be able to help them. Worse still, if the ICT staff use their knowledge in a superior way they may simply intimidate the user, and make it difficult for the users to feel comfortable with the technology.

If a person asks for help with a problem with the computer system or with the use of an application, ideally he or she wants to meet a technical expert who not only sorts out the problem but also explains how to avoid or solve the problem in the future. So technical staff need to be able (a) to listen, (b) to understand the problem from the user's point of view, and (c) to explain how the problem is solved, at the right level of technical detail for the user to understand.

How can Abdul overcome the 'culture gap' within GBW Bank? In the first place, he can try to employ people who can communicate successfully. He can then ensure that his staff are give the same initial training about the business as everyone else who joins GBW Bank. There is a tendency for ICT staff to stick together at lunchtime, so he will encourage his staff to socialise with staff from other departments and to take part in any sporting and leisure activities that GBW Bank organises.

In a large IS department like the one at GBW Bank, some employees – such as the systems manager, helpdesk staff and systems analysts – deal directly with other members of the company. Other staff, such as systems administrator's, do so less frequently; but they do have to communicate with suppliers, so they cannot afford to have poor communication skills.

ICT serving communication in an organisation

Systems and software

ICT systems support many different methods of communication. Voicemail, e-mail, teleconferencing, even the telephone system itself, are all dependent on ICT systems. Written communications are normally prepared using software packages instead of being handwritten. In many organisations, such as GBW Bank, the systems manager has responsibility for all of these communication tools.

In order to provide a useful and effective service to the employees at GBW Bank, Abdul needs to know how these communication systems are used and any shortcomings. He can use system logs to get information about the usage of the phones and of any software packages used on the computer network. He can also carry out surveys, by questionnaire or face-to-face interviews, to find out if there are any problems with the current systems or if there are any new needs.

ICT also provides access to some very useful databases which speed up the process of finding people and places. Organisations can purchase a postcode database, which lists the correct postal address for each postcode in the UK. They can also acquire electronic versions of telephone directories and electoral registers (the lists of people registered to vote in a local authority or constituency). Databases of companies offering goods and services can be searched for business-to-business contacts. Most of this material is also accessible on the Internet.

Work patterns

ICT has had a significant impact on work patterns.

Time displacement

Time displacement refers to the facility to send and to respond to communications at times that suit the people involved. For example, in the past if you wanted to get a message to someone in Australia you could send a letter, although this might take several days to reach its destination. You could, of course, use the phone, but you would probably have to make the call outside normal office hours in order to catch the other person at work. Today you can send a fax, which can be picked up when the recipient arrives at work, or you can e-mail. Both these technologies allow for time-displaced communications, that is, they allow both sender and recipient to communicate within their own normal working hours.

Flexible working

Flexible working, also known as flexi-time, is an increasingly popular mode of working. Employees are required to work a set number of hours per week, or month, but can choose the actual hours for themselves. This method of working is liked by employees as it can reduce travelling times and can free up time during the working day for dealing with domestic matters.

At GBW Bank some of the finance staff are on flexi-time. Some choose to start work early and leave early,

avoiding the rush-hour traffic. Others work longer hours each day, and are able to free up one whole day every week or two. The Head of Finance has stipulated that all staff must be on the premises between the hours of 10am and 3pm (apart from lunchbreaks) and that employees who have 'banked' a free day must negotiate this with their line manager at least a week in advance. Although

Flexi-time has become increasingly popular

there are some minor inconveniences with these arrangements the Head of Finance believes that they are outweighed by the advantages of having a happier and better motivated team.

Once again, time-displaced communications can support these patterns of work. Work in progress which needs to be discussed with colleagues can be stored in a shared workspace on the network; internal e-mails can be sent to people who are not in the office; and messages can be left on voicemail systems.

Teleworking

Teleworking is the name given to the style of working which allows employees to work from home, and at hours that suit them. It is particularly suitable for occupations that do not require daily face-to-face communications with colleagues. The Open University was founded almost entirely as a teleworking institution.

Teleworking is normally dependent on ICT systems such as e-mail and mobile phones. Employees will often have a remote login facility which will allow them to log to the company's networks from anywhere in the world. Laptop computers with modem connections are commonly provided to enable this. Face-to-face meetings can often be replaced with Internet, phone or videoconferencing.

We are also moving towards the concept of a *virtual organisation*. Such an organisation will not be located anywhere in particular, but will consist of a group of people who work together using a range of ICT tools to communicate. This book was produced by a team of writers, who created an informal organisation for the duration of the project. They communicated largely by e-mail, with occasional meetings at 'borrowed' locations. Small workteams like these have no expensive overheads, and the members can live anywhere in the world.

CHAPTER 23

Data communications and networks

This chapter covers some of the technical knowledge that the systems manager at the bank needs to have. It will describe:

● data communications

● networks.

This chapter covers these Technical Knowledge topics in the specification:

T4.3.2   Communications
T4.3.3   Networks and protocols (in part)

Data communications at GBW Bank

At the bank, the Head of IS, Jane Morgan, has overall responsibility for the electronic communications that underpin all the extensive computer systems and networks within the organisation. In practice, the Systems Manager, Abdul Ahmed, and his team prepare specifications for upgrades, carry out any installations, diagnose problems and generally maintain these data communication systems.

Communicating computer data

Data communications (or just simply 'communications') concerns the transfer of computer data from a process on one machine to a process on another machine. Transfer may take place over a very short distance using a cable or other means of connection such as radio, infrared or microwave, or it may involve thousands of miles of transfer using a range of connection equipment. Long-distance communications are sometimes referred to as *telecommunications*.

Essentially all these transfer media are the 'pipes' down which data flows. Each transfer of data involves three basic stages and you can liken this to any kind of communication.

First, a sending device must be physically connected to the receiving device. Second, the two devices must be ready to communicate – the sending device must know that the receiving device is ready and waiting to receive data (e.g. it is switched on and listening for messages). Third, the two devices must engage in transfer so that the sending device knows that the data has arrived and whether it has arrived correctly. This sending and receiving negotiation has to follow an agreed set of rules so that each part of the communication makes sense to both parties. The agreement and use of rules is called a *protocol*.

Activity

Describe how the three stages of communication described above might be applied to the case of two people communicating using a walkie-talkie in a house. What rules would they use?

Computer data is represented as digital information. So a byte of data representing a letter might be 01001011. In order to send this byte of data down a connection such as a copper wire, an agreed way of signalling must be established. This is where international standards bodies come in, as they set out to electronic engineers the agreed rules for transmitting a signal down a wire. For example, to send a single bit representing 1 it might be established that a negative voltage of −5 should be used and a positive voltage of +5 be used for a 0 digit. Another agreement might be how long the signal for each bit should last, so that a receiver can read the changing voltages accurately. For example, if a sender wants to send three 1s then the receiver must be able to read three 1s and not two 1s or four. This is done by the receiver sampling the signal at the same speed as the sender generated it.

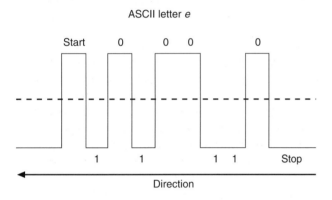

Figure 23.1 *Transmitting a single character using serial transmission*

In Figure 23.1, a letter *e* is being sent down a wire, from right to left. Below the dashed line represents a minus voltage and above it a positive one. In order for the receiver to know when a byte of data is arriving a *start bit* is used. This sets the receiver off reading at fixed time intervals until all eight bits are read. At the end a *stop bit* signals the end of the byte of transmission and ensures that the receiver is ready to receive another character.

Serial and parallel data transmission

Sending a single bit or series of bits down a single wire is called *serial transmission*. This works fine over distances of about 15 metres. However, it is constrained by the fact that each bit has to follow the one in front and is therefore fixed by this configuration. Another way of sending data is to use a group of parallel wires where a group of data can be transmitted at the same time. Imagine sending the letter *e* as in Figure 23.2. If each bit could be sent at the same time down its own individual wire then in one signal length a whole byte can be sent as opposed to just the first bit. This is *parallel transmission*.

In Figure 23.2 you can see that each signal that makes up the letter *e* is carried down its own wire and arrives simultaneously at the receiver. This is going to be about eight times as fast as serial transmission.

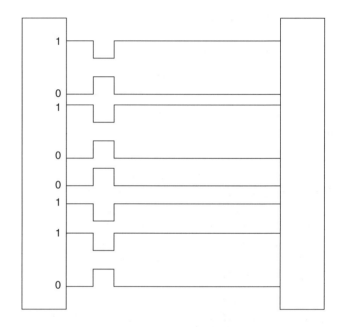

Figure 23.2 *Parallel transmission of a single character*

International standards exist for sending serial and parallel transmissions. The most common standard for serial transmission is called the Recommended Standard 232c, or RS232c for short. This is a standard developed in the US by the Electronics Industry Association. Parallel transmission commonly uses the Centronix interface that is found in devices such as printers.

Analogue–digital interfaces

Sending digital data down a copper wire is successful for short distances. As distances increase the problem of signal deterioration occurs, in addition to the physical problem of needing long cables. Therefore it was decided early on that it would be sensible to use the existing telephone system for longer distances. After all, why lay new copper cable if an existing infrastructure exists? Similarly a system of relay

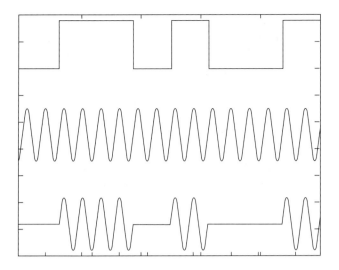

Square-shaped digital signal used within a computer or sent down a serial cable

Wavy analogue signal used on a telephone line to carry voice

Modulated analogue signal – in this example the amplitude (length of a wave) for 1s is modulated (modified) as compared with 0s (it is much flatter). In this way a digital signal can be represented

Figure 23.3 *A simple example of modulation*

stations exists for boosting signals, throughout the telephone network.

However, the type of signal able to travel on a telephone wire is different from that of a serial cable. That is because the signal used to carry voice is analogue and not digital. Therefore, if the square-shaped signal used for digital information is going to be used on an analogue line, the signal has to be converted to a wavy analogue signal. This process is known as *modulation*.

The conversion of the analogue signal to a digital signal and vice versa is carried out by electronics. In the example in Figure 23.3, the electronics and control logic are built into a device called a 'modem'. The origin of the word modem comes from the function it performs – *mod*ulator *dem*odulator. Other kinds of analogue to digital conversion take place as well, for example sound from a microphone into a sound card will be converted from analogue to digital data.

Data transmission protocols

The need for protocols

Communication *protocols* exist to enable different parties, systems and devices to make meaningful communications. In computer networks, heterogeneity is the norm. Communications may take place over a muliplicity of connection media (satellites, microwave, radio, copper; etc.), using a range of organisations (state-owned and private telecoms) and utilising a variety of hardware. Rules governing interchange are therefore essential.

Because of the complexity of providing secure and reliable interconnection over networks, protocols have been developed that break the entire communication process down into a series of different stages or levels. At each stage, protocols carry out processing relevant for that particular step in the communication process. Each computer must use the same protocols and apply the stages consistently so that the rules are applied systematically. The basic procedures for communications can be summarised as follows:

Sending computer
- Breaks the whole data transmission down into a series of data packets.
- Adds addressing information to each packet so that it will be delivered to the correct destination computer.
- Converts the data packet into a transmission format appropriate for the network connection being used. For example, a connection using the phone line will use a modem to convert digital data to an analogue signal or a network adapter card will convert the digital data to a signal, used by the network cable.

Receiving computer
- Intercepts suitably addressed network signals and converts them back into data packets.
- Removes addressing and other control information added by the sending computer.

- Stores the data packets in a temporary storage area where the packets are re-assembled into the original transmission.
- Passes the re-assembled data to an application where it can be processed.

Each stage of the sending operation breaks the transmission process down into more and more basic parts until an actual signal of some kind is generated. Similarly, the receiving computer builds the signal back up using the reverse operations of the same protocols.

Data packets

You will have noticed that the data communication described above refers to 'data packets'. So just what are data packets and why are they used? Data packets are small chunks of data usually made up from a larger collection of data such as a file. However, files are not an appropriate way of sending data over a network. There are two basic reasons why this is so:

- If one computer sends a file over a network it ties up the network to the disadvantage of other users. Other computers cannot interact in a timely way and the sharing of the network becomes disjointed and uneven.
- Breaking a large file into packets means that any errors introduced into the transmission affects only a small proportion of the communication. Those packets affected can be replaced easily by resending them so that overall the transmission is efficient. Also, packets allow different communication paths to be used: if one pathway becomes blocked, packets can be rerouted using other pathways.

Different network protocols use different packet structures. However, whatever the protocol being used there will be a need for the same basic information to be included in the data packet:

- a source address identifying the sending computer
- a destination address identifying the receiving computer
- the data being sent
- sequencing information that allows packets to be re-assembled
- error-checking information which allows the receiving computer to calculate whether data has become corrupted
- possibly other instructions that will be used by parts of the network to assist in delivery.

The Open Systems Interconnection model

In order to provide network designers and manufacturers with a consistent and well-defined set of rules, a network architecture was devised to enable many different types of computer system to exchange information. This architecture was created by the International Standards Organisation (ISO) and is called the *Open Systems Interconnection* (OSI) reference model.

This model is the most widely recognised standard for networked environments. It provides a set of rules governing how network hardware and software should be specified so they can work together at different layers to ensure communication. The OSI model specifies seven layers that make up the activities needed for network communication (see Figure 23.4).

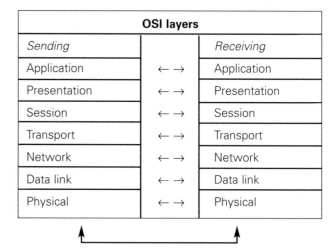

OSI layers		
Sending		*Receiving*
Application	← →	Application
Presentation	← →	Presentation
Session	← →	Session
Transport	← →	Transport
Network	← →	Network
Data link	← →	Data link
Physical	← →	Physical

Figure 23.4 *The seven OSI layers*

It is important to understand the following characteristics of the layered approach:

- Each layer has a clearly defined set of functions (see Figure 23.5). These functions form a coherent set of related tasks.
- Each layer has a clear interface with the layers above and below, so that components (data packets) can be passed up or down the layers. Each layer adds its part of the communication process to the packets received from or going to another layer.
- The lower layers (1 and 2) define the tasks for physical transmission of bits over a network connection using adapter cards and cable. The

Layer	Function	Typical action
7: Application	Provides services to user applications such as Word. Services include access to remote files or e-mail.	A user application needs to send a file across a network.
6: Presentation	Provides data encryption or compression, and any translating needed between data formats; e.g. between ASCII and UNICODE.	The file is converted into a character set used by the network, such as ASCII. It may also be encrypted and compressed.
5: Session	Establishes the connection to the server or peer-to-peer client, agrees the protocols to be used, transfers the data and closes the connection.	Adds connection information so that a communication session can be established and protocols agreed between sending and receiving computers.
4: Transport	Splits the data into suitable packets, determines the actual transmission type that is going to be used, and re-assembles packets.	Breaks the Word file into packets. Determines what kind of network link is going to be used (for instance multiple connections might be used). Decides the connection service (e.g. broadcast or point-to-point).
3: Network	Ensures that data is routed to the correct network address and coordinates travel over different networks. Keeps billing information.	This layer determines how the document packets will be routed from source to destination.
2: Data link	Splits the message into small data frames and sends them to another station on the network.	The packets are broken into smaller sized frames and sent to the physical layer. This layer ensures receipt of frames by sending and receiving acknowledgements and retransmitting frames that are lost.
1: Physical	Binary data signals are coded into the appropriate electrical signals and sent down the cable.	The actual physical stream of 1s and 0s that are sent down a wire.

Figure 23.5 *Functions of the OSI layer*

higher layers coordinate the interchange between applications using available network services.

- Each packet coming from a sending layer has control information added to it. A reciprocal layer on the receiving computer will process this. These are said to be *peer processes,* hence the arrows connecting them in the diagram above.

Example

A German physicist, Erika, works in a laboratory at Imperial College in London and wants to send a draft manuscript of a new research paper she has been working on to Lee Hun, a Chinese colleague in St Thomas' Hospital radiography department. The manuscript has been written in German using a pencil and consists of several chapters, sections, and appendices of figures.

This example simulates the use of the seven OSI layers in a communication setting that we might use. Each stage in the process corresponds to one of the OSI levels. Some of it is a little stretched to fit the model.

Stage 1

Erika contacts her document administration department and requests use of the college's document handling service.

Stage 2

The document department translates all documents into English to make their handling easier, as the people in the document service work in English to standardise their work language. The document is also word-processed and set into an agreed font using both sides of a page. Pages are numbered using our numbering system. This makes the document more compact and in a standard format.

Stage 3

The postal section of the document department receives the manuscript in a large box with a sticker on top saying who requested the transmission and who it is supposed to be sent to. The postal section uses courier firms for sending small packets around town. The postal section sends a message to the hospital asking if it is all right to send the document to Lee Hun, checking he works there and finding out his department and room number. This information is gathered and sent back to the college with the courier. They open a ticket that tracks the transmission of the document through to completion. The postal section then passes the box to its courier liaison person.

Stage 4

Because the manuscript box is too large for couriers, courier liaison breaks the manuscript box down into two chapters at a time that are put into plastic packets. Each packet is labelled with detailed sender and receiver addresses and which packet it is out of the total number of packets being sent (e.g. 3/12). The courier person has to ensure a same-day speedy delivery for the manuscript's packets. He discovers that the usual bicycle courier firm only has two couriers available and they can only carry three packets each. So he contacts a motorcycle courier firm who can deliver the remaining six packets on one motorbike. The packets are passed to despatch who organise the delivery and receipt of packets with the courier substation. Because the college sends a lot of information around town it has a courier substation in the despatch area.

Stage 5

Despatch has many packets to send and many different courier firms come and go. A courier will turn up and request a signature before handing over packets; similarly despatch will require a courier to sign for outgoing packets. This is so that the despatch section and the courier firms can keep a track of billing information. As a courier turns up the despatch person tells the courier the latest road traffic conditions and suggests more suitable routes. This routing information changes as the traffic conditions vary throughout the day and might involve handing over to a different firm (e.g. when they want to go through the Greenwich foot tunnel).

Stage 6

Unknown to despatch, the courier firms actually use lots of relays of bikes around town. In the courier substation, the plastic packets are opened and two sheets of paper are put into a plastic envelope; each envelope has addressing information on it. Each envelope must also say which packet it came from and where in the chapter. These are then carried to intermediate courier substations where they are handed over to another courier. Once they hand them over to the carrier substation courier, couriers go back to the station they started from and report that the sheets were handed on successfully. If they don't come back with news on successful delivery, the sheets are passed on again. This goes on until all the sheets from the packets have been sent.

Stage 7

The couriers physically use a bike with typically 10 gears and they must put their envelopes into a pouch they carry on their backs. They cycle quite fast but must be prepared to stop at zebra crossings and when traffic gets in their way. Sometimes they get lost and have to abandon their envelopes or they lose their pouches – in which case they have to go back and get copies of the pages and take them again. The couriers work from one substation to the next.

Activity

In small groups, work backwards from stage 7, writing down what happens to Erika's document. You must work from an understanding that the receipt of her document will be a mirror image of the sending. Start from when the plastic envelopes arrive at the courier substation based at the hospital. Remember that the sending level in the system is 'virtually' talking to the same level in the receiving system.

You might find it easier to draw all the sending stations and people.

Current methods of data transmission

Dial-up via modem

This is the standard low-cost connection using a phone line. The modem converts digital signals into audio analogue, and vice versa. Data rates are low – with 56Kbps being standard (although this is not often achieved in practice).

ISDN

The Integrated Services Digital Network has been in use for over 25 years. However, its rather high installation and rental costs have kept its use limited to certain business categories. It has also been hampered by the proprietal nature of its availability.

This is a fully digital system so that digital output from the computer is not converted into a tone signal. Instead the system uses a *terminal adapter* to prepare the computer's digital output from a serial port or NIC into the digital signals used on the ISDN line. ISDN can also carry digitised voice signals.

There are two basic ISDN offerings: ISDN30 has six or more channels and is mainly used for Private Branch Exchange (PBX) equipment; ISDN2 provides two channels each at 64Kbps. The two channels can carry a variety of traffic: 2 data, 1 data and 1 voice or 2 voice. ISDN lines using Multilink Point-to-Point Protocol allow several ISDN lines to be used together – so that, for example, a videoconferencing system can be used carrying 384Kbps bandwidth.

Digital Subscriber Line

This technology allows for high-bandwidth data transmission using ordinary copper phone wire. The first of its kind was ISDN, described previously. DSL became feasible when powerful digital signal processing technologies became available at a relatively low price. DSL works by using the unused bandwidth of the telephone line. The human voice needs about 3Hz of bandwidth to be transmitted. However, engineers discovered that the phone cable could support up to 2MHz of bandwidth over distances of about 3km. This means that once voice and signalling bandwidth is removed, enough bandwidth remains to carry between 1.5 and 8Mbps of data.

Asymmetric DSL (ADSL) is used because it helps prevent data loss caused by crosstalk – signals on one cable interfere with signals on an adjacent cable. The sending station can use high-power signals to transmit at higher bandwidth than the upwards pair.

Cable

Cable networks were built primarily for the transmission of television signals. Usually the main backbone cable is fibre-optic while short local distribution uses coaxial cable. As the systems were originally designed for only the *delivery* of traffic, the downstream side is technically easier.

The standard that is currently in force is the Data Over Cable Service Interface Specification 1.1 (DOCSIS 1.1) ratified by the International Telecommunications Union in 1999. The standard covers the 'head end' based in the cable company's distribution centre to the customer's house, where a cable modem connects to the TV in-socket.

In Europe, TV is transmitted in the 65–850MHz range and from this 6MHz channels can be used to carry downstream data at between 27Mbps and 32Mbps. Upstream channels are created below the 65MHz range and are much slower, delivering 500Kbps to 10Mbps. Most cable modems are external devices, although internal ones are now appearing. They use an Ethernet or USB interface and the channel is always on.

Local-area networks

The LANs used within GBW Bank

In Chapter 5 you saw how GBW had set up its computer operations. Each branch has a local-area network on which local processing takes place. Central

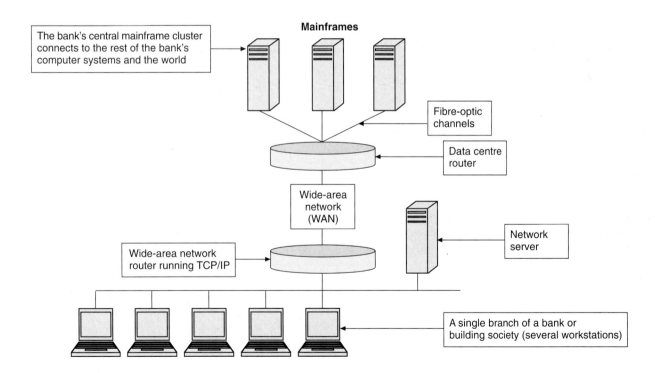

Figure 23.6 *GBW Bank's network topology*

master records are kept on the bank's mainframes that are accessed as part of a wide-area network. Transaction records are transmitted daily to the mainframes for updating master files; interactive queries can be carried out in real time.

The bank's LANs have been standardised around a leading industry network operating system (see Figure 23.6). The LAN topology is an Ethernet bus system using file servers and Ethernet hubs.

Data collision problems

The Ethernet LAN topology is a broadcast system whereby packets of data are sent to all stations connected to the network. Each time a message is sent, the sending computer must be able to transmit without other computers transmitting at the same time. If computers transmit at the same time, signals collide and the messages are lost. The problem is to ensure that many users are able to access and share a single communications channel in a way that does not lead to message collisions and poor performance. In Ethernet systems the solution is to use a method called 'Carrier Sense Multiple Access with Collision Detection' (CSMA/CD).

The way this works is that a station transmits data only when the cable is free of a signal from another computer – it senses the carrier to see whether it is available to transmit. If it is free, then the station sends its data packet (see Figure 23.7).

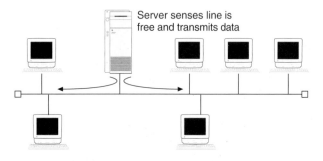

Figure 23.7 *CSMA/CD: the sending computer senses a free line and transmits a signal to the whole LAN*

Inevitably, sometimes two computers detect the line is free and transmit data signals at the same time. If this happens the two signals collide. The collision can, however, be detected – hence the *collision detection*

part of the description. When this happens, the computers involved in sending the signals wait a random amount of time and then attempt to retransmit.

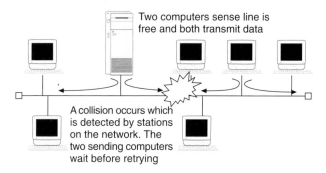

Figure 23.8 *A collision of signals is detected and retransmission will be attempted after a random pause*

Activity

1. The Ethernet access protocol is called a contention protocol. *That means any station wishing to transmit is in contention or competition with any other station. Can you imagine what happens when the number of active users increases on an Ethernet LAN using this protocol?*

   Look at Figure 23.9, which plots the percentage of data throughput on a network using the CSMA/CD protocol against the number of stations on the carrier. The number of stations gets larger from left to right.

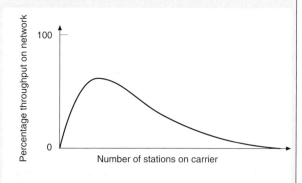

Figure 23.9 *See the Activity*

Discuss this with a colleague. What is happening to the percentage of data able to pass along the data carrier? How is this related to the number of stations on the channel? With this in mind, what in general can you say about the performance of a network that uses CSMA/CD?

2. *Investigate the token ring protocol, which is a non-contention access protocol. Using a series of diagrams and short explanations, explain how multiple stations are able to share the same data carrier.*

Limitations imposed by cabling

There are several types of cabling option available to engineers when connecting together components on a network (as well as the increasingly popular wireless networks). Essentially there are three main categories:

- coaxial
- twisted pair (unshielded or shielded)
- fibre-optic.

With these cabling options, two techniques are used to transmit signals:

- baseband
- broadband.

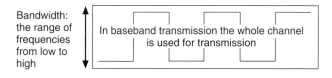

Figure 23.10 *Baseband transmission*

In *baseband* transmission, a single digital signal occupies the whole channel available (see Figure 23.10). Digital signals represent data as discrete pulses of electricity or light. The entire communication capacity of the channel is occupied by a single data signal and therefore the cable's whole bandwidth is used. The cable's bandwidth is the difference between the lowest and highest frequencies that can be used to carry data; the greater the difference, the more channels can be carried.

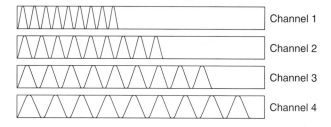

Figure 23.11 *An example of broadband transmission with four channels*

Broadband transmission uses analogue signalling – signals that are made up of continuous waves. The wave path can be in only one direction, so return traffic has to be carried on a different channel. The range of frequencies possible on a cable can be used to carry multiple channels of data.

In the example in Figure 23.11, four frequencies are used to carry four different signals.

All types of signals become weaker as they travel along a cable. In order to boost the signals, baseband systems use *repeaters* while broadband systems use *amplifiers*.

When selecting cabling, the network engineer will take into consideration the following questions:

- How heavy do I expect network traffic to be?
- How secure does the network traffic need to be?
- What distances does my network need to cover?
- What are the cable options?
- How much money can I spend?

All these questions affect the choice of cable because the most secure and fastest cable will be the most expensive. Network designers therefore have to balance the needs of the network with the optimum choices. These factors include:

- *How easy is a particular type of cable to install?* There are thick cumbersome types and thin more flexible ones (e.g. thick versus thin coaxial).
- *How much shielding does the cable require?* The more shielding a cable has then the more expensive it is. Cable that runs through areas where there are high levels of interference will require better shielding. Electrical fields caused by power lines, electric motors, transmitters and a range of electromechanical equipment can cause interference. There is also 'crosstalk'; signals from

Characteristic	Thinnet coaxial (10base2)	Twisted pair (10baseT)	Fibre-optic
Cost	Medium	Low	High
Usable cable length	185 metres	100 metres	2 kilometres
Transmission rate	10Mbps	4–100Mbps	100Mbps and more
Ease of installation	Fairly easy	Easy	Difficult
Protection	Good	Poor	Excellent

Figure 23.12 *Typical cable characteristics*

one data carrier can get mixed with signals on another, causing data corruption.

- *What transmission speeds are required?* Thick cable transmits over longer distances than thin cable but is more expensive and difficult to install. Fibre-optic is the fastest but this requires the greatest expertise to install. Signals that travel down a cable become 'attenuated' – that is they get weaker. However, boosting the signal slows down the speed at which the network can operate.

Figure 23.12 compares different cables with various characteristics

Wide-area (distributed) networks

Outgrowing a LAN

As companies grow larger their need to communicate electronically also grows. Initially a company may start with one network, but then grow to need other networks on a local site. These networks will have to connect to each other, and soon the company may have to send messages, files and transactions to parts of the company based in other towns. Communications will also grow to include other companies and countries. When a network has grown to include users beyond the physical capability of a LAN, then it is called a *wide-area network*.

Any LAN has limitations to its size and the number of users who can use it without major delays occurring. When this happens, the network administrator will have to decide how to overcome these limitations. There are basically three responses to LANs that have outgrown their capacity or which need to communicate with distant users:

- chop them up into smaller segments
- add new LANs
- add the capability to transfer information across wider areas.

This section looks at how networks on one site can communicate with networks on other sites no matter where they are. For the user, operations should be no more difficult than if they were working on their own computer. Most WANs are made up from computer networks that can connect to other networks using a communications link and communications devices that allow computers to connect across the link (see Figure Figure 23.13).

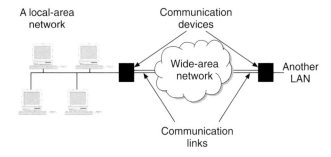

Figure 23.13 *Communication links and devices*

The communications links that are available vary considerably and are usually supplied by telecommunication service providers such as national Telco (telecommunication companies) or private phone companies. The communications equipment used to connect a computer system or network to the link is commonly a *router* or *gateway*. The communication link ensures that traffic destined for external computer systems is routed appropriately and can operate according to the various protocol layers existing on either side of it.

Routers

These are specialised computer systems used to control traffic between networks (see Figure 23.14). Routers operate at the network layer (level 3) of the OSI model (refer back to Figure 23.5). This means they can route packets, exchange protocol information with different networks, and ensure packets are sent to the right network using forwarding rules.

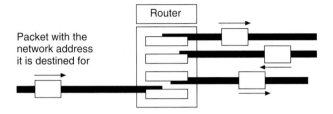

The router is connected to four networks. It reads the network address from data packets it receives and forwards them using the best route from its routing table.

Figure 23.14 *This router is connected to four networks*

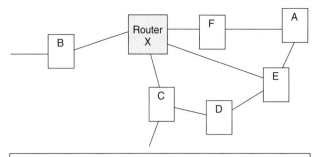

Router X receives packets from four other routers. It examines the addresses and picks the best route for a packet from the information it holds about the other routers.

Figure 23.15 *Router X receives packets from four other routers*

They construct *information tables* on the status of the networks and the routing options available. This means they can find the optimum path for sending packets if traffic through a router in their table shows it to be slow. A router stores the addresses of all networks it is able to communicate with, how to connect to them, and the paths between them. The

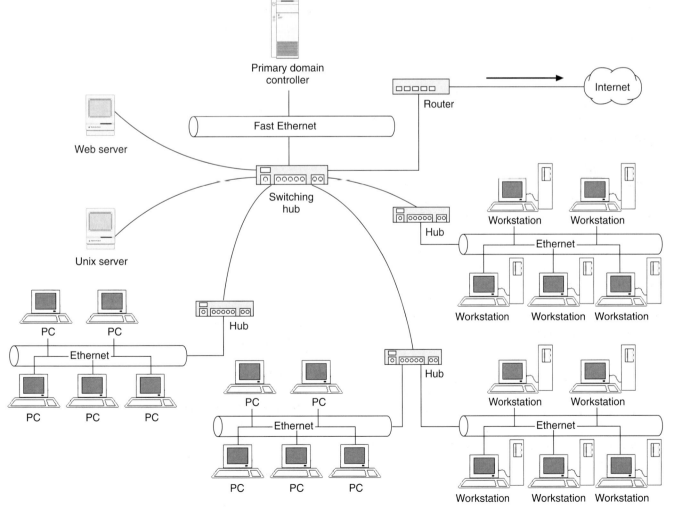

Figure 23.16 *Typical network configuration*

address of each network will be the router that controls packets into it.

Routers create routing tables either dynamically or statically. A *dynamic router* builds up a map of the network routers it has contact with during service, while a *static routing table* fixes the routing information once and for all (unless it is reconfigured).

Figure 23.16 depicts a typical network configuration for a medium-sized organisation. In this case the internal LANs are connected using hubs or switches. The external connection to the WAN is through a router connecting into the Internet.

Gateways

Whereas routers receive and forward packets at the third OSI network layer, transforming if necessary the packet information from one type of protocol to another; gateways carry out a complete transformation of a packet from one network architecture into the format used by another.

This means that networks operating in completely different ways – for example an IBM SNA network and a Novell network – can transfer data from an application on one architecture to an application running on another. A packet will have its various protocol information from different OSI levels stripped off, and will be repackaged to protocol information at levels for the other network architecture.

Gateways are usually dedicated to this kind of activity and are particularly used for connecting mainframes to LANs across WAN links.

Communication links

The types of communication link available today are very varied. They include:

- analogue telecoms lines (telephone)
- digital telecoms lines (various telephone or cable options)
- microwave
- wireless
- satellite links.

Each type of link has advantages and disadvantages, although the main difference is cost. Organisations

that need to have a data link open most of the time will use a dedicated or leased line. This type of line is one where the telecommunications company (telco) maintains the link to be open all the time. This would be the same as connecting your computer to the Internet and keeping online permanently. Leased lines like this are more expensive but generally offer faster and more reliable connectivity.

Common types of dedicated lines are digital connections such and DSL or ISDN that you read about above. Larger businesses use another common point-to-point digital line called T1. This is a transmission technology that uses two pairs of wires, one for receiving and one for transmission. This allows a full duplex signal at a rate of 1.544Mbps. This type of line is expensive to maintain and would only be used as a main line within a WAN. Companies can also choose to use part of a T1 channel, known as 'fractional T1', which uses bandwidth in chunks of 64Kbps. The most expensive dedicated point-to-point line is a T3 line. This operates at speeds between 6Mbps and 45Mbps and transports large amounts of data at high speed between two fixed points.

Depending on the type of router being used to connect to the telecommunication link, all of these digital services require some kind of conversion from the digital signal that comes from the router into the digital signals carried on the telco line. A device that carries out this conversion is called a CSU/DSU (channel service unit/date service unit).

Connection strategies

The basic unit of data transmission used today is the data packet. If a data packet is sent down a dedicated line from one computer system to another computer system within a company, then this is a permanent circuit. However, a company usually pays for part of the bandwidth of a line and joins a WAN made up of many routeing stations controlled by the telco and other operators (see Figure 23.17).

When a packet can be shunted around a network via many routes, that is known as *packet switching*. Packets can follow different routes from source to destination and then be re-assembled for the end-user application. This kind of connection service is cheaper than maintaining a dedicated line because users pay only for the portion of bandwidth their transaction uses.

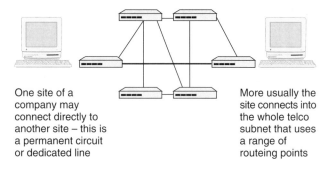

One site of a company may connect directly to another site – this is a permanent circuit or dedicated line

More usually the site connects into the whole telco subnet that uses a range of routeing points

Figure 23.17 *Dedicated versus shared*

Another approach is to use *virtual circuits*. In this method a connection between two users will be formed when communication starts. A circuit along a pathway of routers will be set up and used for the duration of the transmission. Once again only packets will be used, and thus routeing tables at each routeing point will maintain the circuit. Once the transmission is finished the circuit is closed. It is called 'virtual' because again it is not an actual dedicated line but part of the bandwidth of a matrix of connection routes.

Firewalls

Firewalls are security systems designed to provide a single point of entry into or out of an organisation's network (Figure 23.18). This is similar to the drawbridge used to protect a medieval castle. Security personnel can inspect all traffic into and out of the castle. Security breaches may be caused by the

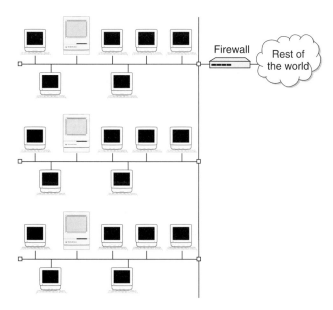

Firewall

Rest of the world

Figure 23.18 *Firewalls are necessary to protect systems against damage from outside*

transmission of confidential information out of the organisation or, more commonly, attempts by others to get in and steal or disrupt systems.

Various services operating on routers use allocated *ports*. These are connection numbers that make up the address of a packet of information. For example, in some systems port 23 is used for Telnet, a TCP/IP application to allow your computer to act as terminal to a remote system. If this port is left unmonitored, unscrupulous agents trying to sneak into a computer network might use it.

A firewall usually consists of a router, or even two routers, that carry out *packet filtering* and an *application gateway*. The router will be set up to filter incoming and outgoing packets based on certain criteria. If packets fail to meet the criteria then they are discarded. The *filter tables* can be set by the network administrator and may include certain categories of address or list sources and destinations that are barred. There will also be some default rules for all packets.

If the packets cross the router then they can be examined by the application gateway. Rather than examining the addressing information of packets, the gateway can look at the application-specific nature of the information. So, for example, mail application messages can be examined and any with programme attachments can be dropped.

Electronic mail (e-mail)

E-mail is a powerful communication tool used in most organisations. It has features that enhance the connectivity of individuals or groups by allowing messages to be shared, distributed, stored, filtered, encrypted and used to carry other files as attachments. Because e-mails are text-based messages, they can be printed and stored to form a record of a particular correspondence. E-mails use the following features:

- *mailboxes*: a delivery location for each user
- *notification*: flags users when a message has arrived
- *return receipt*: tells the sender when a message has been received and opened
- *reply*: allows a recipient to quickly create a new message back to a sender
- *attachments*: allows users to attach files of any sort to messages.

E-mail is set up by a systems administrator and requires an e-mail server to act as post office to the messages being sent in an organisation. The administrator will set the account permissions of people being added to the system, as well as directory information and how the server will communicate with the rest of the world.

The distinction between WAN and LAN protocols

LAN protocols exist to allow multiple users to share a network resource within a local physical environment.

These standards were defined by the American Institute of Electronic and Electrical Engineers (IEEE) and set out in the 802 collection. The 802 collection includes Ethernet, Token Ring and other varieties of LAN. The definition of how the various 802 standards work covers the first two layers of the OSI model: the physical and data link layers (see Figures 23.4 and 23.5). This is in contrast with WAN protocols where communication starts from the point a message leaves a LAN and so includes the top five remaining levels of the OSI model.

CHAPTER 24

Proposals based on performance

This chapter continues to explore the development of EauCo Water, which was introduced in Chapter 6. It will describe:

- how systems software monitors performance of ICT systems
- how performance should be reported to a higher authority
- how the systems manager should make a case for an upgrade.

This chapter covers these Learning Objectives in the specification:

L.O. 4.4   Understand how the appropriate systems software can monitor the use and performance of ICT systems for the purposes of reporting to a higher authority (e.g. a line manager)

L.O. 4.5   Make the case for an upgrade to a specified ICT system based on given performance and user reaction information

The systems manager's role in the development of a business

Andrew Jones is the Operations Manager at EauCo Water (see Chapter 6). He is, in fact, the systems manager, although he has the rather more traditional job title. He works for a management company called Direct Control and through them is under contract to the water company. As we saw in Chapter 6, his responsibilities include:

- maintaining computer operations within EauCo Water
- making sure that all the company's systems are secure
- offering support on the company's computer systems
- purchasing new software
- purchasing new hardware
- evaluating the company's computer equipment.

The company runs a local-area network (LAN) with 120 workstations, controlled by eight servers. The network is used to carry out a mixture of batch processing (for billing) and online processing (for dealing with customer enquiries).

Andrew supports a team of two systems administrators, who each carry out a range of tasks:

- network administration
- direct support to users
- batch processing operations.

The systems manager is in a unique position to help the business to grow and be successful. The systems manager can propose upgrades to the hardware and software, which should ultimately help the business, and can critically assess proposals made by others.

The systems manager can:

- advise the company on strategic developments based on projected system performance and needs
- assess the value for money of proposed new hardware and software systems
- prioritise proposals for upgrades to fit a limited budget

- draw up tender documents for purchases that meet the company's strategic plan
- ensure that projects fall within budget and timescale
- assess the performance of systems according to service level agreements negotiated with contractors and vendors.

Notice that these are all management issues, not technical matters. Andrew Jones knows that new IT systems should be bought only if they can be justified on business grounds. He needs to be on the lookout for problems and inadequacies in the current systems, and be ready to suggest improvements that will benefit EauCo Water.

Managers can influence decisions only if they have good information. The next sections in this chapter examine some of the sources of information that a systems manager can use.

Monitoring system performance

What is monitoring?

The LAN system that Andrew Jones uses at EauCo Water includes a number of useful software tools that monitor the system. These are known as *system diagnostics* as they help the systems manager to identify any problems.

As an example of system diagnostics, it is possible for Andrew to check on a network router across the other side of the building. He can immediately see the load statistics, how many packets of data are flowing through the router, and how many packets of data are being dropped (possibly because the router's memory cannot hold the number of packets arriving for forwarding).

System diagnostics can be used to check how the system is performing and also how it is used. Monitoring is the process of checking on an activity on a planned basis.

The server software automatically generates *system logs*. Every time a user accesses any part of the system the details are recorded in a *log file*. Here is an extract from one of Andrew's system log files:

```
08/23 14:42:03 ─────────────────────────
08/23 14:42:03   NetpValidateName: checking to see if
                 'WORKGROUP' is valid as type 2 name
08/23 14:42:03   NetpCheckNetBiosNameNotInUse: for
                 'WORKGROUP' returned: 0x858
08/23 14:42:03   NetpCheckNetBiosNameNotInUse for
                 'WORKGROUP' [ Workgroup as MACHINE]
                 returned 0x858
08/23 14:42:03   NetpValidateName: name 'WORKGROUP' is valid
                 for type 2
08/23 14:42:04 ─────────────────────────
08/23 14:42:04   NetpValidateName: checking to see if
                 'WORKGROUP' is valid as type 2 name
08/23 14:42:04   NetpCheckNetBiosNameNotInUse: for
                 'WORKGROUP' returned: 0x858
08/23 14:42:04   NetpCheckNetBiosNameNotInUse for
                 'WORKGROUP' [ Workgroup as MACHINE]
                 returned 0x858
08/23 14:42:04   NetpValidateName: name 'WORKGROUP' is valid
                 for type 2
08/23 14:42:04 ─────────────────────────
08/23 14:42:04   NetpDoDomainJoin
08/23 14:42:04   NetpMachineValidToJoin: 'EAUCO_ACCNT56'
08/23 14:42:04   NetpGetLsaPrimaryDomain: status: 0x0
08/23 14:42:04   NetpMachineValidToJoin: status: 0x0
08/23 14:42:04   NetpJoinWorkgroup: joining computer
                 'EAUCO_ACCNT56' to workgroup
                 'WORKGROUP'
08/23 14:42:04   NetpValidateName: checking to see if
                 'WORKGROUP' is valid as type 2 name
08/23 14:42:04   NetpCheckNetBiosNameNotInUse: for
                 'WORKGROUP' returned: 0x858
08/23 14:42:04   NetpCheckNetBiosNameNotInUse for
                 'WORKGROUP' [ Workgroup as MACHINE]
                 returned 0x858
08/23 14:42:04   NetpValidateName: name 'WORKGROUP' is valid
                 for type 2
08/23 14:42:04   NetpSetLsaPrimaryDomain: for 'WORKGROUP'
                 status: 0x0
08/23 14:42:04   NetpControlServices: open service 'NETLOGON'
                 failed: 0x424
08/23 14:42:04   NetpJoinWorkgroup: status: 0x0
08/23 14:42:04   NetpDoDomainJoin: status: 0x0
08/23 14:42:51 ─────────────────────────
08/23 14:42:51   NetpValidateName: checking to see if
                 'EAUCO_ACCNT56' is valid as type 1 name
08/23 14:42:51   NetpCheckNetBiosNameNotInUse for
                 'EAUCO_ACCNT56' [MACHINE] returned 0x0
08/23 14:42:51   NetpValidateName: name 'EAUCO_ACCNT56' is
                 valid for type 1
```

Some system log files are used frequently by systems administrators when sorting out difficulties. For example, if a printer on a network is not printing documents as expected, the administrator can examine the printer log file and see what documents are still waiting in the queue.

This log file is relatively short and changes frequently. Many other system log files are very lengthy and difficult to read. Andrew has purchased system diagnostics software which carries out the tasks of analysing and summarising the contents of the log files. It then produces a report for the systems manager or administrator.

Andrew can configure the system diagnostics software so that the reports contain exactly the content that he requires. The reports are then generated automatically. System reports are not necessarily printed, and often they will simply be viewed on a screen.

Types of system report

In Chapter 22 you met the three types of reports that are commonly used in business: routine, exception and on-demand reports. Those reports were all generated by people, but system software can be configured to generate reports of all three types.

- *Routine system reports* are produced automatically at a specified frequency (daily, weekly, monthly). For example, the system may be configured to produce a weekly report of the number of pages printed by the printers connected to the network.

- *Exception system reports* are also produced automatically, but in response to an event. For example, the system may be required to produce a report whenever a virus is detected.

- *On-demand system reports* are produced in response to a request from the administrator. For example, the administrator may need to know exactly which users are logged in at the time of asking.

What is performance?

We can measure the *performance* of a system and we can measure the *use* of a system. Performance refers to the technical standards achieved. When we discuss the performance of ICT systems we often refer to:

- the time taken to carry out an operation
- the volume of data processed
- the capacity of internal and external memory
- the routeing used through the network.

We will be considering the use of systems in the next section.

System diagnostics used to monitor performance

The speed of a system is crucially important. We may use system diagnostics to measure:

- time taken to boot up a workstation
- time taken to load an application into a workstation
- time taken to access an application
- time taken to access a data item in a database
- time taken to save new data items
- time taken to print a document.

Speed is often dependent on storage and memory capacity. For example, if a hard disk is almost full then the time taken to access data can slow down considerably. System diagnostics can assess:

- spare capacity on a hard disk
- internal memory usage
- the frequency of page swapping between internal memory and hard disk
- size of printer queues.

The Unix server at EauCo Water is used for customer operations, such as billing and customer enquiries. The main database holds records on 225 000 customers. Andrew has decided that he wants weekly reports on:

- speed of access to individual customer records
- hard disk space.

He finds that one report on its own is of limited usefulness, so he combines the weekly reports over a period of time so that he can watch the variations and trends. The system diagnostics tools allow him to create a time-series report, which creates a graph showing values over several weeks or months, or even years.

Andrew needs these reports to make management decisions. He may be able to make changes to the system that will solve an emerging problem. For example, if he finds that the available space on a hard disk is becoming too small, he may decide to defragment the disk. If this does not release enough space then he may archive some old files to release some additional capacity.

But sometimes the reports indicate to Andrew that more substantial changes are needed, requiring the

Proposals based on performance

purchase of new equipment. In fact, the time-series reports on hard disk space have shown that the hard disks are too full. Andrew has been taking regular action to try to solve this, but it is clear that the system does not have the capacity to cope with the demands placed on it. He has also noticed that this has increased the time taken by the system to carry out a number of operations, particularly access to customer records.

Andrew believes these problems could be solved by adding another network server to the system. This could be bridged across to the existing network server. He will have to do some more research before reporting to the senior managers at EauCo.

Activity

What does Andrew need to find out before he can prepare a report for the senior managers?

Monitoring system use

The system diagnostics have already alerted Andrew Jones to the slow access times to customer records on the Unix server. He knows that this problem must have an impact on the online processing system used to handle customer enquiries.

The staff in the customer enquiries team take calls from customers throughout working hours. The team works to a rota which ensures that there are always at least four members on duty at any time, although the system can accommodate six at peak times. Customers phone in with a variety of enquiries. Some want to know how much they owe; some are ready to pay their bills by credit card; others ask about the different tariffs and want advice to identify the one most suited to their needs.

The team members can use the customer enquiries application to look up a customer's record on screen or to check out information about the company and the tariffs it offers. The software gives them read-only access to most of the data in the customer records but does allow them to add notes about each enquiry. Customers who want to pay are transferred to the accounts department which can handle transactions.

System diagnostics used to monitor usage

Andrew can use the Unix® system log files to check how the system is being used as well as how it is performing. He can ask the system to generate reports to show:

- which applications are used the most
- how often an application is accessed
- when an application is used
- which users access an application
- how much time a user spends on an application
- when individual users log on and what applications they use
- how many documents are printed by each user
- how many documents are sent to each of the printers.

Andrew does not have regular reports on the use of the system. Instead he requests reports as and when he needs them. He usually requests a report if a user has complained about a problem, or if he becomes aware of performance problems.

Andrew wants to investigate the use of the customer enquiries application, so he configures the system diagnostics software to produce reports for the next three weeks on the use of the application. At the end of the monitoring period he is astonished to discover that the application is actually being used for 97% of the working day. At many times of the day all the staff on duty are using the system. As soon as one call finishes another begins. This means that staff are working very intensively at their network stations, and are not getting many opportunities to rest their eyes and hands.

He then obtains another report. This time he asks for the length of time spent on each customer enquiry. The system automatically logs the time when a new enquiry begins and the time it ends, so the data is readily available. He discovers that, on average, a customer enquiry takes 4.8 minutes to resolve. If enquiries could be handled faster, then the staff would have to work less intensively. At the moment he does not know whether the time taken could be improved, but he intends to find out.

Helpdesk logs used to monitor use

The end-users at EauCo Water can contact the systems administrators if they have any problems or queries. The company is not big enough to employ full-time helpdesk staff, so Andrew shares the helpdesk role with the two systems administrators.

There is a single helpdesk internal phone number, and this is diverted to the phone line of whichever of the three is on helpdesk duty at the time. Users may also drop in to the Operations Centre at any time to ask for advice.

Andrew knows that each helpdesk request provides valuable information about the use of the network. Helpdesk requests can be classified into certain groups:

- problems with the hardware, including peripherals
- problems with the network system, including access to applications and data
- problems with the use of an application.

Some of these problems result from faults in the hardware or software. Other problems arise because the user does not fully understand the application. In both cases, Andrew can gather valuable information about the use of the system by examining the reported problems.

He has installed a helpdesk logging software application on the system. Every time a user phones the helpdesk line, or calls in to the Operations Centre, the person who handles the problem uses this software. The application prompts for the following information:

- name/user ID
- date and time
- workstation being used by user
- nature of the problem
- advice given

- was the problem solved?
- further action.

The helpdesk software can also generate reports. Although Andrew does not ask for weekly reports, he does find this feature particularly useful when a new application has been installed. He knows that while users are getting used to a new package they will make heavy use of the helpdesk, but that this should tail off over time. He needs to be able to provide enough support for new applications, so he does monitor the helpdesk requests quite carefully during this period.

Andrew is particularly interested to know if the customer enquiry team have been calling the helpdesk. He gets a report detailing calls from the team and sees that there have been a couple of complaints about the slow search time for customer records. He also finds that the staff have put in an unusually high number of requests for help with using the software. He decides to investigate further.

Web statistics used to monitor use of a website

EauCo Water has a small website that provides customers with information about the company and about its charges. It does not, as yet, allow customers to pay bills online. The website address is published on all the letters, bills and leaflets produced by the company.

The website is the responsibility of the Marketing Director, Kostas Papadopoulis. The site is managed inhouse by Lisa Man, and hosted by an Internet service provider (ISP). Lisa is also responsible for the design of all leaflets and other communications from EauCo.

Kostas believes the site could be developed, but cannot at the moment justify employing a full-time Web specialist. He would like to start to monitor the number of visits to the site, feeling that this kind of information will be very useful when he is ready to plan an expansion.

Kostas contacts Andrew to ask him how he can get this information. Andrew tells him that his ISP will be keeping logs of all the requests to the website, and that Andrew can ask for a copy of the log files on a regular basis. These files are commonly known as Web statistics. When Kostas contacts the ISP they agree to e-mail him a weekly log file, but the first time he receives a file he finds that it is a very lengthy text file, with each line recording all the details of a single hit. The following is a typical extract:

```
195.92.198.81    [01/Mar/2000:00:15:51 +0000] "GET / HTTP/1.1"
                 200 3145
195.92.198.81    [01/Mar/2000:00:15:52 +0000] "GET /contents.htm
                 HTTP/1.1" 200 6262
195.92.198.81    [01/Mar/2000:00:15:54 +0000] "GET
                 /rightheader.htm HTTP/1.1" 200 1391
195.92.198.81    [01/Mar/2000:00:15:56 +0000] "GET /home.htm
                 HTTP/1.1" 200 16434
195.92.198.81    [01/Mar/2000:00:15:58 +0000] "GET
                 /buttons/home.jpg HTTP/1.1" 200 1148
195.92.198.81    [01/Mar/2000:00:15:59 +0000] "GET /buttons/how-
                 to-contact-us.jpg HTTP/1.1" 200 1768
195.92.198.81    [01/Mar/2000:00:16:00 +0000] "GET
                 /buttons/tariffs.jpg HTTP/1.1" 200 1574
195.92.198.81    [01/Mar/2000:00:16:00 +0000] "GET
                 /buttons/accounts.jpg HTTP/1.1" 200 1830
195.92.198.81    [01/Mar/2000:00:16:02 +0000] "GET
                 /buttons/about-eauco.jpg HTTP/1.1" 200 1819
195.92.198.81    [01/Mar/2000:00:16:02 +0000] "GET /buttons/all-
                 about-water.jpg HTTP/1.1" 200 1727
195.92.198.81    [01/Mar/2000:00:16:12 +0000] "GET
                 /photos/eauco1.jpg HTTP/1.1" 200 12717
195.92.198.81    [01/Mar/2000:00:16:12 +0000] "GET /clear.gif
                 HTTP/1.1" 200 59
195.92.198.81    [01/Mar/2000:00:16:12 +0000] "GET /accounts.htm
                 HTTP/1.1" 200 13398
195.92.198.81    [01/Mar/2000:00:16:12 +0000] "GET
                 /photos/eauco2.jpg HTTP/1.1" 200 12717
195.92.198.81    [01/Mar/2000:00:16:34 +0000] "GET /how-to-
                 pay.htm HTTP/1.1" 200 13398
195.92.198.81    [01/Mar/2000:00:16:36 +0000] "GET
                 /photos/eauco3.jpg HTTP/1.1" 200 12717
```

Andrew advises him to buy some analysis software which produces reports from the log files. From these reports Kostas can see how many hits the website receives each week.

At first Kostas is delighted with the apparent very heavy use of the site, but Andrew points out that a 'hit' is a *request for a file*, which could be a Web page or a graphical image. The site makes a lot of use of graphics, so the actual number of visitors is very much smaller than he first thought. A more accurate measure of use of the website would be given by the number of front-page hits – that is, the number of times the home page of the site is downloaded by site visitors.

Activity

Try to find a log file for a website and the report produced by an analysis program.

System diagnostics used to monitor usage of other systems

Andrew is also responsible for maintaining the telephone system at EauCo Water. In practice he calls on the expertise of the telephone company if there are any difficult problems.

The digital telephone system that has been installed at EauCo is integrated into the company's LAN. The system records the details of all incoming and outgoing phone calls. It also manages the voicemail systems for all the employees and handles the queueing system for incoming calls.

Andrew is concerned about certain aspects of the telephone system. In particular, from his earlier research he is aware that customers are not always able to get through to the customer enquiries staff. So he requests an on-demand report on voice traffic from the system. The report should include the following details covering the calls in the last month to customer enquiries:

- total number of calls
- average number of calls in the telephone queue during working hours
- average length of time that a call is kept in the queue
- peak times for calls
- dates and times when the telephone queue was full.

The report makes depressing reading. Far too many customers have to wait in the queue to get through to the customer enquiries team. Some customers hang up before getting a reply. At peak times customers have to wait for up to 20 minutes before their call is answered.

Activity

Can you think of other telephone report items that Andrew could request?

Reporting system performance and use

Reporting to senior managers

We have already seen that log files are difficult to interpret in their raw state. The diagnostics software can be used to analyse them to produce system reports, but these are still couched in technical language and are designed to be read by technical staff.

The information presented in a system report can be used for a number of purposes. It can help a systems administrator solve an immediate problem with a peripheral, or it can be used by the systems manager to monitor and plan the use of existing resources. In addition, the systems manager can summarise key pieces of information in a report and use this when discussing the IT systems with senior managers.

Andrew Jones writes a monthly report to Margaret Berman, the Managing Director of EauCo Water. He keeps the report short and succinct, and he avoids using any technical vocabulary whenever possible. In the report he summarises how the IT systems have been functioning and highlights any problems that have been causing concern to staff, like downtimes. He makes sure that he includes warnings about any possible future expenditure.

This is a routine monthly report. If anything goes seriously wrong with the network, to the extent that it might affect the business, then Andrew will prepare an exception report for Margaret. Occasionally, she asks for a report herself – an on-demand report.

The systems manager's influence on company policy

For the last ten years the IT purchasing policy at EauCo Water has been to upgrade all hardware four years after purchase. Redundant equipment is then sold to a second-hand computer agency, and this produces some income for the company. In practice, this means that approximately a quarter of the PCs and peripherals are replaced each year, whilst servers are upgraded (or replaced) every four years.

This policy was drawn up by the Financial Director before Andrew was appointed as Operations Manager, and Andrew has never been very happy with it. He

thinks that the policy is too inflexible at times. He believes that 'hardware must follow software' – in other words, that the company should select the applications that best suit its business needs, and then ensure that the hardware is adequate to support the software.

Andrew feels that the problem he has identified with the customer enquiries system is only the tip of an iceberg. If he were to purchase new software to improve the customer enquiries service, then it would put extra pressure on the Unix® server, which is already barely coping with the demands put on it. Other applications would be affected by this congestion as well. But because the server is only three years old, the policy decrees that it cannot be upgraded for another year.

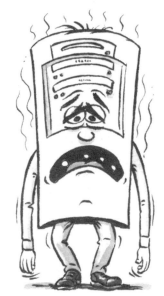

Andrew decides to write a special report to Margaret Berman about the problems with the customer enquiries system. He highlights the slow access to customer records and the long telephone queues that have been building up. He explains that a second server is needed to cope with demand. In the report he asks the Managing Director to change the IT purchasing policy so that all equipment can be upgraded after three years.

Margaret has a meeting with Andrew and the Financial Director, but tells him that a change of policy would have to be discussed by the board of directors. The Financial Director says that the company cannot afford to change all equipment after only three years' use, so he would be unable to recommend a complete change of policy to the board; but he does understand that occasionally hardware will have to be upgraded before the end of the four-year period.

A few weeks later Margaret asks Andrew to meet him, and tells him that the board of directors have agreed some amendments to the IT purchasing policy. The new policy says that hardware will normally be upgraded after four years but that exceptions can be made if they are necessary to achieve business objectives.

Proposals based on performance

Andrew is very happy with this change in the policy. He must now convince the directors that the company needs to upgrade some of its hardware and software. He will begin by gathering some evidence from the end-users who work with the customer enquiries system every day.

Assessing user reactions

Most companies try to assess the reactions of end-users to their systems. There are many methods for doing this. Some of these methods involve direct questioning of the users, whilst other methods rely on indirect evidence.

Finding out what users think of a system is vital. Major software systems costing millions of pounds have been abandoned in the past when they have been found to be difficult to use. A £6 million Home Office project for a case record and management system for the Probation Service was withdrawn when users reported that they had to go through ten screens to open and update a file, that navigation was unpredictable, and that data entered into some fields was lost.

Indirect evidence

A great deal of information about end-users is held in a company. For example:

- Helpdesk logs record all the support requests from each employee and the kinds of problems they had.
- Staff records show how many days employees have been away from work (although information about individuals will be treated as confidential).
- Personnel records also show staff turnover; that is, how many staff leave the company and have to be replaced.
- Training records indicate what training has been provided for employees.

Andrew Jones reads back through the helpdesk logs for the last few months, picking out the requests for help from the customer enquiries staff. He discovers that they have asked more questions about the use of the software than any other section. Most of the questions go like this: 'I've just found the right customer, but how do I check how much she paid last year?', or 'I made a mistake when I typed in my notes for the last enquiry – how do I go back and change it?'

Andrew loads up the application they use and runs it, trying to imagine that he is a new user. He begins to realise just how confusing it is. All selections are made using hot keys. Although this does, theoretically, speed up data entry, the keys to use are not listed on the screen and there are no drop-down menu alternatives. The help screens are far too basic and do not include a problem-oriented troubleshooting section.

He then finds other entries in the helpdesk log containing complaints about the time taken to access customer records, especially during peak times when all the staff are using the system.

Some of the company information can be used to infer the level of satisfaction amongst staff, although it must be used with great care. For example, records may show a high level of staff absence in one department. This could be interpreted as a sign that staff were stressed and unhappy – but it could just be that several employees had, coincidently, suffered illnesses and accidents.

Andrew has noticed that last year he had arranged training for eleven new members in the customer enquiries team, compared with only five in the previous years. He does not have access to personnel records but wonders whether this represents a high turnover due to staff dissatisfaction.

Direct evidence

Indirect evidence should be backed up with direct evidence, in the form of staff surveys and interviews. Survey forms have to be designed carefully. The survey results are valid only if the users have understood the questions correctly, so the questions must be clear and unambiguous.

Surveys are usually analysed and the results presented in a summary form using pie charts or bar charts. Often only a proportion of the survey forms are actually completed, so the results cannot always be taken to be a true representation of everyone's views. Depending on the size of the survey, the results may require careful statistical analysis.

Every year Andrew carries out a user satisfaction survey of all the end-users in the company. He picks out the forms filled in two months ago by the customer enquiries staff, and also finds the similar forms for the previous year. These show that the level of satisfaction with the systems that they use had dropped.

Finally he decides to interview all the customer enquiries staff in person. During these interviews he hears that the software can be very frustrating for users, and that they do not like giving a substandard service to customers. Staff morale is low; they feel that no-one appreciates the problems they are having. Andrew is determined to do something about it.

Activity

These questions were asked in a user satisfaction survey. For each question the interviewees had to tick one of five boxes labelled 'Agree strongly', 'Agree', 'Don't mind', 'Disagree' and 'Disagree strongly'. Are the questions clear and unambiguous?

1. *The helpdesk staff always solve my problems immediately.*

2. *The helpdesk staff deal with me in a courteous manner.*

3. *The helpdesk staff answer the phone within four rings.*

4. *The main application that I use is user-friendly.*

5. *My workstation is satisfactory.*

6. *The memory on my PC is sufficient for my needs.*

Making the case for an upgrade

Identifying the sources of inadequate performance

Andrew Jones summarises what he has found out so far. He has identified a number of problems. The capacity of the hard disks is too small, and this is slowing up a number of operations, especially the processing of customer records. The customer enquiries staff are working over-intensively, raising health and safety issues. Individual enquiries handled by the staff take longer than expected, and customers are kept waiting in the telephone queue. The application used for customer enquiries has a poorly designed user interface, which increases the time spent on each enquiry and is a source of irritation to staff. The employees are not very happy; there has been a high staff turnover in this section and training costs have risen.

The key statistic is the time taken to deal with each customer. If this can be speeded up then customers will spend less time in the queue, and staff will feel they are giving a better service.

How can solutions be identified?

Upgrade solutions can be suggested by users, systems administrators or external suppliers of hardware or software. Anyone who is responsible for purchasing computer hardware, software or consumables receives a large amount of advertising materials through the post and speculative phone calls from suppliers. Relevant material should be filed, so that it can be reviewed when purchases are to be made. Systems managers also try to attend trade shows where new products are displayed and can be tried out.

Caution must be exercised with proposals from external suppliers who will want to market their products and may make extravagant claims, or may try to persuade potential customers that they need something which is not really necessary. Systems managers should always ask themselves these questions about a new product:

- Does it meet a recognised need?
- How is that need prioritised?
- Can the need be met in other ways?
- Is this the most cost-effective solution?

Andrew considers ways of solving this set of problems. He thinks that a combination of new software and hardware is needed. He believes that the speed of access could be improved by adding another server to the system which could be bridged across to the existing network server. At a recent computer show he saw demonstrations of three different software systems that might be suitable replacements for the customer enquiries application. All of them would work satisfactorily only on a more powerful server.

Upgrading the system to meet new business objectives

The Managing Director of EauCo Water, Margaret Berman, has been discussing the future direction of the company with the board of directors. Business has been reasonably steady for the last couple of years, but there are some fast-growing rivals in the field, who are seen as a threat. EauCo needs to be as efficient as possible to remain viable.

The Head of Personnel has reported that more employees than usual left the company during the last year, although she is not sure why. The costs of advertising for new staff, then training them, adds considerably to her department's budget.

The board of directors agree that their main business objectives for the next year will be to:

1. maintain the number of domestic customers
2. reduce the operating costs of the company
3. reduce staff turnover.

Margaret has asked Andrew Jones for his responses to these objectives. He seizes the opportunity to formulate some proposals for improving the customer enquiries system.

As Andrew's proposals will be quite costly, he also looks for ways of saving money elsewhere. Eighteen months ago he negotiated a contract for the supply of paper and cartridges for printers. The contract was with a company called PaperWeight and it specified a price for these consumables, fixed for two years. Although the negotiated prices were already below the normal market rates, Andrew felt sure that he could obtain an even better deal from another supplier.

Making proposals

Once all the necessary information has been gathered the systems manager must prepare an initial proposal. This will include evidence of need and evidence of possible solutions. At some point the true costs of the solutions will have to be given, but broad estimates may be provided at this stage. Senior management may receive proposals from a number of departments, so they will have to prioritise these proposals against the overall aims and current policies of the organisation.

Andrew made out a case for upgrading the hardware and software needed to carry out customer enquiries, as soon as possible. His argument, shown in Figure 24.1, was based entirely on business grounds.

The board of directors met and discussed Andrew's recommendations, and they decided to support his

proposals. Negotiating the contract with a supplier of office consumables would be a relatively straightforward activity. Replacing the customer enquiries system would be a much more interesting challenge.

Activity

Explain these sentences and phrases in Andrew's report, shown in Figure 24.1.

1. *'There is potential for reducing the costs of printer consumables when our two-year contract with PaperWeight Ltd expires in July.'*

2. *'Although [the software application] has all the functionality that is needed, it has very slow search times, and the user interface is less efficient than it could be.'*

3. *'A recent user satisfaction survey ...'*

4. *'A full cost-benefit analysis is required to establish the most effective ways of meeting the three objectives.'*

5. *'... to provide a better service to customers, thus increasing our competitive advantage'.*

6. *'... to reduce physical and workload stress on customer enquiries staff'.*

7. *'... to maintain staff morale, thus reducing staff turnover generally'*

Meeting new business objectives
The ICT perspective
Andrew Jones, July 2000

Objective 1: Maintain the number of domestic customers

The system is accommodating, and will continue to accommodate, the current volume of domestic accounts.

Objective 2: Reduce operating costs

2.1. Billing operations
There is potential for reducing the costs of printer consumables when our two-year contract with PaperWeight Ltd expires.

2.2. Customer enquiries operations
(a) The customer enquiries staff use a software application for logging and solving enquiries. This software was purchased two years ago. Although it has all the functionality that is needed, it has very slow search times, and the user interface is less efficient than it could be.
(b) Since the current customer enquiry system was released other software houses have developed better products, but they cannot be installed on the Unix server as currently configured.
(c) An analysis of the Unix system logs show that the customer enquiry system is in use, on average, for 97% of the working day. This is excessive as staff need short breaks throughout the day to avoid repetitive strain injury.
(d) The telephone logs indicate that at peak times customers are in the telephone queue for up to 20 minutes. This is not satisfactory and customers have been complaining.
(e) Each enquiry takes, on average, 4.8 minutes to resolve. This could be reduced to 2.3 minutes with the new software package.

Objective 3: Reduce staff turnover

3.1. Customer enquiries staff
(a) Last year eleven new customer enquiries staff members had to be trained, compared with five during the previous year.
(b) It appears that staff sickness is particularly high amongst customer enquiries staff.
(c) A recent user satisfaction survey undertaken by Operations revealed that the percentage of staff who were satisfied or very satisfied with the computer systems that they used had fallen from 55% to 32% since last year.

Recommendations

4.1. A full *cost–benefit analysis* is required to establish the most effective ways of meeting the three objectives. Estimated costs are given in the appendix.

4.2. My *initial recommendations* are:

(a) To renegotiate the contract with our supplier of office consumables
Reason:
  • to reduce the considerable printer consumer costs.
(b) Add a new server to support the customer enquiries system, and install the latest version of the customer enquiries software application
Reasons:
  • to provide a better service to customers, thus increasing our competitive advantage
  • to reduce physical and workload stress on customer enquiries staff
  • to reduce the costs of staff turnover.

Figure 24.1 *Andrew Jones' report to the board of directors*

Acquisition options

Andrew Jones knows that he will have to consider a number of options for acquiring the new customer enquiries system. *Acquisition* is a formal term used to describe the process of selecting and acquiring goods and services. When something is acquired it does not necessarily have to be purchased and paid for outright. There are a number ways of financing an acquisition. This section will examine those options.

Proposals based on performance

Insourcing or outsourcing?

When an upgrade is proposed, the hardware, software and related services, such as maintenance and support, have to come from somewhere. In practice these can be either insourced or outsourced.

When an item or service is insourced then it is supplied from another part of the same organisation. If it is outsourced then it is supplied by an external business.

In GBW Bank (see Chapter 21), the Information Systems Department has two sections, each headed up by a middle manager. Abdul Ahmed, the Systems Manager, is responsible for the operation of all the IT systems. His work is very similar to that of Andrew Jones, although on a larger scale. But there is another department within Information Systems at the Bank: Sara Patel is the IT Development Manager, and her section develops software applications. We say that the applications are developed inhouse.

At the bank most software acquisitions and support services are insourced, and most hardware acquisitions are outsourced but maintained internally. At EauCo Water, which is a much smaller business, all hardware and software acquisitions are outsourced.

Outsourcing can be used for operations as well as for acquisition. Andrew is the Operations Manager at EauCo Water, but he is employed by Direct Control, who are under contract to provide management services to EauCo.

The water company decided some years ago to outsource their systems management because they believed they would be buying the expertise of a specialist business. They drew up a facilities management contract based on outcomes, in which Direct Control are obliged to meet certain standards in managing EauCo's systems. Direct Control have to ensure that the network is fully operational. Of course, they cannot avoid occasional system failures, so 'fully operational' is defined in the contract to mean that downtime should last no longer than four hours once a month. If Direct Control does not meet this standard then EauCo Water may reduce the amount they pay for the service.

Activity

1. *What are the advantages and disadvantages of outsourcing software?*

2. *The directors of EauCo Water believe they made a good business decision when they decided to use facilities management for their network system. Why do they think this?*

Software acquisition options

The options for acquiring software are more complex than simply choosing between outsourcing and insourcing. Some of the options are given below.

- *Inhouse applications development.* If the organisation has an IT development function then the design and implementation of the software can be undertaken by its own analysts and programmers.
- *Contract staff working inhouse.* The organisation may employ software development personnel on short-term contracts to complete the software project.
- *Outsourced software which is then customised by inhouse staff.* Some applications software is sold in a form which allows the organisation to tailor it to its own requirements. This will still normally require specialist staff.
- *Outsourced software which is then customised by the supplier.* This is a common approach when software is sold into niche markets. The supplier will customise the application to suit the customer's specific needs. The application will be built out of pre-written modules, so will not be as costly as a bespoke system.
- *Outsourced bespoke system.* An external software house may be asked to produce one-off software that exactly matches the customer's requirements.
- *Outsourced application package.* For simple applications a ready written applications package may be suitable. Very little customisation will be possible with an applications package.

Not all these options are suitable for EauCo Water.

Software services options

The two main software services that have to be considered are software maintenance and user support. Again, there is a range of options.

- *Software maintenance.* Generally, software maintenance will be undertaken in the same way that the original software was developed in the first place. If the software was customised or specially written by an external company, then a software maintenance contract will normally form part of the original agreement between the organisation and the supplier.
- *User support.* There are many options available for the provision of end-user support. Perhaps, for

example, all helpdesk support and training will be carried out by inhouse staff. Alternatively, initial training may be outsourced to a specialist training company, then helpdesk support and additional training is carried out inhouse. A third option is that the software supplier provides all helpdesk support and training from the start.

In each case, the business deal has to be formalised with a contract.

Activity

Under what circumstances should a company outsource training?

Hardware acquisition and maintenance options

Only the largest business organisations will have the facilities to develop hardware inhouse, so most hardware is outsourced. The question then is whether the equipment should be purchased outright, or leased. This is essentially a financial decision, but we will see that there are non-financial advantages to either method.

Leasing

Leasing is a form of rental. The customer pays a monthly or annual fee and has full use of the equipment from the beginning. A lease agreement (contract) will specify who is responsible for maintenance and technical support. The equipment continues to belong to the supplier, who can remove it if the customer does not keep up to date with payments. Leasing has many advantages:

- The customer can acquire the hardware straight away, without capital investment.
- The equipment can be replaced with the latest hardware at any time by renegotiating the leasing agreement.
- Hardware maintenance may be built in to the lease contract. This can specify standards that should be met.

There are some disadvantages too:

- The equipment never belongs to the customer, so never becomes a capital asset of the company.
- After a period of time the total cost of leasing the hardware will be more than purchasing it at the

beginning. However, this has to be calculated with care, to allow for factors such as the cost of borrowing the capital in the first place and the depreciation (reduction) in the value of the hardware.

- The customer is contracted to the supplier for a lengthy period of time and may find it difficult to break the contract if things go wrong.

In addition to the normal leasing arrangements described above, an organisation may rent hardware for a short period. This is normally more expensive than leasing, but is useful for a temporary project, or if hardware has been damaged and needs short-term replacement.

Another option is a purchase-lease (or finance-lease) contract. In this case, the hardware is leased to the customer, but at the end of an agreed period the customer has a right to ownership of the equipment, upon making an additional payment.

Purchasing

When an organisation decides to buy hardware and other equipment outright it does have to find the capital from somewhere. This normally means that the capital must be borrowed, and interest will be payable on the loan. The main advantages of purchasing are:

- The equipment is owned by the customer from the beginning, so can be sold or used in any way.
- The customer is free to choose the supplier, and can change supplier from year to year.

The company has to consider these disadvantages:

- The initial capital costs, and the costs of borrowing the capital, will be high.
- Additional arrangements will have to be made for maintenance.

Sometimes a hardware supplier will offer equipment at reduced price provided the customer makes the company their *preferred supplier*. This normally obliges the customer to make purchases from the supplier in the future. This can often appear to be a very good arrangement for the customer, but they are then tied in with the supplier, sometimes for a long period. Some companies have lived to regret a preferred-supplier contract, especially if the supplier becomes complacent. But others value the good relationship they can build up with a supplier who understands their needs.

CHAPTER 25

Preparing for an upgrade

This chapter continues to explore the use of ICT in EauCo Water, which was introduced in Chapter 6 and discussed further in Chapter 24. It will describe:

● how an upgrade to a system can be planned

● how an upgrade to a system can be properly documented.

This chapter covers these Learning Objectives in the specification:

L.O. 4.6 Understand what is required for the planning of a given upgrade

L.O. 4.7 Demonstrate how the history of an upgrade of an ICT system should be documented

In the previous chapter you read about the proposals put forward by Andrew Jones, the Operations Manager at EauCo Water (see Figure 24.1 on page 277). In this chapter we will concentrate on the major recommendations for upgrading the hardware and software, which were as follows:

Add a new server to support the customer enquiries system, and install the latest version of the customer enquiry software application.

Reasons:

● *to provide a better service to customers, thus increasing our competitive advantage*

● *to reduce physical and workload stress on customer enquiries staff*

● *to reduce the costs of staff turnover.*

Planning an upgrade

Andrew Jones has to plan and manage a major upgrade to the system at the water company. He has to handle all aspects of replacing the server on the customer enquiries system and of installing a major new software application. This has to happen without disrupting the normal business of the company, and Andrew has to make sure that he keeps all the employees happy, including the members of his own department, during the planning and implementation of the changeover.

Project management

The process of introducing new components to an IT system has to be planned in much the same way that any engineering task is planned. You will recall that when a software application is developed a number of steps have to be taken.

Andrew is not intending to develop the software inhouse, nor will his company build the new server from scratch, but he still needs to approach the upgrade in an organised fashion. He is carrying out a project for the company, and the project needs to be managed systematically.

The main steps in a project for acquiring software and hardware upgrades are:

● the proposal

● the specification

● acquisition

● implementation.

Andrew knows that he will need to keep full documentation at every stage of the project.

Risk management

All changes carry risks. Andrew has to be aware of the risks he is taking and try to minimise them. He has to consider these risks in his project:

- running over time
- exceeding its budget
- not performing as intended
- putting extra strain on the organisation
- costs of cancellation.

A research study in the UK in 1992 looked at large IT projects costing over £660 000. It found that 90% went over budget, in 98% the specification was changed during the course of the project, 60% went over time, and 20% even produced an inappropriate solution. Fortunately, Andrew's project is not as large as any of these, but he still has to be aware of the risks.

Many people work on large projects and the communications can sometimes be difficult. Communication between people with different skills and outlooks is easier in smaller teams. Projects are much more likely to be fully successful if they are small, so sometimes large projects are broken down into smaller ones.

Managing change

The customer services staff are pleased that they are going to get new software, plus the hardware to support it. But they still have some concerns about the project. Andrew arranges a meeting with the staff and listens to their questions.

- Will the new system do what we want it to do?
- Will it give us extra work, especially when we are changing over to the new system?
- Will it give us less work? If so, will any of us be redundant?
- Will we have to learn new skills in order to use the new system? If so, how will we learn them?
- Will the job be less satisfying with the new software?

Some of the customer services team are very anxious about coping with change, whilst others are looking forward to it. Personality, experience and training are all factors which affect how people handle change. The project will go much more smoothly if Andrew pays attention to the human issues as well as the technical ones.

> **Activity**
>
> 1. *How would you answer the questions posed to Andrew by the customer enquiries team?*
>
> 2. *Describe other strategies that Andrew could adopt to ensure that staff cope well with changes in their working practices.*

Writing the specification

Andrew Jones prepares two specifications, one for the hardware (and systems software) and one for the application software. His aim is to acquire the product he needs at the best possible price.

Preparing the specification

Hardware and systems software

A specification for new hardware and systems software is described in terms of the system performance and design required.

Performance specification
- capacity (memory size)
- speed
- resolution (for monitors and printers)

Design specification
- operating system
- compatibility with existing hardware and software
- disaster recovery
- environmental considerations – cabling, power, noise levels
- support and maintenance
- reliability.

Andrew needs a server which will support the customer enquiries system, but which is bridged across to the Unix server that is already in use. He writes his specification as shown in Figure 25.1.

Additional network server
Requirements specification

1. Aim
To provide an additional network server.

2. Summary
The current Unix server cannot meet the expected usage that will follow the installation of the new customer enquiry system. A new server is required that can be bridged across to the current one. The new server will, initially at least, be dedicated to serve the terminals used by the customer enquiries staff, but in time additional terminals will be added.

3. Performance (minimum requirements)
3.1. *Capacity*: 4GB RAM and 1MB L2 cache RAM
3.2. *Speed*: four multiple Intel 700MHz processors

The supplier must quote independently verified benchmark tests of performance

4. Design
4.1. *Operating system*: Windows 2000
4.2. *Disaster recovery*: Integrated fast backup system
4.3. *Environmental consideration*: The supplier must specify independently verified decibel levels during normal functioning
4.4. *Support and maintenance*: The supplier must offer
  - minimum 3-year warranty
  - preinstalled and configured operating system
  - 24-hour telephone support

4.5. *Installation*: The supplier must state the delivery lead times and installation schedule

Figure 25.1 Andrew Jones' specification for a new server

Activity

Explain what is meant in the hardware specification by these terms:

(a) 'The supplier must quote independently verified benchmark tests of performance'.

(b) 'The supplier must state the delivery lead times and installation schedule'.

Applications software

There are several options for acquiring applications software and these were discussed in the previous chapter. In a large organisation the software may be developed inhouse. In Andrew's case he intends to purchase the application from an external software house, and it may have to be customised by the supplier to meet his requirements.

A full software application specification must be drawn up, whether the software is likely to be an off-the-shelf package, a customised solution or bespoke software.

Performance specification
- user interface specification – what standards the user interface should meet
- operating system required
- network compatibility
- query language used
- storage requirements

Design specification
- functionality – what functions the application must carry out
- security
- compatibility with existing applications – if necessary
- maintainability
- reliability
- life expectancy
- support – user support, customer support, upgrade path
- installation schedule.

Andrew draws up his specification for the new software, as shown in Figure 25.2.

Customer enquiries system
Requirements specification

1. Aim

To provide software to support the customer enquiries function of the company.

2. Summary

The current Unix server cannot meet the expected usage that will follow the installation of the new customer enquiry system. A new server is required that can be bridged across to the current one. The new server will, initially at least, be dedicated to serve the terminals used by the customer enquiries staff, but in time additional terminals will be added.

3. Performance (minimum requirements)

Customer enquiries staff receive telephone calls from existing customers and potential customers. To respond to these queries they need to be able to:

- advise customers about the status of their accounts
- recommend alternative tariffs where appropriate
- accept credit card payment
- advise potential customers about the service offered and the tariffs available.

3.1. *User interface*

(a) The system must use standard Windows style components.
(b) Users must be able, from any screen, to select any operation with a single keystroke or from an accessible drop-down menu.
(c) It must support up to eight users simultaneously.
(d) It must access a customer account record within 2 seconds at normal times and 4 seconds at peak times.
(e) It must report lockouts on the customer records.

3.2. *Operating system*: The system must run on Windows 2000.
3.3. *Network compatibility*: The software must be compatible with the network as described in the hardware specification.
3.4. *Query language*: The customer accounts and tariff data must be accessed using SQL.

4. Design

4 1 *Functionality*

(a) The system must provide a full voicemail queuing system for enquiries.
(b) The system must provide the user with:
   - read-only access to all customer accounts data
   - capability to record date-stamped notes on enquiries
   - capability to transfer to the accounts payment system for automatic payment
   - capability to transfer to accounts staff for detailed accounts investigation
   - read-only access to tariffs and other information.
(c) The system must maintain a log of all enquiries and the action taken.

4.2. *Compatability*: The system must interface with the SQL-based customer accounts database.

4.3. *Maintainability*: The system must require minimum technical supervision on a day-to-day basis.

4.4. *Support*: The supplier must offer:
   - online help system
   - training packages
   - pre-installation support
   - 24-hour telephone support.

4.5. *Reliability*: The supplier must state what fail-safe security is built in to the software to ensure that hardware failure does not lead to loss of data.

4.6. *Installation*: The supplier must state the delivery lead times and installation schedule.

Figure 25.2 *Andrew Jones' specification for the customer enquiries system*

Acquiring the new system

A hardware or software supplier is sometimes known as a *vendor* – someone who sells goods.

Getting quotations

Andrew sends the software requirements specification to a number of software houses which produce suitable applications. He asks them all to send him a quote within the next two weeks. A *quote* is what the vendor is prepared to sell the software for. It is sometimes referred to as the *asking price*.

Request for tender

Large organisations, especially public bodies, go through a more detailed process for acquiring goods and services. These processes are used when the costs are expected to be substantial, running into many thousands or, in some cases, millions of pounds. The process is known as tendering. A *tender* is a proposal from a vendor to supply the goods and services. Crucially, the vendor specifies what it will all cost.

Before a tender can be received the company has to draw up a request for tender. This is simply a more detailed version of the requirements specification. A request for tender should include:

- *introduction* – reason for the request for tender and deadline for submission

- *background* – information about the company
- *requirements specification* – which should distinguish the essential features from those that are desirable but not essential
- *the form of the proposal* – how the proposal should be submitted (this could include a formal presentation as well as a document)
- *evaluation criteria* – how the company will make its selection.

Tenders are prepared in secret, so that none of the suppliers knows what the others are proposing. The asking price in a tender is known as a *bid*.

At EauCo Water, acquisitions have to be put out to tender if the expected expenditure is greater than £50 000. As Andrew Jones is not expecting to have to spend that amount, he is able to use the simpler process of asking for quotes from known suppliers in this field.

Evaluating quotes and tenders

When quotes or tenders are received the company will evaluate them and *shortlist* the vendors. These will often be the vendors who have submitted the lowest bids; in other words, those who have offered to supply the goods for the lowest prices.

Quotes and tenders have to be evaluated, to ensure that they meet the requirements and that the goods can be purchased with confidence. A quote or tender can be evaluated against these criteria:

- Is the vendor reliable? References, past performance, size and financial viability should be checked.
- Does the product meet the performance specification? Both essential and desirable features should be assessed.
- Does the product meet the design specification? Again, essential and desirable features must be assessed.
- What is the asking price (or bid) and what will be supplied for the asking price?

Some vendors will be eliminated at this stage, and the remaining ones will form the shortlist.

Negotiating and selecting

When you buy goods in a shop, the price displayed on the sales label is the asking price. The shop can actually sell it to you for a lower price, and in some parts of the world it is normal to haggle over the price to be paid in a shop. Haggling is a form of negotiation.

It is normal to negotiate on an asking price, or tender bid, in a business transaction. After the evaluation there will probably be a period of negotiation with the shortlisted vendors. As a result of these negotiations the price may be brought down further or additional services included.

Next a final selling price can be negotiated with the shortlisted vendors, before a final selection is made. Finally a legal contract is drawn up between the company and its selected vendor.

Andrew has received five quotes for the new software. He eliminated one of them because it did not meet his requirements, and he eliminated another one because he was not happy about the viability of the vendor company.

Of the remaining three, the quotes were £13 000, £18 700 and £26 000. Andrew does not usually expect to pay the full asking price in the end. The vendor that quoted the middle price has been established for a number of years and has many satisfied customers, so Andrew thinks they may be a safer bet. But he will try to get them to reduce their price by mentioning that he has received a lower quote.

Andrew has also received four quotes for the new server, ranging from £23 600 to £34 250. He decides to use the vendor that had supplied the other server, as he was very pleased with the support offered and the reliability of their hardware. They were keen to maintain their relationship with EauCo, so had quoted the lowest price.

Planning the implementation

Andrew Jones has chosen the vendors for the new hardware and software. He now begins planning the implementation of the new system. Although the hardware can be delivered immediately, the software house has told him that they require a one-month lead time to customise and test the software.

Andrew plans the implementation over a three-month period. He checks the holiday rotas of the systems administration staff, as he will need all staff available at certain times. He also discusses the timing with the customer enquiries supervisor, so that staff can be trained in readiness for the new system.

Generally, implementation of an upgrade follows this pattern:

- order the hardware and software
- prepare the site
- install and test the hardware and software
- review and rewrite systems and user documentation
- select staff, if necessary
- train the staff
- institute data conversion, if necessary
- make the changeover.

The systems manager must devise and lay down the procedures to be followed through the whole of an upgrade. There are several methods for planning projects like this. The project consists of a set of tasks. Some of these tasks must be completed before others can begin, but some tasks can be carried out in parallel with others. Staff have to be assigned to tasks. In order to plan the project the systems manager needs to establish the sequence of tasks and their duration.

One straightforward method of time planning is known as a Gantt chart, and Andrew decides to create one to plan his upgrade (see Figure 25.3).

> ### Activity
>
> *There are other, more complex, methods for planning projects. One well-known method is known as PERT. Find out what the initials stand for and obtain a sample PERT chart.*

Documenting an upgrade

Andrew Jones knows that he must keep very full records of each stage in the upgrade project. Many things could go wrong (recall Murphy's Law from Chapter 21). For example, the hardware could develop a fault and corrupt the software. The software might

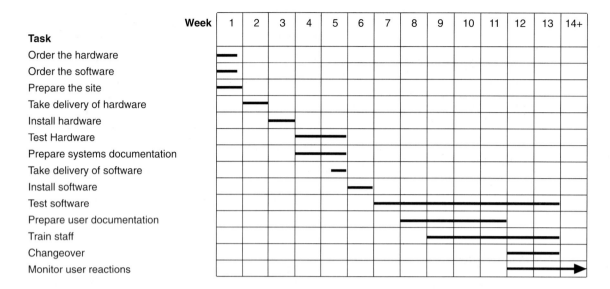

Week	1	2	3	4	5	6	7	8	9	10	11	12	13	14+
Task														
Order the hardware														
Order the software														
Prepare the site														
Take delivery of hardware														
Install hardware														
Test Hardware														
Prepare systems documentation														
Take delivery of software														
Install software														
Test software														
Prepare user documentation														
Train staff														
Changeover														
Monitor user reactions														

Figure 25.3 *An example of a Gantt chart*

interfere with another application. Staff may crash the system during training. Andrew or some of his staff may have to take time off because of illness in the middle of the upgrade. If full documentation is maintained then none of these problems should be catastrophic.

As the plan is carried out, the documentation of the project will form a *history* of the upgrade. If something goes wrong, it should be possible to use the documentation in order to go back to the stage the system was at before the problem arose.

Documenting the stages

Each of the stages in the implementation generates its own documentation, which should be carefully stored. Below is a list of the different types of documentation required throughout an upgrade project (for each stage the person responsible should be named):

- *order the hardware and software* – requirements specification, tenders and bids, evaluation criteria, evaluation assessments, records of negotiations, contracts
- *prepare the site* – plans, furnishings, timetable
- *install hardware and software* – procedures to be followed, action logs
- *test hardware and software* – test plan, results of tests, action taken on errors
- *review and rewrite systems and user documentation* – new and revised manuals

- *select staff* – job descriptions, recruitment procedures
- *train staff* – training materials, timetable for course, arrangements for covering staff on training
- *data conversion* – data model, data formats before and after conversion, data conversion procedures
- *changeover* – method used, acceptance testing, end-user reactions.

Logging procedures

The systems administrators will carry out many of the implementation tasks. They should keep a log, or diary, of every procedure they carry out. The systems administrators' action log could look something like Figure 25.4.

The column headed 'Authorised by' should contain the name of the person who has authorised the procedure. This will usually be the administrator's line manager. The same person must initial the final column when the task is completed satisfactorily.

Activity

Explain why all tasks carried out by the systems administrators should be authorised.

Date	Time	Who	Action	Authorised by	Signed off
10.1.01	10.30	K. Taylor	Prepared location for new server in computer centre	AJ	**AJ**
18.1.01	16.00	K. Taylor	Took delivery of server – checked all components delivered	AJ	**AJ**
23.1.01	17.30	T. Price	Installed server and cabling	AJ	**AJ**
24.1.01	11.15	T. Price	Tested operating system on server	AJ	**AJ**
24.1.01	13.30	T. Price	Set up users on server	AJ	**AJ**
24.1.01	16.30	T. Price	Tested user access to new server	AJ	**AJ**
25.1.01	14.00	T. Price	Tested bridge to Unix server	AJ	**AJ**

Figure 25.4 *Systems administrators' action log*

Reverting to the previous state

You may have had the experience of reconfiguring your PC, then changing your mind about the result. For example, you may change the display resolution and colours. How do you revert to the previous state?

Fortunately, the configuration program will normally enable you to change back – but only if you remember what values you used before. It would be sensible to jot down the original settings before making the changes. This is a simple form of upgrade documentation which enables you to revert to the previous state.

For every one of the procedures followed during the upgrade, the documentation should allow the system to be reverted to the state it was in before the procedure was carried out.

Activity

1. If something goes wrong during one of the tasks, who is held responsible, the administrator or the person who authorised it?

2. You might expect the systems administrators to record their activity logs using a word-processor or other standard software. In practice, this is not a sensible thing to do. Why not?

CHAPTER 26

Managing the changeover

This chapter continues to explore the use of ICT in EauCo Water, which was introduced in Chapter 6 and discussed further in Chapters 24 and 25. It will describe:

- how the systems manager designs the procedures for changing over to an upgraded system

- how the upgraded system should be tested.

This chapter covers these Learning Objectives in the specification:

L.O. 4.8   Design the operational changeover procedures that are necessary when an ICT system is upgraded

L.O. 4.9   Demonstrate a knowledge of the technical testing processes for the upgrade of an ICT system

In the previous chapter we saw how Andrew Jones, the Operations Manager at the EauCo Water, planned an upgrade to the customer enquiries system. The upgrade consisted of a new server and new applications software. The project breaks down to a number of stages:

- the proposal
- the specification
- acquisition
- implementation.

As we saw, the implementation stage itself consists of a number of activities:

Implementation
- order the hardware and software
- prepare the site
- install and test the hardware and software
- review and rewrite systems and user documentation
- select staff, if necessary
- retrain staff
- institute data conversion, if necessary
- make the changeover.

The project will take about three months to complete, and the outline plan for the project can be seen in the previous chapter.

Andrew has to develop detailed plans for certain aspects of the project. In particular, he has to consider how the new systems will be tested and how the changeover to the new system will be managed. These aspects have to be thought about at the beginning of the three-month period, as the choices made will affect the overall planning.

Changeover methods

The aim of the project is to 'go live' successfully with the upgraded system. There are several different ways of managing the switch to a new system. Four common methods are:

- direct changeover
- pilot conversion
- phase-in conversion
- parallel running.

The choice of which method to use depends on the answers to a number of questions, such as:

- How large is the new system?
- Does the new system replace an older similar system, or is it completely new?
- How long will it take for end-users to become familiar with the new system?
- Is the new system safety critical?

Direct changeover

If this method is adopted then, on an agreed date, the old system will be abandoned and the new system will be used. This is the usual method adopted for small systems or simple upgrades. It is the only possible method when replacing faulty hardware, or when installing completely new software in a small system.

Direct changeover can be risky, even for a simple upgrade. Installing a new version of an application must follow careful end-user training. If training is not provided, users may be confused about how to use the software and become very unhappy about the change. Users must have access to quality help facilities. In addition, the systems manager has to ensure that all the data used by the previous version will convert across to the new version.

Andrew Jones has decided to change over directly to the new customer enquiries system.

Pilot conversion

When a large system is installed that will be used by people at a number of locations, it is sometimes

EPOS terminal

advantageous to try it out in one location first. For example, a supermarket chain may want to introduce new EPOS (electronic point-of-sale) terminals supported by enhanced sales software. They may decide to use one store as a guinea pig for the system. That store will pilot the new system for a few months, and if all goes well the supermarket company will eventually roll out the system across all their stores.

Pilot conversion is a cautious way of introducing changes, but it has many advantages over a direct changeover. Any problems with the system will be picked up at the pilot branch. The systems development teams will be able to monitor a functioning system and fix any errors, but they will be able to concentrate their attention on the one branch. In this way, the pilot stage can be treated as an extended testing period.

The pilot branch will probably need extra resources during the pilot phase. The staff will need training. Also, staff will take some time to become accustomed to the new system and the throughput may be slowed up for a while. During this 'bedding in' time, staff may be asked to work overtime. However, these additional costs will be limited to one store.

A further advantage of piloting a new system is that staff across the company can be sent to the pilot location for training.

Phase-in conversion

The phase-in conversion method can be used only for particular types of system. In this approach only part of the system is launched initially, with other parts following later.

A college may want to change to a new student administration system. The full system will handle student admissions, timetabling and student progress (including examination results). This is a very complex system, with three distinct sub-systems, so the college management might decide to introduce the student admissions phase first, then add the timetabling and student progress phases in later years. By phasing in the complete system, the college can ensure that the first phase has been used throughout a full academic year. Any problems with the application or with the hardware can be sorted out and the second phase will begin when the management feel confident.

Training will be important in a major system like this, but it will be spread over the three phases. Users will not be overwhelmed with having to learn a large number of new skills at the beginning.

There is one serious drawback with phased-in conversion. Normally the new system will be replacing an old computer-based system. This means that during the lengthy changeover period parts of the old system will have to work alongside the new. The student admissions phase will still have to interact with the old method of recording student examination results. The application developers may have to write some special software to interface the two systems, and this can be both costly and risky. Also, during this period, users who are having to work with old and new phases may find it confusing to have to switch between the two.

Parallel running

The safest method of changeover is parallel running, although it is often not feasible to do it. The old and the new systems are both run together so that users and technical staff can compare the results. The old system may be a fully manual system or it may already be computer-based. This method can work only if both systems carry out the same tasks.

For example, a small music venue is run as a club. It has always issued tickets for gigs at the door. The box-office staff have books of numbered tickets, which are torn off and given to customers when sold. A stub remains in the book of tickets as a record of each sale. The club management decide to install a ticket sales system, which will allow customers to phone up and pay for tickets by credit card, which they then pick up at the door. A PC, ticket printer and suitable software are purchased.

Although the manager is confident that the ticket-booking application software is reliable, he is afraid that the box-office staff may make mistakes, especially when the system is new. He cannot afford to lose money. He also knows that if he overcrowds the venue, even by mistake, he could lose the club's entertainment licence.

So during the first two weeks the box-office staff issue tickets from the books of tickets in the usual way, but also enter all the details on the computer system. At the end of the trial period the manager compares the ticket stubs with the record of sales on the computer. He finds a few minor errors which he discusses with the box-office staff. After another week of parallel running the manager is happy to drop the old system and work totally with the new one.

The prime advantage of parallel running during changeover is that the old and new can be compared, so that the new software can be fully tested in use. Staff too can check their own accuracy with the new system. But in some cases it is an expensive method, as staff need to do double the work, and this can incur labour costs. The manager at the club was able to use the parallel running method only by helping out in the box office himself.

Parallel running should work to a clear time plan, so that staff know when the changeover will be completed.

Activity

1. *Why did Andrew chose to use the direct changeover method for the customer enquiries system?*

2. *Can you think of any disadvantages of the parallel-running method, apart from the cost?*

Changeover issues

Safety-critical and business-critical systems

A safety-critical system is a system in which a failure could lead to loss of life. Many traffic control systems, such as train signalling or air traffic control, are safety-critical systems, as are the systems that organise the emergency services, or monitor patients in intensive care, or control theme park rides.

When safety-critical systems are installed, the initial period carries a high level of risk. Systems like these have to be tested very thoroughly, and parallel running can be used once the system goes live. The additional expense of parallel running is normally accepted as essential.

A business-critical system is one in which failure could be very damaging to the organisation, even though lives may not be at risk. Organisations which are highly dependent on ICT systems, such as credit card companies, travel agencies and Internet-based retailers, also need to plan changeover very carefully.

Although the new customer enquiries system at the EauCo Water is not safety-critical, it is mildly business-critical. The customer enquiries system is an important link with the general market and with potential new customers. If the system does not function properly for an extended period then the business will suffer.

Andrew Jones is paying a lot of attention to the planning of the changeover period. He will monitor the systems very carefully during this critical time, and is expecting to have to work long hours dealing with problems as they occur. He is particularly careful to design procedures for his department that will ensure that full documentation is kept and that data backups are kept securely throughout.

Data conversion

Data is stored in a variety of formats. This can be a problem during an upgrade, as the systems staff may find that the new system requires the data to be formatted differently from the old. This is a particular problem when a database is transferred to a new database management system.

One of the tasks of the applications developer will be to convert the data into its new format, and a special program may be written to carry this out. When the program is run it will take the old data file as input and generate a new data file. The old data will still be preserved in case any errors occur during the data conversion process.

Occasionally the new system replaces a manual system. This occurred frequently during the last quarter of the last century, but is less common now. If it is ever necessary to convert a large amount of data from a manual to electronic form, temporary data-entry staff are usually employed to carry out the task.

Data migration

If data has to be transferred to a new hardware platform, then this is described as data migration. This cannot be carried out until the changeover period, as the data will be changing constantly on the old system right up to the moment when the system goes live.

For training and testing purposes, a sample of the data, or a complete copy of the data, will be migrated to the new system in advance of the changeover. This will have to be replaced with the correct set of data at changeover.

Sometimes data migration also involves data conversion. As usual, full documentation must be kept and backups generated so that the system can be restored to its previous configuration if necessary.

Upgrading user and systems documentation

Manuals used by end-users and by the systems administrators will have to be reviewed prior to changeover.

Figure 26.1 New manuals will be needed for an upgrade

The hardware supplier will normally provide installation and maintenance instructions for the new equipment. The software developer should have provided the company with user support in the form of help files and user manuals. These should be checked by the systems staff for completeness and intelligibility. During the training period, users will be introduced to the help facility and to the documentation; any shortcomings should be identified at this stage.

Andrew is reasonably satisfied with the online help facilities provided in the customer enquiries application. The company selected to provide the software was unable to provide training materials, and as a result Andrew was able to negotiate a reduced cost for the whole contract.

Andrew employs a training consultant for a few days to develop suitable training guides. He points out to the consultant that the training materials will have to be adapted to meet the needs of Craig Johnson, who is a partially sighted member of the customer enquiries team. Andrew's staff have already adapted Craig's workstation by replacing his standard monitor with a large, high-resolution one, and they have configured the display to make it readable for him. But the printed training materials will have to be scanned in and enlarged for him.

All the paper-based documentation must be date-stamped and its location recorded in a logbook or data file.

Implications for staff

Training is an essential component of any upgrade. The systems manager has to consider the training needs of:

- systems administration staff
- end-users.

The training may be quite brief, but even a short introduction to the system must be planned and delivered to the right people at the right time. The training period also allows the systems staff to monitor the use of the new system and to judge the effectiveness of any support given by the system.

Andrew has arranged for the hardware supplier to provide initial instructions to the systems administration staff about the new server and its integration with the existing server. Since they are not planning to introduce a new operating system at this stage, the systems staff do not require intensive training.

Andrew has also planned training for customer enquiries staff and has discussed this with the training manager in the human resources department. Andrew, as Operations Manager, is not required to provide the training, but he puts in a request for consultants to be brought in to deliver the training. The consultants will need to familiarise themselves with the new system and with the training materials.

Staff morale has to be monitored carefully during the changeover period. Some employees, both systems and users, may have to work longer hours whilst the system is being tested and launched. Staff holidays may have to be postponed until the upgrade is complete. The senior managers may have to develop an incentive scheme and promise a bonus for the staff if they get the system up and running with minimum interruption to the flow of business.

Activity

1. *List all the safety-critical ICT systems that you can think of.*

2. *Can you identify any systems at the water company which are safety-critical?*

Technical testing

The aim of testing is not to show that the system works under normal conditions. The aim of all testing is to find the faults. We are back with Murphy's Law again; the principle 'What can go wrong, will go wrong' is a good one to adopt when carrying out testing.

Hardware testing

There are a number of ways in which a client can test the hardware that has been purchased.

With *burn-in testing*, the components of the new system are run intensively in order to simulate several weeks' operation. Any faults which occur are reported back to the supplier.

With *hardware monitoring*, sensors can be attached to the hardware to measure such factors as the speed of the drives and the use of internal memory. The sensors are attached to a computer known as a *hardware monitor*, which analyses and reports on the performance of the system.

Software testing

An application developer takes the software through several stages of testing, as follows.

Initial testing

The programmers carry out the initial testing of the software. The testing is based on a test plan which includes normal data, extreme data and exceptional (erroneous) data. The test plan should check for accuracy, whether the functionality of the application meets the specification, and the effectiveness of the user interface.

Acceptance testing – alpha testing

The software house carries out further testing, but this time the tests are done by someone other than the original developer. This person will approach the system with fresh and unbiased eyes.

A bespoke application will be tested by the end-users under the guidance of the developer, using dummy data.

Off-the-shelf and customised applications will normally be alpha tested within the software house.

Acceptance testing – beta testing

Finally the application will be used in a real environment. The application developer will want to get feedback from the customer about how the system works under normal circumstances. The end-users will also report on how well the application manages when it is heavily used. Final minor adjustments may be made at this stage – the most carefully developed software can still contain errors, so acceptance testing should push the application to extremes.

Beta testing for off-the-shelf packages is conducted somewhat differently. The software supplier will ask a selected group of customers to look at the software and to use it under normal circumstances. The testers will be expected to report back on any problems with the application and they will normally then be offered a free copy of the software when it is finally released.

Improvements may be added at this stage in response to feedback.

More about acceptance testing

The software house that is supplying EauCo Water has carried out initial and alpha testing in house.

Andrew has planned the beta testing to start a week before training and to carry on during the training period. He refers back to the original specification which, with regard to functionality, stated:

> (a) The system must provide a full voicemail queuing system for enquiries.
> (b) The system must provide the user with:
>   • read-only access to all customer accounts data
>   • capability to record date-stamped notes on enquiries
>   • capability to transfer to the accounts payment system for automatic payment
>   • capability to transfer to accounts staff for detailed accounts investigation
>   • read-only access to tariffs and other information.
> (c) The system must maintain a log of all enquiries and the action taken.

He creates dummy customers on the customer accounts database. During the testing period the real data for the tariffs and other information will be used.

Testing under normal circumstances

Andrew then devises, on paper, a series of test cases which would simulate a series of phone enquiries that might be made by the 'dummy' customers. For example, one customer might ask for their current water consumption, another would want to challenge the last bill, whilst another would be from a new customer wanting to change water supplier. For each test Andrew describes the required outcomes. One of the systems administrators then carries out the tests and checks that the results match the required outcomes.

Testing under extreme and exceptional circumstances

Andrew has to devise further tests that will check that the system will cope in extreme and exceptional circumstances.

An *extreme circumstance* is an unexpected situation that the application should be able to handle, but which is at the outermost limits of acceptability. For example, the daughter of a customer may phone in and explain that she wants to take responsibility for the account from now on, but that the bills must be sent to her overseas address, except during three months during the summer when she will be back in England. This is an unusual request, but the company would want to try to fit in with the customer's requirements.

Some extreme circumstances involve extreme data. For example, if a field in a database is specified as 'text' type this normally means that it can hold up to 256 characters. (The same applies if a variable is declared as a 'string' in programming languages such as Basic.) An extreme example of data to be entered in this field would be a sentence of exactly 256 characters. The test should check two things – does the system accept the data, and can the data be displayed clearly on-screen.

An *exceptional circumstance* is one that you would expect the application to identify as invalid. For example, if two people try to register as customers at the same address, the system should throw up a warning message to the user. Of course, the property at the address may have recently been converted into two self-contained flats, in which case the application should make it possible for the user to enter this new information and to register both customers.

Exceptional data – that is, invalid data – may play a part in an exceptional circumstance. For example, if a customer provides a phone number that has an incorrect number of digits, then we would expect the system to display a helpful message to the user.

End-user errors often give rise to exceptional circumstances, so the test cases should always include some that simulate the kinds of errors that users make when keying in data.

End-user testing

During the training phase, Andrew will be asking customer enquiries staff to note down any difficulties they have with the software. By this stage, the logical errors in the software should have been identified and corrected. End-user testing concentrates on the effectiveness of the user interface.

The user interface can be assessed on a number of features, including:

- screen layout, colour, font style
- menu structures and methods of access (drop-down menus, contextual menus, shortcut keys, etc.)
- speed of access to data (number of keystrokes, search facility, data retrieval times).

The learning curve

When anyone learns a complex skill they often go through an initial period when they find it quite difficult. As they gradually familiarise themselves with the task their learning speeds up. This is described as the *learning curve* and can be illustrated by a simple graph (see Figure 26.2).

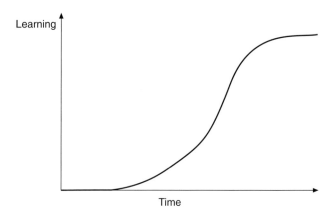

Figure 26.2 *The learning curve*

The height of the curve depicts how many new skills have to be learnt in the time available. A steep learning curve is produced if a person has to learn a lot of new skills in a short time, and this can be quite a stressful process. Steep learning curves can prove too much for some learners, who may become convinced that they can never master the skills. A shallower learning curve is more likely to be successful with most learners.

At EauCo Water, the new customer enquiries system is quite complex and the staff will have to learn a number of new skills. Andrew is aware that training costs money – the company has to pay for the training consultant by the hour, and whilst someone is being trained someone else must be paid to do their day-to-day job. He would prefer that the system can be learnt in a short time, but this will be achievable only if the users do not have to learn too many skills.

The quality of the user interface can have a substantial effect on the time it takes to learn to use the system. A good interface will incorporate methods that the user is already familiar with, for example by using the same shortcut keys that were used in the old application.

Acceptance testing must incorporate a measure of the time taken to learn to use the application. It will also include an assessment of potential improvements to the user interface which could reduce the number of skills to be learnt, and hence reduce the learning time.

Activity

Recall some complex IT skills that you have learnt, such as coming to grips with a new software package or working through a game. Draw a learning curve for each, and comment on how the user interface helped you to master the skills.

Responses to results of acceptance testing

Customised software

The systems manager must collate all the data collected during the acceptance testing stage. If the software has been customised or specially written for the organisation, then the systems manager can

discuss the data with the software developer. The software developer will probably refer back to the specification.

If the specification has been clearly written and the software does not fully meet its requirements then the customer is entitled to ask for corrections and improvements to be made. If these are not completed satisfactorily, the customer is entitled to withhold some of the payment.

If the application already meets the specification, and the systems manager is asking for additional features, then the software developer may want to charge extra. In a large project this can lead to lengthy legal negotiations.

Andrew asks the developer to make some minor adjustments to the menu structure in the software but is otherwise happy that the new application meets the specification.

Off-the-shelf packages

Bought-in packages may be cheaper than customised solutions, but they are unlikely to meet every aspect of the specification. The systems manager should certainly report any logical faults to the software house. The suppliers would then be expected to produce a software *patch*, at no extra charge, to deal with the problem. A software patch is a procedure that can be added to the system to correct an error. It is designed only as a temporary measure, and should be properly incorporated into the next version of the application.

The software developer should also be monitoring the reactions to the package and consider releasing upgrades to meet market demands. See Chapter 14 for more information about upgrade policies.

Test Manager

The holder of this new position will manage the Integration and User-Acceptance testing of code released by the package supplier on a day-to-day basis.

As well as planning and co-ordinating the platforms and environments required for all kinds of testing, you'll ensure the tests themselves are carried out to a consistent standard, with results recorded, stored and approved. You'll make sure that testing proceeds according to predetermined plans and distribute management information. In addition you'll need to liaise extensively with operational managers.

With three to five years' experience of test management – incorporating some strategy development – you'll be familiar with co-ordinating environments and setting up data. Knowledge and understanding of system development lifecycles will prove particularly valuable, as will familiarity with current testing tools. You will need to be a team player with a can-do attitude, and excellent communication skills will contribute to your all-round suitability as a manager.

Activity

Here is the job advertisement for a testing manager in a very large organisation. What are the responsibilities of the testing manager? Who does the testing manager communicate with?

CHAPTER 27

Getting the best out of a large system

This chapter continues to explore the management of the large system in a college, introduced in Chapter 7. It will describe:

- how security policy is developed and how the operational procedures for maintenance of file security are derived from it
- multitasking operating systems
- how systems can be connected to a MAN.

The chapter covers this Learning Outcome in the specification:

L.O. 4.10   Outline a set of maintenance procedures for a specified ICT system

It also covers these Technical Knowledge topics:

T4.1.1   Types of operating system
T4.1.2   Facilities of current operating systems
T4.1.3   Multitasking
T4.1.4   Interrupt handling

Designing security procedures for large systems

Bevan Hughes is the network administrator at Highgate College and as such is responsible for carrying out all the maintenance procedures on the systems. He must ensure that the individual PCs in the networks function properly and that the local-area networks (LANs) themselves work effectively.

In Chapter 6 you saw that the maintenance procedures for a PC tend to concentrate on simple cleaning processes, and on checking that the hard disk is free from errors and superfluous files. Chapter 7 looked in detail at the network maintenance procedures that Bevan has to follow. These focus almost entirely on system security and they take up the majority of the administrator's time.

We now need to look more closely at how the maintenance procedures are themselves designed. Although the systems administrators are responsible for carrying out all the procedures, it is the systems manager who has ultimate responsibility for deciding which procedures should be implemented and what priority should be given to each.

Margaret Roberts is the Head of ICT Services at Highgate College. She is, effectively, the systems manager. It is her job to decide on the maintenance procedures the systems administrators should carry out, which she does in consultation with Bevan Hughes, who is the senior administrator.

The maintenance procedures have to be reviewed every time major changes in hardware or software are introduced. In any case, Margaret always reviews the procedures annually, even if no changes have been made, to ensure that they still meet the requirements of the college's IT security policy.

The need for security policy

Some years ago Margaret drew up a security policy which she presented to the senior management team at the college. After considerable discussion the policy was adopted and it is now reviewed every three years.

Why, then, does an organisation need a security policy? Any ICT system is at risk of failure, which could result in the loss of any combination of:

- *availability* – if the system goes down then the business of the organisation can be severely damaged
- *integrity* – if any of the data held on the system is no longer accurate then this can affect business and it can also reduce confidence in all aspects of the system
- *confidentiality* – if access security is breached then the organisation can be at risk in both business and legal terms.

The possible sources of these risks have to be identified. Any of these security failures could be the result of:

- either accidental or deliberate damage
- either physical or data alteration.

Very tight system security can be achieved, but at considerable cost to the organisation. All security measures have a price, as they can be implemented only by using new hardware, software or human labour, or a combination of all three.

On the other hand, a failure of security – whether failure of availability, integrity or confidentiality – will also have financial implications for the organisation. A major breach of security would kill off most businesses. The costs of correcting even minor damage can be considerable.

So somehow the cost of providing security has to be balanced against the potential costs of not providing it. Managing security is always a matter of *risk assessment*. A security policy is a description of how these risks are to be balanced within the organisation and what steps are to be taken to minimise the risks.

Any security policy will normally include a *security model* and *security procedures*.

The security model

A *security classification* is a category that can be applied to information, such as 'For general use', 'Business sensitive', 'Top Secret'. The security policy should include a list of all the classifications that will be used in an organisation. Each piece of information held on the system will be given one or other of these classifications.

Security clearance is a category which is applied to employees. Each user will be given a level of security clearance depending on what information he or she needs to know to do a job. Someone with a higher level of security clearance will have access to more information than someone with a lower level of clearance.

A *security model* is a list which matches levels of security clearance with security classifications. For example, it might state that only people with security clearance at level 3 are allowed to access information with a 'Business sensitive' security classification.

Security procedures

The systems manager has to design procedures to implement the security model. For example, there would have to be a method for ensuring that each new employee is assigned the correct security clearance. This would be developed in conjunction with the Personnel Department.

Other procedures would determine how passwords are issued to users and which user groups they are assigned to. Each user group will be assigned its own clearance level, which should never be higher than the lowest clearance level of any individual within the group.

Even when the procedures are in place, the systems manager must still check that errors are not creeping in, so *security audit procedures* will be designed. These will normally require the administrators to analyse system logs on a regular basis.

Activity

Find out whether a security policy exists for the networks (academic and administrative) used at your centre. If not, try to draw one up which reflects the current allocations of access privileges.

Multi-programming operating systems

When we examined operating systems in the first section of this book we concentrated on the systems used to manage single-user computer systems, such as normal PCs. We also looked at how network systems are configured – but we did not, at that stage, look in any depth at the operating systems required to manage them.

In this chapter we will be examining operating systems that allow more than one user or process to use them simultaneously, such as those used at Highgate College.

System architecture

Modern operating systems are said to have a *system architecture*. This means they are constructed from various software components and layers that carry out different specialised functions but still operate closely together. The system is also given different operating levels, called *user* and *kernel* mode. In the simplified drawing of an OS architecture in Figure 27.1 you can see how these two modes relate to each other.

The user applications run in user mode and communicate their operating conditions to the rest of the operating system that is running in kernel mode.

The user-mode applications have the following characteristics:

- they are prevented from directly accessing the hardware
- they cannot change their assigned memory space
- they may use space on the hard disk as an extension of their memory space
- they are controlled by the executive.

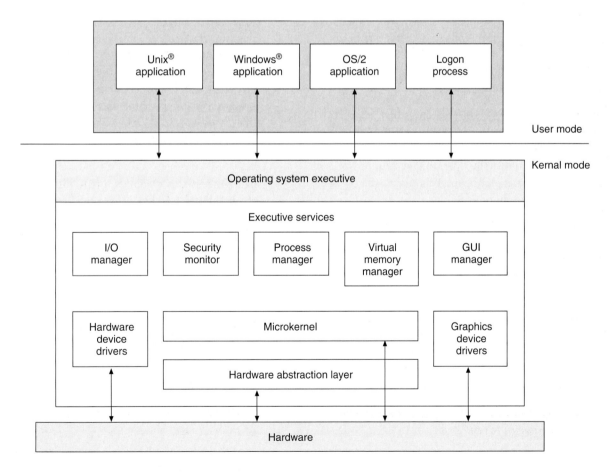

Figure 27.1 *How the user and kernal modes relate to each other*

This architecture is to provide a secure and robust operating environment. Malfunctioning applications should not be able to interfere with other applications that are running and cause a crash. System resources such as hardware are kept under the control of the OS, and unauthorised users will find it harder to carry out malicious activities. User-mode applications are the programs we would use.

The kernel-mode services have a higher priority than user processes, so that the OS is always in charge. The kernel comprises executive services that manage how user applications can access memory, hardware and peripherals. In the example we are looking at here, the kernel mode has three important components: the executive services, the microkernel and the hardware abstraction layer.

The *executive services* comprise managers and device drivers. The managers are software systems that carry out particular jobs for the operating system. In this example there are managers for I/O (input/output), process operations and security, memory management and control of the GUI (graphical user interface). The software services for I/O use device drivers that allow operating systems commands written for a generic device such as a hard drive to work with different manufacturers' equipment that may have different specific operating commands.

The *microkernel* carries out low-level operating services such as process scheduling and responding to interrupts. The *hardware abstraction* layer, like device drivers, allows the operating system to work on different hardware platforms. This makes the operating system more portable.

Processes

We have referred to processes but what exactly do we mean by a process? *A process is essentially any unit of code that is being executed by the computer's central processing unit (CPU).* A computer system may have many working processes, with each one being allocated some time on the CPU when the OS schedules it. Some processes will be the user code that is being executed, while other processes are code that makes up operating system activities.

So a process represents an active portion of code that may be running on a computer. Each process has information related to its operation. Each process has:

- its own program code
- the program counter that says which instruction is being currently executed
- the data section that maintains the state of data being used by the process
- a process stack that maintains temporary data for smaller parts of the process.

Each process has a current 'state' that indicates whether the process is new, running, waiting, ready or terminated (see Figure 27.2). The information about a process is stored by the operating system in a data structure called a process control block. The operating system uses the process control block to store the state of a process; so if it changes from running to waiting, the operating system can restore the process back to running exactly where the process left off.

The process states change due to different circumstances. One process may have used up its

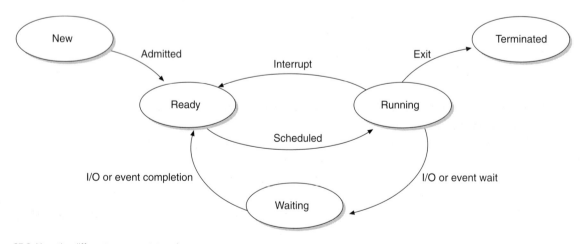

Figure 27.2 *How the different process states change*

allocation of processor time and be suspended; another process may call I/O and be placed in a waiting state until the I/O operation is finished. Another process may be taken from the running state and placed in the ready queue because the OS has interrupted with a job of its own to execute.

Multi-programming systems

A system that allows for many processes to exist and run at the same time is called a *multi-programming system*. In reality, in a single processor system the jobs are not executing at the same time but are in a state where they can execute when their turn comes. The operating system keeps track of all the jobs that are being processed and must select which job should use the processor at any given time. This activity is called *job scheduling*.

Multi-programming allows for maximum utilisation of the processor's time because as one process finishes or is suspended other processes can start. One further complexity is to allow for multi-programming environments to switch between the processes of different users. This system allows users to use a computer system as though it is under their control all

the time. In fact the system is *time-sharing* between different users but at a speed that means the users do not notice any delay. The system is interactive because the response time between a key press or menu selection and the execution of the related code is kept short. Time-sharing systems are also referred to as *multitasking* systems.

Process scheduling

The selection of a process so that is goes from a ready state to a running state is called scheduling. The scheduler selects processes that are waiting to run according to a range of different schemes. One scheme is called non-pre-emptive or *co-operative scheduling* when a process has control of the CPU until it either terminates or goes into a waiting state. This kind of scheduling is easier to build because it does not require specialised hardware.

Another type of scheduling is called *pre-emptive scheduling*. This means that a process can be switched from a running state to a ready state and another process given access to the CPU resources. The pre-emption timing when a process gets allocated processor time can vary a great deal. Some systems use

Activity

Try to organise the following events into an order that corresponds to what would happen when a computer system is called by two people to run two different programs. The underlines indicate where you can identify a process. You may want to use a statement more than once. Write the number down indicating each step in the order in which they happen. Clue: Start from when a user types in a program name for execution.

1. *The disk drive interrupts the OS indicating that the file is open and ready to be read.*
2. *The shell finds program solvit, its code is loaded and executed. Process ___ is started.*
3. *The operating system places Process ___ into its Process Control Block.*
4. *User A types in a program name, solvit, for the shell command interpreter to act on.*
5. *Process ___ is BLOCKED until the requested file is opened.*
6. *The OS responds to system call by running code relevant to the call type.*
7. *User B types in a program name, dolt, for the shell command interpreter to act on.*
8. *Process ___ is now in RUNNING state.*
9. *The shell finds program dolt, its code is loaded and executed. Process ___ is started.*
10. *Process ___ is READY to run but is suspended in a queue until it is allowed to restart.*
11. *Process ___ issues a system call indicating it wants to open a file.*
12. *A Process i.d. is given to the new process.*
13. *Process ___ has used its current allocation of processor time and a timeout occurs. It is moved into the READY queue.*
14. *The current context information of Process ___ is put into Process Control Block.*
15. *Process ___ is taken from the READY queue and restarted.*

a 'first come first served' rule, or else a shortest job first and then there is priority scheduling when processes are ranked in priority for processor time. Another system uses time slices in a round-robin order. A process is selected from the process queue and started running. The scheduler sets a timer going and if the process does not finish running in the allotted time an interrupt occurs and the process is placed at the back of the round-robin queue.

Executive services

Returning now to the diagram of the OS architecture (Figure 27.1), let us examine some of the other executive services, in particular virtual memory management, the I/O and GUI managers.

Virtual memory management

This technique is used to provide a large address space for processes when the physical size of the address space is small. So for example, a system like Windows® NT allows each process to have a 32-bit address giving it in all 4GB of memory. Remember that the total physical address space might be much smaller, say 256MB of RAM, but the process works as though it has been allocated the full 4GB of memory.

Each process has a memory table 1MB in size, divided into 4KB blocks called *pages*. Each 4KB page in the virtual memory space is mapped to physical memory. When a process calls to a part of its memory map, the virtual memory manager makes sure that page of memory is somewhere in the computer's physical memory space. If that page is not actually loaded in physical space then it is loaded into any available memory and the actual addresses mapped to the relevant part of the virtual 4GB space. The process behaves as if it has up to its maximum space and the virtual memory manager juggles the physical space around so that a process's memory space is available, virtually. This means a process's virtual memory space can be in one of three states:

- Most of the pages allocated in the 1MB address space are empty because the process does not need them. They wait to have actual physical pages allocated to them if a demand is made.

- Pages that do exist in the virtual memory map are redirected by a pointer to actual physical space.

- Some pages that have been loaded and not used recently have a pointer indicating that the page is not in memory any more but moved to a 4KB space on the hard drive. If that page is needed again the memory manager locates memory space (it might remove an unused page of space from another process to disk), moves the page into that space, and redirects the virtual memory map to those physical addresses.

I/O management

The operating system is responsible for co-ordinating the movement of data around and to the outside of a computer system. In order for this to be controlled, events – such as a request to send data to a printer – signal the OS that an I/O response is needed. The event is signalled to the OS by an interrupt. Interrupts can be generated by either hardware or software. In the case of the hardware this involves sending a signal to the CPU via the system bus. In the case of software it involves executing a special operation called a *system call* (see Figure 27.3).

Interrupts can be triggered by a range of different events, not just the request for an I/O operation. An invalid access to memory or a request for an OS service trigger interrupts. For each type of interrupt, a service routine exists that is responsible for dealing with the event. When the CPU is interrupted it stops its current processing. Then, using the unique device information generated by the interrupt, it accesses a service routine held in a table. The table holds the identifiers for all the service routines that need to be called by the various interrupts.

Before a service routine is executed the state of the current process must be saved so that it can continue execution later.

You should remember that I/O devices are attached to the system bus of a computer, usually through a bridge or controller chip that allows for signals to be matched and allows for data to be passed between the device and the computer system. To start an I/O operation, the OS loads the registers of a device controller with instructions telling it what kind of operation is needed. The device controller responds to the instructions and then signals the CPU by interrupt once it has finished its task.

The I/O manager carries out requests for I/O in kernel mode; that is, the user application has no access to the

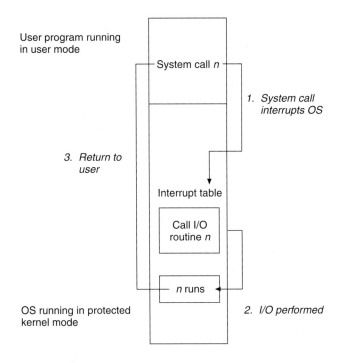

User program running
in user mode

System call *n*

1. *System call
   interrupts OS*

3. *Return to
   user*

Interrupt table

Call I/O
routine *n*

n runs

OS running in protected
kernel mode

2. *I/O performed*

Figure 27.3 *Use of a system call to perform I/O*

device but must signal to the OS the service it requires. This request triggers a system call that is an instruction sent to the CPU indicating what service routine (also known as an interrupt *request* or interrupt *vector*) to use.

GUI managers

There are several ways in which the GUI we use can work (see Figure 27.4).

Microsoft's GUI manager

In Microsoft Windows® the operation of the graphical user interface is managed by the Microsoft's GUI

manager, or *graphics device interface* (GDI) to give it its proper name (see Figure 27.5). This comes as part of the kernel of the OS. Like most GUIs it comprises three parts.

● The *windows manager* provides process calls to specific hardware device drivers that control the graphics devices. The windows manager builds the windows, menus and dialogue boxes that appear on the screen. The device driver then makes these happen.

● The *imaging model* defines the fonts and graphics that appear on the screen.

● The *application program interface* (API) is the means for the application program to specify how and what windows and graphics appear on the screen. An API provides the information from one process to another. In this case it might pass the location of the mouse from the user application to the windows manager that then translates this into the screen you see.

GUIs in Unix®

In other operating environments, most notably Unix® and its spin-off Linux®, there is a similar demarcation between the user applications and the underlying software that manages GUI windows. However, because of the more open nature of the underlying systems, the design approach is quite different.

In order to create the GUI, a system called X-Windows was designed. This has a set of core functions that provide the means of producing GUI systems through APIs. These APIs are the 'glue' under which the windows manager provides the shape, size and feel for the window itself. The interesting feature of the X-

Microsoft® Windows®	Linux® & Unix®
● Part of the OS	● Sits on top of the OS
● Provides hardware independence using different device drivers	● Provides hardware and network independence by using open code (X-Windows and windows managers)
● Applications using the GUI all have same look and feel because they must use the underlying graphics architecture	● Applications may use different GUIs as anyone can write a GUI windows manager
● Graphics system cannot provide a client server model across networks	● Graphics system is independent of location of graphics device and GUI
● Graphics system is an overhead on server machines because it runs with the OS	● Graphics system need not be run on server machine because it is a separate application

Figure 27.4 *Comparison of different GUIs*

Windows system is that it runs as an ordinary application on top of the OS. In other words, it is not part of the kernel, rather it is part of the user space.

X-Windows is not a GUI but it allows commands from the user to be sent as simple character sequences to the process that is going to provide the display. This means that the process that is going to provide GUI support need not reside on the same computer as the user program. Command strings can be sent across a network from a client application on one workstation to a server program on another computer that then provides the functional support for the GUI. The purpose of this approach is to provide hardware and network independence: the application requesting a GUI display need not have any knowledge of how the mouse or VDU works nor where the GUI processes reside.

So if X-Windows provides the means to create the graphical user interface, how does the interface work? Another application is run by X-Windows, called the 'windows manager'. This is the collection of program components that control the size, location and movement for the windows being used. The windows manager contains the hardware-specific information for the platform on which the GUI is being used. Information from the X-Window program is passed to the windows manager using APIs that then creates the specific GUI.

Because the Unix® and Linux® systems are applications running on top of the OS, anyone can write a 'windows manager' using a programming language. As a result there are many different GUIs available for Unix® and Linux®. Because one of the advantages of a GUI is to provide a coherent graphical world in which users interact with their computer programs, it is not surprising that developers have come up with more integrated desktop environments much like MS Windows®. The best known examples of these desktop environments for Linux are KDE and GNOME.

The need for good user interface design

The user interface provides us, the users, with access to the functionality of a program. To us the user interface is the program because that is what we see and use. A bad user interface can therefore lead to an entire application becoming problematic simply because we have difficulty using it.

The user interface is not only the screens we see but also all aspects of the system design that influence the interaction between the user and the system. Therefore the user interface is essentially the bridge between us (seeing, touching, hearing) and the computer system. This includes:

- mapping the tasks we want to do with the features of the program (does it do what we want it to do?)
- the environment we use to control the program (GUIs, command lines)
- the way in which we control the program through buttons, menus, selection boxes
- how we expect these controls to work
- moving within and between windows
- the look and feel of the screen and windows
- the way different applications share a common interface.

Technology trends

Rapidly advancing technology means the way in which we interface with programs can be very different. Many systems operate across networks and people may collaborate in widely dispersed ways. PCs are becoming more powerful, supporting more powerful applications, and there is a wider range of hardware to be used within the overall ICT system.

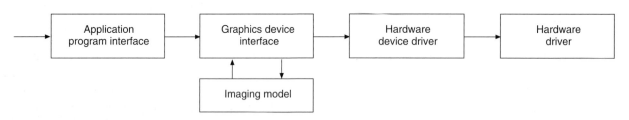

Figure 27.5 *The relationship between components of Microsoft's GUI*

As a result of this the user interface is taking up more and more of the resources when applications are developed. The interface may comprise the largest part of the code and may take as much as 40% per cent of the development effort. Of course there is a reason for this: if a software company does not optimise the users' ability to rapidly use the functionality of a program they will lose out to other developers.

A well-designed user interface means that people can more quickly understand the 'look and feel' of an application and therefore start working quickly with it. This cuts down training and mistakes. The user needs to be able to be productive faster and to be able to have a broader and more customisable approach to his or her work. The impact of good design can lead to:

- improved efficiency
- reduced training time
- reduced system maintenance costs after implementation
- fuller utilisation of system functionality.

A poorly designed user interface can lead to:

- users being unable or unwilling to use an application that is difficult to learn
- a fall of morale, and suspicion that new software will make the job harder
- a program to be simply unusable by the intended users
- a long training period
- much slower working because users have to constantly refer to help functions.

Benefits of good user interface design

There are important benefits of a user-friendly user interface for any business. These include:

- fewer errors
- lower support costs
- lower initial training costs
- smaller loss of productivity when the system is introduced
- quicker return to improved operations
- more focus on tasks to be done, rather than the technology being used
- lower turnover and better morale
- high transfer of skills across applications, further reducing training needs

Activity

If possible, compare the GUI features provided by a Windows®-based application with one based on another operating system. You will still be able to find applications based on the earlier MS-DOS® standards, especially in some commercial locations such as shops, although these will not strictly speaking provide you with a graphical interface. Ask around for examples of Unix®-based applications.

The hardware abstraction layer

The hardware abstraction layer (HAL) in Windows® allows for devices of all kinds to be supported by a windows system. The hardware manufacturer, whether it is for a printer, DVD or video system, has simply to write the code that interfaces with the windows code. In Unix®, new device drivers need to be linked into the code. This entails a re-linking process.

Device drivers, multimedia and plug and play

In Windows®, device drivers are implemented as dynamic link libraries (DLLs). These programs are loaded only when an application needs to use them and can be shared by other programs. This means only one copy of the code need be in memory, which is useful if a number of programs use the same device (e.g. display or mouse drivers).

Another advantage is that a device may be upgraded or require optional drivers depending on who is using it. These can be made available without a lot of trouble.

Plug and play has been introduced in the last few years and is particularly useful when adding non-standard equipment. In the past, adding a device usually meant plugging in some kind of interface card, copying a device driver on to the hard drive, and then playing about with configuration settings, interrupt priorities and command syntax. Now plug and play means adding new equipment is more automatic. It is familiar to users of Windows® and is being developed for other systems such as Unix®.

Devices are added to a computer and then a setup program copies over the required device drivers and configures the driver for the host computer.

Implementing this technology requires the hardware manufacturer to be compliant with the specified architecture, the computer BIOS and operating system. Much co-operation across the industry between Microsoft, IBM, Intel and others means that Microsoft Windows® provides support for it.

Good examples of this are multimedia devices. The operating system is able to take the input stream from, for example, an audio CD and pass the resulting output to the speakers by using the correct DLL device drivers.

BIOS

In Chapter 3 you looked at the operation of the 'basic input–output system' (BIOS). This provides device drivers on read-only (ROM) so that when the operating system loads at boot-up it is able to load the code necessary to carry out basic I/O between the keyboard, monitor, mouse and boot disk. These routines will then be replaced or integrated with other device drivers when normal system operation is working.

Operating system structures

In order for the operating system to manage the many processes it has to contend with, there are a number of ways it can organise both the operations being run and the data being processed. In computing terms, different data organisations are called data structures and these structures have operations that are carried out on them. Their purpose is to make sure resources can be stored, retrieved and otherwise used in a manner that is efficient and safe. You have already come across two of these typical structures, the tree and linked lists. In this section we shall refresh your understanding of these, and introduce another structure called the 'queue'.

Linked lists

Where have you met the concept of the linked list? In Chapter 4, you saw how files may be stored using several clusters across the surface of a disk. In order for each cluster to be accessed in the right order, the operating system stores the address of each cluster in a table. Review this part of Chapter 4 and do the task below.

Activity

1. Five files are stored in a file allocation table:

   - file A occupies 5 clusters
   - file C occupies 1 cluster
   - file E occupies 4 clusters.
   - file B occupies 3 clusters
   - file D occupies 3 clusters

   Draw a portion of a file allocation table (FAT) showing how these files might be stored as a linked list. Only file B occupies contiguous clusters. Underneath explain exactly what the purpose of the pointer is.

2. Next examine Figure 27.6. You will see two files (A and B) in a linked list.

FAT		
Cluster	Data	Pointer
1	File A.0	8
2		9
3	FFFF	4
4	File B.0	5
5	File B.1	7
6		2
7	FFFF	0
8	File A.1	3
9		10
10		−1

FAT pointers	
Free space	6
First file	1

File address	Cluster
File A	1
File B	4

Figure 27.6 Data for the activity

a. You will see there are two FAT pointers: one for showing where the first file starts and the second is the pointer into the first free space. Both work on the FAT table.

When a file is added, the system uses the free space pointer to determine which cluster should be used. All the free space is linked from the cluster pointed to by the free space pointer: –1 indicates the last free space in the FAT; 0 indicates the last cluster in the last file; FFFF, as before, indicates the end of a file.

Have a look at the linked lists above and check you can follow the address path for the files being held and the available free space.

(b) Carry out the following problem; adjust the FAT table and the FAT pointers:

(i) Add a new file C occupying two clusters. (Remember to adjust the first free space pointer)

(ii) What would the table and pointers look like if File A were deleted? Remember both the used file space and the free space need to be linked.

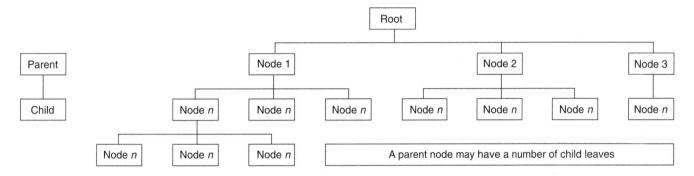

Figure 27.7 *Tree structures*

Trees

These are structures that are used to create indexes or lists. They are easy to search in order to find items based on their alphabetical or numerical order. They are based on the same simple structure made up of root, nodes and leaves (see Figure 27.7).

Every tree must have a starting point and this is the root of the tree. Each branch starts with a node and they may have a number of other nodes or leaves attached. The tree can be searched for leaves lower down by comparing the value of a node with a search target. A common application of trees is for directory or folder structures. Each directory may have a number of other directory or files coming off it.

Activity

1. Draw a tree structure of your document folder and sub-folders.

2. Figure 27.8 shows a directory tree and files.

   • Which directory is the root directory?
   • Each file or directory can be uniquely identified by its path and name. Write out the full path for the file Web Links.htm. Use the standard separator symbol /.
   • If this directory was stored on a shared drive on a network system, what information would you have to add to the path you wrote above?
   • Describe a possible way in which the OS could search its file structure to find Web Links.htm.

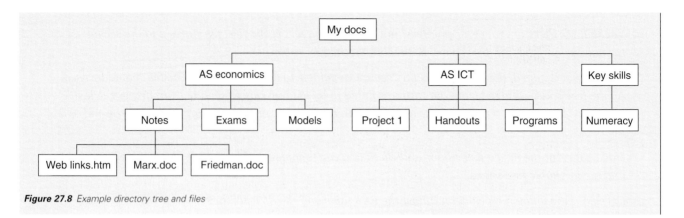

Figure 27.8 Example directory tree and files

Queues

You saw earlier how code is organised into processes, and the state of each process is kept in its process control block. As the processor switches between jobs it must keep processes in various queues ready to be used when that job becomes scheduled. A queue, as you are aware, is a list of items where the next item to be used is taken from the front and any new item is added to the back (see Figure 27.9).

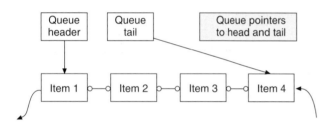

Figure 27.9 The principle of queuing

The OS maintains several queues depending on the state of processes being run and the need to allocate processor time to different jobs and respond to interrupts or I/O states. When a process is first started it is placed in a ready queue. As processes are used they are taken from the front and new ones are placed on the back. The pointers tell the system where to fetch a process and where to add a new process.

Remember that in a multi-programming system the state of processes may change. For example, a process may terminate, be interrupted or have to wait for the outcome of an event such as the completion of an I/O request. As there may be many user processes active, there may well be many requests for an array of I/O devices. Each device, therefore, has a device queue maintained for it.

We can represent the overall process of scheduling using a queuing diagram (see Figure 27.10). Each

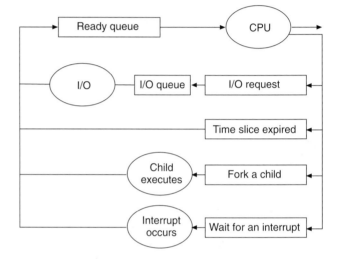

Figure 27.10 Queuing diagram

rectangle represents a queue. Two types of queues are present: queues that are related to I/O devices and queues related to process management. A queue has a circle if it is waiting for a resource to do something. As you can see, the ultimate destination for a process is the ready queue. This is how it works.

A process is created and goes into the ready queue. When it is called it executes until it terminates or else an event occurs:

● The process issues an I/O request and is placed in a request queue. It waits here before being allocated to an I/O queue.

● The process creates (forks) a sub-process (child). It must wait for this to finish execution before continuing its own processing.

● The process is peremptorily removed from execution owing to an interrupt, and placed in the ready queue.

● The process is waiting for an interrupt before continuing execution.

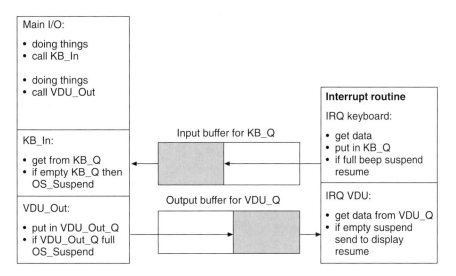

Figure 27.11 *Operation of interrupt service routines*

Whenever a process is ready to run, it moves into the ready queue.

Another example of the use of the queue is for controlling the mismatch of speed between an I/O device and the internal component that might require the I/O stream. For example, a file is arriving via a modem. It needs to be transferred to a file on disk. The modem is vastly slower than the disk write operation, so data from the modem is placed in a queue. This queue acts as a temporary storage area and is otherwise known as a buffer. The I/O system need do nothing until the buffer from the modem is full, and then carry out a single write operation to the file on disk.

This process is further assisted by the use of two buffers, when it is known as *double buffering*. When the first buffer is filled by the modem, the disk write takes over using data in the buffer. Meanwhile the modem continues placing data in a second buffer. In this way the disk write operation takes place at the most appropriate time and the transfer of data from the modem is not interrupted in any way.

Similarly two buffers are used for I/O output between the VDU and keyboard (see Figurer 27.11).

In Figure 27.11 an interrupt service routine on the right of the drawing responds to interrupts from the keyboard, and data is placed into the input buffer for the keyboard. Notice that if the buffer is full then the routine suspends. Meanwhile, if data is arriving in the keyboard buffer then it is removed and placed in the VDU buffer. Again this is serviced by an interrupt routine triggered in a similar way.

More about metropolitan-area networks

Recall that Bevan Hughes, the Network Administrator at Highgate College, is going to connect the college local-area networks to the higher-education network, using a router connection into the London metropolitan-area network (MAN).

Technical connection

A MAN aims to serve a geographic area beyond the scope of LAN technologies, and to support the close relationships of parts of the same organisation or different organisations that see the potential for collaborating and sharing close links. The MAN provides interconnectivity between sites within a local regional or metropolitan area. MANs try to provide performance close to that obtained on LANs whilst coping with the interaction of multiple networking arrangements. As a consequence, the establishment of a successful MAN requires the correct balancing of a number of technical and political factors.

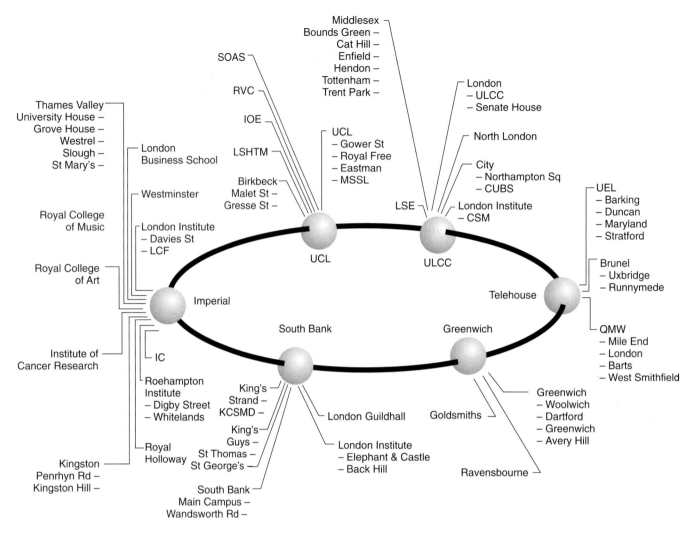

Figure 27.12 *The London MAN*

Bevan Hughes investigates the London MAN and finds out what the existing connections are. He gets a great deal of information from the MAN management centre at University of London Computer Centre (ULCC). Figure 27.12 shows the structure of the London MAN.

The infrastructure consists of six core sites connected by an ATM (asynchronous transfer mode) ring. Local sites are connected as spurs. The network is managed in the following way:

● Where a higher-education institution (HEI) has several sites connected to the same core hub they are managed by that HEI. For these links, the MAN's main function is that of a purchasing consortium.

● Where an institution's sites connect to different core sites they are centrally managed at University of London Computer Centre.

An ATM ring is a development of a token ring, called 'slotted ring'. Like a token ring, it is able to deliver time-critical traffic such as voice and video. Each core site is connected at 155Mbps and is managed by a consortium of cable telecoms companies. They are responsible for the lines that connect the core sites together. Connection to the core sites is shown in Figure 27.13.

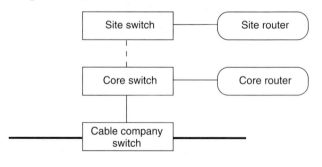

Figure 27.13 *Connection of core to telco switch*

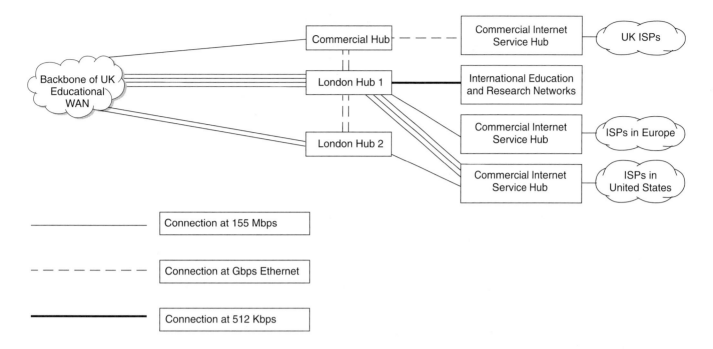

Figure 27.14 *The higher-education network's connections to external networks*

A student or member of staff sitting at a PC on a college LAN might be connecting to the Internet. Firstly, users connect to the college's intranet pages through a local web server. If they want to request an URL for external pages, then the request is sent to the router, which transmits the data packets to the core router. The core router decides whether the packets should go on to the MAN ring or whether they will go back up to a local spur – that is, to another site connected at the local core switch. The London MAN connects through to the Internet by telecoms access sites.

So, for example, you can see from Figure 27.14 that the London Hub 1 connects to the US using 155Mbps leased lines to Commercial Internet Service Hub that routes traffic on to the United States.

Bevan Hughes also finds out how a connection can be carried out by any new site. Highgate College can

Activity

Find out whether your centre is connected to an educational MAN, which may be referred to as a Grid for Learning. Find out what benefits it brings to staff and to students.

either purchase a local router from the academic network agency UKERNA® (United Kingdom Education & Research Networking Association) or buy their own. Leased lines to the router are organised by UKERNA® as they have a bulk deal with telecoms companies. The UKERNA® team can then connect and configure the local router to work on the college's LAN.

CHAPTER 28

Getting value from an ICT system

This chapter continues to explore the management of the network systems in the college that was introduced in Chapters 7 and 27. It will describe:

- how an organisation can generate income from its ICT system
- how the internal market works
- how the systems manager can cost the ICT services provided within the organisation.

This chapter covers these Learning Outcomes in the specification:

L.O. 4.11 Demonstrate an understanding of the market potential of the facilities offered by a specified ICT system

L.O. 4.12 Demonstrate knowledge of the total costs of running and maintaining a specific ICT system

Financial management of ICT

Business units

In a large organisation each department is sometimes structured like a small business in its own right, known as a *business unit*. Each business unit is responsible for its own budget and for setting its own targets for income and expenditure (spending).

Each unit is expected to 'sell' services, and possibly goods, to other departments. These services have to be costed and pricing agreements have to be negotiated. This is known as an *internal market*. The income generated by a business unit through selling goods or services is known as *revenue income*.

Highgate College, which you read about first in Chapters 1 and 7, has adopted this style of financial management. The academic departments – Business, Science and Technology, Visual and Performing Arts, Humanities, Health Studies, Hotel and Catering – all function as business units and each is responsible for its own income and expenditure. Three further

business units in the college provide support to all the academic departments. These are the Administration, Learning Services (which includes the Library and Learning Support) and ICT Services departments.

ICT in an internal market

In an organisation with an internal market the IT department becomes a supplier, with other departments as customers.

This has certain advantages. The IT department is forced to develop good communications with other departments. If the IT staff do not bridge the 'culture gap' then they will not be successful in selling services, so the internal market encourages a good 'customer services' mentality.

The IT department can also use the internal market mechanism to control the use of its services. This is discussed later in the chapter.

There are also disadvantages with this way of working. Other departments are, theoretically, free to choose their supplier for IT services. They may decide to go to another supplier to meet their needs, especially for consultancy. Or they may build up sufficient expertise themselves to meet their own needs. But a department will only outsource its requirements if it can negotiate a better price. This means that the IT department must be seen to be giving value for money.

Margaret Roberts is the ICT Services Manager at Highgate College and is a member of the senior management team of the college. Her job is to ensure that all the other departments are provided with the ICT equipment and services they need. Her department will survive only if it can offer these services at a competitive rate.

Marketing the ICT facilities

Within the ICT Services department, Margaret Roberts acts as line manager for Bevan Hughes and his technical services team. She also employs a Database Manager, who is responsible for the college's administration systems. Recently a new post of Online Services Manager has been created to cover all the Internet and intranet developments. The Administration department buys in the services of the Database Manager and Online Services Manager. The income from the Administration department helps the ICT Services department to pay for their salaries and equipment.

Services that generate income

The ICT Services department has two types of resource – human resources (staff) and physical resources (equipment). Together they can be used to offer a wide range of services to the college.

Any of these services can also be used to generate revenue income for the department. As you have seen, services can be sold internally to other business units within the college. But the department also has the freedom to sell services externally – that is, to businesses outside the college.

The costs of providing services have to be calculated, and then a price negotiated with the customer.

Margaret Roberts can offer most of the services noted below using the resources that she already has. However, the application development services she can offer are limited to database development (using the database management system that is already in place) and website development.

Service level agreements

Unless the service is simple and clearly defined, it is usual to draw up an agreement between the supplier and the customer. This agreement will include a description of the service in some detail, sometimes with targets to be met. It will also specify what should happen if these targets are not met. This is called a service level agreement.

In general, an IT department within an organisation could offer some or all of these services:

- use of networks (both LAN and WAN)
- helpdesk support
- computer operations (e.g. payroll)
- consultancy services (e.g. feasibility study, drawing up specifications for purchase, systems analysis)
- installation of new equipment
- testing new systems
- development and maintenance of computer systems
- development and maintenance of software applications
- training
- user and technical documentation.

All these services exploit the resources of an IT department. Many of them use only the human resources available, especially where consultancy services are being offered. Other services make substantial use of the physical resources.

For example, Margaret provides helpdesk support to the Science and Technology department specifically for engineering students who use a specialised computer-aided design package. The service level agreement says that the ICT Services department will provide this helpdesk support within office hours during term time. But there is only one person in her department who can offer this specialist support. If he is away for a substantial length of time, she will be obliged to employ someone temporarily to cover the absence. But she knows that it could be difficult to find anyone with those particular skills, so she may find that she cannot fulfil the terms of the agreement. The agreement should state what must happen in these circumstances; it will probably mean a refund to her customer, the Science and Technology department.

Developing the external market

Sometimes an IT department may find that it is being particularly successful in selling services to external businesses. Although initially this might have been undertaken in order to profit from underused capacity, the systems manager may suggest that this side of the work be expanded.

This may mean taking on additional staff whose continued employment will depend on the success of finding new clients and selling services. The department, in effect, develops a profit-making consultancy arm.

At Highgate College, Margaret has been developing some profitable business in selling website design and hosting services to local schools, who do not have the same level of technical support. Some years ago, Kris Novak was employed in the Science and Technology department as a lecturer in IT. As his interest and expertise in multimedia systems grew, Kris took on the development of the college's website. Margaret spotted the potential for development and created a new post of Online Services Manager, which was offered to Kris.

As well as developing the website and external mailing lists for the Administration department, Kris has now set up a college-wide intranet. But this work does not take up all his time, so he is able to generate further income for the ICT Services department by taking on some external projects.

Costing ICT services

Margaret has to charge other departments and external organisations for the services and goods that she supplies. To do this she has to:

- calculate the cost of providing the goods and/or services
- decide what price to charge her customers.

Margaret will usually charge her customers a price that covers the costs, as a minimum. In fact, normal practice is to add an extra margin so that services are priced above the actual costs. However, there may be circumstances when she will charge less than the costs.

Costing new systems

When a new system is installed, or an existing system is upgraded, the total cost of the project can be calculated in a fairly straightforward way. But we will see that the total *startup costs* go beyond the obvious costs of acquiring new hardware and software. Once the system has been installed and is functioning properly, there will be ongoing *operational costs*, and these need to be predicted and budgeted for as well.

Startup costs

The startup costs are the one-off costs incurred in order to get a new system up and running. There are both visible and hidden costs.

The *visible costs* of a new system are the actual amounts paid out for:

- development – systems analysis and software development (whether inhouse or externally sourced)
- acquisition – hardware, software, licences, maintenance contracts
- environment – wiring, furniture, lighting, safety, health (e.g. compliance with eye-test regulations).

But in order to launch a new system, a great deal of additional hidden work will have been done by employees in the organisation. This work will be seen as part of the normal work of the employees; but as they are on the organisation's payroll the costs of the labour they have contributed must be taken into account. These labour costs can be quite difficult to calculate, but the usual method is to work out what proportion of an employee's working week was given to the project and then to calculate the equivalent proportion of that person's salary.

The *hidden costs* of a new system are the costs of the work done by employees, such as:

- installation
- acceptance testing costs – by systems administrators and by end-users
- changeover – data entry, data conversion, 'bedding in' costs (that is, costs arising from getting used to the new system)
- training.

If a software application is developed inhouse these hidden costs can add as much as 50 per cent extra to the visible costs. If a package is bought in, the hidden costs would be even higher and could even be double the visible costs.

Sometimes Margaret finds it very difficult to estimate the costs of a project at the outset, especially if it is unlike anything that has been undertaken in the college before. In this case she finds it useful to employ an external consultant who has expertise in the field, to carry out a *feasibility study*. A feasibility study will include an estimate of costs, so that when she reports back to the managers of the 'customer' department they will be in a position to decide whether to go ahead with the whole project. Unfortunately, even a small feasibility study has a cost, which must be borne by the customer.

Activity

Investigate the costs of the network system that you use at your school or college. Use a spreadsheet to estimate the startup costs if the system were to be completely replaced. Do you need any information to complete the task?

Operational costs

Once a system is installed, there will be on-going costs of running it on a day-to-day basis. Operational costs include:

- systems administration – network management, database management, data security management, disaster recovery plans
- systems maintenance – hardware and software maintenance
- consumables – paper, ink, storage media
- external services – power, telephone and broadband lines, subscriptions
- end-user support – helpdesks, training for new staff, upgrading skills.

Many of these costs are actually the costs of employing staff. For example, the bulk of the expense of administering a network is the salaries paid to the technical staff. The remaining costs for administering the network are likely to be normal office expenses.

In most organisations, information systems staff spend about half of their time on maintaining existing software.

The operational costs of IT systems are very high, for a number of reasons.

- Businesses are changing rapidly and have changing information needs.
- IT personnel have high levels of technical skill and can command high salaries.
- Software has become increasingly complex, requiring more maintenance.
- Faults overlooked at the analysis and design stages can be expensive to correct once the software and hardware have been developed.

Activity

Use a spreadsheet to estimate the operational costs of (a) a home personal computer and (b) the network system that you use at school or college.

Human resources

Many of the startup and operational costs of IT systems are for labour. But the cost of employing someone is more than just their salary. Employers also have to pay National Insurance and pension contributions, and they may offer benefits such as a company car and health insurance. There is also the cost of advertising vacancies and interviewing applicants.

In some cases, the organisation will need to take on extra staff to work on the development of the new system, and the costs of employing them will be part of the startup costs. These specialists may be employed on a permanent basis, but it is very common for people to be offered short-term contracts just to cover the expected development time.

Once the system is up and running the organisation may need to employ more personnel either as end-users or as systems administrators. Their time becomes part of the operational costs.

Costing knowledge work

Some of the services offered by an IT department simply require the work of specialist knowledge workers, such as analysts, programmers or helpdesk staff. However, these people can carry out their work only by using the hardware and software resources provided within their department. A proportion of the costs of providing these resources will be included in the overall cost of providing the service.

Activity

Read through job advertisements in the field of ICT and note typical salaries for different roles. How many of these are offering short-term contracts?

Pricing IS services

The internal market

In an internal market, the systems manager will have to calculate the cost of a service requested by another business unit.

Margaret knows that she must, over time, aim to receive back, as a minimum, all the costs of the services that the department provides. This is known as *cost recovery*. But she does not have to charge the exact cost of providing each service. The aim will be to generate enough revenue from all the services to cover the total costs. Some services may be priced below their true cost, and others may be priced above their true cost.

For example, in one of his regular reports Bevan Hughes has noted that the academic network does become overloaded at certain times of the day, particularly in the mornings. Margaret decides that she would like to spread the use of the system more, so she investigates the possibility of charging departments a lower rate for use of the network during the 'twilight' hours between 4.30 pm and 6.30 pm. By adjusting the pricing structure she may be able to achieve a better loading of the whole system.

The external market

In an external market the actual price charged will include an element of markup (profit), so will normally be more than the cost of providing the service.

Negotiating pricing agreements

Services supplied by one business to another are usually called *business-to-business services*. Although you expect to pay the asking price when you buy something in a high street store, this does not always apply in business-to-business deals, where the asking price is often simply the first step in a negotiation.

Most suppliers of IT services are willing to negotiate the final price. They will offer special deals, depending on how much they need the business. They may also offer a low price for a service as an introductory offer, hoping that the customer will return for more once they have experienced the quality of the service provided.

Negotiating service level agreements

As you saw before, a service level agreement is a document that specifies exactly what services the customer is buying, and the penalties incurred by the supplier if these are not provided. This has to be negotiated at the same time as the price, and forms part of the contract between the two parties.

CHAPTER 29

The social, moral, ethical and legal responsibilities of systems managers

This chapter continues to explore the significance of ICT in the medical research centre at Wessex County Hospital that was introduced in Chapter 2. It will also move into the hospital itself to explore the implications of ICT-based applications for society at large. It will describe:

- the social, moral, ethical and legal implications of ICT solutions

- the responsibilities of the systems manager with regard to the provision of ICT services

- how the systems manager should advise seniors to predict and mitigate the consequences of the use of ICT systems.

This chapter covers these Learning Objectives in the specification:

L.O. 4.13   Reflect on the social, moral, ethical and legal implications of an ICT-based solution to a specified problem

L.O. 4.14   Design a report, for a higher authority, presenting a range of possible options that could mitigate the consequences of the use of a defined ICT system

---

In Chapter 9 we considered a number of social, moral and ethical issues. They were all discussed from the point of view of the *impact* that an IT application would have on employee or on the general public. There is further discussion about the implications of an ICT solution in Chapter 36. That concentrates on the *evaluation of software by the developer* before it is implemented.

In this chapter we discuss *the responsibilities of the systems manager*.

ICT within Wessex County Hospital

The medical research department

The medical research department in Wessex County Hospital contributes towards the diagnosis and management of diseases. The researchers publish their findings in medical journals and share their knowledge with the medical staff at the hospital.

Nuria Sanchez has recently been appointed as the Systems Manager at Wessex County Hospital and she recognises the important work done by the medical research department. She accepts that standalone PCs meet the data-logging and analysis needs of the research teams very well. But she would like to offer the team access to the hospital's intranet and e-mail facilities, so she has undertaken a costing exercise to see whether this can be achieved within her budget.

The researchers are pleased that their PCs will be integrated into the hospital's network. They can see the advantages of being able to store their raw data and research findings on the hospital system. They will be able to discuss their results with clinical colleagues and will be able to share early drafts of the papers they intend to publish.

Nuria is aware that she has social, moral, ethical and legal responsibilities towards staff and patients at the hospital. If anyone is harmed, in any way, as a consequence of the way in which the ICT systems function, then she would have to explain the situation to the senior managers. She must also ensure that all data is stored legally and that the system is not being used for illegal purposes. In certain circumstances, she could face disciplinary proceedings and lose her job.

So when Nuria finally manages to link the research department's computers into the main hospital network, she does start to ask some questions about the scope of her responsibilities. Until now the researchers were entirely responsible for their data and for the way they disseminated their findings. Nuria wants to know what her responsibility would be in cases like these:

- The researchers make errors when entering data into their files.
- The network system corrupts the researchers' data during data transfer, but this is not detected.
- Incorrect data is used in a medical trial.
- The network crashes and some of the essential data is lost.
- Someone from another department copies the researchers' results and publishes them under his own name.

Activity

How would you respond to the questions that Nuria posed?

Diagnosis and treatment

ICT plays a very important role in the diagnosis of conditions and also in the treatments that patients are given. Expert systems have been used for some time to support the work of the doctors, but recent developments have opened up some interesting new possibilities.

Cancer specialists at Wessex County have been trialling an application that analyses scans produced by magnetic resonance spectroscopy (MRS). In the past it has often been difficult to interpret scans of tumours, without resorting to surgery, which can be risky. The new system uses artificial-intelligence techniques to analyse the visual images. Doctors know that the same technology can be used to assess certain heart conditions.

Over in the maternity unit, ultrasound scans of babies in the womb can now be converted into 3D images using computer technology. This technique makes it much easier for doctors to identify abnormalities even when the foetus is as young as 10 weeks.

For some time the psychiatric department at Wessex County has been using ICT systems that allow patients to take more control over their treatment. They use a number of specially written computer games to help relax people with stress-related conditions. In another interesting example, a specialist can advise people suffering from certain obsessive–compulsive psychiatric disorders to use an application which helps them to monitor and assess their own moods and behaviour at home. After a few weeks the patients often find they can identify the situations which trigger the unacceptable behaviour and can train themselves to deal with it, without the use of drugs and without having to wait for hospital appointments.

Many aspects of surgery at the hospital have been transformed with the use of ICT systems. Indeed, micro-surgery would be impossible without it. Today many surgical procedures can be carried out with lasers, which have the advantage of not leaving any scars. Lasers often need to be directed very accurately using computer-based scanning techniques.

Activity

Can you add further new developments in diagnosis and treatment that depend on ICT systems?

Responsibilities of the systems manager

Nuria's challenge is to supply and support systems that will meet the main objectives of Wessex County Hospital; namely, to diagnose and treat patients as effectively as possible. In this context, 'effective' must mean both:

- that the treatment of each patient should be successful, and
- that as many patients as possible should be treated.

Nuria is very aware of the pressures on her, which often seem to be pulling in opposite directions. Most of the difficult decisions she has to make are concerned with the allocation of resources. If the hospital had enough money to buy whatever it liked, then many of her worries would be over, but she has to consider dilemmas like these:

- Should money be spent to help a few patients with expensive treatments, or many patients with cheaper treatments?
- How much money should go on ICT to support research, instead of treating patients?
- Should the hospital buy the best (and therefore most expensive) and most up-to-date technical solution to one problem at the expense of a number of cheaper projects?
- Which is more important, security of patient data or improved diagnosis?

In many of these cases it is the senior management who make the final decisions, but Naria has to make convincing recommendations and proposals to them.

Activity

If employees are responsible for aspects of the work of the organisation, then they have to answer to someone for their actions. The systems administrator is accountable to the systems manager and the systems manager is accountable to senior management.

Who are the following people accountable to?

- *a receptionist in the accident and emergency department*
- *a hospital pathologist*
- *a senior manager at the hospital*
- *a member of the Area Health Authority*
- *the Secretary of State for Health.*

Social responsibilities of systems managers

The systems manager has responsibilities towards all the people affected by the work that he or she does. Some of these responsibilities arise directly from the job, but some of these simply arise from her role as a worker and as a citizen.

Nuria Sanchez recognises that, like all IT managers, she has responsibilities towards two specific groups outside her own department:

- IT users within the organisation
- customers (patients) and visitors.

She also accepts that her work is a part of the whole of society and that she must consider her responsibilities towards society at large.

Social responsibilities towards people within the organisation

When Nuria applied for the post at Wessex County she was given a copy of the job description. This spelt out, in detail, the tasks she was supposed to undertake and the areas of responsibility that she would have towards IT users in the hospital. When she started work she was asked to sign a contract of employment which referred explicitly to the *job description*.

A job description for a senior role of this kind would include the duty to provide support services to all users in compliance with both legislation and the internal policies of the organisation.

Whether or not it was explicitly stated in her job description, Nuria accepts that she also has a responsibility to protect all employees from abuses of the IT systems. She is particularly concerned about the possibility of an employee using the internal e-mail system to distribute inappropriate material. Such material could be abusive about another member of staff; it could be racially offensive; it could be politically subversive. Although this has, thankfully, not happened yet at Wessex County, nevertheless Nuria wants to do whatever she can to prevent such abuses from occurring.

She has therefore proposed a policy which states that the hospital computer systems may be used only for legitimate work purposes, that networks will be monitored, and that offenders will subjected to disciplinary procedures. The policy was accepted by the senior management and now random checks are made to ensure that users are using the systems for work purposes only. However, having taken reasonable steps to implement the policy, Nuria cannot be held liable for irresponsible behaviour on the part of employees.

The social, moral, ethical and legal responsibilities of systems managers

Lewd e-mail highlights danger of modern gossip

. . . The e-mail appeared to be from an employee of the London-based solicitors, Norton Rose. Sent nine days ago, it purported to be a quick note to him from "Claire", his girlfriend, complimenting him on his sexual activities.

Sent to four people, who sent it to friends, who sent it to even more friends, the e-mail soon took on a life of its own – and proved Churchill's quip that "a lie can be halfway around the world before the truth has got its boots on". Yesterday, "Claire" was in hiding . . . . Her parents, interviewed at their East Sussex home, said she was "horrified" and, understandably, declined to discuss her sex life.

We are now living in the age of the e-mail avalanche, and these are just the latest victims. The touch of a button can now send a hoax "virus warning", a dirty joke or a complete untruth to a trusted network of contacts who will often forward it unquestioningly in moments. . . .

In this case the original e-mail appears to be a fake, though this could not be confirmed. Norton Rose is now conducting an internal inquiry involving five people . . .

Andrea Turrell, head of communications at Norton Rose, said yesterday: "[This e-mail] is going into circulation around the world, and realistically we're now just on the fringes of what's happening . . . . We're just the firm that employs the people who originally sent it."

Keith Bellamy, of Outrade.com, which specialises in e-mail management, said: "Companies have filters to stop people looking at porn sites on the Web, but tend to have nothing to do the same for e-mail. But if you get a snowball effect and everyone is sending stuff to your company or from it, it can crash your e-mail and that can take a long time to bring back."

The solution? Computer managers should apply word-based filters to e-mail once they hear of avalanches, and put suspect messages aside. Meanwhile, if the e-mail does prove to have been faked, "Claire" can sue its creator.

Source: Modified from an article by Charles Arthur in *The Independent*, 16 December 2000

Figure 29.1

Social responsibilities towards clients and customers

A hospital is a business that offers a service. As a public-sector organisation its prime aim is to provide healthcare to the general public. Its patients are its main customers, although it also provides services to GPs.

As Nuria works in a public-sector service industry she knows that her prime obligation is to patients. It is sometimes easy to forget this, as she rarely meets them. But she does have to assess any ICT developments in the light of this main aim.

Every day members of the public attend the accident and emergency (A&E) department at the hospital, and for many of them it is a distressing experience. Some of these people have been seriously injured and require immediate attention, others have minor damage and their needs are not so urgent. Some people turn up at A&E with non-urgent ailments that could easily have been dealt with at a normal GP's surgery. The problem that the medical staff have is to ensure that patients do not have to wait any longer than necessary.

The ICT system in A&E has been designed to ensure that patients are attended to in order of priority, and that the most effective use is made of the skills of the medical staff. Each newly arrived patient is assessed by a nurse (known as a triage nurse) who decides whether the problem is serious or minor. Serious problems, which amount to about 10% of all cases, are dealt with immediately by the medical staff.

For the remaining cases a nurse enters details about the patient and symptoms into an expert system. The system prompts the nurse to ask further questions and then provides advice on treatment. In many cases the problem does not require the specialist skills of a doctor and can be treated by a nurse. In other cases, the patient is referred back to their own GP. In around 25% of cases the patient is told that there is nothing seriously wrong and they can be shown how to care for the problem themselves. This system has reduced average waiting times from over two hours to 36 minutes.

Patients who are waiting for treatment for minor injuries are given a number and progress is displayed on a screen in the waiting area. The display indicates how long each patient can expect to have to wait.

Social responsibilities towards society as a whole

Major public services do not work in isolation. Sometimes their actions can have profound effects on the general population or on groups within it.

In June 2000, the air traffic computer system at West Drayton collapsed for the second time in two days. This system handles all the planes that fly in UK airspace. Although the fault was repaired within a few hours, many flights were cancelled or diverted and passengers were severely inconvenienced. At Gatwick Airport the interval between flights was slowed from two minutes to five. Flights which did depart were delayed by up to four hours.

In this case, a technical fault affected many thousands of people indirectly. These included passengers who had to wait for flights, incoming passengers who were diverted to other European countries, relatives and friends waiting to meet passengers, and the many staff working at the airports and for the airlines and tour operators. You can imagine some of the human stories behind these delays – someone urgently trying to fly home because of a family bereavement, another person missing an important business meeting or interview.

The systems manager at West Drayton must have been only too aware that sometimes a small computer error can have a catastrophic social impact.

Nuria has to consider the possible effects of a major system collapse at Wessex County Hospital. Many of the systems, such as those used for guiding lasers in operations, are safety-critical systems, and lives can be endangered if they do not function correctly. Faults in other systems, such as the patient administration system, which may not appear to be so critical, can still have disastrous consequences. Corrupted data may affect a patient waiting for urgent surgery; appointments may not be made as requested; prescriptions may be inaccurate.

Many callers to the AA, requesting help on the road, struggled to get through on the phone, said a spokesman. "The AA has spent millions on the technology that allows us to answer calls in seconds and get out to people in half an hour. It was annoying that we couldn't do the job we invested for, simply because the phone wasn't working properly."

British Gas estimates it lost about 35,000 calls. And yesterday the RSPCA's main switchboard was still not operating.

Yesterday, BT said: "We will be keeping a very close eye on things and working to establish the cause. We send apologies to all our customers and will be speaking to them all."

Source: Hester Lacey in *The Independent*, 27 February 2000

Figure 29.3

Twenty-two thousand foreign nationals "trapped" in Britain for up to six months because of computer failure at the UK's main immigration office may now qualify for ex-gratia compensation payments, the Home Office admitted last night.

The breakdown at the headquarters of the Immigration and Nationality Directorate in Croydon, south London, was triggered by the introduction of a new computerised casework system while moving offices earlier this year.

The Home Office admits it is currently holding 22,000 passports of foreign nationals in Britain who are trying to get their visas renewed. The chaos means they face a wait of months to get their visas renewed. Many are business people living and working in London, who have been forced to cancel business and family trips.

®*The Guardian*, extract taken from an article by Alan Travis on 24 March 1999

Figure 29.4

Moral responsibilities of systems managers

Dilemmas

In Chapter 9 we saw that *a moral duty is something that we ought to do, because we are human.* Moral duties tend to fall into two groups – duties to other people as individuals and duties to society at large.

We are looking here specifically at the responsibilities of systems managers. Could a situation ever arise in which there would be a conflict between the moral duties someone has as a person and the duties of the job?

Such conflicts have certainly been experienced by professionals. When two moral duties seem to be in conflict we describe it as a dilemma. Here are some examples of dilemmas in a medical setting:

- A doctor is bound to keep everything that a patient says completely confidential. But what should a doctor do if a patient says that he feels like killing someone?
- A public relations officer at a hospital is instructed to deny that a certain celebrity is undergoing treatment at the hospital, even though it is true. What should the PR person do?
- A scientific researcher is under pressure to complete an important medical project, so pads out the published report with invented data. A colleague is aware of this, but also knows that the invented data had no effect at all on the valuable conclusions reached by the researcher.

Activity

What should they do?

Dilemmas in ICT

Do systems managers ever have to solve moral dilemmas during their work? A systems manager might have to decide between his or her personal responsibility as a member of society and a corporate responsibility as an employee. Cases include conflicts of interest. Sometimes a manager will feel so strongly about a moral issue that he or she resigns.

Conflicts of interest

Nuria Sanchez's brother, Jaime, owns a software company. He specialises in IT solutions for pharmacies. The pharmacy at Wessex County Hospital needs a new system and senior management has commissioned a feasibility study. Nuria has, quite properly, not mentioned this to her brother yet as it is still a confidential business matter.

When the hospital eventually advertises for interested suppliers to put forward formal proposals, Jaime is keen to get the contract. Nuria has a moral duty towards her family and naturally wishes for her brother's business success. But she also has a duty towards the hospital to recommend the best solution, and she will find it difficult to make an objective assessment of all the proposals.

Nuria therefore has a clear conflict of interest. The term 'interest' does not mean 'is interested in', although she is indeed interested in the outcome from the viewpoints of both her brother and the hospital. In a stronger sense she has 'an interest in' the outcome. To 'have an interest in' means that someone stands to gain, probably financially, from the situation. Now although Nuria does not have a direct interest in her brother's earnings, she does have an indirect interest. An indirect interest is one where a close member of the family may gain.

The correct action for her to take, morally and professionally, is to explain the conflict of interest to the senior managers, and then to play no part in the process of awarding the contract.

Activity

Can you think of other situations in which ICT personnel might be faced with a conflict of interest? What should they do?

Taking the blame

Managers are accountable for the actions of their departments. Sometimes they have to take the blame when things go awry.

Nuria has herself known about a difficult case at another hospital. Complaints had been made about the competence of a surgeon at Clayton Manor Hospital, with relatives claiming that patients were damaged or killed by him. Just days before a public inquiry was due to start, vital computer records, containing details of all the doctor's surgical cases during the relevant period, were erased from the database. The records had been in place when the surgeon was suspended, pending the inquiry, and the systems manager, Malcolm Bray, had immediately removed the surgeon's access privileges.

Although he had done nothing wrong himself, nevertheless Malcolm was the person responsible for data security. It may well have been that the security procedures that Malcolm had designed were flawed, allowing unauthorised access to files. Or perhaps the physical security of the IT department had been breached. Malcolm had come to the conclusion that he would have to resign.

Ethical responsibilities of systems managers

In Chapter 9 we considered some of the ethical duties of employees. We saw that professionals in any industry are often governed by *codes of practice* devised by professional bodies.

The term 'ethical' is often used, in philosophical debate as well as in general conversation, to mean the same as 'moral'. In this section we will be concentrating on a particular sub-section of ethical duties, those duties that we might have as workers in the ICT industry. These duties are sometimes referred to as *professional ethics*.

Systems managers have some very specific ethical duties. These tend to coalesce around issues of privacy and access to data, the accuracy of data, and the ownership of electronic data.

Ethical responsibilities towards the whole organisation

The systems manager has a responsibility, as an employee, to work towards the business objectives of the organisation. If employees cannot commit themselves to the objectives then they should not be working for that organisation.

For many businesses, the maintenance of business security, beyond the legal requirements, is of prime importance. The systems manager is responsible for this. Loss of security could refer to lack of access to the system or to parts of it, loss of data integrity, or breaches of confidentiality.

Nuria Sanchez knows that it her responsibility to monitor and report any security lapses that occur at the hospital. But she also has a duty to prevent, as far as possible, the occurrence of such lapses. In practice, Nuria does not completely control the development of the systems that her staff have to administer. Some systems are developed by the National Health Service and then all hospitals have to use them. Nuria is not at all sure to what extent she will be responsible for any failings in these systems.

Activity

Read the extract from the newspaper article reproduced here as Figure 29.5. Use the Internet, and other methods of research, to discover whether NHSNet is currently in use, and whether the potential problems listed in this article in 1999 have been overcome.

Public prescriptions

The National Health Service is failing to address security and privacy concerns as it sets about compiling the largest electronic database of personal information ever seen in the UK, says a study due to be published next week. Computer records, coded with each patient's unique NHS number and accessible via a UK-wide network, NHSNet, will be linked to patients' names by a new tracking system, the NHS Strategic Tracing Service, to be developed by Sema, an IT company under contract to the NHS, over the next six months.

Plans to protect privacy will not work, says Ross Anderson, lecturer in computer security at Cambridge University and editor of the critical study, *Safety and Privacy in Clinical Systems* [Sheffield Academic Press]. The proposed use of smart cards to access the system and firewalls between NHSNet and the Internet will be inadequate because of the large number of health staff involved. Many people will be motivated to abuse the system, he adds, because it will be the first ever up-to-date register of every UK resident.

"Other databases such as tax, national insurance and driver and vehicle licensing capture only some of the population, omitting children and some adults, and are very out of date in many cases. So the police and security services will demand access [to the NHS system], and then the private detective community will get in, whether by using old contacts in the police or bribing a nurse. This will open the system up to everyone prepared to pay: jealous husbands wanting to find runaway wives, gangsters wanting to find runaway witnesses." . . .

One solution, says the study, may lie in extrapolating to a national scale a new model for controlling access to patient data being tested at Conquest Hospital in Hastings, East Sussex. The model sets rules for access and monitors all transactions; for instance, nurses can see only records of patients who have been in their care in the past 90 days. It also sets out which types of clinician can access which types of data, with notes divided into security-coded sections. An override system allows clinicians to access data outside the normal rules, but a clear audit trail is created.

The NHS Executive says security for the tracking system will follow two basic principles of the Hastings trial: access will occur only where there is a clear need, and all transactions will be strictly monitored. A full risk assessment is being carried out, says the executive, and security procedures will be reviewed at least annually. ...

Ten reasons to steal your data
1. Insurance companies may want to know how big a risk you are.
2. Extremist anti-abortionists may want to know who has terminated a pregnancy.
3. Blackmailers could access health records of public figures.
4. Information could be used to make obscene phone calls, or even to identify subjects for stalking or attacks.
5. Lawyers may want to contact certain kinds of patient to suggest litigation.
6. Government departments may be keen to access the data to check their own records.
7. Companies selling drugs and medical appliances could try to market directly to relevant people.
8. Funeral parlours may try to find out who is seriously ill.
9. Banks may try to access records of people to whom they have lent money.
10. Firms may try to obtain records of prospective employees.

©*The Guardian*, extract taken from an article by Dan Jellinek on 28 February 1999

Figure 29.5

Ethical responsibilities towards employees

As a manager, Nuria has a number of professional and ethical responsibilities towards her staff. She should ensure that the hospital's policies that affect staff are interpreted fairly and implemented correctly. Most large organisations will have policies on:

- *equal opportunities* – to ensure that staff are recruited, and when employed, treated in a non-discriminatory way
- *discipline* – to warn, and possibly dismiss, staff who are guilty of misconduct

- *competence* – to deal with staff who are not meeting their contractual duties, either through incompetence or ill-health
- *health and safety* – to maintain legally required standards
- *professional development* – to encourage and support staff to undergo further training.

ICT technologies can be used to support many of these policies. Because computers can be adapted to meet individual users' needs, it is possible to employ people in ICT-related jobs with disabilities ranging from visual impairment to mobility difficulties.

ICT is also used widely in training. DVD- or CD-based training courses can be followed at a time most convenient to the employee, and they can be taken at the user's speed. Nuria can make individualised courses available to raise the competency of staff who need additional support.

Health and safety standards can, in some cases, be monitored directly by ICT systems. At the hospital the environmental conditions (heat, air quality, humidity) in the operating theatres are monitored automatically, and unacceptable variations are alerted to the theatre managers. Routine health and safety checks on the wards are logged and reported to the nursing managers.

Activity

This equal opportunities statement appears at the bottom of recruitment advertisements for the Home Office. What else would count as an 'irrelevant factor'?

'The Home Office is an equal opportunities employer and welcomes applications from candidates regardless of ethnic origin, religious belief, gender, sexual orientation, disability or any other irrelevant factor.'

Compare this with other advertisements or job descriptions that you have seen.

Ethical responsibilities towards clients and customers

The systems manager clearly has a professional responsibility towards customers even though they may never come into direct contact. Lapses in data integrity can have unfortunate or even dangerous effects on customers.

One such incident happened recently at Wessex County Hospital. From time to time the hospital sends out surveys to former patients to gain their views on the quality of the service they received. When the mailing lists were prepared for one of these surveys, the administrative staff included names of a handful of people who had since died. This information was stored on the database, but the mailing list software did not have a suitable filter that would screen out the deceased.

One widower was very distressed when the survey was sent to his wife who had died two months before, and threatened legal action against the hospital. The Chief Executive responded by apologising in person to all the affected relatives. But he also demanded an explanation from Nuria. She has since ensured that the correct filters are in place.

The accuracy of the information held on computer systems is even more significant when it is used to support decisions which may affect people's health or finances.

The medical staff at Wessex County have all been trained to use the patient records system. They all know that if they make an error when they key in the details of a consultation with a patient then they are professionally responsible for the consequences of their mistake. But Nuria has to ensure that the user interface is clear and unambiguous and that effective training is given to staff who use the system.

Activity

Cybermedicine – health advice via the Internet – is growing rapidly. Computer users can log into a website, key in their symptoms and receive an online diagnosis. In some countries they can even receive a prescription for a drug which can be ordered online as well.

You have been asked by a medical friend to design and set up such a website. What ethical issues would you have to discuss before launching the new site?

Legal responsibilities of systems managers

This section examines some of the laws in the UK that affect the work of the systems manager.

See Chapter 9 for more information about the Computer Misuse Act and the Data Protection Act.

Computer Misuse Act 1990

Under the Computer Misuse Act, the systems manager is responsible for the security of computer systems,

The social, moral, ethical and legal responsibilities of systems managers

and in particular for issuing authorisation. Nuria Sanchez has encouraged the hospital to draw up a security policy that defines which data and programs each category of employee is allowed to access. She has then created a security system which enforces the policy. She also uses system log files to check any security lapses.

The law, however, puts the responsibility on the individual. If someone discovers a weakness in the system and uses it to gain unauthorised access, Nuria will not necessarily be held liable in the eyes of the law, although she would certainly be asked for an explanation within the hospital. (But note that under data protection laws Nuria does have a legal duty to prevent unauthorised access to personal data.)

Data Protection Act 1998

The systems manager, as a data controller as defined by the Act, must ensure that the organisation abides by this law. Since Wessex County Hospital stores personal data about patients and about staff, Nuria has checked the notification made to the Data Protection Commissioner. She has reviewed the data held on the systems to make sure that it still complies with the law; in particular she has checked that no irrelevant data is being stored. She has also ensured that a patient or member of staff can be provided with a copy of their entries, and an explanation of why the data is held, on request.

Principle 7, which relates to the security of data, has a direct impact on the technology used in the hospital. In full, this states 'Appropriate technical and organisational measures shall be taken against unauthorised or unlawful processing of personal data and against accidental loss or destruction of, or damage to, personal data.' This means that Nuria has to review all the usual data-security procedures on a regular basis to ensure that they comply with the law. She also has to ensure that the staff who have access to personal data (which includes systems staff as well as data users) are reliable.

Copyright, Designs and Patents Act 1988

Part of this law concerns software piracy, so is very relevant to IT professionals. Before this Act it was not at all clear whether the laws about copyright, which referred to written materials, also applied to software. The 1988 Act made it clear that software is a literary work and should be treated in the same way as books and articles.

The copyright owner of a piece of software is usually the company that has produced it or the organisation that has commissioned it. If an application has been

Activity

Read and comment on the article reproduced here as Figure 30.6.

Patients' right to know threatened

The government is facing growing pressure to rewrite data protection rules which are landing hospitals and GP surgeries with "ridiculously high" copying costs from patients asking for access to their medical records.

Doctors are threatening to force a high court test case over rules introduced this year stating that unlimited amounts of patient records – including x-rays which can cost over £20 a plate – should be available for a maximum fee of £50.

The potential bill to the already pressed national health service was described as "alarming" yesterday by one medico-legal practice serving 15 East Anglian hospitals, which is currently resisting a demand to process £2000-worth of x-ray copying for the £50 fee as "totally unreasonable". The same office had reluctantly photocopied 1900 pages of patient notes for lawyers at the £50 fee a few days earlier, at a cost of £250 in materials and staff time. . . .

The new system imposed the £50 maximum for manual copying, with a £10 limit for computer records and no charge for copies of additions to records requested within 40 days of treatment. It was introduced as part of the government's drive to increase freedom of information, but the majority of record-copying requests stem from personal injury litigation over poor treatment or clinical errors, which is rapidly increasing.

The Department of Health and the Home Office, which oversees data protection law, have both been contacted by NHS trusts appealing for revisions during the law's current transition period, which could see changes when the regulations are reviewed in October next year. But a spokesman for the Department of Health said: "The levels set down are the maximum that should be charged and in many cases patients should be charged less than that."

®*The Guardian*, extract taken from an article by Martin Wainwright on 18 August 2000

Figure 29.6

written independently by an individual, then that person may own the copyright. Only the copyright owner may copy or adapt software.

In order to give permission to someone else to copy the software and install it on another machine, the copyright owner will issue a licence for its use. When you purchase an application you in fact purchase a licence with it, and this gives you permission to make one copy for your own use, plus any necessary backup copies.

Illegal copying and selling of software costs the industry millions of pounds each year in lost sales. This in turn pushes up the price of mass-market software, or in some cases reduces the income of independent software writers.

In any large organisation the systems manager must ensure that staff know about this law. Nuria orders *software audits* from time to time; a software audit is a check on all the software installed on networks and standalone machines. This can be effective only if a scrupulous inventory of software licences is maintained so that discrepancies can be identified.

Health and Safety (Display Screen Equipment) Regulations 1993

These regulations cover work done by employees using a 'workstation' which has any kind of display screen, including a point-of-sale terminal. They are designed to protect the health and safety of employees.

Employers have a duty to evaluate workstations and to make any changes needed to reduce risks to eyesight, physical problems and mental stress, and this task is usually delegated to the systems manager. As well as the main hardware and peripherals, Nuria must assess the software, furniture, lighting and heating, and make sure that these all meet minimum requirements. For example, the work surface must be at the right height and adjustable, allow space in front of the keyboard and be non-reflective.

Employees should be trained and their work should be planned with breaks or changes in activity. Nuria has to arrange regular free eye tests for all employees who work with computers.

Unfortunately, the Display Screen Regulations do not apply to students, as they are not employees at their place of study.

Liability of the systems manager

If a client is unhappy with the service or product provided by a company, they can take the company to court. For example, if a hardware supplier sells faulty computers then the business can be sued. Equally, if a solicitor gives bad advice which results in financial loss to the client, then the firm of solicitors can be sued.

Although a problem may have arisen directly as the result of actions taken by a particular employee, it will still be the company that will be held to be legally responsible. The employee has no personal liability towards the client.

An employer may, in theory, sue an employee for negligence (lack of reasonable care), but in practice this is very rarely done. Instead, the employer is more likely to use disciplinary procedures, which could result in dismissal. The employee could then challenge the dismissal through an Employment Tribunal. In order to justify dismissal, employers do not have to prove that the employee was negligent; it might be sufficient to show that the employee was incompetent.

A systems manager is normally an employee of an organisation. The actions of a systems manager may, unwittingly, result in damage or injury to another employee or to a client. But although the systems manager would not be liable in law for these problems, he or she could be fairly dismissed by the employer.

At the hospital, Nuria realises that some of the computer systems for which she is responsible can possibly cause damage. For example, one day a panel fell from a computer-controlled scanning machine and caused a minor injury to a patient. The previous year, a software application in the pathology laboratory gave false negative results to blood tests. Then the expert system that was tested by the research department was, in its pre-release version, not entirely reliable.

Although Nuria felt personally to blame for the problem with the scanning machine, the hospital would have been legally responsible had the patient decided to sue for damages. In fact, she discovered that the panel fell off the scanning machine because an over-enthusiastic cleaner had accidently loosened it. Nuria has released new instructions to the cleaning staff, identifying those pieces of equipment they should not touch.

Nuria reported her concerns about the pathology software to Peter Harris, the Head of Administration.

The social, moral, ethical and legal responsibilities of systems managers

She had to install a new application in the laboratory, and the technicians then had to retest a large number of blood samples before writing to patients to explain what had happened. Two patients decided to sue the hospital for compensation; they had to face lengthy treatment because their conditions were not diagnosed in the early stages.

Although Nuria had recommended the software, and had arranged for it to be thoroughly tested before it was used, Peter did not believe that she was responsible for the problem that arose. Instead Peter decided to make a claim against the software house that supplied the original application. Although the documentation supplied with the application did state that the software house was not responsible for any damage caused as a result of its use, Peter knew that this argument would not stand up in court.

Mitigating the consequences of the use of an IT system

Whenever a new IT system is installed, the organisation *intends* that consequences will follow. These intended consequences could include increased sales, faster processing, exploitation of new business opportunities, improved patient care, and so on. But the new system may lead to additional consequences other than those intended. Some of these may be of benefit to the organisation, such as improved staff morale, but some consequences may not be welcomed, such as technical problems with existing software.

These unintended consequences need to be *mitigated*; that is, their effect needs to be reduced. In other words, the risks posed by the new system should be minimised. This can be achieved only if the systems manager has considered the implications of the use of the new system, has warned the senior management in a report about possible risks, and has suggested ways of mitigating the consequences.

Types of consequences

Business consequences

These include the impact on sales, which may be much greater (or considerably less) than expected. New methods of trading, such as online retailing, can be very unpredictable; and whilst low sales can be worrying, unexpectedly high sales can place impossible pressures on a company. Rapid growth of a business can require new capital investment, and may mean that the company has to take on further risks.

The performance of the business might affect rival businesses, who may react in unexpected ways – for example by more aggressive marketing, or perhaps by going out of business.

Administrative consequences

These may be seen in the need to recruit new staff or to reduce the number of employees. The administration of supplies and of the production processes may have to be overhauled and streamlined. Substantial changes in sales may make it difficult for the company to fulfil orders in time, or may result in a build-up of unsold stock.

As an organisation grows or contracts it normally needs to adapt its organisational structure. This can take time and requires the professional expertise of human resources personnel. The internal communications of the organisation will have to be examined to check that they meet the current needs.

Technical consequences

These often relate to the integration of a new system with existing systems. The time and costs of this will depend on the compatibility of the new system with the old. If a previous system is completely replaced, the systems manager will have to develop policies and procedures for handling downtime, software errors, viruses, hardware malfunction and user errors.

Environmental consequences

These are often the most difficult to predict but are of increasing significance to the wider community. For example, if a company centralises its warehouses this may result in the increased use of transport, with its consequential costs and environmental impact.

When a replacement hardware system is installed, the systems manager is often left with the problem of disposing of redundant machines. Most of the components of a computer system are not biodegradable.

If there are changes in the work environment for some of the employees, then health and safety risks must be assessed.

Advising superiors

Most of the consequences mentioned above are not technical issues. It is important, therefore, that if a systems manager identifies unwanted consequences then these should be reported to senior managers. A report written for a senior manager should be concise and avoid technical language. It should include the following elements:

- a summary of the problems
- a clear list of recommended solutions
- justifications for the recommendations
- costings, where relevant.

At Wessex County Hospital, the Head of Administration, Peter Harris, has been looking at better ways of charging for meals in the staff dining room. At present a normal cash payment system is used. Medical staff use the dining room at all hours of the day or night, so this means that the Catering Manager has to employ cashiers throughout the full 24 hours each day. It is very difficult to recruit staff for the night shifts.

Peter has seen an automated system in use in another large organisation and he suggests to Nuria Sanchez that the Catering Department should invest in a similar system. Members of staff would be able to buy swipe cards for £10, £30 or £50 from a machine located in the dining room. At the exit from the servery area, the customer would enter the items they have bought on the touch-sensitive screen of an automatic point-of-sale terminal, and then swipe their card to register the sale. The cost of the meal would then be deducted from the value on the swipe card.

Nuria believes that the system is technically feasible, but she does want to warn Peter of some possible consequences that he may not have considered. She prepares some notes for a report to Peter Harris, based on the following:

Possible problems

1. Problem – Technical malfunction of point-of-sale terminal

   Solution – Design alternative manual system that could be used temporarily if this happens

   Justification – Will enable the staff dining room to carry on during downtime

2. Problem – Dishonest staff avoiding entering their purchases

   Solution – Random visible checks

   Justification – Will catch some transgressing staff (who would then be subject to hospital disciplinary procedures) and deter others

3. Problem – Changeover may expose throughput problems and could cause annoyance to staff

   Solution – Change to new system at quiet point in the year; have additional staff on duty during first week

   Justification – Important to maintain level of service during changeover

4. Problem – Disposal of old cash tills

   Solution – Contact specialist recycling company

   Justification – Will be in accordance with hospital's green policy

---

Activity

In each of these cases you should answer the following questions:

1. *What are the intended consequences of adopting the new system?*

2. *What could be the additional consequences of adopting the system?*

3. *Of the additional consequences, which would be beneficial to the organisation and which would pose risks?*

4. *Outline a report to senior management on the range of options for mitigating the consequences of using the new system.*

Case 1

Picton Farm Herbs is a small company in Essex that grows and sells a wide range of herbs, including some unusual varieties. Customers include cooks and herbalists around England. At present it sells its products through the farm shop and through a limited amount of mail order.

As it serves a specialist market, Picton Farm Herbs is keen to reach a wider audience of customers around the country, and possibly around the world. The company has decided to move into e-commerce and has employed an

Internet manager to oversee the development of the system and to manage it once it is running. The Internet manager knows that some aspects of e-commerce are unpredictable so wants to warn the company about possible risks.

Case 2

The directors of Amari Bank are concerned that its ATM machines present a rather old-fashioned image to the public. They want to install a new online system that will present the customer with an attractive graphical interface and that will also offer improved facilities for customers, such as real-time access to balances. The system will require new hardware at each cashpoint as well as new software linking in with the bank's customer account system.

The information systems manager has planned the project, but wants to ensure that the changeover is carried out with the minimum disruption.

CHAPTER 30

Exploiting multimedia and the Internet

This chapter looks at the development of an online car retailing company. It will describe:

● multimedia systems

● the development and maintenance of websites

● network protocols, especially those that are used in the Internet.

This chapter covers these Technical Knowledge topics in the specification:

T4.3.1   Multimedia
T4.3.3   Networks and protocols (in part)

Launching an Internet business

Bethanycars.com

Bethany Price is a young and gifted entrepreneur. She has set up a number of small businesses in the past and has now turned her attention to Internet sales. When she left university she worked for a while for a car dealership, so she understands that market well. She realised that many makes of car could be bought much more cheaply in some European countries than in the UK.

About a year ago Bethany decided to set up a business, called Bethanycars.com, selling imported new cars directly to customers through the Internet. She believed that she would be able to cut up to 40% off the price of new cars. Bethany was also convinced that within five years up to 20% of car sales would be made through the Internet; certainly in 10 years up to 70% of new cars would be purchased this way. Bethany was keen to establish a lead in this fast-moving market.

Bethany discussed her plans with an old university friend, Caroline Russell. Caroline is a marketing expert and she immediately became enthusiastic about the venture. Together they set up a partnership and started looking for venture capital.

During the last six months a number of high-profile Internet-based businesses had collapsed. The main problem for all of them had been to predict the level of sales they might achieve. When a company opens a high street shop they can call on extensive market research to get an idea of how the business is likely to perform. On the Internet this is almost impossible to determine. Some companies failed because they did not attract enough custom; some failed because they attracted too many and could not meet the demand.

Caroline Russell, as the Marketing Manager of Bethanycars.com, had tried to avoid all these pitfalls. She carried out a very careful analysis of the potential market and she used the traditional media (newspapers, magazines, radio and television) to build up a customer base. At first interest from the general public was slow.

Fortunately, Bethanycars.com's business plan allowed for a slow beginning, so it was able to weather the first few months. But then it began to have problems with a major car dealer on the European mainland who did not deliver the cars within the time they had promised to customers. Although this was not Bethanycars.com's fault, customers tended to blame them for delayed deliveries and they got some bad publicity in the national press.

The company rapidly renegotiated its arrangements with dealers and was confident it could now provide customers with their cars within the agreed time period. Bethanycars.com was still surviving, but its chances of rapid growth had been knocked on the head by the negative publicity.

Making a success of an Internet-based business

Caroline felt that the company had learnt a great deal from its earlier trading. She knew that an online retailing operation needs to be planned as carefully as a high-street or out-of-town store.

Caroline also knew that online businesses use their financial resources differently from other retailers. Bethanycars.com did not need expensive premises, but was operating out of a small suite of offices in a low-cost area of the country. They did not have to store any of the products they sold, as the sales were all negotiated with existing car dealers in Europe. But Bethanycars.com's existence depended crucially on the website and the database that supported it, so it was important to get the best possible professional support for this.

As part of their recovery strategy, Bethany and Caroline decide to bring in a top Internet solutions provider, WorldWise. Their immediate recommendation was to relaunch the company with a new trading name and a new website. The business objectives would remain the same: to maximise the profit through importing and selling cars directly to customers.

Commercial websites

Before the new website was designed, Caroline prepared a report for Bethany outlining the factors that should be taken into account. In this report she mentioned that sites can be categorised in a number of ways:

- *Informational/transactional*. Informational sites only give information; transactional sites allow the user to interact with the provider, often by purchasing goods.
- *Target audience*. A website can aim to attract any member of the public, or it can be targeted at a very specific group, such as people who share a particular interest or live in a specific area.
- *Level of innovation*. Some websites are very innovative (either in design or on content) and attract visitors because of this. Visitors may find some sites easy to use because they have many similarities to other sites.

She believed that the new site, which would necessarily be transactional, should be more specific about its target audience. In particular, she recommended that the company should be marketing much more overtly to women.

Caroline also outlined the advantages of selling through the Internet:

- *Global market*. The Internet can be used to sell goods anywhere in the world.
- *User profile*. Internet users tend to have higher levels of income and education than the general public.
- *Internet-based products*. It is possible to develop products and services specifically for Internet users.

Although her market would be confined to the UK, she would be able to reach any corner of the country with equal ease. She recommended that the company looked at the feasibility of providing 'value-added' services, such as offering online comparisons between different models of car, and a search facility which would allow visitors to enter their requirements and would display a list of possible purchases.

Finally, Caroline listed some of the pitfalls, which Bethanycars.com had already acknowledged:

- *Access to the product*. Internet customers often want to see and handle actual products before buying.
- *Prediction of market share*. It is difficult to envisage exactly how much demand a website will generate.
- *Distribution*. The company must be confident that it will be able to deliver goods within an advertised period.

Activity

Find some Internet retailing sites and analyse them according to the factors given above. Can you draw any conclusions about what makes a successful online retailing operation?

Launching UK Cars Direct

So, with the help of WorldWise, Bethanycars.com launched a new subsidiary called UK Cars Direct. Its new website is much easier to use. WorldWise brought in a graphic designer to work on the look of the site and the image they wanted to convey. Some prototypes were tested with small focus groups of potential customers, and the reports suggested that it would appeal to women as well as men, and that it was much easier to navigate than the previous website.

The company, now trading as UK Cars Direct, promoted the new site heavily through the printed media and television over a two-week period. Bethany took on some temporary staff for the launch period and they were able to handle the volume of requests.

So far business has been going well. They have learnt from the earlier experience and are now giving a reliable service to customers. They continue to use temporary staff whenever trade increases.

Multimedia systems

Some definitions

Multimedia is the term used to describe any computer application that uses more than one type of output medium, such as text, graphics, video, animation or sound. Strictly speaking, the term 'media' is the plural of 'medium', just as 'data' is the plural of 'datum'.

A *multimedia system* is a computer system which allows the user to run multimedia applications. Today all new PC systems selling into the home and small business markets support multimedia, to an extent, but some older and specialised commercial systems may not do so. Any PC which supports multimedia can also handle voicemail and fax.

An *interactive multimedia* system is one which allows the user to interact with it in real time. Many games fall into this category. Some interactive systems support sound and video input as well as keyboard and mouse inputs.

A virtual reality system is an interactive multimedia systems which adds touch and position inputs and outputs to sound and vision. Users wear headsets which feed back their position and display computer-generated images. Data gloves can also feed back the position of the hands and can provide a touch sensation to the user. Although you will be familiar with the entertainment uses of virtual reality, it also plays an important role in training for complex skills such as space exploration.

Many multimedia systems use hypertext and hypermedia links. *Hypertext* refers to *links* embedded within text which take the user to another page of text. Many application help files are constructed using hypertext methods. *Hypermedia* extends the idea of hypertext to include all kinds of media. The *WorldWide Web* is a hypermedia system.

Multimedia is exploited in a range of IT products such as CD and DVD ROMs, WAP mobile phones (Figure 30.1), and interactive kiosks. It can also be used to support videoconferencing, training and education.

The Internet was originally a text-only system. Since the World Wide Web protocols were adopted, it has become increasingly a vehicle for multimedia. Protocols for sound and graphics have been widely

Figure 30.1 *a WAP mobile phone*

DVD is a storage medium that is replacing video tape, audio tape, computer diskettes and CDs. In the same way, televisions, radios, computer monitors and screens, and visual displays on telephones, games machines and calculators, will eventually converge into one technology. We have already seen a similar convergence of printing, fax, scanning and photocopying, with the marketing of multifunction machines.

Electronics manufacturers can produce a machine that functions as a PC, an Internet terminal, a television, a telephone and a camera, and combine them all into a videoconferencing tool, so companies will be creating and selling into new markets.

As the technologies converge so do the industries that use and support them. Publishing companies, who in the past produced only paper-based magazines and newspapers, now produce online interactive publications. Similarly, music publishers launch multimedia versions of new tracks. Publishers are becoming multistranded in their products, with multimedia as the core technology.

accepted. Web TV and radio are supported by current browsers and extensions of HTML.

Convergence

In the past we have treated television, computing, graphic design, radio, games machines, music production, telephones, animation, calculators, e-mail, the Web, photography, film and video as separate technologies.

Now that these applications all use digital methods, today's multimedia systems can integrate them using the same hardware. A PC can serve as an interactive television, a voicemail system, a music system, a games machine, and so on. Similarly, the same software can be used on a variety of platforms. For example, computer games producers now develop multimedia games that can be played online on the Internet, or on a television, games machine or telephone, as well as in the normal way on a standalone computer.

We say that these hardware and software technologies have *converged*. Convergence is possible because of the growth in capacity and speed of computer components, high-speed communications, and digitising techniques for all the media.

Activity

By the time you read this book there will have been further developments in multimedia technology, and new applications of it will have been launched. Identify the current trends in multimedia that you have read about. What new technologies can you foresee in the next five years?

Hardware requirements for a multimedia system

Most personal desktop computers now have multimedia capabilities, although other computer formats, such as palmtops, may not be fully configured. A multimedia system will have interfaces and peripherals which permit the full exploitation of sound and video.

The hardware requirements for a system that can run multimedia applications are, as a minimum, a sound card, speakers, a video card and a high-resolution monitor. The system will normally need a CD-ROM or

DVD drive to read the software, or have a broadband Internet connection to capture streaming audio and video.

If the user wants to develop and record multimedia applications, they will also need a microphone or other form of sound recorder and a digital camera (still or video).

Software requirements for a multimedia system

All the hardware devices mentioned above will function only if the relevant *software drivers* have been installed. Specific applications are needed also to display the output from multimedia software. Generic applications have been developed for managing streaming audio and video.

Multimedia software is usually developed using one of several application generators that are available. These are often known as *authoring packages*, as they allow users to generate impressive applications with minimal technical knowledge.

Storage implications of multimedia applications

Sound and graphics are memory-hungry in comparison with text-based data. Recall that, in pure text format, one character requires one byte of storage. An average novel uses about 500 000 characters, so could require about 500 KB (0.5 MB) of storage.

In comparison, in a bit-mapped image, one pixel is represented by anything from 1 bit (monochrome) to 3 bytes (24-bit colour, giving millions of colour values). A 640 x 480 pixel photo taken with a digital camera at a low resolution will need about 1 MB of storage space. It may seem remarkable that a single photo takes up as much memory as two novels, but this is the problem that has to be overcome in multimedia systems.

Similarly, one second of CD quality sound takes about 176 KB of storage space. So a whole minute will require over 10 MB, and an hour of music will need 600 MB.

Even with high-capacity storage and broadband data communications, there is still a problem with the storage and transmission needs of sound and video. Most multimedia data is now transmitted in a compressed form, and increasingly stored in a compressed form as well. Compression reduces the storage needed, but it also allows more sound and pictures to be transmitted in a given time.

User interfaces, including browsers and search tools

All multimedia applications require *user interfaces* which are easy to use. Common features of multimedia user interfaces include:

- hypermedia methods to enable the user to browse through the system
- search engines which allow the user to enter *key words*
- configuration files which record the users' preferences and recent pages visited.

There is no one standard method of programming and describing multimedia pages. There are several types of multimedia authoring software package, each of which uses its own design and technical standards. In addition, individual developers create their own protocols. This has certain disadvantages. For example, if a multimedia encyclopedia is released then only the original publisher can update it.

The one major exception to this is the World Wide Web, which uses a set of common protocols, such as HTML, for describing Web pages. A *browser* is a client application which displays pages written according to these standards. Internet search engines are able to search all documents as they all conform to the same standards.

How can multimedia be used?

Entertainment

Most computer games exploit multimedia techniques to the fullest. Indeed, it has been this sector of the IT industry which has led the way in developing compression and other techniques to get around the inherent limitations of the hardware and communication devices.

Education and training

Computer-aided learning commonly uses CD-based multimedia systems for delivering staged lessons and for testing learning. Individual records of progress can be stored on hard disks. Many reference materials designed for browsing, such as encyclopedias, are now presented in multimedia format.

Presentations

Business presentations can exploit all the multimedia capability by integrating video and sound with graphics developed using presentation packages.

Conferencing

Wide-area networks, including the Internet, offer the possibility of teleconferencing. Online meetings can be carried out in real time with the use of video and live sound. This technology can cut the considerable costs and time of travelling to meet people face to face.

Kiosks

These are multimedia outlets used to provide information in public places such as museums and airports (Figure 30.2). They are usually interactive using touch-screen technology. Kiosks have to be robust to withstand frequent use, and occasional misuse, by the general public. Some kiosks have card swipes for payment. For example, kiosks have been installed in shopping malls in Toronto which allow people to pay local taxes and court fines.

Figure 30.2 An interactive kiosk

> ### Activity
>
> *We have five senses – hearing, sight, touch, smell and taste. Multimedia systems concentrate on hearing and sight. Virtual reality systems explore the use of touch. How will systems develop in the future? Will they integrate smell and taste as well? What kind of applications will they support?*

Market inertia

Any business which sells into the fast-moving multimedia market has to realise that not all customers have the latest technology. Whilst hardware companies may proclaim that the customer cannot survive without their latest device, software companies know that they must make their products compatible with older hardware if they want to sell enough.

Businesses that use multimedia to promote their products must be aware of the likely hardware capabilities of their potential customers. They will be wasting their time if they distribute a sales catalogue on a medium that will run only on the latest player to hit the market. Similarly, when they develop websites they need to be sure that they use techniques that can be displayed with the majority of browsers.

What are the implications for UK Cars Direct?

Caroline Russell, the Marketing Manager at UK Cars Direct, is determined that the company should keep abreast with the latest multimedia technology. But she does not wish to alienate potential customers by requiring them to have the latest technology. Now that the new website has been successfully launched, she decides to examine other business uses of multimedia:

- distribution of information to corporate customers via physical media (CD-ROM, DVD)

- high-quality presentations to dealers, using both presentation software and private websites
- the use of webcams (Web-based cameras) on the website
- videoconferencing with dealers around the country.

Using the Internet

Connecting to the Internet

In order to connect to the Internet, a user's computer must be linked to a network server known as a *host computer*. The host computer is permanently linked to the Internet. It manages all the communications between the computers on its network and all the other computers on the Internet.

A host computer is known as a *point of presence* on the Internet. It handles e-mail, Web space and all the other services provided by the Internet.

Large organisations may have their own host computer. In that case, the user's computer will be part of the organisation's network and will gain access to the Internet through the host computer. Many host computers run on the powerful Unix operating system, which was designed specifically for multi-user systems.

Internet service providers

Many organisations (and all individual users) do not have their own host computer so use the services of an Internet service provider (ISP). An ISP provides a host computer and all the services associated with it to its subscribers.

An individual computer may be temporarily connected to the host computer provided by an ISP by using a dial-up service. This makes use of a telephone line and modem to make the connection. During the time that the computer is linked to the ISP's host computer, it effectively becomes part of the ISP's network.

Alternatively, the user's computer may be connected permanently to the ISP's host computer using a broadband connection (such as an ISDN or ADSL line).

In an organisation with a local-area network (LAN) it is unlikely that individual users will connect directly to an ISP. Instead there will be a terminal server on the

What is the Internet?

The Internet connects together a vast number of computer networks located all over the world. It can be described as a network of networks. The individual networks connected to the Internet can be of any size. The data communications within these networks may also be of any type, from dial-up connections using modems to the fastest broadband links.

The Internet began when a number of large networks linked together to share information. Most of these networks were based at research centres or universities. In the United States, the Advanced Research Projects Agency Network (ARPANET) was set up in 1969 by the US Defense Department to link it with university research centres. The intention was to develop a system that would allow the networks in each of the centres to continue to communicate with others even if part of the ARPANET was destroyed. The techniques developed by ARPANET were then used to run the National Science Foundation Network (NSFNET) in that country.

In the UK, the Joint Academic Network (JANET®) linked universities and research centres, and in time JANET® itself became linked to NSFNET® and to similar academic research networks in other countries. The latest version of JANET® is known as SuperJANET®.

The Internet is often referred to as the **Information Superhighway**.

LAN which can access the Internet when one of the stations requests it. A terminal server usually uses a broadband connection to an ISP, although it may use a dial-up modem instead.

Services offered by the Internet

Although you will probably associate the Internet with the World Wide Web, it is important to realise that the Internet provides more services than the Web itself. Most of these services were available long before the Web was invented.

The Internet offers:

- file transfer
- e-mail
- remote login
- newsgroups
- chat lines
- mailing lists
- search engines, such as Google and Yahoo!
- the World Wide Web.

A later section examines the World Wide Web, and we will look at the other services in this section.

File transfer

Computer files of any type can be copied from one computer to another through the Internet using a method known as the *file transfer protocol* (FTP). This can be used to transfer word-processed files, pictures, sound, software – in fact, any type of digital data. This process is often known as *downloading*.

Electronic mail (e-mail)

An e-mail message must be generated using e-mail client software, which also manages incoming e-mails. E-mails can usually incorporate multimedia elements, such as hypertext, sound and images. Also, users can attach to an e-mail files produced in any format. The *postmaster* is the systems administrator with responsibility for an e-mail system.

Remote login

A computer can be logged in remotely to a network. This is used by employees who need to logon to their employer's system from a distance in order to have access to the organisation's data or applications.

People who travel around the country when they work, and teleworkers (people who work from home), use this method of connection. Whilst they are connected to the network, the computer they are using acts as a terminal of the remote network. The Internet can be used to provide the link between the terminal and the network, using a program such as *Telnet*.

Newsgroups

Users may join one of the many thousands of newsgroups on the Internet. Each newsgroup concentrates on a particular subject. Members send e-mails to the newsgroup and these are all posted at one location. Users can then download all the newsgroup messages to their own computers or read them online. All newsgroups have a moderator, who may censor messages before they are posted to the newsgroup.

Conferences and *bulletin boards* are very similar to newsgroups. All these are generally referred to as *Usenet*.

Chat lines

Chat facilities allow groups of users to have a text-based 'conversation' over the Internet, almost in real time. As soon as one user has finished keying in a message it is displayed for all the members of the group to read. The most common software used for chat is *Internet Relay Chat* (IRC).

Mailing lists

A list server is a system that automatically forwards e-mails to users who have joined a mailing list, which is simply a list of e-mail addresses. The list will be managed by a list owner, or moderator.

With *announcement lists*, e-mails can be sent only by a few nominated persons to the list, so they are often used by commercial companies for advertising purposes. With *discussion lists*, any member can post an e-mail to everyone on the list, so these are used to support groups of people who have a common interest. These are very similar to newsgroups.

Search engines

A search engine is a program that searches the Internet to find a file that matches a user's query. Search engines themselves create huge databases, known as indexes, that identify complete websites or individual web pages. Indexes may be based on domain names, on titles of web pages, on keywords contained in the head of each web page, or on the actual text contained on a page.

Indexes are often generated automatically using *web spiders*. A web spider, or *crawler*, is a program that follows links within websites and from one website to another, recording entries in the index as it goes.

Impact of the Internet

For many years the Internet was used almost entirely by academics and the military. University researchers throughout the world posted research papers, in the form of text files, on their Internet servers. These were then downloaded (using FTP) by colleagues working in the same field, anywhere in the world. This was the first *virtual community*, in which researchers were able to share knowledge and constructively criticise the work of others.

Using the Internet meant that documents became instantly available to anyone using the system. This reduced the costs, time delay and uncertainty of worldwide postal systems, and also made work available to anyone interested. The Internet has been seen by many as a very significant tool in maintaining academic freedom, especially in countries where governments might try to limit free speech.

E-mail enabled cheap and fast global communications. One of its important advantages was its ability to overcome time differences around the world. A message could be sent at any time, in the sure confidence that the receiver would access it at a time that suited that person.

Intranets

An intranet is a miniature version of the Internet which is confined to one organisation. Intranets are accessible only to authorised users.

An intranet offers the same range of facilities as the Internet, such as file transfer, web pages and e-mail, but with the added advantage of good security.

What are the implications for UK Cars Direct?

Although the website is the most significant use of the Internet made by UK Cars Direct, the company does also use some other features. It has set up a mailing

list for customers. Anyone who wants to receive a regular bulletin with news about the car market can provide their e-mail address when online to the website. UK Cars Direct uses standard software to send out an e-mail each week to everyone on the mailing list.

Activity

Discuss the uses that you make of the Internet, other than browsing web pages. How can organisations and individuals exploit these facilities? Consider both commercial and non-commercial organisations.

Protocols used on the Internet

The Internet works only because all the networks connected to it use the same technical standards known as protocols. You are familiar with some protocols already; for example, ASCII is the widely used protocol for encoding characters. The main protocols on the Internet are:

- those for identification of computers and files
- data communication protocols
- file-handling (transfer) protocols
- e-mail protocols.

The protocols used on the Internet are identified by the *Internet Architecture Board*.

Identification of computers and files

Internet protocol (IP) addresses

Every computer linked directly to the Internet is allocated a number, known as its *IP address*. Each IP address occupies 32 bits. This is represented as four 8-bit integers; e.g. 123.67.238.165.

Each computer on the Internet has an IP address; this is not confined to host computers. If a user's computer connects to a host computer using dial-up, then it is usually allocated a temporary IP address by the host computer for the session that it is online.

Domain names

A domain name is the name of a location on the Internet. For example, `www.mydomain.co.uk` is a domain name.

Originally domains were synonymous with IP addresses. In other words, each computer on the Internet had one domain name and one IP address – but the domain name was easier to remember. That is no longer the case. Today a host computer on the Internet can manage any number of domains, so there may be many domains at any one IP address.

The structure of domain names is defined by the *domain name system* (DNS). Domain names are stored on large databases. A program called a *DNS server* searches these databases and couples each domain name with the IP address where it is stored.

Domain names fall into three types:

- a top-level domain name, for example `co.uk`
- a second-level domain name, for example `mydomain.co.uk`
- a third-level domain name, for example `www.mydomain.co.uk`.

The top-level domain name identifies the type of organisation and/or country. Examples include:

- `com`
- `org` (non-profit-making organisations)
- `gov`
- `ac` (educational institutions in the UK)
- `edu` (educational institutions in the US)
- `co` (used in the UK).

Recently new types have been permitted, including `shop` and `tv`. Country codes are added for countries outside the United States; for example:

- `uk` (United Kingdom)
- `au` (Australia)
- `ie` (Ireland)
- `fr` (France)
- `ca` (Canada)
- `nl` (Netherlands)
- `de` (Germany).

Domain names registered in the United States do not have a country code. But certain American domain types, notably `com`, have become very popular and are used by companies all over the world, to the extent that Internet-based businesses are often referred to as 'dot coms'.

Second-level domain names give a recognisable identity to a domain. These names have to be registered with one of the organisations accredited by the *Internet Corporation for Assigned Names and Numbers* (ICANN).

Any further additions, which result in a third-level domain name, are optional. These additions, such as `www`, usually refer to a specific server on the host system. As a third-level name, such as `www.mydomain.co.uk`, refers to an actual host computer it is sometimes known as a *host name*.

Uniform resource locator (URL)

Any file available on the Internet, whether it be a web page, an image or any other kind of file at all, is a *resource*. Each resource has its own unique address, known as its URL. For example:

```
http://www.mydomain.co.uk/welcome.htm
http://www.mydomain.co.uk/images/myphoto.jpg
ftp://archive.myuni.ac.uk/exams/compsci/y2000.zip
news:alt.butterflies
mailto:bloggs@myisp.com
```

Each URL starts with the transfer protocol to be used (such as FTP, HTTP or News). It usually follows this with the domain name. Sometimes a local part, such as `www` or `archive`, is included. This identifies a storage location (probably a particular server) on the host network. Web pages commonly have `www` as the local part of their domain name, but it is not obligatory.

In the case of URLs beginning with HTTP and FTP, the final part (after the first single forward slash, /) is the pathname for the file that is to be downloaded. For example:

`http:`	`//www.mydomain.co.uk`	`/images/myphoto.jpg`
transfer protocol	*domain name*	*file pathname*

In this example, `myphoto.jpg` is a web graphic stored in a directory called `images`, in the domain `www.mydomain.co.uk`.

Most domains have a default file name, such as `index.html` or `home.htm`, which is used if no file name is given. For example, if you enter the URL `http://www.hotmail.com/` in your browser, it automatically loads the file `index.html` at this domain.

Data communication protocols

These protocols determine how signals are sent over the Internet. They allow host computers using all kinds of operating systems and hardware configurations to communicate with each other.

See Chapter 23 for a general account of data communication protocols.

Packets and datagrams

Data is transmitted around the Internet in packages known as *packets* (or *datagrams*). A packet (or datagram) contains the IP addresses of its source and destination computers, and can take any route at all through the Internet.

Transmission control protocol (TCP)

TCP creates the packets of data that are transmitted around the Internet. A file, such as an e-mail file or a Web page, may be quite lengthy, so TCP may divide it into several packets. The individual packets may travel through the Internet on different routes. This means that packets do not necessarily arrive at their destination in the correct order, but TCP will reassemble them into the original file on the destination system.

TCP also adds some error-detection controls to the transmission of data. The packets are routed through a number of computers on the Internet, and error-detection methods are used at each stage. As packets are transmitted, TCP adds *checksums* to the stream of data. A checksum is a number which is calculated by adding together all the integer values of all the bytes in the packet. When the packet is received by a computer on the Internet, the receiver will add up the values of all the bytes and compare it with the checksum. If they match, then it is highly likely that the whole packet was uncorrupted during transmission. The receiver will send an acknowledgement signal to the transmitter, and the transmitter will then send the next packet. If the data received does not match the checksum, then the receiver will send an error signal and the transmitter will retransmit the packet.

TCP is the transport layer of the TCP/IP protocol.

Checksums

The description of a checksum given above omitted some detail. Checksums are used in a number of data transmission contexts, but the way they are calculated varies.

Generally, the bytes of data are first added as though they were integers. The total is then divided by a fixed figure, and the remainder is the actual checksum. For example, suppose the checksum is one byte (8 bits) in length, giving a range of integer values from 0 to 255. The sum of all the bytes will be divided by 256, leaving a remainder that is also a byte in length. This sounds a bit complex, but is very easy to achieve in binary. The checksum is simply the sum of the integers, ignoring any overflow.

The Internet uses a 4-byte (32-bit) checksum.

Activity

A transmission system uses an 8-bit checksum. Calculate the value of the checksum for a packet containing the following values:

102, 99, 251, 6, 187, 23, 67, 79, 198, 247.

Can you show how this will work in binary? (**Hint**: *use the binary function on a calculator.*)

Internet protocol (IP)

IP is the underlying protocol that all computers connected to the Internet must use. It handles the address part in each packet and ensures that each reaches its correct destination. It has two components:

- an address structure (see the earlier section on IP addresses)
- a packet-switching service, which routes packets from one point of presence to another.

IP is the network layer of the TCP/IP protocol.

TCP/IP

On the Internet, TCP always works with IP, so they are usually linked together like this. The acronym is sometimes pronounced 'TCP over IP'.

Point-to-point protocol (PPP)

When two computers are connected directly to each other there is no need to use the full TCP/IP protocol, so the simpler protocol, PPP, is often used instead. PPP uses IP, so it can be used, in certain circumstances, on the Internet.

In particular, PPP is commonly used when a computer is connected to a host computer through a telephone line. PPP handles the data communications between the user's computer and the host computer. The host computer will then access the Internet using TCP/IP.

User datagram protocol (UDP/IP)

TCP/IP is often used on LANs and wide-area networks (WANs), quite independently of any Internet access. UDP/IP is a simple alternative to TCP/IP for networks that already work with the IP protocol. UDP is not used directly on the Internet.

UDP adds a checksum to packets (datagrams), in much the same way as TCP. But the application that is using UDP has to carry out the error-checking process and request retransmission itself, if necessary.

Also, UDP does not reassemble the packets when they arrive at their destination, so it is more suited to the transmission of small files.

UDP is faster than TCP, but offers less functionality.

Transfer protocols

File transfer protocol (FTP)

FTP is a protocol which runs on TCP/IP. It is used to copy files from one computer to another and was designed as the basic method of transferring files across the Internet. The main features of FTP are:

- the data file is divided into blocks of data by the transmitting computer
- the data file is checked for errors by the receiving computer.

To speed up the data transfer times these files are often temporarily compressed (or *zipped*). When the files are opened at the receiving end they have to be decompressed (*unzipped*) back to their original form. Compare this with the compression of sound and picture files, which can be used without loss of quality in their compressed form, and are not usually designed to be decompressed.

Hypertext transfer protocol (HTTP)

HTTP also runs on TCP/IP and is the protocol for requesting and transferring a Web page. If `http:` appears at the beginning of a URL, this identifies the resource as a multimedia page constructed in HTML.

Secure HTTP (SHTTP)

Secure HTTP is an extension of HTTP which ensures that files can be transferred securely. This is achieved by encrypting the files. SHTTP is commonly used for credit card and other financial transactions on the Internet.

Internet e-mail protocols

E-mail addresses and files

An internal e-mail address on a LAN may be in any format at all, determined by the systems administrator, but on the Internet this standard format is used:

$$username@domainname$$

An e-mail file begins with a header which contains the e-mail addresses of the sender and recipient, the time and date when it was sent, and a subject line. The body of the message follows this.

Simple mail transfer protocol (SMTP)

This is part of the TCP/IP protocol. It enables e-mail to be sent from one computer to another. SMTP is usually used to transfer e-mails between host computers on the Internet. SMTP is also used when a user sends an e-mail to a host computer.

Incoming e-mails are stored on the host computer until the user requests them to be downloaded. The area of memory where incoming e-mails is stored is known as a *mailbox*.

Post office protocol (POP3)

POP3 is also an e-mail transfer protocol, which is more complex than SMTP. It is usually used to download e-mails held on a host computer.

Multi-purpose Internet mail extender (MIME)

This is a protocol which allows someone to send an e-mail containing data other than simple text. MIME enables a sender to include *attachments*, which are files of any type. It also allows multimedia e-mails to be sent incorporating hypertext, sound and images.

The World Wide Web

History of the Web

The World Wide Web can be referred to as the Web, WWW, W3 or W3. It is a hypermedia information system, connecting millions of websites.

Since the Internet grew out of the scientific research community, it is not surprising that the Web itself was invented at a research institution. The World Wide Web is a set of protocols invented by CERN (European Organisation for Nuclear Research) and publicly launched in 1991.

These protocols have been universally adopted as the standard for transmitting and displaying pages of information on the Internet. Each page on the Web has its own URL, and can be quickly located and downloaded to any computer in the world that is online to the Internet. The Web standard can also be used within local intranet systems which use the TCP/IP data transmission protocol.

Web protocols

A *website* is a location on the Internet where one or more *web pages* are stored. The *home page* acts as the starting point for the website.

Although each web page has its own URL, most users simply enter the URL of the home page and then browse through the site from there.

The main features of the Web are:

- *HTML* (hypertext mark-up language) – code written in a simple programming language that is transmitted when a web page is downloaded
- *browsers* – client software, such as Internet Explorer and Netscape, which convert the HTML code to a web page
- *hyperlinks* – links embedded in HTML code which are used to jump from one page to another using the URL
- *graphical images* – hyperlinked from web pages and stored in compressed form, as either 'jpg' or 'gif' files
- *other audio and video files* – such as streaming audio and video formats.

Impact of the Web

The advent of the WWW had a significant impact on the use of the Internet. Before its launch, the use of the Internet was limited largely to the academic and military communities and to a few forward-looking industries.

By the end of the last century over 25% of the population in the UK had access to the Internet, and although users also discovered the benefits of other aspects of the Internet, such as e-mail and chat, it is undoubtedly the Web which encouraged the widespread uptake. As a direct result businesses began to use the Internet for commercial activities.

The reasons for these effects are not difficult to find:

- the ease of access to information, compared with FTP
- opportunities for online retailing of goods and services
- the globalisation and democratisation of knowledge
- globalisation of markets
- globalisation of communications
- the growth of virtual communities in 'cyberspace', based around mutual interests
- continuous, 24-hour activity.

Activity

Find out what proportion of the population currently have access to the Internet in the UK and in other countries.

Web servers

A web server is a computer linked to the Internet which stores one or more websites. The web server transfers web pages to other computers, when requested, using HTTP.

How are UK Cars Direct using the Web?

UK Cars Direct is a relatively small organisation. WorldWise gave them some excellent advice when they relaunched the business. Bethany Price and Caroline Russell are very pleased with the outcomes.

WorldWise recommended that they should leave the technical adminstration of the website to their Internet service provider. They have a business account with their ISP and a broadband connection.

The ISP offers a dedicated web server hosting service, which UK Cars Direct subscribes to. This means that a web server, located at the ISP's premises, has been configured specifically for their needs. It holds the website as well as the product database, both of which can be accessed easily from UK Cars Direct's own system. The website uses dynamic techniques to interrogate the database in response to visitors' enquiries.

The ISP also offers secure transfers via a third party, which allow customers to pay deposits on cars with confidence using their credit cards. This means that the company can concentrate on the knowledge side of the business and does not need to employ systems experts. It does, of course, employ a website designer who manages the site, as well as a database manager. The remaining staff work directly with customers and business clients, handling sales and deals.

UK Cars Direct also uses the Web as a customer. A large number of companies now offer business-to-business services through the Internet. These services include recruitment services and IT consultancy as well as the sale of office supplies.

Activity

Carry out some research on the Internet to produce a list of business-to-business services offered online.

CHAPTER 31

Using data formats

This chapter explores some technical issues underpinning a range of office automation tools. Although it does not refer explicitly to any of the organisations that we have been studying, the information is relevant to all of them. It will describe:

- a range of common data formats
- practical considerations when using object-based systems.

A short tutorial on HTML is provided on the website at www.heinemann.co.uk/vocational/it.

This chapter covers these Technical Knowledge topics in the specification:

T4.2.1 Internal representation of data types
T4.2.2 Object types
T4.2.3 The storage implications of objects

Common data formats

The history of computers reveals much innovative development carried out in isolation from other developments. The consequence of this was that data formats differed from machine to machine. This is not acceptable today when computer data is often shared between users.

To overcome the compatibility problem some common data formats have become popular and have developed into protocols in their own right. The simplest of these formats is the *ASCII* (or text) file, but many other more complex common formats have emerged. We will examine some alternative text formats.

Word-processing formats

Figure 31.1 shows a document prepared in Microsoft Word. The Word file for this document contains considerably more than the text that you see. It holds all the style definitions available from the style box as well as all the document formatting instructions.

Drawing perfect shapes

One simple trick enables you to draw perfect squares and circles.

Most vector-mapped drawing packages will produce equilateral shapes if you hold down the Shift key as you drag out the shape with your mouse.

Figure 31.1 *A document prepared in MS Word*

The Word file was opened in a simple *text editor*. Figure 31.2 is an extract from what appeared, although there are several more pages of code after the actual text.

Using data formats

```
_Ï à¡± á  >    _ÿ   !  #  _ÿÿÿÿÿÿÿÿÿÿÿÿÿÿÿÿÿ ÿÿÿÿ ÿÿÿÿ
ÿÿÿÿÿÿÿÿÿÿÿÿÿÿÿÿÿÿÿÿÿÿÿÿÿÿÿÿÿÿÿÿÿÿÿÿÿÿÿÿÿÿÿÿÿÿÿÿÿÿÿ
ÿÿÿÿÿÿÿÿÿÿÿÿÿÿÿÿÿÿÿÿÿÿÿÿÿÿÿÿÿÿÿÿÿÿÿÿÿÿÿÿÿÿÿÿÿÿÿÿÿ
ÿÿÿÿÿÿÿÿÿÿÿÿÿÿÿÿÿÿÿÿÿÿÿÿÿÿÿÿÿÿÿÿÿÿÿÿÿÿÿÿÿÿÿÿÿÿÿÿÿ
ÿÿÿÿÿÿÿÿÿÿÿÿÿÿÿÿÿÿÿÿÿÿÿÿÿÿ¥Á G  ¿   ô bjbj_Ù_Ù
       4 ì_ ì_ î     ÿÿ ÿÿ ÿÿ ] t t t t
   8 X d  _¶| | | | |                       ~  _ $ o ô  c
<                ç "                  5 t t |  | k | 5
5  5   t |¦ |  |~  t t            t  t    ~ 5 è 5  V 2@
à  ,   ~ |  p  >_ÒÕ À       %    r
 Drawing perfect shapes
One simple trick enables you to draw perfect squares and circles.



Most vector-mapped drawing packages will produce equilateral
shapes if you hold down the Shift key as you drag out the shape
with your mouse.

 [  \  _  _  ô  õ ó  6 _ j U h mH  nH              [  ]
^  _  `  î  ï  _  ñ  ò  ó  ô  _  û  û û û û û û û û û û
```

Figure 31.2 *The Word file viewed in a text editor (extract)*

What you can see are the ASCII equivalents of some of the formatting codes that Word uses.

Unfortunately, many word-processing packages have been developed independently of each other and they use completely different formatting codes. This is why documents created in one word-processor are often not compatible with other word-processors.

In practice, different versions of a word-processor may be incompatible with each other as well, although in general a later version should be able to read documents prepared in an older version. Generally, versions of a package are backwards-compatible but not forwards-compatible.

Activity

1. *Can you remember under what circumstances you have opened a document only to be presented by apparent gobbledygook like in Figure 31.2?*

2. *Can you explain why versions of a package are usually backwards-compatible but not forwards-compatible?*

Text files

Text files (also known as ASCII files) consist simply of the ASCII codes for the individual characters. This format can be read by any system at all, so is compatible with all kinds of software, and not just word-processors. Text files are the simplest way of transferring text from one system to another, and have been used in data communications for very many years.

To illustrate this, the original Word document in Figure 31.1 was saved as a text-only file, then viewed in a text editor (Notepad) – see Figure 31.2. Note that the document has lost all the character formatting and alignment as well as the graphic.

Drawing perfect shapes

One simple trick enables you to draw perfect squares and circles.

Most vector-mapped drawing packages will produce equilateral shapes if you hold down the Shift key as you drag out the shape with your mouse.

Figure 31.3 *The text-only file viewed in a text editor*

As a text file contains no formatting information, the file is as small as it could possibly be, so is the fastest option for transmission of text. At one time all e-mail traffic was in text-only format, although today other formats such as HTML are supported.

Text editors, such as Notepad, can only interpret ASCII codes. The code written in a programming language is created as a text file, so a simple text editor could be used for the task. In practice, most high-level programming is done using an enhanced editor which analyses the code and reports syntax errors (that is, incorrect programming code).

Rich text format (RTF)

There is clearly a need for a format which preserves much of the character formatting in a word-processed document, yet can be read by a wide range of software packages. It was for this reason that rich text format was invented.

```
{ \rtf1 \ansi \ansicpg1252 \uc1 \deff0 \deflang1033 \deflangfe1033

{ \fonttbl{ \f0 \froman \fcharset0 \fprq2{ \* \panose
02020603050405020304} Times New Roman;} { \f1 \fswiss
\fcharset0 \fprq2{ \* \panose 020b0604020202020204} Arial;} {
\f3 \froman \fcharset2 \fprq2{ \* \panose 05050102010706020507}
Symbol;} }

\pard \plain \s1 \qc \sb360 \sa60 \sl240 \slmult0 \keepn \nowidctlpar
\outlinelevel0 \adjustright \b \f1 \fs28 \cf1 \lang2057 \kerning28
{Drawing perfect shapes \par }

\pard \plain \qj \sb120 \sl240 \slmult0 \nowidctlpar \adjustright \cf1
\lang2057 {One simple trick enables you to draw perfect squares
and circles.  \par }

{ \lang1024 \cgrid { \shp{ \* \shpinst \shpleft2265 \shptop176
\shpright3450 \shpbottom1361 \shpfhdr0 \shpbxcolumn \shpbypara
\shpwrk0 \shpfblwtxt0 \shpz0 \shplid1042 { \sp{ \sn
shapeType} { \sv 1 } } { \sp{ \sn fFlipH} { \sv 0} } { \sp{ \sn
fFlipV} { \sv 0} } } { \shprslt{ \* \do \dobxcolumn \dobypara
\dodhgt8192 \dprect \dpx2265 \dpy176 \dpxsize1185 \dpysize1185
\dpfillfgcr255 \dpfillfgcg255 \dpfillfgcb255 \dpfillbgcr255
\dpfillbgcg255 \dpfillbgcb255 \dpfillpat1 \dplinew15 \dplinecor0
\dplinecog0 \dplinecob0} } } }

{ \par \par \par \par } {Most vector-mapped drawing packages will
produce equilateral shapes if you hold down the } { \i Shift} { key
as you drag} { out the shape with your mouse. \par } }
```

Figure 31.4 *The RTF file viewed in text editor (extract)*

The Word file used for Figure 31.1 was saved again in RTF. It was then opened in a text editor so that the formatting codes could be viewed – see Figure 31.4.

As you can observe, RTF uses special codes to give instructions about the format of the text. You can probably work out what some of them mean. These codes use the basic ASCII characters and can be read by anyone who knows them. Codes like this are known as *markup codes*.

RTF can be used for a surprisingly large number of word-processing functions. As well as preserving all the features of font styles, it can also convey the properties of a vector graphic, as shown above in the section beginning '{\lang1024\cgrid'.

Also, although not demonstrated in our extract, a full *bitmap* of a graphic can be included in the code. However, some of the more specialist functions of a word-processor, such as tables and mail-merge, cannot be handled by RTF.

The most useful feature of RTF markup codes is that all word-processors can interpret them. When this RTF file is opened by Word, or by any other word-processor, the output will be identical to the original Word document.

Hypertext markup language (HTML)

HTML is, as its name indicates, another set of markup codes. It was specifically developed as the standard method of describing web pages, but it can be used offline to create any hypermedia application.

The Word file used earlier was also saved as an HTML file – see Figure 31.5. However, HTML is not as versatile as RTF and could not reproduce the embedded drawing. All graphics on web pages have to be *linked*, not embedded, and the graphics themselves have to be downloaded as separate files.

The particular feature of HTML is its ability to handle *hyperlinks*. A hyperlink is a 'hotspot' (text or graphic) on a page which when clicked activates a jump to another page. Although hyperlinks are not illustrated in this example, further information about them can be found in the HTML tutorial on the Heinemann website (www.heinemann.co.uk).

```
<html>
 <head>
  <meta http-equiv="content-type"
  content="text/html; charset=windows-1252">
  <meta name="generator" content="Microsoft
  Word 97">
  <title></title>
 </head>
 <body text="#000000">
  <b><font face="arial" size="4">
  <p align="center">Drawing perfect
  shapes</p></b></font>
  <p align="justify">One simple trick enables
  you to draw perfect squares and circles.</p>
  <p align="justify"></p>
  <p align="justify"> </p>
  <p align="justify"> </p>
  <p align="justify"> </p>
  <p align="justify">Most vector-mapped
  drawing packages will produce equilateral
  shapes if you hold down the <i>Shift</i> key
  as you drag out the shape with your mouse.
  </p>
 </body>
</html>
```

Figure 31.5 *The source code for an HTML file*

However, HTML does have the advantage of taking up very little memory compared with RTF and word-processor files, and this enables the pages to download relatively quickly.

The storage implications

The storage requirements for each of the variations on the original document given above are:

Word document	19KB
Rich text format	4KB
HTML	1KB
Text-only	1KB

Object types and object libraries

The term 'object' has a very precise meaning in programming. An object has properties, events and methods. So the declaration of an object consists of the definition of a data structure together with the procedures (methods) for manipulating the data structure and the events which trigger those procedures.

It is tempting to think of objects as visual items such as buttons and forms. Whilst these may indeed be developed as objects, there are many objects which do not have simple visual components. For example, a complete database can itself be treated as an object; so can a macro.

In fact, the programmer can draw on and incorporate many pre-written objects into an application. Some of these are provided by the programming environment. Microsoft Office provides many objects which can be used within applications built using Office environments such as Excel and Access.

Objects are commonly grouped into *libraries*. To find out what libraries of objects are available for you to use, you should select the Object Browser in your programming or application development environment. Figure 31.6 is an example of a small

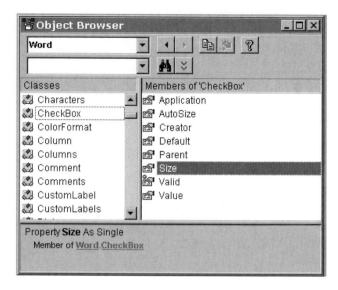

Figure 31.6 *Discovering the range of libraries of objects*

selection of objects available within the Visual Basic editor in Microsoft Word.

In this example, the Word library of objects has been selected. Several other libraries are also offered within this environment, including one for MSForms (the form designer), those for Microsoft Office as a whole, and the Visual Basic library itself.

Each library offers a choice of *classes*. A class is a formal definition of an object; it is effectively a template from which you can create your own objects. So the class Checkbox gives you the structure to enable you to insert a checkbox object, with its associated properties, events and methods. The property Size has been selected.

An object itself has to be declared like any variable within a program. If it has been created using a class in one of the libraries, then it will already have a selection of properties, events and methods associated with it.

The systems manager in an organisation needs to ensure that the right libraries are made available to anyone who needs to develop an application. This can be ascertained only by asking the inhouse developers.

When an application generator or programming environment is first installed, the installation program usually displays a dialogue box which allows the user (systems administrator) to decide which libraries should be installed. In practice, the installation program often offers the systems administrator a choice of 'full installation', 'normal installation' or 'customised installation'. The third option allows the administrator to choose which libraries should be installed.

Embedding and linking objects, and storage implications

Inserting objects into a document

When a graphic is inserted into a document the user can choose between several ways of handling it. It can be:

- copied and pasted
- hyperlinked
- embedded as an object
- linked as an object.

Note that a graphic is treated as a graphical object only in the last two cases. Remember that an object is a data structure together with methods (procedures) for manipulating it. Many instances of graphics are simply data structures (either bit-mapped or vector-mapped), without any related methods.

A copied graphic becomes part of the document. If you select the graphic you can usually make some minor adjustments to it, such as changing its size or position, but you are not able to edit the contents of the graphic itself. This is because the graphic is not being treated as an object, in the technical sense.

When a graphic is hyperlinked, the document notes the file (or web) address where it can be located. The graphic is then loaded into the document, and is treated in much the same way as a copied graphic; that is, not as an object. This is possible only if the browser itself supports the type of file that is downloaded.

In comparison, when an object is *inserted* into a document, it retains its connection with its parent application – that is, the software that was used to create the object. For example, if you insert a graphical object into a word-processed document, and then select it, the application in which it was created will be launched. You will be given the opportunity to edit the graphic and save it again.

There are two ways in which an object can be inserted into a document. These are collectively known as *object linking and embedding* (OLE).

- An *embedded* object is saved with the original document. If the document is passed to another user then the embedded object will automatically be included.
- When a *linked* object is included in a document, only a pointer to the object is contained in the document. The software loads in the object at the time it is viewed. Any changes made to the original object will be visible in the document. If the document is passed on to another user then they must also have separate access to the object.

Embedded objects remain fixed on the document, but linked objects can appear differently each time the document is viewed. This technique makes it possible to produce dynamic documents.

OLE in Microsoft Office documents

Microsoft Office supports both embedding and linking of objects. The objects that are used include the familiar bit-mapped and vector-mapped graphical objects, animations, video clips and sound files. In addition, any Office document may be embedded or linked within another one.

Activity

1. *Explore the range of objects that can be embedded and linked within Microsoft Office documents. Use Insert/Object to view the possibilities.*

2. *Do other software products offer the same range of OLE tools?*

Inserting objects into HTML files

When a simple graphic or sound file is placed on a page developed in HTML, it is hyperlinked and is not usually treated as an object. This means that when a web page is viewed, the actual HTML text is downloaded first, then the browser requests all the remaining files that are referred to in the text.

The advantage of this is that the HTML text file can be kept to a minimum size and can be downloaded relatively quickly. The visitor can then decide whether to wait for all the remaining components to be downloaded before switching to another page.

All the hyperlinked objects must be stored somewhere on the Web, normally in the same web space as the HTML file itself.

It is, however, possible to place embedded objects on a web page, using dynamic HTML (DHTML). These techniques would normally be used for more sophisticated effects such as video clips. When the page is loaded into the browser, the parent application will be launched. These parent applications are sometimes known as plug-ins. The user will be offered the opportunity to download the relevant plug-in if it is not already available.

Implications of OLE

We have looked at linking and embedding objects in documents. Other software applications also make use of both techniques. For example, the Microsoft Office products themselves reuse a large number of graphical icons across the product range. These are all linked objects and are stored in specified directories on the system.

The main disadvantage of linking or embedding objects in a document is that the viewer must have access to the parent application. However, if the author of the document is sure that the parent application will be available to the viewer, then linking or embedding both have advantages over other methods, such as copying or hyperlinking. OLE methods can be used very successfully on a network and allow co-workers to share material with each other.

There are several advantages in linking an object rather than embedding it in an application or document:

- The object can be linked from several applications or documents at the same time.
- The object only needs to be stored once.
- The object can be changed and the changes will show in any application or document which links to it.
- The application or document is smaller than one which contains embedded objects.

The advantages of embedding an object include:

- The application or document and all their objects can be transferred to another system as one file.
- Once embedded, it does not matter if the original object is deleted or moved.

You will see that a number of these points refer to storage issues.

- If a document contains an embedded object, then it will be larger than a virtually identical document in which the same object is linked.
- If a document contains a linked object, then the object must be correctly addressed within the document. If the object is moved to a new location, or is renamed, *the document will not be able to link to it.*
- All embedded and linked objects rely on the availability of the parent application.

When installing an application the systems administrator needs to be aware of linked objects and must ensure that these are installed in the correct directory. Failure to do this may mean that the application will not 'find' the object when it is needed. Normally installation programs ensure that all objects are placed in the correct directories.

The systems administrator must also secure any applications that are likely to be used to generate objects that will be linked or embedded.

CHAPTER 32

How to do Task 3

This chapter gives advice on how to tackle coursework **Task 3.** The task requires you to produce a detailed written report describing the full range of implications of a *major actual* application, with stress on the effect on all the people involved.

You should investigate two or three non-technical aspects of the selected application, chosen from sociological, legal, moral and political aspects.

Before you start on Task 3, you are strongly advised to look back over the social, moral, ethical, legal and political issues covered in Chapters 8 and 29.

A sample report, with comments, can be viewed on the Heinemann website at www.heinemann.co.uk/vocational/it

Do not forget that the examiners will have read this book, so do not attempt to use any of the material from the sample in your own report (see the section below on plagiarism).

This chapter covers the following Learning Outcome in the specification:

L.O. 6.1   Produce a written report on an ICT application

It also relates to:

L.O. 1.8   Demonstrate a critical understanding of the social, ethical and moral implications of the exploitation of an ICT-based solution to a problem

L.O. 4.13   Reflect on the social, moral, ethical and legal implications of an ICT-based solution to a specified problem

L.O. 5.4   Present arguments that relate to the social, moral, ethical and legal implications of a proposed ICT solution to a specified problem

Selecting your subject

You should choose a *major actual* application from one of these areas:

- industry
- commerce
- government
- society
- academia (education and research).

Ideally this should be a custom-built system for one specific application, such as the example given in the sample report of the system for handling passport applications. Alternatively it could be a system that has been customised to meet specific needs, such as student records in a particular college.

You may not be able to see the system at work directly, but you should be in a position to collect as much information as possible about it.

Here are some suggestions, but feel free to choose from many other applications:

- billing for services
- emergency services
- air traffic control

- booking system (for a particular airline, theatre, sports stadium, etc.)
- global positioning systems
- medical support and diagnosis
- travel agency
- online retailing and banking services
- restaurants and fast-food outlets
- manufacturing and production
- public information systems
- disability support systems
- hospital patient records.

You will try to come to some *conclusions* in your report. These should be consistent with your *research findings*.

Selecting the aspects

You should carry out some initial research to discover what the *main issues* are. Once you have identified a number of issues, decide whether they are social, legal, moral or political matters. Some complex issues may cross over these boundaries.

- **Social aspects** – See Chapters 8 and 29 for discussion about the social aspects of ICT solutions.
- **Legal aspects** – See Chapters 8 and 29 for an outline of the main legal constraints on the suppliers and users of ICT systems.
- **Moral aspects** – See Chapters 8 and 29 for discussion about the moral aspects. These chapters also examine the ethical responsibilities of IT professionals.
- **Political aspects** – The political implications of ICT systems are discussed in Chapter 8.

Carrying out your information gathering

Who is affected by the application?

You should consider all the groups of people who are affected, directly or indirectly, by the application. This list may help:

- those who drew up the original specification and monitored the project
- software developers
- technical staff (e.g. systems managers and administrators)
- non-technical staff who support the end-users (e.g. personnel officers)
- end-users (e.g. administrative staff)
- members of the general public who are directly affected by the application (e.g. customers, patients)
- members of the general public who are indirectly affected by the application (e.g. local residents)
- special-interest groups (e.g. disabled, non-English speakers)
- commentators on the system (e.g. journalists)
- lawyers
- politicians.

How do I find information?

Decide how you could obtain information about each group:

- from **primary sources** – by talking directly with them, or reading what they have written
- from **secondary sources** – by discovering what other writers have said or written about them.

Remember that few sources are completely objective. Comment on the possible bias of any source when using it in the report.

How do I provide evidence of my information gathering?

Keep a **research log** with dated notes on every piece of research that you do, *including any unsuccessful attempts to discover information*. The research log is the summary of the history of information gathering.

You should also keep safely any printed documents, notes on interviews, printouts from websites, newspaper cuttings, summaries of written material, etc.

If you have copied a large number of pages from a document, or have collected many pages printed from a website, then you should select the key documents for inclusion in your coursework. You could also summarise lengthy documents.

How can I get information from written sources?

You may want to get information from any of the following written sources: newspapers, magazines, books, leaflets, advertisements, forms, manuals. Cuttings should be annotated with the date and name of publication. If you cannot keep the material, perhaps because you have borrowed it, you should write a summary of the key information.

In each case, note in your research log the name of the publication, date published, author, etc.

How can I get information from the Internet?

Note on your research log the name of the organisation and URL of any site from which you obtain material. Try to decide how trustworthy the information is. Cross-reference with other sites and written material if necessary.

Here are some suggestions for websites that can be searched for up-to-date material:

- BBC and other television channels
- major newspapers
- government, local authorities
- Parliament, European Parliament, regional assemblies.

How can I get information from people?

If you want to interview someone then prepare your interview carefully in advance, and decide how you are going to record the information gained. You could transcribe an interview word for word, but it is usually better to summarise the main points.

You should decide how trustworthy your sources are, and also whether they represent accurately a wider population.

If you decide to carry out a survey, you need to select a set of respondents who will form a representative sample of all the people affected. You can draw general conclusions from your survey only if you are sure your sample is representative. If you have simply gathered a random selection of views, then you can state that the responses are *anecdotal*, but that they may be indicative of widely held views.

Are there any other sources of information?

You may use any other sources of information, such as television programmes that you have seen. Keep a note in your research log of the programme title, date and channel on which it was broadcast, and give a summary of the contents. You should also give the names of anyone you wish to quote. Try to record the programme so you can go back and transcribe interesting comments.

You may want to search multimedia systems, such as encyclopedias. Once again, make sure that you record any useful finds on your research log.

How do I avoid plagiarism?

Plagiarism *is passing off someone else's work as your own.* Submitting a report that was written by someone else is obviously wrong and could lead to disqualification by the Examination Board.

But it is still possible to plagiarise unintentionally, by not adhering to the conventions that apply to academic work. For example, you may want to include a quote from a book you have read. This is always acceptable provided you *make it clear that it is a quote*, and you state where it is from. If you simply copy extracts from a written source and do not credit the original author, then you are plagiarising their work.

The problem becomes more difficult when you read a book, find some useful material and then summarise it in your own words in your report. Even though you are not directly quoting from your source, you should still acknowledge where the material or ideas came from.

Writing the report

How should I present the main report?

The report itself carries only half the total possible marks for Task 3, so you should ensure that you have provided plenty of background material in the first two sections!

Task 3 requires you to write a report, not an essay. This means that you can use any of the following throughout the report:

- headings
- sub-headings

- bullet points
- footnotes
- diagrams and charts
- tables
- headers and footers.

The subject specification makes it clear that you can structure your report however you like. But you should try to make it easy for the examiner to give you marks where you deserve them. If the report is presented in an unorganised way the reader may miss important parts.

When you discuss one of your chosen aspects you should consider at least two points of view. These could be:

- advantages and disadvantages of implementing the application for all involved
- the differing views of groups of people affected by the application
- the intended outcomes of the application compared with any unintentional outcomes
- the short-term and long-term effects.

You should attempt to keep a balance between these alternative views, even though you may have strong opinions of your own.

At the end of the report you should summarise the main arguments and come to a conclusion. If there are any undesirable side-effects you should discuss how these could be handled.

Quality of language and presentation

The main report should be presented clearly and attractively, which also gives you an opportunity to demonstrate your technical skills in word-processing. In the marking scheme, up to 5 marks are awarded for quality of presentation and language. Here is a checklist to use when your main report is complete:

☐ Have I checked the report for spelling and grammar?

☐ Have I checked that the report is readable and makes sense to a new reader?

☐ Have I numbered the pages (preferably in a footer)?

☐ Have I included my name in a header or footer on each page?

☐ Have I selected suitable text styles for headings, the main body of the text, headers and footers? (The styles should be consistent throughout the report, and should be clear and businesslike.)

☐ Have I included a contents page?

Assessment of Task 3

How does the mark scheme work?

Maximum marks are shown in square brackets. The maximum possible total is 40 marks.

- **Preparation for the report**
  - Identification of the major issues [10]
  - History of information gathering [10]

- **The report**
  - Quality of presentation and language [5]
  - Depth of treatment of the identified issues [5]
  - Consistency of argument [5]
  - Validity of conclusions in the context of the arguments given [5]

Writing up Task 3

This coursework task should be presented in two parts, in much the same way as Task 1.

The *preparation for the report* is addressed to the examiner and provides evidence of how you planned, researched and developed the task.

The *report* itself is addressed to an 'audience' other than the examiner. It could be a report for publication in an IT or general interest magazine; or it could be a report for a non-IT senior manager in an organisation. This part should be capable of being read and understood independently of the first part. You may feel that you are repeating some of the material, but because the preparation part is addressed to a different reader from the report, you should not be writing exactly the same in each.

Preparation for the report [20 marks]

1. Identification of the major issues
[10 marks]

The report should make it clear from the outset as to what particular implications of the application are to be considered. Moreover the report should argue why these aspects are identified as being of importance.

1.1 Description of the application
- Describe the application and explain your interest in it.

1.2 Implications of the application
- Identify the particular implications that you will be discussing.
- Identify the aspects (sociological, legal, moral, political) that you will be considering.

2. History of information gathering
[10 marks]

A significant part of this task will be the process of gathering raw information. The nature and the sources of this information are relevant with regard to the credibility of the report; thus it is important that the sources be described.

2.1 Research log
- This contains dated entries of all your research.

2.2 Sources of information
- Identify sources, and comment on their relevance and trustworthiness.

2.3 Information collected
- Provide copies of original documents (where relevant).
- Give summaries of source materials.
- Include notes on interviews and other research findings.

The report (Give it a suitable title)
[20 marks]

Title page

Contents

Acknowledgements

. . .

You may structure the main body of the report in any way you like.

CHAPTER 33

Examination questions and mark schemes for unit 4

This chapter provides examination questions and mark schemes for unit 4: Systems management. Edexcel has given permission for the use here of this copyright material.

Note that some of the questions are not full-length questions. Questions for the current specification will normally be marked out of 19 (although totals of 18 or 20 are possible).

Specimen examination questions

1. There is some evidence that certain specialist ICT systems are better at diagnosing illness than are many highly respected medical consultants.

   (a) Describe *three* features of ICT systems that allow them to out-perform, in certain areas, the intelligent behaviour of human beings.
   [9 marks]

   (b) ICT-based systems exist that enable patients to diagnose their own ailments. Discuss the *social, moral* and *legal* implications of such systems.
   [6 marks]

   (c) Describe, with justification, one other application of ICT that may be challenging the intellectual capabilities of the human species.
   [4 marks]

   Edexcel specimen paper

2. A systems manager of a large company provides a number of ICT facilities, including word-processing, across the company via a network. Recently the users of the word-processing facility have complained that it is out of date and can be slow.

   (a) Describe how the systems manager could devise the criteria for proposing a replacement word-processing facility.
   [3 marks]

   (b) Many modern word-processing packages can work in a multitasking environment.

   Describe one circumstance where the facility to multi-task might be beneficial. [3 marks]

   (c) The systems manager is considering the complaint that the word-processing facility can be slow. She can set the operating system to support either cooperative or pre-emptive multi-tasking. She thinks that pre-emptive multi-tasking would better serve her customers. Explain why the systems manager might think this way. [4 marks]

   (d) State *one* problem disabled people might have using the new word-processing package, and describe a software solution to the problem. [2 marks]

   Edexcel specimen paper

3. A large insurance company contains a specialist unit researching into the insurance claims for personal injury. One reason for this research is that there is a suspicion that some claims are fraudulent.

   Part of the research involves examining a variety of documents to extract specific information that has to be entered on to a pre-designed paper form. The forms are currently analysed manually. The results have to be double-checked for accuracy.

   The person in charge of the unit has approached the company's ICT systems manager about computerising the analysis of the data.

(a) The systems manager has decided to investigate the possible cost implications of the proposed system. Describe *one* benefit of the computerisation of the data analysis. Describe how the benefits may be costed.

[4 marks]

(b) Once the systems manager understands the nature of the data that will have to be stored on the computer system, she has concerns about the legal and moral issues that may be involved. Discuss what these issues might be.

[4 marks]

(c) The computerisation has been given the go ahead but it will involve the purchase of some new equipment. Describe *two* advantages of leasing the necessary equipment rather than buying it. [2 marks]

(d) Once the required hardware and software have been installed, they must be rigorously tested before real data can be entered and analysed. State *five* main tests that must be carried out on the installed system. [5 marks]

(e) The insurance company is a very large organisation using computers for a wide variety of applications, many of which are essential for the smooth running of the organisation. Describe how the systems manager can minimise the risk of computer systems becoming unusable either through user ignorance or hardware malfunction.

[4 marks]

Edexcel specimen paper

4. The management of Safebury's supermarkets has decided to introduce a loyalty card scheme. Customers will earn 'points' according to how much they spend. Points will be redeemed against special offers. When the system is in place, it will operate like this:

- Customers sign up to the scheme by filling in a form with their personal details.

- Each customer is issued with a loyalty card which contains a unique reference number on a magnetic strip.

- When goods are bought, the bar codes are scanned at the checkout and then the customer's loyalty card is 'swiped'.

- Points are credited to the customer.

- A record is made of the transaction.

Safebury's already has a computerised electronic funds transfer at point of sale (EFTPOS) system and stock control system.

(a) Describe *two* advantages to Safebury's of introducing the loyalty card scheme.

[4 marks]

(b) There are contractors who could provide the hardware and software necessary to implement this application. The systems manager invites several contractors to bid for the job. Describe, with reasons, *three* essential items of information that the systems manager needs to supply to prospective contractors. [6 marks]

(c) State and explain *three* criteria that the systems manager could use in order to decide which contractor to recommend to management. [5 marks]

Edexcel pilot specification, Summer 2000

5. Clark, the systems manager of a company, believes that it would be a good idea to change the company's network operating system. He produces a report for the managing director that details his arguments. An extract is given below.

The existing network needs to be upgraded to a 250-workstation star configuration. Our network operating system licences allow up to 100 concurrent users. We shall need to buy more licences. Alternatively, it could be a good time to consider changing to a new operating system, which has no limit on the number of users. Another advantage is that, unlike the existing operating system, it supports the same communications protocol as is used on the Internet.

(a) Describe *two* other essential considerations that Clark would have included in this report.

[4 marks]

(b) (i) Explain the term 'protocol' in this context. [2 marks]

(ii) State *two* advantages of the company's Network Operating System using the same protocol as the Internet. [4 marks]

(c) An upgrade proposal has been agreed. This upgrade includes the installation of additional workstations and a change to the new network operating system. Produce an outline plan for an upgrade, taking into account the tasks that will be performed and how it will have an impact on staff. [5 marks]

Edexcel pilot specification, Summer 2000

6. A company has introduced Internet access for all its employees so that they can carry out research. The systems manager has been told by a department head that Jay has been misusing this facility. The systems manager is asked by management to monitor Jay's Internet activities. Software is installed which maintains a log of Jay's Internet activity.

   (a) State *three* items of data that could be collected in the monitoring process. For each one, comment on how it could contribute to the investigation. [6 marks]

   (b) Discuss the moral implications of the systems manager performing this monitoring process. [4 marks]

   (c) The company's manager is worried that other employees are also misusing the system and asks the systems manager to set up procedures to monitor all the company's Internet users. The systems manager is uneasy about this request. Explain *two* reasons for the systems manager's unease. [4 marks]

   (d) The systems manager suggests that instead of monitoring all users, it would be preferable to draw up guidelines for the employees' use of the Internet. Give *three* distinct points that should be included in the guidelines, with a reasoned justification for each. [6 marks]

Edexcel pilot specification, Summer 2000

Mark schemes

1

This question is about the features of ICT systems that allow them to outperform humans, and not about features that enable the mimicking of humans.

1 (a)
ICT systems can store unlimited knowledge from a range of human sources; thus the ICT system's body of knowledge can be potentially greater than that of any individual. An ICT system can process the knowledge in at least three distinct ways:

- It can be structured as a database that can be interrogated by a number of structured rules.
- It can examine a vast number of combinations of input states and make comparisons with standard possibilities.
- ICT systems can control multimedia delivery systems and thus present a range of stimuli and information in a context that could not be matched by a human.

0–3 marks for each of three distinct points. [9]

1 (b)
Any question at Advanced level that asks the candidate to 'discuss' requires balanced arguments for full marks. Good arguments that are confined to one side of the argument are unlikely to gain more than half marks.

Below are some possible points. Each valid point within a balanced context would gain a maximum of two marks. [6]

- *Social*: Ease of access to knowledge. Large body of knowledge gives in-built second opinions. Potential for social manipulation by suppression of selected information. Reduction of human interaction skills, importance of human comfort.
- *Moral*: Greater equality of opportunity to have access to knowledge (the moral argument that knowledge belongs to all). The dangers of such unlimited access without advice and human interaction.
- *Legal*: Possibility of extensive vetting of the stored knowledge due to the legal obligations of the providers of the system. Individual humans being less accountable.

1 (c)
The examiner must be prepared for a range of responses here. Just a description of two applications, for example chess and financial advice, could gain half the possible marks.

To obtain full marks the candidate must explain how the intellectual capability of a human is challenged. [4]

2 (a)

The candidate is asked about the process of devising criteria, not what the criteria should be. Four distinct relevant information-gathering techniques or processes are required, maybe including: [3]

- Find out problems from user.
- Find out requirements from user.
- Look in press, Internet, ask companies/associates etc. for details of suitable package.
- Send off for literature.
- Arrange for trials/presentations.
- Report on how each package meets the requirements.
- Select package in conjunction with user representatives.

2 (b)

The candidate may describe a circumstance that is totally within the WP environment, for example **when repagination or printing in the background is taking place.** *Alternatively the candidate may describe the use of another application whilst word-processing, for example* **embedding a spreadsheet or a database report.** *For any case the candidate must describe the advantage in the context of what would happen if the facility were not available.* [3]

2 (c)

- Keyboard generates interrupt.
- Background program suspended.
- Input dealt with.
- Background program continues. [2]

The advantage of pre-emptive multi-tasking is that the processor is not taken over by long-running tasks such as complex mathematical analysis. [1]

If the ICT manager provides a general service, then it is likely to be better for most users to have the OS switch the power of the processor to give all applications a chance to use it. [1]

2 (d)

- Trouble distinguishing colours/eyestrain – change colour configuration.
- Difficulty using mouse – change sensitivity/speed.
- Difficulty using keyboard – slow down auto repeat.
[2]

3 (a)

- Much faster analysis of the data, leading to fewer researchers being needed.
- More accurate results, less checking needed, leading to fewer researchers needed.

Two marks each. [4]

3 (b)

The candidate should frame their discussion in the context of the preamble to the question; i.e. the investigation of fraudulent insurance claims. Special issues could include:

- Implications of storing personal information.
- The need for meticulous accuracy of the data in case of use of the data in legal process.
- The concern of possible conflict between her moral responsibilities to the company and to the customers.
- The possibility that data could make indirect reference to other members of staff. Then, from a moral point of view, should they be informed?

Two marks each for any two points in context. [4]

3 (c)

- Does not need large sum of money up front.
- Leasing company responsible for hardware maintenance.
- Often get (fairly) new equipment.

One mark for each of two points. [2]

3 (d)

- Can log on from all workstations.
- Test all login codes allowing access to the network.
- Test login codes allowing access to the right packages.
- Test major options of every package, especially saving and printing.
- Test directory and data file security.
- Test backing up and restoration.

One mark for each point. [5]

3 (e)

- Ensure all new staff are appropriately trained.
- All systems are documented.
- Hardware is regularly serviced.
- All enhancements are tested.

- All systems are secure.
- All systems are protected from viruses.

One mark for each of four points. [4]

---

4 (a)
- *Information*: A record can be made of transactions, thereby learning customer buying habits.
- *Sales*: Customers are likely to return in order to accumulate points. Special offers possible, such as double points.

Two marks for each of two advantages explained. [4]

4 (b)
- Existing file formats – to allow coexistence of new facilities with legacy systems.
- Existing hardware/software – to allow coexistence.
- Budgetary constraints.
- Time frame – to allow contractor to properly plan the project.
- Details of existing network.

Statistics such as:
- Number of transactions per time period/number of customers expected to allow storage to be estimated.
- Quantitative data, such as record sizes to allow storage to be estimated.

Two marks for each of three specific items of information explained. [6]

4 (c)
- Company track record.
- Time quoted to complete job.
- Cost.
- Compatibility with legacy systems.
- Quality of the report.
- Support issues examined.

One mark for each of any three factors. A reasonable explanation of any one factor, such as given below, would attract another two marks. [3]

Examination of previous contracts fulfilled by the company would provide useful indicators as to whether the company would perform well in this case. Company accounts could be looked at.

5 (a)
- Operational advantage, such as less maintenance time and hence cost savings.
- Reference site as demo of system successfully in action.
- Costings.
- Compatibility with applications software.
- Training issues examined.

Two marks for each of two commented issues. [4]

5 (b)
(i) Rules for interconnectivity such as packet sizes/construction/speed of transmission/cabling/data format/error detection/example quoted. [2]

(ii)
- No need for gateways, reducing complexity, costs and skill levels/training required.
- Possible to directly address from outside/management and access considerations.
- Simplicity of management, especially in WAN setting.

Two marks for each of two explained considerations. [4]

5 (c)
Tasks:
- Migrate user accounts.
- Alter configurations of workstations.
- Install NOS software.
- Testing.
- Construct directory structure.
- Arrange print facilities.
- Groups and permissions.
- Organise security.
- Install workstations.
- Retraining.
- Allowances made for disruption.
- Phasing in.
- Any evidence of awareness that stages must be properly sequenced, such as fitting in with other business plans, or idea of first install hardware, then software, then user accounts.

One mark for each of five distinct points. [5]

6 (a)

- Sites visited: to see if they are work-related.
- Examine history files/cookies for evidence of sites visited.
- Time online: to see if this may be excessive.
- Workstation used: to see who was the probable user.
- Login used: identity issues.
- Login time/date: implications for presence at work – during working hours.

Any three items, one mark for item, one mark for reason. [6]

6 (b)

The event is in work time, so no marks for invasion-of-privacy ideas.

- The firm has a right to expect its staff to use company time only for legitimate activities.
- Possibility of company reputation being damaged if unsuitable Internet activity.
- Worker not doing his/her job while misusing facilities.
- Possibility of causing offence to other staff.
- Offence caused to Jay by lack of trust.

Two marks for each of two points. [4]

6 (c)

The main idea is that the systems manager has better things to do than chase misuse, and this is an unpleasant extra burden.

- Unease that time is being spent chasing this problem which could be better spent doing normal job/other cost/resource implications.
- Unease about spying on colleague.
- Possibility of destroying colleague's reputation/ livelihood.

Two marks for each of two reasoned points. [4]

6 (d)

These are guidelines for staff, not system resources/ additions.

- Only use Internet for work-related matters as time is paid for by company.
- No downloading of software/inappropriate material: risk of viruses/excessive use of company resources/illegality issues.
- No visiting chat rooms: time wasted.
- Hints on how to make efficient searches.

Two marks for each of three justified points. [6]

THE IMPLEMENTATION
OF EVENT-DRIVEN
APPLICATIONS

CHAPTER 34

Programming concepts

This chapter develops the fundamental concepts of program development which were introduced in Chapter 16. It introduces these largely through a brief study of BASIC.

This chapter covers this Learning Outcome in the specification:

L.O. 5.1 Demonstrate knowledge of fundamental computer programming constructs

It also covers these Technical Knowledge topics:

T5.1.1   Language and translation
T5.1.2   Static load libraries
T5.1.3   Dynamic link libraries (DLLs)
T5.2.2   Client–server concepts

In Chapter 16 you were introduced to the range of programming languages that have been developed over the years, and to the mechanism by which the source code of a program is edited, complied and linked to create an executable program. In this chapter we will look in more detail at how programs are actually written. You will be shown several different simple programs written in BASIC and C++. This chapter is not a tutorial on these languages, so do not worry if you do not understand everything about the programs. The important thing is to grasp the basic concepts used in writing programs.

Full Solutions, you will recall, is a software house. They write major software applications for public bodies such as hospitals, and have recently branched out into the mass market with a product called 'Fitness Matters'. Programmers employed by Full Solutions have built up experience with a number of programming language. Different languages, and types of language, have different strengths and tend to get used for different purposes. Full Solutions, therefore, do not use one language exclusively.

Introduction to BASIC

Prior to the dominance of windows-based systems in the computing world, most commercial programming, including the projects undertaken by Full Solutions, was done using traditional procedural languages such as COBOL, BASIC and C. Programs written using these languages took their input from the keyboard, and the formatting of their output was entirely up to the programmer (as we shall see later, this is in contrast to windows programming languages).

The BASIC (Beginners' All-purpose Symbolic Instruction Code) language was written specifically as a teaching language, but its simplicity has made it very popular. We shall therefore introduce the major concepts of programming using this language.

Simple programs in BASIC

The examples in this book are written for Quick Basic®, a Microsoft product that was provided with version 5 of MS-DOS®. (If you want to experiment with these programs you may be able to find someone with a set of disks with Quick Basic® on them, or the programs should work with most other versions of BASIC.)

Tradition demands that the first program you write in a new language is the 'hello world' program, so here is the BASIC version:

```
10 REM hello world program, author: Alan Jarvis
20 PRINT "Hello World"
```

BASIC, as we have said, is a simple language, so the 'hello world' program ends up being very simple indeed, with just two instructions. The first of these, using the REM instruction (which stands for 'remark'), is ignored by the computer as it is what is called a *comment*. It is good programming practice to include comments in your programs as it helps other people understand what they do and who wrote them.

Introducing variables

To grasp a little more about how programs work in general, and BASIC in particular, we need to look at a slightly more complex program. This program takes two numbers and adds them together, and conveniently demonstrates the three main things anything but the most simple program must do, that is, accept some input, do some processing and produce some output.

It also demonstrates a fundamental concept of programming, the declaration and use of *variables*. Variables are named areas of memory used to store data while the program is working on it. You have already learned that in database systems data is stored in fields which are given a name and a datatype. Variables are similar in concept in that, like fields, they have a name, chosen by the programmer, and a datatype which is dictated by the type of data they will store (e.g. numeric, text etc.). However, unlike database fields, variables are temporary storage areas which exist only while the program runs (or in some cases, while part of the program runs).

```
10    REM Simple calculator
```

> The next lines declare (create) three variables using the DIM command. Each variable has a name (e.g. number1) and a datatype (in this case they are all Integer – whole numbers).

```
20    DIM number1 As Integer
30    DIM number2 As Integer
40    DIM answer As Integer
```

```
50    PRINT "Enter the first number"
```

> The next lines use the PRINT command to output messages to the screen, and INPUT to collect the user's responses and place them in the variables.

```
60    INPUT number1
70    PRINT "Enter the second number"
80    INPUT number2
```

> The next line does the calculation.

```
90    answer = number1 + number2
```

> This line outputs the result.

```
100   PRINT "The answer is"; answer
```

Activity

Variables can be given any name as long as they start with a letter and do not contain any spaces, so 'x' and 'y' would work just as well as 'number1' and 'number2'. Why might variable names like 'x' and 'y' not be a good idea?

Making choices

In the example above, the program runs from the first line through to the last and then stops. This is not a very typical example of how a real-life program would work.

Programs usually need, at some point, to select between alternative courses of action based on some criteria. For example, the program above could be modified so the user could choose to either add or subtract the two numbers; the program would need to select addition or subtraction based on the choice the user made. This is normally done using the IF command, which is similar to the IF function you have come across in spreadsheets. A modified version of the above program with the functionality added to either addition or subtraction is shown below:

```
10    REM simple calculator, version 2
20    DIM number1 As Integer
30    DIM number2 As Integer
```

```
40    DIM answer As Integer
```

```
50    DIM opcode As String
60    PRINT "Enter the first number"
70    INPUT number1
80    PRINT "Enter the second number"
90    INPUT number2
100   PRINT "Enter + for add, or – for subtract"
110   INPUT opcode
```

The next lines make the choice between addition and subtraction based on the value in opcode.

```
120   IF opcode = "+" THEN answer = number1 + number2
130   IF opcode = "–" THEN answer = number1 – number2
140   PRINT "The answer is"; answer
```

Activity

Modify the program so that it can do multiplication and division as well.

Loops

As well as making selections, programs often need to carry out some commands repeatedly. This is done using a *loop*. For example, the program above will run only once, but what if the user wanted to do a whole series of calculations? Rather than running the program again and again it could be modified to run until the user indicated that it was to stop.

There are a number of commands that can be used to put loops into BASIC programs. The following uses the WHILE command which loops until some condition is met:

```
10    REM Simple calculator with loop
20    DIM number1 As Integer
30    DIM number2 As Integer
40    DIM answer As Integer
50    DIM opcode As String
```

A variable is needed to store the user's response as to whether or not they want to exit. 'Exit' is the variable name, and its datatype is STRING.

```
60    DIM exit As String
```

The DO WHILE command puts the lines of the program between here and the LOOP command (line 190) into a loop until the exit variable is set to 'X'.

```
70    DO WHILE exit <> "X"
80       PRINT "Enter the first number"
90       INPUT number1
100      PRINT "Enter the second number"
110      INPUT number2
120      PRINT "Enter + for add, or – for subtract"
130      INPUT opcode
140      IF opcode = "+" THEN answer = number1 + number2
150      IF opcode = "-" THEN answer = number1 – number2
160      PRINT "The answer is"; answer
```

The next line asks the user whether he or she wants to exit the program. If the user types an 'X' then the condition in line 70 will be true and the loop will end.

```
170      PRINT "Type X to exit, or any other key to do another sum"
180      INPUT exit
190   LOOP
200   PRINT "Good bye"
```

Summary

In these simple examples you have seen that programs do three fundamental things:

- *input* – using the INPUT instruction in BASIC
- *output* – using the PRINT instruction in BASIC
- *processing* – using a variety of instructions.

The path the program follows through the instructions can be:

- *sequence* – in other words the instructions simply follow one after another
- *selection* – a choice is made between several paths based on some criteria
- *loop* – a series of instructions are repeated.

Introduction to C++

The BASIC language in the form shown in the previous section is no longer widely used for commercial programming. One traditional language that is still widely used is C++. The calculator program described above, but written in C++, is shown below:

```
#include <iostream.h>
int number1;
int number2;
int answer;
char opcode;
char exit;
void main()
{
   while (exit != 'X')
   {
      cout << "Enter first number";
      cin >> number1;
      cout << "Enter second number";
      cin >> number2;
      cout << "Enter + for add, or – for subtract";
      cin >> opcode;
      if (opcode == '+')
      {
         answer = number2 + number1;
      }
      if (opcode == '-')
      {
         answer = number2 – number1;
      }
      cout << "The answer is " << answer << "\n";
      cout << "Type X to exit, or any other key to do another sum";
      cin >> exit;
   }
   cout << "goodbye\n";
}
```

Apart from the use of 'cin' and 'cout' rather than INPUT and OUTPUT the two examples look pretty similar. However, C++ and BASIC are really quite different languages. The reason they look similar is because we have used only the basic features. It is only when you write large and complex programs that the differences between the languages really begin to show.

There are a couple of other things to bear in mind about C++, before we look at some more features of programming languages:

- Unlike BASIC, C++ is case-sensitive. All the instructions must be in *lower case*, and as far as variable names are concerned 'number1' and 'Number1' are different. Notice also that C++ does not use line numbers.

- Sections of C++ programs are divided up by pairs of curly brackets – {like this}. So where you have the instruction

  While (exit != 'X')

it is followed by a curly bracket. This instruction means *do everything between the matching set of curly brackets while the variable exit is not set to X.* This might sound straightforward, but then a few lines down in the program we find this instruction:

```
if (opcode == '+')
{
```

This means *if the variable opcode is set to '+' then do everything between the next set of curly brackets.* So you end up with curly brackets within curly brackets. This can be confusing, which is why C++ programs should always be indented as in the example shown, and at each new opening curly bracket the instructions are indented further. At an ending curly bracket the indent is reduced again.

Just to prove that the curly brackets are in pairs, go though the program and number each pair of curly brackets; you should find four pairs.

- Something else that you may have noticed as odd is the 'if' instruction, as in:

  if (opcode == '+')

  Why does it have two equals signs instead of just one? The answer is that one equals sign and two equals signs have different meanings:

  (opcode = '+') is an *assignment*; it sets the variable opcode to the value '+'

  (opcode == '+') is a *comparison*; it compares the value in opcode with '+'

- Each instruction in C++ ends with a semi-colon, unless it is followed by a curly bracket.

As you can see from just this small program, the syntax of C++ is more complex than that of BASIC, which makes it a more difficult language to learn. However, the trade-off is that the more complex syntax and sophisticated facilities give C++ greater flexibility and power, which is why it is often the choice of professional programmers.

Activity

Have a look at a website that specialises in jobs for computer programmers – there is a section on www.yahoo.co.uk for this, but there are many more. See which programming languages are in the most demand.

Using C++

You might imagine that, with the dominance of Windows®, traditional languages are no longer used. However this is not the case as there are many situations where programs need to be written which do not have significant (or, in some cases, any) interaction with the end-user. Networking control software, device drivers, and database management control software are just some examples of low-level (i.e. closer to the complex internal workings of the computer rather than the user) software which would normally be written using a traditional programming language such as C++. Such languages are powerful, create efficient code (i.e. programs that run quickly), and allow the programmer to manipulate the internal workings of the computer.

As previously described, Full Solutions developed and launched the 'Fitness Matters' software. The majority of the application is written in the event-driven, windows-based programming language called Visual Basic®. However, when they wanted to interface the software to electronic weighing scales and heart-rate monitors, they needed to write device drivers to communicate with these microprocessor-controlled devices. They used the C++ language as it gave them greater control over the hardware interface.

Programming constructs

To grasp the fundamental concepts of program writing we will continue to look at some programming examples written in BASIC. In the next chapter, however, we will move on to look at a widely used commercial language, Visual Basic®, which – as its name suggests – has its roots in the BASIC we are looking at here.

Variables and arrays

We have already come across the concept of variables – these are the named memory areas that the program uses to store data. Suppose you worked for a small company and you wanted to write a program to store the number of hours that each of the company's employees worked each week, and calculate their wages. If the company had five employees you could have five different variables in the program to store their hours, like this (the Single datatype defines a floating point number that is stored using 32 bits (as opposed to the double-data type which uses 64 bits)):

```
10      DIM emp1 As Single
20      DIM emp2 As Single
```

```
30      DIM emp3 As Single
40      DIM emp4 As Single
50      DIM emp5 As Single
```

This would work but it is not very efficient, especially if your company had 50 employees. In these situations you need an *array*. An **array** provides more than one memory area for the variable, each one of which is numbered. So to define an array for the five employees you would type:

```
10      DIM employee(4) As Single
```

This defines a five-element array, which can be referenced as 'employee(0)', 'employee(1)' and so on.

The number by which each element of the array is referenced is called the *array index*. This can be a variable itself so, for example, the whole array could be printed using a loop. Programming languages number their arrays from zero; but since real-world objects, such as employees, are normally numbered from 1, the example program that follows uses a six-element array but element 0 is not used.

This program allows the user to enter the hours for all the employees, then prints them all out. This program uses a new type of loop. We have already seen the WHILE loop which runs while some condition is true. The FOR loop runs a fixed number of times, and uses a variable to count the number of times the program goes around the loop (called the *loop counter*). The general form of the FOR loop is:

```
50      FOR loop_counter = 1 TO 10
60          Instruction
70          Instruction
80      NEXT loop_counter
```

Here, 'loop_counter' is the name of the variable used as the loop counter. The loop will start at 1 and run to 10 (as controlled by the expression 'loop_counter = 1 TO 10'). The instruction at line 80 ends the loop. Each time the program reaches this point the 'loop counter' will be incremented, so the first time around the loop the 'loop_counter' variable will be set to 1, the second time around the loop it will be set to 2 and so on until it reaches 10. The program looks like this:

```
10      REM Example of an array
20      DIM employee(5) As Single
30      DIM counter As Integer
40      PRINT "Wages calculator"
50      FOR counter = 1 TO 5
60          PRINT "Enter hours for employee"; counter
70          INPUT employee(counter)
```

The loop counter is used as the array index counter.

```
80      NEXT counter
90      PRINT "Hours list"
100         FOR counter = 1 TO 5
110             PRINT "Employee number",counter; employee(counter)
120     NEXT counter
```

The FOR loop doesn't end with LOOP, like a WHILE loop. It ends with NEXT and the loop counter variable.

The output of the program looks is shown in Figure 34.1.

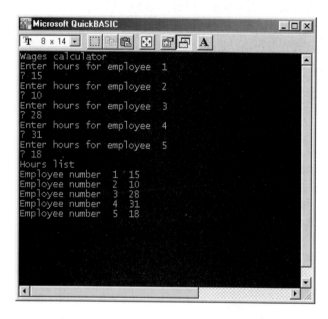

Figure 34.1 *The screen output of the wages calculator example*

Arrays are powerful data structures and are widely used in commercial programming.

Activity

What is a two-dimensional array? Try to find out, and see whether you can think of an application for one.

More about the IF instruction

We have already looked, in the previous program, at how the programming construct of selection can be coded using the IF instruction. However, we used only a one-line IF instruction, like this:

```
130     IF opcode = "+" THEN answer = number1 + number2
```

In most circumstances there is more than one instruction to be carried out if the result of the comparison is true. There may also be instruction to be carried out if the comparison is not true. In BASIC the ELSEIF and END IF instructions are used. These instructions are used like this:

```
100     IF x=1 THEN
120         Instruction
130         Instruction
150     ELSEIF x=2 THEN
160         Instruction
130         Instruction
140     END IF
```

Let us see how this works in a real program. The following is another version of the wages calculator, but this time the user can enter the hours for each employee in any order, rather than using a FOR loop as in the last example. The program displays a simple menu, with three choices, and it is in processing the choice the user makes that the IF, ELSEIF and END IF instructions are used:

```
10      REM Wages calculator
20      DIM hours(5) As Single
30      DIM choice As Integer
40      DIM rate As Integer
50      DIM empno As Integer
60      DIM counter As Integer
70      PRINT "Wages calculator"
80      rate = 2
90      DO WHILE choice <> 3
100         PRINT "Type 1 to enter hours, 2 to calculate wages or 3 to
                exit"
110         INPUT choice
120         IF choice = 1 THEN
130             PRINT "Enter employee number"
140             INPUT empno
150             PRINT "Enter hours"
160             INPUT hours(empno)
170         ELSEIF choice = 2 THEN
180             PRINT "Wages are:"
190             FOR counter = 1 TO 5
200                 PRINT "Employee"; counter; "£"; hours(counter) * rate
210             NEXT counter
220         END IF
230     LOOP
240     PRINT "Goodbye"
```

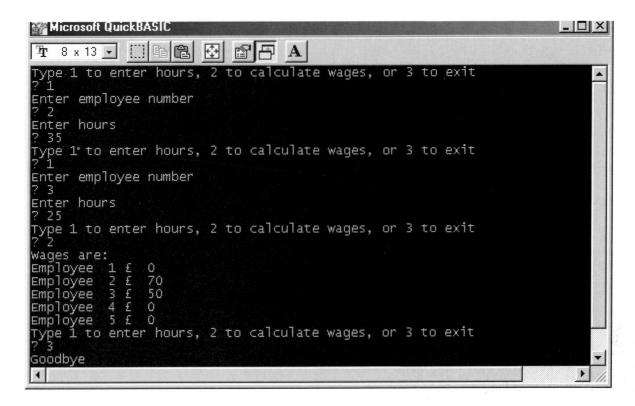

Figure 34.2 *The screen output of the enhanced wages calculator example*

The output of this program would look something like Figure 34.2.

Runtime errors

The program shown above works fine as long as the user follows the on-screen instructions and obeys certain rules.

However, in real life the user can rarely be relied upon to keep to these restrictions. For example, the array used to store the employee hours has only five elements, but what happens if you type in 6 for the employee number? There isn't an element 6 in the array, so the program crashes with an error message. This would not be acceptable in a commercial program, so code must be added to prevent operator errors like this causing the program to crash.

In fact quite a high proportion of the code included in commercial programs is there to protect the user from the consequences of erroneous actions. What is needed here is something that will check what the user has entered; if it is greater than 5, it should display an error message and ask for the employee number again. This can be done with a DO WHILE loop which exits

the loop only when the employee number is less than 6. If the user enters an employee number less that 6 the first time, the loop never runs; but if a number over 5 is entered a message is displayed and the employee number must be input again.

```
120    PRINT "Enter employee number"
130    INPUT empno
140    DO WHILE empno > 5
150        PRINT "Employee number must be between 1 and 5"
160        INPUT empno
170    LOOP
180    PRINT "Enter hours"
190    INPUT hours(empno)
```

Activity

The solution, given above, to the problem of entering the employee number incorrectly does not solve the problem completely. There are still several ways in which operator error (or deliberate misuse!) while entering the employee number would crash the program. Can you think what they might be?

User-defined datatypes

The technique of defining names and datatypes for variables has already been described, but so far we have used only the pre-defined datatypes (such as Integer, String and Single) that are part of the BASIC language. It is also possible to create your own, so-called user-defined, datatypes. This facility is useful when you are dealing with a group of variables that naturally fit together but have different datatypes. To create a user-defined datatype you use the TYPE and END TYPE instructions, like this:

```
TYPE emptype
        idnumber As Integer
        empname As String * 20
        rate As Single
    END TYPE
```

This creates a new datatype called 'emptype', which can store data on the employee's i.d. number, name ('STRING * 20' reserves memory space for 20 characters) and pay rate. Once a new datatype has been created it can be used to create a variable like any other:

```
DIM manager As emptype
```

You can reference the individual components of the datatype like this:

```
manager.empname = "Wendy Smith"
```

When creating a variable using a user-defined datatype, you can, of course, create an array, as shown in the program below, which is a version of the one described earlier, this time utilising a user-defined datatype.

```
10      REM user-defined datatypes
20      TYPE emptype
            idnumber As Integer
            empname As String * 20
            rate As Single
        END TYPE
```

Next, an array of six of the variables called 'employee' are created with the datatype of 'emptype'.

```
30      DIM employee(5) AS emptype
40      DIM counter As Integer
50      FOR counter = 1 TO 5
60          employee(counter).idnumber = counter
70          PRINT "Enter name of employee number"; counter
80          INPUT employee(counter).empname
90          PRINT "Enter pay rate"
100         INPUT employee(counter).rate
110     NEXT counter
```

```
120     PRINT "Employee List"
130     FOR counter = 1 TO 5
140         PRINT "Employee number"; counter
150         PRINT "Name"; employee(counter).empname
160         PRINT "Rate: £"; employee(counter).rate
170     NEXT counter
180     PRINT "Goodbye"
```

Modular programming

So far the programs we have looked at have been linear – that is, they start at the beginning, they go through the various instructions (perhaps with some repetition and selection), and they reach the end and stop. That is fine for simple programs, but as programs get more complex it is good practice to split them into a number of self-contained sections, called *procedures* (some programming languages call them *functions* or *sub-routines*).

Procedures

Procedures have a number of benefits:

- Procedures are *reusable*. Typically, there are a number of times within a program when a particular function needs to be carried out – e.g. displaying an error message or validating user input such as a date. By putting the instructions for this function into a procedure, the instructions only have to be written once. The procedure can then be run as many times as desired within the program.

- Procedures are *easier to write*. A program that is split into a number of procedures is easier to write, especially if it is written by a team of programmers because each person can be allocated a particular procedure to work on.

- Procedures are *easier to understand*. Programs that are split into procedures are easier for programmers to read and understand than one long program. This makes it easier to spot mistakes and to solve programming errors.

Well-written procedures are self-contained, rather like a program within a program. They carry out a clearly defined function and they don't rely on other parts of the program. This means that, when there is more than one programmer working on a suite of programs, one programmer can use the functions that a procedure written by another programmer provides, without having to understand how the procedure works.

The programs we have looked at so far are so simple that it is hardly worth dividing them into procedures; however we will look at an example to see how this important programming technique actually works. The latest version of the wages calculator we looked at did three basic things:

- It provided a menu for the user to choose the required options.
- It allowed the user to input the hours worked by employees.
- It calculated and displayed the wages due to all the employees.

A sensible way to divide the program into procedures would be to construct the main program out of the loop that displays the menu and then processes the user's choice. Then two procedures can be created. The first procedure is called ENTER and it allows entry of the hours worked; the other procedure is called CALC and displays the wages bill. The main program, rewritten using procedures, is shown below:

```
10      DECLARE SUB enter ()
20      DECLARE SUB calc ()
```

The DECLARE instructions above are used to tell the program that these two procedures are being used.

```
30      DIM SHARED hours(5) As Single
40      DIM choice As Integer
50      PRINT "WAGES CALCULATOR"
60          DO WHILE choice <> 3
70          PRINT "Type 1 to enter hours, 2 to calculate wages or 3 to exit"
80          INPUT choice
90          IF choice = 1 THEN CALL enter
```

Instead of having the actual instructions to carry out the user's choice, a CALL instruction is used to transfer control to the proccedure.

```
100         IF choice = 2 THEN CALL calc
110     LOOP
120     PRINT "Goodbye"
```

The 'calc' procedure looks like this. (Quick Basic® called procedures SUBs, which is short for sub-program, another name for a procedure):

```
10      SUB calc
20      DIM counter As Integer
30      DIM rate as Single
40      rate = 5.8
50      PRINT "Wages Are:"
60      FOR counter = 1 TO 5
```

```
70          PRINT "Employee"; counter; "£"; hours(counter) * rate
80      NEXT counter
90      END SUB
```

The enter procedure looks like this:

```
10      SUB enter
20      DIM empno As Integer
30      PRINT "Enter employee number"
40      INPUT empno
50      PRINT "Enter hours"
60      INPUT hours (empno)
70      END SUB
```

There are important aspects to the way procedures work. First, when the program runs and the CALL instruction is reached, control is then passed to the procedure that is named in the CALL instruction. The instructions in that procedure are executed. At the end of the procedure, control is returned to the program from where the CALL instruction was issued, and execution continues at the next instruction after the CALL.

Second, unless you say otherwise, variables in the main program do not exist in the procedures, and vice-versa. You may have noticed that the procedures have their own variables and these variables and their contents exist only during each execution of the procedure. However there are situations where you want variables to be available to both the main procedure and to the procedures it calls. Such variables are generally known as *global* variables, and to create them in BASIC you use the SHARED qualifier with the DIM instruction. Because the array used in the program above to hold the employees' hours worked must be available to both the procedures, it is made a global variable with the instruction:

```
30      DIM SHARED hours(5) as Single
```

Variables in the program that calls the procedure (i.e. the main program) and the procedure itself are completely separate, even if they have the same names. This makes writing complex programs easier because it reduces the likelihood that variables will be modified accidentally. It is therefore good programming practice to keep the number of global variables to a minimum.

Parameters

As you have seen, one way to pass information between the calling program and the procedure is to use a global variable. Another important way to do this is to use *parameters*. Passing parameters to a procedure is often regarded as the preferred method because it does not require the use of global variables.

To demonstrate the technique of a parameter passing, a procedure which calculates the volume of a cylinder will be used. To calculate the volume of a cylinder you need to know its radius and its height; these are two of the parameters passed to the procedure, a third parameter is used to return the result. The main program is shown below:

```
10      REM Main program
```

> The DECLARE statement now lists the parameters after the name of the procedure.

```
20      DECLARE SUB cvolume (radius, height, volume)
30      PRINT "The volume of a cylinder"
40      PRINT "Enter the radius of the cylinder"
50      INPUT radius
60      PRINT "Enter the height of the cylinder"
70      INPUT height
80      CALL cvolume (radius, height, volume)
90      PRINT "Volume is"; volume
```

The code for the procedure is also below. Note that the parameters have been given different names (r, h and v), this is not a requirement, but is done to point out that the variables used in the procedure are different (even if they had the same names) from the ones used in the main program.

```
10      REM Procedure to calculate the volume of a cylinder
20      SUB cvolume (r, h, v)
30      DIM pi As Single
40      DIM area As Single
50      pi = 3.1415
60      area = pi * r ^ 2
70      v = area * h
80      PRINT "test"; v
90      END SUB
```

These simple programs do not really demonstrate that one of the main advantages of using procedures is that they can be called as many times as needed from the main program. However, you should have gained a basic understanding of how procedures work, and you should bear in mind that most programs make extensive use of the technique.

Functions

Functions are facilities provided to the programmer to carry out certain tasks. BASIC has a number of built in functions, such as SQR() which provides the square root of a number supplied to it, and INT() which returns an integer, so:

```
PRINT INT (4.2)
```

will print 4.

As well as the in-built functions, you can write your own – which in many ways are similar to the procedures described above. However, there are two important differences:

- Functions are used by simply including their name in an expression (like PRINT INT (4.2) above), whereas procedures must be called using the CALL instruction.

- The way parameters are passed from a function is different to the way they are passed to a procedure. When a procedure is called, parameters are passed to it using one or more variables, as in the example above which calculates the volume of a cylinder. Changes made to the values in those variables within the procedures are passed back to the main program. This is known as parameter passing *by reference*. However, with functions the parameters are passed *by value*; that is, the actual value is passed to the function and no changes are made to the contents of the variable.

This is probably best explained by two simple examples. The first program shows how to create a user-defined function, called FNexample (all user-defined functions must begin with the letters FN). All this function does is add 1 to the parameter which is passed to it:

```
10      REM function example
```

> Lines 20–50 are the function definition, which must be at the start of the program.

```
20      DEF FNexample (x)
30        x = x + 1
40        FNexample = x
50      END DEF
60      DIM y As Integer
70      y = 0
80      PRINT FNexample (y)
90      PRINT y
```

This program sets a variable called y to 0 (line 70), the FNexample function is called, using the expression PRINT FNexample (y). This passes the *value* of y to the function which will add 1 to it, so the program will print 1. The next instruction (line 90) prints the variable y, and since this has been left unchanged by the function it will print 0.

However if we write this program using a procedure, we can see the difference between passing parameters by reference (as in a procedure) and by value (as in a function). First the main program is

```
10    DECLARE SUB example (y)
20    y = 0
30    CALL example (y)
40    PRINT y
```

and the procedure is

```
100   SUB example (x)
110   x = x + 1
120   PRINT x
130   END SUB
```

In the main program, once again, the variable y is set to 0 (line 20). Then the example procedure is called, the variable y is passed to the procedure by reference, (i.e. the address of the variable y in the main program, and x in the procedure, are set to the same memory location). One is added to the variable x (line 110) and it is printed (line 120). Then control returns to the main program and when the variable y is printed the number 1 appears. So, unlike in a function, the value in the variable of the main program has been altered by the procedure.

Modules

A *module* is a procedure, or a collection of procedures, which can be compiled and stored independently of the main program. The program can then call the module when needed.

Unlike procedures which are internal to a specific program, a module may be made available to other programs.

As you saw in Chapter 16, pre-compiled modules can be stored in libraries, so that they are readily accessible by programmers. These libraries may be provided by the supplier of the programming environment, or may be collections of modules built up by the programmers themselves.

Libraries fall into two types: *static load* libraries and *dynamic link* libraries.

Static load libraries

The load libraries that were described in Chapter 16 are referred to as static load libraries. If a program uses a module from a load library, then the module is incorporated into the code by the linker loader. The linker loader takes the object code that has been

generated by the compiler and adds in the lines of code that make up the module.

The final program contains all the code that is needed in order for it to be run, so is known as *executable code*.

This method of enlarging a program by including the code of all its modules was commonly used in the past. But as applications became more complex, the programs themselves became very long indeed, and alternative methods of supporting modularisation began to be employed.

Dynamic link libraries

A dynamic link library (DLL) is a collection of modules that is supplied alongside the executable code. This means that when an application is installed it will consist of one or more executable programs plus a number of DLLs. When the executable code is run, it will call upon the DLLs when they are needed. When a DLL is called it is linked to the main program.

DLLs were developed specifically for modules that are used across a range of applications. For example, the common interface modules in Microsoft Office®, such as the Save or Open dialogues, appear in most, if not all, of the components that make up this family of application generators. There are many of these common modules, and each consists of quite a lengthy set of program statements. If they had each been incorporated individually into each of the programs in which they appear, the programs would become unfeasibly large. Instead, only one copy of the DLL is stored and it is called as needed at runtime.

There are many advantages in using DLLs :

- Programs can be maintained at a manageable length.
- In a multitasking environment the user may load up several applications at the same time, and these may have modules in common. By using a DLL, only one copy of the module has to be in memory.
- The module is loaded only at the point when it is needed, thus reducing the pressures on memory.
- If the supplier improves a DLL then it only needs to provide an upgrade for the DLL itself. The main programs will be unchanged.

The only disadvantage with using DLLs is that the program code for an application is split into several files and these must all be installed correctly. Usually the application is sold with an installation program which places all the component files in their correct directories. The systems administrator has to ensure that all the DLLs that are needed have been installed, and must make sure that the access privileges assigned to end-users include access to these DLLs.

Activity

Check through the files on the computer you are using and identify some DLL files. You will usually find them within the program directories.

Client–server relationships

You have met the concept of a client–server relationship in the context of a network (see page 8). A client terminal makes use of the facilities held on the server station. A similar concept can be applied to software products.

When an application can use a module that is part of another application we say that the first application is the *client* and the second is the *server*. A client always receives some kind of service from the server.

As an example, you may like to open a Word document and then insert a spreadsheet object (select Object from the Insert menu). The end-user is given the impression that Word contains full spreadsheet facilities. When the spreadsheet object is selected, the menu bar and toolbars change to the ones associated with Excel, and the user can carry out the usual range of spreadsheet processes. When the text outside the object is selected again, the menu and toolbars revert to those for Word, and the spreadsheet appears as a table of values. In this example, Word is the client and Excel is the server.

One very common client–server relationship is that between a database management system (DBMS) and the user interface that is presented to the user. The user interface is the client and the DBMS is the server. The user interface may be developed in a spreadsheet or a word-processor, or it may be developed in a multimedia tool such as presentation graphics. A website is a familiar user interface for a database, and you will be able to find many examples of websites which interact with databases, especially on Internet retailing sites. The user interface is sometimes referred to as the *front-end system*, and the DBMS as the *back-end system*.

There are obvious advantages in using a client–server relationship over developing a single integrated application:

- The two applications can be maintained separately and upgraded as needed.
- Each application can be built with industry-standard software tools.
- The applications do not have to be stored on the same hardware system.

The main issue, in practice, is the provision and use of software which enable the developer to create and maintain the client–server link.

CHAPTER 35

Programming object-based event-driven systems

This chapter follows on from Chapter 34. It introduces Microsoft's object-based event-driven language Visual Basic®, and discusses its programming environment.

The chapter covers these Learning Outcomes in the specification:

L.O. 5.2 Demonstrate knowledge of the fundamentals of object-based event-driven systems
L.O. 5.3 Demonstrate an understanding of the facilities and advantages of an integrated programming environment (IPE)

It also covers this Technical Knowledge topic:

T5.2.1 Macros

Object-based event-driven languages

The Windows® computing environment requires a different approach from the traditional programming languages, such as BASIC, that we looked into in the last chapter. Programs today consist of screen forms, menus, pop-up dialogue boxes, buttons and the like. Input comes not just from the keyboard but from the mouse too. Programs running in the Windows® environment need to respond to events, such as a button or menu option being clicked, or the mouse being moved over a certain area.

Another important aspect of Windows® programming is that many screen objects are reusable. For example, take a simple object like a button. There is no point in every programmer writing his or her own code for creating a button. Programming languages such as Delphi™, Visual Basic® and Visual C++® all come with the code for the standard screen objects built in. This principle does not apply just to simple objects such as text boxes or buttons; it also applies to standard dialogue boxes such as the Save As box (see Figure 35.1), which is used by a wide range of programs.

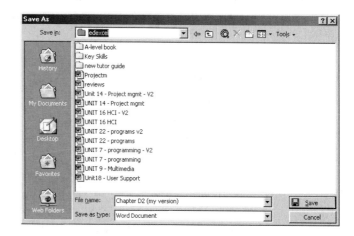

Figure 35.1 *The Windows® Save As dialogue box*

As the programming for these objects is already built into the language, professional-looking applications can be built relatively quickly. Programs therefore consist, for a large part, of reusable modules.

Activity

Can you think of other dialogue boxes which are widely used in Windows® programs?

Software houses that have been around for many years have had to adapt to the new styles of programming. The software developer Full Solutions likes to fill any job vacancies with young graduates who have learnt to use the latest tools. They also send their more experienced employees on training courses to ensure that their expertise is kept up to date.

Introduction to Visual Basic®

In this chapter we will look at Microsoft's Visual Basic®, (which we will often shorten to VB). It is a widely used commercial Windows® programming language. VB is supplied as an integrated programming environment, rather than with a separate editor, compiler, linker, debugging tool etc. It has one integrated suite of programs which provide all these functions and a number of others as well.

This chapter is an introduction to the basic concepts of event-driven programming in general, and VB in particular. It is not a 'how to program in Visual Basic' tutorial. There are many excellent books which provide this, including *Visual Basic V6 Made Simple* by Stephen Morris (ISBN 075065189X).

Objects

Within event-driven languages there are a number of concepts that do not apply to the traditional languages we have looked at so far. The main one of these is that of *objects*. Everything displayed by a Windows® program, such as labels, buttons and text boxes, is referred to as an object. A simple program might look like the one in Figure 35.2, which consists of a number of objects.

Objects have names and they have *properties*, which control the way the object looks and behaves. So a form has a colour property, which might be set to blue; a label has a caption property which in the example is set to 'Calculator'. Properties can be set default values before the program runs and they can be changed by the program while it is running.

When modifying properties at runtime the so-called *dot notation* is used. So, for example, to set the caption property of a label called 'Label1' you would use the instruction

    Label1.Caption = "Hello"

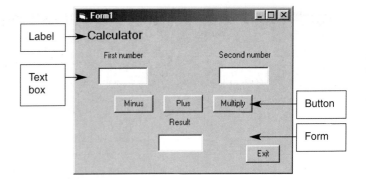

Figure 35.2 *A simple program*

Events

Another important concept is that of *events*. Objects can respond to certain events by running a series of instructions (in a procedure, as described in the previous chapter) when that event occurs. Different objects can respond to different events. Some of the major ones are shown in the box.

Some simple events

Object	Event	Occurs when
Form	Load	The form is first loaded (i.e. displayed)
Button	Click	The button is clicked
Text box	Change	When the contents of the text box change
Text box	Gotfocus	When the text cursor moves into the text box

Creating a program in Visual Basic®

Let us now look at how a simple VB program is created. The example we will use is the simple calculator from Chapter 34.

After starting the VB program, and selecting a standard '.exe' program, you will then see the main screen with a form object (called *Form1*) already created for you (see Figure 35.3).

Objects, such as buttons and text boxes, are created using the *controls* in the toolbox on the left. When a particular object is selected, an alphabetical list of its properties is displayed on the right side of the screen. You can modify the default property setting for an object using this list.

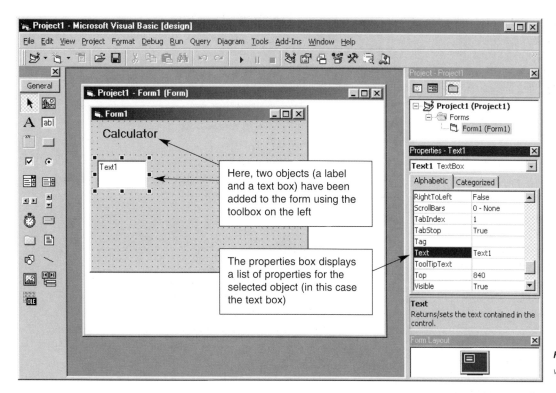

Figure 35.3 *What you see when starting Visual Basic®*

To create the calculator, three text boxes will be needed, two to enter the two numbers to be added together and one to show the result. A button will be needed to carry out the calculation. They should look something like Figure 35.4.

The user will need to type numbers in the first two boxes, but should not type in the third one, where the answer will appear. The enabled property of the third text box should be set to 'false' so that it does not accept input. Note that Visual Basic® automatically names the

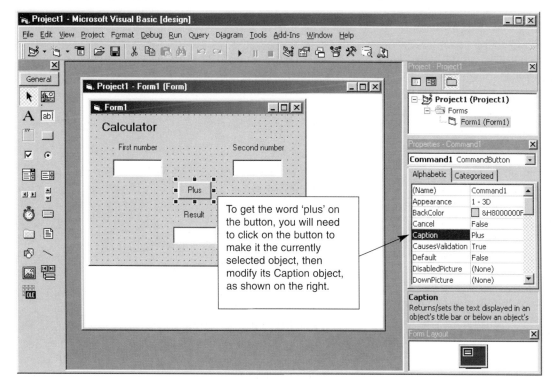

Figure 35.4 *Modifying the function button*

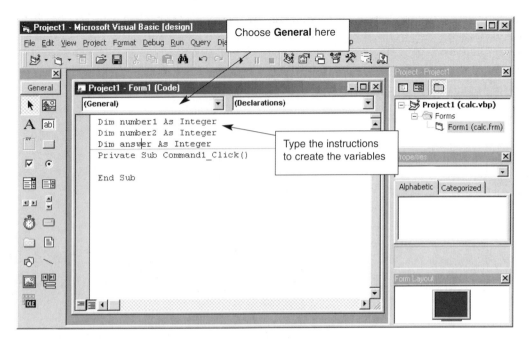

Figure 35.5 *Creating variables*

objects you create, so the first text box you create will be called 'Text1', the second 'Text2' and so on. These default names are fine for simple programs, but when creating more sophisticated programs it is good practice to name the objects something more meaningful.

Having completed the form design, the programming code is now added. This needs to be associated with an event, which in this case is the event that triggers when the button is clicked, known as the *Click* event. This is the most commonly used event for buttons, and all you have to do is double-click the button and this will open the code window with a skeleton procedure already created.

Having opened the code window, the first thing you need to do is create the required variables. Because you may want to add a subtract and a multiply button at a later date, it is sensible to make these variables available to all procedures, rather that local to just this one. To do this, select *General* from the object drop-down menu at the top of the code window, and enter the instructions in that section, as shown in Figure 35.5.

Once the variables have been created, instructions are added in between the start and end statements of the click procedure in order to make the button work (see Figure 35.6).

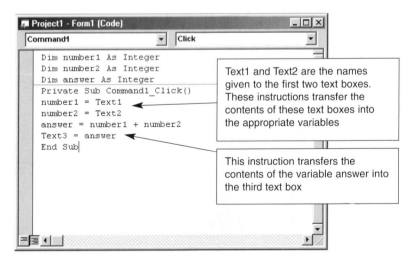

Figure 35.6 *Adding instructions*

The program will now run when you can click the Run button in the top toolbar or choose the *Start* option from the *Run* menu. Type a number in each of the top two text boxes, click the plus button and the result will be displayed in the lower text box.

Activity

Work out how you could add buttons (and associated code) to do subtraction, multiplication and division.

Modifying objects at runtime

While the program above provides a simple example of using event procedures and setting default object properties, it does not demonstrate how to modify object properties at runtime.

Adding a clear button to the calculator gives that opportunity. First, create a new button and set its Caption property to 'Clear'. Double-click the button to open the code window, and type the code shown in Figure 35.7 in the Click event procedure for the button.

This program suffers the same problems as the one written earlier in traditional BASIC, in that if you type something other than a number in the text box the program will display an error when you click the plus button. The solution to this problem in Visual Basic® is neater as it uses an in-built function, called 'IsNumeric', to trap any non-numeric entry. The function takes the form

IsNumeric(expression)

It returns the value 'true' if the expression is numeric or 'false' if it is not. So by combining the IsNumeric function with an IF instruction, the text boxes can be tested for numeric entries before attempting to add their contents together. The required code goes in the event procedure for the plus button (see Figure 35.8).

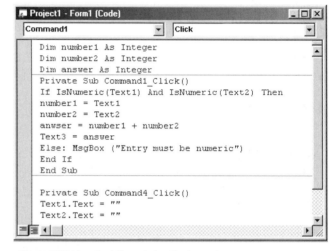

Figure 35.8 *How the IsNumeric function is used*

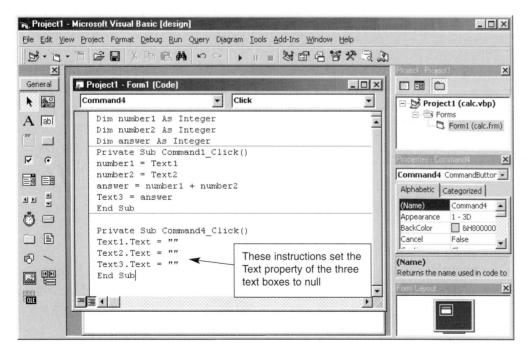

Figure 35.7 *Setting up a clear button*

Note the use of logical operator 'And' to allow the two variables to be tested together. There are three other logical operators which can be used with a conditional instruction like 'If':

- And – if both tests are true then the result is true
- Or – if either tests are true then the result is true
- Not – if the test is true then the result is false, and vise-versa
- Xor – if one of the tests is true then the result is true; if both are true or both are false then the result is false.

'MsgBox' is another function which, as its name suggests, displays a message box, with the text contained in brackets displayed in it.

Integrated programming environments

It has already been mentioned that Visual Basic® provides an integrated programming environment (IPE), which is designed to make it easier to develop programs. IPEs have a number of features, some of which you many have noticed already if you have been using VB.

Context-sensitive editor

In the past, before IPEs became commonly used, programmers would type the code for their programs using a simple text editor, like Notepad. These text editors know nothing about the syntax of the language, so they give the programmer no assistance in writing the program.

Context-sensitive editors, like the one found in VB, 'know' about the syntax rule of the language so they help the programmer in a number of ways. For example, when you are typing an instruction VB presents a list of available options. So if you are writing an instruction to modify the properties of an object (using the dot notation described earlier) the editor will display a list of properties which apply to the object in question, as shown in Figure 35.9.

Context-sensitive help

Most integrated programming environments also provide context-sensitive help. This means that when the help key (F1) is pressed the Help topic provided is relevant to what you are doing at that time, rather than you having to search for the topic.

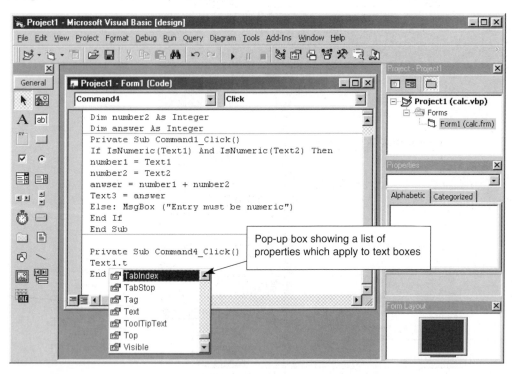

Figure 35.9 Context-sensitive editing

Colour coding and tooltips

Visual Basic® colour-codes your instructions to make them easier to read. Tooltips are also provided. If the mouse pointer is kept over a toolbar button for a short period, a small message box is displayed describing the purpose of the button.

Toolbars, toolboxes and windows

In common with other Windows® programs, Visual Basic® provides a range of toolbars, boxes and windows which are designed to provide the programmer with the required facilities without having to search through countless menus (see Figure 35.10). Additional toolbars, such as the Debug and Form Editing toolbars, can be displayed as required.

In addition to the form-editing, code and properties windows that we have already used, VB provides the Form Layout window, for setting the location of a form when it runs, and the Project window which allows you to select for display the various parts of your program (e.g. different forms and modules). Both the toolbox and toolbars are customisable, so the programmer can add those buttons which he or she finds most useful.

Debugging

Writing programs, even for an experienced programmer, is a complex and difficult process, and programs rarely if ever work correctly at the first attempt. The process of finding and correcting errors in programs is called *debugging*. As you saw in Chapter 12, there are basically three types of error that can occur in a program: syntax errors, logic errors and runtime errors.

- *Syntax errors* are mistakes in the instructions entered in the code window, such as a misspelled property, that break the rules (syntax) of VB. The VB editor examines each line as it is typed for several types of syntax errors, and displays an error message if it detects them. The program cannot be executed until this type of error is corrected.

- *Logic errors* are mistakes in the logic of the instructions which cause the program to produce the wrong results. This type of error can be the most difficult to identify, and most debugging efforts are focused on tracking down logic errors.

- *Runtime errors* cause the program to stop unexpectedly during execution. We have already described several circumstances which have this effect.

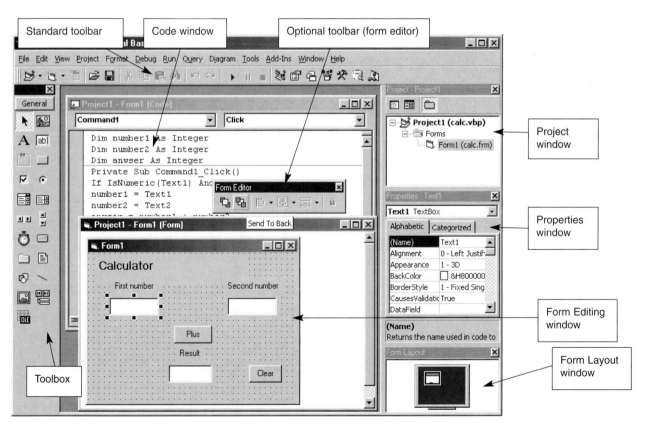

Figure 35.10 *The VB window is customisable*

The VB integrated programming environment provides debugging facilities to help identify the causes of runtime and logic errors. *Break mode* allows the programmer to execute the program one line at a time and to examine the contents of variables and properties as they change.

Activity

Examine an IPE with which you are familiar. Identify the following features, if they exist, and comment on how useful and effective you find them to be in use:

- *context-sensitive editor*
- *context-sensitive help*
- *colour-coding*
- *tooltips*
- *toolbars*
- *toolboxes*
- *windows*
- *debugging tools*

Arrays and methods

The concept of an array has already been introduced (see page 369). It applies to Visual Basic® just as it does to traditional BASIC. However, in VB you can create arrays of screen objects as well as variables. So-called *control arrays* (this type of object is also known as a *container* as the object 'contains' several controls) can be very useful as they allow a series of related controls to be processed together, for example by a FOR … NEXT loop.

Another concept than needs to be introduced is that of *methods*. These are statements that perform some action or service for a particular object in a program. Methods use the dot notation, as previously described, such as:

```
List1.AddItem "Friends"
```

where List1 is the name of a list-box object, AddItem is the method (which adds a text item to a list box), and "Friends" is the text that is added.

These concepts are best understood with the aid of a simple example program. This program displays a group of three images when you click a button, like a simple slide projector. It could be used as the basis for a multimedia program or game. To make this program work, the three images must already exist, and have filenames in a numerical series, such as image1.jpg, image2.jpg and image3.jpg.

An image box should be created on the form, using the image-box control (at the bottom right of the toolbox). Set the *Stretch* property of the image box to 'true' so that the images will be zoomed to fit the image box. Then copy and paste the image box. When you do this a dialogue will appear asking if you want to create a control array; click the Yes button. Paste another copy of the image box to create three in all, and space them out across the form. Using this technique a control array with three elements, Image1(0), Image1(1) and Image1(2), has been created. Now add a button to the form and double-click it to open the code window, with the skeleton procedure for the click event already created. A loop can now be used to fill each of the elements of the control array with a picture. The code to do this is

```
Private Sub Command1_Click()
DIM counter as Integer
FOR counter = 0 to 2
Image1 (counter).Picture = LoadPicture("C:\images\image" & counter
+ 1 & ".jpg")
NEXT counter
END Sub
```

The FOR … NEXT loop is used to loop through each of the three image boxes. The LoadPicture function is used to place an image in each box, as in the fourth line of the code. The & operator is used to build up the name of each file by concatenating (joining) the string 'image' with the loop number and the string '.jpg'. The counter variable needs to be incremented by 1 because the loop runs from 0 to 2, while the images' names are image1.jpg, image2.jpg and image3.jpg.

When the program is run and the button is clicked, the three images will be loaded into the image boxes (see Figure 35.11).

Figure 35.11 *The result of running the program*

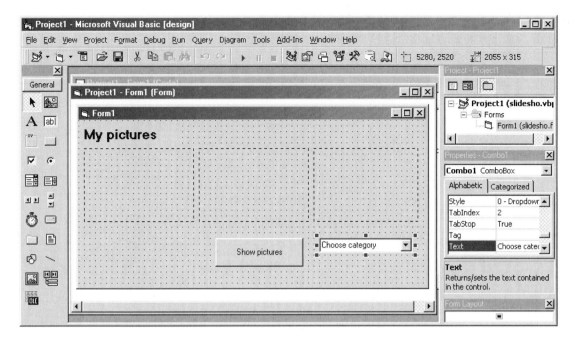

Figure 35.12 *Using the combo-box control*

The next stage with this program is to add an option that allows the user to choose what category of pictures to view. To do this, a drop-down box (or *combo box* as VB calls it) needs to be added using the combo-box control. The Text property of the combo box should be set to 'Choose category' or something similar (see Figure 35.12).

To demonstrate the use of *methods*, the options listed in the combo box will be added at runtime. The event

that will be used to add these options will be the Load event for the form; this occurs when the forms load, as soon as the program starts.

Double-click the form background to open the code, with the skeleton Load event module already created. The method that is used to add an item to a combo box list is called AddItem. The completed code is shown in Figure 35.13.

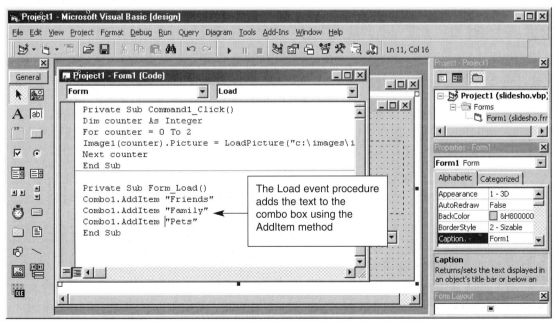

Figure 35.13 *Using the AddItem method with a combo box*

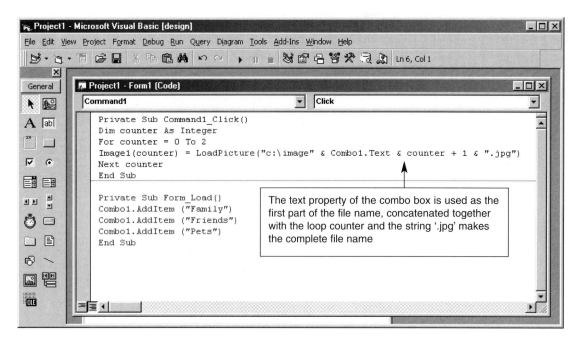

Figure 35.14 *The finished code*

Now the categories of the pictures have been added to the combo box, the code to process the user's choice must be added. This version of the program depends on naming the image files with their category name and number as before (so images in the pets category need to be named pets1.jpg, pets2.jpg, pets3.jpg and so on). Rather than using the fixed string 'image' and adding the loop number to it, as before, the file name string is selected based on the choice made in the combo box (see Figure 35.14). The program will now display different sets of pictures depending on the choice the user makes in the combo box.

This program has one major fault, however. If the user clicks the button before making a choice in the combo box the program will fail, because the text property of the combo box will be set to 'Choose a category'. There are a number of possible ways around this. An IF instruction could be introduced which tests the text property of the combo box, and if it finds it set to 'Choose a category' the MsgBox function could be used to display an appropriate error message. An alternative, and possibly neater way, is to do away with the button altogether. The button click module code could instead be used in the Click event for the combo box, so that as soon as the user selects a category in the combo box the pictures will appear.

Activity

Experiment with both techniques described above to solve the problem of clicking the combo box before the button. Which do you think is the best?

User interface design

Features

One of the advantages of using visual Windows® programming environments like Visual Basic® is that it makes building user interfaces relatively easy. However while these interfaces may be easy to construct they are not necessarily easy to use. The programmer must bear in mind the end-user when designing forms. End-users may not be computer professionals and may have little IT knowledge or experience. Therefore the forms designed by the programmer must have certain features.

● They must be *easily understood*. Labels on the forms must be informative and meaningful to the end-user, as must the captions for buttons and boxes. Error messages and other message box text also needs careful wording. Consideration also needs to be given to how to provide the user with help, and also to the wording of Help topics.

- They must be *logical*. The order in which forms are presented and the layout of controls on forms must follow the logical workflow of the user. The most commonly used controls and options must be the most easily accessible.

- They must be *consistent*. The forms that make up the program must be consistent in the way they are laid out and how the controls are labelled. The use of colour, for example, should be consistent so if an error message box has a red background, then all error message boxes should have red backgrounds. In a similar way, if a button is provided to close a form and it is labelled 'Close', yet on another form a button with the same function is labelled 'Exit', users may find this confusing.

When the 'Fitness Matters' software was being developed, Ian McPherson, the Project Manager, paid especial attention to the development and prototyping of the user interface. This application was going to be used by members of the general public in leisure centres, and there would be no opportunity to train the end-users in how to use the software. It was therefore very important that the user interface would guide the user step-by-step through the activities, provide clear instructions at all stages, and handle any user errors appropriately.

Graphical versus text-based interfaces

The Windows® graphical user interface gives the programmer the opportunity to provide the end-user with a graphical representation of the real-world task he or she is attempting to complete. Right from the start, in an attempt to make computing accessible and easy to understand the Windows® operating system itself used the *metaphor* of an office desktop. It allows the user to drag and drop icons (which represent files) into folders (which represent directories or a recycle bin). Depending on the application, the use of a metaphor in the user interface may be appropriate. For example, a computer system used to control security in a building might use a graphical representation of each floor of the building. In order to remotely lock a door the user could drag an icon of a key on to a picture of the door in question.

Such user graphical interfaces are in contrast to the multiple menus or function keys of a DOS (i.e. text) based application. However, text-based user interfaces

should not be underestimated. Graphical interfaces, unless carefully designed, can be complex and confusing for users, and there are many circumstances where a text-based user interface may be preferable. Some work situations (such as supermarket checkouts) do not easily lend themselves to the use of a mouse, for example; and, once learnt, function keys are quicker to use than clicking buttons. In many cases text-based systems are sometimes preferable.

User interface design is a big topic, to which whole books have been devoted, so we have only scratched the surface here. In most cases programmers will need to have a good understanding of the users of the system, so they can create a user interface that is easy to navigate. Since user interfaces are relatively easy to create with VB, programmers may find it helpful to create a prototype of the interface and have the end-users review it before the final version in created.

Activity

Speak to friends or family who use computers at home or work. Do they find them easy to use? What type of user interface do they use (text or windows-based)? Does the interface they use comply with the guidelines given above (easily understood, consistent and logical). Could it be improved? If so, how?

Macros

Macros are small programs that automate the functions of application programs like Microsoft® Word or Excel. They allow customised facilities to be built into these programs, permitting, for example, a complex series of actions to be automated and attached to a button.

Macro recording and macro languages

You will probably already have come across the macro recording facility found in Excel. When a macro is recorded, a Visual Basic® code module is created, which can be edited to enhance the functionality of the macro. You can, of course, create a macro from scratch by typing in the VB code without using the macro recorder at all, if you so wish.

All of the products in the Office suite that support macros (including Word, Excel and Access) use VB as their macro language. In the past different applications had their own macro languages, but this harmonisation has the obvious advantage that anyone familiar with VB can write macros for any of the Office applications. Writing a VB macro is a little different from writing a standalone program like the ones discussed in the rest of the chapter. For example, there are no forms to deal with, and new functions and properties are used to interact with the application interface.

Writing a macro

The following simple example shows how to use a macro to create a customised application in Excel. Returning to our wages calculator example, a spreadsheet has been created with formulas to calculate each person's gross wages and the total wages bill (see Figure 35.15).

However, the wages clerk has never used a spreadsheet before so it must be modified to make data entry easier and reduce the likelihood of mistakes being made or other parts of the spreadsheet being overwritten. The macro recorder is used to start with, recording a simple macro that involves placing the cursor in cell C6 and typing a value. When this macro is edited it looks something like this:

```
Sub Macro1()
'
' Macro1 Macro
' Macro recorded 16/09/2001 by Alan
'
```

    The next line selects cell C6.

```
Range ("C6") .Select
```

    The active cell object is the cell on the sheet that is currently selected. The FormulaR1C property controls the contents of the cell.

```
    ActiveCell.FormulaR1C1 = "37"
    Range ("C7").select
End Sub
```

This macro can now be edited to provide an input box so any value can be typed into the cell:

```
Sub Macro1()
'
' Macro1 Macro
' Macro recorded 16/09/2001 by Alan
'
    Dim hours_worked As Single
    hours_worked = InputBox ("Enter hours worked")
    Range ("C6") .Select
    ActiveCell.FormulaR1C1 = hours_worked
    Range ("C7") .Select`
End Sub
```

In this edited version a variable is created (hours_worked) to hold this data and the InputBox function is used to

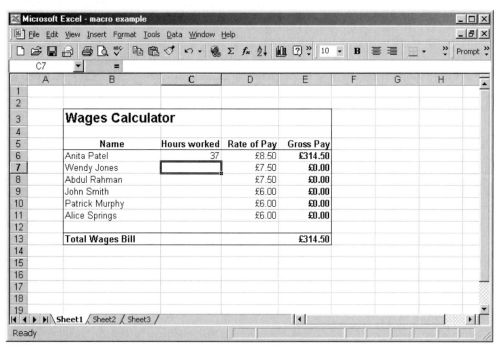

Figure 35.15 The wages calculator spreadsheet

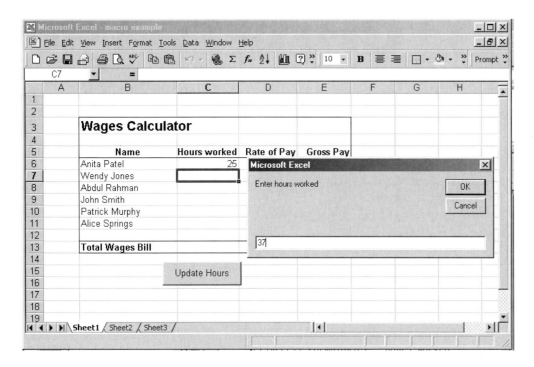

Figure 35.16 *The operation of the edited macro*

display an input box so the user can type in the value required. The FormulaR1C1 property of the ActiveCell object is then set using the variable.

This modified macro can now be attached to a button on the spreadsheet – which, when clicked, displays the input box and inserts the entered value into cell C7 (see Figure 35.16).

This simple example demonstrates the basic concept of macro writing. The example is not complete, of course, as the hours for the other employees need to be added,

perhaps using a loop. Error-checking numeric (probably using the IsNumeric function) is also needed to make sure the values entered are numbers.

Activity

Using the knowledge you have already gained about Visual Basic®, modify the macro, as suggested, so it requests hours for every employee and rejects non-numeric entries.

This chapter describes the processes involved in turning a user's requirements into a design specification from which software can be developed.

The chapter covers these Learning Outcomes in the specification:

L.O. 5.4   Present arguments that relate to the social, moral, ethical and legal implications of a proposed ICT solution to a specific problem

L.O. 5.5   Critically appraise a given specification for an ICT-based solution to a specified problem as it relates to the needs of specified users

L.O. 5.10   Demonstrate knowledge of the costs of generating, customising and maintaining software solutions to specified problems

An ICT project at GBW Bank

In this chapter and the next, the focus will be on the development of a bespoke application by the IS department of GBW Bank.

The project description

The Premises Maintenance Supervisor at the bank, Eric Thompson, has been to see Sara Patel, the IT Development Manager. He wants Sara to look into the possibility of developing a database that will help them with their electrical testing programme.

The bank uses a great deal of electrical equipment – computers, photocopiers, fax machines etc. The Health and Safety at Work Act 1974 places a legal obligation on an employer to ensure that electrical equipment is safe. In order to check that this equipment is safe it must be tested regularly. Testing is done using a machine called a portable appliance tester (PAT). Records of this testing need to be kept so the bank can be sure that it has been done properly and regularly. If there is an accident or a problem with a piece of equipment, then records of the testing will be needed and could be used as evidence in an enquiry or court of law.

PAT tester

The electricians have attempted to keep track of the testing programme using a simple spreadsheet, but this is proving too complex and does not provide the functionality required. They want to use new PAT testers that can be attached to a computer so details of equipment to be tested can be downloaded into the tester. When the testing is done the PAT tester is attached to the computer again so the results of the tests can be uploaded.

User requirement specification

As with any software development project, the first step is for the Estates Manager (the 'client' in this case, even though they work for the same company) to write a user requirement specification. To do this Eric sits down with his electricians and discusses what they need. They identify what the primary goals of the system should be, and then list the functions that the application needs to provide.

The primary goals they decide on are:

- keep accurate details of the testing that has been done (thereby complying with the legal requirements)
- produce schedules of equipment to be tested
- reduce the amount of time that is spent keeping the records.

The *functions* the application needs to perform are:

- interface with the database the Estate Management department use to keep records of equipment installed in branches (the asset register)
- produce schedules of equipment that needs testing
- interface with testing equipment used to record results of tests
- provide facilities to search for and print reports on any piece of equipment or testing session.

Eric takes these basic goals and functions and writes them up into a more detailed report that he submits to Sara.

Cost considerations

Sara needs to estimate how long it will take to write the program. Although Eric and Sara work for the same company, the Estates Department must pay the IS department for the work it will do for them. When Eric knows how much the IS department will charge for this work he can add on the cost of the new PAT testers and then submit a budget to the Estates Manager for approval. Until he has the approval to spend this money he cannot tell Sara to go ahead with the project.

Sara allocates the project to one of her system analysts, Jamie Soomary. Jamie has a vital role to play in the development of the system. He needs to understand what is required from the point of view of the domain experts (the electricians) and then turn that into a technical design that the programmers can follow. He also has the difficult task of estimating how long the program will take to write (and therefore how much it will cost). This task is difficult because there are many unknowns involved in developing software. Jamie investigates the system in a number of ways:

- He speaks to Eric and his team to clarify various points from the user requirements specification.
- He looks at the spreadsheet that the electricians have been using.
- He talks to the company that produces the PAT testers. They have some software that could be used to record the testing, but when Jamie takes a look at it he discovers it is very basic and could not work with the bank's asset management database.

Having gained a better understanding of the system required, Jamie now needs to write a proposal, which will include the cost of producing the system, which Eric can then take back to the Estates Manager for approval. There is no point in Jamie starting work on the detailed system design until this approval is given.

Detailed costing

Estimating the cost of a software development project is notoriously difficult. Often, due to natural optimism and enthusiasm to go ahead with the project, estimates of the costs are made which turn out to be inadequate. It is not uncommon for software projects to go 'over budget', often owing to an inadequate understanding of how complex the problem is, and therefore how long it will take to solve.

Techniques for estimating the cost of a project are more of an art than a science, and depend heavily on the previous experience and knowledge of the person doing the estimating. The major component of any project will be human resource costs, but other components such as hardware and software need to be taken into account.

In order to estimate how long this software development project will take, Jamie needs to produce an outline project plan that identifies all the steps that will be taken in the development process. Then, drawing on his experience from other projects, he allocates a number of days work to each task. He includes a certain amount of contingency into some of the tasks in case they prove more difficult that he expects (in other words, he adds in some extra days in case things don't go to plan). This would apply in particular to tasks that the IS department may not have had much experience with before, such as writing the programs that will interface to the PAT tester to download and upload data.

Jamie decides to break the project down into the following steps:

- system design
- module design
- prototyping
- coding
- module testing
- integration testing
- acceptance testing
- implementation
- user training.

It should also be borne in mind that the costs involved do not stop when the system is implemented. Maintaining the software and providing support for the users will also cost money.

For each stage, not only does he need to estimate how long it will take, but he also needs to estimate how many people will work on each stage and what combination of managers, senior staff and junior staff

will be required. This is important because staff are paid differently. A junior member of staff might cost the company £100 a day, while a more senior manager might cost £250 a day.

Jamie will also have to consider the availability of staff. If they are all fully occupied working on other projects he may have to consider employing temporary staff, or contractors. Using contractors is more expensive (around £400 a day), but at the end of the project the company does not have to go on paying them as they do with full-time staff.

As well as staffing costs Jamie must include the cost of any additional hardware and software that may be required. IT development staff may also need to be sent on training courses if any new products or techniques are to be used in the project.

Using project management software

All in all, the cost estimating process is a complex one. Jamie uses project management software (such as Microsoft's Project) to assist in the process. This software is designed to plan projects. It allows him to create a calendar showing the dates and durations of all the tasks, and how they are interrelated. It also allows him to create resources (such as members of staff) and allocate them to the various tasks. He can also allocate a daily cost for each member of staff, so that the program will automatically calculate the human resource costs of each step and of the whole project.

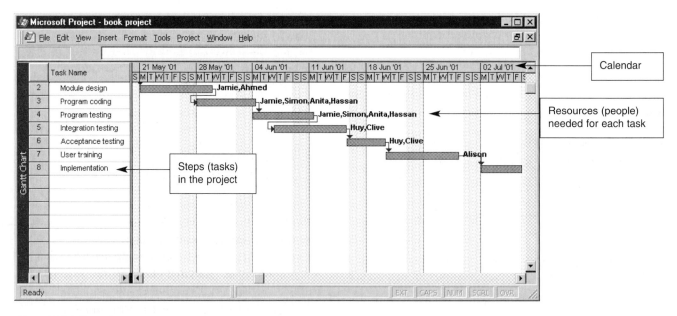

Figure 36.1 A Gantt chart

Microsoft® Project produces a Gantt chart, which is a type of graph showing different tasks as bars plotted along a calendar. The chart Jamie is using is shown in Figure 36.1.

Although using this type of software helps, Jamie still needs to use his judgement and experience to estimate the length of the tasks involved.

Making the decision

Having produced his outline project plan and costing, Jamie has a meeting with Sara to discuss his response to Eric's user requirements spec. They run through the plan and the costing and, after making some minor adjustments to the figures, they agree that the proposal can be sent to Eric.

Once Eric has received the proposal Jamie has produced, he takes it to the Estates Manager to gain approval. Unlike a system developed for the bank's core business, this is not a situation where there is a decision to be made about the return on investment; the system will not make any money for the bank. Instead the decision on whether to spend the money is based on two main factors:

- Will it increase the efficiency of support staff (the electricians)?
- Will it protect the company from litigation?

The second question is probably the most important. If there is an accident with some electrical equipment the bank could be heavily fined if it could not prove it had taken reasonable care to ensure the equipment was safe. It could also face compensation claims from anyone who was injured in the accident.

It is also important to increase the efficiency of support staff, as these are an overhead, who do not produce any revenue for the bank.

The Estates Manager has an annual budget for IT expenditure, and fortunately Eric mentioned to him at the beginning of the year, when he was setting his annual budget, that he would have to do something about software for PAT testing. This means that the Estates Manager has made provision in his budget for expenditure in this area. Having taken these factors into account, the proposal is approved, and Eric telephones Jamie to give him the good news.

Writing the design specification

Writing the design specification involves taking the system as described from the user's perspective and analysing how it can be achieved from a technical point of view. The end result should be a document that a programmer (or team of programmers) can use to write the required programs. Some work has already been done in this area to produce the outline project plan from which the costing has been derived, but now more detail needs to be added.

The basic stages in working towards the system spec are:

- *Investigation.* Some fact-finding has already been done, but further investigation will be needed to capture the detail of the way the system will work.
- *Use of various analysis tools.* These model the flow of data and the relationships in the system. The programs or modules that are identified are then designed and things like screen designs and report layout are produced.

Investigation

Information already gathered from the electricians needs to be formalised and documented. In particular the following information needs to be recorded.

The people involved

Different people or groups may have different requirements, and the system must attempt to meet them all. For example, consider the possible requirements these people or groups may have:

- Electricians – want a system that is easy to use and does not create extra work
- Estates Manager – wants a system that will increase the efficiency of the electricians so they can test more equipment in less time.
- Health & Safety Executive – in the case of an investigation into an accident they will want

Specification

reliable, detailed evidence of testing that has taken place.

Data sources and capture methods

The data listing the equipment to be tested will be extracted from the existing assets register database. Now more technical detail must be gathered about exactly how this can be done. Data must also be downloaded and uploaded to the PAT tester machines.

Decisions taken and types of processing

Every system (both computerised and manual) will have rules about how the input data is processed and how different circumstances are dealt with. Many of these rules are unwritten, but the analyst must identify and formalise them all. Talking to the end-users and developing a detailed understanding of the processes involved in the existing system will be required.

Outputs

Most of these should have been identified in the user requirements and will mostly consist of printed reports.

Use of analysis tools

There are a number of methods than can be used to develop an understanding of how a system can be constructed, most of which involve modelling the real-world system using diagrams. The use of entity relationship diagrams and normalisation in data modelling have already been discussed (see Chapter 13), and these techniques are well matched to this kind of data-orientated system.

Modelling tools such as data flow diagrams can be used to decompose the system into more and more detailed processes until the basic functions of individual programs or modules have been defined. As well as designing the underlying data structure and the processing required, attention must also be paid to the user interface.

Jamie has spent several weeks collecting information and analysing it, and his first draft of the system specification is now ready. The document he produces is divided into the following sections:

- *introduction* – an overall description of the purpose and the goals of the new system

- *user requirements* – a summary of the user requirements document
- *data design* – description of the database design that will support the system, including entity relationship diagrams, data dictionaries etc.
- *data flow* – using data flow diagrams the system is decomposed into more detail
- *process specifications* – the processes are designed using pseudo-code
- *input and output specifications* – including details of screen designs, data validation and report layouts.

Jamie is satisfied with the document he has produced, but it needs to be carefully evaluated before the work of creating the system can start.

Verifying the specification

The specification is a vital document. If the analyst has misunderstood any aspect of what the user requires, then, no matter how skilled the programmer is in writing the programs, the system will not fully meet the needs of the users and will need modifications (which may prove expensive) before it can be used successfully.

As well as capturing the user requirements accurately, the specification needs to describe the way the system should be programmed in a way that will actually work, protecting the integrity of the data as it is processed and stored.

The difficulty of successfully achieving this task should not be underestimated. The history of software development is littered with many examples of expensive failures and projects that took a great deal longer (and therefore cost a lot more) than was originally estimated.

The specification therefore needs to be correct (or as near correct as you can make it). A systems analyst will usually have worked in the IT industry for quite a few years, often spending time first as a programmer before moving on to the analyst role. The experience the analyst gains over the years working on other projects is therefore important in helping him or her to produce a good specification, but this on its own is not enough.

There are a number of ways in which the specification can be *verified*.

Verification against the user requirements specification

One obvious way to check the design specification is to compare it with the user specification. It needs to be checked, for example, that all the requirements the user has outlined are covered in the design. The user may ask for five different types of reports to be produced by the system. Is the design of all five of those reports covered in the design specification? Such checking should be obvious, but often things are simply left out.

Verification against the organisation's standards

Most organisations have quality standards that define how certain tasks should be carried out. An IT department would have a quality manual which describes how, amongst other things, design specifications and programs are written and how programs are tested.

The information contained in a quality manual is general – it doesn't apply to a specific project, instead it lays down guidelines on how the various tasks an IT department undertakes should be carried out. The guidelines contained in the quality manual are normally developed from two sources:

- *Past experience*. IT departments of all but new companies will have had experience of previous projects (and even newly created companies will employ people with experience). The organisation will learn from its past experience, and this learning should be encompassed in the quality manual. Some of that learning will be generalised and apply to any IT project (programs must be commented to certain standards, there must be regular project reviews, and the like). In other cases past experiences will be specific to the environment the organisation operates in (product *xyz* does not have sufficient security to use in the banking industry, a wealth of experience has been gained in using Visual Basic® so this should be the preferred language, etc.).
- *External standards*. There are quite a range of international, national and industry standards that

apply to software engineering. For example, there is a standard called *ISO 9001* (ISO stands for International Standards Organisation, 9001 is just a number they give to the standard) which defines general guidelines on how any industry (not just IT) should set up a quality management system. It includes sections on how an organisation should produce, approve and issue specification documents. Organisations can apply for certification (a bit like an exam for a whole company!) that they comply with the requirements of the ISO 9001 standard.

The design specification should be checked to see that is complies with the organisation's standards as outlined in the quality manual.

Activity

Find out more about the requirements of ISO 9001. What would an organisation need to do to gain certification? The ISO website is a good place to start.

Verification against the modelling rules

Most specifications will use one or more modelling or design techniques. Entity relationship diagrams, normalisation and data flow diagrams have all been mentioned, and there are many other methods which are widely used.

All these methods have rules about how they are used and how the diagrams are drawn. In data flow diagrams, for example, one rule states that a data store must have both a data flow going in and one coming out. These rules are not there just to make the diagrams look neat; they are there to prevent inconsistencies and errors in the design. What would be the point of storing an item of data that was never read?

If errors are found in the way the techniques have been used they would suggest that an error or omission has been made in the design. In the example of a missing data flow from a data store, this might mean that a process to read (or write) the data from the data store has also been omitted. Omitting a process from a specification is clearly a serious flaw.

Design review and prototyping at GBW Bank

Verification is usually best done by someone other than the person who wrote the specification. Authors are notoriously bad at spotting errors in their own work.

There are two main group methods that can be used to verify a specification and ensure, as far as possible, that the system the specification describes will meet the users' requirements and that there are no flaws in the design of the programs.

- *Design review* involves drawing together a small team of people, made up of domain and technical experts, to review the specification critically. They use the verification techniques described above to check the correctness of the specification.

- *Prototyping* involves building part of the intended system (usually including only limited functionality) and then asking the users to review the prototype to see whether their requirements have been interpreted correctly. Prototyping is often used to verify the design of the user interface.

A design review

First Jamie Soomary arranges a design review, for which he needs to assemble a small team of reviewers. Sara, his boss, has already identified a senior programmer, Rosalind Lawson, to head a small team of programmers who will write the software for the system.

She will bring programming expertise to the team as she has worked on many database projects in the past.

Joseph Cohen, one of the electricians, is reasonably computer literate (he put together the spreadsheet they currently use to track the testing).

Although he won't understand some of the program design sections of the specification, his domain knowledge is vital to the success of the review. Finally, Jennifer Murphy is the IS department's Quality Manager. She will be looking at the specification to see whether it complies with the relevant standards detailed in the department's quality manual.

Jamie sends them an copy of his draft specification for them to read through, and arranges a time and place for them to meet. When they meet they go though the specification page by page, discussing every aspect of the design to check that it will meet the users' needs and will be technically workable. They also look for errors and omissions.

Joseph looks at it from the users' point of view. For example, he spots a potential problem. The specification requires that the system will download a list of all the items to be tested in a particular location (perhaps a local branch of the bank) into the PAT tester. The electrician then takes the tester to the location. But suppose he finds that one of the items listed is not there (the asset register in not always 100 per cent accurate, or it may be that an item has been sent away for repair)? Conversely, the electrician may find equipment at the location that should be tested but is not listed. Neither of these eventualities is covered in the spec. Jamie questions Joseph about how these situations should be dealt with and makes notes so he can add this information into his design.

Rosalind, on the other hand, reviews the specification from a programming perspective. She checks the entity relationship and the data flow diagrams carefully for any inconsistencies. She has implemented several similar projects in the past and uses her experience of those projects to check that what Jamie is proposing is feasible.

Jennifer, as the Quality Manager, compares the specification structure and content to the guidelines in the department's quality manual. She looks to see whether anything has been omitted and that the guidelines have been properly followed.

The meeting takes all day, but investment in time at this stage is well worthwhile as errors can be costly to fix later on. By the end of the meeting a list of changes to the specification has been made; it's nothing really major, mostly just minor omissions and errors. However, the need to deal with the situation where a piece of equipment to be tested is not where it should be is an important one. Without the review the software would have been written without this functionality. It would not have been until much later, perhaps not until the software was in use, that this omission would have been noticed.

Another important point arises from the meeting. Joseph is concerned that some of the other electricians may find the system difficult to use. He has looked at the screen designs and thinks that some of the buttons and menu options seem a bit confusing. Jamie listens to his concerns and then speaks to Sara and Rosalind. They agree that creating a prototype of the user interface would be a good idea.

In the meantime, Jamie uses the feedback from the specification review meeting to correct the errors and omissions in his spec. He then sends the updated copy to each member of the review team and they all confirm that they are now happy with the spec.

Prototyping

Prototyping is a popular method of verifying that what the designer has in mind (as described in the design specification) meets the users' needs. End-users find it difficult to express their real requirements (often because they don't know, or can't imagine, how the application will look when the software is completed). There is often no substitute for trying out an initial version of the software system. By creating a prototype concepts can be demonstrated, design options can be tried out, and problems and solutions can be investigated. There are a number of different ways of prototyping.

- *Evolutionary prototyping.* With this technique an initial prototype of the system is developed and evaluated by the users. Using this evaluation another prototype is developed and evaluated. This process continues, with each prototyping and evaluation cycle bringing the system closer to what is required until an optimal version of the system has been developed.

- *Throw-away prototyping.* In this case a prototype is developed and evaluated, but the prototype is not used as part of the final system. It is thrown away, as the name suggests. It is only the things learnt about how the system should work that are incorporated in the final system.

In both cases, for it to be successful, the prototyping activity has to be treated rather like a complete, miniature, software development process. Typically, the stages involved would be as follows:

- *Planning.* What exactly is the prototype intended to achieve? It may be to validate some functional requirement of the system (is this what you want it to do?), to test out the user interface (is this how you want it to look and feel?), or to demonstrate some other aspect of the system. It is important that users understand the purpose of the prototype, otherwise they may not get what they are expecting.

- *Definition.* What functionality will the prototype have? It may also be important to consider what is to be left out of the prototype. In order to speed the development of the prototype, some aspects of the system, such as error handling or response times, may be ignored or only partly addressed.

- *Development.* The prototype program code is written and tested.

- *Evaluation.* In many ways this is the most important stage. Evaluation is normally carried out by the end-users, either all of them or – if that is not practicable – a representative sub-set. If, for example, you were evaluating the ease of use of the user interface using a prototype, then you would need to make sure the group of users contained both novices and experienced people. The evaluation having been completed, the results need to be analysed and recommendations made.

Prototyping has become increasingly popular in software development because of its ability to verify that the software designer has understood what the user requires. However, it is not without its own problems. Prototyping can create uncertainty because the designer may not be able to predict how much time (and therefore cost) the project will take until the prototype is complete. In many circumstances the user will want a fixed price for completing the development project and will want to know this cost before the project starts. This can be a drawback when prototyping is being used because the design of the system may need to change after the prototyping process has been completed.

Prototyping takes time (and therefore costs money), so a project that uses this method may cost more and take longer (particularly if throw-away prototyping is used). On the other hand, where evolutionary prototyping is used the compromises made to produce the early prototypes (ignoring issues such as error checking and performance) may adversely affect the quality of the eventual system.

A prototyping activity

Jamie and Rosalind plan a prototyping activity. The aim of the prototype is to assess the user interface they have designed. They create the forms they have designed using Visual Basic® and write some simple code behind the forms so they work in a limited fashion. They then select a small group of electricians, with a range of computer literacy, to try out the forms.

Having produced the prototype, the evaluation session proves interesting. Although the electricians generally cope well with the forms, there are quite a number of areas where they would like things done differently. Jamie and Rosalind note all the comments the electricians make during the session and discuss them in detail afterwards. Although quite a few changes are requested, fortunately none of them requires a major redesign of the system and all can be implemented quite easily.

The forms are modified in line with the suggestions made by the electricians and then shown to them again, to check that their comments have been understood correctly.

Overall, the effect of the prototyping activity is positive. The electricians feel involved in the development process because their views have been taken into consideration. Jamie and Rosalind also feel good, although they have more work to do redesigning the forms. They know that what they produce will meet the needs of the users.

CHAPTER 37

Testing, implementation and file maintenance

This chapter describes the processes involved in testing and implementing a programmed solution.

The chapter covers these Learning Outcomes in the specification:

L.O. 5.6   Describe how the technical testing of a programmed solution to a stated problem should be carried out

L.O. 5.7   Distinguish between technical documentation and user documentation

L.O. 5.8   Comment on the user training requirements for a stated programmed solution

L.O. 5.9   Describe sensible maintenance procedures for a stated programmed solution

Testing issues

Once the development of the software is well under way, consideration needs to be given to testing it. Although the concept of testing is simple, the reality is much more complex. There are two main things that testing is intended to discover:

- whether there are any defects in the written programs
- whether the system correctly matches the users' requirements.

To produce high-quality, reliable software, testing must be carried out according to a well-defined plan. The reliability of a piece of software generally increases with the amount of testing done. However, testing takes time and therefore costs money, so there is often a trade-off to be made. Some types of software need to be more reliable that others. Safety-critical systems such as aircraft control need to be tested much more rigorously than most business software, for example.

It is also worth noting that testing cannot turn a poorly designed software program into a good one. Conversely, a well-designed system, with reusable modules, is likely to be easier to test.

You have seen that the early stages of program development involve decomposing the users' requirements into the detail of a program or module. Once the program has been written, testing is carried out at each stage as the different modules are put together into sub-systems, and then as the sub-systems are integrated into a complete system. Testing is therefore done at each stage:

- *Component testing.* Individual modules or programs are tested to ensure they operate correctly.
- *Integration testing.* Modules and programs are tested together to ensure compatibility and to check that the interfaces between the programs work correctly.
- *Acceptance testing.* This is the final stage before the system is accepted for operational use. It involves testing by the users, usually in the real environment that the software is designed for, with live data rather than test data.

Component testing

In most cases component testing is carried out informally by the programmer responsible for writing the individual programs or modules, and is sometimes called *debugging*. Integration and acceptance testing is a more formal affair with a test plan used to define what is to be tested, and how. Testing at these stages is not normally carried out by the programmer who wrote the software; instead an independent quality assurance team is brought in.

Another issue that needs to be addressed is how we define what 'working properly' means. This might seem obvious, but there are several ways one can interpret the phrase. For example, 'working properly' might mean that the program runs without crashing or locking up. This is a straightforward definition: provided the programmer can test all the parts of the program to check there are no circumstances that cause it to fail (not as easy as it sounds!), there should not be a problem.

Alternatively, 'working properly' might mean that *the program produces the correct results*. This is a more complex definition, because the programmer must have some way of identifying what the 'correct results' are. The program specification is the place where this definition can be found and the programmer must refer back to that document to ensure the program works correctly. He or she may also need to ask the systems analyst for clarification on some points.

Testing techniques

Testing anything other than the simplest program is a complex affair. The problem is that there is a very wide range of possible combinations of input values, menu options and circumstances and it is not feasible to test all of them.

In general, testing is done by producing *test cases*. These are scenarios that are meant to match how the software will be used in the real world. The person doing the testing follows the scenarios (choosing particular options, entering the test data that is provided as part of the test case etc.) and notes the results obtained. These test results are compared with the anticipated (or correct) results, and if they are different then modifications need to be made to the program.

There are two main approaches to producing suitable test cases:

- Using knowledge about the functions the program is supposed to perform, test cases can be generated to discover whether the program performs these functions correctly. This is known as *black-box testing* (sometimes called *functional testing*) since the person doing the testing takes no account of the internal workings of the system (it is assumed to be a 'black box').

- Using knowledge about the internal workings of the software, test cases can be generated that make sure every part of the program has been adequately exercised. This is known as *white-box testing* (sometimes called *structural testing*) since it takes an opposite approach to black-box testing.

In general, white-box testing is done in the early stages, whereas black-box testing is appropriate for integration and acceptance testing.

Equivalence classes

As already stated, exhaustive testing is impracticable and probably unnecessary. With this in mind, the concept of *equivalence classes* is important to understanding how test cases can be generated in black-box testing.

For example, imagine an input field for a person's age, which according to the specification should be validated to ensure that entries are in the range 18 to 65. To exhaustively test this field to check that all valid entries are accepted, the tester would need to enter 18,19, 20, 21 and so on up to 65. However, that would be a waste of time since there is a high probability that if the two values at the boundaries are accepted (18 and 65), and any other value in the mid range (38 say), then all the others will work. All the numbers between 18 and 65 are therefore said to be in the same equivalence class because the program handles them all in the same way.

Equivalence classes come in two types, *valid* and *invalid*. In the example above, the numbers 18 to 65 represent a valid equivalence class. Invalid equivalence classes in this example would include numbers outside the range, as well as non-numeric entries.

Recording and correcting faults

Finding faults is only part of the task of system testing. At the component testing stage, most of the faults identified by the developer will be programming errors. The programmer will often fix them without reference to anyone else. However, it is possible that design errors will be discovered at this stage. It is important that the design of the system should be kept accurate and consistent, so if changes in the design are required, even if they are minor, there must be some kind of *change control procedure* governing how they are carried out.

A change control procedure will generally involve a number of steps:

- a method to record the nature of the problem – either a printed form or some kind of database
- an analysis of how the problem can be solved – this will normally involve the system analyst and the programmer
- implementation of the agreed change, in both the program(s) and design documentation.

When the integration testing phase is reached (discussed below), the programmer who wrote the code does not normally carry out the testing. Therefore all faults (programming and design) must be accurately recorded on an error report form (or database). Those faults that are deemed to be programming errors (or situations where the program does not conform to the design) will be routed back to the programmer to investigate and correct. Problems that relate to the design will have to go through a similar change control procedure as outlined above.

Activity

What should an error report form look like? Try to design one, including all the fields you think will be necessary.

Integration testing

Once the individual components have been tested, they need to be integrated into a partial or complete system. Integration testing involves checking the system for problems that arise from the way the different modules interact with each other.

Integration of the system should be done in stages, starting with a minimal system and then adding components, testing at each increment. The reason for this incremental approach is that the interactions between the various modules can be complex and errors can be difficult to pin-point. Starting with a

minimal system and adding modules one (or a few) at a time makes identifying errors easier.

There are two approaches to integrating the different modules, which are known as *top-down* and *bottom-up* testing.

- In top-down integration, the high-level components of a system are integrated and tested before the lower-level components have been completed.
- In bottom-up integration, lower-level components are integrated and tested before the higher-level components have been developed.

There are advantages and disadvantages to both approaches, and they are summarised below.

Top-down testing is more likely to discover problems with the system architecture and high-level design at an early stage in the development process. Also, with top-down testing a basic working system which can be used for demonstration and feasibility purposes is available earlier than with bottom-up testing. Top-down testing also fits well with prototyping as described earlier.

However, when using the top-down technique there may be problems getting the higher-level modules to work without the services that the lower-level modules provide. This may mean that special software has to be written, which is basically a simple version of the lower-level modules, to simulate the services they provide. The technical name for these is *program stubs*.

Conversely, with bottom-up testing special software may also be required to exercise the low-level modules, in place of the high-level modules which have yet to be completed. The technical name for this software is a *test driver*.

In reality the choice between top-down and bottom-up testing will probably not be a clear-cut one, and a combination of both approaches may be used. Since different modules will be completed at different times, and not always to schedule, the testing team on a project will have to work with whatever modules are ready for testing.

Integration testing at GBW Bank

Sara Patel, the IT Development Manager, has put Huy Lee in charge of testing the electrical safety system. He is a veteran of many software development projects and has been organising the testing of new products for several years.

Huy heads up a team of three test engineers. They have to decide which modules to integrate and test first, and then create a plan which will define exactly how the testing will be carried out. The modules that Huy needs to integrate and test are shown in Figure 37.1.

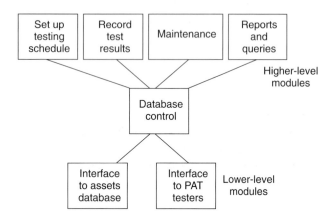

Figure 37.1 *Identification of the modules to be integrated and tested*

The approach

Since an incremental prototyping activity had already been carried out on the high-level modules for setting up testing and recording results, these modules are ready for integration testing first. Fortunately the database control module is ready for integration as well, so these three modules form the first stage of the integration testing.

Since the modules which interface to the assets database and the PAT testers are not yet ready for integration testing, the team have to simulate the way they would provide and accept data from the modules under test. In this case it is not really necessary to write program stubs, as an end-user database program such as Microsoft Access® can be used to input the required data and inspect the data that the modules under test write to the database.

The lower-level interface modules are ready for testing next so they can be integrated with the other modules and the whole system tested again. Finally the maintenance and reports/queries modules are completed so the whole system can be integrated and

tested. Note that in this case the integration was not completed in strict top-down order.

The test plan and execution

Huy Lee creates a test plan in order to ensure that testing is done in a systematic and thorough fashion. Using the system design specification as a guide, the test plan details exactly what is to be tested, and how. At this stage Huy is concerned with testing the functions of the system that the users require; in other words this is black-box testing.

Huy's test plan will consist of a number of scenarios that mimic the way the users will use the system. In the choice of test data he uses the concept of equivalence classes to reduce the amount of testing. His plan also organises which member of his team will be carrying out which test, and when.

One of the functions that must be tested is to allow the engineers to set up a series of electrical equipment checks at a particular location (perhaps a high street branch of the bank). A test plan is created for this function, and test data is chosen. For example, one of the input screens they have to test is the form used to select a location where equipment will be tested (see Figure 37.2)

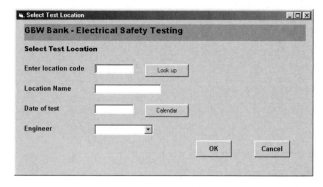

Figure 37.2 *Example of a form to be tested*

When an equipment check needs to be arranged, the engineer will fill in the location code of the building (all the bank's buildings have unique location code numbers). If the engineer does not know the location code, clicking the 'Look up' button will display a list. When the location code has been entered, the Location Name will automatically appear in the text box. The date of the test is entered in the appropriate box. If the engineer is not sure of the date, clicking the Calendar button will display a calendar from which the engineer can choose a date. The name of the engineer who will carry out the testing is selected from the drop-down box.

We shall look at just that part of the plan that deals with the input fields for the location code and the date of the test. The choice of test data for the location code fields is fairly straightforward as there are only two equivalence classes: invalid codes and valid codes. Within these two classes a single value in each should therefore be sufficient.

The choice of test data for the date of the test is slightly more complex. Three equivalence classes can be defined, since the program should handle each situation differently:

- *Invalid dates.* These are dates that do not exist, such as 31–02–01.
- *Weekends.* These are valid dates, but testing is not normally carried out at weekends (although it is done in special circumstances). When a date is entered that falls on a Saturday or Sunday, the program should display a message box warning the user that this date is a weekend.
- *Weekdays.* These are valid dates that fall between Monday and Friday inclusive.

The part of the test plan that deals with these two fields (location and date) is shown in Figure 37.3.

Remember, this is only a very small part of the whole test plan. The member of the test team doing the testing will follow the plan as the testing is carried out. If, when the test data is entered, the actual result is the same as the expected result, the tester will enter a 'Y'

in the correct column; if not an 'N' will be entered and an error report form completed. The code number of the error report form is entered in the column labelled 'Error report no.', so that the error reports and the test plan can be cross-referenced.

Activity

How would the rest of the form be tested? Is more test data needed?

Acceptance testing

Once the system has been tested by the test team and deemed to be stable, it is time to release the system to a user test group. This group carries out acceptance testing on the system to see whether it meets user requirements under operating conditions.

This is probably one of the most important stages in software development. It is when the development team find out whether all the work they have put into the development of the system has been worthwhile. If the system they have produced does not meet the users' needs, their efforts will have been wasted.

It is worth noting that, where prototyping has been used, the users will have already seen and had an influence on the design of the software – which should give the system developers more confidence that what has been produced will be acceptable.

Test plan for:	Electrical safety testing			Document no: EST0941	
Function:	Set test location				
Author:	W. Johnson				
Date:	12/04/01				
Input Field	**Test data**	**Expected result**		**Correct? Y/N**	**Error report no.**
Location code	A142	Accepted, location name displayed (Dunstable High Street Branch)			
Location code	X099	Error message displayed (Invalid location code)			
Date of test	24-04-01	Accepted			
Date of test	4-08-01	Warning message displayed (Date is a weekend, do you want to continue?)			
Date of test	31-02-02	Error message displayed (Invalid date)			

Figure 37.3 Some sample report results

Testing, implementation and file maintenance

As with all the other testing that needs to be done, acceptance testing must be carefully planned and controlled. The basis for the acceptance testing must be the requirement specification that the users produced right at the beginning of the development process. That is the yardstick against which the system should be measured.

Acceptance testing for a bespoke application is often done in two stages:

- *Alpha testing* is done in the users' work environment but with people from the software development team present, to assist if necessary, and to observe the system in use, recording any errors or problems.

- Following successful alpha testing, *beta testing* is conducted, with no members of the development team present. The users record any errors or problems themselves and report them back to the development team periodically.

Activity

The software industry, like every industry, aims to produce a 'quality product'. What attributes should a piece of quality software possess? How can software developers ensure the software they produce possesses these attributes? What might the consequences be if a piece of software does not possess one or more of these attributes?

Implementation

Technical documentation

Once the testing of the system is well under way, the programmers who have been writing the software will need to turn their attention to completing the technical documentation.

Many software systems are long-lived. Throughout their life changes and improvements may need to be made, and it may be the case that some errors and problems surface only after many years of use (as was the case with the so-called millennium bug). The programmers who originally wrote the software will probably have moved on to new projects or perhaps

new companies. In view of the need to change or correct software written some time ago by someone else, technical documentation is vital.

If the programs are written well in the first place, including adequate comments for example, certain aspects will be self-documenting. Also, in a well-run software development project, where the software produced closely follows the design specification (or, where changes are necessary, the design specification has been updated to reflect the changes), the need for further technical documentation will be reduced.

The content of technical documentation

In order to ensure consistency, each project should state *standards* (usually in the project quality manual). These define exactly what should be contained in the technical documentation (and other types of documentation too), and the format and style of the documents produced.

Typically, technical documentation for each module or program should include:

- listings of the code
- lists of the modules and forms etc. that are used in the program
- details of inputs to and outputs from the module
- the design specification for the program
- details of testing carried out.

In addition, the technical documentation will need to include details of (a) how the overall system works (the database design, including data dictionaries for example) (b) how the different modules integrate with each other, and (c) other technical information like for what hardware and operating system software the system is designed.

User training requirements

Another important aspect of implementing a new system is to train the users. Without proper training the users will probably not gain the full benefits of the software. There may be resistance to using it (because they don't know how to) and that would create support problems. Arranging training for users involves a number of steps.

First, the training requirements of the users need to be analysed. Different people will have different requirements. For example, there may be some users who have never used a computer. They may need to be sent on an introductory course for first-time computer users before receiving training with the new software. Some users may need to know how to use different parts of the software. It may be necessary to organise different types of training courses that cover particular parts of the software.

Once the training requirements have been analysed, the training program can be planned. Again, there are a number of decisions to be made. There are various ways in which the training can be delivered. Questions that need to be asked include:

- Do we do all the training ourselves, or do we involve an external training organisation?
- Do we deliver the training at the site where the users work, or should we hold a central training course?
- Do we use traditional training methods (with a trainer and a classroom), or do we develop a computer-based training package?

Activity

What do you think would be the advantages and disadvantages to each of these options?

Training materials need to be developed. If the traditional method of classroom training is used, the tutor needs to make himself or herself familiar with the software, work out the structure of the course (what to cover, and in what order) and create support materials such as a training manual and practical exercises.

Finally, the training programme needs to be delivered, courses need to be arranged, with facilities (rooms, computers etc.) booked and users notified when and where their training will take place.

You might have noticed that creating the training programme is almost like a miniature software development process – with analysis, development and implementation all required.

Developing the training programme at GBW Bank

Sara Patel has to consider how to develop a training programme. She asks the IT development section's training specialist, Alison Wilson, to develop one. When the project was initially agreed, the costing included a budget for training, so Alison must now work within that budget.

In order to accurately assess the training requirements of all the users, Alison creates a 'skills analysis' questionnaire. This is a multiple-choice questionnaire that asks questions about the users' current computer skills and what aspects of the new software they will need to use. The questionnaire is sent to all the people who will be using the software.

From the analysis of this questionnaire, Alison decides that three different types of training course will be required:

- an introduction to using Microsoft® Windows® for some of the users who have not used a computer before
- an electricians' course
- a managers' course.

The introductory course will be required for only a small number of users, so Alison decides to send these people on an externally provided course, even though this is quite expensive.

The electricians are spread around offices all over the country, but the bank has an IT training room in each of its four regional centres (London, Bristol, Manchester and Glasgow) where courses can be run. Alison therefore produces a schedule that shows when each electrician can attend one of the courses she is planning.

There are not many managers' training courses needed. From past experience Alison knows it can be difficult to get the managers to attend training courses away from their offices. She therefore decides to provide them with on-site training.

Having decided the type of training needed, Alison spends several days with the developers learning all she needs to know about the software. She then spends several more days deciding on the structure and content of the courses and writing the course material.

She now needs to finalise the training plan. It is important that the training takes place at the right time. On their return from training, the electricians and the managers need to have the new software available and begin using it at once, otherwise they will forget much of what they have learnt. Careful co-ordination is therefore needed with the project manager. Alison also needs to make sure the training rooms are booked, send out letters to the users telling them when and where their training courses will take place, get the training materials photocopied, and arrange to have the software installed on the computers that will be used for the training. She also needs to arrange the externally provided beginners' courses.

File maintenance

Once a system has been through the acceptance testing process and come into everyday use, responsibility for the software moves from the development team to the support and maintenance team.

Maintaining the integrity of the data stored on the system is an important task. A computer system is usually only as good as the data it contains. If the data is full of errors and inconsistencies the system will not be able to deliver the benefits it was designed to produce. For example, one of the expected benefits of GBW Bank's electrical safety system is that it will improve the efficiency of the electricians. If the data in the system is full of errors, electricians may waste time being sent to check equipment that is not where the system says it is or which has already been tested.

Backup

The data in the system needs to be protected from loss due to hardware or software faults or physical threats (such as fire or flood). To do this the support team must ensure that it is backed up regularly and the backup disks or tapes stored safely.

Error reporting

A mechanism needs to be put in place to allow users to report data problems (inconsistencies, errors etc.) so that its quality can be improved. This will probably be part of the system set up to allow users to report other errors, such as program bugs, to the user support team.

Reconciliation checks

In some cases it may be necessary to carry out a *reconciliation check* on the database. This involves printing out the records on the database and comparing the items listed with the actual real-world items. A stock check is an example of this. Another, in the electrical safety system, would be for a list of all the electrical items printed out to be sent to each branch for the staff to physically check whether the equipment is actually there.

Data integrity

The design of the database system should take into account the need to maintain *data integrity*. It is important that, for example, should a hardware, software or power failure cause the computer to crash, the data on the system is left in a consistent state.

The concept of a *transaction* is important here. Normally, in database systems a single transaction consists of several data updates. For example, a transaction at an online music store would involve at least two data updates, one printing off a despatch note in the warehouse to send the CDs purchased to the customer, and another transferring money from the purchaser's bank account. To maintain the integrity of the data it is vital that *either* the whole transaction takes place *or* none of it takes place. The situation where a system failure in the middle of a transaction means that some updates are done but not others must be avoided at all costs. For example, the person buying the CDs may get them delivered but not be charged for them.

At GWB Bank, electricians are paid monthly by computerised bank transfer. These transactions involve two data updates. The first update involves subtracting the amount the electrician is to be paid out of the bank's wages account; the second one adds the same amount to the electrician's account. Should the computer which does these wage transfers crash in the middle of this transaction, the situation could arise where a particular electrician's wages have been deducted from the bank's wages account but not transferred to the electrician's account. That situation should not be allowed to occur.

The normal method used to avoid these types of data inconsistencies is to write the data updates to a temporary file (sometimes called an *update log*) until the end of the individual transaction is reached. Then the updates are copied from the temporary file into the real database all at once. This is called *committing* the transaction. The benefit of this approach is that if the transaction fails half way through, no changes have been made to the real database.

This chapter gives advice on how to tackle coursework **Task 4**. The task requires you to produce and document an ICT solution to a significant problem that involves the use of an object-based event-driven programming language.

A Visual Basic® tutorial can be downloaded from the Heinemann website (www.heinemann.co.uk/vocational).

The chapter covers the following Learning Outcome in the specification:

L.O. 6.2   Document and implement an ICT-based solution

Solve a problem using an object-based event-driven programming language

At first glance the requirements for Task 4 seem very similar to those for Task 2 (covered in Chapter 18). You have to carry through a project which will result in (hopefully) a working application designed to meet a specific need.

The major difference is that this time you are expected to use a programming language for implementation. It is expected that most of you will use Visual Basic®, and that many of you will use it to interact with the components of Microsoft® Office. You will find a Visual Basic® tutorial on the website.

However, you may already have skills in another suitable language, and alternative software tools may become available during the lifetime of Edexcel's specification. In either case, you should check that they cover the constructs listed on pages 43–44 of the specification before deciding to use them.

You are advised to read through Chapter 18 again, to remind yourself of the basic constraints on any practical project, which are not repeated here.

What do I have to submit to the examination board?

You will submit a report that will appear very similar to the one you did for Task 2. Note, however, that if your project does not involve a substantial amount of programming then it will be assessed within the Foundation level mark range.

How do I select a problem?

The comments in Chapter 18 about choosing a problem also apply to Task 4, with one exception. You may, if you like, enhance the solution that you have already developed for Task 2. Of course, if you choose to do this you cannot simply resubmit the same specification and analysis as you wrote before; you will be producing a new solution so will need to rethink every single section in the coursework report.

But you may decide to start afresh with a new problem, and that is acceptable as well.

Can I use the features of an application generator?

You may certainly use an application generator to set up the basic structure of your solution, but you should then ensure than you exploit the built-in programming facilities to develop it further.

Assessment of Task 4

The mark scheme looks very similar to that used for Task 2, but note that the criteria for awarding marks in some sections differ from those used in Task 2.

Maximum marks are shown in square brackets below. The maximum possible total is 60 marks.

- **Requirements stage**
  - Specification (user specification, or proposal) [9]
  - Facilities [3]
  - Analysis [9]

- **Design stage**
  - Design [9]

- **Implementation and testing stage**
  - Implementation [9]
  - Testing [9]

- **Operations and maintenance stage**
  - Documentation for the systems administrator [3]
  - Documentation for the user [3]
  - User training needs [3]
  - Evaluation [3]

The differential mark ranges still apply to each section, depending on whether the project is rated at Foundation, Intermediate or Higher levels of difficulty. This judgement will be largely based on the amount of programming you have attempted.

Writing up Task 4

- **Title page**
- **Contents**
- **Acknowledgements**

1. *Specification* [9 marks]

Give a clear description of the problem that has to been identified and the context in which it has arisen.

Give a description of a proposed solution from a user's point of view.

Give a description of the processing requirements and systems implications.

1.1 Description of the task
- Summarise the overall problem.
- Describe the context in which the problem has arisen.

1.2 The proposed solution from a user's point of view
- Outline the solution that the potential user would like to have implemented.
- Identify the existing IT skills of the potential user.
- Describe the user interface requirements of the user.

1.3 Processing requirements
- Describe the processing required by the user.
- Describe the systems implications of implementing the new application.

1.4 Justification of ICT solution
- Explain why an ICT solution is appropriate.
- Consider wider (social, organisational, legal etc.) implications of providing an ICT solution to the problem.

2. *Facilities [3 marks]*
Discuss the suitability of specific hardware and software required as they relate to the task in hand.

Make particular reference to the programming system that it is intended to use.

2.1 Hardware
- Discuss minimum and optimum hardware requirements.

2.2 Software
- Discuss operating system requirements.
- Identify the programming system to be used.
- Discuss the suitability of the programming system for generating the application, and identify alternatives.

3. *Analysis [9 marks]*
Provide evidence that a thorough investigation of the background to the task has taken place in relationship to the potential users of the product. This should include an analysis of any existing system and users, and indications of from where the evidence that defines the needs of the new environment has been gathered.

Give a description of the complete information requirements of the proposed system and indications of the sources of this information.

3.1 Investigation
- Describe your investigation into the problem, using interviews, questionnaires, background research and observation, as appropriate, with evidence.
- If an existing system is in use, describe it in detail, with evidence.

3.2 Proposed system
- Identify the objectives of the proposed system.
- Identify and describe each process in the proposed system, and identify whether it will be a manual or computer-based process.
- Describe the input and output data requirements for each process.
- Identify the sources of data for each process.

4. *Design [9 marks]*

Provide a top view of the proposed system showing the sources of the information, the information flow paths, the relationships with any existing system and the general nature of the processing required related to appropriate programming tools.

Show complete designs of all proposed input and output interfaces; for example, screen designs, report structures, and details of input signals if it is a real-time application.

Show complete designs of any required processing structures; for example, file structures, database structures, spreadsheet functions, hypertext connections, OLE sources and destinations.

Show complete designs of any procedures (event and general) that may be required, together with an indication of how events may be dependent; e.g. spider diagrams.

4.1 System design
- Draw a diagram showing the information flow in the proposed system.
- Describe how the facilities of a programming language can be exploited in order to implement each process.
- Draw a menu diagram to show how users will access the computer-based processes.

4.2 Software design – user interface design
- Sketch designs for paper-based data collection forms (if needed).
- Sketch designs for screen layouts, including forms for inputting and/or displaying data, forms for providing instructions or help.
- Sketch layouts for menus and toolbars.
- Sketch designs for printed reports.

4.3 Software design – design of data structures
- Specify data structures and data types (including a full description of the data model for a relational database, if used).
- Discuss data validation requirements and how these will be implemented.

4.4 Software design – design of procedures
- Design event procedures, using structured English or a similar method.
- Design general procedures, using structured English or a similar method.
- Give diagrams to show the dependency of events.

4.5 Choice of programming tool
- Explain why the programming tool you have chosen is suitable for implementing this design.

5. *Implementation [9 marks]*

Give detailed evidence of the implementation of the design. It is important that the relationship between the design and the implementation is clear and this may include reporting any iteration between design and implementation that takes place (prototyping).

It could be an advantage to implement a system in a modular fashion and ensure that the documentation reflects this approach, as it may assist in the awarding of deserved marks.

Annotated listings of all program procedures should be produced.

Sensible program structure within procedures should be evident.

Any requirement to use given dynamic linked libraries should be described, together with a copy of the standard documentation of the routine used.

This section provides the evidence for the way in which you have implemented your solution. All the printouts should be annotated (either by hand or in a word-processor).

You should build up Sections 5 and 6 at the same time. You should test each process as you complete it.

5.1 History of the implementation

- Give a description of the sequence in which the solution was implemented.
- Give a description of any prototyping that took place and how the design was modified in response to feedback.
- Give a description of any technical problems encountered and how they were solved.
- Provide an explanation for any variations from the original design.

5.2 User interface

- Provide a printout of paper-based data collection forms (if needed).
- Provide screen dumps of all screen forms.
- Provide screen dumps showing customised pull-down menus, toolbars or menu (switchboard) forms.
- Produce printouts of printed reports.

5.3 Procedures

- Give an annotated listing of all procedures/modules, to include evidence of data structures and data validation.
- Provide standard documentation of any library modules used.

6. Testing [9 marks]

It is good practice to perform technical testing as integral with implementation. Nevertheless, to help you maximise credit for testing it is sensible to give evidence, in a separate section, of what tests you have designed and carried out, including evidence of results, which show that the components of your implementation work as expected.

6.1 Test plan

- Provide a set of test cases to test the individual modules in the system.

6.2 Testing

- Provide annotated screen dumps or printouts to show the effects of following through the test plan with individual modules.

- Provide annotated screen dumps or printouts to demonstrate integration testing.

6.3 Comments on testing

- Comment on the success, or otherwise, of the testing procedures.
- Identify any limitations or shortcomings in the application.

7. Documentation for the systems administrator [3 marks]

Produce documents that will assist a systems administrator install, test and troubleshoot the implemented system.

7.1 Installation

- Outline the system requirements.
- Provide installation instructions.
- Describe security measures.
- Describe how to back up and recover files.

7.2 Testing

- Describe the technical testing that should be carried out prior to use.

7.3 Troubleshooting

- Describe common technical problems and their solutions.

8. Documentation for the user [3 marks]

You have to demonstrate that you appreciate what is likely to be understandable to a potential user.

Use suitable software to produce an attractive guide to the product for the end-user. Include screen dumps where appropriate. Do not duplicate information in Section 7 nor anything required for Section 9.

The guide may be in the form of a tutorial, or it could be related directly to each of the processes that the user has to carry out.

9. User training needs [3 marks]

Make statements concerning any prior knowledge and skills the user may require.

9.1 Prior knowledge and skills

- Identify the knowledge and skills that users should have before they start any training with the application.

- Describe the structure of a suitable training programme for end-users.

9.2 Training materials – walkthrough example
- Take an end-user through a straightforward session with the application.

9.3 Training materials – self-evaluation test
- Provide a set of questions (perhaps using a tick list) to enable users to check whether they have used and understood the application correctly.

10. Evaluation [3 marks]
Provide reflective statements on how the final system meets the expectations of the specification with reference to reported reactions of users of the system.

10.1 Comparison of specification with final system
- Compare the developed application with the specification in Section 1.

10.2 Report on reactions of users
- Provide users with copies of the documents from Sections 8 and 9 and ask them to work through the software and comment on it.
- Ask other people to comment on the final system.

10.3 Evaluation of final system
- Give your comments overall on the success of the implementation.

CHAPTER 39

Examination questions and mark schemes for unit 5

This chapter provides examination questions and mark schemes for unit 5: The implementation of event-driven applications. Edexcel has given permission for the use here of this copyright material.

Note that some of the questions are not full-length questions. Questions for the current specification will normally be marked out of 19 (although totals of 18 or 20 are possible).

Specimen examination questions

1. Part of the user interface of a particular application is a screen form that contains a number of visible interactive objects.

   (a) Describe four characteristics of visual interactive objects that allow the design of a good user interface. [4 marks]

   (b) One of these objects is an area that displays information in Rich Text Format (RTF).

      (i) Discuss the advantages and disadvantages of designing user interfaces that use Rich Text Format objects. [4 marks]

      (ii) Describe how Rich Text Format is achieved from a technical point of view. [3 marks]

   (c) Integral to the user interface is a Help facility that is provided by files in hypertext format.

      (i) Explain why information structured as hypertext is particularly suited to Help facilities. [4 marks]

      (ii) Describe another major ICT application where information is structured as hypertext. [4 marks]

Edexcel specimen paper

2.
   (a) Object-based event-driven applications are usually developed using an integrated development environment (IDE). Describe four facilities that might be provided by an IDE, illustrating each description with an example of use. [8 marks]

   (b) Luis is developing an application to simulate games that use dice. The programs that Luis is developing seem to work but they are giving results that he does not expect. Abeda, a friend of Luis, comments: '*The problem may be than you allow some variables more scope than they need.*' Explain why some programmers may be tempted to give variables more scope than is required. [3 marks]

   (c) Luis limits the scope of the variables as much as is possible. When he tries to run the application, he gets several identical error messages.

      (i) State what the error message is likely to be. [2 marks]

      (ii) Explain why the application that appeared to work before now produces error messages. [3 marks]

   (d) Luis finds the reasons for the error message and is happy to find that the test results are as expected. However, he is disappointed with the performance of the application with respect to speed. Abeda comments: '*There are many long loops in your program. What* about the data types of the loop control variables?' Explain why the data type of a loop control variable could affect the performance of the application.   [3 marks]

Edexcel specimen paper

3. The country of Datalia has a comprehensive bus service run by a company named Whippet Travel.

   ● Bus routes are divided into fare stages.

   ● All buses have just 44 passenger seats arranged in two pairs across the bus to a length of 11. Thus the seats are numbered A1, B1, C1, D1, ..., A11, B11, C11, D11.

   ● All seats on every bus must be booked in advance.

   ● The seat booking system is ICT-based and includes the use of spreadsheet and relational database software that can communicate with each other.

   (a) Describe, in general terms, *three* of the base tables that are essential to the underlying database of the booking system.   [5 marks]

   (b) The screen interface for seat booking has been implemented via a spreadsheet where one cell maps to one seat. The booking clerks of Whippet Travel have requested an improved screen interface. In particular they want to be able to use drag-and-drop operations to change seat allocations, and they want to retrieve the full details of a passenger by double-clicking on the appropriate cell. Explain why event procedures are necessary if the improvements to screen interface are to be implemented.   [4 marks]

   (c) It has been decided to scrap the use of the spreadsheet software and use a general-purpose event-driven programming language to implement the new interface. Explain how the programming language and the database software should relate to each other.   [4 marks]

   (d) Describe how the event procedures required to implement the drag-and-drop effects are best implemented for this application.   [6 marks]

Edexcel specimen paper

4. A software developer has been engaged to produce an IT-based system to handle car service bookings at a garage. After discussions with the owner, he decides that the system will store details of customers, their cars and their service histories. Information about the cars to be serviced needs to be accessed both from the reception area and the workshop. The developer produces two prototype interfaces for the owner to consider.

Interface A

Interface B

   (a) Comment on the two interfaces in terms of:

   (i)   ease of use;
   (ii) ease of modification.   [3 marks]

   (b) In event-driven applications, a variety of programmable objects will be used. These objects have properties and methods. With the help of examples, explain the difference between object *properties* and object *methods*.   [4 marks]

   (c) Interface A is adopted. It is required that:
   ● workshop staff can indicate the completion of a job by transferring the

car's registration number from the left to the right side of the screen form;

- reception staff can access full customer details in order to telephone the customer.

For two distinct screen objects in Interface A, specify the event procedures that would have to be written. [8 marks]

Edexcel pilot specification, Summer 2000

---

5. A university receives information about new students from a central agency. Each day, the details of more applicants are received. The data is held by the university in a number of files. Each field is separated by a comma and each record by a carriage return character. A new file is created each day as data is received from the agency.

The data contains the applicant's reference number, name, address and course code. Three records are shown below.

456,Mr Linus Gates,21 Linux Road,Hexham,NN6 7AA,E678
678,Ms Ada Lovelace,48 Byron Road,Winchester, SO4 6CA,E678
1029,Ms Lisa Macintosh,101 Super Highway,Appleby,GR5 6BG,G564

It is required to display the contents of this file in a suitable screen control or controls such that each field is individually accessible.

(a) Describe a type of screen control which could be used for this purpose and why it would be suitable. [3 marks]

(b) Different files will need to be accessed from disk for display in this way. State and justify which control could be used to select the file required. [3 marks]

(c) The university wants to be able to edit and validate any field in any file. Describe the event procedures needed to trigger and complete the validation and file updating processes. [5 marks]

(d) Outline a suitable strategy to enable the finished application to be tested. [4 marks]

Edexcel pilot specification, Summer 2000

---

6. A Formula 1 car, while it is being driven in a race, transmits data to the data control engineers by radio link. The data includes items such as the height of the car above the track, how much fuel is remaining and the temperature of the tyres. A programmer writes an application to collect this data and store it in a computer file so that it can be analysed. The programming language used supports only data types byte, integer, real (floating point) and string.

(a) Explain why the programmer should use integers or bytes instead of real data types for the processing of this data. [4 marks]

(b) The programmer creates a *user-defined data type* to handle the file processing required.

   (i) Explain what is meant by a user-defined data type. [2 marks]

   (ii) Explain why a file record is a suitable data structure to be addressed by a user-defined data type. [2 marks]

   (iii) Describe the main advantage of programming such user-defined data types rather than programming for individual data items. [2 marks]

(c) The finished program makes extensive use of dynamic link libraries (DLLs).

   (i) Explain the meaning of 'dynamic link library'. [2 marks]

   (ii) Explain how the use of DLLs can reduce programming effort. [2 marks]

   (iii) Some programmers try to alter the behaviour of existing DLLs. Explain why this practice is inadvisable. [4 marks]

Edexcel pilot specification, Summer 2000

---

7. A school uses its relational database application to administer examination entries. The application produces from the database:

- individual statements of entry for each candidate;
- lists of candidate examination entries, for transmission to the Examination Board.

(a) The Examinations Officer is using the examination entry system and is alarmed to see the message:

Error: referential integrity violation

Describe *three* different circumstances that could have resulted in this message.[6 marks]

(b) The Examinations Officer is disappointed with the speed of response of the database examinations entry system. It is found that the problem is *not* related to the performance of the hardware. Describe a possible cause of this problem and how it can be rectified.

[3 marks]

(c) It is proposed to upgrade the database application using an event-driven programming language. The Examinations Officer wants to be able to produce a seating plan for each examination session, showing the location of each student according to candidate number. This is needed on-screen. It may sometimes be necessary to check and edit the student details from the screen.

(i) Sketch a possible design of the main screen display. On your diagram label the screen objects required. [6 marks]

(ii) Describe *two* event procedures associated with these objects, relating their visible behaviour to any necessary actions taken on the associated data tables. [4 marks]

Edexcel pilot specification, Summer 2000

Mark schemes

1 (a)

The candidate must indicate the relationship between a characteristic of a visual interactive object and the advantage to a user interface that it presents.

Ability to:

- be programmed to respond to a number of distinct events,
  encouraging the multiple use of controls;
- visually respond to certain events,
  thus distinguishing actions (down/up);
- be hidden and shown,
  allowing multiple use of the same form;

- to be enabled and disabled,
  thus allowing the forcing of a sequence of events;
- to change appearance (colour, border style, 3D),
  allowing a visual indication of a recent history of interactions;
- to have their position programmed,
  for redirecting priority of interaction;
- to be members of a control array,
  to use the opportunities of subscripting;
- to be created at runtime,
  to produce precisely positioned and sized families of visual objects.

Any four characteristics and reference to interface. [4]

1 (b)(i)
Possible points:
- Rich text has all its formatting information embedded.
- The total text, including formatting, consists of ASCII characters.
- Thus it can be edited by conventional means.
- Many applications can interpret rich text; thus it is easy to move selections of rich text from one application to another.
- The main disadvantage is the memory taken to store all the formatting information and thus the capacity of rich text-compatible visible objects may be limited.

Any four sensible points. [4]

1 (b)(ii)
Each character or group of characters is preceded by a sequence of 'commands' that define the format, font, colour, size etc. of that group. [2] The object that displays the rich text has the functionality to interpret these commands to affect the display appropriately. [1]

1 (c)(i)
A Help facility requires non-sequential searching [1]; direct connections between related topics and a user interface that turns these connections into a browser [1]. Hypertext can provide this.

In particular, hypertext creation systems allow the highlighting [1] of key words (often by colour) that allow the user to jump to a connected topic [1].

1 (c)(ii)
The candidate must describe an application where nonlinear searching of text is essential for the sensible exploitation of the application [2]. For example, any

form of interactive encyclopaedia or Internet browsing [2].

---

2 (a)

The example of use of each screen object must be plausible to gain the second mark.

- *Toolbox of available screen components*: To allow the easy placing of screen objects and set up the event procedure templates. [2]
- *Contex-sensitive editor*: It provides windows in which code can be written and edited using normal editing facilities but in addition is aware of the syntax of the language being used and will indicate when a syntax error has been made. [2]
- *Context sensitive-help*: It allows the programmer to select any statement and requests a description of its function by a single key depression. [2]
- *Contextual debugging facilities*: When a run error is detected the IDE displays the appropriate procedure and highlights the statement from where the detection has been activated. In addition, the current values of some variables can be displayed by the action of mouse pointing. [2]

Any other combination of four IDE facilities.

2 (b)

In the extreme it is tempting to declare all variable as global; for example, as the programmer can refer to them from any procedure and can simplify procedure parameter lists. [3]

The candidate may answer the question in the context of the inadequate facilities of a particular language; such an approach would gain a maximum of two marks.

2 (c)(i)

'Undeclared variable' or similar. [2]

Only 1 mark for 'Undeclared'.

2 (c)(ii)

A variable that has been mistakenly addressed [1] in a sub-procedure has now gone out of scope [1] because of the removal of a global or public declaration [1].

2 (d)

During the execution of a long loop the arithmetic required on the loop control variable would have to take place many times [1]. If it can be arranged that,

for example, arithmetic can be achieved with integer variables rather than real variables [1]; then the process would be quicker because there are less complex processes to be carried out [1].

---

3 (a)

The candidate who looks deeply into the possible interpretations of the scenario might produce a range of plausible base tables and the assistant examiner will have to make judgements. The three most likely to be discussed are:

- routes;
- buses;
- passengers. [3]

For full marks the candidate should indicate the means of relating these tables by a discussion of suitable primary and foreign keys. [2]

3 (b)

The proposed interface improvements require that there is an object on the screen that represents a seat on the bus [1]. That object must be able to distinguish between events that it suffers [1]. These different events will have to activate other actions in the system, maybe some complex database manipulation [1]. This is possible only if complex event procedures can be written [1].

3 (c)

The programming language and the database management system should be able to establish a client–server relationship [2] in the sense that the user interface created in the programming language is the client [1] which demands services from the server database [1].

3 (d)

The candidate must indicate that using actual dropping of the selected object requires quite precise mouse actions.

It would be better for the user if the programmer used the mouse down, mouse up and the drag–drop event procedures [2] to swap the objects' captions [1] and update the underlying database [1], thus giving the impression of precise dropping [1].

A correct answer that involves direct dropping would gain a maximum of four marks.

4 (a)(i)

Some specific comment on menu structure visible from one screen in either case, such as:

- familiarity of typical windows menu;
- use of hot keys in menu-driven interface;
- intuitive nature of data layout in tabbed interface.

NB: Not comments on aesthetics. Any one suitable comment as above. [1]

4 (a)(ii)

Any one briefly explained idea which refers to development, such as:

- new tabs easily added with no need to change existing ones;
- new items on menu will require menu editing and new procedures.

One idea explained. [2]

4 (b)

Object property – *adjective* idea – a state of an object that can be tested or set; e.g. mouseover = true. [1 + 1]

Object method – *verb* idea – an action which can be carried out on or by an object; e.g. mycombobox.additem. [1 + 1]

4 (c)

Two objects identified such as text box, label, check box, grid object.

Two objects, one mark each. [2]

Completion of job
- drag and drop, involving mouse-down/mouse-up events;
- which would access procedures to change status of job in data table;
- display required data.

Access details
- (e.g.) double-click event on car registration in text box or other suitable object;
- leading to procedure to call up search or dynaset;
- to isolate individual owner data;
- display details. [6]

5 (a)
- Text box – accommodate reasonable amount of text – updatable – individual field access

- List box – easy presentation line by line for each record
- Grid control – natural way to present tabulated data – each cell editable

A suitable object/control named: one mark then described: two marks. [3]

5 (b)
Controls
- Common dialog box
- File selection control
- Drive selection control

Any one suitable, one mark [1]

Justification
- Drives are selectable
- Directories are selectable
- Files
- Paths
- Allows selection of file by clicking
- Standard format that is familiar to user

Two reasons, one mark each [2]

5 (c)
Consider file displayed in a grid:
- Select cell (click) – no code
- Enter new field value
- Terminate with CRLF

leads to validation routine:

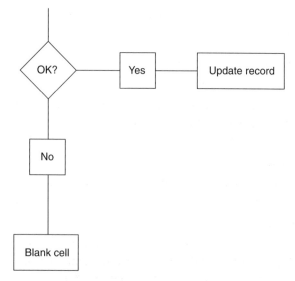

- Access record and field
- Display field
- Allow edits
- Validation procedure described, such as length check
- If OK then update
- Else blank cell
- Close.

Any five correct stages, one mark each. [5]

5 (d)
Test that:
- new file is correctly opened and positioned in controls;
- editing possible;
- edits correctly saved;
- edits correctly validated;
- correct/erroneous/extreme data;
- close file – reopen;
- data still correct;
- beta testing;
- module testing.

Any four points, one mark each. [4]

6 (a)
- Integers/bytes take less storage: program more efficient
- Transmission of data faster
- Integer/byte arithmetic requires less processing so program runs faster.

Two points, two marks each. [4]

6 (b)(i)
When the programmer needs a data type not provided by the language, a new type can be constructed from pre-existing ones. [2]

6 (b)(ii)
A complete record, made of various fields, can be constructed as a single unit. [2]

6 (b)(iii)
A number of variables can be declared which inherit the type definition. File read/write operations can be coded as a single statement instead of several.

One explained point: two marks. [2]

6 (c)(i)
- Precompiled code
- Linked at runtime
- May be called by different programs.

Two points: one mark each. [2]

6 (c)(ii)
- Modules written for one application/function can be accessed by others without the need for rewriting
- Testing time reduced as DLLs already tested
- Ease of updating more than one dependant program.

One reasoned point: two marks. [2]

6 (c)(iii)
- Alteration will affect all dependent programs
- Unexpected effects
- Possible impact on OS functions.

Two reasoned points: two marks each. [4]

7 (a)
- A value has been entered in the foreign key field that does not exist in the primary key of the primary table.
- An attempt has been made to delete a record from a primary table when matching records exist in a related table.
- An attempt has been made to change the value of a primary key data item when there are related records.

Three reasoned points: two marks each. Marks can be gained by suitable examples. [6]

7 (b)
- Lack of an index can slow down operations – create index for a field that is being searched.
- On the other hand, the existence of an index can slow down performance when records are being modified and the index has to be recreated – remove index in this case.
- Too many fields may be used to create the index – keep these to a minimum.
- File fragmentation – perform a defrag.

One mark for the problem plus up to two marks for the remedy. [3]

7 (c)(i)

The sketch:

- Orientation of room given (e.g. which is the front?)
- Provision for candidate location (e.g. spaces/boxes mapped out)
- Provision for candidate identification (e.g. evidence of candidate number/other id).

One mark each.   [3]

The objects:

Three suitable *labels* such as text box; label; list box; grid object; data object; command button.

One mark each.   [3]

7 (c)(ii)

An event and underlying operations *on data tables* such as:

- Double-click event on a text box showing candidate number will access the student table and display the necessary details on a form for editing.
- Drag-and-drop operation involving mouse-down and mouse-up events to move the seating position of a student, access the student table and adjust the seat number field.

In each case, one mark for the event and one mark for a correct action on a data table.   [4]

INDEX